From *Grassroots: The Writer's Workbook,* Eleventh Edition
by Susan Fawcett

If found, please return to:

Name: _____

Phone: ( ) _____

Personal Error Patterns Chart

Error Type & Symbol	Specific Error	Correction	Rule or Reminder	Assignment & Number of Errors

Proofreading Strategies

Many writers have found that the proofreading strategies described below help them see their own writing with a fresh eye. You will learn more strategies throughout *Grassroots.* Try a number of methods and see which ones work best for you.

Proofreading Strategy: Allow enough time to proofread.

Many students don't proofread at all, or they skim their paper for grammatical errors two minutes before class. This just doesn't work. Set aside enough time to proofread slowly and carefully, searching for errors and hunting especially for your personal error patterns.

Proofreading Strategy: Work from a paper copy.

People who proofread on computers tend to miss more errors. If you write on a computer, do not proofread on the monitor. Instead, print a copy of your paper, perhaps enlarging the type to 14 point. Switching to a paper copy seems to help the brain see more clearly.

Proofreading Strategy: Read your words aloud.

Reading silently makes it easier to skip over small errors or mentally fill in missing details, whereas listening closely is a great way to hear mistakes. Listen and follow along on your printed copy, marking errors as you hear them.

    a. Read your paper aloud to *yourself.* Be sure to read *exactly* what's on the page, and read with enthusiasm.

    b. Ask a *friend* or *writing tutor* to read your paper out loud to you. Tell the reader you just want to hear your words and that you don't want any other suggestions right now.

Proofreading Strategy: Read "bottom up," from the end to the beginning.

One way to fool the brain into taking a fresh look at something you've written is to proofread the last sentence first. Read slowly, word by word. Then read the second-to-last sentence, and so on, all the way back to the first sentence.

Proofreading Strategy: Isolate your sentences.

If you write on a computer, spotting errors is often easier if you reformat so that each sentence appears isolated, on its own line. Double-space between sentences. This visual change can help the brain focus clearly on one sentence at a time.

Proofreading Strategy: Check for one error at a time.

If you make many mistakes, proofread separately all the way through your paper for each error pattern. Although this process takes time, you will catch many more errors this way and make real progress. You will begin to eliminate some errors altogether as you get better at spotting and fixing them. You will learn more recommended proofreading strategies in upcoming chapters.

Two million students have become stronger and more confident writers with Susan Fawcett's *Grassroots with Readings: The Writer's Workbook*

"…*Grassroots* is the single most effective text for this level of student on the current market."

> — Beverly Dile,
> Elizabethtown Community
> and Technical College

"The eye-catching, innovative, and user-friendly *Grassroots* textbook makes the writing task less daunting for developing writers."

> — Jennifer Bubb,
> Illinois Valley Community College

NEW! Focus on Academic Skills

Grassroots, 11e, features unprecedented writing coverage, with two new writing chapters; 23 new models written by students and professionals; expanded critical-thinking coverage throughout; 70 new practices to hone students' academic skills; and a stronger Unit 9, Reading Selections, with eight new readings that explore ideas and current issues.

Get Students Up to Speed Quickly with College-Level Writing Coverage

Greatly expanded writing instruction prepares your students for academic success.

Two new chapters 5 and 6, "Thinking Through Paragraph Patterns, 1 and 2," guide students step by step through the nine most common paragraph patterns in academic and workplace writing.

With her trademark clarity and creativity, Fawcett provides for each pattern two model paragraphs (one student and one professional), engaging paced practices, a collaborative critical-thinking or viewing task, and a graphic organizer to help students write their paragraphs.

Instructors can easily tailor this material to their course, assigning only the patterns they wish to cover.

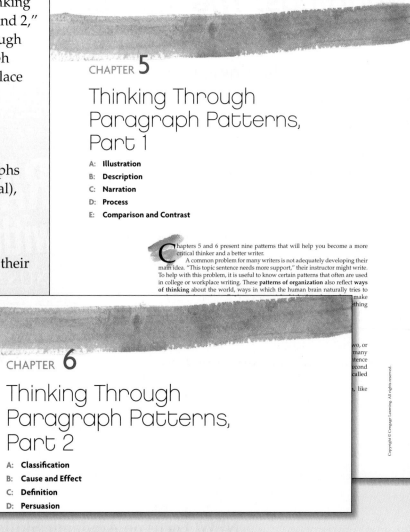

CHAPTER **5**

Thinking Through Paragraph Patterns, Part 1

A: **Illustration**
B: **Description**
C: **Narration**
D: **Process**
E: **Comparison and Contrast**

Chapters 5 and 6 present nine patterns that will help you become a more critical thinker and a better writer.
A common problem for many writers is not adequately developing their main idea. "This topic sentence needs more support," their instructor might write. To help with this problem, it is useful to know certain patterns that often are used in college or workplace writing. These **patterns of organization** also reflect **ways of thinking** about the world, ways in which the human brain naturally tries to make ... thing

CHAPTER **6**

Thinking Through Paragraph Patterns, Part 2

A: **Classification**
B: **Cause and Effect**
C: **Definition**
D: **Persuasion**

"These are excellent chapters that I will definitely utilize in my courses. Kudos to Susan Fawcett."

— Cindy Pierce, Northwest Community College

"I really like the approach and the style of the explanations . . . The setup of the book is a model in how to read and write effectively."

— Spencer Green, Penn State Harrisburg

Get Students Up to Speed Quickly with College-Level Writing Coverage

Students learn more with step-by-step instruction and practice for every writing pattern.

PRACTICE 4 — Teamwork: Critical Viewing and Writing

Sometimes a writer notices specific examples first, sees a pattern, and then comes up with a generalization. In your group, discuss the three examples pictured and then craft your generalization into a topic sentence that includes all three.

Writing an Illustration Paragraph

Pick a topic from the list below or one that your instructor assigns. Draft a topic sentence that you can support well with examples. Now prewrite to get as many examples as possible and think critically as you pick the best three or four. Many students find it helpful to use a graphic organizer as they plan their paragraph. In your notebook, draw an organizer like the one below and fill it in as you think, or use the illustration organizer on the *Grassroots* website.

- offensive "reality" television shows
- best places to study on campus
- people you most admire
- traditions typical of one culture or area
- people whose attitude is their worst
- what not to wear for a job interview
- mistakes first-year college students make
- ads that use humor effectively
- ways to handle difficult customers
- best apps for a student (or sports or

ILLUSTRATION PARAGRAPH ORGANIZER

Topic Sentence	In box 1, write a topic sentence that clearly states your topic and point of view.
Example 1	In box 2, write your first example. Brainstorm details and specifics to explain this example
Example 2	In box 3, write your second example. Brainstorm details and specifics to explain this example.
Example 3	In box 4, present your third example. Brainstorm details and specifics to explain this example.
Conclusion	

PRACTICE 1 — Read this student's paragraph and answer the questions.

As a proud Californian, I separate glass, plastic, and paper and do what I can for the environment. Even if, like me, you rent and don't own a home, you can take simple actions that will help the earth and save money. For example, replace all your incandescent lightbulbs with compact fluorescents (CFLs). CFLs use 75 percent less electricity, last ten times longer, and save money. Another way to make a difference is water use. Homeowners might install low-flow toilets, but renters can save water with a simple trick. Fill a one-liter plastic bottle with water and put it in the toilet tank. The bottle will displace enough water to save almost a gallon a flush—around ten gallons a day. Next, if you're handy, install a water filter on the kitchen faucet. By refilling stainless-steel bottles instead of buying plastic, a family of four can save $1000 a year and keep 600 plastic bottles out of landfills. Finally, even if your landlord won't weather strip those old windows, it is worth $50 or so to do it yourself. You will save a fortune in winter heating bills. Actions like these take a couple hours on a weekend, but the benefits last much longer.

James Lam, Student

1. Underline the topic sentence of this paragraph. Hint: It is not the first sentence.

2. How many examples of renters' actions are discussed?
   four

3. What transitional expressions does Mr. Lam use?
   For example, Another way, Next, Finally

"Susan's textbooks stand out from the rest because she gets that students can be intelligent and insightful even if they still need instruction in subject/verb agreement "

— Dr. Karen Cox, San Francisco City College

"I like the group exercises and the step-by-step method of developing the paragraphs."

— Anne Smith, Northwest Mississippi Community College

Help Students Develop Vital Critical-Thinking Skills

Superior critical-thinking exercises help students meet college and career challenges.

Author Susan Fawcett expands her much-praised critical thinking and viewing program. Based on her research into how to increase comprehension with dual verbal and visual coding, these activities reinforce writing lessons with verbal group tasks or "images worth looking at."

- 11 new Teamwork: Critical Thinking and Writing activities
- 10 new Teamwork: Critical Viewing and Writing activities
- Many visual images with critical-thinking captions

Shoe designer D'Wayne Edwards at the launch of his Air Jordan XX2

PRACTICE 4   **Teamwork: Critical Thinking and Writing**

In a group with four or five classmates, discuss the personal qualities or actions that helped D'Wayne Edwards get his first design job and, later, many promotions. Are there any lessons you can learn for yourself from the story of Edwards's career? Take notes for a composition.

EXPLORING ONLINE

TEACHING TIP
Instructor tools for *Grassroots* include a computerized Test Bank, PowerPoint slides, an Instructor's Resource Manual with teaching tips, and more, and can be accessed at ‹login .cengage.com›.

<http://grammar.ccc.commnet.edu/grammar/cgi-shl/quiz.pl/spelling_add1.htm>
Interactive quiz: Choose the correctly spelled words.

<http://grammar.ccc.commnet.edu/grammar/cgi-shl/quiz.pl/lie_lay_quiz.htm>
Interactive quiz: Practice *lie/lay*, *sit/set*.

<http://a4esl.org/q/h/homonyms.html> Practice sound-alikes, like *night/knight*, that may confuse ESL students. Pick easy, medium, or difficult, and test yourself.

- 70 new idea-based practices engage students in current topics like the signs of video game addiction, concussions and the fate of football, the effects of music on learning, futurists' predictions for 2050, negative effects on children of too much screen time, Roadtrip Nation as a career resource, growth careers, experiences of awe in child development, sexy news anchors, and plastic pollution in our oceans.
- Exploring Online sites showing students how to research help and information

"Generally, the practices are more oriented toward critical thinking than usual in textbooks at the developmental level. That is a MAJOR good thing."

— Craig Bartholomaus, Metropolitan Community College

Challenge Your Students with Issues-Based Reading Selections by Top Contemporary Authors

Eight new expository and persuasive articles and essays engage students and explore current ideas and issues.

Grassroots' diverse and provocative array of 20 quality essays now places more emphasis on third-person writing, not personal narrative, to better prepare students for academic work.

NEW to this 11th Edition: John Quiñones on everyday moral heroes, Scott Smith challenging students to a day without media, Leonard Pitts on why people still text and drive, Amy Chua's controversial views on parenting, MP Dunleavy on why we keep buying "stuff," Martin Lindstrom on freshness as a sales gimmick, Melissa Seligman's discovery that letters, not Skype, could save a military marriage, and Susan Cain's surprising research on introverts.

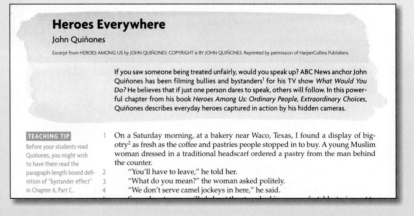

A Day without Media: Heaven or Hell?
Scott Smith

Smith, Scott "An entire day without media: Heaven or hell?" Copyright © The Pueblo Chieftain, Colo. Adapted by permission of the author.

Could you survive 24 hours with no media at all? At the University of Maryland, 200 horrified college students were given this challenge. Newsman Scott Smith of the *Pueblo Chieftain* in Colorado reports in this article on the Maryland challenge, the results, and what our dependency on social media might mean about how we live and how we relate to each another.

1 Imagine a media-free day. No computer. No television. No cell phone. No car radio. No iPod. No newspapers or magazines. No texting. No Facebook. No e-mails. No instant messaging. No tweeting. Nada. Could you do it? Could you spend an entire day pondering your own thoughts, creating your own diversions[1] and interacting only with real people, face to face?

2 That was the recent challenge posed by the International Center for Media and the Public Agenda, which asked 200 journalism students at the University of Maryland to abstain[2] from using all media for 24 hours. After their unplugged day, the students blogged about their experiences, and the center compiled the results. The findings: No surprise. Most college students are flat-out hooked on their social-media security blankets. Wrote one student: "I clearly am addicted, and the dependency is sickening."

1. diversions: distractions, entertainments
2. abstain: *not* do something

Heroes Everywhere

John Quiñones

Excerpt from HEROES AMONG US by JOHN QUIÑONES. COPYRIGHT © BY JOHN QUIÑONES. Reprinted by permission of HarperCollins Publishers.

If you saw someone being treated unfairly, would you speak up? ABC News anchor John Quiñones has been filming bullies and bystanders[1] for his TV show *What Would You Do?* He believes that if just one person dares to speak, others will follow. In this powerful chapter from his book *Heroes Among Us: Ordinary People, Extraordinary Choices,* Quiñones describes everyday heroes captured in action by his hidden cameras.

TEACHING TIP
Before your students read Quiñones, you might wish to have them read the paragraph-length boxed definition of "bystander effect" in Chapter 6, Part C.

1 On a Saturday morning, at a bakery near Waco, Texas, I found a display of bigotry[2] as fresh as the coffee and pastries people stopped in to buy. A young Muslim woman dressed in a traditional headscarf ordered a pastry from the man behind the counter.

2 "You'll have to leave," he told her.

3 "What do you mean?" the woman asked politely.

4 "We don't serve camel jockeys in here," he said.

"[One of the outstanding features of *Grassroots* is] the strength and quality of the readings."

— Spencer Green, Penn State Harrisburg

Bolster Academic Success with Reading, Writing, and Thinking Activities that Students Enjoy

New and enhanced instruction, practices, and assignments challenge students to think through college tasks.

- Clear, step-by-step lessons based on Fawcett's inductive MAP (model-analysis-practice) strategy for student learning.

- Spotlights on Reading and Writing launch each unit with a professional paragraph.

- Collaborative Writers' Workshops conclude units with guided peer-review and revision.

- Many more continuous-discourse practices model third-person prose while engaging students in much-needed grammar and writing review.

- Many new student and professional models throughout the text show students how it's done.

- Eight new readings by eminent writers inspire analysis of ideas and issues.

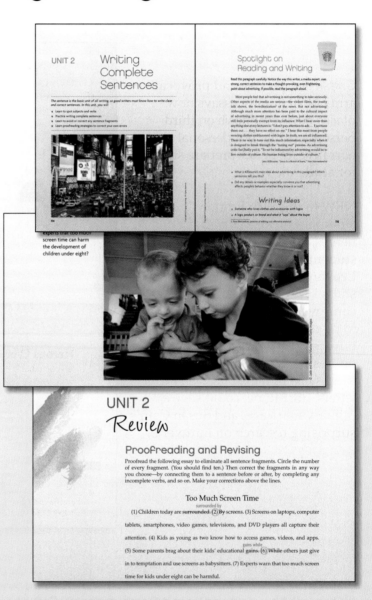

"**The emphasis on writing and critical thinking is a plus.**"

– Christopher Morelock, Walters State Community College

Student Resources

aplia™

Aplia for *Grassroots* is an online learning solution that helps your students become stronger writers. Aplia's clear, succinct, and engaging instruction and practice help students build the confidence they need to master basic writing and grammar skills with ongoing individualized practice, access to an electronic version of *Grassroots* and terminology and concepts that match the textbook, high-interest examples that demonstrate the principles of writing, and thought-provoking multimedia content that engages students in the writing process. Learn more by visiting *www.aplia. com/developmentalenglish*.

Instructor Resources

 MindTap™

MindTap is a customizable, total course solution that supports your instruction and makes coursework more effective, affordable, and easily accessible for students. It combines myriad learning tools—readings, multimedia, activities and assessments—into one easy-to-use platform that guides students through the curriculum with a fully customizable learning path based on the book's Table of Contents. MindTap for *Grassroots* includes unit overview videos; grammar videos; and the full text of all chapters, with interactive versions of the practice exercises that may be completed on-screen. Results are reported to the Progress Tracker, which informs students and instructors of their progress and targets areas for improvement. Find out more at *www.cengage.com/ mindtap*.

Annotated Instructor's Edition

The **Annotated Instructor's Edition** includes answers to every practice in the text. In addition, margin annotations provide Teaching Tips with teaching suggestions for specific text sections or practice exercises, new Learning Styles Tips with suggestions for reaching students with particular learning styles, and ESL Tips with suggestions for teaching English Language Learners.

Instructor Companion Site

Visit login.cengage.com to access the **Instructor's Manual and Test Bank**, online testing management tool Cognero, Creative Classroom Links, customizable rubrics for every paragraph and essay type, and chapter-specific PowerPoint slides for classroom use.

Revised Instructor's Manual and Test Bank

The Instructor's Manual and Test Bank offer suggestions for the new instructor looking for support or the more experienced teacher looking for ideas. Instructional ideas, assignments, and ways to use the book's features are based on the author's many years of classroom teaching experience. Notes on each chapter, unit, and reading provide an overview of concepts and skills addressed, plus specific teaching suggestions. A revised and reorganized Test Bank with diagnostic and mastery tests, chapter tests, and unit tests offers instructors ample supplementary assessments to provide additional practice or monitor students' progress. With Cengage Learning Testing Powered by Cognero, tests can also be created, edited, and managed online.

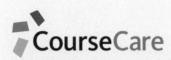

CourseCare connects you with people. Available exclusively through Cengage Learning, CourseCare is a revolutionary program designed to provide you with exceptional services and support to integrate Aplia and other online resources into your course, including a conversion program that maps Aplia content to your syllabus. CourseCare provides you with one-on-one service every step of the way—from finding the right solution for your course to training to ongoing support. Visit *www.cengage.com/coursecare*.

Our **TeamUP** program provides a range of services to help you implement new ideas and learning tools into your courses. To connect with your TeamUP Faculty Programs Consultant, call 1-800-528-8323 or visit *www.cengage.com/teamup*.

Grassroots with Readings:
The Writer's Workbook

Eleventh Edition

Annotated Instructor's Edition

Grassroots
with Readings
The Writer's Workbook
ELEVENTH EDITION

Annotated Instructor's Edition

Susan Fawcett

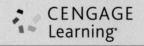

CENGAGE
Learning·

Australia • Brazil • Mexico • Singapore • United Kingdom • United States

CENGAGE Learning·

Grassroots with Readings: The Writer's Workbook, Eleventh Edition

Susan Fawcett

Product Director: Annie Todd

Senior Content Developer: Leslie Taggart

Development Editor: Laurie Dobson

Associate Content Developer: Elizabeth Rice

Product Assistant: Luria Rittenberg

Marketing Brand Manager: Lydia LeStar

Senior Content Project Manager: Aimee Chevrette Bear

Art Director: Faith Brosnan

Manufacturing Planner: Betsy Donaghey

Rights Acquisition Specialist: Ann Hoffman

Production Service: Lachina Publishing Services

Cover Designer: LMA/Leonard Massiglia

Cover Image: © Radius Images/CORBIS

Compositor: Lachina Publishing Services

For product information and technology assistance, contact us at **Cengage Learning Customer & Sales Support, 1-800-354-9706**

For permission to use material from this text or product, submit all requests online at **www.cengage.com/permissions**. Further permissions questions can be emailed to **permissionrequest@cengage.com**.

Library of Congress Control Number:

ISBN-13: 978-1-285-43077-5

ISBN-10: 1-285-43077-8

Annotated Instructor's Edition:

ISBN-13: 978-1-285-45159-6

ISBN-10: 1-285-45159-7

Cengage Learning
200 First Stamford Place, 4th Floor
Stamford, CT 06902
USA

Cengage Learning is a leading provider of customized learning solutions with office locations around the globe, including Singapore, the United Kingdom, Australia, Mexico, Brazil and Japan. Locate your local office at **international.cengage.com/region**.

Cengage Learning products are represented in Canada by Nelson Education, Ltd.

For your course and learning solutions, visit **www.cengage.com**.

Purchase any of our products at your local college store or at our preferred online store **www.cengagebrain.com**.

Instructors: Please visit **login.cengage.com** and log in to access instructor-specific resources.

Printed in the United States of America
1 2 3 4 5 6 7 17 16 15 14 13

Brief Contents

Contents

UNIT 1   Writing Effective Paragraphs   2

Spotlight on Reading and Writing: Alice Walker   3

UNIT 2   Writing Complete Sentences 114

Spotlight on Reading and Writing: Jean Kilbourne 115

UNIT 3   Using Verbs Effectively 146

Spotlight on Reading and Writing: Darcy Frey 147

UNIT 4 Joining Ideas Together 222

Spotlight on Reading and Writing: Brent Staples 223

UNIT 5 Choosing the Right Noun, Pronoun, Adjective, Adverb, or Preposition   278

Spotlight on Reading and Writing: David G. Myers and Ed Diener   279

24 Adjectives and Adverbs   308

25 Prepositions   321

UNIT 6   Revising for Consistency and Parallelism   336

Spotlight on Reading and Writing: Julia Alvarez   337

26 Consistent Tense   338

27 Consistent Person   343

28 Parallelism   347

UNIT 9 Reading Selections and Quotation Bank 436

Reading Strategies for the Writer 437

Preface

L
ike many college professors these days, I have been pondering the recent seismic shifts in higher education and the increased demands on our students to master higher level material, often within an accelerated time frame. Colleges and states are reconfiguring courses in an effort to prepare students for college within stringent budgets. Although *Grassroots with Readings* has remained the top-selling first-level developmental writing text in the United States, winning juried awards for excellence, I knew that this eleventh edition needed be the most significant revision I have ever done.

To ensure that this new edition would best serve the changing needs of students and instructors, my publisher and I solicited more in-depth commentary than ever before from faculty across the country. The consistency of comments was striking. Specifically, professors wanted much more writing instruction to expose developmental students to more expository and persuasive writing and less personal narrative. Likewise, they wanted their students to handle more academically challenging reading selections and third-person passages on current issues and ideas. These instructors praised *Grassroots'* innovative critical-thinking program but asked me to expand it even further. And to make room for this enriched coverage, they welcomed judicious streamlining of selected grammar chapters.

These thoughtful comments inspired the major changes in this edition, all geared to preparing students for more rigorous academic challenges while maintaining the user-friendly, innovative approach that has helped so many *Grassroots* students learn.

WHY I WROTE *GRASSROOTS*

Grassroots with Readings grew out of my experience teaching and directing the writing lab at Bronx Community College of the City University of New York. Existing texts labeled correct forms, the way handbooks do, but failed to teach my underprepared students how to write correctly. *Grassroots* is designed for a range of students—native and non-native speakers, diverse in age, ethnicity, and background—who have not yet mastered the basic writing skills so crucial for success in college and most careers. The hallmarks of *Grassroots'* successful pedagogy are its clear, inductive lessons in writing and grammar; its modular organization; inspiring student and professional models; numerous engaging practices and writing assignments; top-quality reading selections; and ESL coverage that is seamlessly integrated throughout the text.

IMPORTANT NEW FEATURES TO ADDRESS CHANGING COURSE NEEDS

New! Greatly expanded writing instruction, with two new chapters on writing patterns

New Chapters 5 and 6 teach nine common writing patterns—illustration, description, narration, process, comparison and contrast in Chapter 5, and classification, cause and effect, definition, and persuasion in Chapter 6. Each pattern includes two model paragraphs (one student and one professional), engaging practice exercises, writing prompts, a visual image for analysis, and a graphic organizer. Because each section is a self-contained module, the instructor can assign only those patterns relevant to the course. In addition, a new essay model enriches Chapter 7, Moving from Paragraph to Essay, and throughout the text, more well-crafted paragraphs, essays, and practices inspire students and model various techniques. Two of eight unit openers—Spotlights on Reading and Writing that feature professional paragraphs—are new to this edition, and all are enhanced with visual images.

New! More critical-thinking coverage to bolster academic skills

Grassroots' unique critical-thinking program engages students and hones their ability to think through verbal and visual material. This edition features 11 new collaborative *Teamwork: Critical Thinking and Writing* activities, 10 new *Teamwork: Critical Viewing and Writing* activities, and many more visuals with critical-thinking captions. These tasks reflect recent research on dual brain coding as a tool to enhance comprehension and connect instruction or provocative practice topics with "visual images worth looking at."

New! 70 practice exercises to build students' academic skills

Grassroots' superior high-interest practices set it apart from competitors. Not only does *Grassroots* have more practice exercises than any other text, but many more engaging paragraph- and essay-length practices on absorbing topics that are relevant to students' lives, education, or cultural literacy. Engagement with the text leads to persistence, and persistence is key to success in basic writing courses. Fresh subjects chosen to make students *want* to keep reading include:

the signs of video game addiction ● futurists' predictions for 2050 ● concussions and the fate of football ● child beauty pageants ● Roadtrip Nation as a career resource ● the effects on children of too much screen time ● how to confront your fears ● antibiotic resistance ● sexy news anchors ● star shoe designer and mentor D'Wayne Edwards ● growth careers ● driverless cars on highways now ● experiences of awe in child development ● girls' education advocate Malala Yousufzai ● netiquette in Korean schools ● the effects of music on learning

New! 8 expository and persuasive reading selections

Grassroots' diverse and powerful array of 20 essays by top authors now includes eight fresh selections focused on contemporary issues and sure to spark discussion: John Quiñones on everyday moral heroes, Scott Smith challenging students to a day without media, Leonard Pitts on why people still text and drive, Amy Chua's controversial views on parenting, MP Dunleavy on why we keep buying stuff, Martin Lindstrom on freshness as a sales gimmick, Melissa Seligman's discovery that letters, not a webcam, could save a military marriage, and Susan Cain's surprising research on introverts. Instructor and student favorites from the last edition have been retained to round out this thought-provoking collection.

Expanded! Visual program with 120 high-quality visual images

The rich visual-image program that students so enjoy has been expanded to more than 120 photographs, advertisements, paintings, graphs, and cartoons—64 of them new to this edition. Reflecting the author's belief that developmental students deserve exposure to the highest quality visual images as well as written models and readings, all visuals are tied to and augment the instruction at hand.

Highlighted! Flexible, modular organization

The modular organization of *Grassroots with Readings* allows instructors or departments to tailor the book to nearly any course design or approach. Fawcett's inductive MAP method (Model, Analysis, Practice) helps students learn quickly. Each chapter and part is a self-contained lesson, so instructors may teach these modules in any sequence. For example, many instructors weave together each week, according to the needs of the class, some writing instruction, a grammar lesson, and a reading, perhaps a long selection from Unit 9 and/or shorter ones from the writing or grammar chapters. This flexibility makes *Grassroots* adaptable to almost any teaching and learning situation: classroom, laboratory, or self-teaching.

Improved! Other improvements in this edition

Several long grammar chapters have been streamlined to facilitate accelerated coverage of the material, including Present Tense, Past Participle in Action, Pronouns, and Look-Alikes/Sound-Alikes. At the request of faculty, many sentence exercises were replaced by continuous-discourse practices exploring one topic. *Grassroots* is unique in including vetted URLs that teach students to search out additional help or do basic research; many such Exploring Online features were added. Finally, to support adjuncts or inspire seasoned instructors with fresh ideas, the author has written many new Teaching Tips for the Instructor's Annotated Edition of *Grassroots*.

THE BEST OF *GRASSROOTS*

Grassroots with Readings, Eleventh Edition, retains the features that have made it the most popular first-level developmental writing text in the country:

- Clear, step-by-step lessons based on Fawcett's MAP (Model, Analysis, Practice) strategy for student learning

- 383 thought-provoking practices that keep students involved

- Thought-provoking activities, assignments, and reading selections

- Strong unit openers, Spotlights on Reading and Writing, showcasing a professional paragraph

- Strong unit closers, Writers' Workshops, featuring student writing for guided peer review and writing

- Modular organization and flexible flow of chapters

- Dynamic, clear design that supports basic readers and writers

- Hundreds of quality photos, paintings, cartoons, and graphics

- Critical thinking and viewing opportunities throughout the text

- Integrated ESL coverage, with typical problems anticipated in the text

- "Exploring Online" web links for mini-research and self-initiated practice

- Instructor's Annotated Edition with answers and the author's "Teaching Tips" and "ESL Tips" to guide a new instructor or adjunct and inspire even seasoned instructors

- Student answer key for faculty who want students to self-check

- Extensive, updated Test Bank, web and computer resources

Ebook and Comprehensive Support

This text is also available as an **interactive eBook**, available with the print text, on its own, with Aplia, or with MindTap. These options offer you and your students online homework, automatic grading solutions, and more.

- **aplia** **Aplia for** *Grassroots* is an online learning solution that helps your students become stronger writers. Aplia's clear, succinct, and engaging instruction and practice help students build the confidence they need to master basic writing and grammar skills with ongoing individualized practice, access to an electronic version of *Grassroots* and terminology and concepts that match the textbook, high-interest examples that demonstrate the principles of writing, and engaging multimedia content that engages students in the writing process. Learn more by visiting *www.aplia.com/developmentalenglish*.

- **MindTap** **MindTap** is a customizable, total course solution that supports your instruction and makes coursework more effective, affordable, and easily accessible for students. It combines myriad learning tools—readings, multimedia, activities and assessments—into one easy-to-use platform that guides students through the curriculum with a fully customizable learning path based on the book's Table of Contents. MindTap for *Grassroots* includes unit overview videos; grammar videos; and the full text of all chapters, with interactive versions of the practice exercises that may be completed on-screen. Results are reported to the Progress Tracker, which informs students and instructors of their progress and targets areas for improvement. Find out more at *www.cengage.com/mindtap*.

- **Annotated Instructor's Edition.** The Annotated Instructor's Edition includes answers to every practice in the text. In addition, marginal Teaching Tips provide teaching suggestions for specific text sections or practice exercises, new Learning Styles Tips with suggestions for reaching students with particular learning styles, and ESL Tips with suggestions for teaching English Language Learners.

- **Instructor Companion Site.** Visit login.cengage.com to access the Instructor's Manual and Test Bank, online testing management tool Cognero, Creative Classroom Links, customizable rubrics for every paragraph and essay type, and chapter-specific PowerPoint slides for classroom use.

- Updated **Instructor's Manual and Test Bank.** The Instructor's Manual and Test Bank offer suggestions for the new instructor looking for support or the more experienced teacher looking for ideas. Advice about instructional methods, assignments, and uses of the book's features are based on the author's many years of classroom teaching experience. Notes on the book's units provide an overview of concepts and skills addressed in each chapter along with some specific teaching suggestions. A robust and revised Test Bank including diagnostic and mastery tests, chapter tests, and unit tests offers instructors a wide array of supplementary assessments that can be used as additional practice or a way to monitor students' progress. With Cengage Learning Testing Powered by Cognero, tests can also be created, edited, and managed online.

ACKNOWLEDGMENTS

The author wishes to thank these astute reviewers and colleagues. Their thoughtful comments and suggestions in both written reviews and focus group interviews helped strengthen this eleventh edition:

Nelly Aguilar, *Westwood College*

Craig Bartholomaus, *Metropolitan Community College-Penn Valley*

Lynette Bowen, *South Plains College*

Ashlee Brand, *Cuyahoga Community College*

Jennifer Bubb, *Illinois Valley Community College*

Ethan Saul Bull, *Portland Community College*

Jennifer Felts Call, *Cape Fear Community College*

Julie A. S. Cassidy, *City University of New York*

Laura Caudill, *Sullivan University*

Dale Davis, *Northwest Mississippi Community College*

Kelly L. Dedmon, *Isothermal Community College*

Beverly Dile, *Elizabethtown Community and Technical College*

Patricia Dungan, *Austin Community College*

Deborah Paul Fuller, *Bunker Hill Community College*

Lilian Gamble, *Delgado Community College*

Robert B. Galin, *University of New Mexico at Gallup*

Phyllis E. Gowdy, *Tidewater Community College*

Spencer Green, *Penn State Harrisburg*

Curtis Harrell, *Northwest Arkansas Community College*

Gina Henderson, *Tallahassee Community College*

Lisa Jones, *Hillsborough Community College*

Lourdes Marx, *Palm Beach State College*

Sharon May, *Midlands Technical College*

Sara C. McCorkendale, *Westwood College*

Jennifer McCue, *Hodges University*

Rachel McDermott, *Palm Beach State College*

Zeba Mehdi, *Central Piedmont Community College*

Ronda Mehrer, *Black Hills State University*

Jack Miller, *Normandale Community College*

Christopher Morelock, *Walters State Community College*

Karen L. Newman, *University of Indianapolis*

Karen Owen-Bogan, *Central Carolina Community College*

Cindy Pierce, *Northwest Community College*

Kathleen Perryman, *Joliet Junior College*

Jessica G. Rabin, *Anne Arundel Community College*

Joan Reeves, *Northeast Alabama Community College*

Anne Smith, *Northwest Mississippi Community College*

Carrie Thompson, *Palm Beach State College*

Terri Walker Degenhardt, *Augusta Technical College*

Laurel S. Watt, *Inver Hills Community College*

Jeana West, *Murray State College*

Audrey A. Wick, *Blinn College*

Lisa Williams, *Kirkwood Community College*

I am indebted to the team at Cengage who helped make this the best revision of *Grassroots* yet despite many obstacles. My deep thanks to Annie Todd, Director of Developmental Studies, for her brains, creativity, and support of my work; to Laurie Dobson, Development Editor, who hung in with me day by day through a complex revision process, earning her place in our ultimate Happy Dance; Leslie Taggart, Senior Content Developer, who generously shared her thoughts on everything from our grand revision plan to individual reading and photo selections; Beth Rice, Associate Content Developer, who did her usual stellar job of tracking *Grassroots'* supplements and making sure they are as excellent as the text itself; Jeff Hahn for his truly amazing market research during this time of uncertainty and upheaval in higher education; and Aimee Bear, Content Product Manager, and Whitney Thompson, Lachina Publishing Services, who supervised the great new design and production of this book; Ann Hoffman, Rights Acquisition Specialist, for work above and beyond to secure permissions on time and maintain *Grassroots'* singular excellence; Priya Subbrayal, PreMediaGlobal Image Research Project Manager; Sunetra Mukundan, PreMediaGlobal Text Permissions Project Manager; Luria Rittenberg, Product Assistant, and Liz Kendall, Product Manager.

My special thanks to two people: first, Marcy Kagan, my photo researcher, design consultant, and sometime alter ego, whose artist's eye helped make an exceptional book even better and whose ethics and friendship I treasure. Deep gratitude as well to Dr. Karen Cox of San Francisco City College, my brilliant colleague and friend across the miles, who leapt in to help research topics, review ideas, and draft some of the record number of new practices that make this edition shine. Thanks also to Ann Marie Radaskiewicz, Dean of the Developmental Education Division at Western Piedmont Community College, who helped me find great reading selections, cut some grammar coverage, and update *Grassroots'* many supplements, whose usefulness and excellence owe a debt to Ann Marie. Finally, I am grateful to Emmy Smith Ready for taking time from her doctoral studies and new motherhood to make sure that *Grassroots* is as error-free as it is beautiful.

My love and profound gratitude to the friends who supported me during this tumultuous year—especially Maggie Smith, Elaine Unkeless, Laraine Flemming, Colleen Huff, and Trisha Nelson. I dedicate the 11th Edition to my beloved family: my husband and best friend, Professor Richard Donovan; my dear brother David Fawcett; and his partner, Edward Brown. The book's design is a tribute to our mother, the watercolorist Harriet Fawcett, who died in 2010. My deepest wish is that this book will achieve the goal of teaching and uplifting those students whose aspirations and determination to succeed are a force of nature.

Grassroots with Readings:
The Writer's Workbook

Eleventh Edition

UNIT 1

Writing Effective Paragraphs

The goal of Grassroots is to make you a better writer, and Unit 1 is key to your success. In this unit, you will

- Learn the importance of subject, audience, and purpose
- Learn the parts of a good paragraph
- Practice the paragraph-writing process
- Learn how to revise and improve your paragraphs
- Apply these skills to exam questions and short essays
- Learn proofreading strategies to find and correct your own errors

Spotlight on Reading and Writing

Here, writer Alice Walker recalls her mother's extraordinary talent. If possible, read the paragraph aloud.

My mother adorned with flowers whatever shabby house we were forced to live in, and not just your typical straggly country stand of zinnias, either. She planted ambitious gardens—and still does—with over fifty different varieties of plants that bloom profusely from early March until late November. Before she left home for the fields, she watered her flowers, chopped up the grass, and laid out new beds. When she returned from the fields, she might divide clumps of bulbs, dig a cold pit, uproot and replant roses, or prune branches from her taller bushes or trees—until night came and it was too dark to see.

Alice Walker, "In Search of Our Mothers' Gardens"

- Ms. Walker's well-written paragraph brings to life her mother's passion for flowers. Are any words and details especially vivid? Why do you think Walker's mother worked so hard on her gardening?

- Good writing can make us remember, see, feel, or think in certain ways. Unit 1 will guide you through the steps of writing well and give you tools to improve your writing.

Writing Ideas

- *An activity that you or someone close to you passionately enjoys*
- *Someone who inspires you with her or his ambition or creativity*

CHAPTER 1

Exploring the Writing Process

A: The Writing Process

B: Subject, Audience, and Purpose

C: Guidelines for Submitting Written Work

Did you know that the most successful students and employees are people who write well? In fact, many good jobs today require excellent writing and communication skills in fields as varied as computer technology, health sciences, education, and social services.

The goal of this book is to help you become a better and more confident writer. You will realize that the ability to write well is not a magical talent that some people possess and others don't but rather a life skill that can be learned. I invite you now to make a decision to excel in this course. It will be one of the best investments you could ever make in yourself, your education, and your future. Let *Grassroots* be your guide, and enjoy the journey.

A. The Writing Process

This chapter will give you an overview of the writing process, as well as some tips on how to approach your writing assignments in college. Many people have the mistaken idea that good writers just sit down and write a perfect paper or assignment from start to finish. In fact, experienced writers go through a **process** consisting of steps like these:

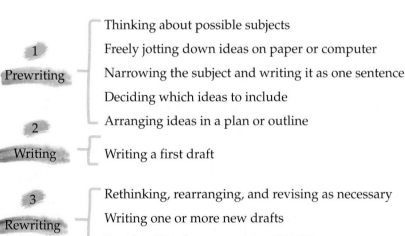

1 Prewriting
- Thinking about possible subjects
- Freely jotting down ideas on paper or computer
- Narrowing the subject and writing it as one sentence
- Deciding which ideas to include
- Arranging ideas in a plan or outline

2 Writing
- Writing a first draft

3 Rewriting
- Rethinking, rearranging, and revising as necessary
- Writing one or more new drafts
- Proofreading for grammar and spelling errors

Writing is a personal and often messy process. Writers don't all perform these steps in the same order, and they may have to go through some steps more than once. However, most writers **prewrite**, **write**, **rewrite**—and **proofread**.

It is important that you set aside enough time to complete every step in the writing process. A technique called **backwards planning** helps many students manage their writing time. Begin with the assignment's due date and plan to complete each step on a different day. Using the calendar below, one student first wrote down the Friday deadline for her paragraph assignment. Then, working backwards, she decided to proofread on Thursday and again Friday morning, to revise her paragraph on Wednesday, write her first draft on Tuesday, and start jotting and organizing her ideas on Monday.

SUNDAY	MONDAY	TUESDAY	WEDNESDAY	THURSDAY	FRIDAY	SATURDAY
1	2	3	4	5	6	7
	Jot down and organize ideas for paragraph.	*Write first draft of paragraph.*	*Revise paragraph.*	*Proofread.*	*Proofread again. Final draft due!*	

PRACTICE 1

Self-Assessment

Choose something that you wrote recently for a class or for work and think about the *process* you followed in writing it. With a group of three or four classmates, or in your notebook, answer these questions:

1. Did I do any planning or prewriting—or did I just start writing the assignment?
2. How much time did I spend improving and revising my work?
3. Was I able to spot and correct my own grammar and spelling errors?
4. What ideas or beliefs do I have about writing? (Examples: *In my field, I won't need to write,* or *English teachers make a bigger deal about errors than anyone else.*) Do any of my beliefs get in the way of my progress?
5. What one change in my writing process would most improve my writing? Spending more time for prewriting? Spending more time revising? Improving my proofreading skills?

TEACHING TIP

Encourage students to perform similar self-assessments each time they receive feedback on their writing and to use self- and instructor assessment to set personal goals in this course.

PRACTICE 2

Bring in several newspaper help-wanted sections. In a group with four or five classmates, study the ads in career fields that interest you. Next, count the number of ads that stress writing and communication skills. Alternatively, if you have Internet access, you could visit a job-search website like ‹**http://www.monster.com**› and perform the same exercise. Be prepared to present your findings to the class.

PRACTICE 3

Using a calendar, employ the *backwards planning technique* to plan the steps needed to complete your next writing assignment.

B. Subject, Audience, and Purpose

As you begin a writing assignment, give some thought to your **subject**, **audience**, and **purpose**.

When your instructor assigns a broad **subject**, try to focus on one aspect that interests you. For example, suppose the broad subject is *music*, and you play the conga drums. You might focus on why you play them rather than some other instrument or on what drumming means to you. Whenever possible, choose subjects you know and care about: observing your neighborhood come to life in the morning, riding a dirt bike, helping a child become more confident, learning more about your computer. Your answers to questions like those listed below will suggest promising writing ideas. Keep a list of the best ones.

To find or focus your subject, ask

- What special experience or knowledge do I have?

- What angers, saddens, or inspires me?

- What campus, job, or community problem do I have ideas about solving?

- What story in the news affected me recently?

How you approach your subject will depend on your **audience**, your readers. Are you writing for classmates, a professor, people who know about your subject, or people who do not? For instance, if you are writing about weight training, and your readers have never been inside a gym, you will approach your subject in a simple and basic way, perhaps stressing the benefits of weightlifting. An audience of bodybuilders, however, already knows these things; for bodybuilders, you would write in more depth, perhaps focusing on how to develop one muscle group.

To focus on your audience, ask

- For whom am I writing? Who will read this?

- Are they beginners or experts? How much do they know about the subject?

- Do I think they will agree or disagree with my ideas?

Finally, keeping your **purpose** in mind helps you know what to write. Do you want to *explain* something to your readers, *convince* them that a certain point of view is correct, *describe* something, or just *tell a good story*? If your purpose is to persuade parents to support having school uniforms, you can explain that uniforms lower clothing costs and may reduce student crime. However, if your purpose is to convince students that uniforms are a good idea, you might approach the subject differently, emphasizing how stylish the uniforms look or why students from other schools feel that uniforms improve their school atmosphere.

PRACTICE 4

List five subjects you might like to write about. Consider your audience and purpose. For whom are you writing? What do you want them to know about your subject? For ideas, reread the boxed questions.

	Subject	Audience	Purpose
EXAMPLE:	how to make a Greek salad	inexperienced cooks	to show how easy it is to make a great Greek salad

	Subject	Audience	Purpose
1.	_____	_____	_____
2.	_____	_____	_____
3.	_____	_____	_____
4.	_____	_____	_____
5.	_____	_____	_____

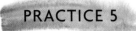

PRACTICE 5

With a group of three or four classmates, or on your own, jot down ideas for the following two writing tasks. Notice how your points and details differ depending on your audience and purpose. (If you are not employed, write about a job with which you are familiar.)

1. For a new co-worker, you plan to write a description of a typical day on your job. Your purpose is to help train this person, who will perform the same duties you do. Your supervisor will need to approve what you write.

2. For one of your closest friends, you plan to write a description of a typical day on your job. Your purpose is to make your friend laugh because he or she has been feeling down recently.

PRACTICE 6

Teamwork: Critical Viewing and Writing

Study the advertisement shown below and then answer these questions: What *subject* is the ad addressing? Who do you think is the target *audience*? What is the ad's intended *purpose*? In your view, how successful is the ad in achieving its purpose? Explain.

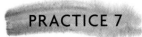

In a group with three or four classmates, read the following classified ads from real city newspapers around the country. The *subject* of each ad is a product or service that is for sale, the *audience* is the potential customer, and the *purpose* is to convince that customer to buy the product or service. How does each ad writer undercut his or her purpose? How would you revise each ad so that it better achieves its apparent purpose?

1. Do you need a dramatic new look? Visit our plastered surgeons.
2. We do not tear your clothing with machinery. We do it carefully by hand.
3. Now is your chance to have your ears pierced and get an extra pair to take home free.
4. Tired of cleaning yourself? Let me do it.
5. Auto repair service. Try us once, and you'll never go anywhere again.

What's wrong with this picture?

AP Photo/Post Register, Robert Bower

C. Guidelines for Submitting Written Work

Learn your instructor's requirements for submitting written work, as these may vary from class to class. Here are some general guidelines. Write in any special instructions.

1. Choose sturdy, white, 8½-by-11-inch paper, lined if you write by hand, plain if you use a computer.
2. Clearly write your name, the date, and any other required information, using the format requested by your instructor.
3. If you write by hand, do so neatly in black or dark blue ink.
4. Write on only one side of the paper.
5. Double-space if you write on a computer. Some instructors also want handwriting double-spaced.
6. Leave margins of at least one inch on all sides.
7. Number each page of your assignment, starting with page 2. Place the numbers at the top of each page, either centered or in the top right corner.

Other guidelines: _____

_____

_____

Chapter Highlights

Tips for Succeeding in this Course

- Remember that writing is a process: prewriting, writing, rewriting, and proofreading.
- Before you write, always be clear about your subject, audience, and purpose.
- Follow your instructor's guidelines for submitting written work.
- Practice.

EXPLORING ONLINE

TEACHING TIP

Instructor tools for *Grass-roots* include a computerized Test Bank, PowerPoint slides, an Instructor's Manual with teaching tips, and more, and can be accessed at ‹**login .cengage.com**›.

Throughout this text, the Exploring Online feature will suggest ways that you can use the Internet to improve your writing and grammar skills. You will find that if you need extra writing help, online writing centers (called OWLs) can be a great resource. Many provide extra review or practice in areas in which you might need assistance. You will want to do some searching to find the best sites for your needs, but here are two excellent OWL sites to explore:

‹http://owl.english.purdue.edu/› Purdue University.

‹http://grammar.ccc.commnet.edu/grammar/› Capital Community College.

CHAPTER 2

Prewriting to Generate Ideas

A: Freewriting

B: Brainstorming

C: Clustering

D: Keeping a Journal

The author of this book used to teach ice skating. On the first day of class, her students practiced falling. Once they knew how to fall without fear, they were free to learn to skate.

Writing is much like ice skating: the more you practice, the better you get. If you are free to make mistakes, you'll want to practice, and you'll look forward to new writing challenges.

The problem is that many people avoid writing. Faced with an English composition or a report at work, they put it off and then scribble something at the last minute. Other people sit staring at the blank page or computer screen—writing a sentence, crossing it out, unable to get started. In this chapter, you will learn four useful prewriting techniques that will help you jump-start your writing process and generate lots of ideas: **freewriting**, **brainstorming**, **clustering**, and **keeping a journal**.

A. Freewriting

Freewriting is a method many writers use to warm up and get ideas. Here are the guidelines: For five or ten full minutes, write without stopping. Don't worry about grammar or about writing complete sentences; just set a timer and go. If you get stuck, repeat or rhyme the last word you wrote, but keep writing nonstop until the timer sounds. Afterward, read what you have written, and underline any parts you like.

Freewriting is a wonderful way to let your ideas pour out without getting stuck by worrying too soon about correctness or "good writing." Sometimes freewriting produces nonsense, but often it provides interesting ideas for further thinking and writing. **Focused freewriting** can help you find subjects to write about.

Focused Freewriting

In *focused freewriting*, you try to focus your thoughts on one subject as you freewrite. The subject can be one assigned by your instructor, one you choose, or one you discover in unfocused freewriting.

Here is one student's focused freewriting on the topic *someone who strongly influenced me*:

Thin, thinner, weak, weaker. You stopped cooking for yourself—forced yourself to choke down cans of nutrition. Your chest caved in; your bones stuck out. You never asked, Why me? With a weak laugh you asked, Why not me? I had a wonderful life, a great job, a good marriage while it lasted. Have beautiful kids. Your wife divorced you—couldn't stand to watch you die, couldn't stand to have her life fall apart the way your body was falling apart. I watched you stumble, trip over your own feet, sink, fall down. I held you up. Now I wonder which one of us was holding the other one up. I saw you shiver in your summer jacket because you didn't have the strength to put on your heavy coat. Bought you a feather-light winter jacket, saw your eyes fill with tears of pleasure and gratitude. You said they would find you at the bottom of the stairs. When they called to tell me we'd lost you, the news wasn't unexpected, but the pain came in huge waves. Heart gave out, they said. Your daughter found you crumpled at the foot of the stairs. How did you know? What else did you guess?

Daniel Corteau, student

- This student later used his freewriting as the basis for an excellent paragraph.

- Underline any words or lines that you find especially striking or powerful. Be prepared to discuss your choices.

- How was the writer influenced by the man he describes?

PRACTICE 1

1. Set a timer for ten minutes, or have someone time you. Freewrite without stopping for the full ten minutes. Repeat or rhyme words if you get stuck, but keep writing! Don't let your pen or pencil leave the page or your fingers leave the keyboard.

2. When you finish, write down one or two words that describe how you feel while freewriting. _____

3. Now read your freewriting. Underline any words or lines you like—anything that strikes you as powerful, moving, funny, or important. If nothing strikes you, that's okay.

PRACTICE 2

Now choose one word or idea from your freewriting or from the following list. Focus your thoughts on it, and do a ten-minute focused freewriting. Try to stick to the topic, but don't worry too much about it. Just keep writing! When you finish, read and underline any striking lines or ideas.

1. home
2. a good student
3. the biggest lie
4. a dream
5. someone who influenced you
6. your experiences with writing
7. the smell of _____
8. strength

PRACTICE 3

Try two more focused freewritings at home, each one ten minutes long. Do them at different times of the day when you have a few quiet moments. If possible, use a timer: set it for ten minutes, and then write fast until it rings. Later, read your freewritings, and underline any ideas or passages you might like to write more about.

B. Brainstorming

Brainstorming means freely jotting down ideas about a topic on paper or on a computer. As in freewriting, the purpose of brainstorming is to get as many ideas down as possible so that you will have something to work with later. Just write down everything that comes to mind about a topic—words and phrases, ideas, details, examples, little stories. Once you have brainstormed, read over your list, underlining any ideas you might want to develop further.

Here is one student's brainstorming list on *an interesting job*:

chechele/iStock.com

> midtown messenger
>
> frustrating but free
>
> I know the city backward and forward
>
> good bike needed
>
> fast, ever-changing, dangerous
>
> drivers hate messengers—we dart in and out of traffic
>
> old clothes don't get respect
>
> I wear the best Descente racing gear, a Giro helmet
>
> people respect you more
>
> I got tipped $100 for carrying a crystal vase from the showroom to Wall Street in 15 minutes
>
> other times I get stiffed
>
> lessons I've learned—controlling my temper
>
> having dignity
>
> staying calm no matter what—insane drivers, deadlines, rudeness
>
> weirdly, I like my job

As he brainstormed, this writer produced many interesting facts and details about his job as a bicycle messenger, all in just a few minutes. He might want to underline the ideas that most interest him—perhaps the time he was tipped $100—and then brainstorm again for more details.

PRACTICE 4

Choose one of the following topics that interests you, and write it at the top of your page. Then brainstorm! Write anything that comes into your head about the topic. Let your ideas flow.

1. a singer or a musician
2. the future
3. an intriguing job
4. a story in the news
5. the best/worst class I've ever had
6. making a difference
7. a place to which I never want to return
8. a community problem

After you fill a page with your list, read it over, underlining the most interesting ideas. Draw arrows to connect related ideas. Do you find one idea that might be the subject of a paper?

C. Clustering

Some writers find *clustering* or mapping an effective way to get ideas onto paper. To begin clustering, write one idea or topic—usually one word—in the center of your paper. Then let your mind make associations, and write those ideas down, branching out from the center. When one idea suggests other ideas, details, or examples, jot down those around it in a cluster, like this:

Once this student filled a page with clustered ideas about the word *sports*, his next step was choosing the cluster that most interested him and writing further. He might even have wanted to freewrite for more ideas.

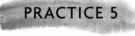

PRACTICE 5

Read over the clustering map above. If you were giving advice to the writer, which cluster or branch do you think would make the most interesting paper? Why?

PRACTICE 6

Choose one of these topics or another topic that interests you. Write it in the center of a piece of paper and then try clustering. Keep writing down associations until you have filled the page.

1. movies
2. a pet
3. a lesson
4. sports

5. my hometown
6. self-esteem
7. a relative
8. someone I don't understand

D. Keeping a Journal

Keeping a journal is an excellent way to practice your writing skills and to discover ideas for future writing. Most of all, your journal is a place to record your private thoughts and important experiences. Open a journal file on your computer, or get yourself a special book with 8½-by-11-inch lined paper. Every night, or several times a week, write for at least ten minutes in your journal.

What you write about will be limited only by your imagination. Here are some ideas:

TEACHING TIP

Ask students who are already in the habit of keeping a journal to share with the class the benefits of journaling.

- Write in detail about things that matter to you—family relationships, falling in (or out of) love, an experience at school or work, something important you just learned, something you did well.

- List your personal goals, and brainstorm possible steps toward achieving them.

- Write about problems you are having, and "think on paper" about ways to solve them.

- Comment on classroom instruction or assignments, and evaluate your learning progress. What needs work? What questions do you need to ask? Write out a study plan for yourself and refer to it regularly.

- Write down your responses to your reading—class assignments, newspaper items, magazine articles, websites that impress or anger you.

- Read through the quotations at the end of this book until you find one that strikes you. Then copy it into your journal, think about it, and write. For example, Agnes Repplier says, "It is not easy to find happiness in ourselves, and it is not possible to find it elsewhere." Do you agree with her?

TEACHING TIP

Explain to students that although they may prefer one prewriting technique, they should try using several techniques if they need to generate more ideas about a topic.

- Be alert to interesting writing topics all around you. If possible, carry a notebook during the day for "fast sketches." Jot down moving or funny moments, people, or things that catch your attention—an overworked waitress in a restaurant, a scene at the day-care center where you leave your child, a man trying to persuade an officer not to give him a parking ticket.

You will soon find that ideas for writing will occur to you all day long. Before they slip away, capture them in words. Writing is like ice skating. You have to practice.

PRACTICE 7

Write in your journal for at least ten minutes three times a week.

At the end of each week, read what you have written. Underline striking passages, and mark interesting topics and ideas that you would like to explore further.

As you complete the exercises in this book and work on the writing assignments, try all four techniques—freewriting, brainstorming, clustering, and keeping a journal—and see which ones work best for you.

PRACTICE 8

From your journal, choose one or two passages that you might want to rewrite and allow others to read. Put a check beside each of those passages or mark them with sticky notes so that you can find them easily later. Underline the parts you like best. Can you already see ways you might rewrite and improve the writing?

Chapter Highlights

To get started and to discover your ideas, try these techniques.

- Focused freewriting: freewriting for five or ten minutes about one topic

- Brainstorming: freely jotting down many ideas about a topic

- Clustering: making word associations on paper

- Keeping a journal: writing regularly about things that interest and move you

EXPLORING ONLINE

<http://owl.english.purdue.edu/owl/resource/673/1/> If you still feel stuck when you start to write, try these techniques from Purdue University's famous OWL (Online Writing Lab).

<http://www.gallaudet.edu/TIP/English_Works/Writing/Pre-Writing_Writing_ and_Revising/Prewriting_Strategies.html> Look at numbers 2 and 3 for ways to graph your ideas visually, to see if these strategies might help you.

CHAPTER 3

Developing Effective Paragraphs

A: Defining the Paragraph and the Topic Sentence

B: Narrowing the Topic and Writing the Topic Sentence

C: Generating Ideas for the Body of the Paragraph

D: Selecting and Dropping Ideas

E: Arranging Ideas in a Plan or an Outline

F: Writing and Revising the Paragraph

G: Proofreading and Writing the Final Draft

The paragraph is the basic unit of writing. This chapter will guide you through the process of writing paragraphs.

A. Defining the Paragraph and the Topic Sentence

A *paragraph* is a group of related sentences that develop one main idea. Although a paragraph has no definite length, it is often four to twelve sentences long. A paragraph usually appears with other paragraphs in a longer piece of writing—an essay, a letter, or an article, for example.

A paragraph looks like this on the page:

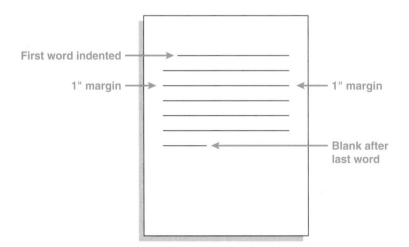

First word indented

1" margin — 1" margin

Blank after last word

- Clearly **indent** the first word of every paragraph about 1 inch (or one tab on the computer).

- Extend every line of a paragraph as close to the right-hand margin as possible.

- If the last word of the paragraph comes before the end of the line, however, leave the rest of the line blank.

Topic Sentence and Body

Most paragraphs contain one main idea to which all the sentences relate. The **topic sentence** states this main idea. The **body** of the paragraph supports this main idea with specific details, facts, and examples.

> When I was growing up, my older brother Joe was the greatest person in my world. If anyone teased me about my braces or buckteeth, he fiercely defended me. When one boy insisted on calling me "Fang," Joe threatened to knock his teeth out. It worked—no more teasing. My brother always chose me to play on his baseball teams though I was a terrible hitter. Even after he got his driver's license, he didn't abandon me. Instead, every Sunday, the two of us went for a drive. We might stop for cheeseburgers, go to a computer showroom, drive past some girl's house, or just laugh and talk. It was one of childhood's mysteries that such a wonderful brother loved me.
>
> *Jeremiah Woolrich, student*

- The first sentence of this paragraph is the *topic sentence*. It states in a general way the main idea of the paragraph: that *Joe was the greatest person in my world*. Although the topic sentence can appear anywhere in the paragraph, it is often the first sentence.

- The rest of the paragraph, the *body*, fully explains this statement with details about braces and buckteeth, baseball teams, Sunday drives, cheeseburgers, and so forth.

- Note that the final sentence provides a brief conclusion so that the paragraph *feels* finished.

PRACTICE 1

Read this paragraph and answer the questions.

Millions of people play video games as a way to relax and have fun. Yet because video game addiction is a growing problem, gamers and their loved ones should know the warning signs. One warning sign of video game addiction is abandoning former interests. A gamer who stops participating in activities or social events he or she once enjoyed to play video games may be in the grip of a harmful addiction. Another indication of possible addiction is constantly thinking or talking about a game even while doing other things. If thoughts about the next gaming session prevent someone from paying attention to commitments, coursework, or other people, that player could be in trouble. A final warning sign is fighting with or lying to loved ones about the amount of time spent gaming. Neglecting relationships with family and friends is a classic sign of addiction. As with gambling and other addictive behavior, people close to the addict often spot these signs first while the addict vigorously denies having a problem.

1. Is the topic sentence of this paragraph sentence 1 or 2? Which of these best states the main idea explained by the rest of the paragraph?

   sentence 2

2. How many supporting points does this writer provide?

   three

3. What words help introduce each of the three warning signs of gaming addiction?

   One warning sign; Another indication of possible addiction; A final warning sign

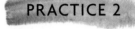

PRACTICE 2

ESL TIP

Because ways of organizing ideas and language vary from culture to culture, Practice 2 is very important. Teachers should explicitly point out the *topic sentence (main idea)* and *support* organizational pattern to ESL students.

TEACHING TIP

Practice 2 works well in class.

Each group of sentences below can be arranged and written as a paragraph. Circle the letter of the sentence that would be the best topic sentence. REMEMBER: The topic sentence states the main idea of the entire paragraph and includes all the other ideas.

EXAMPLE:
a. Speed-walking three times a week is part of my routine.
b. Staying healthy and fit is important to me.
c. Every night, I get at least seven hours of sleep.
d. I eat as many fresh fruits and vegetables as possible.

(Sentence b is more general than the other sentences; it would be the best topic sentence.)

1. a. Some colleges are experimenting with using iPods to deliver instructional material, complete with musical clips, news, and even video.
   b. Runners, hikers, and bicyclists sometimes use their iPods as personal trainers that plan a route and then provide maps, distances, and time goals.
   c. Although most people still think of the iPod as a digital music player, others are using these gadgets in creative and innovative ways.
   d. Video iPod owners can search for their soul mates using PodDater software to download short video clips and profiles of available singles.

2. a. Each prisoner in the program receives a puppy, which he feeds, cares for, and trains to be a service dog for a combat veteran.
   b. The convicted felons often feel, many for the first time, a sense of responsibility, compassion for other creatures, and the power of unconditional love.
   c. The successful Puppies Behind Bars program improves the lives of both inmates and disabled war veterans.
   d. When a dog "graduates," each trainer presents his dog to a vet who returned from Iraq or Afghanistan with brain or bodily injuries.
   e. The disabled soldiers say that the dogs not only open doors, turn on lights, and dial 911 on special phones but greatly ease their anxiety and depression.

AP Photo/Tim Rooke/Rex Features

3. a. To protect her little boy from the streets, Will's mother encouraged his obsession with music and got him into better Los Angeles schools.
   b. In 1987, twelve-year-old Will met schoolmate Alan Pineda, known as *apl.de.ap*, and they began rapping and performing in L.A. clubs.
   c. Will.i.am is now a seven-time Grammy winner, producer, and consultant to American corporations on "cool" new products.
   d. Atbann Klann, renamed the Black Eyed Peas, recruited Fergie in 2001 and soon exploded in popularity worldwide.

e. An early focus on music and performing launched rapper will.i.am on the path to stardom.

f. In 1988, Will and Pineda formed Atbann Klan, a "backpack rap" group that was signed by Ruthless Records in 1992.

4. a. Physical courage allows soldiers or athletes to endure bodily pain or danger.

 b. Those with social courage dare to expose their deep feelings in order to build close relationships.

 c. Those rare people who stand up for their beliefs despite public pressure possess moral courage.

 d. Inventors and artists show creative courage when they break out of old ways of seeing and doing things.

 e. Psychologist Rollo May claimed that there are four different types of courage.

5. a. In middle school, she devoured books about detective Nancy Drew, a strong female role model of courage and character.

 b. Born to Puerto Rican parents in the Bronx, NY, Sotomayor fell in love with comics like *Archie*, *Spiderman*, and *Batman* in elementary school.

 c. Sonia Sotomayor, the first Hispanic U.S. Supreme Court Justice, says that books were her "rocket ship out of the projects" and into a meaningful life.

 d. When she was weighing job offers, great novels like George Orwell's *1984* opened her eyes to the dangers of too much government and right use of the law.

 e. When teenaged Sotomayor saw *West Side Story*, a modern *Romeo and Juliet* about rival Puerto Rican gangs, a lightbulb came on—that great books dealing with human emotion are always relevant.

6. a. Many old toys and household objects are now collectors' items.

 b. A 1959 Barbie doll still in its original box recently sold for $3,552 on the eBay auction website.

 c. Many collectors now hunt for Fiesta dinnerware, made in the 1930s, in garage sales and resale shops.

 d. Star Wars action figures and vintage baseball cards are among the ten most wanted collectibles.

7. a. In our increasingly global economy, employees who can communicate with non-English-speaking customers and overseas colleagues are in demand at many American companies.

 b. People who can speak and write two languages fluently possess a valuable professional, social, and mental asset.

 c. Studies confirm that bilingualism boosts brain power because adults who grew up speaking two languages stay sharper and quicker later in life.

 d. Bilingualism brings personal rewards, such as the ability to bridge cultural boundaries and broaden one's social network to include people of other nationalities and ethnic groups.

8. a. You should read the ingredients on every package of food you buy.

 b. Children should not eat mandelona, which is made from peanuts soaked in almond flavoring.

 c. Avoid buying food from bins that do not list ingredients.

 d. If your child is allergic to peanuts, you need to be constantly on the alert.

 e. In a restaurant, tongs may have been used to pick up items containing peanuts.

B. Narrowing the Topic and Writing the Topic Sentence

The rest of this chapter will guide you through the process of writing paragraphs of your own. Here are the steps we will discuss:

1. Narrowing the topic and writing the topic sentence
2. Generating ideas for the body
3. Selecting and dropping ideas
4. Grouping ideas in a plan
5. Writing and revising the paragraph
6. Proofreading and writing the final draft

Narrowing the Topic

Often your first step as a writer will be **narrowing** a broad topic—one assigned by your instructor, one you have thought of yourself, or one suggested by a particular writing task, like a letter. That is, you must cut the topic down to size and choose one aspect that interests you.

Assume, for example, that you are asked to write a paragraph describing a person you know. The trick is to choose someone you would *like* to write about, someone who interests you and would probably also interest your audience of readers.

At this point, many writers find it helpful to think on paper by *brainstorming**, *freewriting*, or *clustering*. As you jot down or freely write ideas, ask yourself questions. Whom do I love, hate, or admire? Who is the funniest or most unusual person I know? Is there a family member or friend about whom others might like to read?

Suppose you choose to write about your friend Beverly. *Beverly* is too broad a topic for one paragraph. Therefore, you should limit your topic further, choosing just one of her qualities or acts. What is unusual about her? What might interest others? Perhaps what stands out in your mind is that Beverly is a determined person who doesn't let difficulties defeat her. You have now *narrowed* your broad topic to *Beverly's determination*.

You might visualize the process like this:

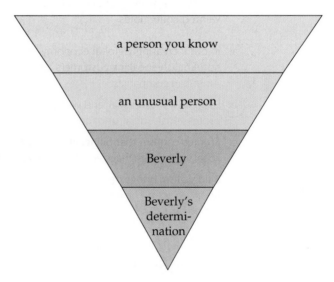

a person you know

an unusual person

Beverly

Beverly's determination

---

* Brainstorming is discussed further in Part C. Also see Chapter 2 for more information about prewriting.

PRACTICE 3

Good writers need a clear understanding of general and specific—that is, which ideas are general and which are specific. Number the items in each group below, with 1 being the most specific and limited, 2 being the second most specific, and the highest number being the most general.

1. 2 chairs
    3 furniture
    1 Grandma's oak rocking chair
    4 household contents

2. 1 Malian singer Habib Koité
    4 music
    3 African music
    2 music of Mali, West Africa
    5 sound

3. 2 rose
    3 flowering plants
    5 living things
    4 plants
    1 the Betty Boop rose

4. 1 *Union-Tribune* sports writer Jim Jackson
    3 California
    4 North America
    2 *San Diego Union-Tribune* office building
    5 Earth

5. 5 athletes
    1 Brodeur's agility
    4 hockey players
    3 goalies
    2 New Jersey Devils goalie Martin Brodeur

6. 3 actresses
    4 movie stars
    1 Helen Mirren
    2 successful older actresses
    5 human beings

Writing the Topic Sentence

The next step is to write your **topic sentence**, which clearly states, in sentence form, your narrowed topic and a point about that topic. This step helps you further focus your topic by forcing you to make a statement about it. That statement sets forth one main idea that the rest of your paragraph will support and explain. A topic sentence can be very simple (*Beverly is very determined*), or, better yet, it can state your attitude or point of view about the topic (*Beverly's determination inspires admiration*).

Think of the topic sentence as having two parts: a **topic** and a **controlling idea**. The controlling idea states the writer's attitude, angle, or point of view about the topic.

topic	controlling idea

Topic sentence: Beverly's determination inspires admiration.

All topics can have many possible topic sentences, depending on the writer's interests and point of view. The controlling idea helps you focus on just one aspect. Here are three possible topic sentences about the topic *attending college*:

TEACHING TIP
Suggest that students who write on computers test out different versions of a topic sentence—with different controlling ideas—until they find the one they like best.

(1) Attending college has revolutionized my career plans.

(2) Attending college has put me in debt.

(3) Attending college is exhausting but rewarding.

- These topic sentences all explore the same topic—attending college—but each controlling idea is different. The controlling idea in topic sentence (1) is *has revolutionized my career plans*.

- What is the controlling idea in topic sentence (2)?

  has put me in debt

- What is the controlling idea in topic sentence (3)?

  is exhausting but rewarding

- Notice the way each controlling idea lets the reader know what that paragraph will be about. By choosing different key words, a writer can angle any topic in different directions. If you were assigned the topic *attending college*, what would your topic sentence be?

  _____

  _____

PRACTICE 4

Read each topic sentence below. Circle the topic and underline the controlling idea.

EXAMPLE: (Computer games) improved my study skills.

1. (Hybrid cars) offer monetary advantages over gasoline vehicles.

2. (White-water rafting) increased my self-confidence.

3. (Ed Bradley) achieved many firsts as a television journalist.

4. (Immigrants) frequently are stereotyped by native-born Americans.

5. (A course in financial planning) should be required of all college freshmen.

Writing Limited and Complete Topic Sentences

Check to make sure your topic sentence is *limited* and *complete*. Your topic sentence should be **limited**. It should make a point that is neither too broad nor too narrow to be supported in a paragraph. As a rule, the more specific and well defined the topic sentence, the better the paragraph. Which of these topic sentences do you think will produce the best paragraph?

(1) My recent trip to Colorado was really bad.

(2) My recent trip to Colorado was disappointing because the weather ruined my camping plans.

- Topic sentence (1) is so broad that the paragraph could include almost anything.

- Topic sentence (2), on the other hand, is *limited* enough to provide the main idea for a good paragraph: how terrible weather ruined the writer's camping plans.

> (3) The Each-One-Reach-One tutoring program encourages academic excellence at Chester Elementary School.
>
> (4) Tutoring programs can be found all over the country.

- Topic sentence (3) is limited enough to provide the main idea for a good paragraph. Reading this topic sentence, what do you expect the paragraph to include?

  It might explain ways in which the program encourages academic excellence at Chester.

  _____

- Topic sentence (4) lacks a limited point. Reading this sentence, someone cannot guess what the paragraph will be about.

In addition, the topic sentence must be a **complete sentence**; it must contain a subject and a verb and express a complete thought.* Do not confuse a topic with a topic sentence. For example, *the heroism of Captain "Sully" Sullenberger* cannot be a topic sentence because it is not a complete sentence. Here is one possible topic sentence: *Because Captain "Sully" Sullenberger landed a packed airplane on the Hudson River and saved 155 lives, he is a true hero.*

For now, it is best to place your topic sentence at the beginning of the paragraph. After you have mastered this pattern, you can try variations. Placed first, the topic sentence clearly establishes the focus of your paragraph and helps grab the reader's attention. Wherever the topic sentence appears, all other sentences must relate to it and support it with specific details, facts, examples, arguments, and explanations. If necessary, you can revise the topic sentence later to make it more accurately match the paragraph you have written.

Caution: Do not begin a topic sentence with *This paragraph will be about . . .* or *I am going to write about . . . .* These extra words contribute nothing. Instead, make your point directly. Make every word in the topic sentence count.

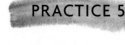 **PRACTICE 5**

Put a check beside each topic sentence that is limited enough to be the topic sentence of a good paragraph. If you think a topic sentence is too broad, limit the topic according to your own interests; then write a new, specific topic sentence. Sample answers

_____

* For more work on writing complete sentences, see Chapters 9 and 10.

EXAMPLES:

✔   Texting has changed my life in three ways.

Rewrite: _____

I am going to write about cell phones.

Rewrite: *Talking on a cell phone can distract drivers to the point of causing accidents.*

✔ 1.   Working in the complaint department taught me tolerance.

Rewrite: _____

2.   A subject I want to write about is money.

Rewrite: Saving money requires discipline but has unexpected rewards.

_____

3.   This paragraph will discuss food.

Rewrite: It is hard to change some of the attitudes about food that we learn as children.

_____

4.   Some things about college have been great.

Rewrite: Being able to set my own study schedule in college has improved my attitude

toward studying.

✔ 5.   Living in a one-room apartment forces a person to be organized.

Rewrite: _____

_____

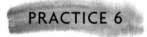

PRACTICE 6   Here is a list of topics. Choose one that interests you from this list or from your own list in Chapter 1 on page 7. Narrow the topic, and write a topic sentence limited enough to provide the main idea for a good paragraph. Make sure that your topic sentence is a complete sentence.

A talented musician	An act of courage
Why get an education?	Advertising con jobs
AIDS	Clothing styles on campus

Narrowed topic: _____

Topic sentence: _____

_____

C. Generating Ideas for the Body of the Paragraph

Rich supporting detail is one key to effective writing. A good way to generate ideas for the body of a paragraph is by *brainstorming*, freely jotting down ideas. This important step may take just a few minutes, but it gets your ideas on paper and may pull ideas out of you that you didn't even know you had.

Freely jot down anything that might relate to your topic—details, examples, little stories. Don't worry at this point if some ideas don't seem to belong. For now, just keep jotting them down.

Here is a possible brainstorming list for the topic sentence *Beverly inspires admiration because she is so determined.*

1. saved enough money for college
2. worked days, went to school nights
3. has beautiful brown eyes
4. nervous about learning to drive but didn't give up
5. failed road test twice—passed eventually
6. her favorite color—wine red
7. received degree in accounting
8. she is really admirable
9. with lots of will power, quit smoking
10. used to be a heavy smoker
11. married to Virgil
12. I like Virgil too
13. now a good driver
14. never got a ticket
15. hasn't touched another cigarette

As you saw in Part B, some writers brainstorm or use other prewriting techniques *before* they write the topic sentence. Do what works best for you.

PRACTICE 7

Now choose the topic from Practice 5 or Practice 6 that most interests you. Write your limited topic sentence here.

Topic sentence: _____

_____

Next, brainstorm, freewrite, or cluster for specific ideas to develop a paragraph. On paper or on a computer, write anything that comes to you about your topic sentence. Just let ideas pour out—details, memories, facts. Try to fill at least one page.

PRACTICE 8

Many writers adjust the topic sentence after they have finished drafting the paragraph. In a group of three or four classmates, study the body of each of the following paragraphs. Then, working together, write the most exact and interesting topic sentence you can. Answers will vary.

1. Topic sentence: Students who are the first in their families to attend college often face special challenges.

TEACHING TIP

If many in your class are first-generation college students, you might recommend these sites for resources, videos, and inspiration: ‹**http://www.firstinthefamily.org/**› and ‹**http://latinosincollege.com/**›

One challenge is a lack of knowledge about how to apply, register for classes, and obtain financial aid. Students who are first in their families to attend college often lack an experienced guide to help them navigate these procedures. After they do enroll, first-generation college students may also find that their high school classes did not adequately prepare them for the academic demands of college work. Consequently, they may have to take courses to strengthen their reading, writing, or math skills. Even as they improve academically and progress through their studies, students whose relatives and friends never attended college must deal with a range of difficult emotions. They may feel anxious about pleasing proud relatives with high hopes for their success. They may fear losing old friends who undercut or even mock their college goals. They may experience stress from the constant struggle to find enough time to study. When they finally receive their college degrees, however, they always swell with pride, knowing that their accomplishment is worth every obstacle they have overcome.

Inocencia Colon, student

2. Topic sentence: <u>My hero is my father, who taught me what it is to be a man.</u>

_____

Despite his pressured schedule, he always found time to play with my sisters and me, tell us stories, and make us feel loved. From his example, I learned that men can be loving and show affection. In addition, he often sat with me and discussed the responsibilities of being a man. He instilled in me principles and morals that I would not have learned from the guys on the corner. My hero felt that a man should be the provider for his family. He demonstrated this by working two jobs, seven days a week. After many years, my father saved enough money to make a down payment on a three-bedroom house next to a park. He accomplished all this with only a sixth-grade education. The values on which I now base my life were given to me by my hero, an unknown man who deserves to be famous.

Robert Fields, student

3. Topic sentence: <u>Winter mornings in Minnesota were bitterly cold but beautiful.</u>

_____

Frigid air would hit us in the eyes when we stepped out the door to catch the school bus. Even though our faces were wrapped in scarves and our heads covered with wool caps, the cold snatched our breath away. A thin layer of snow crunched loudly under our boots as we ran gasping out to the road. I knew that the famous Minnesota wind chill was pulling temperatures well below zero, but I tried not to think about that. Instead, I liked to see how everything in the yard was frozen motionless, even the blades of grass that shone like little glass knives.

Ari Henson, student

D. Selecting and Dropping Ideas

This may be the easiest step in paragraph writing because all you have to do is select those ideas that best support your topic sentence and drop those that do not. Also drop ideas that just repeat the topic sentence and add nothing new to the paragraph.

Here is the brainstorming list for the topic sentence *Beverly inspires admiration because she is so determined.* Which ideas would you drop? Why?

1. saved enough money for college
2. worked days, went to school nights
3. has beautiful brown eyes
4. nervous about learning to drive but didn't give up
5. failed road test twice—passed eventually
6. her favorite color—wine red
7. received degree in accounting
8. she is really admirable
9. with lots of will power, quit smoking
10. used to be a heavy smoker
11. married to Virgil
12. I like Virgil too
13. now a good driver
14. never got a ticket
15. hasn't touched another cigarette

    You probably dropped ideas 3, 6, 11, and 12 because they do not relate to the topic. You also should have dropped idea 8 because it merely repeats the topic sentence.

PRACTICE 9

Read through your own brainstorming list in Practice 7. Select the ideas that best support your topic sentence, and cross out those that do not. In addition, drop ideas that merely repeat the topic sentence. You should be able to give good reasons for keeping or dropping each idea in the list.

TEACHING TIP

Organizing ideas is a key skill that many students lack. You might illustrate the process by "thinking aloud" as you reason out the best order of ideas for a paragraph. That is, model the mental process that writers go through when they plan.

ESL TIP

Emphasize to ESL and other students that they should include specific details in their paragraphs. How might the writer of this paragraph about Beverly add more specific details (e.g., the specific name of her college or workplace, her job title, and so forth)?

E. Arranging Ideas in a Plan or an Outline

Next, choose an **order** in which to arrange your ideas. First, group together ideas that have something in common, that are related or alike in some way. Then decide which ideas should come first, which second, and so on. Many writers do this by numbering the ideas on their list.

    Here is a plan for a paragraph about Beverly's determination.

Topic sentence: Beverly inspires admiration because she is so determined.

    worked days, went to school nights
    saved enough money for college
    received degree in accounting

    nervous about learning to drive but didn't give up
    failed road test twice—passed eventually
    now a good driver
    never got a ticket

    used to be a heavy smoker
    with lots of will power, quit smoking
    hasn't touched another cigarette

● How are the ideas in each group related?   The first group of ideas deals with school,

the second with driving, and the third with smoking.

● Does it make sense to discuss college first, driving second, and smoking last?

Why?   Yes, it makes sense. This may be the order of importance to the writer.

_____

Keep in mind that there is more than one way to arrange ideas. As you group your own brainstorming list, think of what you want to say; then arrange your ideas accordingly.*

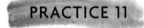

PRACTICE 10   On paper or on a computer, make a plan or outline from your brainstormed list of ideas. First, group together related ideas. Then decide which ideas will come first, which second, and so on.

F. Writing and Revising the Paragraph

Writing the First Draft

By now, you should have a clear plan or outline from which to write the first draft of your paragraph. The **first draft** should contain all the ideas you have decided to use, in the order in which you have chosen to present them. Writing on every other line will leave room for later changes.

Explain your ideas fully, including details that will interest or amuse the reader. If you are unsure about something, put a check in the margin and come back to it later, but avoid getting stuck on any one word, sentence, or idea. If possible, set the paper aside for several hours or several days; this step will help you read it later with a fresh eye.

PRACTICE 11   On paper or on a computer, write a first draft of the paragraph you have been working on.

Revising

Whether you are a beginning writer or a professional, you must **revise**—that is, rewrite what you have written in order to improve it. You might cross out and rewrite words or entire sentences. You might add, drop, or rearrange details.

As you revise, keep the reader in mind. Ask yourself these questions:

ESL TIP

Emphasize that revising is an essential follow-up to writing a first draft. This checklist of revising questions will help students focus as they revise.

● Is my topic sentence clear?

● Can the reader easily follow my ideas?

● Is the order of ideas logical?

● Will this paragraph keep the reader interested?

In addition, revise your paragraph for *support* and for *unity*.

_____

* For more work on choosing an order, see Chapter 4, Part A.

Revising for Support

Make sure your paragraph contains excellent **support**—that is, specific details, facts, and examples that fully explain your topic sentence.

Avoid simply repeating the same idea in different words, especially the idea in the topic sentence. Repeated ideas are just padding, a sign that you need to brainstorm or freewrite again for new ideas. Which of the following two paragraphs contains the best and most interesting support?

A.   Every Saturday morning, Fourteenth Street is alive with activity. From one end of the street to the other, people are out doing everything imaginable. Vendors sell many different items on the street, and storekeepers will do just about anything to get customers into their stores. They will use signs, and they will use music. There is a tremendous amount of activity on Fourteenth Street, and just watching it is enjoyable.

B.   Every Saturday morning, Fourteenth Street is alive with activity. Vendors line the sidewalks, selling everything from DVD players to wigs. Trying to lure customers inside, the shops blast pop music into the street or hang brightly colored banners announcing "Grand Opening Sale" or "Everything Must Go." Shoppers jam the sidewalks, both serious bargain hunters and families just out for a stroll, munching chili dogs as they survey the merchandise. Here and there, a panhandler hustles for handouts, taking advantage of the Saturday crowd.

- The body of *paragraph A* contains vague and general statements, so the reader gets no clear picture of the activity on Fourteenth Street.

- The body of *paragraph B*, however, includes many specific *details* that clearly explain the topic sentence: *vendors selling everything from DVD players to wigs, shops blasting pop music, brightly colored banners.*

- What other details in *paragraph B* help you see just how Fourteenth Street is alive with activity?

serious bargain hunters

strolling families

chili dogs

a panhandler

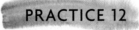 **PRACTICE 12**

Check the following paragraphs for strong, specific support. Mark places that need more details or explanation, and cross out any weak or repeated words. Then revise and rewrite each paragraph *as if you had written it*, inventing and adding support when you need to. Answers will vary.

Paragraph A: Aunt Alethia was one of the most important people in my life. She had a strong influence on me. No matter how busy she was, she always had time for me. She paid attention to small things about me that no one else seemed to notice. When I was successful, she praised me. When I was feeling down, she gave me pep talks. She was truly wise and shared her wisdom with me. My aunt was a great person who had a major influence on my life.

Paragraph B: Just getting to school safely can be a challenge for many young people. Young as he is, my son has been robbed once and bullied on several occasions. The robbery was very frightening, for it involved a weapon. What was taken was a small thing, but it meant a lot to my son. It angers me that just getting to school is so dangerous. Something needs to be done.

Revising for Unity

TEACHING TIP

Stress to students that out-lining first and then using the outline as a guide while writing will help prevent problems with unity.

While writing, you may sometimes drift away from your topic and include information that does not belong in the paragraph. It is important, therefore, to revise your paragraph for **unity**—that is, to drop any ideas or sentences that do not relate to the topic sentence.

This paragraph lacks unity:

> (1) Franklin Mars, a Minnesota candy maker, created many popular candy snacks. (2) Milky Way, his first bar, was an instant hit. (3) Snickers, which he introduced in 1930, also sold very well. (4) Milton Hershey developed the very first candy bar in 1894. (5) M&Ms were a later Mars creation, supposedly designed so that soldiers could enjoy a sugar boost without getting sticky trigger fingers.

- What is the topic sentence in this paragraph? <u>sentence (1)</u>
- Which sentence does *not* relate to the topic sentence? <u>sentence (4)</u>
- Sentence (4) has nothing to do with the main idea, that *Franklin Mars created many popular candy snacks*. Therefore, sentence (4) should be dropped.

PRACTICE 13

Check the following paragraphs for unity. If a paragraph is unified, write U in the blank. If it is not, write the number of the sentence that does not belong in the paragraph.

TEACHING TIP

Practice 13 is fun to do in class.

1. <u>U</u> (1) Families who nourish their children with words as well as food at dinnertime produce better future readers. (2) Researchers at Harvard University studied the dinner conversations of sixty-eight families. (3) What they found was that parents who use a few new words in conversation with their three- and four-year-olds each night quickly build the children's vocabularies and their later reading skills. (4) The researchers point out that children can learn from eight to twenty-eight new words a day, so they need to be "fed" new words. (5) Excellent "big words" for preschoolers include *parachute, emerald, instrument,* and *education,* the researchers say.

2. <u>3</u> (1) Personalized license plates have become very popular. (2) These "vanity plates" allow car owners to express their sense of humor, marital status, pet peeves, or ethnic pride. (3) Of course, every car must display a plate on the rear bumper or in the back window. (4) Drivers have created messages such as ROCK ON, NT GUILTY, and (on a tow truck) ITZ GONE. (5) In some states, as many as one in seven autos has a personalized plate. (6) Recently, *Parade* magazine chose the nation's top ten vanity plates, including XQQSME on a Massachusetts plate, ULIV1S on an Arkansas plate, and on an SUV in Missouri, a message to be read in the rearview mirror—TI-3VOM.

3. _5_   (1) Swimming is excellent exercise. (2) Swimming vigorously for just twelve minutes provides aerobic benefits to the heart. (3) Unlike jogging and many other aerobic sports, however, swimming does not jolt the bones and muscles with sudden pressure. (4) Furthermore, the motions of swimming, such as reaching out in the crawl, stretch the muscles in a healthy, natural way. (5) Some swimmers wear goggles to keep chlorine or salt out of their eyes whereas others do not.

Peer Feedback for Revising

You may wish to show your first draft or read it aloud to a respected friend or classmate. Ask this person to give an honest reader response, not to rewrite your work. Having another pair of eyes inspect your writing can alert you to issues you missed and help you think like a reader. To elicit useful responses, ask specific questions of your own, or use the Peer Feedback Sheet on the following page. You may want to photocopy the sheet rather than write on it so that you can reuse it.

PRACTICE 14   Now read the first draft of your paragraph with a critical eye. Revise and rewrite it, checking especially for a clear topic sentence, strong support, and unity.

PRACTICE 15   Exchange *revised* paragraphs with a classmate. Ask specific questions or use the Peer Feedback Sheet on page 32.

When you *give* feedback, try to be as honest and specific as possible; saying a paper is "good," "nice," or "bad" doesn't really help the writer. When you *receive* feedback, think over your classmate's responses. Do they ring true?

Now revise a second time, with the aim of writing a fine paragraph.

Did you know that even professional writers often show their work to a friend as they revise? These two college students are using the same technique, giving each other feedback on their writing.

Hill Street Studios/Blend Images/Corbis

PEER FEEDBACK SHEET

To _____ From _____ Date _____

1. What I like about this piece of writing is _____

   _____

   _____

2. Your main point seems to be _____

   _____

   _____

3. These particular words or lines struck me as powerful.

   Words or lines: I like them because

   _____   _____

   _____   _____

   _____   _____

   _____   _____

4. Some things aren't clear to me. These lines or parts could be improved (meaning not clear; supporting points missing; order mixed up; writing not lively):

   Lines or parts: Need improving because

   _____   _____

   _____   _____

   _____   _____

   _____   _____

5. The one change you could make that would most improve this piece of writing is

   _____

   _____

   _____

G. Proofreading and Writing the Final Draft

When you are satisfied with your revisions, recopy your paper. Be sure to include all your corrections, and write neatly and legibly—a carelessly scribbled paper seems to say that you don't care about your work.

The first draft of the paragraph about Beverly, with the writer's changes, and the revised final draft follow. Compare them.

First Draft with Revisions

(1) Beverly inspires admiration because she is so determined. (2) Although
doing what? add details
she could not afford to attend college right after high school, she worked to save
How long?! Better support needed—show her hard work!
money. (3) It took a long time, but she got her degree. (4) She is now a good driver.

(5) At first, she was very nervous about getting behind the wheel and even failed
The third time,
the road test twice, but she didn't quit. (6) She passed ~~eventually~~. (7) Her husband,
Drop Virgil—he doesn't belong
Virgil, loves to drive; he races cars on the weekend. (8) Anyway, Beverly has never
how long?
gotten a ticket. (9) A year ago, Beverly quit smoking. (10) For a while, she had a
too general—add details here
rough time, but she hasn't touched a cigarette. (11) Now she says that the urge to
better conclusion needed
smoke has faded away. (12) She doesn't let difficulties defeat her.

> *Guide the reader better from point to point! Choppy—*

Final Draft

(1) Beverly inspires admiration because she is so determined. (2) Although she could not afford to attend college right after high school, she worked as a cashier to save money for tuition. (3) It took her five years working days and going to school nights, but she recently received a BS in accounting. (4) Thanks to this same determination, Beverly is now a good driver. (5) At first, she was very nervous about getting behind the wheel and even failed the road test twice, but she didn't give up. (6) The third time, she passed, and she has never gotten a ticket. (7) A year ago, Beverly quit smoking. (8) For a month or more, she chewed her nails and endless packs of gum, but she hasn't touched a cigarette. (9) Now she says that the urge to smoke has faded away. (10) When Beverly sets a goal for herself, she doesn't let difficulties defeat her.

● This paragraph provides good support for the topic sentence. The writer has made sentences (2) and (3) more specific by adding *as a cashier*, *for tuition*, *five years working days and going to school nights*, and *recently received a BS in accounting*.

- What other revisions did the writer make? How do these revisions improve the paragraph? The writer made sentence (6) more exact and combined it with sentence (8),

  dropped the sentence about Virgil, added details to sentence (10), and expanded sentence (12) to

  relate it to the topic sentence. The paragraph is now more unified and specific.

- *Transitional expressions* are words and phrases that guide the reader smoothly from point to point. In sentence (5) of the final draft, *at first* is a transitional expression showing time. What other transitional expressions of time are used?

  The third time, a year ago, for a month or more, now

- What phrase provides a transition from sentence (3) to (4)?

  Thanks to this same determination

- Note that the last sentence now provides a brief *conclusion* so that the paragraph *feels* finished.

Proofreading

Finally, carefully **proofread** your paper for grammatical and spelling errors, consulting your dictionary and this book as necessary. Errors in your writing will lower your grades in most college courses, and they may also limit your job opportunities. The more writing errors you tend to make, the more you need to proofread.

Chapter 8 of this book will teach you tools and proofreading strategies to help you find and correct your own errors. Then Units 2 through 8 will help you improve your grammar, punctuation, and spelling skills and proofread for specific errors.

Meanwhile, allow yourself enough time to proofread; read your work slowly, word by word. Some students find it useful to point to each word and read it aloud softly; others place a blank index card or ruler under the line they are reading. These methods help them catch mistakes as well as "hear" any words they might have left out as they wrote, especially little words like *and*, *at*, and *of*.

In which of these sentences have words been omitted?

(1) Texting while driving is an easy way cause accident.

(2) Plans for the new gym were on display the library.

(3) Mr. Sampson winked at his reflection in the bathroom mirror.

- Words are missing in sentences (1) and (2).
- Sentence (1) requires *to* before *cause* and *an* before *accident*.
- What word is omitted in sentence (2)? _____*in*_____
- Where should this word be placed? _____*after display*_____

PRACTICE 16

Proofread these sentences for omitted words. Add the necessary words above the lines. Some sentences may already be correct.

    EXAMPLE: Many people listen ^to^ music at work.

1. Radios, headphones, and earbuds are a common sight ^in^ many offices.

2. Yet ^a^ recent study found that music almost always makes people less productive.

3. Quite simply, words and melodies distract the brain from its task.   Correct

4. Therefore, learning any new material should ^be^ done with no music at all.

5. Students reading a textbook or studying for ^a^ test remember far less with a soundtrack.

6. Music can, however, relax ^a^ person before work or before class.

7. Playing a favorite artist ^is^ a great way to calm nerves and get ready to focus.

8. But when work starts, turn off the tunes.   Correct

9. Researchers found one case when music improves performance.   Correct

10. A well-practiced expert ^like^ a surgeon might focus better during surgery when music plays.

PRACTICE 17

Proofread the final draft of your paragraph, checking for grammar or spelling errors and omitted words.

PRACTICE 18

Teamwork: Critical Viewing and Writing

In a group with several classmates, look closely at the photo on the following page. It shows James Blake Miller, a Marine in Fallujah, Iraq, 2004. Choose someone to take notes. What *general impression* does this photo convey? Together, craft a topic sentence that states this general impression. Now brainstorm five to ten details from the picture that support this general impression. Working separately, each group member should choose the best details and write a paragraph that captures this iconic image for readers who have never seen it. Conclude the paragraph; don't just stop.

This U.S. soldier, photographed in Iraq, became famous as the "Marlboro Marine." See Practice 18.

PRACTICE 19

Writing and Revising Paragraphs

The assignments that follow will give you practice in writing and revising basic paragraphs. In each assignment, aim for (1) a clear topic sentence and (2) sentences that fully support and explain the topic sentence. As you write, refer to the checklist in the Chapter Highlights on page 37.

Paragraph 1: Describe a public place. Reread paragraph B on page 29. Then choose a place in your neighborhood that is "alive with activity"—a park, street, restaurant, or club. In your topic sentence, name the place and say when it is most active; for example, "Every Saturday night, the Blue Dog Café is alive with activity." Begin by freewriting or by jotting down as many details about the scene as possible. Then describe the scene. Arrange your observations in a logical order. Revise for support, making sure that your details are so lively and interesting that your readers will see the place as clearly as you do.

TEACHING TIP

If you assign paragraph 2, you might wish to discuss the prompt in class and help students identify strengths that could apply to their writing. Because many students have only a generalized sense of inadequacy as writers, knowing specific strengths (as well as error patterns) will help them.

Paragraph 2: Evaluate your strengths as a writer. In writing as in life, it helps to know your true strengths as well as your weaknesses. You may not realize it, but you probably already possess several skills and personality traits that can nourish good writing. These include being observant and paying attention to details, imagining, feeling deep emotions, wanting to learn the truth, knowing how and where to find the answers to questions, thinking creatively, being well organized, and being persistent. Which of these abilities do you already possess? Do you possess other skills or traits that might help your writing? Describe three of your strengths as a writer. As you revise, make sure your ideas follow a logical order. Proofread carefully.

Paragraph 3: Choose your time of day. Many people have a favorite time of day—the freshness of early morning, 5 P.M. when work ends, late at night when the children are asleep. In your topic sentence, name your favorite time of day. Then develop the paragraph by explaining why you look forward to this time and exactly how you spend it. Check your work for any omitted words.

Chapter Highlights

Checklist for Writing an Effective Paragraph

- Narrow the topic: Cut the topic down to one aspect that interests you and will probably interest your readers.

- Write the topic sentence. (You may wish to brainstorm or freewrite first.)

- Brainstorm, freewrite, or cluster ideas for the body: Write down anything and everything that might relate to your topic.

- Select and drop ideas: Select those ideas that relate to your topic, and drop those that do not.

- Group together ideas that have something in common; then arrange the ideas in a plan.

- Write your first draft.

- Read what you have written, making any necessary corrections and additions. Revise for support and unity.

- Write the final draft of your paragraph neatly and legibly or print a fresh copy, using the format preferred by your instructor.

- Proofread for grammar, punctuation, spelling, and omitted words. Make neat corrections in ink.

TEACHING TIP

For downloadable rubrics for the basic paragraph and essay, go to the *Grassroots* instructor website at ‹**login** **.cengage.com**›.

EXPLORING ONLINE

TEACHING TIP

Instructor tools for *Grass-roots* include a computerized Test Bank, PowerPoint slides, an Instructor's Manual with teaching tips, and more, and can be accessed at ‹**login** **.cengage.com**›.

<http://grammar.ccc.commnet.edu/grammar/paragraphs.htm> Review paragraph unity and topic sentences at this excellent OWL.

<http://owl.english.purdue.edu/owl/resource/606/01> A review of paragraph writing from the famous Purdue University OWL.

CHAPTER 4

Improving Your Paragraphs

A: **More Work on Organizing Ideas: Coherence**

B: **More Work on Revising: Exact and Concise Language**

C: **Turning Assignments into Paragraphs**

In Chapter 3, you practiced the steps of the paragraph-writing process. This chapter builds on that work. It explains several skills that can greatly improve your writing: achieving coherence; choosing exact, concise language; and turning assignments into paragraphs.

A. More Work on Organizing Ideas: Coherence

Every paragraph should have **coherence**. A paragraph *coheres*—holds together—when its ideas are arranged in a clear and logical order.

Sometimes the order of ideas flows logically from your topic. However, three basic ways to organize ideas are **time order**, **space order**, and **order of importance**.

Time Order

Time order means arranging ideas chronologically, from present to past or from past to present. Careful use of time order helps avoid such confusing writing as *Oops, I forgot to mention before that . . .*

Most instructions, histories, processes, and stories follow the logical order of time.

Mary Pope Osborne's lifelong zest for travel and reading inspires her best-selling *children's* books. From ages 4 to 15, Mary bounced with her family from one army base to another, in Europe and the States. Unlike many military kids, she loved these adventures, and upon returning to North Carolina, took imaginary trips through books and community theater. After graduating from the University of North Carolina, Chapel Hill, she took off traveling the world, finally settling in New York. In 1976, she married Will Osborne, a writer of children's plays. Over the next four years, she started writing children's stories that explored other cultures or time periods: ancient Egyptian mummies, Amazon rain forests, Greek myths, mermaid tales from around the world, and endangered animals. In 1992, she wrote her first Magic Treehouse book about 8-year-old Jack and his 7-year-old sister Annie, who time travel back to the dinosaurs. More Magic Treehouse books followed, and children around the world loved them. By 2013, Mary Pope Osborne had written 45 books and sold 45 million copies in 30 countries. Parents and teachers praised her work. Refreshingly, she refuses to license Magic Treehouse toys, clothing, and games, explaining that her only goal is to ignite in children the joy of reading.

- The paragraph moves in time from Mary Pope Osborne's travel in a military family to her hugely successful writing career.

- Note how some transitional expressions—for example, *from ages 4 to 15*, *after graduating…*, *over the next four years*, *in 1992*, and *by 2013*—show time and connect the events in the paragraph.

Transitional Expressions to Show Time
first, second, third
then, next, finally
before, during, after
soon, the following month, the next year

PRACTICE 1

Arrange each set of sentences in time order, numbering them 1, 2, 3, and so on. Be prepared to explain your choices.

ESL TIP

If students have difficulty ordering paragraphs chronologically, have them do Practice 1 in groups. An enjoyable ESL technique is to cut the sentences in a time-order paragraph into strips and have groups re-create the paragraph.

1. In eighty years, the T-shirt rose from simple underwear to fashion statement.
   - ___2___ During World War II, women factory workers started wearing T-shirts on the job.
   - ___3___ Hippies in the 1960s tie-dyed their T-shirts and wore them printed with messages.
   - ___4___ Now, five billion T-shirts are sold worldwide each year.
   - ___1___ The first American T-shirts were cotton underwear, worn home by soldiers returning from France after World War I.

2. The short life of Sadako Sasaki has inspired millions to value peace.
   - ___1___ Sadako was just two years old in 1945 when the atom bomb destroyed her city, Hiroshima.
   - ___3___ From her sickbed, Sadako set out to make 1,000 paper cranes, birds that, in Japan, symbolize long life and hope.
   - ___4___ Although she died before making 1,000, classmates finished her project and published a book of her letters.
   - ___2___ At age eleven, already a talented runner, she was crushed to learn that she had leukemia, caused by radiation from the bomb.
   - ___5___ Now, every year, the Folded Crane Club places 1,000 cranes at the foot of a statue of Sadako, honoring her wish that all children might enjoy peace and a long life.

3. Scientists who study the body's daily rhythms can suggest the ideal time of day for different activities.
   - ___1___ Taking vitamins with breakfast helps the body absorb them.
   - ___4___ Allergy medication should be taken just before bedtime to combat early-morning hay fever—usually the worst of the day.

__3__ The best time to work out is 3 P.M. to 5 P.M., when strength, flexibility, and body temperature are greatest.

__2__ Ideal naptime is 1 P.M. to 3 P.M., when body temperature falls, making sleep easier.

PRACTICE 2

Writing Assignment

Have you ever been through something that lasted only a few moments but was unforgettable—for example, a sports victory, an accident, or a kiss? Write a paragraph telling about such an event. As you prewrite, pick the highlights of the experience and arrange them in time order. As you write, try to capture the drama of what happened. Use transitional expressions of time to make the story flow smoothly.

Space Order

Space order means describing a person, a place, or a thing from top to bottom, from left to right, from foreground to background, and so on.

Space order is most often used in descriptions because it moves from detail to detail, like a camera's eye.

LEARNING STYLES TIP

Visual and other learners often find it helpful to draw or diagram a subject described using space order, for instance, sketching what this writer sees from his mango tree: coconut palms, valley, hills, and sea.

> When the city presses in on me, I return in my mind to my hometown in St. Mary, Jamaica. I am alone, high in the mango tree on our property on the hilltop. The wind is blowing hard as usual, making a scared noise as it passes through the lush vegetation. I look down at the coconut growth with its green flooring of banana plants. Beyond that is a wide valley and then the round hills. Farther out lies the sea, and I count the ships as they pass to and from the harbor while I relax on my special branch and eat mangoes.
>
> *Daniel Dawes, student*

- The writer describes this scene from his vantage point high in a tree. His description follows space order, moving from the plants below him, farther out to the valley and the hills, and then even farther, to the sea.

- Notice how *transitional expressions* indicating space—*beyond that*, *then*, and *farther out*—help the reader follow and "see" the details.

Transitional Expressions to Show Space Order
to the left, in the center, to the right
behind, beside, in front of
next, beyond that, farther out

PRACTICE 3

Arrange each set of details according to space order, numbering them 1, 2, 3, and so on. Be prepared to explain your choices.

1. After the party, the living room was a mess.

   __2 (3)__ greasy pizza boxes on the coffee table

   __1 (4)__ empty soda cans on the floor

   __4 (1)__ deflated balloons on the ceiling light

   __3 (2)__ pictures hanging at odd angles on the wall

2. The nurse quietly strode into my aunt's hospital room.

   _3 (3)_ black and silver stethoscope draped around his neck

   _2 (4)_ crisp, white cotton pants and short-sleeved tunic

   _4 (2)_ reassuring smile

   _1 (5)_ blue paper covers on his shoes

   _5 (1)_ kind, dark brown eyes

3. The taxicab crawled through rush-hour traffic in the rain-drenched city.

   _3 (3)_ fare meter on the dashboard ticking relentlessly

   _1 (5)_ headlights barely piercing the stormy, gray dusk

   _2 (4)_ windshield wipers losing their battle with the latest cloudburst

   _5 (1)_ backseat passengers frantically checking their watches

   _4 (2)_ driver wishing hopelessly that he could be home watching the news

PRACTICE 4

Writing Assignment

Study this portrait of Dr. Mae Jemison, who in 1992 became the first woman of color ever to soar into space. Notice her facial expression, posture, clothing, equipment, and other details. Then describe the photograph to someone who has never seen it. In your topic sentence, state one feeling, impression, or message this picture conveys and then choose details that support this idea. Arrange these details in space order—from left to right, top to bottom, and so on. As you revise, make sure that your sentences flow clearly and smoothly.

To learn more about the life of this remarkable astronaut, visit ‹**http://space.about .com/cs/formerastronauts/a/jemisonbio.htm**›.

Astronaut Mae Jemison

JSC Digital Image Collection/NASA

Gehry's Disney Concert
Hall in Los Angeles

Richard Cummins/CORBIS

Order of Importance

Order of importance means arranging your ideas from most to least important—
or vice versa.

> Frank Gehry is one of the greatest living architects. There are at least three
> reasons for his worldwide influence. Most important, Gehry has created new
> shapes for buildings, literally moving outside the boxes in which we often live
> and work. He has found ways to build walls that look like mountains, sails, and
> wings. In addition, Gehry uses new materials—or old materials in new ways.
> Going beyond plaster and wood, Gehry's buildings have rounded metal walls,
> curves made of glass, and stone in strange places. Third, because of its striking
> looks, a Gehry building can bring tourist dollars and international attention
> to a town or city. This happened when Gehry designed the now-famous
> Guggenheim Museum building in the little town of Bilbao, Spain. And like the
> latest blockbuster movie, the Disney Concert Hall in Los Angeles opened to
> rave reviews.

- The three reasons in this paragraph are discussed from the most important
  reason to the least important.
- Note that the words *most important*, *in addition*, and *third* help the reader move
  from one reason to another.

You might visualize order of importance like this:

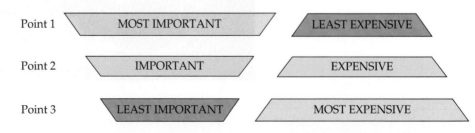

Sometimes you may wish to begin with the least important idea and build toward a climax at the end of the paragraph. Paragraphs arranged from the least important idea to the most important idea can have dramatic power.

> Although my fourteen-year-old daughter learned a great deal from living with a Pennsylvania Amish family last summer, adjusting to their strict lifestyle was difficult for her. Kay admitted that the fresh food served on the farm was great, but she missed her diet colas. More difficult was the fact that she had to wear long dresses—no more jeans and bomber jackets. Still worse in her view were the hours. A suburban girl and self-confessed night person, my daughter had to get up at 5 A.M. to milk cows! By far the most difficult adjustment concerned boys. If an Amish woman is not married, she cannot spend time with males, and this rule now applied to Kay. Yes, she suffered and complained, but by summer's end, she was a different girl—more open-minded and proud of the fact that all these deprivations put her more in touch with herself.
>
> *Lucy Auletta, student*

- The adjustment difficulties this writer's daughter had are arranged from least to most important. How many difficulties are discussed? _____four_____

- Note how the words *more difficult*, *still worse*, and *by far the most difficult adjustment* help the reader move from one idea to the next.

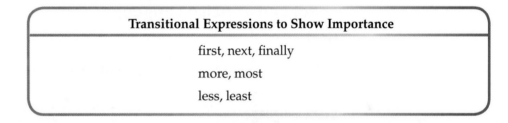

Transitional Expressions to Show Importance
first, next, finally
more, most
less, least

TEACHING TIP

After students learn the three types of order, have each student choose one type of order and write a paragraph using it. Bring in the most successful examples of each type, and ask the authors to read them aloud.

PRACTICE 5

Arrange the ideas that develop each topic sentence in order of importance, numbering them 1, 2, and 3. Begin with the most important idea, or reverse the order if you think that a paragraph would be more effective if it began with the least important idea. Be prepared to explain your choices. Then, on a separate sheet of paper, write the ideas in a paragraph.

1. Sixty-eight percent of things Americans throw in the trash should be recycled or composted
   - __1 (3)__ Twenty-nine percent of all garbage in landfills is recyclable paper like newspapers and product packaging.
   - __3 (1)__ Plastic bottles, bags, and packaging make up twelve percent of landfill waste.
   - __2 (2)__ Twenty-seven percent of the trash in landfills is food scraps, leaves, grass clippings, and yard waste that could go into compost piles.

2. A hidden epidemic of steroid use among young women—for weight control or enhanced athletic performance—is causing serious consequences.
   - __3 (1)__ Steroid use, which has been linked to heart attacks, strokes, and some cancers, can be fatal.
   - __1 (3)__ Many female steroid users not only lose hair on their heads but also grow extra body hair.
   - __2 (2)__ Steroids prematurely stop bones from lengthening, so developing girls who take the drug may permanently stunt their growth.

3. Undiagnosed or untreated diabetes can cause serious problems.

__4 (1)__ The diabetic's craving for sweets can lead to a house littered with candy wrappers.

__2 (3)__ If diabetes is not properly managed, blindness and other serious health problems, such as ulcers and gangrene, can result.

__1 (4)__ Ignoring a diabetes diagnosis can result in premature death.

__3 (2)__ Untreated diabetes often causes dry, itchy skin and intense thirst.

PRACTICE 6

Writing Assignment

Write a paragraph to persuade a certain group of people to do something they don't do now. For example, you could write to convince couch potatoes to begin exercising, senior citizens to take a free class at your college, or nonvoters to register and cast a ballot. Discuss the three most important reasons why your readers should follow your advice, and arrange these reasons in order of importance—least to most important or most to least important, whichever you think would make a better paragraph. Don't forget to use transitional expressions. If you wish, use humor to win over your audience.

B. More Work on Revising: Exact and Concise Language

Good writers do not settle for the first words that spill onto their paper or computer screen. Instead, they revise what they have written, replacing vague words with exact language and repetitious words with concise language.

Exact Language

As a rule, the more specific, detailed, and exact the language is, the better the writing. Which sentence in each of the following pairs contains the more vivid and exact language?

TEACHING TIP

For an effective class exercise in close observation and exact language, choose one or more photographs from this book (or elsewhere); consider those on pages 87, 136, 177, and 336. Ask students to pick key details and then express them vividly in writing.

(1) The office was noisy.
(2) In the office, phones jangled, faxes whined, and copy machines hummed.
(3) What my tutor said made me feel good.
(4) When my tutor whispered, "Fine job," I felt like singing.

- Sentence (2) is more exact than sentence (1) because *phones jangled, faxes whined, and copy machines hummed* provide more vivid information than the general word *noisy*.

- What *exact* words does sentence (4) use to replace the general words *said* and *made me feel good*? whispered, "Fine job," I felt like singing.

You do not need a large vocabulary to write exactly and well, but you do need to work at finding the right words to fit each sentence.

PRACTICE 7

These sentences contain vague language. Revise each one, using vivid and exact language wherever possible. Sample answers

EXAMPLE: A man went through the crowd.

Revise: _A man in a blue leather jacket pushed through the crowd._

1. An automobile went down the street.

    Revise: A late-model Infiniti roared down Maple Street.

2. This apartment has problems.

    Revise: This apartment has peeling paint and leaky water pipes.

3. My job is fun.

    Revise: Selling toe rings and ear cuffs to enthusiastic teenagers lifts my spirits.

4. This magazine is interesting.

    Revise: This issue of *National Geographic* has beautiful photographs of wolves.

5. The expression on his face made me feel comfortable.

    Revise: His reassuring eyes and warm smile made me feel comfortable.

6. When Allison comes home, her pet greets her.

    Revise: When Allison walks in the door, her cat meows and rubs up against her leg.

7. There was a big storm here last week.

    Revise: A freak electrical storm swept through Cleveland last week.

8. The emergency room has a lot of people in it.

    Revise: Crying children, people with broken bones, and busy nurses fill the emergency room.

Concise Language

Concise writing never uses five or six words when two or three will do. It avoids repetitious and unnecessary words that add nothing to the meaning of a sentence. As you revise your writing, cross out unnecessary words and phrases.

Which sentence in each of the following pairs is more concise?

> (1) Because of the fact that Larissa owns an antiques shop, she is always poking around in dusty attics.
>
> (2) Because Larissa owns an antiques shop, she is always poking around in dusty attics.
>
> (3) Mr. Tibbs entered a large, dark blue room.
>
> (4) Mr. Tibbs entered a room that was large in size and dark blue in color.

- Sentences (2) and (3) are concise; sentences (1) and (4) are wordy.

- In sentence (1), *because of the fact that* is a wordy way of saying *because*.

- In sentence (4), *in size* and *in color* just repeat which ideas?

    large and dark blue

Of course, conciseness does not mean writing short, choppy sentences. It does mean dropping unnecessary words and phrases.

PRACTICE 8

The following sentences are wordy. In a group with two or three others, make each sentence more concise by deleting unnecessary words, rewording slightly as necessary. Write your revised sentences on the lines provided, making sure not to change the meaning of the original. Answers will vary.

EXAMPLE: Many people wonder what life will be like in the future in years to come.

Revise: _Many people wonder what life will be like in the future._

1. Experts make the prediction that by 2050 some people will live to a ripe old age of 130 or even 150 years old.

    Revise: _Experts predict that by 2050 some people will live to 130 or even 150._

2. The reason why we will be healthier is because replacement organs and parts of the human body will be grown if needed.

    Revise: _We will be healthier because replacement organs and body parts will be grown if needed._

3. Tiny earbud computers in our ears will make us smarter and more intelligent, translating languages and linking to large, enormous databases.

    Revise: _Tiny earbud computers will make us smarter, translating languages and linking to large databases._

4. Most of our food that we eat will come from high-rise farms rising many stories straight up to the sky.

    Revise: _Most of our food will come from high-rise farms._

Sophisticated robots, already in use, will be part of everyday life in 2050.

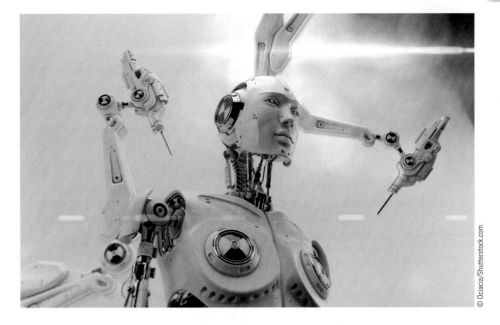

© Ociacia/Shutterstock.com

5. The Internet will connect human beings, homes where they live, places they work, and pets that they own in one vast grid.

   Revise: The Internet will connect humans, their homes, workplaces, and pets in one vast grid.

6. Three-dimensional TV and computer images will seem real, with odors to smell, textures to touch, and tastes.

   Revise: Three-dimensional TV and computer images will seem real, with odors, textures, and tastes.

7. Friendly robot nannies will care for children who are still young and the elderly who are getting on in years.

   Revise: Friendly robot nannies will care for children and the elderly.

8. Experts also give a warning of future dangers like extreme, severe weather and new ethical challenges that people will think about and face.

   Revise: Experts also warn of future dangers like extreme weather and new ethical challenges.

9. Because of the fact that human cloning will be a reality, some groups might create clones to be slaves or soldiers.

   Revise: Because human cloning will be a reality, some groups might create clones to be slaves or soldiers.

10. In 2050 of the future, we could face hard and difficult questions about what it means to be human in a world of machines.

    Revise: In 2050 we could face hard questions about what it means to be human in a world of machines.

EXPLORING ONLINE

<http://www.futuretimeline.net/> Visit Future Timeline to learn more about what the experts see in our future.

<http://www.wfs.org/> To read predictions of the future and perhaps research for your own writing, visit the World Future Society.

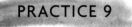
PRACTICE 9

Teamwork: Critical Thinking and Writing

Following are statements from real accident reports collected by an insurance company. As you will see, these writers need help with more than their fenders!

TEACHING TIP

Practice 9 makes an amusing in-class activity and underscores the relevance of clear writing to everyday life and to business.

In a group with four or five classmates, read each statement and try to understand what each writer meant to say. Then revise each statement so that it says exactly and concisely what the writer intended.

1. "The guy was all over the place. I had to swerve a number of times before I hit him."
2. "The telephone pole was approaching fast. I was attempting to swerve out of its path when it struck my front end."
3. "Coming home, I drove into the wrong house and collided with a tree I don't have."
4. "I was on my way to the doctor's with rear-end trouble when my universal joint gave way, causing me to have an accident."
5. "I was driving my car out of the driveway in the usual manner when it was struck by the other car in the same place it had been struck several times before."

PRACTICE 10

Review

Choose a paragraph or paper you wrote recently. Read it with a fresh eye, checking for exact and concise language. Then rewrite it, eliminating all vague or wordy language.

C. Turning Assignments into Paragraphs

In Chapter 3, Part B, you learned how to narrow a broad topic and write a specific topic sentence. Sometimes, however, your assignment may take the form of a specific question, and your job may be to answer the question in one paragraph.

For example, this question asks you to take a stand for or against a particular issue.

> Are professional athletes overpaid?

You can often turn this kind of question into a topic sentence:

> (1) Professional athletes are overpaid.
> (2) Professional athletes are not overpaid.
> (3) Professional athletes are sometimes overpaid.

- These three topic sentences take different points of view.
- The words *are*, *are not*, and *sometimes* make each writer's opinion clear.

Sometimes you will be asked to agree or disagree with a statement:

> (4) Salary is the most important factor in job satisfaction. Agree or disagree.

- This is really a question in disguise: *Is salary the most important factor in job satisfaction?*

In the topic sentence, make your opinion clear and repeat key words.

> (5) Salary is the most important factor in job satisfaction.
> (6) Salary is not the most important factor in job satisfaction.
> (7) Salary is only one among several important factors in job satisfaction.

- The words *is*, *is not*, and *is only one among several* make each writer's opinion clear.
- Note how the topic sentences repeat the key words from the statement—*salary, important factor, job satisfaction*.

Once you have written the topic sentence, follow the steps described in Chapters 2 and 3—freewriting, brainstorming, or clustering; selecting; grouping—and then write your paragraph. Be sure that all ideas in the paragraph support the opinion you have stated in the topic sentence.

PRACTICE 11

Here are four exam questions. Write one topic sentence to answer each of them. REMEMBER: Make your opinion clear in the topic sentence and repeat key words from the question. Answers will vary.

1. Should computer education be required in every public high school?

   Topic sentence: Computer education should be required in every public high school.

   _____

2. Would you advise your best friend to buy a new car or a used car?

   Topic sentence: A late-model used car can have all the advantages of a new car and save people

   a lot of money.

3. Is there too much bad news on television news programs?

   Topic sentence: There is too much bad news on television news programs.

   _____

4. How have your interests changed in the past five years?

   Topic sentence: I have become more interested in both local and national politics in the past five

   years.

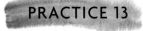 **PRACTICE 12** Imagine that your instructor has just written the exam questions from Practice 11 on the board. Choose the question that most interests you and write a paragraph answering that question. Prewrite, select, and arrange ideas before you compose your paragraph. Then read your work, making neat corrections in ink.

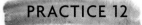 **PRACTICE 13** Here are four statements. Agree or disagree, and write a topic sentence for each.
Answers will vary.

1. All higher education should be free. Agree or disagree.

    Topic sentence: All high school graduates should be able to obtain their higher education free of

    charge.

2. Expecting one's spouse to be perfect is the most important reason for the high divorce rate in the United States. Agree or disagree.

    Topic sentence: Expecting one's spouse to be perfect is one of the most important reasons for

    the high divorce rate in the United States.

3. Parents should give children money when they need it rather than give them an allowance. Agree or disagree.

    Topic sentence: Parents should give children an allowance so that they can learn how to handle

    money.

4. Silence is golden. Agree or disagree.

    Topic sentence: It is usually better to speak out on important issues than to remain silent.

 **PRACTICE 14** Choose the statement in Practice 13 that most interests you. Then write a paragraph in which you agree or disagree.

Chapter Highlights

To improve your writing, try these techniques:

- Organize your ideas by time order.
- Organize your ideas by space order.
- Organize your ideas by order of importance, either from the most important to the least or from the least important to the most.
- Use language that is exact and concise.
- Turn assignment questions into topic sentences.

EXPLORING ONLINE

TEACHING TIP

Instructor tools for *Grass-roots* include a computerized Test Bank, PowerPoint slides, an Instructor's Manual with teaching tips, and more, and can be accessed at ‹**login .cengage.com**›.

<http://lrs.ed.uiuc.edu/students/fwalters/cohere.html> Review ways to add coherence to your writing.

<http://grammar.ccc.commnet.edu/grammar/quizzes/wordy_quiz.htm> Practice making wordy sentences lean and mean.

CHAPTER 5

Thinking Through Paragraph Patterns, Part 1

A: **Illustration**

B: **Description**

C: **Narration**

D: **Process**

E: **Comparison and Contrast**

Chapters 5 and 6 present nine patterns that will help you become a more critical thinker and a better writer.

A common problem for many writers is not adequately developing their main idea. "This topic sentence needs more support," their instructor might write. To help with this problem, it is useful to know certain patterns that often are used in college or workplace writing. These **patterns of organization** also reflect **ways of thinking** about the world, ways in which the human brain naturally tries to make sense of experience. For instance, we might think of good *examples* to make our meaning clear or *compare* two things or search for the *reasons why* something happened. This chapter will teach you five useful patterns.

A. Illustration

TEACHING TIP

Point out that knowing how to choose excellent examples to develop a point will serve students well in college and on the job.

One effective way to make your writing more specific is by thinking of one, two, or three **examples**. Someone might write, "Divers in Monterey Bay can observe many beautiful fish. For instance, tiger-striped treefish are common." The first sentence makes a general statement about the beautiful fish in Monterey Bay. The second sentence gives a specific example of such fish: *tiger-striped treefish*. This is called **illustration**.

Illustration is especially useful in fields requiring careful observation, like science, psychology, sociology, medicine, and design.

Topic Sentence

Here is the topic sentence of an illustration paragraph:

> Many of the computer industry's best innovators were young friends working in pairs when they first achieved success.

- The writer begins this paragraph with a topic sentence that makes a general statement.

- What generalization about many computer innovators does this sentence make?

  When they were young, they worked together to achieve success.

Paragraph and Plan

Here is the entire paragraph:

> Many of the computer industry's best innovators were young friends working in pairs when they first achieved success. For example, buddies David Filo and Jerry Yang were graduate students at Stanford when they realized that their hobby of listing the best pages on the World Wide Web might become a business. They created Yahoo!, a Web index now logging 647 million visits a month. Two more youthful examples are Google founders Larry Page and Sergey Brin. They were students in their twenties when they got the idea for one of the Internet's most popular search engines. In 2004, just six years after launching their new company, Page and Brin became multibillionaires by selling Google shares to the public. A third pair of young computer geniuses created the video-sharing website YouTube.com. Chad Hurley and Steven Chen worked in Hurley's garage to solve a personal problem: they wanted to figure out an easier way to share video clips with each other via the Internet. The popularity of their site exploded, and just one year later, Hurley and Chen sold YouTube to Google for $1.65 billion. Youth and collaboration, it seems, are common factors in digital breakthroughs.

- What three examples does this writer provide as support?

Example 1: David Filo and Jerry Yang

Example 2: Larry Page and Sergey Brin

Example 3: Chad Hurley and Steven Chen

- Note that the topic sentence, examples, and concluding sentence make a rough **outline** for the paragraph. In fact, before drafting, the writer probably made just such an outline.

The simplest way to tell a reader that an example will follow is to say so, using **transitional expressions**: *For example, David Filo . . . .*

Transitional Expressions for Illustration	
for instance	another instance of
for example	another example of
one illustration is	another illustration of

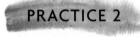

PRACTICE 1 Read this student's paragraph and answer the questions.

As a proud Californian, I separate glass, plastic, and paper and do what I can for the environment. Even if, like me, you rent and don't own a home, you can take simple actions that will help the earth and save money. For example, replace all your incandescent lightbulbs with compact fluorescents (CFLs). CFLs use 75 percent less electricity, last ten times longer, and save money. Another way to make a difference is water use. Homeowners might install low-flow toilets, but renters can save water with a simple trick. Fill a one-liter plastic bottle with water and put it in the toilet tank. The bottle will displace enough water to save almost a gallon a flush—around ten gallons a day. Next, if you're handy, install a water filter on the kitchen faucet. By refilling stainless-steel bottles instead of buying plastic, a family of four can save $1000 a year and keep 600 plastic bottles out of landfills. Finally, even if your landlord won't weather strip those old windows, it is worth $50 or so to do it yourself. You will save a fortune in winter heating bills. Actions like these take a couple hours on a weekend, but the benefits last much longer.

James Lam, Student

1. Underline the topic sentence of this paragraph. Hint: It is not the first sentence.

2. How many examples of renters' actions are discussed?

   four

3. What transitional expressions does Mr. Lam use?

   For example, Another way, Next, Finally

PRACTICE 2 Each example in a paragraph must clearly relate to and explain the topic sentence. Each of the following topic sentences is followed by several examples. Circle the letter of any example that does *not* clearly illustrate the topic sentence. Be prepared to explain your choices.

EXAMPLE:

Some animals and insects camouflage themselves in interesting ways.
   a. Snowshoe rabbits turn from brown to white in winter, thus blending into the snow.
   b. The cheetah's spotted coat makes it hard to see in the dry African bush.
   c. The bull alligator smashes its tail against the water and roars during mating season.
   d. The walking stick is brown and irregular, much like the twigs among which this insect hides.

1. Many people are unaware that comic book superheroes include a number of Native American characters with special powers.
   a. Navaho Jason Strongbow became American Eagle, a comics hero with superhuman strength, through exposure to sonic energy and radiation.
   b. Female superhero Danielle Moonstar of the X-Men series is a Cheyenne who can create illusions with her thoughts.
   c. Writer Louise Erdrich, the author of thirteen novels, identifies as Chippewa.
   d. The GI Joe series produced Spirit Iron-Knife, a Native American superhero highly attuned to nature.

2. Mrs. Makarem is well loved in this community for her generous heart.
   a. Her door is always open to neighborhood children, who stop by for lemonade or advice.

b. When the Padilla family had a fire, Mrs. Makarem collected clothes and blankets for them.

c. "Hello, dear," she says with a smile to everyone she passes on the street.

(d.) Born in Caracas, Venezuela, she has lived on Bay Road for thirty-two years.

3. Several players from Japanese baseball leagues have achieved success in the United States's major leagues.

   a. Outfielder Hideki Matsui, a New York Yankee since 2003, won the World Series MVP award in 2009.

   b. Pitcher Yu Darvish of the Texas Rangers made the all-star team during his 2012 rookie season in the major leagues, a rare achievement.

   c. The Seattle Mariners' all-star outfielder, Ichiro Suzuki, holds the single-season record for 262 hits and has won nine Gold Gloves for his stellar defense.

   (d.) Baseball has been played and loved in Japan for many years.

4. A number of unusual, specialized scholarships are available to college students across the United States.

   a. The Icy Frost Bridge Scholarship at Indiana's DePauw University is awarded to female music students who sing or play the national anthem "with sincerity."

   (b.) Brighton College, a secondary school for boys and girls in England, pays the full tuition of a student with the last name of *Peyton*.

   c. Left-handed, financially needy students can get special scholarships at Juniata College in Pennsylvania.

   d. The Collegiate Inventors Competition awards $25,000 to the undergraduate with the most original, socially useful invention.

5. Throughout history, artists, scientists, and inventors have gotten new ideas or solved problems in dreams.

   a. In 1816, after a nightmare about a scientist bringing a hideous corpse back to life, Mary Shelley wrote *Frankenstein*, her famous horror story.

   b. Biologist James Watson dreamed about spiral staircases, leading him to discover the structure of DNA and win the Nobel Prize.

   (c.) Two weeks before he was shot and killed, President Abraham Lincoln dreamed he saw the body of a president lying in the White House.

   d. The entire melody for the Beatles' hit song "Yesterday" came to Paul McCartney in a dream.

PRACTICE 3

The secret of good illustration lies in well-chosen and well-written examples. Think of one example that illustrates each of the following general statements. Write out the example in sentence form—one to three sentences—as clearly and exactly as possible. Answers may vary.

1. Some professional athletes inspire young people with talent as well as good character.

   Example: _____

   _____

2. Certain unique foods are served in my culture (or family).

   Example: _____

   _____

3. Many films today have amazing special effects.

Example: _____

_____

PRACTICE 4 — Teamwork: Critical Viewing and Writing

Sometimes a writer notices specific examples first, sees a pattern, and then comes up with a generalization. In your group, discuss the three examples pictured and then craft your generalization into a topic sentence that includes all three.

PRACTICE 5 — Writing an Illustration Paragraph

Pick a topic from the list below or one that your instructor assigns. Draft a topic sentence that you can support well with examples. Now prewrite to get as many examples as possible and think critically as you pick the best three or four. Many students find it helpful to use a graphic organizer as they plan their paragraph. In your notebook, draw an organizer like the one below and fill it in as you think, or use the illustration organizer on the *Grassroots* website.

- offensive "reality" television shows
- best places to study on campus
- people you most admire
- traditions typical of one culture or area
- people whose attitude is their worst enemy

- what not to wear for a job interview
- mistakes first-year college students make
- ads that use humor effectively
- ways to handle difficult customers
- best apps for a student (or sports or fashion lover)

ILLUSTRATION PARAGRAPH ORGANIZER

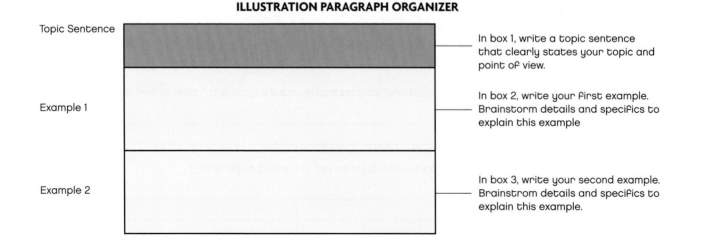

Topic Sentence — In box 1, write a topic sentence that clearly states your topic and point of view.

Example 1 — In box 2, write your first example. Brainstorm details and specifics to explain this example

Example 2 — In box 3, write your second example. Brainstrom details and specifics to explain this example.

Example 3   In box 4, present your third example. Brainstorm details and specifics to explain this example.

Conclusion   Jot ideas for a lively concluding sentence or two, a final thought about your illustration.

Now write the best draft you can. Use transitional expressions of illustration to guide your reader from point to point. Let your draft cool for an hour or a day; then read it like a thoughtful stranger. Think critically as you read. Is the topic sentence clear and interesting? Does it "set up" the paragraph for the reader? Does each example develop the main idea? Proofread for grammar and spelling.

B. Description

Good **description** creates such a vivid word picture of a person, place, or object that a reader can experience it too. While detailed, exact language adds spark to any writing, it is the lifeblood of great description. Descriptive language appeals to our *senses*—sight, sound, smell, taste, and touch.

Imagine, for example, that you want your friends to try the creative new ice cream shop in town. You could say, "The ice cream is to die for," or you could describe one flavor that is startling purple, tastes a bit like sweet potatoes, and is called "Yam I Am." As you practice describing, you'll discover an amazing thing: The more you look, the more you see!

Descriptive ability is important in journalism, architecture, science, engineering, medicine, design, and many other fields.

Topic Sentence

Here is the first sentence of a descriptive paragraph:

> The windows at either end of the laundry room were open, but no breeze washed through to carry off the stale odors of fabric softener, detergent, and bleach.

- The topic sentence of a descriptive paragraph indicates what will be described. What will be the subject of this description?

  a laundry room

- The topic sentence often also gives the reader an *overall impression* of the person, place, or thing to be described. Does this topic sentence give an overall impression of the laundry room?

  It implies that the room is stale and perhaps neglected.

Paragraph and Plan

Here is the entire paragraph:

> The windows at either end of the laundry room were open, but no breeze washed through to carry off the stale odors of fabric softener, detergent, and bleach. In the small ponds of soapy water that stained the concrete floor were stray balls of multicolored lint and fuzz. Along the left wall of the room stood ten rasping dryers, their round windows offering glimpses of jumping socks, underwear, and fatigues. Down the center of the room were a dozen washing machines, set back to back in two rows. Some were chugging like steamboats; others were whining and whistling and dribbling suds. Two stood forlorn and empty, their lids flung open, with crudely drawn signs that said "Broke!" A long shelf partially covered in blue paper ran the length of the wall, interrupted only by a locked door. Alone, at the far end of the shelf, sat one empty laundry basket and an open box of Tide. Above the shelf at the other end was a small bulletin board decorated with yellowed business cards and torn slips of paper: scrawled requests for rides, reward offers for lost dogs, and phone numbers without names or explanations. On and on the machines hummed and wheezed, gurgled and gushed, washed, rinsed, and spun.
>
> *Richard Nordquist*

- Do the details in this description help you see and feel this laundry room? The overall impression seems be that this is a stale and shabby place.

- List at least three details or sections that support this overall impression:

  "ponds of soapy water," "stray balls of multicolored lint and fuzz," "dribbling suds," "crudely drawn

  signs that said, 'Broke!'"

- How many senses does the writer appeal to in this paragraph? Underline your favorite descriptive words or parts.

  sight, sound

- Like many descriptive paragraphs, this one is arranged according to space order.[†] Underline at least four transitional expressions that the writer uses to show where things are.

- Before composing this paragraph, the writer probably brainstormed or freewrote to gather the best details and then organized them into a rough **outline**.

---

*© 2013 Richard Nordquist (http://grammar.about.com/). Used with permission of About Inc., which can be found online at www.about.com. All rights reserved.

[†]For more work on space order, see Chapter 4, "Improving Your Paragraphs," Part A.

If your teaching goals include creative nonfiction—or if you just want to add a bit of poetry or poetic prose to your course—this "Where I'm From" exercise produces powerful writing and helps students approach description in a new way: ‹**http://www.george ellalyon.com/where.html**›.

Transitional expressions for descriptive paragraphs usually help readers "see" where things are.

Transitional Expressions Indicating Place or Position	
above, below	on top, underneath
near, far	to the left, right, in the center
next, to, near	behind, beside
up, down, between	front, back, middle

PRACTICE 6

Read this student's descriptive paragraph and answer the questions.

It is about two inches wide and two inches in height. It has three peaks on the top and one peak at the bottom center. Words are written across the top half, and in the middle are engravings of two men standing with a shield and an eagle between them. The lower half of this metal object displays numbers. On the back is a pin. This object carries a powerful meaning that calls up mixed feelings in some people. It is a symbol of authority and identifies a group of people who represent respect and discipline. You must attend an academy in order to enter this group, and then you can wear this object proudly on your chest or carry it in a wallet. It is a symbol of law enforcement, and sometimes good people die because of it.

Steven Rodriguez, Student

1. Rather than start with a general impression, this student describes an object in detail and puts his topic sentence at the end. Underline the topic sentence. Did you guess the object being described?

   yes, a police badge

2. Does keeping the object a mystery add to or take away from the effectiveness of the paragraph?

   Answers will vary.

3. The first five sentences give physical details. What kinds of details are given in the second half?

   The writer discusses the meaning of the badge, how it is earned, and what it might cost in sacrifice.

PRACTICE 7

The details in a descriptive paragraph should support the *overall impression* stated or implied in the topic sentence. In each of the following plans, one detail has nothing to do with the topic sentence and should be dropped. Find the irrelevant detail and circle its letter.

1. The patient presents with a painful rash down the left side of her head.
   a. patient well-dressed, designer handbag
   b. no fever, temperature 97.8 degrees
   c. vertical line of raised red blisters behind left ear to neck
   d. complains that left head and neck have hurt increasingly for three days

2. For two months every summer, Abuelita's house in the Dominican Republic was my tropical paradise.

   a. outdoor and courtyard walls painted pink

   b. giant banyan tree near the kitchen, my castle to play in

   c. huge vines and tiny lizards climbing the walls

   (d.) Haiti on one end of the island, DR on the other

   e. delicious smells of flowers and Abuelita's cooking

3. The pelican was oil-drenched and greatly distressed.

   a. weak from weight loss and dehydration

   b. feathers matted, separated, and glossy black with oil

   c. beak open, panting

   (d.) eighty-six oil spills since 2000

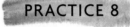

PRACTICE 8

Teamwork: Critical Viewing and Writing

In a group with four or five classmates, study these photos of a tropical hotel that your marketing firm has been hired to promote. Your audience is adult couples who want a weekend away from it all without the children. Your goal is to describe this hotel—location, pool, views, guest rooms—in such enticing detail that guests will rush to make reservations and your team will retire on your bonus checks. Ask one group member to take notes as you brainstorm. Then organize and craft your masterpiece of verbal salesmanship. Be prepared to share with the class.

PRACTICE 9

Writing a Descriptive Paragraph

Pick a topic from this list or one your instructor assigns. Think of one overall impression you wish to convey, and draft a topic sentence stating this impression. Prewrite to get rich descriptive details to support your topic sentence. Many students find it useful to use a graphic organizer as they plan their paragraph. In your notebook, draw a blank 8½-by-11-inch organizer like the one below or use the descriptive paragraph organizer on the *Grassroots* website.

- a workplace
- an object that says to you: *I have arrived*
- someone you know well
- a device or piece of equipment you use
- a sad (intense, dirty, quiet, historic, inspiring) place

- a photograph from the news
- your favorite meal (or worst meal)
- an animal at the zoo
- an object that deserves attention
- a "worthless" object that you treasure

DESCRIPTIVE PARAGRAPH ORGANIZER

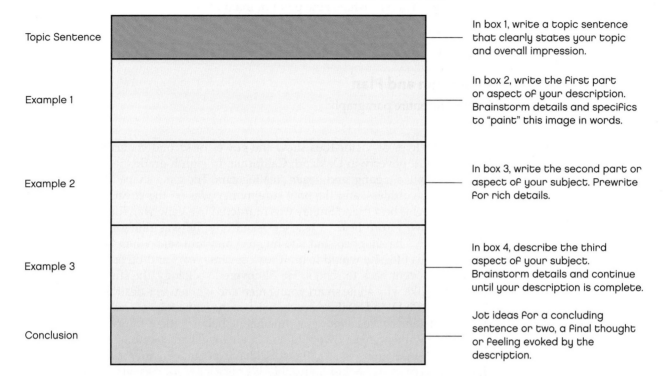

Now write the best draft you can. Use transitional expressions of description to guide your reader from detail to detail. Let your draft cool for an hour or a day. Then read it like a thoughtful stranger. Think critically as you read. Is the topic sentence clear and interesting? Does it "set up" the paragraph for the reader? Does each detail develop the main idea? Proofread for grammar and spelling.

C. Narration

From childhood on, most people love a good story. To **narrate** is to tell a story—to explain what happened, when it happened, and who was involved. When you tell a friend or relative about a funny, frightening, or annoying incident, you are sharing a narrative. Many writers and public speakers use stories to connect with their audiences and bring ideas to life. The key to a good narrative is that it has a clear **point**. The critical-thinking task of narrative is to ask "What is the point of this story? Why do I want to tell it?"

Narrative is a useful skill in any field that requires reports, such as sociology, psychology, business, nursing, and police work.

Topic Sentence

Here is the topic sentence of a narrative paragraph:

> The two lives of Victor Rios show the power of second chances.

● The topic sentence should indicate the subject or main idea of the narrative. Before you write, you should think about the *point* of your story. What do you want your readers to learn from reading your story? Do you hope to teach a lesson, to make them laugh, or perhaps inspire them to take action?

- The writer begins this paragraph with a topic sentence that reveals the point of the narrative. What is the point or main idea?

  Victor Rios's life story shows the power of second chances.

Paragraph and Plan

Here is the entire paragraph:

> The two lives of Victor Rios show the power of second chances. Rios grew up in squalid poverty in Oakland, California. In eighth grade, he dropped out of school, joined a gang, and began stealing cars. The gang shaped his thinking: school was worthless, and the only sure money was on the streets. Then when Rios was 15, his best friend Smiley was murdered in a gang war. Rios saw clearly what his own future held. A teacher asked how he was doing after Smiley's death. "Fine," he snapped, but she hugged him and said when he was ready to change his life, she would help. It took several years and other mentors, but at last Rios went back to school. He discovered sociology, the study of human behavior—like why some smart young men and women self-destruct. Rios went on to earn a Ph.D. and a college teaching job at the University of California. Today he mentors and writes about gang members, helping them transform. In 2012, Rios told TV interviewer Gwen Ifill that if an angel had said to him as an angry teen, "hang in there because at 34, you'll have an amazing life," he would have laughed. His message to kids in trouble: it's not a joke; your second chance exists.

TEACHING TIP

Ask students how they would explain why some smart young men and women self-destruct. Do they agree with Rios that mentors and education are two lifelines?

- The body of a narrative is made up of small events or actions told in the order they occurred. Arranging these details in time, or chronological, order helps readers follow more easily.[*]

- List the smaller events in this paragraph in chronological order:

  dropped out; joined a gang and stole cars; best friend murdered; teacher offered help;

  returned to school; earned Ph.D. and teaching job; helps gang members now

- Underline at least three transitional expressions of time in this paragraph.
- Note that the topic sentence, events, and concluding sentences make a rough *outline* for the paragraph. Before drafting, the writer probably made just such an outline.

Using transitional expressions of time can help your readers follow the narrative.

Transitional Expressions of Time for Narratives		
afterward	first	next
currently	later	soon
finally	meanwhile	then

---

[*]For more work on time order, see Chapter 4, "Improving Your Paragraphs," Part A.

PRACTICE 10

Here are three plans for narrative paragraphs. The events in the plans are not in chronological order, and they each contain an event or detail that does not relate to the story. Number the events in time order and cross out the irrelevant one.

1. The invention of cornflakes was a happy accident.

   _3_ Will decided to bake the boiled wheat flakes, liked the taste, and found that the patients loved them.

   _1_ In the late 1800s, Dr. John Kellogg ran a health retreat, helped in the kitchen by his "slow" brother Will, a sixth-grade dropout.

   _4_ Will had the brilliant idea of baking cornflakes as he had baked the wheat, and orders poured in.

   ___ ~~Eating oatmeal might be good for the heart.~~

   _2_ One day in 1894, after Will accidentally boiled some wheat too long, it fell into flaky pieces.

   _5_ After John resigned, Will ran the W. W. Kellogg Company, proving himself to be a business and advertising genius.

2. I learned the hard way that a friend's envy is a serious warning sign.

   _2_ After that conversation, we became best friends in high school.

   ___ ~~Many students share apartments to keep costs down.~~

   _3_ We shared an apartment in college, and after I decorated my bedroom, I was hurt when she just said, "I'd kill for this room" and walked out.

   _1_ The first thing Lara said to me in high school was, "I want your hair," which I took as a compliment.

   _4_ When Lara secretly interviewed for a job she knew I desperately wanted, I was shocked to realize that this woman was not my friend.

TEACHING TIP

You and your students can view the stolen artworks at ‹http://www.gardner museum.org/resources /theft›.

3. The largest unsolved art heist in history occurred quietly in Boston in 1990.

   _3_ Working fast, the thieves removed 13 masterpieces from the walls, including paintings by Vermeer and Rembrandt, and then slipped into the night.

   _4_ Art detectives, the FBI, and a five million dollar reward never turned up the missing works, which are valued at five hundred million dollars.

   _1_ Around midnight on March 18, two men posing as Boston police entered the security door of the small Isabella Stewart Gardner Museum.

   _2_ They ordered the security guard to come away from his desk and then handcuffed him and the one other guard on duty.

   ___ ~~Almost four hundred years after his death, Vermeer is admired for the way he painted light.~~

PRACTICE 11

Teamwork: Critical Thinking and Writing

Like many fairy tales, fables were told to convey a life lesson. In a small group, have someone read this fable, "The Frog and the Scorpion," aloud and then discuss what you and your groupmates think the story is about and answer the questions on page 64. Finally, write the missing topic sentence.

The Frog and the Scorpion
by Heidi Taillefer

Once you have read the fable below, can you explain why you think this artist painted partial armor on the frog? (There are no wrong answers in art.)

The ancient fable of the frog and the scorpion teaches a lesson about ___believing___

someone's words yet ignoring his or her actions.

A poisonous scorpion wanted to cross a rushing river, but he could not swim. Spotting a frog sitting on the riverbank, the scorpion called to him, politely asking for a ride on the frog's back. "I'm sorry," said the frog, "but you will sting me, and then we will both die." The scorpion replied, "That makes no sense because I want to cross the river." This sounded reasonable, but the frog had a nagging worry. "Well, you might wait until we are almost across and then sting me." But the scorpion protested, "Never! Because I would be so grateful for your help." So the frog agreed, the scorpion hopped on his back, and off they went. About halfway across the river, the scorpion suddenly stung the frog hard. The frog's body started going numb, and he knew he was dying. "Why did you do that?" he gasped. The scorpion said, "Because it's my nature," and they both sank.

Does this story relate to your experience? Have you ever been a "frog" and let yourself get stung despite your common sense? Have you ever stung somebody else and then regretted it? Do we all have a bit of self-defeating frog or scorpion hiding in us? Discuss what you think is the lesson or point of this fable. Then complete the topic sentence so that it clearly states this point.

PRACTICE 12

Writing a Narrative Paragraph

Pick a topic from this list or one your instructor assigns. Draft a topic sentence that will get the reader's attention and/or states the point of your story. Prewrite to get as many narrative details as possible. Many students find it helpful to use a graphic organizer as they plan their paragraph. In your notebook, draw a blank 8½-by-11-inch organizer like the one shown on the next page or use the narrative paragraph organizer on the *Grassroots* website.

- something I am (not) proud of
- a family story
- a parenting lesson
- a key event in history or science
- a lesson in dignity

- a career insight
- becoming a volunteer
- a cautionary college tale
- a decision to change jobs
- a turning point

Now write the best draft you can. Use transitional expressions of narration to guide your reader from event to event. Let your draft cool for an hour or a day. Then read it like a thoughtful stranger. Think critically as you read. Is the topic sentence clear and interesting? Does it "set up" the paragraph for the reader? Does each event or detail develop the main idea? Proofread for grammar and spelling.

NARRATIVE PARAGRAPH ORGANIZER

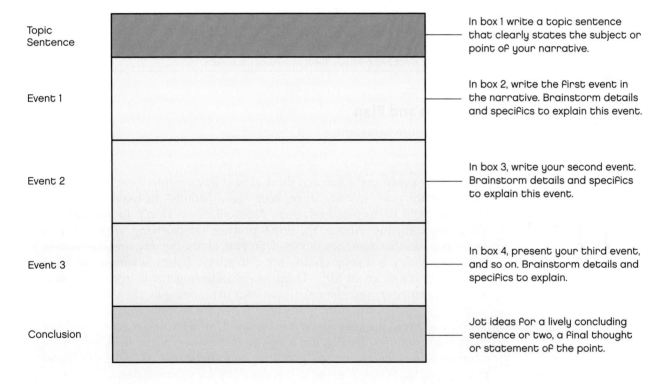

Topic Sentence — In box 1 write a topic sentence that clearly states the subject or point of your narrative.

Event 1 — In box 2, write the first event in the narrative. Brainstorm details and specifics to explain this event.

Event 2 — In box 3, write your second event. Brainstorm details and specifics to explain this event.

Event 3 — In box 4, present your third event, and so on. Brainstorm details and specifics to explain.

Conclusion — Jot ideas for a lively concluding sentence or two, a final thought or statement of the point.

D. Process

A **process** paragraph explains *how to do something* or *how something gets done*. A recipe for cherry pie, the directions for your new scanner, or the stages in becoming a U.S. citizen are all processes. The goal of such directions is a delicious pie, a scanner that scans, and an understanding of the citizenship process. After reading a process paragraph, the reader should be able to do something or understand how something works. The process writer must think like the reader and not leave out a step.

Process writing is useful in technology, psychology, history, the sciences, business, and many other fields.

Topic Sentence

Here is the topic sentence of one student's process paragraph:

> In just five easy steps, you can flunk almost any job interview.

- The topic sentence should clearly state the goal of the process. What should the reader be able to do once he or she finishes reading this paragraph?

  flunk a job interview

- Based on the topic sentence, do you think this writer is being serious? What audience, or group of readers, is she addressing?

  The writer is not being serious. She is addressing job seekers.

Paragraph and Plan

Here is the entire paragraph:

> In just five easy steps, you can flunk almost any job interview. First, during the important pre-interview stage, keep these "don'ts" in mind. Don't take down the wild party pics from your Facebook page. Don't do any research about the company. Above all, don't practice interviewing with a friend, answering possible questions out loud. Second, on the big day, dress to express. Your team jersey is a solid choice, but a hilarious T-shirt is better, like "TXT Queen" or "It's all about ME." Third, make an unforgettable first impression. Arrive late without your résumé. Leave your tongue ring in; chewing gum will keep it flashing. Fourth, during the interview, it's important to act as detached as possible. Avoid the interviewer's eyes, say "Um" a lot, and check your phone every three minutes. Finally, the way you leave can seal the deal. Forget the interviewer's name as you say goodbye, and afterwards, skip the old-school thank you note. You will be the talk of the office for weeks to come.
>
> *Yesenia Ramos, Student*

- The body of a process paragraph consists of the steps to be completed in the order they should be done. Arranging these steps in time, or chronological,[*] order helps your readers understand the directions more easily.

- How many steps are there in this how-to paragraph and what are they?

  Five steps: don't take pre-interview actions to prepare; dress inappropriately; make a terrible first

  impression; act detached when you leave, forget the interviewer's name; and don't send a note.

---

[*]For more work on time order, see Chapter 4, "Improving Your Paragraphs," Part A.

- Note that the topic sentence, five main steps, and concluding sentence make an outline of the paragraph. In fact, after brainstorming or freewriting for ideas, the writer made just such an outline before she wrote.

To help readers follow the steps in a process, transitional expressions of time are useful.

Transitional Expressions of Time for Process		
Beginning a Process	**Continuing a Process**	**Ending a Process**
first	next, then	finally
initially	after that	last
the first step (or stage)	the second step (or stage)	the final step

Just as this series of photos depicts the stages of a butterfly's development, your process paragraphs should clearly describe each step or stage for the reader. Before writing, try to visualize the process as a series of clear steps.

PRACTICE 13   Read this student's process paragraph carefully and answer the questions.

Properly shooting a basketball is a four-step process. First, position your body by squaring your shoulders in the direction of the hoop, holding the ball above your eyes, and aiming your shooting elbow at the basket. Next, bend your knees and explode upwards to transfer power from your legs through your back to your shooting shoulder and arm, pushing the ball upward and forward toward the rim. Third, using only the fingertips of the shooting hand, apply a consistent and straight backspin as you release the basketball from your hands; your non-shooting hand should grip the ball as lightly as possible to stabilize it. Finally, snap your wrist as you release the ball. This fourth step not only ensures a tight rotation but also helps control the path of the shot. Mastering these four steps will help your shots float to the hoop with a nice arc and a tight, consistent backspin. Swish.

Jared Cohen, Student

1. What process is described in this paragraph?

   shooting a basketball
   _____

2. How many steps does the writer present?

   four
   _____

3. What transitional expressions does this writer use to signal each new step in the process?

first, next, third, finally

 **PRACTICE 14**

Here are three plans for process paragraphs. The steps for the plans are not in the correct chronological order, and they contain irrelevant details that are not part of the process. Number the steps in the proper time sequence and cross out any irrelevant details.

1. Opening a Twitter account is as easy as one, two, three.

____4____ Finally, type the security code, read the Terms of Service (or not) and click "I accept."

____2____ Once on the site, click the green box that says "Join the conversation."

_____ ~~Family Leaf is like a mini Facebook just for relatives.~~

____1____ Go to ‹**http://twitter.com**›.

____3____ Create your Twitter user name and type in your email address.

____5____ Start tweeting!

2. Stress, so common in modern life, is actually a process, with symptoms that will keep progressing if they are not addressed.

_____ ~~Not getting enough sleep causes stress.~~

____3____ After a time, a person enters the final phase, exhaustion, characterized by poor performance, lowered immunity, and a loss of zest for life.

____1____ In the first, or alarm, stage, a threatening situation triggers strong "fight or flight" reactions—a racing heart, high blood pressure, and muscle tension.

____2____ The second stage, resistance, occurs as the person anxiously attempts to keep coping with the stress, perhaps turning to overeating or drinking too much caffeine.

3. The creation of a woodblock print has four stages.

____3____ Paper is laid over the inked block and is rubbed all over the raised design with a spoon.

____1____ The artist sketches a design on a block of wood and then carves away all the wood around the design.

____2____ Next the artist rolls ink across the raised surface of the design.

_____ ~~Other prints are lithograph prints and silkscreens.~~

____4____ When the paper is lifted away, the inked design is printed on it.

PRACTICE 15

Teamwork: Critical Thinking and Writing

If you have ever tried to diet or quit smoking, you know how hard change can be. Behavioral change is actually a *process*, not an event. In a small group, look closely at this graphic on the *five stages of change*. Discuss each stage and what a person might think or do at this stage. Which stages are most likely to cause trouble for a person hoping to change a behavior? Why do some people try to change but fail? Share examples if you wish.

Private journal assignment: Think of an important change you made or tried to make. Did you want to exercise more, quit drinking, or study more regularly? Describe your change process. Which stages were the hardest for you? What if anything did you learn?

THE STAGES OF BEHAVIORAL CHANGE

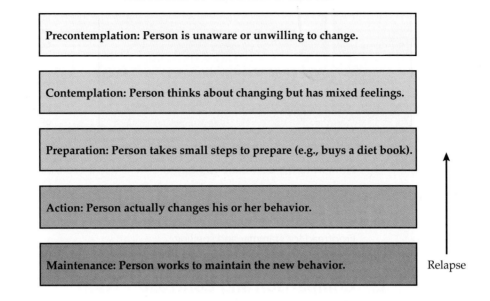

Precontemplation: Person is unaware or unwilling to change.

Contemplation: Person thinks about changing but has mixed feelings.

Preparation: Person takes small steps to prepare (e.g., buys a diet book).

Action: Person actually changes his or her behavior.

Maintenance: Person works to maintain the new behavior.

Relapse

PRACTICE 16   ## Writing a Process Paragraph

Pick a topic from this list that interests you or one your instructor assigns. Draft a topic sentence to introduce your paragraph and catch the readers' interest. Visualize or go through the process, jotting facts and details. Don't leave out any steps. Many students find it helpful to use a graphic organizer as they plan the paragraph. Fill in this graphic organizer with your ideas, or in your notebook, draw a blank 8½-by-11-inch organizer like the one shown here. You might also use the process paragraph organizer on the *Grassroots* website.

- how to turn a failure into success
- how to find (or get rid of) a roommate
- how to survive a night of babysitting (or other)
- how to groom a dog
- how to become more _____

- how to use Instagram
- how to study for a test
- how to motivate yourself (or overcome resistance)
- how to choose a major
- how to find a job

PROCESS PARAGRAPH ORGANIZER

Topic Sentence	In box 1 write a topic sentence that clearly states your topic and point of view.
Step 1	In box 2, write the first step or stage in the process. Include details that clearly explain the step.
Step 2	In box 3, write your second step or stage. Include details that clearly explain this step

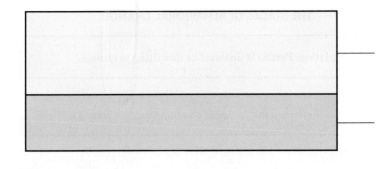

Step 3 — In box 4, present your step, and so on until the process is complete.

Conclusion — Jot ideas for a lively concluding sentence or two, a final thought about the importance of the process.

Now write the best draft you can. Use transitional expressions of process to guide your reader from step to step. Let your draft cool for an hour or a day. Then read it like a thoughtful stranger. Think critically as you read. Is the topic sentence clear and interesting? Does it "set up" the paragraph for the reader? Does each detail develop the main idea? Proofread for grammar and spelling.

E. Comparison and Contrast

To **contrast** two people, places, or things is to examine the ways in which they are different. To **compare** them is to examine the ways in which they are similar.

Contrast and comparison are extremely useful thinking skills in daily life, college, and work. When you shop, you might contrast two brands of running shoes or two flat screen TVs to get the better value or style. In courses like English, history, psychology, and art, you will often be required to write comparison/contrast essays. Your employer might ask you to compare two overnight delivery services, two office chairs, or two child-care programs.

Topic Sentence

Here is the topic sentence of a contrast paragraph:

> Extroverts and introverts are two personality types that differ in important ways.

- The writer begins a contrast paragraph with a topic sentence that clearly states what two people, things, or ideas will be contrasted.

- What two things will be contrasted in this paragraph?

  extroverts and introverts

- What word or words tell you that the writer will contrast, not compare?

  differ

Paragraph and Plan

Here is the entire paragraph:

> Extroverts and introverts are two personality types that differ in important ways. Extroverts are outgoing "people persons" who draw energy from social situations, noise, and action. They usually have many friends and love parties.

TEACHING TIP

Students are fascinated by this subject and want to know whether they are introverts or extroverts. You might link this paragraph with a discussion of Susan Cain's article "Introverts Run the World, Quietly" in Unit 9. Her 20-question quiz helps students see where they fall on the introvert-extrovert continuum; scroll down at ‹**http://www.npr.org/2012/01/30/145930229/quiet-please-unleashing-the-power-of-introverts**›.

Working on teams appeals to them, so the emphasis on teamwork in many businesses favors extroverts. In fact, American culture is geared to extroverts, whose ranks include Oprah Winfrey and Bill Clinton. Introverts, on the other hand, tend to be more inward people who need private time to recharge. They often prefer a few close friendships and dislike parties though they can be charming and fun in social gatherings if they choose. Introverts enjoy working alone, taking time to think deeply about a task. Recent books have highlighted the career strengths of introverts, whose traits make them good scientists, writers, doctors, and quiet leaders. Microsoft founder Bill Gates, actress Gwyneth Paltrow, and writer Toni Morrison are introverts. Understanding which type we are can help us make more satisfying career and life choices.

● To develop the topic sentence, the writer first provides information about (A) *extroverts* and then gives contrasting parallel information about (B) *introverts*.

● In column (A) list the main points given about extroverts, and in column (B) list the parallel points about introverts.

	(A)	(B)
sociability	outgoing "people persons"	inward, need private time
friends	many friends, love parties	close friends, dislike parties
work	like to work on teams	enjoy working alone
advantages	American culture geared to them	good scientists, writers, doctors, leaders
examples	Winfrey, Clinton	Gates, Paltrow, Morrison

● When the writer makes a point about (A), he or she makes a similar point about (B). For example, "many friends" is balanced by "a few close friendships."

● Can you see why the contrast writer needs to make an *outline* before writing? Otherwise, keeping track of all the points would be too confusing, and important information might be left out. In fact, this writer's outline probably looked a lot like the chart you just filled in: two columns of balanced points presented in the same order.

● What *transitional expression* indicates that the writer has completed (A) and now is moving on to (B)?

on the other hand

● The concluding sentence suggests how this information might help the reader. Could knowing about extroverts and introverts help you in life or work? Which personality type are you?

There are two ways to organize the details in comparison or contrast writing. You can visualize the first way like this:

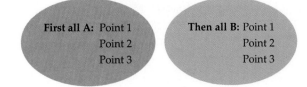

First all A: Point 1
Point 2
Point 3

Then all B: Point 1
Point 2
Point 3

The other way to organize your points of contrast or comparison is to move back and forth between A and B. Present one point about A and then the parallel point about B. Move to the next point and do the same:

First A, Point 1	Then B, Point 1
First A, Point 2	Then B, Point 2
First A, Point 3	Then B, Point 3

Transitional expressions in contrast paragraphs stress *differences*:

Transitional Expressions for Contrast	
however	on the contrary
in contrast	on the one hand
nevertheless	on the other hand

Transitional expressions in comparison paragraphs stress *similarities*:

Transitional Expressions for Comparison	
also	in a similar way
as well	in the same way
likewise	similarly

PRACTICE 17 Read this student's paragraph carefully and answer the questions.

"Two birds of a feather," so the family describes my mother and me, and it's true that we have much in common. First, we share the same honey-colored skin, hazel eyes, and pouting mouth. In addition, I like to think I've inherited her creative flair. Though we were poor, she taught me that beauty requires style, not money, and I see her influence in my small apartment, which I have decorated with colorful batiks and my paintings. A third similarity, I'm sorry to say, is procrastination. When I was growing up, we teased mom about waiting until the last minute to do the taxes, send out Christmas cards, or prepare for a family party. Once, the relatives were actually arriving at our house as she raced in, out of breath, with a grocery bag holding the chickens she had to cook. Now I'm the one who starts too many assignments the night before and decides to get gas when the tank is almost empty. Mostly, I thank my mother for the gift of who I am.

Cheri Baldwin, Student

1. What words in the topic sentence does this writer use to indicate that a comparison will follow?

    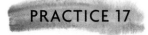 much in common

2. In what ways are the writer and her mother similar?

similar appearance, creative flair, and tendency to procrastinate

3. Does the writer use the all A, then all B pattern or the AB, AB, AB pattern?

AB, AB, AB

4. Why do you think the writer saves procrastination for last?

She presents the first two positive traits and saves the one negative trait for last.

PRACTICE 18

Below are three plans for contrast paragraphs. The points of contrast in the second column do not follow the same order as the points in the first column. In addition, one detail is missing. First, number the points in the second column to match those in the first. Then fill in the missing detail.

1. Standard camera

1. takes great close-ups, clear shots
2. heavy to carry around
3. can be very expensive
4. some expertise required

Smartphone camera

<u>4</u> no special expertise needed
<u>3</u> price built into cost of phone
<u>1</u> can't take close-up shots
<u>2</u> light and easy to carry

2. Beyoncé

1. 33, music veteran
2. stays true to R&B roots
3. focuses more on albums
4. started in group, Destiny's Child
5. married to Jay-Z

Rihanna

<u>3</u> dominates radio with hit singles
<u>4</u> started as solo artist
<u>5</u> unmarried
<u>2</u> more trendy pop, less R&B
<u>1</u> 26, still on the way up

3. CT Scan

1. costs $1200–$3200
2. takes about 5 minutes
3. radiation of 1000 X-rays
4. some risk of harm from radiation

MRI

<u>3</u> no radiation, works magnetically
<u>4</u> no risk of radiation
<u>1</u> costs $1200–$4000
<u>2</u> takes about 30 minutes

PRACTICE 19

TEACHING TIP

You might ask students to read nutritional labels on sodas or other products like cookies or cereals, look at serving sizes, take notes, and write about their findings.

Teamwork: Critical Viewing and Writing

Nutrition expert Dr. Marion Nestle, a professor at New York University, writes about ways that "Big Soda" manufacturers take advantage of legal loopholes to avoid giving consumers the facts. In a group with four or five classmates, study the two soda labels on the following page. The label on the left is from a 20-ounce bottle of a popular cola. The new label on the right is proposed by consumer groups like the Center for Science in the Public Interest and by Dr. Nestle. List the six differences between the two labels. Do any facts on the proposed label surprise you? In what ways is the proposed label more honest? When you buy a can or bottle of soda, do you think of it as one serving—to drink all at once—or as 2½ servings? Be prepared to write about your findings.

CURRENT LABEL

Nutrition Facts

Serving Size 8 fl oz (240 mL)
Servings Per Container about 2.5

Amount Per Serving		
Calories 110		
		% Daily Value*
Total Fat 0g		0%
Sodium 70mg		3%
Total Carbohydrate 32g		10%
Sugars 30g		
Protein 0g		

*Percent Daily Values are based on a 2,000 calorie diet.

PROPOSED LABEL

Nutrition Facts

Serving Size 1 bottle (600 mL)
Servings Per Container 1

Amount Per Serving	% Daily Value*
Calories 275	14%
Total Fat 0g	0%
Sodium 175mg	7%
Total Carbohydrate 78g	26%
Sugars 75g	
Protein 0g	

*Percent Daily Values are based on a 2,000 calorie diet.

PRACTICE 20   Here are ten topics for either contrast or comparison paragraphs. Choose your three favorites, and on a separate sheet of paper, compose one topic sentence of either comparison or contrast for each of the three.

- two members of your family
- two cars you'd consider buying
- paper textbook vs. e-textbook
- two TV shows of the same type
- soccer and American football

- two places you have lived
- a phone call and FaceTime
- weeknight dinners and holiday dinners
- two teachers who have inspired you
- two careers you have considered

PRACTICE 21   ## Writing a Comparison or Contrast Paragraph

Choose either the best topic sentence you wrote in Practice 20 or a topic your instructor assigns. Think and jot about the differences or similarities between A and B. Don't be satisfied with the first points you write; keep jotting to get as many ideas as possible. Now decide whether you will use the all A, all B pattern or AB, AB, AB. Many students find it helpful to use a graphic organizer as they plan their paragraph. Try it. In your notebook, draw a blank 8½-by-11-inch organizer like the one that follows or use the comparison or contrast paragraph organizer on the *Grassroots* website.

COMPARISON-CONTRAST PARAGRAPH ORGANIZER

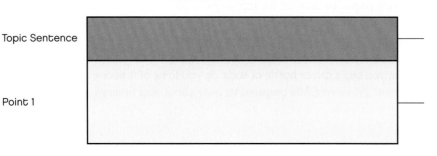

Topic Sentence

In box 1 write a topic sentence that clearly states the two things you will compare or contrast.

Point 1

In box 2, write your first point of contrast or comparison. Brainstorm details to support this point for A and B.

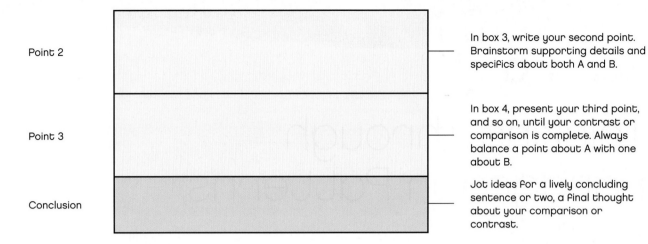

Point 2

In box 3, write your second point. Brainstorm supporting details and specifics about both A and B.

Point 3

In box 4, present your third point, and so on, until your contrast or comparison is complete. Always balance a point about A with one about B.

Conclusion

Jot ideas for a lively concluding sentence or two, a final thought about your comparison or contrast.

Now write the best draft you can. Use transitional expressions of comparison or contrast to guide your reader from point to point. Let your draft cool for an hour or a day. Then read it like a thoughtful stranger. Think critically as you read. Is the topic sentence clear and interesting? Does it "set up" the paragraph for the reader? Does each point develop the main idea? Proofread for grammar and spelling.

Chapter Highlights

These paragraph patterns are often used in college and the workplace. They reflect different ways of thinking about a subject.

- The illustration paragraph develops the topic sentence with one, two, three, or more specific examples.

- The descriptive paragraph paints a vivid word picture of a person, place, or object.

- The narrative paragraph tells a story that makes a clear point.

- A process paragraph explains step by step how to do something or how something gets done.

- The comparison or contrast paragraph examines the ways in which two people, places, or things are alike or different.

EXPLORING ONLINE

<http://writesite.cuny.edu/projects/keywords/example/hand2.html> Fill in the boxes to help you develop your idea with examples.

<http://video.about.com/grammar/How-to-Write-a-Descriptive-Paragraph.htm> This short video reviews the basics of a good descriptive paragraph.

<http://lrs.ed.uiuc.edu/students/fwalters/compcontEx1a.html> Practice the transitional expressions for contrast writing, and get instant feedback online.

CHAPTER 6

Thinking Through Paragraph Patterns, Part 2

A: **Classification**

B: **Cause and Effect**

C: **Definition**

D: **Persuasion**

This chapter will teach you four more paragraph patterns that will help you become a more critical thinker and a better writer.

A. Classification

To **classify** is to sort things into types or categories, according to one basis of division. For example, you might classify the music on your iPod by purpose (music for relaxing, music for working out, and so on). Dealers divide cars by body type into sedans, sports cars, SUVs, and convertibles. Experts rate hurricanes based on their wind speed and destructive force as category 1 through 5. In fact, classification is so common because it reflects one way our brains organize information.

For anyone in the sciences, medicine, retail, engineering, psychology, and many other fields, classification will be especially important.

Topic Sentence

Here is the topic sentence of a student's classification paragraph:

> Couples can be classified on the basis of their public displays of affection as get-a-room gropers, G-rated romantics, or cold customers.

- The writer begins a classification paragraph with a topic sentence that clearly states what group of people or things will be classified.

- What group of people will be classified in this paragraph? Into how many categories will they be divided?

  couples; three categories

- Based on just the topic sentence, do you think the writer's tone is serious or humorous?

  humorous

Paragraph and Plan

Here is the entire paragraph:

> Couples can be classified on the basis of their public displays of affection as get-a-room gropers, G-rated romantics, or cold customers. Get-a-room gropers take public displays of affection to insane extremes. They can turn a kiss in a crowded elevator into an ear, nose, and throat exam. They grind and grab while disgusted parents cover their children's eyes. The next type, G-rated romantics, are affectionate but appropriate for general audiences. Strangers might feel that love is in the air as these two stroll down the street with their arms around each other, and G-rated romantics may kiss now and then, mouths closed, but they know when to quit. Walking with their hands in each other's back pockets is about as steamy as it gets. The last group is the cold customers. These pairs could pass for strangers except that they stay side by side for hours. In a restaurant, they can eat a whole meal in total silence. It's easy to wonder what put the chill in their relationship, but maybe they're just reacting to the gropers pawing each other at the next table.
>
> *Deirdre Chaudry, Student*

- What information does she provide about the first type, get-a-room gropers?

  They take public displays of affection to extremes.

- What information does she provide about the second type, G-rated romantics?

  They are affectionate but appropriate.

- What information does she provide about the third type, cool customers?

  They can pass for total strangers.

- Note that the topic sentence, the three types, and the concluding sentence form an **outline** of this paragraph. In fact, the student brainstormed or freewrote to gather ideas and then made just such an outline.

Transitional expressions in classification paragraphs stress *divisions* and *categories*:

Transitional Expressions for Classification	
can be divided	the first type (or class)
can be classified	the second kind (or group)
can be categorized	the last category

PRACTICE 1

Read the following classification paragraph carefully and answer the questions.

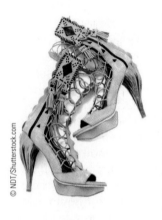

Everett Rogers' theory of consumer trends and how they spread is useful information for every business student. Rogers divided shoppers into five types, based on how quickly they respond to new products. The first type of shoppers, the innovators, are those techies, adventurers, or fashionistas who are first to stand in line for an iPad Mini, a new snowboard, or edgy gladiator boots. While these cool leaders introduce a trend, the second group, the early adopters, establish the trend by joining it early on. Think of them as the popular crowd at school. Third comes the early majority, a large group of buyers who wait to buy their iPads until the trend is a sure thing. The late majority is even more cautious; they won't commit money to a snowboard until snowboarding has become an Olympic event. Finally come the laggards. These folks at last get the courage to buy gladiator boots when the trend is almost over, and innovators are already wearing the next hot thing. Marketers still rely on Rogers' categories to help them target buyers, create ad campaigns, and squeeze all the profit they can from a trend.

TEACHING TIP

Students often enjoy placing themselves in one of Rogers' categories. Ask how many are innovators, early adopters, laggards, and so forth. Let them provide examples of products that they bought early or late on the trend curve.

1. What group of people does Everett Rogers classify? Which sentence tells you this?

   shoppers; the second sentence

2. On what basis does he classify shoppers?

   how quickly they respond to new products

3. How many categories does he name and what are they?

   five categories: innovators, early adopters, early majority, late majority, laggards

4. Make an outline of this paragraph on a separate sheet of paper.

PRACTICE 2

Each group of things or people has been divided according to *one basis of classification* However, one item in each group does not belong—it does not fit in that single basis of classification.

Read each group of items carefully; then circle the letter of each item that does not belong. Next, write the single basis of classification that includes the rest of the group.

EXAMPLE:

Jeans

a. skinny

b. bootcut

c. colorful

d. flares

style or cut

1. Professors
   a. tough graders
   b. easy graders
   (c.) online graders
   d. moderate graders
   <u>toughness of their grading</u>

2. Teenagers
   a. send fewer than 50 texts a day
   b. 50–150 daily texts
   c. daily send more than 150 texts
   (d.) 64% of teens text during class
   <u>texting frequency</u>

3. Credit-card users
   a. pay in full monthly
   (b.) pay with another credit card
   c. never pay total amount due
   d. sometimes pay in full
   <u>amount of payments</u>

4. Breakfast cereals
   a. 7–14 grams sugar per cup
   b. 1–6 grams sugar per cup
   c. 15 grams sugar or more in a cup
   (d.) 30 grams sugar or more in a soda
   <u>amount of sugar in cereal</u>

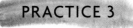 **PRACTICE 3**

Any group can be classified in different ways, depending on the basis of classification. For example, you might classify home-team football fans on the basis of how upset they are when their team loses (very upset, mildly upset, unfazed) or how many home games they attend (TV only, 1–3 games, 4 or more). Both are valid classifications.

For each group below, think of two ways in which each of the following groups could be classified. Answers will vary.

Group	Basis of Classification
EXAMPLE: Home team football fans	(A) *how upset they are when they lose*
	(B) *number of home games they attend*
1. Clothes in your closet	(A) _____
	(B) _____
2. Facebook users	(A) _____
	(B) _____
3. Fast-food burgers	(A) _____
	(B) _____

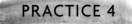 **PRACTICE 4**

Teamwork: Critical Thinking and Writing

In a group with several classmates, plan online categories for a retail website. Ugly Christmas sweaters are now a hot item, and your group's goal is to make extra money by selling 35 ugly Christmas sweaters you have collected from your parents' and grandparents' homes, garage sales, and thrift shops. To help your customers find what they are looking for online, your sweaters will be photographed and classified into various groups on at least three bases (for example, one basis would be *size*—small, medium,

Ugly Christmas sweaters awaiting classification for the retail website described in Practice 4

large, and extra-large). Decide what your *bases of classification* will be and then *name your types or categories*. Make sure all your ugly Christmas sweaters are included in your classifications.

You might search the photo above for ideas about ways to classify the ugly Christmas sweaters in your collection.

PRACTICE 5

Writing a Classification Paragraph

Pick a topic from the list below or one your instructor assigns. Draft a topic sentence, using this form: "_____ *can be classified on the basis of* _____ *as A, B, C, and D.*" Think carefully as you plan your categories, which should cover the whole group. Then prewrite to get as many juicy details as possible. Many students find it helpful to use a graphic organizer as they plan their paragraph. Try it. In your notebook, draw a blank 8½-by-11-inch organizer like the one below or use the classification paragraph organizer on the *Grassroots* website.

- parenting styles
- detectives (or doctors) on TV
- attitudes toward saving money
- reactions to success (or failure)
- students in this class (or at this college)

- annoying co-workers
- jobs for college grads
- bosses
- YouTube videos
- dog (cat, or other pet) owners

CLASSIFICATION PARAGRAPH ORGANIZER

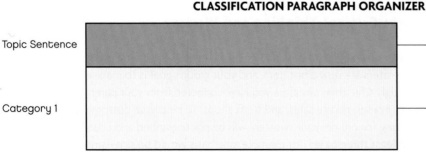

Topic Sentence

In box 1 write a topic sentence that clearly states the group you will classify and your basis of the classification.

Category 1

In box 2, write your first category or type. Brainstorm details and specifics to explain this group.

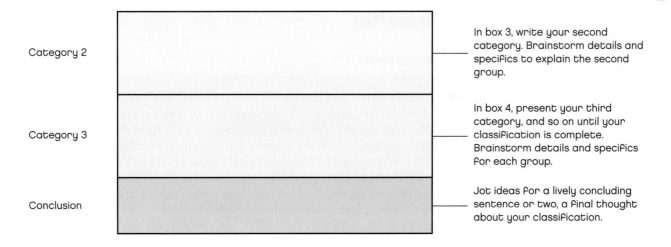

Category 2

In box 3, write your second category. Brainstorm details and specifics to explain the second group.

Category 3

In box 4, present your third category, and so on until your classification is complete. Brainstorm details and specifics for each group.

Conclusion

Jot ideas for a lively concluding sentence or two, a final thought about your classification.

Now write the best draft you can. Use transitional expressions of classification to guide your reader from category to category. Let your draft cool for an hour or a day. Then read it like a thoughtful stranger. Think critically as you read. Is the topic sentence clear and interesting? Does it "set up" the paragraph for the reader? Does each category develop the main idea? Proofread for grammar and spelling.

B. Cause and Effect

Causes are the *reasons* for events. Humans naturally look for causes; we want to know *why*: Why am I afraid of public speaking? Why is my child diabetic? The mature human mind also tries to anticipate *effects*. **Effects** are the *results* or *consequences* of a cause or causes. If my nephew drops out of high school, what effects will it have on his life? If I take out this loan, how will it affect my finances going forward? You can see that ability to think critically about causes and effects is a vitally important skill in college, work, and daily life.

Cause and effect writing is particularly useful in medicine, pharmacy, psychology, science, electronics, business, history, and nearly every field.

Topic Sentence

Here is the topic sentence of a student's cause and effect paragraph:

> Although my parents don't believe it, online gaming has had positive effects on my life.

● The writer begins a cause and effect paragraph by clearly stating the subject and indicating whether causes or effects will be stressed.

● Will causes or effects be the focus? What words tell you this?

  effects; the phrase "positive effects"

● Does this topic sentence make you want to read on? Why or why not?

  Answers will vary.

Paragraph and Plan

Here is the entire paragraph:

> Although my parents don't believe it, online gaming has had positive effects on my life. For the last couple years, I have spent two hours every night playing World of Warcraft, an online role-playing game, with a team of eleven other people. I have always been a shy person, but having to communicate clearly with my team has developed my public-speaking skills and helped me become an effective team player. Our team bought special microphones so we can speak to each other directly during raids. Another important result might be hard to measure, but I believe I have become a better problem solver. As a guild leader, I have to make quick decisions that affect my entire team, and I'm learning to make critical choices with confidence. Finally, the most important effect is that gaming reduces my stress. As a new college student, I need that release each evening in order to face all the responsibilities waiting for me when I sign off with my team and join the real world again—studying, doing chores, and hearing my parents worry out loud that their "American" daughter must be addicted to the Internet.
>
> *Talia Bahari, Student*

- How many effects does the writer discuss? What are they?

  three effects: development of public-speaking and teamwork skills; improvement in problem-

  solving skills; stress reduction

- Do you play video games? Has this activity had positive or negative effects in your life?

  Answers will vary.

- Note that the topic sentence, three effects, and conclusion make a kind of *outline* for this paragraph. Indeed, this student jotted just such an outline before she started to write.

Transitional expressions in cause and effect paragraphs often imply order of importance or time order. Remember that the words *causes* and *reasons* refer to causes; the words *effects*, *results*, and *consequences* refer to effects.

Transitional Expressions for Cause and Effect	
To Show Causes	**To Show Effects**
the first cause (second, third)	one important effect
the first reason (second, third)	another result (or outcome)
yet another factor	consequently

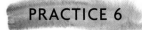 **PRACTICE 6**   Read this student's cause-effect paragraph and answer the questions.

I never wanted to be a vegetarian. Pulled-pork sandwiches were my friends. But in this year of big personal changes, for three reasons, I decided to become a "veg head." The most important reason was saving money. Returning to college has me on a tight budget.

Tuition, books, and rent are expenses I cannot control, but when I wrote down where my extra money was going, big items were meat, chicken, and fast food. I am saving at least $500 a year by cutting out meat and limiting fast food. Another motivation was weight. I gained ten pounds in the first six months of college, all packed around my gut. It is so easy to eat pepperoni pizza while studying, Taco Bell with friends, and beef jerky when I'm stressed. A friend told me to research vegetarian diets online and see how people who eat vegetables, fruits, whole grains, and beans usually weigh less than meat eaters. Then, a final reason pushed me over the edge. My doctor made a big point this year about my family history of heart disease. Now that I am over 30, he said, this puts me at greater risk, but cutting saturated fat out of my diet now will help protect me from serious problems down the road. So goodbye, pulled pork. Goodbye, bacon cheeseburgers. Once I got the hang of eating green, I actually liked it and don't miss meat most of the time.

Ivan Akerstrom, Student

1. Underline the topic sentence. Hint: It is not the first sentence. Will this paragraph discuss causes or effects? How do you know?

   causes: The phrase "for three reasons" suggests causes.

2. How many causes are discussed? What are they?

   three: money, weight, and health

3. On a separate sheet of paper, make an outline of this paragraph.

PRACTICE 7

To practice separating cause from effect, write the cause and the effect contained in each statement below.

EXAMPLE: Because it snowed during rush hour, there were several fender benders this morning.

   Cause: _snow during rush hour_

   Effect: _several fender benders_

1. With so many musicians in the family, I grew up with a love of music.

   Cause: many musicians in the family

   Effect: love of music

2. Three in ten young adults are moving back home with their parents, a trend experts blame on the weak economy.

   Cause: weak economy

   Effect: 3 in 10 young adults moving back home

3. People who do strenuous cardiovascular exercise three or four times a week score higher on intelligence tests.

   Cause: cardio exercise 3 or 4 times a week

   Effect: higher intelligence scores

4. Medical students who take art appreciation classes become better at observing and diagnosing their patients, according to Harvard University.

Cause: art appreciation classes

Effect: better doctors

5. When white sunlight is split by rain or mist into colors, observers see a rainbow.

Cause: rain splits white sunlight

Effect: rainbow

 **PRACTICE 8**

On a sheet of paper, list three causes or three effects that could support each topic sentence below. First, read the topic sentence to see whether causes or effects are called for. Then, think, jot, and list your three best ideas.

1. Public speaking courses would benefit nearly all college students.

2. Concerned citizens point to a number of factors to explain the empty storefronts downtown.

3. Dropping out of school often results in negative consequences.

This upbeat sign is based on research studies showing the positive effects of playing a musical instrument. What are some of these effects?

EXPOSURE TO MUSIC MAY CAUSE SUDDEN OUTBURSTS OF **JOY ENERGY CREATIVITY AND SPONTANEOUS HEALING**

© Cengage Learning

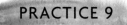 **PRACTICE 9**

Teamwork: Critical Thinking and Writing

In a group with four or five classmates, discuss the fact that more and more companies are now declaring one day each week an e-mail–free day. On that day employees cannot use email and must walk to each other's desks or pick up the phone to make contact. Why do you think this is being done? What issues with e-mail might have *caused* employers to take this step? What *effects* do you think executives are hoping to achieve with this policy? Take notes and list the most important three causes or effects of the no-e-mail policy. Be prepared to present your conclusions to the class.

PRACTICE 10   ## Writing a Cause and Effect Paragraph

Pick a topic from this list that interests you or one your instructor assigns. Draft a topic sentence that states your subject and indicates whether causes or effects will be discussed. Prewrite to get as many points and details as possible. Many students find it helpful to use a graphic organizer as they plan their paragraph. In your notebook, draw a blank 8½-by-11-inch organizer like the one below, or use the cause and effect paragraph organizer on the *Grassroots* website.

- causes for making a key decision
- why violent movies are popular
- reasons why some people text so much
- what makes you (or another) happy
- why some people exercise regularly

- effects of teasing (or bullying) on the victim
- consequences of speaking two languages
- effects of traveling to another country
- effects of a relationship on one partner
- consequences of passing a certain course

CAUSE AND EFFECT PARAGRAPH ORGANIZER

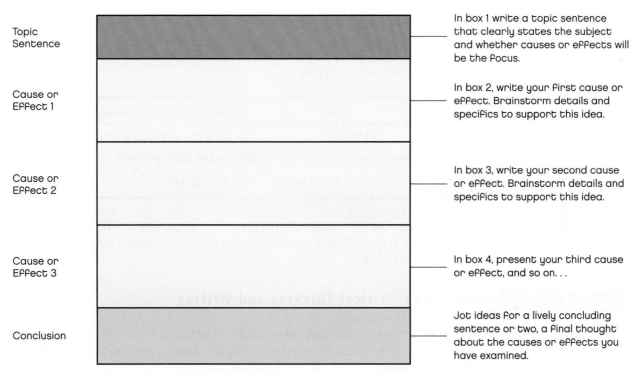

Topic Sentence

In box 1 write a topic sentence that clearly states the subject and whether causes or effects will be the focus.

Cause or Effect 1

In box 2, write your first cause or effect. Brainstorm details and specifics to support this idea.

Cause or Effect 2

In box 3, write your second cause or effect. Brainstorm details and specifics to support this idea.

Cause or Effect 3

In box 4, present your third cause or effect, and so on. . .

Conclusion

Jot ideas for a lively concluding sentence or two, a final thought about the causes or effects you have examined.

Now write the best draft you can. Use transitional expressions of cause and effect to guide your reader from point to point. Let your draft cool for an hour or a day. Then read it like a thoughtful stranger. Think critically as you read. Is the topic sentence clear and interesting? Does it "set up" the paragraph for the reader? Does each point develop the main idea? Proofread for grammar and spelling.

C. Definition

To **define** is to explain clearly what a word or term means. As you write for college and work, you will need to define words or terms your readers may not know. Often, a one-sentence definition will do. For example, *"diligent* means hardworking" or "*malware* is malicious software like viruses, worms, or spyware." Other terms, however—like *self-esteem*, *Custer's last stand*, and *climate change*—are harder to define. They challenge you to think and write with care so the reader understands exactly what you mean, and they usually require a paragraph or more.

Definition becomes more important as you advance in college or in fields like medicine, computer programming, science, psychology, sociology, and others because every field has its own vocabulary.

One-Sentence Definitions

To define a term, a one- or two-word definition is often sufficient. For instance, definitions by **synonym**, a word that means the same thing, are common in the dictionary:

> *Indolent* means lazy.
> A *fluke* is a chance event or coincidence.
> To *exult* means to rejoice greatly.

In college courses and work settings, however, **class definitions** may be necessary. A class definition has two parts: (1) the larger group or class in which the word belongs and (2) the particular details that set it apart from others in that group. Here are some examples:

Word	Class	Distinguishing Details
A *cupcake* is	a small cake	that is baked in a cup-shaped container.
Cargo pants are	casual trousers	with many large pockets.
A *Yorkie* is	a very small terrier	with a long, glossy, tan and gray coat.

Notice that the definitions all have two parts: the class (small cake, casual trousers, and very small terrier) followed by details that make that one different or special in its class.

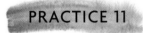

PRACTICE 11

Teamwork: Critical Thinking and Writing

In a group with several classmates, discuss and then write a *class definition* for each of the following words. You will see how much thinking is required just to define things we know well! Use this form:

A _____ is a _____
       (noun)   (class or group)

that _____.
         (distinguishing details)

1. turkey burger
   A turkey burger is a sandwich consisting of two buns with a turkey patty in between.

2. laptop
   A laptop is a computer that is small and light enough to be portable.

3. lemonade

   Lemonade is a nonalcoholic drink made of lemons, water, and sugar.

4. goalie

   A goalie is a player on an athletic team whose job is to tend the goal.

5. tricycle

   A tricycle is a cycle with pedals and three wheels.

Tornado by Mario Carreno, MOMA, NY

Class definition of the event pictured: A tornado is a violent, whirling column of wind that is accompanied by a funnel cloud and cuts a narrow path of destruction across the land. How does the painting's "definition" differ from the verbal one?

EXPLORING ONLINE

<http://grammar.ccc.commnet.edu/grammar/definition_list.htm> Learning just a few "college words" a day will strengthen your vocabulary and your writing. This excellent website, A Year's Worth of Words, is one of many vocabulary-building resources online.

<http://quizlet.com/1070674/100-words-every-college-students-should-know-flash-cards/> 100 Words Every College Student Should Know

The Definition Paragraph: Topic Sentence

When a word is complex or important, a paragraph or essay may be needed to define it well. Here is the topic sentence of a definition paragraph:

> The bystander* effect is the passive reaction of people in groups who see someone in trouble but do nothing to help them.

---

*bystander: a person who watches an event but does not participate.

- The topic sentence of a definition paragraph should identify the word being defined along with its meaning.

- What word or term is defined in this paragraph?

  bystander effect

Paragraph and Plan

Here is the rest of the paragraph.

TEACHING TIP

This subject often spurs animated discussion. Consider covering the definition of *bystander effect* along with John Quinones's strong essay, "Heroes Everywhere" on page 444 of Unit 9. Based on his television series "What Would You Do?" the essay focuses on the rare bystanders who *do* act when they see someone in trouble.

> The bystander effect is the passive reaction of people in groups who see someone in trouble but do nothing to help them. The first famous example was the 1964 murder of Kitty Genovese in Queens, NY—her neighbors supposedly heard her screams but did not call police. Although it now appears that some of Kitty's neighbors did call, psychologists say the bystander effect is real. In fact, the larger the crowd, the more likely it is that bystanders will assume someone else will take responsibility. For instance, hundreds of people might drive past a serious traffic accident, all assuming that someone else called 911. At schools across the country, many students witness verbal or physical bullying but fail to speak up. A current example of bystander effect is teenagers bullied on social media. Online witnesses who remain silent, like all bystanders, unknowingly encourage the bully. Successful new anti-bullying programs are focusing on the key role of the bystander. They teach people not to wait for someone else to act but to imagine the victim's feelings and find the courage to say something. Just one person taking action often stops a bully and might even save a life.

- One effective way to help your reader understand a definition is to provide *examples*. What four examples does the writer choose to explain *bystander effect*?

  1964 murder of Kitty Genovese, traffic accident, verbal or physical bullying at school,

  bullying via social media

- After giving examples of "bystander effect," the writer discusses new anti-bullying programs. What do anti-bullying programs have to do with bystander effect?

  They teach people to have the courage to speak up or act to stop the problem.

- Were you ever a silent bystander? What kept you from speaking up? Have you ever been the bystander who did speak up? Why did you take action?

Note that the topic sentence, examples, point about anti-bullying programs, and concluding sentence form an *outline* for the paragraph. In fact, before drafting, the writer probably prewrote and then made just such an outline.

There are no transitional expressions specifically for definition paragraphs, but phrases like "can be defined as . . ." and "means that . . ." alert the reader that a definition follows.

PRACTICE 12   Read this student's definition paragraph carefully and then answer the questions.

Stress is an inner experience of pressure building up. Have you ever shaken up a bottle of soda pop and then opened it right afterwards? I have, and it explodes all over everything. When I think of stress, this picture is the first thing that comes to mind. For example, imagine it is Thursday and you have two important tests coming up on Monday, but you also have just realized your research paper is due on Friday. A bill just arrived that you thought was taken care of three months ago, and relatives from out of town decide to drop by at the last minute. Therefore, when you aren't working, your relatives expect you to spend time with them. Exhausted yet? Well, just when you think nothing else could come up, someone backs right into the driver's door of your car! By now your entire inside is so shaken up, it feels as though it is going to explode. This is what I call "stress."

Peggy Wheeler, Student

1. Underline the topic sentence.

2. How does this student develop her definition?

She compares stress to a soda and then gives examples of stressful events piling up.

PRACTICE 13   ## Teamwork: Critical Thinking and Writing

In a group with four or five classmates, define the word *bully* or *bullying*. Write a one-sentence definition, and take notes for a composition about this important subject. What are typical behaviors of a bully? What motivates the bully? Who are the bully's ideal victims? What is the best way to stop a bully?

To learn more, try ‹**http://www.pacer.org/bullying/about/media-kit/stats.asp**› or The Bully Project, with a powerful trailer from the documentary film, at ‹**http://www .thebullyproject.com/#prettyPhoto/1/**›. Take notes for further writing.

PRACTICE 14   Here are three topic sentences for definition paragraphs. Choose one that interests you, brainstorm or freewrite for ideas to develop the definition, and, on a separate sheet of paper, make a plan for a possible paragraph.

1. *Unemployed* means so much more than "out of work at the present time."

2. A *nurse* is the patient's guardian, cheerleader, and lifeline.

3. *Motivation* is the drive or incentive to act in ways that will advance one's goals.

PRACTICE 15   ## Writing a Definition Paragraph

Pick a topic from this list that interests you, one from Practice 14, or one your instructor assigns. Draft a topic sentence that defines the word or term and introduces your paragraph. Think and freewrite about your term and what it really means. You might also discuss the term with a smart friend. Many students find it helpful to use a graphic organizer as they plan. In your notebook, draw a blank 8½-by-11-inch organizer like the one that follows or use the definition paragraph organizer on the *Grassroots* website.

- work ethic
- working mom (or dad)
- gossip
- veteran
- success
- AIDS or other illness
- wealth (or poverty)
- rap, country (or other music)
- honor

DEFINITION PARAGRAPH ORGANIZER

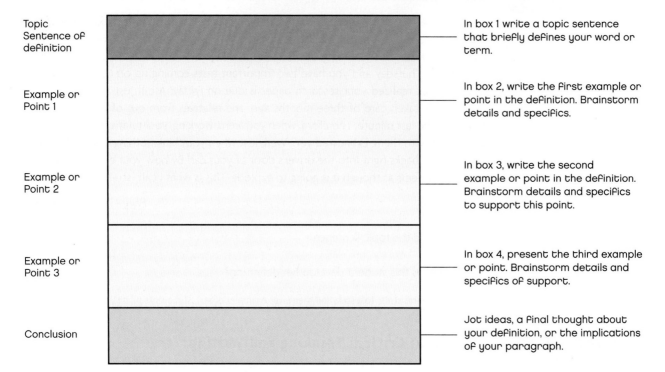

Now write the best draft you can. Use transitional expressions of illustration to guide your reader from point to point. Let your draft cool for an hour or a day. Then read it like a thoughtful stranger. Think critically as you read. Is the topic sentence clear and interesting? Does it "set up" the paragraph for the reader? Does each example develop the main idea? Proofread for grammar and spelling.

D. Persuasion

To **persuade** is to convince someone that a particular opinion or plan of action is the correct one. Persuasion is probably the most important thinking and writing pattern in college, work, and life. Any time you argue with a friend, champion a cause, write a college paper or a report at work, or broadcast a message on Twitter, you are trying to persuade people to agree with you, give you an A, or support your ideas.

Fair arguments are **logical and direct**, not emotional. This chapter will teach you basic techniques of logical persuasion that you will use again and again in college and in nearly every career. Understanding logical persuasion also will help you think critically about the ads, messages of bias, and even brainwashing that bombard us every day.

Topic Sentence

Here is the topic sentence of a persuasive paragraph:

> Parents should not enter their little girls in children's beauty pageants.

- The topic sentence of a persuasive paragraph clearly states what you are arguing for or against. It takes a **strong stand**.

- What will this persuasive paragraph argue against?

entering little girls in children's beauty pageants

● Words like *should* and *must* (or their negatives, *should not* and *must not*) are especially effective in the topic sentence of a persuasive paragraph because they show that the writing is taking a strong stand.

Paragraph and Plan

Here is the entire paragraph:

> Parents should not enter their little girls in children's beauty pageants. The first and most important reason to avoid these pageants is that they sexualize little girls. The "glitz pageants" in particular require contestants to wear heavy makeup and elaborate hairstyles, just like tiny adults. They encourage parents to dress their children in revealing costumes and teach them to gesture and dance suggestively. Little girls have no business prancing around on stage, winking at the judges, blowing kisses, and swinging their hips. A second reason to avoid these pageants is that girls who participate often develop unhealthy body images later on. Dr. Syd Brown, a child psychologist in Maryland, says that child beauty contestants are more likely either to hate their bodies in adolescence or to overvalue physical beauty. Third, costs can grow alarmingly if families commit to the pageant life. Costumes, props, coaching, and travel quickly add up to thousands of dollars per pageant. For example, Rick and Misty Simon of Atlanta, Georgia, told reporters that their credit card debt rose to $30,000 after two years of entering their daughter in a series of local pageants. Finally, most pageant moms claim that their daughters "just love dressing up" and want to enter pageants. They are fooling themselves. No four-year-old or seven-year-old is capable of wise life choices, whether it's choosing what food to eat, what time to go to bed, or whether to waste their childhoods in the ugly world of beauty contests.

TEACHING TIP

This topic often elicits vigorous class discussion. You might have students write more about child beauty pageants or about the parents who push them to participate.

● The first reason in this argument states some facts. What *facts* are given?

Contestants wear heavy make-up, elaborate hairstyles, and revealing costumes.

● The second reason supports the topic sentence by *referring to an authority*. Who is this authority and what does he say?

Dr. Syd Brown, child psychologist, says that child contestants develop poor body images.

● The third reason in the argument *predicts a consequence*. If parents commit to the pageant life, what will the consequence be?

They will spend thousands of dollars and may end up in debt.

● The last reason *answers the opposition*. That is, this writer has tried to imagine what opponents in this argument might say. What point does the writer answer?

Little girls love dressing up and entering pageants.

● Persuasive paragraphs either begin or end with the most important reason. Does this writer start with the most or least important reason? How do you know?

Most important; the first reason is introduced with "the first and most important reason."

Before writing this paragraph, the writer made a plan that included the topic sentence and all the reasons in an order that seemed most persuasive.

Transitional expressions for persuasion signal each supporting point or reason. Sometimes, they also indicate the relative importance of a reason.

> ### Transitional Expressions for Persuasion
>
> | | |
> |---|---|
> | first, another, next | first (second, third) |
> | another reason | last, finally, most important |

When you argue or persuade, always keep your audience in mind. Who are your readers? What approach might convince them that you are right? Because people on both sides of an argument can have strong feelings, it is especially important to use logic, not emotional attack, to win over your opposition. Emotional attacks only make the other person angry, encouraging him or her to reject your views. As you compose an argument, a good memory prompt is **FAPO** (reminding you to include facts, authorities, prediction, and an answer to your opposition).

> ### FAPO: Strategies of Persuasion
>
> **Facts** Facts are statements of what is. Be sure to include the source of your facts (magazine article and date, for example), unless you are describing something widely known.
>
> **Authority** Make sure any authority you quote is an expert in the subject you are discussing. Lebron James is an authority on basketball, but you would not quote him in support of your argument that cooking classes should be required in high schools.
>
> **Predicting the Consequence** Think critically about what really might happen if your opponent's ideas become reality: *If scholarship money is cut at this college, we will lose many bright students.* Do not exaggerate, which will undercut your credibility: *If women receive combat pay, the U.S. military will collapse.*
>
> **Answering the Opposition** This might be the hardest and most important persuasive strategy. It is difficult to sympathize with opponents, but to reach them with logic, you must put yourself in their shoes, get inside their minds, and try to understand why they passionately hold the beliefs they do. Let's say you are arguing for certain gun restrictions. If your opposition believes that any gun control means all their firearms will be taken away, how can you answer them respectfully and convincingly?

PRACTICE 16   Read this student's persuasive paragraph and answer the questions.

Unpaid internships are not worth the effort. First, advisors tell students like me that an unpaid internship will give them work experience and a chance to show off their skills. I have had two unpaid internships in two years, one at a retail store and one at a newspaper, but my jobs had nothing to do with my associate degree in business. Instead, I made copies, got coffee, and broke down boxes to put in the trash. The second reason unpaid internships are a bad idea is the obvious: They are unpaid. With no money coming in, the bills add up, and there is less time to look for a paying job. Finally, the most important reason not to become an unpaid intern is that it won't help you get a full-time job. I interviewed Tara Cano, a career coach in Charlotte. She showed me the results of a 2012 survey by NACE, the National Association of Colleges and Employers. This survey found that 37 percent of unpaid interns get job offers, but 36 percent of students who were never unpaid interns also get job offers, so there is no advantage for an unpaid intern. On the other hand, 60 percent of paid interns get job offers. You do the math.

Domingo Reyes, Student

1. What is this paragraph arguing for or against?

   against unpaid internships

2. What audience does the writer seem to be addressing?

   college students or recent graduates

3. How many reasons does the author provide? List them.

   three: internships don't really give job experience; lack of pay; internships don't result in paid jobs

4. Which reason is an answer to the opposition?

   reason 1

5. Which reason combines quoting an authority with facts? How did the student find these facts?

   reason 3; he interviewed Ms. Cano

6. Do you have any revision advice for this writer? What do you like best about his argument? Would you recommend any changes?

   Answers will vary.

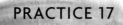

PRACTICE 17

Teamwork: Critical Thinking and Writing

In a group with four or five classmates, choose one of the three topics below. Working as a group, take a stand in answer to the question and express your stand in a strong topic sentence. Write four supporting sentences to build your argument—each sentence using one of the four FAPO methods: *facts, referring to an authority, predicting the consequences,* and *answering the opposition.* If you don't know the facts or an authority, just for this practice— never in real life—you can invent facts or an authority in support of your argument.

1. Should sugary drinks and snacks be taxed heavily, like cigarettes?
2. Should cell phones be banned in all restaurants and theaters?
3. Should all parents-in-waiting in this state be required to take parenting classes?

PRACTICE 18

Teamwork: Critical Viewing and Writing

In a group with four or five classmates, look closely at this public service ad from *discovertheforest.org*. Like many advertisements, this one is trying to *persuade* the viewer to adopt a certain point of view or to take action. What is the subject of the ad? Who is the intended audience? What is the persuasive message? Working with classmates, write down the ad's "topic sentence" and argument. How persuasive is this ad?

PRACTICE 19 Writing a Persuasive Paragraph

Pick a topic from Practice 17, from this list of questions, or a topic your instructor assigns. Then take a stand by answering the question in a topic sentence that you can support with reasons. Prewrite to get as many ideas and reasons as possible, referring to the FAPO chart. Many students find that using a graphic organizer as they plan helps them build a strong paragraph. Fill your ideas and details in an organizer. In your notebook, draw a blank 8½-by-11-inch organizer like the one below or use the persuasive paragraph organizer on the *Grassroots* website.

- Do teachers treat males and females differently in the classroom?
- Is Michael Jordan the greatest athlete who ever lived?
- Should little boys play with dolls?
- Should two years of college be mandatory?
- Should colleges allow drinking on campus?
- Should public schools require uniforms?
- Should citizens be required by law to vote?
- Should contact sports be banned for children under 15?
- Do violent video games lead to violent behavior?
- Should any athlete who takes performance-enhancing drugs be banned from the sport for life?

PERSUASIVE PARAGRAPH ORGANIZER

Topic Sentence	In box 1 write a topic sentence that clearly states your topic and point of view.
Reason 1	In box 2, write your first reason. Include details that clearly explain this reason.
Reason 2	In box 3, write your second reason. Include details that clearly explain this reason.
Reason 3	In box 4, present your third reason. Include details that clearly explain this reason.
Conclusion	Jot ideas for a lively concluding sentence or two, a final thought about the issue and its importance.

Now write the best draft you can. Use transitional expressions of persuasion to guide your reader from reason to reason. Let your draft cool for an hour or a day. Then read it like a thoughtful stranger. Think critically as you read. Is the topic sentence clear and interesting? Does it "set up" the paragraph for the reader? Is each reason suited to the audience? Proofread for grammar and spelling.

Chapter Highlights

These paragraph patterns are often used in college and the workplace. They reflect different ways of thinking about a subject.

- The classification paragraph sorts things into types or categories, according to one basis of division.

- The cause and effect paragraph develops the topic sentence by explaining the causes (reasons for) or effects (results of) events.

- The definition paragraph explains the meaning of a word or term.

- The persuasive paragraph takes a stand, providing reasons to convince the reader that a particular opinion or plan of action is correct.

EXPLORING ONLINE

<http://www.youtube.com/watch?v=wm3ObvB0mLE> Excellent short video walks you through classification: how to divide your subject, create your topic sentence, and discuss your types.

<http://lrs.ed.uiuc.edu/students/fwalters/cause.html> See a sample of cause-effect writing of the type you will be expected to write on tests, in college, and on the job.

<http://www.une.edu.au/tlc/aso/students/factsheets/paragraph-argument.pdf> Tips on persuasive writing and two examples of persuasive paragraphs required in science courses and careers.

TEACHING TIP

Instructor tools for *Grassroots* include a computerized Test Bank, PowerPoint slides, an Instructor's Resource Manual with teaching tips, and more, and can be accessed at ‹**login .cengage.com**›.

CHAPTER 7

Moving from Paragraph to Essay

A: Defining the Essay and the Thesis Statement

B: The Process of Writing an Essay

So far, you have written single paragraphs, but to succeed in college and at work, you will need to handle longer writing assignments as well. This chapter will help you apply your paragraph-writing skills to planning and writing short essays.

A. Defining the Essay and the Thesis Statement

An **essay** is a group of paragraphs about one subject. In many ways, an essay is like a paragraph in longer, fuller form. Both have an introduction, a body, and a conclusion. Both explain one main idea with details, facts, and examples.

An essay is not just a padded paragraph, however. An essay is longer because it contains more ideas.

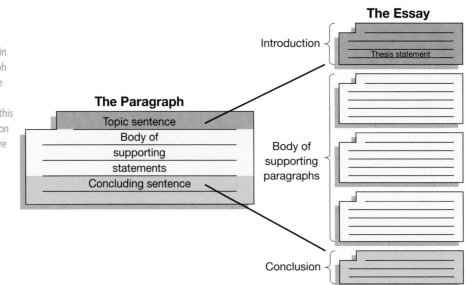

The paragraphs in an essay are part of a larger whole, so each one has a special purpose.

- The **introductory paragraph** opens the essay and tries to catch the reader's interest. It usually contains a **thesis statement**, one sentence that states the main idea of the entire essay.

- The **body** of an essay contains one, two, three, or more paragraphs, each one making a different point about the main idea.

- The **conclusion** brings the essay to a close. It might be a sentence or a paragraph long.

Here is a student essay:

Tae Kwon Do

Wineth Williams

(1) Tae kwon do is a Korean martial art. It is a way of fighting and self-defense based on an understanding of both body and mind. As a college student, I discovered tae kwon do. Even though I was physically fit and planned to become a police officer, I thought that women needed special skills to protect themselves. Tae kwon do teaches these skills and much more. The person who practices tae kwon do gains discipline, maturity, and a changed self-concept.

(2) First, the discipline of tae kwon do helps the student outfight and outsmart her opponent. For a while, I didn't appreciate the discipline. We had to move in certain ways, and we had to yell. Yelling made me laugh. Our teacher told us to shout with great force, "Keeah!" Yelling keeps the mind from focusing on being tired and helps the fighter call out the life force, or "chi," from inside her. Once we started sparring, I also had to get past not wanting to hurt anyone. Later I understood that if I punched or kicked my opponent, it meant that he or she should have been blocking and was not using good skills.

(3) Second, with practice, tae kwon do increases maturity. I have a hot temper. Before tae kwon do, I would walk dark streets and take chances, almost daring trouble. I reacted to every look or challenge. Practicing this martial art, I started to see the world more realistically. I developed more respect for the true danger in the streets. I spoke and behaved in ways to avoid trouble. My reactions became less emotional and more rational.

(4) Finally, after a year or so, tae kwon do can change the student's self-concept. This happened to me. On one hand, I became confident that I had the skills to take care of business if necessary. On the other hand, the better I got, the more I acted like a pussycat instead of a lion. That may sound strange, but inside myself, I knew that I had nothing to prove to anybody.

(5) Friends who do not work out are often surprised when I describe the way that tae kwon do changed me, but a serious exercise routine can do this for anyone. By committing to a routine or "practice," a person is setting a self-loving goal and working toward it. As I discovered firsthand, the rewards are discipline, the maturity to keep going despite discomfort, and finally, new confidence and self-respect.

- The last sentence in the introduction (underlined) is the *thesis statement*. The thesis statement must be general enough to include the topic sentence of every paragraph in the body of the essay.

- Underline the topic sentences of paragraphs (2), (3), and (4). Note that the thesis statement and the topic sentences make a rough plan of the entire essay.

TEACHING TIP

Encourage students to read and study effective essays as models of good writing. The Reading Selections in Unit 9, the Writers' Workshops concluding each unit, and even some practices in this text offer excellent examples.

TEACHING TIP

Using color coding to highlight parts of an essay or other written structures can help students—especially *visual learners*—understand.

● **Transitional expressions** are words and phrases that guide the reader from point to point and from paragraph to paragraph. What transition does this student use between paragraphs (1) and (2)? Between (2) and (3)? Between (3) and (4)?

First, Second, Finally

● The last paragraph provides a brief *conclusion.**

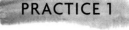

PRACTICE 1

To help you understand the structure of an essay, complete this plan for "Tae Kwon Do." Under each topic sentence, jot down the writer's two or three main supporting points as if you were making a plan for the essay. (In fact, the writer probably made such a plan before she wrote her first draft.)

Paragraph 1. INTRODUCTION
Thesis statement: The person who practices tae kwon do gains discipline, maturity, and a changed self-concept.

Paragraph 2. Topic sentence: First, the discipline of tae kwon do helps the student outfight and outsmart her opponent.

Point 1: didn't appreciate discipline

Point 2: yelling made me laugh

Point 3: didn't want to hurt people

Paragraph 3. Topic sentence: Second, with practice, tae kwon do increases maturity.

Point 1: before—reacted to challenges

Point 2: after—saw danger realistically

Paragraph 4. Topic sentence: Finally, after a year or so, tae kwon do can change the student's self-concept.

Point 1: more confident

Point 2: pussycat, not lion

Point 3: nothing to prove

Paragraph 5. CONCLUSION

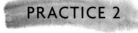

PRACTICE 2

Discuss with several classmates or write your answers to these questions.

1. Did Wineth Williams's introduction (paragraph 1) catch and hold your interest? Would this essay be just as good or better if it had no introduction but started right in with the thesis statement? Why or why not?

2. In paragraph (4), the writer says she now can "take care of business." Is this language appropriate for a college essay? Will readers know what this means?

3. Is the conclusion effective, or is it too short?

* To read essays by other students, see the Writers' Workshops in Units 3, 6, 7, and 8.

4. Williams's audience was her English class. Her purpose (though not directly stated in the essay) was to let people know some of the benefits that come from practicing tae kwon do. Did she achieve her purpose?

5. What did you like best about the essay? What, if anything, would you change?

PRACTICE 3   Read this student's essay and answer the questions.

Confronting My Fear

ANGEL LINARES

(1) What brought me to this college was my dream of becoming a Physician Assistant. Having childhood asthma meant that I grew up spending a lot of time in doctors' offices. It was the kindness, caring, and helpful advice of my pulmonologist's PA that inspired me to pursue this career. In high school, I researched the requirements for a PA degree. I arrived on this campus with my goal and with good study habits, but I almost defeated myself with negative thoughts.

(2) The first thoughts of failure sneaked into my brain when I heard other students talking about Bio 23. I had always known that my curriculum would require hard work and that some of the subject matter would be tedious or difficult to learn. I also knew that biology was one of the hardest subjects. But the students I overheard said the course was so hard that very few students last term even passed it. On campus, I heard more testimonials from students who either failed Bio 23 or withdrew because they were failing. I began to doubt my own abilities. What if I failed Bio? I needed the course to achieve my dream.

(3) These negative ideas grew like mold. The more I let them stay in my head, the stronger and more toxic they got. I was scaring myself with my own thoughts. I started changing the mental channel, over and over again. Instead, I focused on my goal of becoming a Physician Assistant. I pushed all my fears to the back of my mind and registered for Bio 23. Once I entered the class, I studied all the material day and night. I took every pop quiz and test and poured my best effort into every assignment. In the end, I passed with a B.

(4) This experience increased my self-confidence. It taught me an important lesson that I will teach my children someday. I turned my self-destructive fear into victory because I tried.

1. Underline this writer's thesis statement. Based on this sentence, what do you expect this essay to be about?

   details of writer's near self-defeat by doubt

2. What is the main idea of paragraph 2? What is the main idea of paragraph 3?

   2: how thoughts of failure started; 3: changing the mental channnel

3. How effective is the conclusion? Is it too short, or does brevity give it power?

   Answers will vary.

4. Have you ever had the experience of defeating (or almost defeating) yourself with negative thinking? What happened?

   Answers will vary.

B. The Process of Writing an Essay

Whether you are writing a paragraph or an essay, the writing process is the same. Of course, writing an essay will probably take longer. In this section, you will practice these steps of the essay-writing process:

- Narrowing the subject and writing the thesis statement
- Generating ideas for the body of the essay
- Selecting and arranging ideas in a plan
- Writing and revising your essay

Narrowing the Subject and Writing the Thesis Statement

While an essay subject should be broader than a paragraph topic, a good essay subject also must be narrow enough to write about in detail. For example, the topic *jobs* is broad enough to fill a book. But the far narrower topic *driving a bulldozer at the town dump* could make a good essay. Remember to select or narrow your subject in light of your intended audience and purpose. Who are your readers, and what do you want your essay to achieve?

Writing the *thesis statement* forces you to narrow the topic further: *Driving a bulldozer for the Department of Highways was the best job I ever had.* That could be an intriguing thesis statement, but the writer could focus it even more: *For three reasons, driving a bulldozer for the Department of Highways was the best job I ever had.* The writer might discuss one reason in each of three paragraphs.

Here are two more examples of the narrowing process:

Provide students with additional thesis statements that are too broad or too vague, and demonstrate how they can be improved.

TEACHING TIP

(1) Subject:	music
Narrowed subject:	Cuban singer Lucretia
Thesis statement:	In talent and style, Cuban singer Lucretia might be the next Celia Cruz.
(2) Subject:	pets
Narrowed subject:	pains and pleasures of owning a parrot
Thesis statement:	Owning a parrot will enrich your life with noise, occasional chaos, and lots of laughs.

- On the basis of each thesis statement, what do you expect the essays to discuss?

Essay 1 will show how Cuban singer Lucretia's talent and style might make her the

next Celia Cruz. Essay 2 will discuss the noise, chaos, and laughs of parrot ownership.

Although the thesis statement must include all the ideas in the body of the essay, it should also be **clear** and **specific**. Which of these thesis statements is specific enough for a good essay?

(1) Three foolproof techniques will help you avoid disastrous first dates.

(2) NBA basketball is the most exciting sport in the world.

(3) Dr. Villarosa is a competent and caring physician.

- Thesis statements (1) and (3) are both specific. From (1), a reader might expect to learn about the "three foolproof techniques," each one perhaps explained in a paragraph.

- On the basis of thesis statement (3), what supporting points might the essay discuss?

  1. Dr. Villarosa's competence _____

  2. his or her caring ways _____

- Thesis statement (2), however, is too broad for an essay—or even a book. It gives the reader (and writer) no direction.

PRACTICE 4

Choose one of these topics for your own essay. Then narrow the topic and write a clear and specific thesis statement.

The benefits of a sport or practice

The most fascinating (or boring or important) job I ever had

How to overcome fear (or laziness or negative family and friends)

Narrowed subject: _____

_____

Thesis statement: _____

_____

Generating Ideas for the Body of the Essay

Writers generate support for an essay just as they do for a paragraph—by prewriting to get as many interesting ideas as possible. Once you know your main point and have written a thesis statement, use your favorite prewriting method—freewriting, for example. If you feel stuck, change to brainstorming or clustering. Just keep writing.

PRACTICE 5

Generate as many good ideas as possible to support your thesis statement. Fill at least one or two pages with ideas. As you work, try to imagine how many paragraphs your essay will contain and what each will include.

Selecting and Arranging Ideas in a Plan

Next, underline or mark the most interesting ideas that support your thesis statement. Cross out the rest.

Make a rough **plan** or **outline** that includes an introductory paragraph, two or three paragraphs for the body of the essay, and a brief conclusion. Choose a logical order for presenting your ideas. Which idea will come first, second, third?

For example, the bulldozer operator might explain why that job was "the best" with three reasons, arranged in this order: 1. *On the job, I learned to operate heavy equipment. 2. Working alone at the controls gave me time to think. 3. One bonus was occasionally finding interesting items beside the road.* This arrangement moves logically from physical skills to mental benefits to a surprising bonus.

PRACTICE 6

Read over your prewriting pages, selecting your best ideas and a logical order in which to present them. Make an outline or a plan that includes an introduction and a thesis statement; two or three supporting paragraphs, each with a clear topic sentence; and a brief conclusion.

Writing and Revising Your Essay

Draft.   Now write your first draft. Try to express your ideas clearly and fully. If a section seems weak or badly written, put a check in the margin and go on; you can come back to that section later, prewriting again if necessary for fresh ideas. Set aside your draft for an hour or a day.

Revise.   Revising may be the most important step in the writing process. Reread your essay as if you were reading someone else's work, marking it up as you answer questions like these:

ESL TIP

Alert ESL students to Appendix 2, "Guidelines for Students of English as a Second Language," at the end of this text and to the excellent resources—quizzes and links—available online—for instance, ‹http://a4esl.org›.

- Are my main idea and my thesis statement clear?

- Have I supported my thesis in a rich and convincing way?

- Does each paragraph in the body clearly explain the main idea?

- Does my essay have a logical order and good transitions?

- Are there any parts that don't belong or don't make sense?

- What one change would most improve my essay?*

You also might wish to ask a respected friend to read or listen to your essay, giving peer feedback before you revise.**

Proofread.   Now, carefully proofread your essay for errors in grammar, punctuation, and spelling. It is all-important not to skip or rush through this step. Read slowly, word by word, line by line.

The next chapter is devoted entirely to proofreading, teaching you some proven proofreading techniques that you will practice in Units 2 through 8. The units to come are your *proofreading handbook*, showing you how to spot and correct a wide range of serious errors.

PRACTICE 7

Now read your first draft to see how you can improve it. Trust your instincts about what is alive and interesting and what is dull. Take your time. As you revise, try to make this the best paper you have ever written.

Finally, write a new draft of your essay, using the format preferred by your instructor. Proofread carefully, correcting any grammar or spelling errors.

PRACTICE 8

Exchange essays with a classmate. Write a one-paragraph evaluation of each other's work, saying as specifically as possible what you like about the essay and what might be improved. If you wish, use the Peer Feedback Sheet (page 32).

For downloadable rubrics corresponding to each rhetorical mode, go to the *Grassroots* instructor website at ‹**login** .**cengage.com**›.

Possible Topics for Essays

1. Three surefire ways to relax
2. A major decision
3. Should football be banned because it endangers players?

---

* See Chapter 3, Part F, for more revising ideas.
** See Chapter 3, page 32, for a sample Peer Feedback Sheet.

4. Should couples live together before marriage?

5. Tips for the new parent (college student, parent, driver, and so forth)

6. A valuable (or worthless) television show

7. A good friend

8. Can anger be used constructively?

9. How I fell in love with reading (German shepherds, nursing, rock climbing, programming, and so forth)

10. What childhood taught me about _____.

Chapter Highlights

Checklist for Writing an Effective Essay

- Narrow the topic in light of your audience and purpose. Be sure you can discuss the topic fully in a short essay.

- Write a clear thesis statement. If you have trouble, freewrite or brainstorm first; then narrow the topic and write the thesis statement.

- Freewrite, brainstorm, or cluster to generate facts, details, and examples to support your thesis statement.

- Plan or outline your essay, choosing two or three main ideas to support the thesis statement.

- Write a topic sentence that expresses each main idea.

- Decide on a logical order in which to present the paragraphs.

- Plan the body of each paragraph, using all you have learned about support and paragraph development.

- Write the first draft of your essay.

- Revise as necessary, checking your essay for support, unity, and coherence.

- Proofread carefully for grammar, punctuation, and spelling.

EXPLORING ONLINE

<http://www.powa.org/index.php/explain/subject-to-thesis> For help turning your subject into a good thesis statement, read "Subject to Thesis."

<http://owl.english.purdue.edu/owl/resource/685/01/> Purdue University's composition site reviews essay writing. At the bottom, click "Expository Essays" and "Argumentative Essays," the two essay types most assigned in college.

CHAPTER 8

Proofreading to Correct Your Personal Error Patterns

A: **Identifying and Tracking Your Personal Error Patterns**

B: **Proofreading Strategies**

The important last step in the writing process is **proofreading**: slowly reading your revised paragraph or essay in order to find and correct any errors in grammar, punctuation, and spelling.

It is essential that you proofread work before turning it in because grammatical and other mistakes distract readers and give a negative impression of your skills and even intelligence. Often, employers won't interview a candidate whose letter or résumé contains errors. Yet many new writers avoid proofreading or rush through it so quickly that they set themselves up for failure.

In fact, the more mistakes you tend to make, the more important proofreading is for you. This chapter will give you tools to enhance your skills as an error detective and writer. Then Units 2 through 8 will further develop your proofreading skills, teaching you how to understand, spot, and correct many specific errors. In every coming chapter, you will practice a proofreading strategy that targets a particular mistake.

A. Identifying and Tracking Your Personal Error Patterns

Knowing what errors you tend to make and then proofreading for these errors will boost your success in college and at work.

Learn Your Error Patterns

An **error pattern** is any error you make two, three, or more times. For example, if a teacher has noted that one of your papers has several comma splices or numerous verb errors, those are *error patterns* that you need to work on. The first step in getting rid of these errors is becoming aware of them.

Here are four ways to discover your error patterns:

Papers. Study recently returned papers, making sure you understand the errors that have been marked. Check the inside back cover of this book for proofreading symbols your instructor might use, like *frag* for sentence fragment. Count the number of times each mistake appears.

Instructor. Ask your instructor to identify your error patterns. List them. Ask which three are the most serious.

Textbook. As you work through this book, notice chapters or practices where you keep making mistakes or writing incorrect answers. These are your error patterns.

Writing lab. Go to the writing lab with a paper you recently wrote. Ask a tutor to help identify the kinds of errors you make. Ask which three are the most serious.

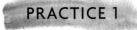

PRACTICE 1

Consult your instructor, or bring a recent paper to the college writing lab. Seek help in identifying your error patterns and start a written list. Ask which three error patterns most harm your written communication and your grade.

Create a Personal Error Patterns Chart

Let's say your instructor marks twelve errors on your English paper, and eight of them are verb agreement errors. This means that eight of your errors are really one error repeated eight times! Mastering this one error pattern would certainly improve your grade.

An excellent tool for tracking and beginning to master your errors is an **error chart** or **log**. This tool will show you what to study and what mistakes to watch for in your writing. Here is an example of one student's chart:

Personal Error Patterns Chart				
Error Type & Symbol	**Specific Error**	**Correction**	**Rule or Reminder**	**Assignment & Number of Errors**
Apostrophe error apos	My brothers fundraiser was a success.	My brother's fundraiser was a success.	's shows ownership by ONE brother.	Paper 1: 4 apos
Run-on ro	Jada is always late she can't decide what to wear.	Jada is always late because she can't decide what to wear.	Check for the end of each complete sentence. Join two sentences with a period or conjunction. See Ch. 18!	Paper 1: 5 ro #2: 3 ro #3: no run-ons!
Adverb adv	The patient did good.	The patient did well.	Good is an adjective; well is the adverb form.	#1: 4 adv #2: 3 adv

- Each time you receive a marked paper, write every *error name* or *type* in column 1 (like *apostrophe error* or *run-on*). Check the inside back cover to understand your instructor's proofreading symbols; for instance, *apos* for apostrophe error.

- In column 2, copy the error as you wrote it.

- In column 3, correct the error. If you have trouble understanding what you did wrong, ask the instructor, or search the index of this book for the pages you need.

- In column 4, jot the rule or ideas for fixing this type of mistake.

- In column 5, write the assignment number or date, plus the number of times you made this error. Add the error count for every later paper. Any error that appears in paper after paper will need a special plan of attack.

Continue to add errors from future papers, instructor conferences, and tests. As you work in this textbook, add to your chart any grammatical concepts that still confuse you. Whenever you master the correction of an error, cross it off the chart and celebrate your achievement.

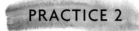 **PRACTICE 2**   Using a recent paper of yours that was graded by an instructor, begin your Personal Error Patterns Chart. You can use the blank chart in this book or create your chart as a Word file, adding rows as you need them. Some students design and draw their own charts. Follow this format:

Personal Error Patterns Chart				
Error Type & Symbol	**Specific Error**	**Correction**	**Rule or Reminder**	**Assignment & Number of Errors**

B. Proofreading Strategies

Whenever you write, honor your own writing process by setting aside enough time to perform each step, including proofreading. Just as it helps to take a break of hours or days between writing your first draft and revising, taking a break *before you proofread* is beneficial. Go for a walk. Call a friend. You cannot do a good job proofreading when you are tired. You will catch more errors with a rested mind and fresh outlook.

If possible, proofread in a quiet place where you won't be distracted—not at a dance club, not standing in the kitchen fixing dinner with the kids.

Many writers have found that the **proofreading strategies** described below help them see their own writing with a fresh eye. You will learn more strategies in subsequent chapters of this book. Try a number of methods and see which ones work best for you.

Proofreading Strategy: Allow enough time to proofread.

Many students don't proofread at all, or they skim their paper for grammatical errors two minutes before class. This just doesn't work. Set aside enough time to proofread slowly and carefully, searching for errors and hunting especially for your personal error patterns.

Proofreading Strategy: Work from a paper copy.

People who proofread on computers tend to miss more errors. If you write on a computer, do not proofread on the monitor. Instead, print a copy of your paper, perhaps enlarging the type to 14 point. Switching to a paper copy seems to help the brain see more clearly.

Proofreading Strategy: Read your words aloud.

Reading silently makes it easier to skip over small errors or mentally fill in missing details, whereas listening closely is a great way to hear mistakes. Listen and follow along on your printed copy, marking errors as you hear them.

TEACHING TIP

Students might wish to have *the computer* read aloud. *ReadPlease* is a free software download for the PC; *TextEdit* comes installed on MACs.

a. Read your paper aloud to *yourself*. Be sure to read *exactly* what's on the page, and read with enthusiasm.

b. Ask a *friend* or *writing tutor* to read your paper out loud to you. Tell the reader you just want to hear your words and that you don't want any other suggestions right now.

Proofreading Strategy: Read "bottom up," from the end to the beginning.

One way to fool the brain into taking a fresh look at something you've written is to proofread the last sentence first. Read slowly, word by word. Then read the second-to-last sentence, and so on, all the way back to the first sentence.

Proofreading Strategy: Isolate your sentences.

If you write on a computer, spotting errors is often easier if you reformat so that each sentence appears isolated, on its own line. Double-space between sentences. This visual change can help the brain focus clearly on one sentence at a time.

Proofreading Strategy: Check for one error at a time.

If you make many mistakes, proofread separately all the way through your paper for each error pattern. Although this process takes time, you will catch many more errors this way and make real progress. You will begin to eliminate some errors altogether as you get better at spotting and fixing them. You will learn more recommended proofreading strategies in upcoming chapters.

PRACTICE 3

Win your Academy Award! In a group with several classmates, role-play discussions between Waldo (or Wanda) and several friends. The friends are committed to getting A's in their writing class, but Waldo is getting Ds and Fs. He *says* he wants to earn a nursing degree, but his actions say otherwise. Last night the friends saw him "proofreading" his paper in a Mexican restaurant over margaritas with a buddy.

Pick someone to play W. Then, one at a time, each member of the group in turn should try to persuade him to take his writing seriously, and especially to work on his proofreading skills. At the end, ask W if anyone's argument got through to him. Be prepared to report to the class.

PRACTICE 4

Print out or make a photocopy of something you wrote recently for college or work. Ask someone to read the original out loud as you listen. On your copy, underline or highlight sentences or places that sound wrong. Also mark any places where the reader stumbles verbally. Rewrite the marked sentences.

PRACTICE 5

Choose a paper you wrote recently. Select one of the proofreading strategies and try it out on this paper. Read with full attention, keenly watching for your personal error patterns. Put a check in the margin beside each error. Then correct them neatly above the lines.

Chapter Highlights

- Proofreading for errors in grammar, punctuation, and spelling is a crucial step in the writing process. Proofreading skills can be learned.

- Keeping a Personal Error Patterns Chart helps writers spot and correct the errors that they habitually make.

- Using proofreading strategies can help writers recognize the errors in their own work. These strategies help many writers:

  - Allow enough time to proofread.
  - Work from a paper copy, not the monitor.
  - Read your words aloud.
  - Read "bottom up," from the last sentence to the first.
  - Isolate your sentences.
  - Read for one error at a time.

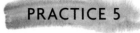

EXPLORING ONLINE

TEACHING TIP

Instructor tools for *Grass-roots* include a computerized Test Bank, PowerPoint slides, an Instructor's Manual with teaching tips, and more, and can be accessed at ‹**login .cengage.com**›.

‹http://writing.wisc.edu/Handbook/Proofreading.html› Excellent proofreading advice from the University of Wisconsin OWL.

‹http://owl.english.purdue.edu/owl/resource/561/01/› Proofreading tips from the Purdue University OWL, plus advice on correcting common errors made by college students.

UNIT 1
Writing Assignments

As you complete each writing assignment, remember to perform these steps:

- Write a clear, complete topic (or thesis) sentence.
- Use freewriting, brainstorming, or clustering to generate ideas for the body of your paragraph or essay.
- Arrange your best ideas in a plan.
- Revise for support, unity, coherence, and exact language.
- Proofread for grammar, punctuation, and spelling errors.

Writing Assignment 1 *Discuss one requirement for a happy family life.* Complete this topic sentence: "A basic requirement for a happy family life is _____." What do you believe a family should have? Is it something material, like a house or a certain amount of money? Is it related to the number or types of people in the family? Does it have to do with nonmaterial things, like communication or support? Begin by jotting down all the reasons why you would require this particular thing. Then choose the three most important reasons and arrange them in order of importance—either from the least to the most important or the reverse. Explain each reason, making clear to the reader why you feel as strongly as you do.

Writing Assignment 2 *Interview a classmate about an achievement.* Write about a time your classmate achieved something important, like winning a sales prize at work, losing thirty pounds, or helping a friend through a bad time. To gather interesting facts and details, ask your classmate questions like these and take notes: *Is there one accomplishment of which you are very proud? Why was this achievement so important? Did it change the way you feel about yourself?* Keep asking questions until you feel you have enough information to give your reader a vivid sense of your classmate's triumph.

In your first sentence, state the person's achievement—for instance, *Getting her first A in English was a turning point in Jessica's life.* Then explain specifically why the achievement was so meaningful.

Writing Assignment 3 *Develop a paragraph with examples.* Below are topic sentences for possible paragraphs. Pick the topic sentence that most interests you and write a paragraph, using one to three examples to explain the topic sentence. If you prefer, choose a quotation from the Quotation Bank at the end of this book and explain it with one or more examples.

a. A sense of humor can make difficult times easier to bear.

b. Mistakes can be great teachers.

c. Television commercials often insult my intelligence.

Writing Assignment 4 *Counsel a young person.* A young friend who is considering dropping out of high school urgently needs your advice. You have read the depressing statistics: more than 30 percent of dropouts end up trapped in poverty, as opposed to 13 percent of college graduates. As you plan your paragraph or essay, put yourself in this teenager's shoes. What pressures is he or she facing that brought on this crisis? What approach is most likely to be helpful to this particular teenager? You might wish to employ one of the paragraph types you learned in this unit, like persuasion, illustration, cause-effect, or contrast. REMEMBER: Keep your young reader firmly in mind as you write.

UNIT 1
Review

Choosing a Topic Sentence

Each group of sentences could be unscrambled and written as a paragraph. Circle the letter of the sentence that would be the best topic sentence.

1. a. Rooftops and towers made eye-catching shapes against the winter sky.

   b. Far below, the faint sounds of slush and traffic were soothing.

   c. From the apartment-house roof, the urban scene was oddly relaxing.

   d. Stoplights changing color up and down the avenues created a rhythmic pattern invisible from the street.

2. a. Service members are eligible for insurance and retirement benefits.

   b. Financial support for a college education is a major advantage of military service.

   c. Being trained by the military can instill discipline and self-esteem.

   d. Many servicemen and -women get to travel to new places and experience new cultures.

   e. Military service, despite its risks, offers many advantages.

Selecting Ideas

Here is a topic sentence and a brainstormed list of ideas for a paragraph. Check "Keep" for ideas that best support the topic sentence and "Drop" for ideas that do not.

Topic sentence: Oprah Winfrey is a force for tremendous good in the United States.

Keep	Drop	
✔		1. on her TV show, featured experts who helped people with relationships or finances
✔		2. through her book club, inspired millions to start reading and periodically introduces a vast audience to new and old authors
✔		3. proves that women don't need to be thin to be beautiful, popular, famous, and greatly loved
	✔	4. was born in 1954 on a farm in Mississippi
	✔	5. at age six was sent to Milwaukee; kept cockroaches in a jar as substitute for farm animals
✔		6. is a well-known example of someone who overcame many obstacles, including childhood abuse and racial prejudice

110

_____ ✔ 7. another example of someone who has overcome abuse and prejudice is actress Halle Berry

_____ ✔ 8. physical abuse by a former boyfriend caused Berry to lose 80 percent of her hearing in one ear

✔ _____ 9. Winfrey gives millions to such causes as helping South African children orphaned by AIDS

✔ _____ 10. her website, magazine, and TV and radio networks encourage women to develop their spirituality and pursue personal goals

Examining a Paragraph

Read this paragraph and answer the questions.

(1) Students at some American colleges are learning a lot from trash by studying "garbology." (2) Wearing rubber gloves, they might sift through the local dump, counting and collecting treasures that they examine back at the laboratory. (3) First, they learn to look closely and to interpret what they see, thus reading the stories that trash tells. (4) More important, they learn the truth about what Americans buy, what they eat, and how they live. (5) Students at the University of Arizona, for instance, were surprised to find that low-income families in certain areas buy more educational toys for their children than nearby middle-income families do. (6) Most important, students say that garbology courses can motivate them to be better citizens of planet Earth. (7) One young woman, for example, after seeing from hard evidence in her town's landfill how many people really recycled their glass, cans, and newspapers and how many cheated, organized an annual recycling awareness day.

1. Write the number of the topic sentence in the paragraph. ____1____

2. What kind of order does this writer use? ____order of importance____

3. Students learn three things in garbology courses. (a) Write the numbers of the sentences stating these. (b) Which two ideas are supported by examples?

   (a) ____3, 4, 6____   (b) ____4 and 6____

On Earth Day, garbology students at Western Kentucky University examine the contents of campus dumpsters to raise awareness about the impact of waste.

Reprinted with permission of Western Kentucky University Office of Sustainability

UNIT 1
Writers' Workshop

Discuss Your Name

Good writers are masters of exact language and thoughtful observation. Read this student's paragraph about her name. Underline any words or details that strike you as well written, interesting, or powerful.

~~In this paragraph I will write about my name.~~ My name YuMing is made up of two Chinese characters that mean "the universe" and "the crow of a bird." This may seem like a strange name to an American, but in fact it has a special meaning for me. In ancient Chinese literature, there is a story about a bird that was owned by God. This bird was rumored to have the most beautiful voice in the universe. A greedy king wanted this bird, so he had it captured and placed in a big cage. He sat next to this cage day after day waiting for the bird to sing, but the bird stayed silent. After three years, the impatient king threw open the cage door and set the bird free. As the bird flew up toward the heavens, it made its first crow in three years. The sound shocked everyone in the kingdom because they realized the legend was true—they had never heard such a beautiful voice before! My parents told me that they gave me this name because they want me to be like the bird in the story. Though I may stay silent for a while as I establish myself in society, they hope that I will "crow" one day when it is the right time for me, and crow loudly so everyone in the universe can hear.

YuMing Lai, student

TEACHING TIP

If you don't have time to reproduce good student writing for class discussion, you can use the Writers' Workshops at the end of each unit for group work and peer editing. This student's subject—the meaning of her name—makes a fine assignment. Refer students to the intriguing website mentioned in Writing and Revising Idea 2.

1. How effective is YuMing Lai's paragraph about the meaning of her name?

   __N__ Good topic sentence?   __Y__ Rich supporting details?

   __Y__ Logical organization?   __Y__ Effective conclusion?

2. Underline the words, details, or sentences you like best. Put a check beside anything that needs improvement.

3. Now discuss your underlinings with your group or class. Try to explain as exactly as you can why you like something. For example, in the last sentence, the way that the writer ties her parents' wish for her to the meaning of the story is moving and surprising.

4. Is YuMing's topic sentence as good as the rest of her paragraph? If not, how might she change it? No, she should drop the first sentence and begin with "My name YuMing . . ."

112

5. Did YuMing's thoughts about her name make you think about your own name? Do you like your name? Why or why not? Do you know why your parents chose it?

6. What order does this paragraph employ? time order

Writing and Revising Ideas

1. Write about the meaning of your name or the name of someone close to you.

2. Visit the government's website below, which lists the most popular baby names in the United States, year by year. Do you see any patterns? How popular is your name? Your parents' names?
   <http://www.ssa.gov/OACT/babynames/>

For help with writing your paragraph, see Chapter 3 and Chapter 4, Parts A and B. As you revise, pay special attention to writing a clear, catchy topic sentence supported by interesting details.

UNIT 2

Writing Complete Sentences

The sentence is the basic unit of all writing, so good writers must know how to write clear and correct sentences. In this unit, you will

- Learn to spot subjects and verbs
- Practice writing complete sentences
- Learn to avoid or correct any sentence fragments
- Learn proofreading strategies to correct your own errors

114

Spotlight on Reading and Writing

Read this paragraph carefully. Notice the way this writer, a media expert, uses strong, correct sentences to make a thought-provoking, even frightening, point about advertising. If possible, read the paragraph aloud.

Most people feel that advertising is not something to take seriously. Other aspects of the media are serious—the violent films, the trashy talk shows, the bowdlerization[1] of the news. But not advertising! Although much more attention has been paid to the cultural impact of advertising in recent years than ever before, just about everyone still feels personally exempt from its influence. What I hear more than anything else at my lectures is: "I don't pay attention to ads . . . I just tune them out . . . they have no effect on me." I hear this most from people wearing clothes emblazoned with logos. In truth, we are all influenced. There is no way to tune out this much information, especially when it is designed to break through the "tuning out" process. As advertising critic Sut Jhally put it, "To *not* be influenced by advertising would be to live outside of culture. No human being lives outside of culture."

Jean Kilbourne, "Jesus Is a Brand of Jeans," *New Internationalist*

- What is Kilbourne's main idea about advertising in this paragraph? Which sentences tell you this?

- Did any details or examples especially convince you that advertising affects people's behavior whether they know it or not?

Writing Ideas

- *Someone who loves clothes and accessories with logos*

- *A logo, product, or brand and what it "says" about the buyer*

---

1. bowdlerization: process of editing out offensive material

CHAPTER 9

Subjects and Verbs

A: **Defining and Spotting Subjects**

B: **Spotting Singular and Plural Subjects**

C: **Spotting Prepositional Phrases**

D: **Defining and Spotting Action Verbs**

E: **Defining and Spotting Linking Verbs**

F: **Spotting Verbs of More Than One Word**

A. Defining and Spotting Subjects

TEACHING TIP

Grassroots' proven approach to grammar is based on its **MAP** method: illustrative **model**, brief inductive **analysis**, and lots of **practice**. Bulleted thinking questions help students actively analyze each boxed model, leading them to a rule. Varied practices then build from easy to harder for every concept taught. Writing and proofreading practices conclude each chapter.

ESL TIP

Pair same-language ESL students to discuss differences between their language and English—such as word order or singulars and plurals—that might confuse them as they write sentences in English.

The sentence is the basic unit of all writing. To write well, you need to know how to write correct and effective sentences. This chapter will show you how. A **sentence** is a group of words that expresses a complete thought about something or someone. It contains a **subject** and a **verb**.

> (1) _____ jumped over the black Buick, scaled the building, and finally reached the roof.
>
> (2) _____ needs a new coat of paint.

These sentences might be interesting, but they are incomplete.

- In sentence (1), *who* jumped, scaled, and reached? Spider-Man, Alicia Keys, the English teacher?

- Depending on *who* performed the action—jumping, scaling, or reaching—the sentence can be exciting, surprising, or strange.

- What is missing is the *who* word—the *subject*.

- In sentence (2), *what* needs a new coat of paint? The house, the car, the old rocking chair?

- What is missing is the *what* word—the *subject*.

   For a sentence to be complete, it must contain a *who* or *what* word—a *subject*. The subject tells you *who* or *what* does something or exists in a certain way.

   The subject is often a *noun*, a word that names a person, place, or thing (such as *Alicia Keys, English teacher,* or *house*).* However, a *pronoun (I, you, he, she, it, we,* or *they)* also can be the subject.**

---

* For more work on nouns, see Chapter 22.

** For more work on pronoun subjects, see Chapter 23, Part F.

PRACTICE 1

In each of these sentences, the subject (the *who* or *what* word) is missing. Fill in your own subject to make the sentence complete. Sample answers

EXAMPLE: A(n) _____*fox*_____ dashed across the road.

1. The _____hockey puck_____ skidded across the ice.

2. The _____student_____ was eager to begin the semester.

3. Because of the crowd, the _____spy_____ slipped out unnoticed.

4. For years, _____comic books_____ piled up in the back of the closet.

5. The cheerful yellow _____wallpaper_____ brightened Sheila's mood.

6. _____Papers_____ and _____pencils_____ were scattered all over the doctor's desk.

7. The _____singer_____ believed that his _____voice_____ would return someday.

8. The _____farmhouse_____ was in bad shape. The _____ceiling_____ was falling in, and the _____downstairs windows_____ were all broken.

As you may have noticed, the subject can be just one noun or pronoun. This single noun or pronoun is called **the simple subject**. The subject also can include *words that describe the noun or pronoun* (such as *the*, *cheerful*, or *yellow*). The noun and pronoun plus the words that describe it are called **the complete subject**.

> (3) Three scarlet roses grew near the path.
>
> (4) A large box was delivered this morning.

- The complete subject of sentence (3) is *three scarlet roses*.

- The simple subject is the noun *roses*.

- What is the complete subject of (4)? _____a large box_____

- What is the simple subject of (4)? _____box_____

Try This To find the subject, try turning the sentence into a question: *Who or what* grew near the path? *Three scarlet roses*. *Who or what* was delivered this morning? *A large box*.

PRACTICE 2

Circle the *simple* subject in each sentence. (A person's complete name—though more than one word—is considered a simple subject.)

EXAMPLE: (Stacie Ponder) blogs about horror movies.

(1) Many (people) love scary films. (2) (Psychologists) want to know why. (3) (Dr. Leon Rappoport) studies this fear factor among moviegoers. (4) (Humans) have always liked to explore their feelings of fear and anxiety, according to Rappoport. (5) Frightening (movies) allow them to master those emotions and work through them. (6) (People) do not wish to meet Hannibal Lecter in daily life. (7) (They) like to watch him onscreen, however, in

Movie poster, 1958

Horror movies allow people to face their fears in a safe way, claim psychologists.

the absence of any real danger. (8) Horror films and stories provide opportunities for such experiences. (9) Also, some moviegoers like to explore their uncivilized, antisocial nature in safe settings. (10) Many teenagers, in particular, need to test their tolerance for threatening situations. (11) In addition, parents often declare horror movies inappropriate. (12) Therefore, adolescents want to see this forbidden entertainment more than ever.

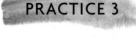

PRACTICE 3

In these sentences, the complete subject has been omitted. You must decide where it belongs and fill in a complete subject (a *who* or *what* word along with any words that describe it to make a complete sentence). Write in any complete subject that makes sense.

EXAMPLE: Raced down the street

My worried friend raced down the street.

1. trained day and night for the big event

   The gymnasts trained day and night for the big event.

2. has a dynamic singing voice

   Bruno Mars has a dynamic singing voice.

3. landed in the cornfield

   A small plane landed in the cornfield.

4. after the show, applauded and screamed for fifteen minutes

   After the show, the crowd applauded and screamed for fifteen minutes.

5. got out of the large gray van

   Mr. Sandhurst got out of the large gray van.

B. Spotting Singular and Plural Subjects

Besides being able to spot subjects in sentences, you need to know whether a subject is singular or plural.

> (1) The man jogged around the park.

- The subject of this sentence is *the man*.
- Because *the man* is one person, the subject is *singular*.

Singular means only one of something.

> (2) The man and his friend jogged around the park.

- The subject of sentence (2) is *the man and his friend*.
- Because *the man and his friend* refers to more than one person, the subject is *plural*.

Plural means more than one of something.*

PRACTICE 4

Here is a list of possible subjects of sentences. If the subject is singular, write *S* next to it; if the subject is plural, write *P* next to it.

EXAMPLES: an elephant   _S_
children   _P_

1.	our cousins	_P_	5. women	_P_
2.	a song and a dance	_P_	6. a rock star and her band	_P_
3.	Kansas	_S_	7. his three pickup trucks	_P_
4.	their website	_S_	8. salad dressing	_S_

PRACTICE 5

Circle the complete subjects in these sentences. Then, in the space at the right, write *S* if the subject is singular or *P* if the subject is plural.

EXAMPLE: (This young cartoonist) is getting national attention.   _S_

1. (Aaron McGruder) was a student at the University of Maryland.   _S_
2. (Comic books and hip-hop music) intrigued him.   _P_
3. To Aaron, (existing comics) did not capture racial diversity in a real way.   _P_
4. (McGruder) decided to create a comic strip called *Boondocks*.   _S_
5. (The characters) were African American city kids in suburbia.   _P_
6. (The strip) appeared in the college's student paper, *The Diamondback*, in 1997.   _S_
7. (Rave reviews and a few angry letters) poured in.   _P_
8. (A major music magazine) soon began publishing *Boondocks* every day.   _S_

* For much more on singulars and plurals, see Chapter 22, Nouns.

9. (Aaron's goal) was to expand racial dialogue by using humor. ___S___

10. (The strip and TV series) have become iconic, with fans awaiting McGruder's next move. ___P___

C. Spotting Prepositional Phrases

A **preposition** is a word like *on, through,* and *before.* Prepositions usually indicate location, direction, or time. For example, the plane sat *on the runway,* flew *through a thunderstorm,* and landed *before dark.* These humble words can be confusing, so it's important to be able to recognize them.

Common Prepositions			
about	beneath	inside	through
above	beside	into	throughout
across	between	like	to
after	beyond	near	toward
against	by	of	under
along	despite	off	underneath
among	down	on	until
around	during	onto	up
at	except	out	upon
before	for	outside	with
behind	from	over	within
below	in	past	without

One group of words that may confuse you as you look for the subjects of sentences is the prepositional phrase. A **prepositional phrase** contains a *preposition* and its *object* (the noun or pronoun that follows the preposition). Here are some prepositional phrases:*

Prepositional Phrase	=	Preposition	+	Object
at work		at		work
behind her		behind		her
of the students		of		the students
on the blue table		on		the blue table

The object of a preposition *cannot* be the subject of a sentence. Therefore, crossing out prepositional phrases can help you find the real subject.

(1) On summer evenings, girls in white dresses stroll under the trees.

(2) ~~On summer evenings,~~ girls ~~in white dresses~~ stroll ~~under the trees.~~

(3) ~~From dawn to dusk,~~ we hiked.

(4) The president ~~of the college~~ will speak tonight

● In sentence (1), you may have trouble spotting the subject. Is it *evening, girls,* or *dresses?*

---

* For more work on prepositions and a list of many English expressions containing prepositions, see Chapter 25, Prepositions.

- However, once the prepositional phrases are crossed out in (2), the subject, *girls*, is easy to see.

- Cross out the prepositional phrase in sentence (3). What is the subject of the sentence? _____we_____

- Cross out the prepositional phrase in sentence (4). What is the subject of the sentence? _____the president_____

Try This   If you have trouble finding prepositional phrases, circle all the prepositions, referring to the prepositions list. Then locate the rest of the words in each prepositional phrase.

PRACTICE 6

Underline all the prepositional phrases in the following sentences. Some sentences include more than one prepositional phrase.

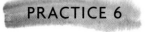

1. In college or the workplace, a knowledge of your learning style can help you master any subject.

2. A learning style is a person's preferred way of learning new information.

3. The four types of learning styles are visual, auditory, reading/writing, and hands-on.

4. Most people learn in all four ways, with one favored style.

5. People with a visual learning style understand best from diagrams, images, or videos.

6. Auditory learners, on the other hand, learn by reading aloud, talking, and listening.

7. Learners with a reading/writing style absorb information easily through written words.

8. After a class, they should write notes and summaries of the material.

9. Hands-on learners show a strong preference for movement and action.

10. For example, they handle objects, perform, or conduct experiments.

PRACTICE 7

Now cross out the prepositional phrase or phrases in each sentence. Then circle the *simple* subject of the sentence.

EXAMPLE: (Millions) of people walk on the Appalachian Trail each year.

1. That famous (trail) stretches from Springer Mountain in Georgia to Mount Katahdin in Maine.

2. One (quarter) of the trail goes through Virginia.

3. The (majority) of walkers hike for one day.

4. Of the four million trail users, two hundred (people) complete the entire trail every year.

5. For most hikers, the (trip) through fourteen states takes four or five months.

6. In the spring, many hardy (souls) begin their 2,158-mile-long journey.

7. These (lovers) of the wilderness must reach Mount Katahdin before winter.

8. On the trail, (men and women) battle heat, humidity, bugs, blisters, muscle sprains, and food and water shortages.

9. After beautiful green scenery, the (path) becomes rocky and mountainous.

10. (Hikers) in the White Mountains of New Hampshire struggle against high winds.

TEACHING TIP

After students have completed Parts A, B, and C, they might highlight all subjects in a recent paragraph of their own, exchange work, and check each other's answers.

11. A pebble from Georgia is sometimes added to the pile of stones at the top of Mount Katahdin.

12. At the bottom of the mountain, the conquerors of the Appalachian Trail add their names to the list of successful hikers.

D. Defining and Spotting Action Verbs

> (1) The pears _____ on the trees.
>
> (2) Robert _____ his customer's hand and _____ her dog on the head.

These sentences tell you what or who the subject is—*the pears* and *Robert*—but not what each subject does.

● In sentence (1), what do the pears do? Do they *grow, ripen, rot, stink,* or *glow*?

● All these *action verbs* fit into the blank space in sentence (1), but the meaning of the sentence changes depending on which action verb you use.

● In sentence (2), what actions did Robert perform? Perhaps he *shook, ignored, kissed, patted,* or *scratched*.

● Depending on which verb you use, the meaning of the sentence changes.

● Some sentences, like sentence (2), contain two or more action verbs.

For a sentence to be complete, it must have a *verb*. An *action verb* tells what action the subject is performing.

PRACTICE 8

Fill in each blank with an action verb. Sample answers

1. Kevin Durant _____sailed_____ through the air for a slam dunk.

2. An artist _____sketched_____ the scene at the waterfront.

3. When the rooster _____crowed_____, the dogs _____barked_____.

4. A fierce wind _____raged_____ and _____howled_____.

5. The audience _____clapped_____ while the conductor _____bowed_____.

6. This new kitchen gadget _____chops_____ and _____slices_____ any vegetable you can imagine.

7. When the dentist _____broke_____ his drill, Charlene _____cheered_____ .

8. Justin Timberlake _____slides_____ and _____glides_____ across the stage.

PRACTICE 9

Circle the action verbs in these sentences. Some sentences contain more than one action verb.

(1) Sometimes the combination of talent and persistence explodes into well-deserved fame and fortune. (2) For almost a year, J. K. Rowling survived on public assistance in Edinburgh, Scotland. (3) Almost every day that year, she brought her baby to a coffee

shop near their damp, unheated apartment. (4) In the warmth of the café, the divorced, unemployed mother (sat) and (wrote). (5) Almost at the end of her endurance, she finally (finished) her first book. (6) Today, Rowling's *Harry Potter* books (sell) hundreds of millions of copies in sixty languages. (7) Each book (tells) about Harry's adventures, both in the everyday world (the Muggles' world) and at a new grade level at Hogwarts School of Witchcraft and Wizardry. (8) The imaginative and very funny series about the courageous young wizard-in-training (attracts) and (enthralls) adults as well as children. (9) In fact, the *New York Times* (began) a children's bestseller list for the first time—after months of *Harry Potter* books in slots 1, 2, and 3 on the adult bestseller list!

E. Defining and Spotting Linking Verbs

The verbs you have been examining so far show action, but a second kind of verb simply links the subject to words that describe or rename it.

(1) Aunt Claudia sometimes seems a little strange.

● The subject in this sentence is *Aunt Claudia*, but there is no action verb.

● Instead, *seems* links the subject, *Aunt Claudia*, with the descriptive words *a little strange*.

Aunt Claudia	*seems*	*a little strange.*
↓	↓	↓
subject	linking verb	descriptive words

(2) They are reporters for the newspaper.

● The subject is *they*. The word *reporters* renames the subject.

● What verb links the subject, *they*, with the word *reporters*? _____are_____

For a sentence to be complete, it must contain a *verb*. A *linking verb* links the subject with words that describe or rename that subject.

Here are some linking verbs you should know:

Common Linking Verbs	
be (am, is, are, was, were)	look
act	seem
appear	smell
become	sound
feel	taste
get	

- The most common linking verbs are the forms of *to be*—*am, is, are, was, were*—but verbs of the senses, such as *feel, look,* and *smell,* also may be used as linking verbs.

PRACTICE 10

The complete subjects and descriptive words in these sentences are underlined. Circle the linking verbs.

1. Jerry (sounds) sleepy today.
2. Sunetra always (was) the best debater on the team.
3. His brother often (appeared) relaxed and happy.
4. By evening, Harvey (felt) confident about the exam.
5. Mara and Maude (became) talent scouts.

PRACTICE 11

Circle the linking verbs in these sentences. Then underline the complete subject and the descriptive word or words in each sentence.

1. The sweet potato pie (tastes) delicious.
2. You usually (seem) energetic.
3. During the summer, she (looks) calm.
4. Under heavy snow, the new dome roof (appeared) sturdy.
5. Raphael (is) a gifted animal trainer.
6. Lately, I (feel) very competent at work.
7. Luz (became) a medical technician.
8. Yvonne (acted) surprised at her baby shower.

F. Spotting Verbs of More Than One Word

All the verbs you have dealt with so far have been single words—*look, walked, saw, are, were,* and so on. However, many verbs consist of more than one word.

> (1) Sarah is walking to work.

ESL TIP

Ask nonnative students how verbs in their language differ from verbs in English.

- The subject is *Sarah.* What is *Sarah* doing?
- Sarah is walking.
- *Walking* is the *main verb. Is* is the *helping verb;* without *is, walking* is not a complete verb.

> (2) Should I have written sooner?

- The subject is *I.*
- *Should have written* is the *complete verb.*
- *Written* is the *main verb. Should* and *have* are the *helping verbs;* without *should have, written* is not a complete verb.

(3) Do you eat fish?

- What is the subject? _____you_____
- What is the main verb? _____eat_____
- What is the helping verb? _____do_____

The *complete verb* in a sentence consists of all the helping verbs and the main verb.

PRACTICE 12

TEACHING TIP

Practices 12 and 13 make enjoyable full-class exercises.

ESL TIP

ESL students may be confused by the variety of verb forms and tenses in Practice 12. Be prepared to refer the students to the appropriate chapters in Unit 3 for explanations.

The blanks following each sentence tell you how many words make up the complete verb. Fill in the blanks with the complete verb; then circle the main verb.

EXAMPLE: Language researchers at the University of Arizona have been studying parrots.

_____have_____   _____been_____   _____(studying)_____

1. Dr. Irene Pepperberg has worked with Alex, an African Gray parrot, for years.

   _____has_____   _____(worked)_____

2. Nearly one hundred words can be used by this intelligent bird.

   _____can_____   _____be_____   _____(used)_____

3. Alex is believed to understand the words, not just "parrot" sounds.

   _____is_____   _____(believed)_____

Alex, the talking parrot, with his trainer, Dr. Irene Pepperberg

Rick Friedman/Corbis

4. For example, from a tray of objects, Alex can select all the keys, all the wooden items, or all the blue items.

       _____can_____   ____(select)____

5. Dr. Pepperberg might show Alex a fuzzy cloth ball.

       _____might_____   ____(show)____

6. The bird will shout, "Wool!"

       _____will_____   ____(shout)____

7. Alex has been counting to six.

    _____has_____   _____been_____   ____(counting)____

8. Currently, he and the other parrots are learning letters and their sounds.

       _____are_____   ____(learning)____

9. Can these birds really be taught to read?

    _____can_____   _____be_____   ____(taught)____

10. Scientists in animal communication are excited by the possibility.

       _____are_____   ____(excited)____

PRACTICE 13

Box the simple subject, circle the main verb, and underline any helping verbs in each of the following sentences.

EXAMPLE: Most [people] have (wondered) about the beginning of the universe.

1. [Scientists] have (developed) one theory.
2. According to this theory, the [universe] (began) with a huge explosion.
3. The [explosion] has been (named) the Big Bang.
4. First, all [matter] must have been (packed) into a tiny speck under enormous pressure.
5. Then, about 15 billion years ago, that [speck] (burst) with amazing force.
6. [Everything] in the universe has (come) from the original explosion.
7. In fact, the [universe] still is (expanding) from the Big Bang.
8. [All] of the planets and stars are (moving) away from each other at an even speed.
9. Will [it] (expand) forever?
10. [Experts] may be (debating) that question for a long time.

Chapter Highlights

- **A sentence contains a subject and a verb, and expresses a complete thought:**

     S   V

  Jennifer swims every day.

         S   V

  The two students have tutored in the writing lab.

- **An action verb tells what the subject is doing:**

  Toni Morrison *writes* novels.

- **A linking verb links the subject with words that describe or rename it:**

  Her novels *are* bestsellers.

- **Don't mistake the object of a prepositional phrase for a subject:**

       S   PP

  The red car [in the showroom] is a Corvette.

    PP   S

  [In my dream,] *a sailor and his parrot* were singing.

Proofreading Strategy

Being able to recognize subjects and verbs will help you know whether or not your sentences are complete. To test for completeness, **cross out** and **color code**:

1. Read each sentence slowly, crossing out any prepositional phrases.

2. Then either circle the subject and underline the verb or *color code your subjects and verbs,* using two different highlighters, like this:

   My hometown has been hit very hard ~~by the recession~~.

   Many ~~of my neighbors~~ have lost their jobs, including both ~~of my brothers~~.

3. Finally, read each sentence slowly to make sure it expresses a complete thought and ends with a period.

WRITING AND PROOFREADING ASSIGNMENT

Whether you have just graduated from high school or have worked for several years, the first year of college can be difficult. Imagine that you are writing to an incoming student who needs advice and encouragement. Pick one serious problem you had as a first-year student and explain how you coped with it. State the problem clearly. Use examples from your own experience or the experience of others to make your advice more vivid. After you write and revise your composition, take a break before you proofread. Then, cross out your prepositional phrases and mark or highlight every subject and verb. Check each sentence for completeness.

CHAPTER REVIEW

Circle the simple subjects, crossing out any confusing prepositional phrases. Then underline the complete verbs. If you prefer, color code the subjects and verbs. If you have difficulty with this review, consider rereading the lesson.

Target Practice: Setting Attainable Goals

(1) Successful people know an important secret about setting and reaching goals. (2) These high achievers break their big goals into smaller, more manageable steps or targets. (3) Then they hit the targets, one by one. (4) Otherwise, a huge goal might seem impossible.

(5) To turn a major goal into smaller steps, many achievers think backward. (6) Dillon, for example, wanted to lose twenty pounds by graduation. (7) That much weight must be lost gradually. (8) So Dillon decided to set smaller targets for himself. (9) First, Dillon eliminated between-meal snacks. (10) On the new plan, he might eat an occasional apple, but only in emergencies. (11) Second, Dillon gave up second helpings at any meal—no matter what. (12) His third target was a walk after dinner. (13) Every night, this purposeful dieter would check off the day's successes.

(14) Even high achievers do not complete a major goal, like losing a lot of weight, every day. (15) Yet they can feel satisfaction about moving forward one step at a time. (16) The photographer at Dillon's graduation captured his beaming smile. (17) Under that cap and gown, Dillon's weight had dropped by twenty-two pounds.

EXPLORING ONLINE

<http://grammar.ccc.commnet.edu/grammar/quizzes/subjector.htm>
Interactive quiz: Identify the subjects.

<http://grammar.ccc.commnet.edu/grammar/quizzes/verbmaster.htm>
Interactive quiz: Identify verbs of one or more words.

CHAPTER 10

Avoiding Sentence Fragments

A: **Writing Sentences with Subjects and Verbs**

B: **Writing Sentences with Complete Verbs**

C: **Completing the Thought**

A. Writing Sentences with Subjects and Verbs

Which of these groups of words is a sentence? Be prepared to explain your answers.

(1) People will bet on almost anything.

(2) For example, every winter the Nenana River in Alaska.

(3) Often make bets on the date of the breakup of the ice.

(4) Must guess the exact day and time of day.

(5) Recently, the lucky guess won $300,000.

- In (2), you probably wanted to know what the Nenana River *does*. The idea is not complete because there is no *verb*.

- In (3) and (4), you probably wanted to know *who* often makes bets on the date of the breakup of the ice and *who* must guess the exact day and time of day.

    The ideas are not complete. What is missing? _____the subjects_____

- But in sentences (1) and (5), you knew *who did what*. These ideas are complete. Why? __They have a subject and a verb, and they express a complete thought.__

Below are the same groups of words written as complete sentences:

(1) People will bet on almost anything.

(2) For example, every winter the Nenana River in Alaska freezes.

(3) The townspeople often make bets on the date of the breakup of the ice.

(4) Someone must guess the exact day and time of day.

(5) Recently, the lucky guess won $300,000.

Every *sentence* must have both a subject and a verb—and must express a complete thought.

A *fragment* is not a complete sentence because it lacks either a subject or a complete verb—or does not express a complete thought.

PRACTICE 1

All of the following are *fragments* because they lack a subject, a verb, or both. Add a subject, a verb, or both to make the fragments into sentences. Answers will vary.

EXAMPLE: Raising onions in the backyard.

Rewrite: *Charles is raising onions in the backyard.*

1. Melts easily.

   Rewrite: On a hot day in Alabama, butter melts easily.

2. That couple on the street corner.

   Rewrite: That couple on the street corner just won the lottery.

3. One of the fans.

   Rewrite: One of the fans caught a fly ball.

4. Manages a Software City store.

   Rewrite: My next-door neighbor manages a Software City store.

5. The tip of her nose.

   Rewrite: The tip of her nose was red from the cold.

6. DVR players.

   Rewrite: DVR players are replacing DVD players in many homes.

7. Makes me nervous.

   Rewrite: Parking my car at the airport all week makes me nervous.

8. A person who likes to take risks.

   Rewrite: Edgardo is a person who likes to take risks.

Sentence fragments are considered a serious and distracting error in college and at work, so it is important that you learn to eliminate them from your writing.

B. Writing Sentences with Complete Verbs

Do not be fooled by incomplete verbs.

(1) She leaving for the city.

(2) We done that chapter already.

- *Leaving* seems to be the verb in (1).
- *Done* seems to be the verb in (2).

But . . .

- An *-ing* word like *leaving* is not by itself a verb.
- A word like *done* is not by itself a verb.

> (1) She $\begin{Bmatrix} is \\ was \end{Bmatrix}$ leaving for the city.
>
> (2) We $\begin{Bmatrix} have \\ had \end{Bmatrix}$ done that chapter already.

- To be a verb, an *-ing* word (called a *present participle*) must be combined with some form of the verb *to be*.*

ESL TIP

Encourage ESL students to bookmark this *helping verb +
main verb* chart for future use. Quiz them on uses of *be* helping verbs with simple verbs to avoid errors like these: *I am
come from Vietnam. I was live
here a long time.*

Helping Verb		Main Verb
am	were	
is	has been	
are	have been	jogging
was	had been	

- To be a verb, a word like *done* (called a *past participle*) must be combined with some form of *to have* or *to be*.**

Helping Verb		Main Verb
am	have	
is	had	
are	has been	
was	have been	forgotten
were	had been	
has		

PRACTICE 2

All of the following are fragments; they have only a partial or an incomplete verb. Complete each verb in order to make these fragments into sentences. Answers will vary.

EXAMPLE: Both children grown tall this year.

Rewrite: *Both children have grown tall this year.*

1. The Australian winning the tennis match.

   Rewrite: The Australian is winning the tennis match.

2. Her friends seen her at the mall every Saturday.

   Rewrite: Her friends have seen her at the mall every Saturday.

---

* For a detailed explanation of present participles, see Chapter 14.
** For a detailed explanation of past participles, see Chapter 13.

3. Steve's letter published in the *Miami Herald*.

   Rewrite: Steve's letter was published in the *Miami Herald*.

4. My physics professor always forgetting the assignment.

   Rewrite: My physics professor is always forgetting the assignment.

5. You ever been to Hawaii?

   Rewrite: Have you ever been to Hawaii?

PRACTICE 3

Fragments are most likely to occur in paragraphs or longer pieces of writing. Proofread the paragraph below for fragments; check for missing subjects, missing verbs, or incomplete verbs. Circle the number of every fragment; then write your corrections above the lines. Answers will vary.

(1) On a routine day in 1946, a scientist at the Raytheon Company put his hand into his pants pocket for a candy bar. (2) The chocolate, however, was a messy, sticky mass of gunk. (3) Dr. Percy Spencer had been testing a magnetron tube. (4) Could the chocolate have melted from radiation leaking from the tube? (5) Spencer sent out for a bag of popcorn kernels. (6) He put Put the kernels near the tube. (7) Within minutes, corn was popping wildly onto the lab floor. (8) Within a short time, Raytheon was working on the development of the microwave oven. (9) Microwave cooking became the first new method of preparing food since the discovery of fire more than a million years ago. (10) It was Was the first cooking technique that did not directly or indirectly apply fire to food.

PRACTICE 4

Proofread the paragraph below for fragments; check for missing subjects, missing verbs, or incomplete verbs. Try combining some sentences. Circle the number of every fragment; then write your corrections above the lines. Answers will vary.

(1) The next time you are about to toss an empty plastic bottle in a trash can, picture it floating in ocean waves. waves (2) Littered littered with plastic trash. (3) Plastic pollution in our oceans has become a serious problem in recent years. (4) Every square mile of ocean now contains 46,000 pieces of floating plastic. plastic like (5) Like water bottles, margarine containers, six-pack rings, bottle caps, and plastic bags. (6) Some of this marine debris litters the world's beaches. (7) Even more drifts in the sea, where it will injure or kill millions of seabirds, sea turtles, fish, and marine mammals. (8) These creatures mistake it for food or get tangled up and slowly die. (9) Because plastic cannot biodegrade, it remains in the sea. sea, breaking (10) Breaking down into

smaller and smaller pieces full of dangerous chemicals. (11) These toxins may wind up in the fish dinner you order at your favorite seafood restaurant. (12) The next time you consider trashing some plastic, think for a moment and keep it for a recycling bin instead. (13) Even better, stop buying bottled water and other single-use plastic items. ⟨14⟩ One sturdy, refillable water bottle ~~to~~ _will_ significantly reduce plastic waste. (15) Take home your groceries in reusable cloth bags. ⟨16⟩ ~~Instead~~ of plastic bags. _bags instead_ ⟨17⟩ Through reducing, reusing, and recycling plastics, our oceans _will be_ cleaner and safer for all.

Plastic-littered scenes like this ocean beach in Hong Kong are common all over the world.

© Ron Yue/Alamy

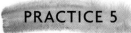 **PRACTICE 5**

Teamwork: Critical Thinking and Writing

Plastic in our oceans has become a global threat to wildlife and, increasingly, human health. Over a billion plastic bags are given out every day in the United States alone; less than 3 percent of them are recycled. In a group with several classmates, answer this question: If more people were educated about the horrible deaths of so many seabirds, fish, and mammals caused by plastic bags and objects, would they be motivated not to toss away plastic carelessly? If not, what can be done to reverse the damage to our oceans?

C. Completing the Thought

Can these ideas stand by themselves?

(1) Because oranges are rich in vitamin C.

(2) Although Sam is sleepy.

ESL TIP

Many ESL students begin sentences with subordinators like *because* and *although*, so this type of fragment is a common problem. Some are copying the oral speech patterns they hear. Others come from language backgrounds, like Japanese, in which this construction is accepted written practice.

- These ideas have a subject and a verb (find them), but they cannot stand alone because you expect something else to follow.

- Because oranges are rich in vitamin C, *then what*? Should you *eat them*, *sell them*, or *make marmalade*?

- Although Sam is sleepy, what will he do? Will he *wash the dishes*, *walk the dog*, or *go to the gym*?

(1) Because oranges are rich in vitamin C, *I eat one every day*.

(2) Although Sam is sleepy, *he will work late tonight*.

- These sentences are now complete.

- Words like *because* and *although* make an idea incomplete unless another idea is added to complete the thought.

You will learn more about words like this, called *subordinating conjunctions*, in Chapter 17, but here is a list of the most common ones.*

Common Subordinating Conjunctions

after	because	though	whenever
although	before	unless	where
as	if	until	whether
as if	since	when	while

Fragments often begin with these *subordinating conjunctions*. When you spot one of these words in your writing, check to make sure you have completed the thought.

PRACTICE 6

Make these fragments into sentences by adding some idea that completes the thought. Answers will vary.

EXAMPLE: Because I miss my family, *I am going home for the weekend.*

1. As May stepped off the elevator, she bumped into her old boyfriend.

2. If you are driving to Main Street, please take me with you.

3. While Kimi studied chemistry, Maurie did his math homework.

4. Because you believe in yourself, you will succeed.

5. Although spiders scare most people, I find them fascinating.

LEARNING STYLES TIP

For Practices 6 and 7, which require students to add their own thoughts, have students discuss their answers in pairs or groups or write them on the board. These activities enhance comprehension for *visual, auditory,* and *kinesthetic learners.*

Can these ideas stand by themselves?

(3) Graciela, who has a one-year-old daughter.

(4) A course that I will always remember.

(5) Vampire stories, which are popular now.

* For more work on this type of sentence, see Chapter 17, Subordination.

- In each of these examples, you expect something else to follow. Graciela, who has a one-year-old daughter, *is doing what?* Does she *attend town meetings*, *knit sweaters*, or *fly planes*?

- A course that I will always remember *is what?* The thought must be completed.

- Vampire stories, which are popular now, *do what?* The thought must be completed.

(3) Graciela, who has a one-year-old daughter, *attends Gordon College.*

(4) A course that I will always remember *is documentary filmmaking.*

(5) Vampire stories, which are popular now, *exist in cultures all over the world.*

- These sentences are now complete.*

> *Try This*   Try this "fragment test," which works for some people. Ask, "Is it true that . . ." followed by the test sentence:
>
> Is it true that __The horoscopes that appear in the daily papers__ ?   NO
>
> Is it true that __The horoscopes that appear in the daily papers make me laugh__ ?   YES

If the answer is *no*, this is a fragment. If the answer is *yes*, the sentence is correct.

PRACTICE 7

Make these fragments into sentences by completing the thought. Sample answers

EXAMPLE: Kent, who is a good friend of mine, __rarely writes to me.__

1. The horoscopes that appear in the daily papers __make me laugh.__

2. Couples who never argue __seem unreal.__

3. Alonzo, who is a superb pole vaulter, __will compete in the Olympics.__

4. Satellite radio, which offers hundreds of channels, __is worth the fee.__

5. A person who has coped with a great loss __often can help others.__

6. My dog, which is the smartest animal alive, __starts to bark five minutes before I arrive.__

PRACTICE 8

Proofread the paragraph below for fragments. Circle the number of every fragment, and then write your corrections above the lines.

(1) The word *meditate* might call to mind the image of a spiritual seeker. ⟨seeker sitting⟩ (2) Sitting for hours in a cross-legged pose. (3) According to psychologists, however, you ⟨are⟩ practicing meditation any time you quiet your mind, focus on your breath, let thoughts and feelings occur without judging them, and ignore all distractions around you. (4) Engaging in this form of "mindfulness" for just five minutes a day can produce remarkable benefits. (5) Small

* For more work on this type of sentence, see Chapter 20, Part A.

function, including
daily doses of meditation can improve intellectual ~~function. (6) Including~~ concentration

and memory. (7) In one study, a group that practiced mindfulness 20 minutes a day for four

tests than
days performed significantly better on brain ~~tests. (8) Than~~ a group of people who did not

meditate. (9) Meditation also shifts brain activity toward more positive emotional states.

regularly report
(10) Many people who meditate ~~regularly. (11) Report~~ a decrease in feelings of depression,

anxiety, anger, and stress. (12) Finally, meditation appears to have beneficial physical ~~effects.~~

effects such
(13) ~~Such~~ as pain management, lower blood pressure, improved cardiovascular fitness, and

a stronger immune system. (14) Try mindfulness meditation the next time you are sitting

quietly—on the bus, in a waiting room, in the bathtub, or anywhere. (15) Sink into the

alive, body
present moment and come ~~alive. (16) Body,~~ mind, and spirit.

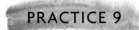

PRACTICE 9

Proofread the paragraph for fragments. Circle the number of every fragment, and then
write your corrections above the lines.

300C, which
(1) Ralph Gilles won fame as the designer of the Chrysler ~~300C. (2) Which~~ earned

many design awards. (3) Raised in Canada by Haitian parents, Gilles was in awe of his

mother because
~~mother. (4) Because~~ she gave her all to various thankless jobs and still told her children

Designer Ralph Gilles
poses with a Dodge
Challenger, one of
Chrysler's "muscle cars."

success stories. (5) When he was a ~~boy.~~ (6) ~~Gilles~~ loved to draw futuristic cars in his

boy, Gilles

notebooks. (7) An aunt noticed his design gifts and urged him to write to Lee

Iacocca, who

~~Iacocca.~~ (8) ~~Who~~ was then chairman of the Chrysler Corporation. (9) Amazingly, after

sketches, an

the embarrassed fourteen-year-old sent a letter and some ~~sketches.~~ (10) ~~An~~ executive

encouragement and

responded with ~~encouragement.~~ (11) ~~And~~ a list of colleges from which Chrysler hired designers.

(12) Later Gilles took the advice, attended Detroit's College for Creative Studies, and landed his

first job at Chrysler. (13) Talent and hard work earned him promotions, the titles of Senior Vice

President of Design and President and CEO of the SRT Brand and media stardom. (14) While

vehicles, he

Gilles is designing the next generation of ~~vehicles.~~ (15) ~~He~~ is also inspiring the next generation

of young people. (16) He tells the kids who write him or attend his talks, "Dream out loud."

TEACHING TIP

Suggest that students try the "bottom-up" proofreading technique—reading the last sentence first, then the second to last, and so on until they reach the first sentence.

Chapter Highlights

A sentence fragment is an incomplete sentence because it lacks

- **a subject:** Was buying a gold ring. (*incorrect*)
  Diamond Jim was buying a gold ring. (*correct*)

- **a verb:** The basketball game Friday at noon. (*incorrect*)
  The basketball game *was played* Friday at noon. (*correct*)

- **a complete thought:** While Teresa was swimming. (*incorrect*)
  While Teresa was swimming, she lost a contact lens. (*correct*)

  The woman who bought your car. (*incorrect*)
  The woman who bought your car is walking down the highway. (*correct*)

Proofreading Strategy

Sentence fragments are a serious error. To spot and correct them more easily in your writing, try the **bottom-up proofreading technique**. Start by reading the last sentence of your paper, slowly, word by word. Then read the second-to-last sentence, and so on, all the way from the "bottom to the top." For each sentence, ask:

1. Does this sentence have a *subject*, a *complete verb*, and express a *complete thought*?

2. Is this an incomplete thought beginning with a word like *because*, *although*, or *when*? If so, such fragments often can be fixed by connecting them to the sentence before or after.

3. Is this an incomplete thought containing *who*, *which*, or *that*? If so, such fragments often can be fixed by connecting them to the sentence before or after.

If sentence fragments are one of your error patterns, log them in your Personal Error Chart and proofread every paper once through just for fragments.

WRITING AND PROOFREADING ASSIGNMENT

Working in a small group, choose one of the sentences below that could begin a short story.

1. As soon as Sean read the text message, he knew he had to take action.
2. Suddenly, the bright blue sky turned dark.
3. The boss's heels clicked down the hallway toward my pathetic cubicle.

Next, each person in the group should write his or her own short story, starting with that sentence. First decide what type of story yours will be—science fiction, romance, action, comedy, murder mystery, and so on; perhaps each person will choose a different type. It may help you to imagine the story later becoming a TV show. As you write, be careful to avoid fragments, making sure each sentence has a subject and a complete verb—and expresses a complete thought.

Then exchange papers, using the bottom-up technique to check each other's work for fragments. If time permits, read the papers aloud to the group. Are you surprised by the different ways in which that first sentence was developed?

CHAPTER REVIEW

TEACHING TIP

Because fragments are most likely to occur in longer pieces of writing, proof-reading exercises like these are particularly helpful to students.

Circle the number of each fragment. Correct it in any way that makes sense, changing it into a separate idea or adding it to another sentence. You might try the bottom-up proofreading strategy.

A.   (1) In our fast-paced society, we often turn to ~~multitasking.~~ (2) ~~Which~~ *multitasking, which* is doing two or more things at once. (3) For example, we might check our email while talking on the ~~phone.~~ *phone* (4) ~~Because~~ we want to save time. (5) Ironically, multitasking often takes ~~longer.~~ (6) ~~Than~~ *longer than* completing each task separately. (7) The reason is simple. (8) Each task requires attention, and switching our attention back and forth is time-consuming. (9) According to recent research, multitasking also can be ~~dangerous.~~ (10) ~~Especially~~ *dangerous, especially* when one of the tasks is driving. (11) In laboratory studies with college students, students who simulated driving in a city and talking on a hands-free cell ~~phone.~~ (12) ~~Crashed~~ *phone crashed* four times more often than other students. (13) An even more frightening study videotaped truck drivers on the road. (14) Some of these truck drivers *were* sending text messages as they drove. (15) Because they switched their attention back and forth from texting to ~~driving.~~ (16) ~~Their~~ *driving, their* reaction times were slow. (17) The texting drivers were an amazing 23 times more likely to crash than other drivers.

**Katrina Cottage,
448 square feet**

B.   (1) Growing up in ~~Alaska.~~ (2) ~~Marianne~~ *Alaska, Marianne* Cusato disliked the trashy, manmade strip malls surrounded by glorious mountain scenery. (3) She decided to be an ~~architect.~~ (4) ~~Who~~ *architect who* would build practical, beautiful buildings. (5) In fact, Cusato achieved her goal. (6) After Hurricane Katrina in 2005, the young architect entered and won a contest to create an alternative to the ugly FEMA ~~trailers.~~ *trailers, which* (7) ~~Which~~ disaster victims often live in temporarily. (8) Her Katrina Cottage won many admirers. (9) Adapting the pastel colors and white trim of Caribbean ~~architecture.~~ *architecture, Cusato* (10) ~~Cusato~~ gave her Katrina Cottages compact living spaces, charming porches, and hurricane windows. (11) The smallest cottage was just 330 square feet. (12) Soon regular families wanted to build these inexpensive and attractive homes. (13) Lowe's *began* selling the houses in prefabricated kits to the public. (14) Cusato believes that small, well-designed houses often feel ~~cozier.~~ *cozier than* (15) ~~Than~~ large, pricey ~~homes.~~ *homes, which* (16) ~~Which~~ have pushed many Americans into debt. (17) Her designs and books promote these ~~values.~~ *values, but* (18) ~~But~~ not strip malls.

C. (1) Many people seem to forget all about good ~~manners.~~ *manners when* (2) ~~When~~ they use a cell phone. (3) They rudely allow the ringing phone to interrupt conversations, meetings, appointments, performances, and romantic dinner dates. (4) The ringtones, which range from roaring motorcycles to mooing ~~cows.~~ *cows, blare* (5) ~~Blare~~ out in classrooms and concert halls. (6) Many people even answer these calls in church or at ~~funerals.~~ *funerals and* (7) ~~And~~ then proceed to talk ~~loudly.~~ *loudly, forcing* (8) ~~Forcing~~ others to listen or wait for them to finish talking. (9) Public relations consultant Carol Page, known as the "Miss Manners of Cell ~~Phones."~~ *Phones," believes* (10) ~~Believes~~ we can stop cell rudeness. (11) We should fix a "cell glare" on any cell phone user who is behaving badly. (12) If that doesn't ~~work.~~ *work, we* (13) ~~We~~ can interrupt and gently ask if the phone conversation might be postponed. (14) Setting a good example when you use your own cell phone *is* probably the best way to teach good cellular phone manners to others.

D. (1) As the demand for paralegals, or legal assistants, ~~grows.~~ *grows, more* (2) ~~More~~ students nationwide are majoring in paralegal studies. (3) Because many different types of law firms and businesses hire ~~paralegals.~~ *paralegals, a* (4) ~~A~~ paralegal's duties vary with the job setting. (5) For

instance, because Denise Cunningham is the only paralegal at a small law firm in Louisville,
Kentucky, she
Kentucky. (6) ~~She~~ has many duties. (7) Cunningham relishes being at the center of ~~things.~~ things,
researching
(8) ~~Researching~~ cases, doing client intake interviews, writing, and even managing the office.

(9) When she was earning her associate's degree in paralegal studies from the University
Lousiville, Cunningham
of ~~Louisville.~~ (10) ~~Cunningham~~ learned about immigration law, real estate law, family law,

and criminal law. (11) Drawn to criminal law, she was hired in 1980 by the attorney with
salary and
whom she still works today. (12) Her professional rewards include a good ~~salary.~~ (13) ~~And~~ the

satisfaction of helping people. (14) In 2006, her boss nominated her for Paralegal of the Year.

EXPLORING ONLINE

<http://www.bls.gov/oco/> Visit this helpful career website, which describes
the duties and future outlook for hundreds of professions. Choose one
career that interests you, research it, take notes, and write a report on the
pros and cons of the job for you.

E. (1) Braille, which is a system of reading and writing now used by blind people all over
world, was
the ~~world.~~ (2) ~~Was~~ invented by a fifteen-year-old French boy. (3) In 1824, when Louis Braille
Paris, he
entered a school for the blind in ~~Paris.~~ (4) ~~He~~ found that the library had only fourteen books

for the blind. (5) These books used a system that he and the other blind students found

hard to use. (6) Most of them just gave up. (7) Louis Braille devoted himself to finding a
night writing, he
better way. (8) Working with the French army method called ~~night-writing.~~ (9) ~~He~~ came
Braille, it was
up with a new system in 1829. (10) Although his classmates liked and used ~~Braille.~~ (11) ~~It~~ not

widely accepted in England and the United States for another hundred years.

EXPLORING ONLINE

TEACHING TIP
Instructor tools for *Grass-roots* include a computerized Test Bank, PowerPoint slides, an Instructor's Manual with teaching tips, and more, and can be accessed at ‹login.cengage.com›.

<http://grammar.ccc.commnet.edu/grammar/cgi-shl/quiz.pl/fragments_add2.htm> Interactive quiz: Find the correct sentence in each group.

<http://grammar.ccc.commnet.edu/grammar/quizzes/fragment_fixing.htm> Try your skills with this interactive fragment test. Can you find and fix all the fragments?

UNIT 2
Writing Assignments

As you complete each writing assignment, remember to perform these steps:

- Write a clear, complete topic sentence.
- Use freewriting, brainstorming, or clustering to generate ideas for your paragraph, essay, or memo.
- Arrange your best ideas in a plan.
- Revise for support, unity, coherence, and exact language.
- Proofread for grammar, punctuation, and spelling errors.

Writing Assignment 1 *Plan to achieve a goal.* Did you know that nearly all successful people are good goal-planners? Choose a goal you would truly love to achieve, and write it down. Next, write down three to six smaller steps or targets that will lead you to your goal. Arrange these in time order. Have you left out any crucial steps? To inspire you and help you plan, reread "Target Practice: Setting Attainable Goals" on page 128, or try out the interactive goal-planner from Paradise Valley Community College at <https://igoal.pvc.maricopa.edu/igoal/images/smart.swf>.

Writing Assignment 2 *Describe your place in the family.* Your psychology professor has asked you to write a brief description of your place in the family— as an only child, the youngest child, the middle child, or the oldest child. Did your place provide you with special privileges or lay special responsibilities on you? For instance, youngest children may be babied; oldest children may be expected to act like parents. Does your place in the family have an effect on you as an adult? In your topic sentence, state what role your place in the family played in your development: *Being the _____ child in my family has made me _____.* Proofread for fragments.

Writing Assignment 3 *Write about someone who changed jobs.* Did you, someone you know, or someone you know about change jobs because of a new interest or love for something else? Describe the person's first job and feelings of job satisfaction (or lack of them). What happened to make the person want to make a job switch? How long did the switch take? Was it difficult or easy to accomplish? Describe the person's new job and feelings of job satisfaction (or lack of them). Proofread for fragments.

Writing Assignment 4 *Ask for a raise.* Compose a memo to a boss, real or imagined, attempting to persuade him or her to raise your pay. In your first sentence, state that you are asking for an increase. Be specific: note how the quality of your work, your extra hours, or any special projects you have been involved in have made the business run more smoothly or become more profitable. Do not sound vain, but do praise yourself honestly. Use the memo style shown here. Proofread for fragments.

MEMORANDUM

DATE: Today's date

TO: Your boss's name

FROM: Your name

SUBJECT: Salary Increase

UNIT 2
Review

Proofreading and Revising

Proofread the following essay to eliminate all sentence fragments. Circle the number of every fragment. (You should find ten.) Then correct the fragments in any way you choose—by connecting them to a sentence before or after, by completing any incomplete verbs, and so on. Make your corrections above the lines.

Too Much Screen Time

(1) Children today are ~~surrounded.~~ <u>surrounded by</u> (2) ⃝By screens. (3) Screens on laptops, computer tablets, smartphones, video games, televisions, and DVD players all capture their attention. (4) Kids as young as two know how to access games, videos, and apps. (5) Some parents brag about their kids' educational ~~gains.~~ <u>gains while</u> (6) ~~While~~ others just give in to temptation and use screens as babysitters. (7) Experts warn that too much screen time for kids under eight can be harmful.

(8) First, excessive time with electronic devices deprives kids of the kind of play that really does develop young brains and creativity. (9) According to child development experts, children learn best by interacting with people and things in the real world. (10) They need to move their bodies and manipulate ~~objects.~~ <u>objects using</u> (11) ~~Using~~ all their senses and letting their imaginations run free. (12) They need to explore outdoors, ride bikes, build ~~forts.~~ <u>forts, and</u> (13) ~~And~~ dream up their own ways to play. (14) Even the most advanced educational apps and games cannot duplicate the brain-building effects of playing with real blocks, sticks, cardboard boxes, ~~sand.~~ <u>sand, and</u> (15) ~~And~~ other children.

(16) Second, too much screen time inhibits the development of relationships, social skills, and coping skills. (17) When children are absorbed in hours of solitary digital ~~play.~~ <u>play, they</u> (18) ~~They~~ interact less with family, friends, and classmates. (19) This limits their opportunities to develop communication and conflict management skills. (20) Even worse, if parents give kids electronic gadgets to distract them from difficult emotions

© Jade and Bertrand Maitre/Flickr/Getty Images

like boredom, grief, or frustration, children are robbed of chances to learn to cope with these feelings. (21) When a screen is always within ~~reach.~~ reach, a (22) ~~A~~ child may never learn to sit quietly and explore his or her own thoughts.

(23) For all these reasons, the American Academy of Pediatrics recommends keeping children two and under away from any screens at ~~all.~~ all and (24) ~~And~~ limiting older children's screen time. (25) Experts urge parents to entice kids away from screens with trips to the playground and toys that require ~~imagination.~~ imagination, such (26) ~~Such~~ as dolls, Play-Doh, and musical instruments. (27) When it comes to raising happy, well-adjusted ~~humans.~~ humans, screens (28) ~~Screens~~ are no substitute for old-fashioned play and personal interaction.

EXPLORING ONLINE

http://www.screenfree.org/ Visit the website and read for ideas. Click "In Your Home" to plan a screen-free week in your home. Keep notes on any reactions or changes. Use these notes to write about the experience.

UNIT 2
Writers' Workshop

Discuss an Event that Influenced You

Readers of a final draft can easily forget that they are reading the *end result* of someone else's writing process. The following paragraph is one student's response to the assignment *Write about an event in history that influenced you*.

In your class or group, read it aloud if possible. As you read, underline any words or lines that strike you as especially powerful.

Though the Vietnam War ended almost before I was born, it changed my

life. My earliest memory is of my ~~father. A~~ father, a grizzled Vietnam warrior who came

back spat upon, with one less brother. He wore a big smile playing ball with

my brother and me, but even then I felt the grin was a coverup. When the

postwar reports were on, his face became despondent. What haunted his heart

and mind, I could not know, but I tried in my childish way to reason with him.

A simple "It'll be all right, Dad" would bring a bleak smirk to his face. When

he was happy, I was happy. When he was down, I was down. Soon the fatherly

horseplay stopped, and once-full bottles of liquor were empty. He was there

in ~~body. Yet~~ body, yet not there. Finally, he was physically ~~gone. Either~~ gone, either working a sixty-

hour week or out in the streets after a furious fight with my mother. Once they

divorced, she moved us to another state. I never came to grips with the turmoil

inside my father. I see him as an intricate puzzle, missing one piece. That piece

is his humanity, tangled up in history and blown up by a C-19.

Brian Pereira, student

1. How effective is Brian Pereira's paragraph?

   __Y__ Good topic sentence?   __Y__ Rich supporting details?

   __Y__ Logical organization?   __Y__ Effective conclusion?

2. Discuss your underlinings with the group or class. Did others underline the same parts? Explain why you feel particular words or details are effective. For instance, the strong words *bleak smirk* say so much about the father's hopeless mood and the distance between him and his young son.

144

3. The topic sentence says that the writer's life changed, yet the body of the paragraph speaks mostly about his troubled father. Does the body of the paragraph explain the topic sentence? yes

4. What order, if any, does this writer follow? time order

5. If you do not know what a "C-19" is in the last sentence, does that make the conclusion less effective for you?

6. Would you suggest any changes or revisions?

7. Proofread for grammar and spelling. Do you notice any error patterns (two or more errors of the same type) that this student should watch out for? yes; sentence fragments

Brian Pereira's fine paragraph was the end result of a difficult writing process. Pereira describes his process this way:

> The floor in my room looked like a writer's battleground of crumpled papers. Before this topic was assigned, I had not the slightest idea that this influence even existed, much less knew what it was. I thought hard, started a sentence or two, and threw a smashed paper down in disgust, over and over again. After hours, I realized it—the event in history that influenced me was Vietnam, even though I was too young to remember it! That became my topic sentence.

Writing and Revising Ideas

1. Discuss an event that influenced you.

2. Choose your best recent paper and describe your own writing process—what you did well and not so well.

For help with writing your paragraph, see Chapter 3 and Chapter 4, Part A (see "Time Order"). Give yourself plenty of time to revise. Stick with it, trying to write the best possible paper. Pay special attention to fully supporting your topic with interesting facts and details.

UNIT 3

Using Verbs Effectively

Every sentence contains at least one verb. Because verbs often are action words, they add interest and punch to any piece of writing. In this unit, you will

- Learn to use present, past, and other verb tenses correctly
- Learn when to add -s or -ed
- Recognize and use past participle forms
- Recognize -ing verbs, infinitives, and other special forms
- Learn proofreading strategies to find and correct your own errors

Spotlight on Reading and Writing

Notice how vividly this writer describes this solitary athlete and the court at dusk. His verbs are underlined.

Russell Thomas <u>places</u> the toe of his right sneaker one inch behind the three-point line. Inspecting the basket with a level gaze, he <u>bends</u> twice at the knees, <u>raises</u> the ball to shoot, then suddenly <u>looks</u> around. What <u>is</u> it? <u>Has</u> he <u>spotted</u> me, watching from the opposite end of the playground? No, something else <u>is</u> up. He <u>is</u> <u>lifting</u> his nose to the wind like a spaniel; he <u>appears</u> to be gauging air currents. Russell <u>waits</u> until the wind <u>settles</u>, bits of trash feathering lightly to the ground. Then he <u>sends</u> a twenty-five-foot jump shot arcing through the soft summer twilight. It <u>drops</u> without a sound through the dead center of the bare iron rim. So <u>does</u> the next one. So <u>does</u> the one after that. Alone in the gathering dusk, Russell <u>begins</u> to work the perimeter against imaginary defenders, unspooling jump shots from all points.

Darcy Frey, *The Last Shot*

- Simple but well-chosen *verbs* help bring this description to life. Which verbs most effectively help you see and experience the scene?

- Do you think that the writer realistically captures this young athlete at practice? What, if anything, do you learn about Russell Thomas—his abilities, personality, even his loves—from reading this short passage?

Writing Ideas

- *A person practicing or performing some sport, art, or task*

- *A time when you watched or overheard someone in a public place*

CHAPTER **11**

Present Tense (Agreement)

A: Defining Agreement

B: Troublesome Verbs in the Present Tense: TO BE, TO HAVE, TO DO (+ NOT)

C: Changing Subjects to Pronouns

D: Practice in Agreement

E: Special Problems in Agreement

A. Defining Agreement

ESL TIP

Many ESL students have trouble with verbs and verb tenses in English. You can tailor this comprehensive unit to your needs by assigning some chapters and parts to the full class and other parts selectively.

ESL TIP

In many languages—such as Chinese, Japanese, and Korean—subject-verb number agreement does not exist. Thus, ESL students may need extra help with the concept.

A subject and a present tense verb **agree** if you use the correct form of the verb with each subject. The chart below shows which form of the verb to use for each kind of pronoun subject (we discuss other kinds of subjects later).

Verbs in the Present Tense *(example verb: to write)*			
Singular		**Plural**	
If the subject is ↓	the verb is ↓	If the subject is ↓	the verb is ↓
1st person: I	write	1st person: we	write
2nd person: you	write	2nd person: you	write
3rd person: he she it	writes	3rd person: they	write

PRACTICE 1

Fill in the correct present tense form of the verb.

1. You *ask* questions.
2. They *decide*.
3. I *remember*.

1. He ___asks___ questions.
2. She ___decides___.
3. He ___remembers___.

148

LEARNING STYLES TIP

Students who mispronounce verbs are more likely to write them incorrectly. Have a little fun making this point: have the class recite the answers to Practice 1 aloud, exaggerating the enunciation of each word. *Aural and kinesthetic learners* will benefit.

4. They *wear* glasses.

5. We *hope* so.

6. I *laugh* often.

7. We *study* daily.

8. He *amazes* me.

4. She __wears__ glasses.

5. He __hopes__ so.

6. She __laughs__ often.

7. He __studies__ daily.

8. It __amazes__ me.

Add -*s* or -*es* to a verb in the present tense only when the subject is *third person singular (he, she, it).*

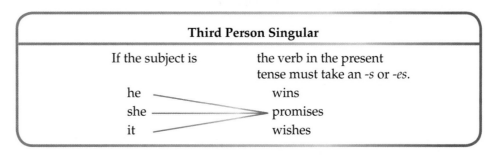

Third Person Singular

If the subject is	the verb in the present tense must take an -*s* or -*es*.
he	wins
she	promises
it	wishes

PRACTICE 2

First, underline the subject (always a pronoun) in each sentence below. Then circle the correct verb form. REMEMBER: If the subject of the sentence is *he, she,* or *it* (third person singular), the verb must end in -*s* or -*es* to agree with the subject.

TEACHING TIP

Consider doing Practice 2 with the whole class or let smaller groups complete it, competing for the best verb-agreement score. Ask students whether Tannen's analysis is accurate or sexist.

1. According to researcher Deborah Tannen, we sometimes (fail, fails) to understand how men and women communicate on the job.

2. When working together, they sometimes (differ, differs) in predictable ways.

3. In Tannen's book *Talking from 9 to 5: Women and Men at Work*, she (describe, describes) the following misunderstanding between Amy, a manager, and Donald, her employee.

4. She (read, reads) Donald's report and (find, finds) it unacceptable.

5. She (meet, meets) with him to discuss the necessary revisions.

6. To soften the blow, she (praise, praises) the report's strengths.

7. Then, she (go, goes) on to explain in detail the needed revisions.

8. The next day, he (submit, submits) a second draft with only tiny changes.

9. She (think, thinks) that Donald did not listen to her.

10. He (believe, believes) that Amy first liked his report, then changed her mind.

11. According to the author, they (represent, represents) different communication styles.

12. Like many women supervisors, she (criticize, criticizes) gently, adding positive comments to protect the other person's feelings.

13. Like many male employees, he (expect, expects) more direct—and to him, more honest—criticism.

14. Tannen says that both styles make sense, but they (cause, causes) confusion if not understood.

15. Stereotypes or truth? You (decide, decides) for yourself about the accuracy of Tannen's analysis.

B. Troublesome Verbs in the Present Tense: TO BE, TO HAVE, TO DO (+NOT)

A few present tense verbs are formed in special ways. The most common of these verbs are *to be, to have,* and *to do.*

Reference Chart: TO BE *(present tense)*				
Singular			**Plural**	
If the subject is	the verb is		If the subject is	the verb is
1st person: I	am		1st person: we	are
2nd person: you	are		2nd person: you	are
3rd person: he she it	is		3rd person: they	are

PRACTICE 3

Use the chart to fill in the present tense form of *to be (am, is, are)* that agrees with the subject.

1. She _____is_____ a member of the Olympic softball team.
2. We _____are_____ both carpenters, but he _____is_____ more skilled than I am.
3. I _____am_____ sorry about your accident; you _____are_____ certainly unlucky with rollerblades.
4. They _____are_____ salmon fishermen.
5. He _____is_____ a gifted website designer.
6. I _____am_____ too nervous to sleep because we _____are_____ having an accounting exam tomorrow.
7. So you _____are_____ the one we have heard so much about!
8. If it _____is_____ sunny tomorrow, they _____are_____ going hot-air ballooning.

Reference Chart: TO HAVE *(present tense)*				
Singular			**Plural**	
If the subject is	the verb is		If the subject is	the verb is
1st person: I	have		1st person: we	have
2nd person: you	have		2nd person: you	have
3rd person: he she it	has		3rd person: they	have

PRACTICE 4

Fill in the present tense form of *to have* (*have*, *has*) that agrees with the subject. Use the chart.

1. We _____ have _____ to taste these pickled mushrooms.
2. It _____ has _____ to be spring because the cherry trees _____ have _____ pink blossoms.
3. She _____ has _____ the questions, and he _____ has _____ the answers.
4. You _____ have _____ a suspicious look on your face, and I _____ have _____ to know why.
5. They _____ have _____ plans to build a fence, but we _____ have _____ plans to relax.
6. You _____ have _____ one ruby earring, and she _____ has _____ the other.
7. It _____ has _____ to be repaired, and I _____ have _____ just the person to do it for you.
8. If you _____ have _____ $50, they _____ have _____ an offer you can't refuse.

Reference Chart: TO DO *(present tense)*			
Singular		**Plural**	
If the subject is ↓	the verb is ↓	If the subject is ↓	the verb is ↓
1st person: I	do	1st person: we	do
2nd person: you	do	2nd person: you	do
3rd person: he she it	does	3rd person: they	do

PRACTICE 5

Use the chart to fill in the correct present tense form of *to do* (*do*, *does*).

1. She always _____ does _____ well in math courses.
2. I always _____ do _____ badly under pressure.
3. They most certainly _____ do _____ sell muscle shirts.
4. You _____ do _____ the nicest things for people!
5. If you _____ do _____ the dishes, I'll _____ do _____ the laundry.
6. He _____ does _____ seem sorry about forgetting your dog's birthday.
7. _____ Do _____ they dance the tarantella?
8. _____ Does _____ she want to be a welder?

To Do + Not

Once you know how to use *do* and *does*, you are ready for *don't* and *doesn't*.

$$do + not = don't$$
$$does + not = doesn't$$

PRACTICE 6

Fill in each blank with either *doesn't* or *don't*.

1. If they ___don't___ turn down that music, I'm going to scream.
2. It just ___doesn't___ make sense.
3. He ___doesn't___ always lock his door at night.
4. We ___don't___ mind the rain.
5. If she ___doesn't___ stop calling collect, I ___don't___ want to talk to her.
6. He ___doesn't___ know the whole truth, and they ___don't___ want to know.
7. Although you ___don't___ like biking five miles a day to work, it ___doesn't___ do your health any harm.
8. When I ___don't___ try, I ___don't___ succeed.

PRACTICE 7

U.S. Navy photo by Mass Communication Specialist 2nd Class Stephanie Tigner

Review

As you read this paragraph, fill in the correct present tense form of *to be*, *to have*, or *to do* in each blank. Make sure all your verbs agree with their subjects.

(1) He ___has___ the expertise of an action hero, but he ___is___ a real-life member of the U.S. Navy SEALs. (2) After 35 weeks of brutal "adversity" training, he ___does___ whatever the mission requires. (3) Right now, he ___is___ calm although he ___is___ ready to leap from the open door of a Navy aircraft. (4) On his back, he ___has___ an oversized parachute capable of supporting both him and the extra hundred pounds of special equipment packed in his combat vest. (5) When he ___does___ hit the water, he ___is___ ready to face the real challenge: finding and defusing a bomb sixty feet under rough and frigid seas. (6) He ___has___ a mission and a tight time frame, and he ___does___ not want to let the enemy know he ___is___ there. (7) Swimming underwater in special scuba gear, he ___does___ not release any air bubbles to mark the water's surface. (8) Working in semi-darkness, performing dangerous technical tasks, he quickly ___does___ the job. (9) However, unlike video heroes, he ___does___n't work alone. (10) It ___is___ precise teamwork for which the SEALs ___are___ famous. (11) Among the most respected special forces in the world, they ___are___ commando divers prepared for hazardous duty on sea, air, and land.

C. Changing Subjects to Pronouns

So far, you have worked on pronouns as subjects (*I, you, he, she, it, we, they*) and on how to make verbs agree with them. Often, however, the subject of a sentence is not a pronoun but a noun—like *dog, banjo, Ms. Callas, José and Robert, swimming* (as in *Swimming keeps me fit*).

To be sure that your verb agrees with your subject, *mentally* change the subject into a pronoun and then select the correct form of the verb. The chart below will show you how.

Reference Chart: Subject-Verb Agreement

If the subject is   **it can be changed to the pronoun**

1. the speaker himself or herself ─────────────────────▶ I
2. masculine and singular ─────────────────────────────▶ he
   (*Bill, one man*)
3. feminine and singular ──────────────────────────────▶ she
   (*Sondra, a woman*)
4. neither masculine nor feminine
   and singular (a thing or an action) ────────────────▶ it
   (*this pen, love, running*)
5. a group that includes the speaker (I) ──────────────▶ we
   (*the family and I*)
6. a group of persons or things not including
   the speaker ──▶ they
   (*Jake and Wanda, several pens*)
7. the person or persons spoken to ────────────────────▶ you

PRACTICE 8   **Review**

Change each subject into a pronoun. Then circle the present tense verb that agrees with that subject. (Use the reference chart on this page if you need to.)

EXAMPLES: Harry = ____he____   Harry (whistle, (whistles)).

   Sam and I = ___we___   Sam and I ((walk,) walks).

1. Camilla = ___she___

1. Camilla (own, (owns)) a horse farm.

2. Their concert = ___it___

2. Their concert ((is,) are) sold out.

3. You and Ron = ___you___

3. You and Ron ((seem,) seems) exhausted.

4. The men and I = ___we___

4. The men and I ((repair,) repairs) potholes.

5. This blender = _____it_____

6. Folk dancing = _____it_____

7. The museum and garden = _____they_____

8. Aunt Lil and I = _____we_____

5. This blender (grate, (grates)) cheese.

6. Folk dancing ((is,) are) our current passion.

7. The museum and garden (is, (are)) open.

8. Aunt Lil and I ((like,) likes) Swedish massages.

D. Practice in Agreement

PRACTICE 9

Review

First identify the subject in each sentence. Then circle the correct verb, making sure it agrees with its subject.

Project Runway: Keeping It (Sort of) Real

(1) *Project Runway* ((entertains,) entertain) viewers, but the television show also ((teaches,) teach) some valuable life and work lessons. (2) This combination ((does,) do) not occur often in American television, especially in "reality" TV. (3) On *Project Runway*, designers, tailors, and dressmakers (competes, (compete)) for the ultimate $100,000 prize. (4) For every new challenge, they (tries, (try)) to design the winning outfit. (5) Sometimes contestants (creates, (create)) clothes out of paper or leaves, or they (redesigns, (redesign)) U.S. postal uniforms. (6) Fashion expert Tim Gunn ((serves,) serve) as the designers' mentor, cheerleader, and guide. (7) Professionals like designer Michael Kors, editor Nina Garcia, and host Heidi Klum (judges, (judge)) the work. (8) At home, the viewer ((guesses,) guess) the outcome as contestants (reacts, (react)) to brutally honest criticism.

(9) *Project Runway* ((differs,) differ) from other "reality" shows because the contestants ((are,) is) talented professionals. (10) They already (knows, (know)) how to design and sew. (11) The challenges (tests, (test)) their ability to rise to another level. (12) The show ((tells,) tell) the personal story of each designer, so the viewer ((observes,) observe) contestants dealing with low self-esteem, anger problems, or even addiction. (13) Week after week, the designers (struggles, (struggle)) to turn criticism into improvement. (14) The viewer ((sees,) see) how hard professionals work, even in a glamorous field. (15) According to critics,

Winner of Project Runway 2012, Michelle Franklin, shows off one of her winning designs.

Project Runway (feeds, feed) unrealistic dreams of quick success, but for admirers, the show

(exposes, expose) the creative process in a realistic and helpful way.

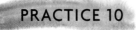

PRACTICE 10   **Review**

In each blank, write the *present tense* form of one of the verbs from this list. Your sentences can be funny; just make sure that each verb agrees with each subject.

leap	spin	yip	woof	attend	win	compete
go	love	try	prance	wiggle	fly	encourage

(1) Dogs of every size and shape, their owners, and visitors all _____attend_____ the Great American Mutt Show. (2) Sponsored by Tails in Need, the Mutt Show _____encourages_____ people to adopt mixed-breed dogs instead of buying pure breeds. (3) Pooches _____compete_____ in categories like Mostly Terrier, Most Misbehaved, Best Kisser, and Best Lap Dog Over 50 Pounds. (4) In one event, a shepherd mix named Top Gun _____leaps_____ through the air to be crowned Best Jumper while a beagle named Jack _____spins_____ his stumpy tail, energetically claiming the coveted trophy for

Best Wag. (5) Four-legged hopefuls _____yip_____ and _____woof_____ trying to snag

the award for Best Bark. (6) The proud winner of Best in Show _____goes_____ home with

a trophy designed by Michael Graves—a red fire hydrant topped by a golden bone.

PRACTICE 11   Review

The sentences that follow have singular subjects and verbs. To gain skill in verb agreement, rewrite each sentence, changing the subject from *singular* to *plural*. Then make sure the verb agrees with the new subject. Keep all verbs in the present tense.

EXAMPLE: The train stops at Cold Spring.

Rewrite: _*The trains stop at Cold Spring.*_____

1. The movie ticket costs too much.

   Rewrite: _The movie tickets cost too much._____

2. The pipeline carries oil from Alaska.

   Rewrite: _The pipelines carry oil from Alaska._____

3. A white horse grazes by the fence.

   Rewrite: _White horses graze by the fence._____

4. My brother knows American Sign Language.

   Rewrite: _My brothers know American Sign Language._____

5. The family needs good health insurance.

   Rewrite: _The families need good health insurance._____

The sentences that follow have plural subjects and verbs. Rewrite each sentence, changing the subject from *plural* to *singular*. Then make sure the verb agrees with the new subject. Keep all verbs in the present tense.

6. The inmates watch *America's Most Wanted*.

   Rewrite: _The inmate watches *America's Most Wanted*._____

7. Overhead, seagulls ride on the wind.

   Rewrite: _Overhead, a seagull rides on the wind._____

8. Good card players know when to bluff.

   Rewrite: _A good card player knows when to bluff._____

9. On Saturday, the pharmacists stay late.

   Rewrite: _On Saturday, the pharmacist stays late._____

10. The jewels from Bangkok are on display.

    Rewrite: _The jewel from Bangkok is on display._____

PRACTICE 12   Review

This paragraph is written in the past tense. Rewrite it in the present tense by changing all the verbs. Write the present tense form of each verb above the lines. (Hint: You should change eighteen verbs.)

    (1) At a rink in Chicago's inner city, two-year-old Shani Davis ~puts~ put on his first pair of roller skates. (2) Before long, he ~skates~ skated so fast that the rink guards ~chase~ chased him and ~warn~ warned him to slow down. (3) Then, at 6, Davis ~discovers~ discovered ice skating, and the future star ~takes~ took off. (4) His mother ~recognizes~ recognized her son's gifts, moving the family to be near a speed skating rink. (5) With his huge talent and grueling work ethic, Davis soon ~becomes~ became the first U.S. junior to make both the short-track and long-track national teams. (6) He not only ~flies~ flew across frozen finish lines winning medals, but he ~is~ was the first African American to join the U.S. Olympic speed-skating team. (7) Fans around the world ~praise~ praised his fine technique and form. (8) Taller than other U.S. skaters, he ~bends~ bent low and ~holds~ held his upper body very still. (9) At the 2006 Winter Olympics in Turin, Italy, Davis ~scores~ scored a gold medal in the 1000-meter and a silver in the 1500. (10) At the Vancouver Olympics in 2010, he ~earns~ earned gold again in the 1000-meter. (11) In 2012, he ~wins~ won his ninth Overall World Cup title. (12) In addition to his achievements on ice, Shani Davis ~is~ was a founder of Inner City Excellence, a skating program for urban children, and he ~finds~ found time to attend Northern Michigan University.

Speed skater Shani Davis flashes through the 1500-meter, Calgary, Canada, 2013.

E. Special Problems in Agreement

So far, you have learned that if the subject of a sentence is third person singular (*he, she, it*) or a word like *Sasha, sister,* or *car* that mentally can be changed into *he, she,* or *it,* the verb takes *-s* or *-es* in the present tense.

In special cases, however, you will need to know more before you can make your verb agree with your subject.

Focusing on the Subject

(1) A box of chocolates sits on the table.

- *What* sits on the table?

- Don't be confused by the prepositional phrase before the verb—*of chocolates.**

- Just one *box* sits on the table.

- *A box* is the subject. *A box* takes the third person singular verb—*sits.*

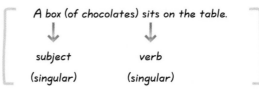

(2) The children in the park play for hours.

- *Who* play for hours?

- Don't be confused by the prepositional phrase before the verb—*in the park.*

- *The children* play for hours.

- *The children* is the subject. *The children* takes the third person plural verb—*play.*

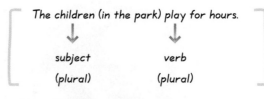

(3) The purpose of the exercises is to improve your spelling.

- *What* is to improve your spelling?

- Don't be confused by the prepositional phrase before the verb—*of the exercises.*

---

* For a detailed explanation of prepositional phrases, see Chapter 9, Part C, and Chapter 25.

- *The purpose* is to improve your spelling.

- *The purpose* is the subject. *The purpose* takes the third person singular verb—*is*.

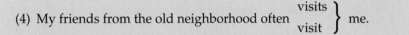

The purpose (of the exercises) is to improve your spelling.

↓ ↓

subject verb

(singular) (singular)

As you can see from these examples, sometimes what seems to be the subject is really not the subject. Prepositional phrases (groups of words beginning with *of, in, at,* and so on) *cannot* contain the subject of a sentence. One way to find the subject of a sentence that contains a prepositional phrase is to ask yourself *what makes sense as the subject.*

(4) My friends from the old neighborhood often $\left.\begin{array}{l}\text{visits} \\ \text{visit}\end{array}\right\}$ me.

- Which makes sense as the subject of the sentence: *my friends* or *the old neighborhood*?

(a) My friends . . . visit me.

(b) The old neighborhood . . . visits me.

- Obviously, sentence (a) makes sense; it clearly expresses the intention of the writer.

PRACTICE 13

TEACHING TIP

If your class is quite diverse, you might use this practice as a springboard for cultural sharing.

In each of these sentences, cross out any confusing prepositional phrases, locate the subject, and then circle the correct verb.

1. Greetings ~~around the world~~ (differs, (differ)) from culture to culture.
2. A resident ~~of the United States~~ ((shakes,) shake) hands firmly to say hello.
3. Kisses ~~on each cheek~~ (is, (are)) customary greetings in Latin America and southern Europe.
4. Natives ~~of Hawaii~~ (hugs, (hug)) and (exchanges, (exchange)) breaths in a custom called *alo ha* (sharing of life breath).
5. The Maori people ~~of New Zealand~~ (presses, (press)) noses to greet each other.
6. A person ~~in traditional Japanese circles~~ ((bows,) bow) upon meeting someone.
7. A custom ~~among Pakistanis~~ ((is,) are) the *salaam*, bowing with the right hand on the forehead.
8. Hindus ~~in India~~ (folds, (fold)) the hands and (tilts, (tilt)) the head forward.
9. The Hindi word ~~for the greeting~~ ((is,) are) *namaste*.
10. This word ((means,) mean) "The divine ~~in me~~ ((salutes,) salute) the divine in you."

Spotting Special Singular Subjects

Either of the students
Neither of the students
Each of the students } seems happy.
One of the students
Every one of the students

- *Either, neither, each, one,* and *every one* are the real subjects of these sentences.
- *Either, neither, each, one,* and *every one* are special singular subjects. They always take a singular verb.
- REMEMBER: The subject is never part of a prepositional phrase, so *of the students* cannot be the subject.

PRACTICE 14

Mentally cross out the prepositional phrases and then circle the correct verb.

1. One ~~of the forks~~ (is, are) missing.
2. Each ~~of my brothers~~ (wear, wears) cinnamon after-shave lotion.
3. Each ~~of us~~ (carry, carries) a snakebite kit.
4. Neither ~~of those excuses~~ (sound, sounds) believable.
5. One ~~of the taxi drivers~~ (see, sees) us.
6. Either ~~of the watches~~ (cost, costs) about $30.
7. Neither ~~of those cities~~ (is, are) the capital of Brazil.
8. One ~~of the butlers~~ (commit, commits) the crime, but which one?

PRACTICE 15

On a separate sheet of paper, write five sentences using the special singular subjects. Make sure your sentences are in the present tense.

Using THERE to Begin a Sentence

(1) *There* is a squirrel in the yard.
(2) *There* are two squirrels in the yard.

- Although sentences sometimes begin with *there, there* cannot be the subject of a sentence.
- Usually, the subject *follows* the verb in sentences that begin with *there*.

To find the real subject (so you will know how to make the verb agree), mentally drop the word *there* and rearrange the sentence to put the subject at the beginning.

(1) *There is a squirrel in the yard.*

becomes

A squirrel   is in the yard.
↓   ↓
subject   verb
(singular)   (singular)

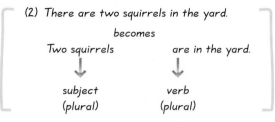

(2) *There are two squirrels in the yard.*

becomes

Two squirrels   *are in the yard.*

↓   ↓

subject   verb
(plural)   (plural)

BE CAREFUL: Good writers avoid using *there* to begin a sentence. Whenever possible, they write more directly: *Two squirrels are in the yard.*

PRACTICE 16

In each sentence, mentally drop the word *there* and rearrange the sentence to put the subject at the beginning. Then circle the verb that agrees with the subject of the sentence.

Answers to Practice 16 are above the lines.

A daycare center is on campus.
1. There (**is**, are) a daycare center on campus.

A scarecrow hangs near the barn.
2. There (**is**, are) a scarecrow near the barn.

Two scarecrows are near the barn.
3. There (is, **are**) two scarecrows near the barn.

One good reason to quit this job is my supervisor.
4. There (**is**, are) one good reason to quit this job—my supervisor.

Six customers are waiting ahead of you.
5. There (is, **are**) six customers ahead of you.

A water fountain is in the lounge.
6. There (**is**, are) a water fountain in the lounge.

A house and a barn stand in the wheat field.
7. There (is, **are**) a house and a barn in the wheat field.

Only two shopping days are left before my birthday.
8. There (is, **are**) only two shopping days left before my birthday.

PRACTICE 17

On paper or on a computer, rewrite each sentence in Practice 16 so that it does not begin with *there is* or *there are*. (You may add or change a word or two if you like.) Sentences (1) and (2) are done for you. Answers to Practice 17 are above the lines in Practice 16. Answers will vary.

EXAMPLES: *1.   A daycare center is on campus.*

　　　　　　　　2.   A scarecrow hangs near the barn.

Choosing the Correct Verb in Questions

(1) Where is Lucas?

(2) Where are Lucas and Jay?

(3) Why are they singing?

(4) Have you painted the hall yet?

- In questions, the subject usually *follows* the verb.

- In sentence (1), the subject is *Lucas*. *Lucas* takes the third person singular verb *is*.

- In sentence (2), the subject is *Lucas and Jay*. *Lucas and Jay* takes the third person plural verb *are*.

- What is the subject in sentence (3)? _____they_____ What verb does it take?

  third person plural verb *are* + *singing*

- What is the subject in sentence (4)? _____you_____ What verb does it take?

  second person plural verb *have* + *painted*

If you can't find the subject, mentally turn the question around:

> (1) Lucas is . . .
>
> (2) Lucas and Jay are . . .

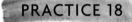

PRACTICE 18

Circle the correct verb.

1. Where (**is**, are) my leather bomber jacket?
2. (Have, **Has**) our waiter gone to lunch?
3. How (is, **are**) your children enjoying computer camp?
4. Who (is, **are**) those people on the fire escape?
5. Which (**is**, are) your day off?
6. Why (do, **does**) she want to buy another motorcycle?
7. (**Have**, Has) you considered taking a cruise next year?
8. Where (is, **are**) Don's income tax forms?

PRACTICE 19

On paper or on a computer, write five questions of your own. Make sure that your questions are in the present tense and that the verbs agree with the subjects.

Using WHO, WHICH, and THAT as Relative Pronouns

When you use a **relative pronoun**—*who, which,* or *that*—to introduce a dependent idea, make sure you choose the correct verb.*

> (1) I know a woman *who* plays expert chess.

- Sentence (1) uses the singular verb *plays* because *who* relates or refers to *a woman* (singular).

> (2) Suede coats, *which* stain easily, should not be worn in the rain.

- Sentence (2) uses the plural verb *stain* because *which* relates to the subject *suede coats* (plural).

---

* For work on relative pronouns, see Chapter 20.

> (3) Dishwashers *that* talk make me nervous.

- Sentence (3) uses the plural verb *talk* because *that* relates to what word?

dishwashers
_____

 **PRACTICE 20**

Write the word that *who*, *which*, or *that* relates or refers to in the blank at the right; then circle the correct form of the verb.

EXAMPLE: I like people who (is, (are)) creative.   *people*
_____

1. My office has a robot that (fetch, (fetches)) the mail.   robot
_____
2. Never buy food in cans that ((have,) has) dents in them.   cans
_____
3. My husband, who (take, (takes)) marvelous photographs,
    won the Nikon Prize.   husband
_____
4. He likes women who (is, (are)) very ambitious.   women
_____
5. The old house, which (sit, (sits)) on a cliff above the sea, is
    called Balston Heights.   house
_____
6. Students who ((love,) loves) to read usually write well.   students
_____
7. I like a person who (think, (thinks)) for himself or herself.   person
_____
8. The only airline that (fly, (flies)) to Charlottesville is booked solid.   airline
_____

PRACTICE 21   ## Review

Proofread the following paragraph for a variety of verb agreement errors. First, locate the subject in each sentence. Then underline all present tense verbs and correct any errors above the lines.

    (1) Each year, millions of people <u>watches</u> the films that Lauren Lazin <u>produces</u>   *[watch above watches]*

and <u>directs</u>. (2) Her name <u>is</u> not well known, but her TV shows and movies certainly <u>is</u>.   *[are above is]*

(3) Lazin, a documentary filmmaker, <u>works</u> for channels such as MTV, PBS, and Bravo.

(4) Her creative spark <u>bring</u> popular shows to these networks each season, including the   *[brings above bring]*

wildly successful MTV shows *Cribs* and *True Life*. (5) Her work <u>explore</u> the lives of high-   *[explores above explore]*

profile celebrities, but she also <u>champions</u> important causes for the network, such as racial

justice and AIDS awareness. (6) There <u>are</u> a long list of shows on Lazin's résumé, but she also   *[is above are]*

<u>makes</u> films independently. (7) *Tupac: Resurrection* <u>probe</u> the complex life of rapper Tupac   *[probes above probe]*

Shakur. (8) Many <u>considers</u> it one of Lazin's best movies. (9) Another powerful film, *I'm Still*   *[consider above considers]*

Here, <u>weaves</u> together diary excerpts from teenagers during the Holocaust. (10) Lazin <u>wants</u>

to create documentary films that <u>appeals</u> to young adults and <u>makes</u> them think. (11) She   *[appeal above appeals; make above makes]*

<u>hope</u> that each of her films <u>engage</u> and <u>educates</u> her viewers.   *[hopes above hope; engages above engage]*

Chapter Highlights

- **A subject and a present tense verb must agree:**

    The light flickers. (*singular subject, singular verb*)

    The lights flicker. (*plural subject, plural verb*)

- **Only third person singular subjects (*he, she, it*) take verbs ending in *-s* or *-es*.**

- **Three troublesome present tense verbs are *to be, to have,* and *to do*.**

- **When a prepositional phrase comes between a subject and a verb, the verb must agree with the subject.**

    The *chairs* on the porch *are* painted white.

- **The subjects *either, neither, each, one,* and *every one* are always singular.**

    Neither of the mechanics *repairs* transmissions.

- **In a sentence beginning with *there is* or *there are*, the subject follows the verb.**

    There are three *oysters* on your plate.

- **In questions, the subject usually follows the verb.**

    Where are *Kimi and Fred*?

- **Relative pronouns (*who, which,* and *that*) refer to the word with which the verb must agree.**

    A *woman who* has children must manage time skillfully.

Proofreading Strategy

If present tense verb agreement is one of your error patterns, you might **isolate and color code**. First, if you are writing on a computer, *isolate each sentence* on its own line. This will help your brain and eye focus on one sentence at a time. Next, find the subject and verb in each sentence; use highlighters to *color code* subjects yellow and verbs green. Cross out any confusing prepositional phrases.

Now check each color-coded pair for subject-verb agreement. (1) If you aren't sure, *change the subject to a pronoun*, and see if it agrees with the verb. (2) Do a final "audio check" and read the sentence aloud. Here are two examples:

       it   *serves*

The cafeteria ~~at my son's school~~ serve sweet-potato fries.

          they   *want*

Most parents wants the cafeteria to offer more fresh vegetables and fruits.

WRITING AND PROOFREADING ASSIGNMENT

In a group of three or four classmates, choose an area of the building or campus that contains some interesting action—the hallway, the cafeteria, or a playing field. Go there now and observe what you see, recording details and using verbs in the present tense.

Choose as many dynamic action verbs as you can. Keep observing and writing for ten minutes. Then head back to the classroom and write a first draft of a paragraph. Proofread for subject-verb agreement, using the strategy described above.

Next, exchange papers within your group. The reader should check for verb agreement and tell the writer what he or she liked about the writing and what could be improved.

CHAPTER REVIEW

Proofread this essay carefully for verb agreement. First, underline all present tense verbs. Then correct each verb agreement error.

Roadtrip to a Satisfying Career

(1) *Roadtrip Nation* is a documentary series on public television that aim [aims] to help people think about their career choices. (2) The program feature [features] small teams of roadtrippers, ages 18 to 40, that travels [travel] across country in a van and interview career leaders they admires [admire]. (3) These leaders and role models, some famous and some not, represents [represent] a range of fascinating jobs. (4) Both the episodes and the *Roadtrip Nation* website is [are] valuable resources for any job seeker or job changer.

(5) Each of the *Roadtrip* travel teams choose [chooses] its role models, interviews them, and film [films] the whole process. (6) The show emphasizes "meaningful conversations" between the career leaders and their interviewers, whose questions and comments inevitably raise key issues: "How do you handle your fear?" "How does [do] you define success?" "My parents doesn't [don't] approve of my goals, but I want to please them." "Does hard work create passion?"

(7) The *Roadtrip Nation* website offer [offers] a bank of over 3500 videos, each one full of information and career advice. (8) The videos is [are] classified in three ways: by leader, by interest, and by theme. (9) Clicking "leaders" brings up a list of hundreds of successful career men and women, including broadcast journalist Soledad O'Brien; forensic anthropologist Bill Bass; Starbucks founder Howard Schultz; comedian Wanda Sykes; and inventor Ray Kurzweil. (10) Clicking "interests" help [helps] you search by fields such as science, travel, education, engineering, film, sports, journalism, and more. (11) Finally, clicking "themes" let [lets] you search for words that feels [feel] right, like *determination, risk, regrets, societal pressures,* and *inspiration.*

EXPLORING ONLINE

http://roadtripnation.com/ See whether the Roadtrip Nation website might be useful to your job search or interest. Click "Explore" to access the collection of interviews, cross-classified as "leaders," "interests," and "themes."

EXPLORING ONLINE

TEACHING TIP

Instructor tools for *Grass-roots* include a computerized Test Bank, PowerPoint slides, an Instructor's Manual with teaching tips, and more, and can be accessed at ‹**login .cengage.com**›.

<http://a4esl.org/q/h/9807/km-thereisare.html> Interactive quiz: *There is* or *there are*? Test your verb agreement skills.

<http://www.new.towson.edu/ows/exercisesub-verb.htm> This interactive quiz from Towson University is a tricky one. Test yourself.

CHAPTER 12

Past Tense

A: **Regular Verbs in the Past Tense**

B: **Irregular Verbs in the Past Tense**

C: **Troublesome Verb in the Past Tense: TO BE**

D: **Review**

A. Regular Verbs in the Past Tense

Verbs in the past tense express actions that occurred in the past. The italicized words in the following sentences are verbs in the past tense.

> (1) They *noticed* a dent in the fender.
> (2) She *played* the guitar very well.
> (3) For years I *studied* yoga.

- What ending do all these verbs take? ___-d or -ed___
- In general, what ending do you add to put a verb in the past tense? ___-d or -ed___
- Verbs that add *-d* or *-ed* to form the past tense are called regular verbs.

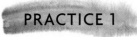

PRACTICE 1

Some of the verbs in these sentences are in the present tense; others are in the past tense. Circle the verb in each sentence. Write *present* in the column at the right if the verb is in the present tense; write *past* if the verb is in the past tense.

1. Ricardo (stroked) his beard.	past
2. Light (travels) 186,000 miles in a second.	present
3. They (donate) blood every six months.	present
4. Magellan (sailed) around the world.	past
5. The lake (looks) as calm as glass.	present
6. Yesterday, Rover (buried) many bones.	past
7. Mount St. Helens (erupted) in 1980.	past
8. That chemical plant (pollutes) our water.	present
9. A robin (nested) in the mailbox.	past
10. He (owns) two exercise bikes.	present

ESL TIP

Verb tense can be a difficult concept for nonnative writers, requiring extra help and practice. Try using conversations or writings to elicit accounts of the past (e.g., *Where were you born? What was life like in your hometown?*), noting correct verbs.

TEACHING TIP

For students who don't pronounce or hear the *-ed* ending on regular verbs, these forms can be more problematic than irregulars. Help such students see that this is their error pattern.

PRACTICE 2

Change the verbs in this paragraph to past tense by writing the past tense form above each italicized verb.

(1) Again this year, Carnival *transforms* [transformed] Rio de Janeiro, Brazil, into one of the most fantastic four-day parties on the planet. (2) On the Friday before Ash Wednesday, thousands of visitors *pour* [poured] into the city. (3) They *watch* [watched] all-night parades and *admire* [admired] the glittering costumes. (4) They *cheer* [cheered], *sweat* [sweated], and *dance* [danced] the samba. (5) Of course, preparation *starts* [started] long before. (6) For months, members of the samba schools (neighborhood dance clubs) *plan* [planned] their floats, *practice* [practiced] samba steps, and *stay* [stayed] up for nights making their costumes. (7) Using bright fabrics, sequins, feathers, and chains, both men and women *create* [created] spectacular outfits. (8) Each samba school *constructs* [constructed] a float that *features* [featured] a smoke-breathing dragon or a spouting waterfall. (9) During Carnival, judges *rate* [rated] the schools on costumes, dancing, and floats, and then they *award* [awarded] prizes. (10) Together, Brazilians and their visitors *share* [shared] great music, drink, food, fun, and the chance to go a little bit crazy.

As you can see from this exercise, many verbs form the past tense by adding either -*d* or -*ed*.

Furthermore, in the past tense, agreement is not a problem, except for the verb *to be* **(see Part C of this chapter). This is because verbs in the past tense have only one form, no matter what the subject is.**

PRACTICE 3

The verbs have been omitted from this paragraph. Choose verbs from the list below and write a past tense form in each blank space. Do not use any of the verbs twice. Answers will vary.

arrive	cry	walk	help
install	climb	pound	learn
grab	hug	smile	work
paint	thank	shout	hurry

(1) Last month, Raoul and I ___helped___ build a Habitat for Humanity house as part of our college's service learning program. (2) On the first day, we ___arrived___ at the construction site at dawn. (3) With three other volunteers, we ___grabbed___ our hammers and ___climbed___ onto the roof. (4) We ___pounded___ nails for hours while other volunteers ___installed___ the Sheetrock walls. (5) For three weeks, we ___worked___ hard and ___learned___ a lot about plumbing, wiring, and

interior finishes. (6) On our last day, the new homeowners _____cried_____ with joy and

_____thanked_____ the whole crew.

PRACTICE 4

Fill in the past tense of each verb.

1. Erik Weihenmayer, blinded at age thirteen, _____dreamed_____ (dream) for years of climbing Mount Everest.

2. Mountaineers _____laughed_____ (laugh) at the idea of a blind man scaling the world's tallest peak—a death trap of rock, wind, and cold.

3. But in 2001, Erik _____gathered_____ (gather) a climbing team and _____started_____ (start) the trek up Everest.

4. Before the climbers _____reached_____ (reach) the first of several camps on the way to the top, Erik _____slipped_____ (slip) into a crevasse, but he _____survived_____ (survive).

5. When he finally _____stumbled_____ (stumble) into the first camp, weak and dehydrated, Erik _____wondered_____ (wonder) whether he had made a serious mistake.

6. Nevertheless, he and his teammates _____vowed_____ (vow) to continue the climb.

7. The group _____battled_____ (battle) upward through driving snow and icy winds.

8. Erik _____managed_____ (manage) to keep up and even _____edged_____ (edge) across the long, knife-blade ridge just below the peak, taking tiny steps and using his ice ax as an anchor.

9. Months after he began his journey, the blind mountaineer _____stepped_____ (step) onto Everest's summit and _____stayed_____ (stay) for ten minutes to savor his victory.

10. For many people around the world, this achievement _____symbolized_____ (symbolize) the nearly unstoppable human power to reach a goal.

Blind mountaineer Erik Weihenmayer successfully scaled Mount Everest.

Didrik Johnck/CORBIS/Sygma

B. Irregular Verbs in the Past Tense

Instead of adding -*d* or -*ed*, some verbs form the past tense in other ways.

ESL TIP

Irregular verbs can be a problem for ESL students and speakers of languages that do not include irregular verbs (e.g., Chinese). Suggest that students make flashcards to study the forms of irregular verbs.

> (1) He *threw* a knuckle ball.
> (2) She *gave* him a dollar.
> (3) He *rode* from his farm into the town.

- The italicized words in these sentences are also verbs in the past tense.
- Do these verbs form the past tense by adding -*d* or -*ed*? _____no_____
- *Threw, gave,* and *rode* are the past tense of verbs that do not add -*d* or -*ed* to form the past tense.
- Verbs that do not add -*d* or -*ed* to form the past tense are called *irregular verbs.*

A chart listing common irregular verbs follows.

Reference Chart: Irregular Verbs

Simple Form	Past	Simple Form	Past
be	was, were	lose	lost
become	became	make	made
begin	began	mean	meant
blow	blew	meet	met
break	broke	pay	paid
bring	brought	put	put
build	built	quit	quit
burst	burst	read	read
buy	bought	ride	rode
catch	caught	ring	rang
choose	chose	rise	rose
come	came	run	ran
cut	cut	say	said
dive	dove (dived)	see	saw
do	did	seek	sought
draw	drew	sell	sold
drink	drank	send	sent
drive	drove	set	set
eat	ate	shake	shook
fall	fell	shine	shone (shined)
feed	fed	shrink	shrank (shrunk)
feel	felt	sing	sang
fight	fought	sit	sat
find	found	sleep	slept
fly	flew	speak	spoke
forget	forgot	spend	spent
forgive	forgave	spring	sprang
freeze	froze	stand	stood
get	got	steal	stole
give	gave	strike	struck
go	went	swim	swam
grow	grew	swing	swung

Reference Chart: Irregular Verbs (*continued*)

Simple Form	Past	Simple Form	Past
have	had	take	took
hear	heard	teach	taught
hide	hid	tear	tore
hold	held	tell	told
hurt	hurt	think	thought
keep	kept	throw	threw
know	knew	understand	understood
lay	laid	wake	woke
lead	led	wear	wore
leave	left	win	won
let	let	wind	wound
lie	lay	write	wrote

Learn the unfamiliar past tense forms by grouping together verbs that change from present tense to past tense in the same way. For example, some irregular verbs change *ow* in the present to *ew* in the past:

bl<u>ow</u>	bl<u>ew</u>	kn<u>ow</u>	kn<u>ew</u>
gr<u>ow</u>	gr<u>ew</u>	thr<u>ow</u>	thr<u>ew</u>

Another group changes from *i* in the present to *a* in the past:

beg<u>i</u>n	beg<u>a</u>n	s<u>i</u>ng	s<u>a</u>ng
dr<u>i</u>nk	dr<u>a</u>nk	spr<u>i</u>ng	spr<u>a</u>ng
r<u>i</u>ng	r<u>a</u>ng	sw<u>i</u>m	sw<u>a</u>m

As you write, refer to the chart. If you are unsure of the past tense form of a verb that is not in the chart, check a dictionary. For example, if you look up the verb *go* in the dictionary, you will find an entry like this:

go \ went \ gone \ going

The first word listed is used to form the *present* tense of the verb (I *go*, he *goes*, and so on). The second word is the *past* tense (I *went*, he *went*, and so on). The third word is the *past participle* (*gone*), and the last word is the *present participle* (*going*).

Some dictionaries list different forms only for irregular verbs. If no past tense is listed, you know that the verb is regular and that its past tense ends in *-d* or *-ed*.

TEACHING AND ESL TIP

Tell students that many irregular verbs fall into one of three categories: 1. do not change (*cut/cut, hit/hit*); 2. change their vowel (*ride/ rode, get/got, drink/drank*); 3. change completely (*teach/ taught, think/thought*). Have students work with a partner to categorize irregular verbs into the three groups.

PRACTICE 5

TEACHING TIP

Students enjoy discussing job-search techniques like these. Stress that lively verbs help get the job. Have students list action verbs for their respective résumés. For résumé verb lists, search "action verbs, résumés" online, or try ‹http://www.quintcareers .com/action_skills.html›.

Circle the correct past tense form of each verb. If you aren't sure, check the chart.

(1) Emma (began, begun) her job search in an organized way. (2) She (thought, thinked) carefully about her interests and abilities. (3) She (spended, spent) time in the library and (readed, read) books like *What Color Is Your Parachute?* and *Job Hunting Online*. (4) She (did, done) online research about interesting professions at sites like Occupational Outlook Handbook from the Bureau of Labor Statistics (‹**http://www.bls.gov/ooh/**›). (5) She (spoke, spoken) to people with jobs that (had, have) special appeal for her. (6) After Emma (understanded, understood) her own goals, she (writed, wrote) a straightforward,

one-page, error-free résumé. (7) Her clear objectives statement (telled, told) prospective employers about her job preferences. (8) After listing her educational experience, she (gave, gived) her past employment, with the most recent job first. (9) She (choosed, chose) lively action verbs like *organized*, *filed*, *oversaw*, and *inspected* to describe her responsibilities at each job. (10) Her references (was, were) four people who (knowed, knew) her work well. (11) At last, Emma (felt, feeled) ready to answer newspaper ads, search for jobs online, and explore every lead she (got, gotten). (12) She (putted, put) her résumé on the *Monster.com* site so that hundreds of companies would see it. (13) Then, she (took, taked) a friend's good suggestion that they interview each other to practice their skills. (14) A few days later, the phone (rang, ringed) and Emma (made, maked) preparations for her first job interview.

PRACTICE 6

Look over the list of irregular verbs on pages 170–171. Pick out the ten verbs that give you the most trouble and list them here.

Simple	Past	Simple	Past
_____	_____	_____	_____
_____	_____	_____	_____
_____	_____	_____	_____
_____	_____	_____	_____
_____	_____	_____	_____

Now, on paper or on a computer, write one paragraph using *all ten* verbs. Your paragraph may be humorous; just make sure your verbs are correct.

C. Troublesome Verb in the Past Tense: TO BE

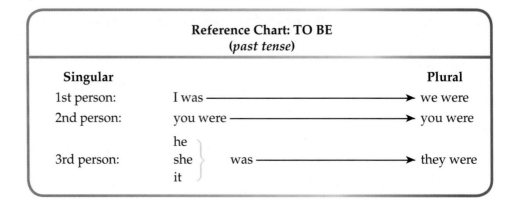

Reference Chart: TO BE
(*past tense*)

	Singular		Plural
1st person:	I was	⟶	we were
2nd person:	you were	⟶	you were
3rd person:	he she it } was	⟶	they were

● Note that the first and third person singular forms are the same—*was*.

PRACTICE 7

In each sentence, circle the correct past tense of the verb *to be*—either *was* or *were*.

1. Our instructor (**was**, were) a pilot and skydiver.
2. You always (was, **were**) a good friend.
3. Jorge Luis Borges (**was**, were) a great twentieth-century writer.
4. Why (was, **were**) they an hour early for the party?
5. I (**was**, were) seven when my sister (**was**, were) born.
6. Carmen (**was**, were) a Republican, but her cousins (was, **were**) Democrats.
7. The bride and groom (was, **were**) present, but where (**was**, were) the ring?
8. (Was, **Were**) you seasick on your new houseboat?
9. Either they (**was**, were) late, or she (**was**, were) early.
10. At this time last year, Sarni and I (was, **were**) in Egypt.

To Be + Not

Be careful of verb agreement if you use the past tense of *to be* with *not* as a contraction.

$$
\begin{array}{l}
was + not = wasn't \\
were + not = weren't
\end{array}
$$

PRACTICE 8

In each sentence, fill in the blank with either *wasn't* or *weren't*.

1. The printer cartridges _____weren't_____ on sale.
2. That papaya _____wasn't_____ cheap.
3. He _____wasn't_____ happy about the opening of the nuclear power plant.
4. This fireplace _____wasn't_____ built properly.
5. The parents _____weren't_____ willing to tolerate drug dealers near the school.
6. That _____wasn't_____ the point!
7. My pet lobster _____wasn't_____ in the aquarium.
8. That history quiz _____wasn't_____ so bad.
9. He and I liked each other, but we _____weren't_____ able to agree about music.
10. Many young couples _____weren't_____ able to afford homes.

D. Review

PRACTICE 9 Review

All main verbs in this paragraph are underlined to help you spot them. Proofread the paragraph, checking every verb in this paragraph and correcting any past tense errors or incorrect verbs above the lines.

(1) Mohawk Indians <u>played</u> a major role in constructing American cities. (2) They <u>builded</u> ^{built}

skyscrapers all over the United States and Canada, earning fame as skillful ironworkers.

(3) Almost 150 years ago, Mohawks first <u>began</u> to "walk high steel" when they <u>work</u> ^{worked} on a

Mohawk Indians and other ironworkers eat lunch on a beam during construction of Rockefeller Center. New York City, 1932.

did
bridge over the St. Lawrence River in Canada. (4) They done well at this dangerous job.

said   had
(5) Some people sayed that Mohawks haved no fear, but in fact they just handled their

moved   were
fear better than others. (6) Mohawk ironworking families move where the jobs was.

put
(7) They putted up the Sears Tower in Chicago (now the Willis Tower) and the San Francisco

took
Bay Bridge. (8) In New York City, they proudly taked their place in history, working on the

Chrysler Building, the Empire State Building, and the George Washington Bridge. (9) In the

went
1960s, the call wented out for ironworkers willing to climb the tallest buildings in the world.

(10) Five hundred Mohawks signed up to build the World Trade Center. (11) In 2001, after the

fell   came
Twin Towers falled, a new generation of Mohawk steelworkers come back to dismantle the

twisted beams.

PRACTICE 10   **Review**

This paragraph is written in the present tense. Underline every main verb. Then change the paragraph to the past tense by changing all the verbs, writing the past tense form of every verb above the lines.*

worked was   went
   (1) Above the office where I work is a karate studio. (2) Every day as I go through my email,

made   wrote   heard
make out invoices, and write letters, I hear loud shrieks and crashes from the studio above

---

* See also Chapter 26, "Consistent Tense," for more practice.

me. (3) All day long, the walls <u>tremble</u> *[trembled]*, the ceiling <u>shakes</u> *[shook]*, and little pieces of plaster <u>fall</u> *[fell]* like snow onto my desk. (4) Sometimes, the noise <u>does</u> *[did]* not bother me; at other times, I <u>wear</u> *[wore]* earplugs. (5) If I <u>am</u> *[was]* in a very bad mood, I <u>stand</u> *[stood]* on my desk and <u>pound</u> *[pounded]* out reggae rhythms on the ceiling with my shoe. (6) However, I <u>appreciate</u> *[appreciated]* one thing. (7) The job <u>teaches</u> *[taught]* me to concentrate no matter what.

Chapter Highlights

- **Regular verbs add** *-d* **or** *-ed* **to form the past tense:**

  We *decided.*

  The frog *jumped.*

  He *outfoxed* the fox.

- **Irregular verbs in the past tense change in irregular ways:**

  We *took* a marketing course.

  Owen *ran* fast.

  Jan *brought* pineapples.

- *To be* **is the only verb that takes more than one form in the past tense:**

I *was*	we *were*
you *were*	you *were*
he	
she } *was*	they *were*
it	

Proofreading Strategy

To proofread for past tense verb errors, especially if these are one of your error patterns, **highlight** and **read aloud**. First, read slowly through the text, underlining or highlighting the *main verb* in every sentence.

- Make sure that every *regular past tense verb* ends in *-d* or *-ed*.

- Carefully consider every *irregular past tense verb* to make sure it is in the correct form. If you aren't sure, check the past tense chart. Here are two examples:

  In 2008, Barack Obama <u>become</u> *[became]* the first African American president of the United States. Almost 53 percent of Americans who participated in the election <u>vote</u> *[voted]* for him.

WRITING AND PROOFREADING ASSIGNMENT

With three or four classmates, invent a group fairy tale. Take five minutes to decide on a subject for your story. On a clean sheet of paper, the first student should write the first sentence—in the past tense, of course. Use vivid action verbs. Each student should write a sentence in turn until the fairy tale is finished.

Now proofread. Underline or highlight every main verb. Then have a group member read your story aloud. As you listen, make sure the verbs are correct. Should any verbs be replaced with livelier ones?

CHAPTER REVIEW

Proofread carefully for past tense verbs. Check every verb in this essay, correcting any past tense errors or incorrect verbs above the lines.

TEACHING TIP

The story of Majora Carter suggests several discussion and writing ideas: growing up in a tough area, moving back with one's parents, eco-issues in poor neighborhoods, and the power of one determined person.

Homegrown Warrior

grew
(1) Majora Carter growed up in a rough neighborhood of New York's South Bronx.

went
(2) When she gone to college, she vowed never to return. (3) Like many inner-city areas, it

was an industrial wasteland, with decaying buildings and gray air. (4) Yet a strange twist of

brought   inspired
fate bringed Carter home and inspire an amazing career.

had   worked
(5) For financial reasons, Majora have to move back with her parents while she work on a

master's degree in writing. (6) She soon heard about the city's plan to build yet another solid

discussed
waste treatment plant in the South Bronx. (7) She and her neighbors discuss this pattern

learned
of dumping unwanted waste in poor areas. (8) They learnt that the toxic effects of sewage

plants already in the South Bronx added to the plague of local health problems, especially

rallied
asthma. (9) Angry and determined, Carter rallyed the residents to fight. (10) Incredibly, they

defeated the city's plan.

saw   needed
(11) Inspired by this success, Carter seen how much more need to be done. (12) Her group

wanted
want clean air, waterfront development, and environmentally friendly jobs. (13) In 2001, she

created Sustainable South Bronx (SSB), an organization dedicated to community restoration.

assembled   built
(14) The group assemble a workforce, builded a park on the site of an old cement plant, and

explored
explores the idea of a four-mile-long greenway along the waterfront. (15) With new respect

pushed
from local officials and businesses, SSB push for economic development, too. (16) The slow

but sure revival attracted other activists and artists to the neighborhood.

studied
(17) Carter further studyed the connection between environment and health. (18) Her group

took
taked steps to improve residents' fitness, recreation, and nutrition. (19) But the "green roof"

became   demonstrated
become one of her proudest achievements. (20) Carter demonstrate how growing plants on

Green roofs like this one in New York City reduce urban heat and pollution.

city roofs cleans the air, cools buildings, provides healthy food, and reduces water pollution.

                                 caught
(21) The idea of green roofs ~~catched~~ on and got national attention.

(22) In 2005, at age 38, Majora Carter received a MacArthur "Genius" Grant for profoundly

                                                        planned   kept
improving her community's quality of life. (23) A career she never ~~plan~~ just ~~keeped~~ blooming.

EXPLORING ONLINE

TEACHING TIP

Instructor tools for *Grass-roots* include a computerized Test Bank, PowerPoint slides, an Instructor's Manual with teaching tips, and more, and can be accessed at ‹**login .cengage.com**›.

<http://iteslj.org/cw/1/em-past3.html> Past tense crossword. Write the correct verbs and solve the puzzle.

<http://grammar.ccc.commnet.edu/grammar/quizzes/chute.htm> Change present tense verbs to past in this passage from a famous book.

CHAPTER 13

The Past Participle in Action

A: Past Participles of Regular Verbs

B: Past Participles of Irregular Verbs

C: Using the Present Perfect Tense

D: Using the Past Perfect Tense

E: Using the Passive Voice

F: Using Past Participles as Adjectives

A. Past Participles of Regular Verbs

Every verb has one form that can be combined with helping verbs like *has* and *have* to make verbs of more than one word. This form is called the **past participle**.

> (1) She ⟨has⟩ solved the problem.
>
> (2) I ⟨have⟩ solved the problem.
>
> (3) He ⟨had⟩ solved the problem already.

- Each of these sentences contains a two-part verb. Circle the first part, or *helping verb*, in each sentence, and write each helping verb in the blanks that follow:

  (1) _____has_____

  (2) _____have_____

  (3) _____had_____

- Underline the second part, or *main verb*, in each sentence. This word, a form of the verb *to solve*, is the same in all three. Write it here: _____solved_____

- *Solved* is the past participle of *to solve*.

The past participle never changes, no matter what the subject is and no matter what the helping verb is.

Fill in the past participle in each series below:

		Helping Verb + Past Participle
Present Tense	**Past Tense**	
(1) Beth dances.	(1) Beth danced.	(1) Beth has _____danced_____.
(2) They decide.	(2) They decided.	(2) They have _____decided_____.
(3) He jumps.	(3) He jumps.	(3) He has _____jumped_____.

- Are the verbs *to dance*, *to decide*, and *to jump* regular or irregular?

  _____regular_____ How do you know? _____The past tense ends in -*d* or -*ed*._____

- What ending does each verb take in the past tense? _____-*d* or -*ed*_____

- Remember that any verb that forms its past tense by adding -*d* or -*ed* is a *regular* verb. What past participle ending does each verb take? _____-*d* or -*ed*_____

The past participle forms of regular verbs look exactly like the past tense forms. Both end in -*d* or -*ed*.

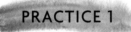

PRACTICE 1

The first sentence in each of these pairs contains a one-word verb in the past tense. Fill in the past participle of the same verb in the blank in the second sentence.

EXAMPLE: She designed jewelry all her life.

She has _____designed_____ jewelry all her life.

1. Several students worked in the maternity ward.

   Several students have _____worked_____ in the maternity ward.

2. The pot of soup boiled over.

   The pot of soup has _____boiled_____ over.

3. The chick hatched.

   The chick has _____hatched_____.

4. We congratulated Jorgé.

   We have _____congratulated_____ Jorgé.

5. Nelson always studied in the bathtub.

   Nelson has always _____studied_____ in the bathtub.

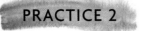
PRACTICE 2

Write the missing two-part verb in each of the following sentences. Use the helping verb *has* or *have* and the past participle of the verb written in parentheses.

EXAMPLE: ____*Have*____ you ever ____*wished*____ (to wish) for a new name?

1. Some of us ____have____ ____wanted____ (to want) new names at one time or another.

2. Many famous people ____have____ ____fulfilled____ (to fulfill) that desire.

3. Some ____have____ ____used____ (to use) only their first names.

4. Robyn Rihanna Fenty ____has____ ____dropped____ (to drop) everything but Rihanna.

5. Beyoncé Knowles ____has____ ____shortened____ (to shorten) her name to Beyoncé.

6. Other celebrities ____have____ ____retained____ (to retain) their first names and taken new last names.

7. For example, comedian Jonathan Leibowitz ____has____ ____renamed____ (to rename) himself Jon Stewart.

8. Changing three names, Peter Gene Hernandez ____has____ ____turned____ (to turn) himself into Bruno Mars.

9. Replacing all her names, Stefani Joanne Angelina Germanotta ____has____ ____transformed____ (to transform) herself into Lady Gaga.

10. What new name would you ____have____ ____picked____ (to pick) for yourself?

B. Past Participles of Irregular Verbs

Present Tense	Past Tense	Helping Verb + Past Participle
(1) He sees.	(1) He saw.	(1) He has seen.
(2) I take vitamins.	(2) I took vitamins.	(2) I have taken vitamins.
(3) We sing.	(3) We sang.	(3) We have sung.

- Are the verbs *to see*, *to take*, and *to sing* regular or irregular? ____irregular____

- Like all irregular verbs, *to see*, *to take*, and *to sing* do not add *-d* or *-ed* to show past tense.

- Most irregular verbs in the past tense are also irregular in the past participle—like *seen*, *taken*, and *sung*.

BE CAREFUL: Past participles must be used with helping verbs.*

Because irregular verbs change their spelling in irregular ways, there are no easy rules to explain these changes. Here is a list of some common irregular verbs.

_____

* For work on incomplete verbs, see Chapter 10, Part B.

Reference Chart: Irregular Verbs

Simple Form	Past	Past Participle
be	was, were	been
become	became	become
begin	began	begun
blow	blew	blown
break	broke	broken
bring	brought	brought
build	built	built
burst	burst	burst
buy	bought	bought
catch	caught	caught
choose	chose	chosen
come	came	come
cut	cut	cut
dive	dove (dived)	dived
do	did	done
draw	drew	drawn
drink	drank	drunk
drive	drove	driven
eat	ate	eaten
fall	fell	fallen
feed	fed	fed
feel	felt	felt
fight	fought	fought
find	found	found
fly	flew	flown
forget	forgot	forgotten
forgive	forgave	forgiven
freeze	froze	frozen
get	got	gotten (got)
give	gave	given
go	went	gone
grow	grew	grown
have	had	had
hear	heard	heard
hide	hid	hidden
hold	held	held
hurt	hurt	hurt
keep	kept	kept
know	knew	known
lay	laid	laid
lead	led	led
leave	left	left
let	let	let
lie	lay	lain

(continued)

Reference Chart: Irregular Verbs (*continued*)

Simple Form	Past	Past Participle
lose	lost	lost
make	made	made
mean	meant	meant
meet	met	met
pay	paid	paid
put	put	put
quit	quit	quit
read	read	read
ride	rode	ridden
ring	rang	rung
rise	rose	risen
run	ran	run
say	said	said
see	saw	seen
seek	sought	sought
sell	sold	sold
send	sent	sent
set	set	set
shake	shook	shaken
shine	shone (shined)	shone (shined)
shrink	shrank (shrunk)	shrunk
sing	sang	sung
sit	sat	sat
sleep	slept	slept
speak	spoke	spoken
spend	spent	spent
spring	sprang	sprung
stand	stood	stood
steal	stole	stolen
strike	struck	struck
swim	swam	swum
swing	swung	swung
take	took	taken
teach	taught	taught
tear	tore	torn
tell	told	told
think	thought	thought
throw	threw	thrown
understand	understood	understood
wake	woke (waked)	woken (waked)
wear	wore	worn
win	won	won
wind	wound	wound
write	wrote	written

You already know many of these past participle forms. One way to learn the unfamiliar ones is to group together verbs that change from the present tense to the past tense to the past participle in the same way. For example, some irregular verbs change from *ow* in the present to *ew* in the past to *own* in the past participle.

blow	blew	blown
grow	grew	grown
know	knew	known
throw	threw	thrown

Another group changes from *i* in the present to *a* in the past to *u* in the past participle:

begin	began	begun
drink	drank	drunk
ring	rang	rung
sing	sang	sung
spring	sprang	sprung
swim	swam	swum

As you write, refer to the chart. If you are unsure of the past participle form of a verb that is not on the chart, check a dictionary. For example, if you look up the verb *see* in the dictionary, you will find an entry like this:

see \ saw \ seen \ seeing

The first word listed is the present tense form of the verb (I *see*, she *sees*, and so on). The second word listed is the past tense form (I *saw*, she *saw*, and so on). The third word is the past participle form (I *have seen*, she *has seen*, and so on), and the last word is the present participle form.

Some dictionaries list different forms only for irregular verbs. If no past tense or past participle form is listed, you know that the verb is regular and that its past participle ends in *-d* or *-ed*.

 **PRACTICE 3**

Write the missing two-part verb in each of the following sentences. Use the helping verb *has* or *have* and the past participle of the verb in parentheses.

EXAMPLE: These drugs ___*have changed*___ the world.

1. Since their discovery in 1927, antibiotics ___have fought___ (fight) serious bacterial infections like tuberculosis and pneumonia and ___have made___ (make) humans healthier.

2. Overuse of these "miracle drugs" ___has led___ (lead) to a medical crisis, however.

3. At the first sign of a child's runny nose, some parents ___have run___ (run) to the clinic for antibiotics.

4. Doctors ___have given___ (give) antibiotics to patients with colds or flu, conditions that antibiotics cannot help.

5. Worse, farmers ___have fed___ (feed) large doses of these drugs to poultry and animals, so the public ___has taken___ (take) antibiotics hidden in eggs, milk, and meat.

6. As a result, our bodies ___have become___ (become) tolerant of these drugs, which then may not help us when we need them.

7. Now, some bacteria ___have grown___ (grow) into dangerous "superbugs" resistant to all known antibiotics.

8. The number of deaths from incurable infections ___has risen___ (rise) to 60,000 a year in the United States alone.

9. Fearing a deadly plague of superbugs, many doctors <u>have begun</u> (begin) to limit their antibiotic prescriptions.

10. Doctors like Mehmet Oz and Sanjay Gupta <u>have told</u> (tell) consumers, especially parents, to buy antibiotic-free eggs, milk, and meat if at all possible.

PRACTICE 4

Review

For each verb in the chart that follows, fill in the present tense (third person singular form), the past tense, and the past participle. BE CAREFUL: Some of the verbs are regular, and some are irregular.

ESL AND TEACHING TIP

Alert students to online drills on irregular English verb forms. ESL students in particular may find these helpful. Try ‹**http://a4esl.org/q/j/ ck/fb2-irregularverbs.html**›.

Simple	Present Tense (he, she, it)	Past Tense	Past Participle
know	knows	knew	known
catch	catches	caught	caught
stop	stops	stopped	stopped
break	breaks	broke	broken
reach	reaches	reached	reached
bring	brings	brought	brought
fly	flies	flew	flown
fall	falls	fell	fallen
feel	feels	felt	felt
take	takes	took	taken
go	goes	went	gone

PRACTICE 5

Review

TEACHING TIP

Point out to students that this practice essay is developed with examples. For more information on using examples, see Chapter 5.

Carefully proofread for verb errors in this essay, which contains both *regular* and *irregular* verbs. In every sentence, find and check any verbs containing a *helping verb* (*has* or *have*) and a *past participle*. Cross out the errors and make your corrections above the lines. Hint: thirteen verbs are incorrect.

EXAMPLES: Millions h̶a̶s̶ *have* heard them sing.

They have u̶s̶e̶ *used* words and music to connect with others.

Latinas Break Through

(1) Recently, a new generation of Latina crossover stars has b̶r̶o̶k̶e̶ *broken* musical barriers, bringing

to American music and films new talent and a Latin flavor. (2) The performer who started it all,

Jennifer Lopez as Selena

Cuban-born Gloria Estefan, now has ~~establish~~ established herself as a hugely successful crossover singer. (3) Her albums, with hits like "Conga" and "Rhythm of the Night," have ~~sell~~ sold millions of copies. (4) In addition to being the first Latina to win Broadcast Music's "Songwriter of the Year" award, she ~~have receive~~ has received five Grammies.

(5) Since then, many young singers ~~has~~ have crossed over to English from a range of Spanish-speaking backgrounds. (6) Selena, for instance, established herself as the first female superstar of Tejano music, a Tex-Mex style that has ~~came~~ come to blend rock, country, conjunto, norteno, and blues. (7) Selena's 1991 hit "Ven Conmigo" was the first Tejano record to go gold, and in 1993, she became the first Tejano artist to win a Grammy. (8) In addition, five Spanish-language albums on the *Billboard 200* have ~~earn~~ earned her another first. (9) Although her tragic murder in 1995 cut short a brilliant career, Selena's recordings have ~~encourage~~ encouraged North Americans to appreciate the beauty, exuberance, and variety of Latino music.

(10) Ironically, a film about Selena's life launched the next Latina superstar into the spotlight. (11) Since her 1997 role as the slain Tejana singer, Puerto Rican Jennifer Lopez ~~have win~~ has won acclaim in both her acting and singing careers. (12) In fact, she was the first U.S. performer to have the number one album (*Love Don't Cost a Thing*) and the number one movie (*The Wedding Planner*) during the same week. (13) Today, commanding top fees for her films and creating her own perfume and clothing lines, JLo has ~~became~~ become a producer and a judge on *American Idol*, in addition to releasing new albums.

(14) These breakthrough stars ~~has help~~ have helped to blend Hispanic and Anglo cultures and have ~~open~~ opened doors for a new crop of singers and actresses. (15) Latina film and TV stars who ~~has~~ have rushed through those doors include Salma Hayek, Kate Del Castillo, and Sofía Vergara, who has become the most highly paid actress on television.

PRACTICE 6   ## Review

Check your work in the preceding exercises or have it checked. Do you see any *patterns* in your errors? Do you tend to miss regular or irregular verbs? To help yourself learn, copy all four forms of each verb that you missed into your notebook in a chart like the one that follows. Add specific mistakes to your Personal Error Patterns chart.

Personal Review Chart

Simple	Present Tense (he, she, it)	Past Tense	Past Participle
go	goes	went	gone

C. Using the Present Perfect Tense

The **present perfect tense** is composed of the present tense of *to have* (*has* or *have*) plus the past participle.

ESL TIP

The perfect tenses are not unique to English, but they are difficult for ESL students. Extra help and discussion of the differences between their native language and English may help.

Present Perfect Tense	
Singular	**Plural**
I *have* spoken	we *have* spoken
you *have* spoken	you *have* spoken
he	
she } *has* spoken	they *have* spoken
it	

Let us see how this tense is used.

(1) They *sang* together last Saturday.

(2) They *have sung* together for three years now.

● In sentence (1), the past tense verb *sang* tells us that they sang together on one occasion, Saturday, but are no longer singing together. The action began and ended in the past.

● In sentence (2), the present perfect verb *have sung* tells us something entirely different: that they have sung together in the past and *are still singing together now*.

(3) Janet *sat* on the beach for three hours.

(4) Valerie *has* just *sat* on the beach for three hours.

● Which woman is probably still sunburned? _____Valerie_____

● In sentence (3), Janet's action began and ended at some time in the past. Perhaps it was ten years ago that she sat on the beach.

● In (4), the present perfect verb *has sat* implies that although the action occurred in the past, it *has just happened*, and Valerie had better put some lotion on her sunburn *now*.

● Notice how the word *just* emphasizes that the action occurred very recently.

Use the *present perfect tense* **to show either (1) that an action began in the past and has continued until now or (2) that an action has just happened.**

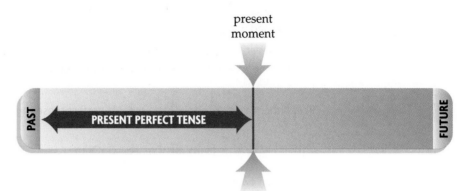

In writing about an action that began in the past and is still continuing, you will often use time words like *for* and *since*.

> (5) We have watched the fireworks *for* three hours.
> (6) John has sung in the choir *since* 2002.

In writing about an action that has just happened, you will often use words like *just*, *recently*, *already*, and *yet*.

> (7) I have *just* finished the novel.
> (8) They have *already* gone to the party.

PRACTICE 7

Paying close attention to meaning, circle the verb that best completes each sentence.

EXAMPLES: Years ago, he (wanted, has wanted) to know how things worked. Since then, not much (changed, has changed).

1. Even as a young boy in New York City, Dean Kamen (loved, has loved) science and invention.

2. While just a teenager, he (got, has gotten) the job of automating the Times Square ball drop for New Year's Eve.

3. Since that time, Kamen (invented, has invented) many amazing machines, including a stair-climbing wheelchair, a robotic scooter, and a small dialysis machine.

4. For several years now, he (lived and worked, has lived and worked) in a huge, six-sided house in New Hampshire.

5. Inside and out, the house (began, has begun) to look like a fabulous science museum.

6. The collection (expanded, has expanded) to include helicopters, a steam engine, a special Humvee, and a wind turbine.

7. Some years ago, Kamen (decided, has decided) to encourage children to enter science careers through FIRST (For Inspiration and Recognition of Science and Technology).

8. In 2012, he (joined, has joined) forces with musician will.i.am to get more kids involved with FIRST.

9. In a recent speech, Kamen (said, has said), "Teenagers think they will become NBA stars and make millions, but their odds [of doing so] are less than 1 percent."

10. "However, many, many scientists and inventors (made, have made) big money and big contributions as well," he added. "Think about it."

PRACTICE 8

Fill in either the *past* tense or the *present perfect* tense form of each verb in parentheses.

(1) In 1976, the town of Twinsburg, Ohio, _____ began _____ (to begin) hosting a gathering of twins from around the world. (2) Every year since then, more and more twins _____ have attended _____ (to attend), wearing matching outfits, crazy hats, and posing for photographers. (3) Last year, 2,064 sets of twins from the United States, Africa, Europe, and South America _____ registered _____ (to register) for Twins Days. (4) Over the years, fascinated tourists _____ have doubled _____ (to double) the fun. (5) More important, the annual event _____ has offered _____ (to offer) scientists a rare research opportunity. (6) For example, researchers _____ have studied _____ (to study) identical twins (with identical genes) to see how DNA and environment affect diseases, hair loss, and even personality traits like shyness. (7) By the way, in the 1990s, researchers _____ found _____ (to find) that shyness is inherited. (8) Many twins _____ have assisted _____ (to assist) scientists by standing in line for hours to answer questions, take tests, and donate their DNA. (9) The twins festival _____ has afforded _____ (to afford) them the chance not only to meet other twins but also to contribute to human knowledge.

D. Using the Past Perfect Tense

The **past perfect tense** is composed of the past tense of *to have* (*had*) plus the past participle.

Past Perfect Tense	
Singular	**Plural**
I *had* spoken	we *had* spoken
you *had* spoken	you *had* spoken
he	
she } *had* spoken	they *had* spoken
it	

Let us see how this tense is used.

> (1) Because Bob *had broken* his leg, he *wore* a cast for six months.

● The actions in both parts of this sentence occurred entirely in the past, but one occurred before the other.

● At some time in the past, Bob *wore* (past tense) a cast on the leg that he *had broken* (past perfect tense) at some time before that.

When you are writing in the past tense, use the *past perfect tense* **to show that something happened at an even earlier time.**

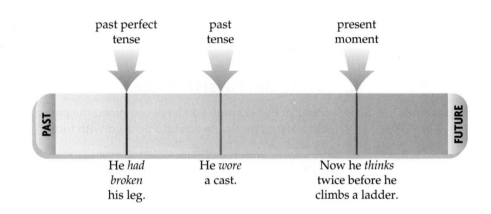

As a general rule, the present perfect tense is used in relation to the present tense, and the past perfect tense is used in relation to the past tense. Read the following pairs of sentences and note the time relation.

> (2) Sid *says* (present) he *has found* (present perfect) a good job.
>
> (3) Sid *said* (past) he *had found* (past perfect) a good job.
>
> (4) Grace *tells* (present) us she *has won* (present perfect) first prize.
>
> (5) Grace *told* (past) us she *had won* (past perfect) first prize.

PRACTICE 9

Choose either the present perfect or the past perfect tense of the verb in parentheses to complete each sentence. Match present perfect tense with present tense and past perfect tense with past tense.

1. The newspaper reports that the dictator _____has_____ _____left_____ (to leave) the country.

2. The newspaper reported that the dictator _____had_____ _____left_____ (to leave) the country.

3. I plan to buy a red convertible; I _____have_____ _____wanted_____ (to want) a convertible for three years now.

4. Last year, I bought a red convertible; I _____had_____ _____wanted_____ (to want) a convertible for three years before that.

5. Mel _____had_____ _____chosen_____ (to choose) the steepest trail up the mountain; he was thoroughly worn out.

6. Mel _____has_____ _____chosen_____ (to choose) the steepest trail up the mountain; he is thoroughly worn out.

7. I am worried about my cat; she _____has_____ _____drunk_____ (to drink) bubble bath.

8. I was worried about my cat; she _____had_____ _____drunk_____ (to drink) bubble bath.

9. Sam told us that he _____had_____ _____decided_____ (to decide) to major in restaurant management.

10. Sam tells us that he _____has_____ _____decided_____ (to decide) to major in restaurant management.

E. Using the Passive Voice

So far in this chapter, you have combined the past participle with forms of *to have*. But the past participle can also be used with forms of *to be* (*am, is, are, was, were*).

(1) That jam was made by Aunt Clara.

TEACHING TIP

To help students improve their writing style, use these and other examples to show that passive voice sentences are often wordier than active voice sentences. Passive voice also allows for omission of the subject—desirable only when the subject is unknown or diplomacy is required (e.g., *The situation was mishandled*).

- The subject of the sentence is *that jam*. The verb has two parts: the helping verb *was* and the past participle *made*.

- Note that the subject, *that jam*, does not act but is acted on by the verb. *By Aunt Clara* tells us who performed the action.

That jam *was made* by Aunt Clara.

When the subject is acted on or receives the action, it is passive, and the verb (*to be + past participle*) **is in the** *passive voice.*

Now compare the passive voice with the active voice in these pairs of sentences:

(2) **Passive voice:** Free gifts are given by the bank.

(3) **Active voice:** The bank gives free gifts.

(4) **Passive voice:** We were photographed by a tourist.

(5) **Active voice:** _____A tourist photographed us._____

- In sentence (2), the subject, *free gifts*, is passive; it receives the action. In sentence (3), *the bank* is active; it performs the action.

- Note the difference between the passive verb *are given* and the active verb *gives*.

- However, the tense of both sentences is the same. The passive verb *are given* is in the present tense, and so is the active verb *gives*.

- Rewrite sentence (4) in the active voice. Be sure to keep the same verb tense in the new sentence.

Write in the *passive voice* only when you want to emphasize the receiver of the action rather than the doer. Usually, however, write in the *active voice* because sentences in the active voice are livelier and more direct.

PRACTICE 10

Underline the verb in each sentence. In the blank to the right, write *A* if the verb is written in the active voice and *P* if the verb is in the passive voice.

EXAMPLE: Nelson Mandela <u>is respected</u> worldwide as a leader.   *P*

1. Nelson Mandela <u>was born</u> in South Africa on July 18, 1918, a member of the Xhosa tribe.   P

2. Under the apartheid government, only whites, not the black majority, <u>enjoyed</u> basic rights.   A

3. As a young lawyer, Mandela <u>defended</u> many black clients.   A

4. They <u>were charged</u> with such crimes as "not owning land" or "living in the wrong area."   P

5. Several times, Mandela <u>was arrested</u> for working with the African National Congress, a civil rights group.   P

6. In 1961, he sadly <u>gave</u> up his lifelong belief in nonviolence.   A

7. Training guerrilla fighters, he <u>was imprisoned</u> again, this time with a life sentence.   P

8. Twenty-seven years in jail <u>did not break</u> Mandela.   A

9. Offered freedom to give up his beliefs, he <u>said</u> no.   A

10. Finally released in 1990, this man <u>became</u> a symbol of hope for a new South Africa.   A

11. In 1994, black and white South Africans <u>lined</u> up to vote in the first free elections.   A

12. Gray-haired, iron-willed Nelson Mandela <u>was elected</u> president of his beloved country.   P

PRACTICE 11

Whenever possible, write in the active, not the passive, voice. Rewrite each sentence, changing the verb from the passive to the active voice. Make all necessary verb and subject changes. Be sure to keep each sentence in the original tense.

EXAMPLE: Good medical care is deserved by all human beings.

   All human beings deserve good medical care.

1. Doctors Without Borders was created by a small group of French doctors in 1971.

   A small group of French doctors created Doctors Without Borders in 1971.

2. Excellent health care was provided by them to people in poor or isolated regions.

   They provided excellent health care to people in poor or isolated regions.

3. Soon they were joined by volunteer doctors and nurses from all over the world.

   Soon volunteer doctors and nurses from all over the world joined them.

Doctors Without Borders provides urgently needed HIV-AIDS care at clinics like this one in Myanmar.

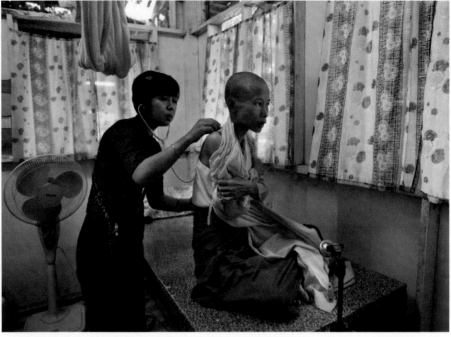

4. Today drugs and medical supplies are brought by the organization to people in need.

Today the organization brings drugs and medical supplies to people in need.

5. Vaccinations are received by children in eighty countries.

Children in eighty countries receive vaccinations.

6. Crumbling hospitals and clinics are restored by volunteers.

Volunteers restore crumbling hospitals and clinics.

7. Victims of wars also are treated by the DWB staff.

The DWB staff also treats victims of wars.

8. Information about humanitarian crises is gotten by the world.

The world gets information about humanitarian crises.

9. Each year, thousands are given the gifts of health and life by these traveling experts.

Each year, these traveling experts give the gifts of health and life to thousands.

F. Using Past Participles as Adjectives

Sometimes a past participle is not a verb at all but an *adjective*, a word that describes a noun or pronoun.*

(1) Jay is *married*.

(2) The *broken* window looks terrible.

(3) Two *tired* students slept in the hall.

---

*For more work on adjectives, see Chapter 24.

- In sentence (1), *married* is the past participle of the verb *to marry*, but here it is not a verb. Instead, it describes the subject, *Jay*.

- *Is* links the subject, *Jay*, with the descriptive word, *married*.

- In sentence (2), *broken* is the past participle form of *to break*, but it is used as an adjective to describe the noun *window*.

- In sentence (3), what past participle is an adjective? _____tired_____

- Which word does it describe? _____students_____

Past participles like *married*, *broken*, and *tired* are often used as adjectives.

Some form of the verb *to be* usually links descriptive past participles with the subjects they describe, but here are a few other common linking verbs that you learned in Chapter 9, Part E.

Subject	Linking Verb (simple form)	Past Participle (used as adjective)
They	act appear become feel get look seem sound	surprised.

PRACTICE 12

Underline the linking verb in each sentence. Then circle the descriptive past participle or participles that complete the sentences.

EXAMPLES: The window <u>was</u> (polish, (polished)).

Paolo <u>seems</u> very (worry, (worried)) these days.

1. This product <u>is</u> (guarantee, (guaranteed)) not to explode.
2. Nellie <u>seems</u> (qualify, (qualified)) for the job.
3. Your aunt <u>appears</u> (delight, (delighted)) to see you again.
4. After we read the chapter, we <u>were</u> still (confuse, (confused)).
5. The science laboratory <u>is</u> (air-condition, (air-conditioned)).
6. Dwayne <u>feels</u> (appreciate, (appreciated)) in his new job.
7. Did you know that one out of two American couples <u>gets</u> (divorce, (divorced))?
8. We <u>were</u> (thrill, (thrilled)) to meet Venus and Serena Williams.
9. During the holidays, Paul <u>feels</u> (depress, (depressed)).
10. Are the potatoes (fry, (fried)), (bake, (baked)), or (boil, (boiled))?

PRACTICE 13

Proofread the following ad copy for past participle errors. First, underline all the past participles. Then make any corrections above the line.

            created
(1) First <u>create</u> in 1959, Barbie is the world's best-selling doll. (2) Changes in society

         reflected
have been <u>reflect</u> in Barbie's looks, clothes, and career options. (3) Although ethnically

_{introduced}
diverse Barbies were <u>introduce</u> over the years by Mattel, many parents grew <u>tire</u> of seeing _{tired}

_{designed}
brown-skinned dolls with Caucasian features. (4) They wanted dolls <u>design</u> to look more

like their daughters. (5) Stacey McBride-Irby was an <u>experienced</u> designer working at

Mattel. (6) She also happened to be African American and the mother of a young girl.

_{Motivated}
(7) <u>Motivate</u> by what she wanted for her own child, McBride-Irby pitched an idea to

_{interested}
Mattel executives. (8) They were immediately <u>interest</u>. (9) The result is McBride-Irby's "So

_{pronounced}
in Style" line of Barbies with fuller lips, wider noses, and more <u>pronounce</u> cheekbones.

_{tinted}
(10) One doll's skin is <u>tint</u> caramel and another's, chocolate brown. (11) Their hair ranges

_{named}
from curly to straight. (12) The dolls are <u>name</u> Grace, Kara, and Trichelle. (13) Each one

_{inspired}
has a little sister she mentors, because, says McBride-Irby, "I want girls to be <u>inspire</u>

_{dressed} _{accessorized}
and dream big." (14) Like all Barbies, these can be <u>dress</u> and <u>accessorize</u> until parents

_{pleased}
wince, and some critics aren't <u>please</u> that their long hair and plastic-surgery proportions

_{loved}
send harmful messages. (15) Despite the controversy, these Barbies are <u>love</u> by a new

group of girls.

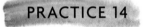

PRACTICE 14

Combine each pair of short sentences. First, find and underline the past participle. Then rewrite the two short sentences as one smooth sentence, using the past participle as an adjective.

EXAMPLE: The book is <u>lost</u>. It is worth $1,000.

The lost book is worth $1,000.

1. This rug has been <u>dry-cleaned</u>. It looks new.

   This dry-cleaned rug looks new.

2. His grades have <u>fallen</u>. He can bring them up.

   He can bring up his fallen grades.

3. The envelope was <u>sealed</u>. Harriet opened it.

   Harriet opened the sealed envelope.

4. The weather forecast was <u>revised</u>. It calls for sunshine.

   The revised weather forecast calls for sunshine.

5. These gold chains are <u>overpriced</u>. Do not buy them.

   Do not buy these overpriced gold chains.

**PRACTICE 15**   The sentences in the left column are in the present tense; those in the right column are in the past tense. If the sentence is shown in the present tense on the left, write the sentence in the past tense on the right, and vice versa. REMEMBER: Only the *linking verb*, never the past participle, changes to show tense.

EXAMPLES: Smoking is forbidden.   *Smoking was forbidden.*

Lunches are served.   Lunches were served.

Present Tense	**Past Tense**
1. Your car is repaired.	1. *Your car was repaired.*
2. *The store looks closed.*	2. The store looked closed.
3. *My feelings are hurt.*	3. My feelings were hurt.
4. The seats are filled.	4. *The seats were filled.*
5. She is relaxed.	5. *She was relaxed.*
6. *You seem qualified for the job.*	6. You seemed qualified for the job.
7. He is supposed to meet us.*	7. *He was supposed to meet us.*
8. They are used to hard work.*	8. *They were used to hard work.*
9. *It is written in longhand.*	9. It was written in longhand.
10. You are expected at noon.	10. *You were expected at noon.*

Chapter Highlights

- **Past participles of regular verbs add *-d* or *-ed*, just like their past tense forms:**

Present	**Past**	**Past Participle**
decide	decided	decided
jump	jumped	jumped

- **Past participles of irregular verbs change in irregular ways:**

Present	**Past**	**Past Participle**
bring	brought	brought
see	saw	seen
take	took	taken

---

* For more work on *supposed* and *used*, see Chapter 35, "Look-Alikes/Sound-Alikes."

- **Past participles can combine with** *to have*:

  He *has edited* many articles for us. (*present perfect tense*)

  He *had edited* many articles for us. (*past perfect tense*)

- **Past participles can combine with** *to be*:

  The report *was edited* by Mary. (*passive voice*)

- **Past participles can be used as adjectives:**

  The *edited* report arrived today. (*adjective*)

Proofreading Strategy

If past participle problems are among your error patterns, read your draft one word at a time and **search for the helping verbs *has, have, had, is, am, are, was, and were***. Every time you find a helping verb, highlight or underline it. If you are using a computer, use the *"Find"* feature to locate these words in your draft. Whenever these helping verbs are part of a past participle verb, **check the past participle form**. If it's a regular verb, it should end in *-d* or *-ed*. If it's an irregular verb and you aren't sure, check the verb chart. How should the writer correct the two incorrect past participles in these examples?

CORRECT   INCORRECT
I have registered for classes next semester, but I haven't yet buy my textbooks.

INCORRECT   CORRECT
The floor was stain a rich brown and polished to a high gloss.

WRITING AND PROOFREADING ASSIGNMENT

In a group of four or five classmates, write a wacky restaurant menu, using all the past participles that you can think of as adjectives: *steamed* fern roots, *fried* cherries, *caramel-coated* hamburgers, and so forth. Brainstorm. Get creative. Then arrange your menu in an order that makes sense (if that is the correct term for such a menu!). Don't forget to proofread.

CHAPTER REVIEW

Proofread this student's essay for past participle errors. Correct each error above the line.

Three Ways to Be a Smarter Learner

(1) Once in a great while, a person is born with a photographic memory, allowing him or her

to memorize a lot of information with almost no effort. (2) However, most of us have ~~struggle~~ struggled

on our own to find the best ways to learn. (3) We have stayed up all night studying. (4) We

have ~~mark~~ marked up our textbooks, highlighting and underlining like ~~skill~~ skilled tattoo artists. (5) Maybe, in

frustration, we have even questioned our own intelligence. (6) Although everyone has his or her own learning style, three techniques have ~~make~~ made me and others better learners.

(7) The first technique is simple—sit at the front of the class! (8) A student who has ~~choose~~ chosen to sit up front is more likely to stay alert and ~~involve~~ involved than students at the back and sides. (9) By sitting away from windows or talkative friends, many students discover that they take a greater interest in the classroom subject and take better notes. (10) An extra benefit of sitting up front is that teachers are often ~~impress~~ impressed by students with whom they make eye contact, students whose behavior says, "I care about this class."

(11) Second, make a smart friend. (12) During the first week of class, exchange phone numbers with another front-row student. (13) You are looking for an intelligent, responsible classmate who seems committed to learning—not for a pizza buddy or a date. (14) Students who have ~~agree~~ agreed in advance to help each other can call if they miss a class. (15) What was ~~discuss~~ discussed that day? (16) Was homework ~~assign~~ assigned or a test announced? (17) Two students who "click" might want to become study partners, meeting regularly to review material and prepare for tests.

(18) Third, ask questions. (19) The student who has ~~sit~~ sat up front, made a study friend, and ~~pay~~ paid close attention in class should not be worried about asking the professor questions. (20) Learning a subject is like building a tower. (21) Each new level of understanding must be ~~build~~ built solidly on the level below. (22) If an important point or term is unclear, ask for help, in or after class.

(23) Students who use these techniques will be rewarded with ~~increase~~ increased understanding and better grades—even before they have ~~pull~~ pulled out their pastel highlighters.

Maurice Jabbar, student

EXPLORING ONLINE

<http://a4esl.org/q/j/ck/fb2-irregularverbs.html> Fill in the blanks and test your past tense and past participle skills.

<http://grammar.ccc.commnet.edu/grammar/quizzes/passive_quiz.htm>
Interactive quiz: Revise these passive sentences. Make them active.

TEACHING TIP

Instructor tools for *Grassroots* include a computerized Test-Bank, PowerPoint slides, an Instructor's Manual with teaching tips, and more, and can be accessed at ‹**login .cengage.com**›.

CHAPTER 14

Progressive Tenses (TO BE + -*ING* Verb Form)

A: **Defining and Writing the Present Progressive Tense**

B: **Defining and Writing the Past Progressive Tense**

C: **Using the Progressive Tenses**

D: **Avoiding Incomplete Progressives**

A. Defining and Writing the Present Progressive Tense

Verbs in the *present progressive tense* have two parts: the present tense form of *to be* (*am, is, are*) plus the *-ing* (or present participle) form of the main verb.

Present Progressive Tense (*example verb: to play*)	
Singular	**Plural**
I *am playing*	we *are playing*
you *are playing*	you *are playing*
he	
she } *is playing*	they *are playing*
it	

Compare the present tense with the present progressive tense below.

TEACHING TIP

Make sure students understand that the present progressive tense indicates ongoing or continuing action. Refer them to Part C for a more detailed explanation.

(1) Luria works at the bookstore.

(2) Luria is working at the bookstore.

- Sentence (1) is in the present tense. Which word tells you this? _____works_____

- Sentence (2) is also in the present tense. Which word tells you this? _____is_____

- Note that the main verb in sentence (2), *working*, has no tense. Only the helping verb *is* shows tense.

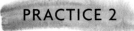

PRACTICE 1   Change each one-word present tense verb in the left-hand column to a two-part present progressive verb in the right-hand column. Do this by filling in the missing helping verb (*am*, *is*, or *are*).

EXAMPLES: I fly.   I _____*am*_____ flying.

He wears my sweater.   He _____*is*_____ wearing my sweater.

Present Tense	**Present Progressive Tense**
1. Elsa and I set goals together.	1. Elsa and I _____*are*_____ setting goals together.
2. They eat quickly.	2. They _____*are*_____ eating quickly.
3. He plans the wedding.	3. He _____*is*_____ planning the wedding.
4. Our work begins to pay off.	4. Our work _____*is*_____ beginning to pay off.
5. We pose for the photographer.	5. We _____*are*_____ posing for the photographer.
6. Maryann smiles.	6. Maryann _____*is*_____ smiling.
7. Sal does his Elvis impression.	7. Sal _____*is*_____ doing his Elvis impression.
8. I speak Portuguese to Manuel.	8. I _____*am*_____ speaking Portuguese to Manuel.
9. My grandson gets silly.	9. My grandson _____*is*_____ getting silly.
10. You probably wonder why.	10. You _____*are*_____ probably wondering why.

REMEMBER: **Every verb in the present progressive tense must have two parts: a helping verb (*am*, *is*, or *are*) and a main verb ending in -*ing*. The helping verb must agree with the subject.**

PRACTICE 2   Below are sentences in the regular present tense. Rewrite each one in the present progressive tense by changing the verb to *am*, *is*, or *are* plus the -*ing* form of the main verb.

EXAMPLE: We play cards.

We are playing cards.

1. The cell phone rings.

   The cell phone is ringing.

2. Dexter wrestles with his math homework.

   Dexter is wrestling with his math homework.

3. James and Sylvia work in the emergency room.

   James and Sylvia are working in the emergency room.

4. I keep a journal of thoughts and observations.

   I am keeping a journal of thoughts and observations.

5. We polish all our old tools.

   We are polishing all our old tools.

B. Defining and Writing the Past Progressive Tense

Verbs in the *past progressive tense* have two parts: the past tense form of *to be* (*was* or *were*) plus the *-ing* form of the main verb.

Past Progressive Tense (*example verb: to play*)	
Singular	**Plural**
I *was playing*	we *were playing*
you *were playing*	you *were playing*
he she *was playing* it	they *were playing*

Compare the past tense with the past progressive tense below.

> (1) Larry worked at the bookstore.
>
> (2) Larry was working at the bookstore.

- Sentence (1) is in the past tense. Which word tells you this? _____worked_____

- Sentence (2) is also in the past tense. Which word tells you this? _____was_____

- Notice that the main verb in sentence (2), *working*, has no tense. Only the helping verb *was* shows tense.

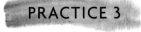

PRACTICE 3

Change each one-word past tense verb in the left-hand column to a two-part past progressive verb in the right-hand column. Do this by filling in the missing helping verb (*was* or *were*).

EXAMPLES: I flew.   I _____was_____ flying.

He wore my sweater.   He _____was_____ wearing my sweater.

Past Tense	**Past Progressive Tense**
1. Elsa and I set goals together.	1. Elsa and I _____were_____ setting goals together.
2. They ate quickly.	2. They _____were_____ eating quickly.
3. He planned the wedding.	3. He _____was_____ planning the wedding.
4. Our work began to pay off.	4. Our work _____was_____ beginning to pay off.
5. We posed for the photographer.	5. We _____were_____ posing for the photographer.
6. Maryann smiled.	6. Maryann _____was_____ smiling.
7. Sal did his Elvis impression.	7. Sal _____was_____ doing his Elvis impression.
8. I spoke Portuguese to Manuel.	8. I _____was_____ speaking Portuguese to Manuel.

9. My grandson got silly.

9. My grandson _____was_____ getting silly.

10. You probably wondered why.

10. You _____were_____ probably wondering why.

PRACTICE 4

Below are sentences in the past tense. Rewrite each sentence in the past progressive tense by adding the helping verb *was* or *were* and changing the form of the main verb to the *-ing* form.

EXAMPLE: You cooked dinner.

You were cooking dinner.

1. The two linebackers growled at each other.

The two linebackers were growling at each other.

2. Leroy examined his bank receipt.

Leroy was examining his bank receipt.

3. We watched the news.

We were watching the news.

4. Mila read the *Wall Street Journal* online.

Mila was reading the *Wall Street Journal* online.

5. He painted like a professional artist.

He was painting like a professional artist.

C. Using the Progressive Tenses

As you read these sentences, do you hear the differences in meaning?

> (1) Lenore *plays* the piano.
>
> (2) Dave *is playing* the piano.

● Which person is definitely at the keyboard right now?

● If you said Dave, you are right. He is *now in the process of playing* the piano. Lenore, on the other hand, *does* play the piano; she may also paint, write novels, and play center field, but we do not know from the sentence what she *is doing right now.*

● The present progressive verb *is playing* tells us that the action is *in progress.*

Here is another use of the present progressive tense:

> (3) Tony *is coming* here later.

● The present progressive verb *is coming* shows *future* time: Tony is going to come here.

(4) Linda *washed* her hair last night.

(5) Linda *was washing* her hair when we arrived for the party.

ESL TIP

ESL speakers may be confused by the progressive tenses or use them when simple present or past would be preferable. For extra quizzes on simple present vs. present progressive tense, see ‹http://ww2.college-em .qc.ca/prof/epritchard/ pcvspsqk.htm›.

- In sentence (4), *washed* implies a completed action.

- The past progressive verb in sentence (5) has a special meaning: that Linda was *in the process* of washing her hair when something else happened (we arrived).

- To say, "Linda *washed* her hair *when* we arrived for the party" means that first we arrived, and then Linda started washing her hair.

Writers in English use the progressive tenses *much less often* than the present tense and past tense. Use the progressive tense only when you want to emphasize that something is or was in the process of happening.

Use the *present progressive tense* (am, is, are + -ing) to show that an action is in progress now or that it is going to occur in the future.

Use the *past progressive tense* (was, were + -ing) to show that an action was in progress at a certain time in the past.

PRACTICE 5

Read each sentence carefully. Then circle the verb or verbs that best express the meaning of the sentence.

EXAMPLE: Right now, we (write, (are writing)) letters.

1. Thomas Edison ((held,) was holding) 1,093 patents.

2. Where is Ellen? She (drives, (is driving)) to Omaha.

3. Most mornings we ((get,) are getting) up at seven.

4. Believe it or not, I (thought, (was thinking)) about you when you phoned.

5. My dog Gourmand ((eats,) is eating) anything.

6. At this very moment, Gourmand (eats, (is eating)) the sports page.

7. Max (fried, (was frying)) onions when the smoke alarm ((went,) was going) off.

8. Please don't bother me now; I (study, (am studying)).

9. Newton (sat, (was sitting)) under a tree when he ((discovered,) was discovering) gravity.

10. The *Andrea Doria*, a huge pleasure ship, ((sank,) was sinking) on July 25, 1956.

D. Avoiding Incomplete Progressives

Now that you can write both present and past progressive verbs, avoid mistakes like this one:

We having fun. (*incomplete*)

- Can you see what is missing?

- All by itself, the *-ing* form *having* is not a verb. It has to have a helping verb.

● Because the helping verb is missing, *we having fun* has no time. It could mean *we are having fun* or *we were having fun*.

● *We having fun* is not complete. It is a fragment of a sentence.*

PRACTICE 6

Each group of words below is an incomplete sentence. Put an X over the exact spot where a word is missing. Then, in the Present Progressive column, write the word that would complete the sentence in the *present progressive tense*. In the Past Progressive column, write the word that would complete the sentence in the *past progressive tense*.

	Present Progressive	Past Progressive
EXAMPLE: He ˣhaving fun.	*is*	*was*
	(He is having fun.)	(He was having fun.)
1. Fran and I ˣwatching the sunrise.	are	were
2. You ˣtaking a computer course.	are	were
3. A big log ˣfloating down the river.	is	was
4. Her study skills ˣimproving.	are	were
5. I ˣtrying to give up caffeine.	am	was
6. Fights about money ˣgetting me down.	are	were
7. Thick fog ˣblanketing the city.	is	was
8. That child ˣreading already.	is	was
9. Your pizza ˣgetting cold.	is	was
10. They ˣdiscussing the terms of the new contract.	are	were

Chapter Highlights

● **The progressive tenses combine** *to be* **with the** *-ing* **verb form:**

present progressive tense: I *am reading*. He *is reading*.

past progressive tense: I *was reading*. He *was reading*.

● **The** *-ing* **verb form must have a helping verb to be complete:**

She playing the tuba. (*incorrect*)

She *is playing* the tuba. (*correct*)

● **The present progressive tense shows that an action is in progress now:**

Aunt Belle *is waxing* her van.

● **The present progressive tense can also show that an action will take place in the future:**

Later today, Aunt Belle *is driving* us to the movies.

● **The past progressive tense shows that an action was in progress at a certain time in the past:**

Aunt Belle *was waxing* her van when she heard thunder.

---

* For more on this type of fragment, see Chapter 10, Part B.

Proofreading Strategy

If you make progressive tense errors, you are probably leaving out one of the verb's two parts: either the helping verb (*am, is, are, was,* or *were*) or the main verb ending in *-ing*.

First, check for sentences in which the verb needs to express ongoing, continuous action. **Underline or highlight** those verbs and make sure that the **main verb ends in *-ing*.**

CORRECT   INCORRECT

The clock was striking midnight, but they still moving furniture into the house.

Then, check the helping verb. If the **helping verb** is missing, add one, making sure that it **agrees** with the subject of the sentence.

were

The clock was striking midnight, but they still moving furniture into the house.

WRITING AND PROOFREADING ASSIGNMENT

Write a brief account that begins, "We are watching an amazing scene on TV. A man/woman/child/couple/group/animal is trying to _____." Fill in the blank, and then write four or five more sentences describing the unfolding action in the *present progressive* tense—as if the action is taking place right now. Now carefully proofread what you have written, checking the verbs.

Now rewrite the whole account in the *past progressive* tense. The new version will begin, "We were watching an amazing scene on TV. A man/woman/child/couple/group/animal was trying to _____."

CHAPTER REVIEW

Proofread this paragraph for incomplete progressive verbs. Write the missing verbs above the lines.

LEARNING STYLES TIP

Have students read this paragraph aloud to better hear where the missing helping verbs belong.

(1) The sluggish economy ˄is prompting many people to seek new career directions. (2) They ˄are hoping to find jobs with bright futures. (3) By checking trusted sources like the U.S. Bureau of Labor Statistics at ‹http://www.bls.gov/oco/›, job-seekers ˄are learning about opportunities in fields like health care. (4) People always need doctors, nurses, and other medical professionals to help them stay healthy, but now, as baby boomers are aging, many jobs in the health sciences ˄are experiencing higher than average growth. (5) Some of these require only a two-year degree. (6) One example is the position of dental hygienist. (7) After they pass biology, science, and other courses, dental hygienists earn an associate's degree and must pass a certification exam. (8) Then they work in dentists' offices, cleaning patients' teeth and teaching them how to maintain oral health. (9) A typical full-time dental hygienist

is
now earning an annual income of about $60,000 or less in some areas. (10) The number of

are
positions will likely increase by 36 percent before 2018, so economists predicting excellent

employment opportunities for these technicians.

Excellent exployment opportunities exist for dental hygienists and other medical professionals.

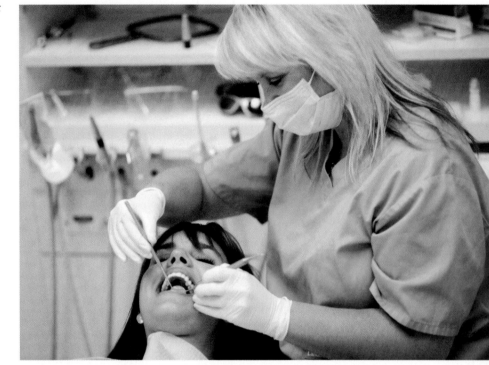

© Tracy Whiteside/Shutterstock.com

EXPLORING ONLINE

TEACHING TIP

Instructor tools for *Grass-roots* include a computerized Test Bank, PowerPoint slides, an Instructor's Manual with teaching tips, and more, and can be accessed at ‹**login .cengage.com**›.

<http://ww2.college-em.qc.ca/prof/epritchard/verblis9.htm> Interactive quiz: Practice progressive tense verbs as you visit Old Montreal.

<http://ww2.college-em.qc.ca/prof/epritchard/presconf.htm> Present tense or present progressive? Take the Used Car quiz and hone your skills.

CHAPTER 15

Fixed-Form Helping Verbs and Verb Problems

A: Defining and Spotting the Fixed-Form Helping Verbs

B: Using the Fixed-Form Helping Verbs

C: Using CAN and COULD

D: Using WILL and WOULD

E: Writing Infinitives

F: Revising Double Negatives

A. Defining and Spotting the Fixed-Form Helping Verbs

You already know the common—and changeable—helping verbs: *to have, to do,* and *to be*. Here are some helping verbs that do not change:

Fixed-Form Helping Verbs	
can	could
will	would
may	might
shall	should
must	

The fixed-form helping verbs do not change, no matter what the subject is. They always keep the same form.

 **PRACTICE 1**

Fill in each blank with a fixed-form helping verb. Answers will vary.

1. You _____can_____ do it!

2. This _____must_____ be the most exciting presidential debate ever held.

206

3. I _____will_____ row while you watch for crocodiles.

4. Rico _____might_____ go to medical school.

5. In South America, the elephant beetle _____may_____ grow to twelve inches in length.

6. If the committee _____can_____ meet today, we _____will_____ have a new budget on time.

7. We _____should_____ rotate the crops this season.

8. Violent films _____may_____ cause children to act out violently.

9. You _____should_____ have no difficulty finding a sales position.

10. Janice _____may_____ teach users to do research on the Internet.

B. Using the Fixed-Form Helping Verbs

> (1) Al will stay with us this summer.
>
> (2) Harper can shoot a rifle well.

- *Will* is the fixed-form helping verb in sentence (1). What main verb does it help? _____stay_____

- *Can* is the fixed-form helping verb in sentence (2). What main verb does it help? _____shoot_____

- Notice that *stay* and *shoot* are the simple forms of the verbs. They do not show tense by themselves.

When a verb has two parts—a fixed-form helping verb and a main verb—the main verb keeps its simple form.

 **PRACTICE 2**

In the left column, each sentence contains a verb made up of some form of *to have* (the changeable helping verb) and a past participle (the main verb).

Each sentence in the right column contains a fixed-form helping verb and a blank. Write the form of the main verb from the left column that correctly completes each sentence.

Have + **Past Participle**	**Fixed-Form Helping Verb + Simple Form**
EXAMPLES:	
I have talked to him.	I may _____talk_____ to him.
She has flown to Ireland.	She will _____fly_____ to Ireland.
1. Irena has written a song.	1. Irena must _____write_____ a song.
2. We have begun.	2. We can _____begin_____.
3. Joy has visited Graceland.	3. Joy will _____visit_____ Graceland.
4. He has slept all day.	4. He could _____sleep_____ all day.
5. I have run three miles.	5. I will _____run_____ three miles.

6. We have seen an eclipse.

7. It has drizzled.

8. Avery has gone on vacation.

9. Has he studied?

10. Della has been promoted.

6. We might _____see_____ an eclipse.

7. It may _____drizzle_____.

8. Fred could_____go_____ on vacation.

9. Should he _____study_____?

10. Della might _____be_____ promoted.

C. Using CAN and COULD

> (1) He says that I *can* use any tools in his garage.
>
> (2) He said that I *could* use any tools in his garage.

- What is the tense of sentence (1)? _____present_____
- What is the tense of sentence (2)? _____past_____
- What is the helping verb in sentence (1)? _____can_____
- What is the helping verb in sentence (2)? _____could_____
- As you can see, *could* may be used as the past tense of *can*.

> **Present tense:** Today, I *can* touch my toes.
>
> **Past tense:** Yesterday, I *could* touch my toes.

Can means *am/is/are able*. **It may be used to show present tense.**

Could means *was/were able* **when it is used to show the past tense of** *can*.

TEACHING TIP

The modal auxiliary verbs are complex, so you might wish to explain their more nuanced meanings, based upon the preparedness of your class.

> (3) If I went on a diet, I *could* touch my toes.
>
> (4) Rod wishes he *could* touch his toes.

- In sentence (3), the speaker *could* touch his toes *if* . . . . Touching his toes is a possibility, not a certainty.
- In sentence (4), Rod *wishes* he *could* touch his toes, but probably he cannot. Touching his toes is a wish, not a certainty.

Could **also means** *might be able*, **a possibility, a wish, or a request.**

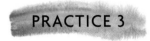 **PRACTICE 3**

Fill in the helper *can* or the helper *could*, whichever is needed. To determine whether the sentence indicates the present or the past, look at the other verbs in the sentence or look for words like *now* and *yesterday*.

1. When I am rested, I _____can_____ study for hours.

2. When I was rested, I _____could_____ study for hours.

3. Jorge insists that he _____can_____ play the trumpet.

4. Jorge insisted that he _____could_____ play the trumpet.

5. A year ago, Zora _____could_____ jog for only five minutes at a time.

6. Now Zora _____can_____ jog for nearly an hour at a time.

7. If you're so smart, how come you _____can_____ never find your own socks?

8. If you were so smart, how come you _____could_____ never find your own socks?

9. When the air was clear, you _____could_____ see the next town.

10. When the air is clear, you _____can_____ see the next town.

PRACTICE 4

Circle either *can* or *could*.

1. Hiliaria thinks that she ((can,) could) carry a tune.
2. Yesterday, we (can, (could)) not go to the town meeting.
3. I wish I (can, (could)) pitch like Johan Santana.
4. You should meet Naveed: he ((can,) could) lift a two-hundred-pound weight.
5. Everyone I meet ((can,) could) do a cartwheel.
6. Until the party, everyone thought that Harry (can, (could)) cook.
7. She ((can,) could) ice skate better now than she (can, (could)) last year.
8. On the night that Smithers disappeared, the butler (can, (could)) not be found.
9. When my brother was younger, he (can, (could)) name every car on the road.
10. I hope that the snow leopards ((can,) could) survive in captivity.

PRACTICE 5

On a separate paper, write five sentences using *can* to show present tense and five sentences using *could* to show past tense.

D. Using WILL and WOULD

(1) You know you *will* do well in that class.

(2) You knew you *would* do well in that class.

● Sentence (1) says that *you know* now (present tense) that you *will* do well in the future. *Will* points to the future from the present.

● Sentence (2) says that *you knew* then (past tense) that you *would* do well after that. *Would* points to the future from the past.

Would **may be used as the past tense of** *will*, **just as** *could* **may be used as the past tense of** *can*.

(3) *If* you studied, you *would* pass physics.

(4) Juanita wishes she *would* get an A in French.

● In sentence (3), the speaker *would* pass physics *if* . . . . Passing physics is a possibility, not a certainty.

● In sentence (4), Juanita *wishes* she *would* get an A, but this is a wish, not a certainty.

***Would* can also express a possibility, a wish, or a request.**

PRACTICE 6

Fill in the *will* or the *would*. To determine whether the sentence is in the present or the past, look at the other verbs in the sentence.

1. The meteorologist predicts that it _____will_____ snow on Friday.

2. The meteorologist predicted that it _____would_____ snow on Friday.

3. Hernan said that he _____would_____ move to Colorado.

4. Hernan says that he _____will_____ move to Colorado.

5. Roberta thinks that she _____will_____ receive financial aid.

6. Roberta thought that she _____would_____ receive financial aid.

7. I _____will_____ marry you if you propose to me.

8. Unless you stop adding salt, no one _____will_____ want to eat that chili.

9. Hugo thinks that he _____will_____ be a country and western star someday.

10. Because she wanted to tell her story, she said that she _____would_____ write an autobiography.

PRACTICE 7

Circle either *will* or *would*.

1. You (will, would) find the right major once you start taking courses.

2. When the house is painted, you (will, would) see how lovely the old place looks.

3. Yolanda wishes that her neighbor (will, would) stop raising ostriches.

4. The instructor assumed that everyone (will, would) improve.

5. They insisted that they (will, would) pick up the check.

6. The whole town assumed that they (will, would) live happily ever after.

7. When we climb the tower, we (will, would) see for miles around.

8. If I had a million dollars, I (will, would) buy a big house on the ocean.

9. Your flight to Mars (will, would) board in fifteen minutes.

10. Because we hated waiting in long lines, we decided that we (will, would) shop somewhere else.

E. Writing Infinitives

Every verb can be written as an **infinitive**. An infinitive has two parts: *to* + the simple form of the verb—*to kiss, to gaze, to sing, to wonder, to help*. Never add endings to the infinitive form of a verb: no *-ed*, no *-s*, no *-ing*.

(1) Quinn has *to take* a course in environmental law.

(2) Neither dictionary seems *to contain* the words I need.

● In sentences (1) and (2), the infinitives are *to take* and *to contain*.

● *To* is followed by the simple form of the verb: *take, contain*.

Don't confuse an infinitive with the preposition *to* followed by a noun or a pronoun.

(3) Tamara spoke *to Sam*.

(4) I gave the award *to her*.

● In sentences (3) and (4), the preposition *to* is followed by the noun *Sam* and the pronoun *her*.

● *To Sam* and *to her* are prepositional phrases, not infinitives.*

PRACTICE 8

Find the infinitives in the following sentences and write them in the blanks at the right.

Infinitive

EXAMPLE: Many people don't realize how hard
it is to write a funny essay.

to write

1. Our guests started to leave at midnight.

to leave

2. Marlena has decided to run for mayor.

to run

3. Han has to get a B on his final exam or he
will not transfer to Wayne State.

to get

4. It is hard to think with that radio blaring!

to think

5. The man wanted to buy a silver watch to
give to his son.

to buy, to give

PRACTICE 9

Write an infinitive in each blank in the following sentences. Use any verb that makes sense. Remember that the infinitive is made up of *to* plus the simple form of the verb.

Sample answers

1. They began _____ to dance _____ in the cafeteria.

2. Few people know how _____ to shake _____ well.

3. Would it be possible for us _____ to meet _____ again later?

4. He hopes _____ to become _____ an operating-room nurse.

5. It will be easy _____ to learn _____   _____ to knit _____.

F.   Revising Double Negatives

The most common **negatives** are *no, none, not, nowhere, no one, nobody, never,* and *nothing.*

The negative *not* is often joined to a verb to form a contraction: *can't, didn't, don't, hasn't, haven't,* and *won't,* for example.

However, a few negatives are difficult to spot. Read these sentences:

(1) There are hardly any beans left.

(2) By noon, we could scarcely see the mountains on the horizon.

● The negatives in these sentences are *hardly* and *scarcely.*

_____

* For more work on prepositions, see Chapter 9, Part C, and Chapter 25.

● They are negatives because they imply that there are *almost* no beans left and that we *almost couldn't* see the mountains.

Use only one negative in each idea. The double negative is an error you should avoid.

> (3) **Double negative:** I *can't* eat *nothing*.

● There are two negatives in this sentence—*can't* and *nothing*—instead of one.
● Double negatives cancel each other out.

To revise a double negative, simply drop one of the negatives.

> (4) **Revised:** I *can't* eat anything.
>
> (5) **Revised:** I can eat *nothing*.

● In sentence (4), the negative *nothing* has been changed to the positive *anything*.
● In sentence (5), the negative *can't* has been changed to the positive *can*.

When you revise double negatives that include the words *hardly* and *scarcely*, keep those words and change the other negatives to positives.

> (6) **Double negative:** They couldn't hardly finish their papers on time.

● The two negatives are *couldn't* and *hardly*.

> (7) **Revised:** They could hardly finish their papers on time.

● Change *couldn't* to *could*.

TEACHING TIP

Double negatives may not make the grade in college and work, but they add flavor to some songs and class discussions. Three examples are "(I Can't Get No) Satisfaction," "Ain't No Mountain High Enough," and Pink Floyd's "We don't need no education, we don't need no thought control" from "Another Brick in the Wall." Have your students bring in more examples; ask them whether double negatives work in pop culture.

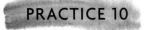 **PRACTICE 10**

Revise the double negatives in the following sentences. Answers will vary.

EXAMPLE: I don't have no more homework to do.

Revised: _I don't have any more homework to do._

1. I can't hardly wait for Christmas vacation.

   Revised: _I can hardly wait for Christmas vacation._

2. Ms. Chandro hasn't never been to Los Angeles.

   Revised: _Ms. Chandro has never been to Los Angeles._

3. Fido was so excited that he couldn't scarcely sit still.

   Revised: _Fido was so excited that he could scarcely sit still._

4. Nat won't talk to nobody until he's finished studying.

    Revised: _Nat won't talk to anybody until he's finished studying._

5. Yesterday's newspaper didn't contain no ads for large-screen television sets.

    Revised: _Yesterday's newspaper didn't contain any ads for large-screen television sets._

6. Alice doesn't have no bathing suit with her.

    Revised: _Alice doesn't have a bathing suit with her._

7. If Vasily were smart, he wouldn't answer no one in that tone of voice.

    Revised: _If Vasily were smart, he wouldn't answer anyone in that tone of voice._

8. Kylie claimed that she hadn't never been to a rodeo before.

    Revised: _Kylie claimed that she had never been to a rodeo before._

9. Some days, I can't seem to do nothing right.

    Revised: _Some days, I can't seem to do anything right._

10. Umberto searched, but he couldn't find his gold bow tie nowhere.

    Revised: _Umberto searched, but he couldn't find his gold bow tie anywhere._

Chapter Highlights

- **Fixed-form verbs do not change, no matter what the subject is:**

    I *can*.

    He *can*.

    They *can*.

- **The main verb after a fixed-form helping verb keeps the simple form:**

    I will *sleep*.

    She might *sleep*.

    Sarita should *sleep*.

- **An infinitive has two parts,** *to* + **the simple form of a verb:**

    to drive

    to exclaim

    to read

- **Do not write double negatives:**

    I didn't order no soup. (*incorrect*)

    I didn't order any soup. (*correct*)

    They couldn't hardly see. (*incorrect*)

    They could hardly see. (*correct*)

Proofreading Strategy

To proofread for the errors discussed in this chapter, **isolate your sentences** and **find key words.** If you write on a computer, reformat your draft to isolate your sentences, one sentence on each line. This can trick your eye and brain into seeing your words anew.

Now use your eyes or the *"Find"* feature to focus on terms related to your problem areas. For instance, if you have trouble with **fixed-form helping verbs** like *can, could, will,* and *would,* search for and highlight these words; then check the main verb following each one. If you write **double negatives,** find all the "negatives" in your paper (words like *no, none, not, nowhere, no one, nobody, never, nothing*) and check for correctness. Here is an example:

any

Make sure your paper doesn't have no fixed-form errors or double negatives.

WRITING AND PROOFREADING ASSIGNMENT

Review this chapter briefly. What part was most difficult for you? Write a paragraph explaining the difficult material to someone who is having the same trouble you had. Your purpose is to make the lesson crystal clear to him or her. As you proofread, search for key words that help you see your trouble spots.

CHAPTER REVIEW

Proofread the following essay for errors in fixed-form verbs, infinitives, and double negatives. Cross out each incorrect word and correct the error above the line.

Man of Honor

(1) According to public opinion polls, the most influential Hispanic American in the country is Edward James Olmos. (2) Olmos is someone who couldn't *could* never be happy promoting only himself. (3) He has tried to setting *set* an example for others through his choice of movie roles. (4) Olmos decided early in his career that he would not take no *any* parts in *Rambo-* and *Terminator*-style movies just to get rich. (5) Instead, he wanted his life's work to be something that he and his descendants will *would* be proud of.

(6) As a result, his film projects have included *American Me*, an examination of gang members and life in prison. (7) Young people have told him that this film convinced them that they should not have nothing *anything* to do with gangs. (8) Olmos is also famous for his portrayal of teacher Jaime Escalante in *Stand and Deliver*. (9) Other projects, from an anti–domestic violence documentary to a film about Brazilian political activist Chico Mendes called *The Burning Season*, aimed to educating *educate* the public.

Actor Edward James Olmos joins Latino leaders to support funding for early childhood education.

(10) Olmos also hopes that he ~~would~~ *will* change lives through his community activism. (11) He gives antidrug speeches. (12) In addition, Olmos visits public schools and promotes projects that help Latinos. (13) For example, he cofounded and now codirects the Los Angeles Latino International Film Festival. (14) The actor also supports the Latino Book and Family Festival and oversees Latino Public Broadcasting. (15) Olmos knows from experience that one person ~~could~~ *can* make a difference.

EXPLORING ONLINE

TEACHING TIP

Instructor tools for *Grassroots* include a computerized Test Bank, PowerPoint slides, an Instructor's Manual with teaching tips, and more, and can be accessed at ‹**login .cengage.com**›.

<http://www.bbc.co.uk/skillswise/game/en31vari-game-double-negatives>
Click the picture and "start" and play the double negatives game!

<http://leo.stcloudstate.edu/grammar/doubneg.html> Good review of double negatives from St. Cloud State University.

UNIT 3
Writing Assignments

As you complete each writing assignment, remember to perform these steps:

- Write a clear, complete topic sentence.
- Use freewriting, brainstorming, or clustering to generate ideas for the body of your paragraph, essay, or letter.
- Arrange your best ideas in a plan.
- Revise for support, unity, coherence, and exact language.
- Proofread for grammar, punctuation, and spelling errors.

Writing Assignment 1 *Tell a family story.* Many of us heard family stories as we were growing up—how our great-grandmother escaped from Poland, how Uncle Chester took his sister for a joy ride in the Ford when he was six. Assume that you have been asked to write such a story for a scrapbook that will be given to your grandmother on her eightieth birthday. Choose a story that reveals something important about a member of your family. As you revise, make sure that all your verbs are correct. Consider sharing your story online at a website that invites viewers to share their personal experiences. Try <http://www.africanaheritage.com/familystories.asp> or <http://www.ellisisland.org/Story/tellstory.asp>.

TEACHING TIP
Your students might wish to expand Assignment 2 and to nominate someone as a CNN Hero. Visit this site and click "Nominate": <http://www.cnn.com/SPECIALS/cnn.heroes/index.html>.

Writing Assignment 2 *Describe a person who takes a risk to help others.* In this unit, you might have read about Majora Carter, who vastly improved the quality of life for her South Bronx neighbors. She stood up and fought for the common good. Do you know someone who is a community crusader, a champion of children, or a person who otherwise helps others? Write a verbal portrait of this person, describing his or her activities and contributions. Select vivid verbs that capture his or her actions for the greater good.

Writing Assignment 3 *Describe a lively scene.* To practice choosing and using verbs, go where the action is—to a sports event, a busy store, a club, a public park, even the woods or a field. Observe carefully as you take notes and freewrite. Capture specific sounds, sights, colors, actions, and smells. Then write a description of what takes place, using lively verbs. Choose either present or past tense and make sure to use that tense consistently throughout.

Writing Assignment 4 *Describe a few intense moments.* Read paragraph A on page 217, which uses lively verbs to describe the saving of someone's life at a health club. This writer uses the present tense, as if the action is happening now. Describe some brief but dramatic event—the birth of a child, the opening of an important letter, the arrival of a blind date, or the reaction of the person to whom you just proposed. Decide whether present or past tense would be better, and choose varied, interesting verbs. As you revise, make sure the verbs are correct.

UNIT 3

Review

Transforming

A. Rewrite this paragraph, changing every *I* to *she*, every *me* to *her*, and every *us* to *them*. Do not change any verb tenses. Be sure all verbs agree with their new subjects, and make any other necessary changes.

(1) ~~I am~~ [She is] at the gym, training a client. (2) A man near ~~us~~ [them] gets off the treadmill and suddenly collapses onto the floor. (3) ~~I know~~ [She knows] that ~~I~~ [she] must act quickly. (4) ~~I shout~~ [She shouts], "Call 911!" (5) ~~I dash~~ [She dashes] to the portable defibrillator on the wall, ~~open~~ [opens] the box, and ~~remove~~ [removes] the device. (6) ~~I press~~ [She presses] the green start button and quickly ~~tear~~ [tears] off the unconscious man's T-shirt. (7) ~~I place~~ [She places] the two electrode pads on his chest and ~~plug~~ [plugs] them into the machine. (8) The defibrillator analyzes the man's heartbeat to determine whether his heart needs to be shocked. (9) It does. (10) The machine charges itself and warns ~~me~~ [her] not to touch the patient. (11) When ~~I press~~ [she presses] the orange button, the machine delivers a jolt and then checks to see if the patient needs another. (12) One is enough. (13) The man's skin almost instantly turns from gray to pink, and he has a pulse. (14) When the paramedics arrive, they tell ~~me~~ [her] that the defibrillator and ~~I~~ [she] probably saved his life.

Marcel Alfonso, student

TEACHING TIP

Ask students to think critically, discuss, and perhaps write about the "disturbing questions" left in Katrina's aftermath. Has enough been done to rebuild New Orleans?

B. Rewrite this paragraph, changing the verbs from present tense to past tense.

(1) It ~~is~~ [was] the morning of August 29, 2005. (2) Hurricane Katrina ~~churns~~ [churned] over the warm waters of the Gulf of Mexico and ~~bears~~ [bore] down on the coasts of Louisiana and Mississippi. (3) When it ~~makes~~ [made] landfall at 6:10 A.M., it ~~is~~ [was] a monster storm, packing 125-mile-an-hour winds and dumping 10 to 15 inches of rain. (4) Hurricane-force winds ~~rage~~ [raged] 120 miles outward from its center. (5) In the city of New Orleans, the storm ~~whips~~ [whipped] up huge waves in Lake Pontchartrain. (6) These waves ~~slam~~ [slammed] into the levees around the city, causing the levees to break. (7) Lake water ~~pours~~ [poured] into the city and ~~floods~~ [flooded] low-lying areas. (8) Winds and torrents ~~rip~~ [ripped] down telephone and power lines, ~~wash~~ [washed] away streets and bridges, and ~~level~~ [leveled] whole neighborhoods. (9) Many of the people still in their homes ~~swim~~ [swam] for their lives. (10) Others ~~scramble~~ [scrambled] to their rooftops, where they ~~wait~~ [waited], sometimes in vain, for rescue. (11) One of the greatest disasters in U.S. history, Hurricane Katrina ~~costs~~ [cost]

217

                             left   shattered

over \$100 billion in damages. (12) Far worse, it ~~leaves~~ over 1,800 people dead, ~~shatters~~

raised
millions of lives, and ~~raises~~ deeply disturbing questions.

Proofreading

The following essay contains both past tense errors and past participle errors. First, proofread for verb errors, underlining all the incorrect verbs. Then correct the errors above the lines. (You should find a total of thirteen errors.)

Protector of the Chimps

                          done
(1) Dr. Jane Goodall, DBE*, has <u>did</u> more than anyone else to understand the lives

of chimpanzees. (2) Always an animal lover, she was too poor to go to college to

study animals. (3) She worked as a waitress until the age of twenty-five. (4) Then she

                                    went
fufilled a lifelong dream and <u>gone</u> to East Africa. (5) There she was thrilled by the

beauty of the land and the wild animals.

                        met   recognized
(6) In Africa, she <u>meet</u> Louis Leakey, a famous naturalist. (7) Leakey <u>recognize</u>

Goodall's curiosity, energy, and passion for the natural world. (8) He hired her for a six-

month study of the wild chimpanzees in a national park in Tanzania. (9) Despite malaria,

primitive living conditions, and hostile wildlife, this determined woman followed

                                                            watched
the activities of a group of chimps in the Gombe Forest. (10) For months, she <u>watch</u>

the chimps through binoculars. (11) She moved closer and closer until she eventually

became
<u>become</u> part of their lives. (12) Dr. Goodall named the chimps and recorded their

* DBE: Dame of the British Empire, an honorary title in England, like "Knight."

Dr. Jane Goodall, DBE, Founder of the Jane Goodall Institute, communicates with a chimpanzee

daily activities. (13) She learned that chimps was [were] capable of feeling happiness, anger, and pain. (14) They formed complex societies with leaders, politics, and tribal wars. (15) One of her most important discoveries were [was] that chimps made and used tools. (16) Dr. Goodall expected to stay in Gombe for six months; instead she studied the chimps there for almost forty years. (17) Her studies lead [led] to a totally new understanding of chimps, and she became world famous.

(18) However, her life changed completely in 1986. (19) She attend [attended] a conference in Chicago, where she heard horrible stories about the fate of chimps outside Gombe. (20) She learned about the destruction of the forests and the wildlife of Africa. (21) From that day on, Dr. Goodall committed herself to education and conservation. (22) Since then, she has traveled, lectured, gave [given] interviews, and met with people. (23) She established both the Jane Goodall Institute and a young people's group, Roots & Shoots, and is a UN Messenger of Peace. (24) These worldwide organizations have already carry [carried] out many important conservation and educational projects. (25) The author of remarkable books and the subject of inspiring television specials, Dr. Goodall is knowed [known] for her total commitment to chimps and to a healthy natural world.

EXPLORING ONLINE

<http://www.janegoodall.org>

<http://www.worldwildlife.org> Visit the Jane Goodall Institute or the World Wildlife Fund to learn more about endangered species.

219

UNIT 3
Writers' Workshop
Tell a Family Story

A **narrative** tells a story. It presents the most important events in the story, usually in time order. Here, a student tells of her mother-in-law's inspiring journey to self-realization.

In your group or class, read this narrative essay aloud, if possible. As you read, underline any words or details that strike you as vivid or powerful.

Somebody Named Seeta

(1) Someone I deeply admire is my mother-in-law, Seeta, who struggled for years to become her best self. She was born in poverty on the sunny island of Trinidad. Seeta's father drank and beat his wife, and sadly, her mother accepted this lifestyle. Her parents did not believe in sending girls to school, so Seeta's daily chores began at 4:00 A.M. when she milked the cows. Then she fed the hens, scrubbed the house, cooked, and tended babies (as the third child in a family of ten children). During stolen moments, she taught herself to read. At age sixteen, this skinny girl with long black hair ran away from home.

(2) Seeta had nowhere to go, so her friend's family took her in. They believed in education, yet Seeta struggled for years to catch up and finish school. Even so, she calls this time her "foot in the door." She married my father-in-law and had four children, longing inside to become "somebody" someday. When their oldest was nine and the youngest two months, Seeta's husband died. She had to get a job fast. She cut sugar cane in the fields, wrapping her baby in a sheet on the ground. In the evenings, she hiked home to care for the other children. Word got around on the sugar estate that she was bringing a baby to work, so she was given a job indoors. All the while, Seeta stayed patient and hopeful that God would help her someday.

(3) In fact, after seven years, she moved with her children to America. She was so poor that she owned only one pot and one spoon. After she finished

cooking, the children would all gather around the pot, and sitting on the floor, they passed the spoon from one to another. My mother-in-law got a job at a department store, selling by day and cleaning offices at night. All the time, in the back of her head, she wanted to be somebody. A plan was taking shape. Eight years ago, my mother-in-law enrolled at this college, first for her GED and then for a college degree. She graduated and became a registered nurse.

(4) When I first met Seeta, I thought she did not like me. Was I wrong! She was just checking me out to see what I was made of. Did I too have goals to be conquered? She taught me that patience is a virtue but that one should never give up. She told me that even in modern America where women have their independence, she had to fight to hold on to hers. Today my mother-in-law is attending Lehman College at night for her master's degree in surgical nursing.

Rosalie Ramnanan, student

1. How effective is Rosalie Ramnanan's essay?
   _____Y_____ Clear thesis statement?   _____Y_____ Rich supporting details?
   _____Y_____ Logical organization?   _____Y_____ Effective conclusion?

2. Underline the thesis statement (main idea sentence) for the whole essay. The rest of the paper—a narrative—develops this idea.

3. Ramnanan uses different action verbs to help the reader see and hear the story, especially in paragraphs (1), (2), and (3). Can you identify them?

4. Why do you think the writer chose the title she did? How effective is it?

5. Proofread for grammar and spelling. Do you notice any error patterns (two or more errors of the same type) that this student should watch out for?
   No errors

Writing and Revising Ideas

1. Tell an inspiring story about one or more of your family members.

2. Use narrative to develop this topic or thesis sentence: Poverty or difficult circumstances can make some people stronger and more ambitious.

For help writing your paragraph or essay, see Chapters 3 to 7. As you revise, make sure that your main idea is clear and that your paper explains it. To add punch to your writing as you revise, replace *is, was, has,* and *had* with action verbs whenever possible.

UNIT 4

Joining Ideas Together

Too many short, simple sentences can make your writing sound monotonous. This unit will show you five ways to create interesting sentences. In this unit, you will

- Join ideas through *coordination* and *subordination*
- Use semicolons and conjunctive adverbs correctly
- Spot and correct run-ons or comma splices
- Join ideas with *who, which,* and *that*
- Join ideas by using *-ing* modifiers
- Learn proofreading strategies to find and correct your own errors

Spotlight on Reading and Writing

Here, writer Brent Staples uses several methods of joining ideas as he describes his first passionate kiss (at least, he was passionate). If possible, read the paragraph aloud.

I stepped outside and pulled the door closed behind me, and in one motion encircled her waist, pulled her to me, and whispered breathlessly that I loved her. There'd been no rehearsing this; the thought, deed, and word were one. "You do? You love me?" This amused her, but that didn't matter. I had passion enough for the two of us. When I closed in for the kiss, she turned away her lips and offered me her cheek. I kissed it feverishly and with great force. We stood locked this way until I came up for air. Then she peeled me from her and went inside for the flour.

Brent Staples, *Parallel Time*

- Brent Staples mixes simple sentences with sentences that join ideas in different ways. Sentences 2, 4, 6, and 8, for example, combine ideas in ways you will learn in this unit.

- Can you recognize what any of these methods are?

- How do you think the writer now feels about this incident from his youth? Does his tone seem angry, frustrated, or amused? Which sentences tell you?

Writing Ideas

- *Your first crush or romantic encounter*

- *A time you discovered that a loved one's view of the relationship was very different from your view of it*

CHAPTER 16

Coordination

As a writer, you will sometimes want to join short, choppy sentences to form longer sentences. One way to join two ideas is to use a comma and a **coordinating conjunction**.

(1) This car has many special features, and it costs less than $20,000.

(2) The television picture is blurred, but we will watch the football game anyway.

(3) She wants to practice her Italian, so she is going to Italy.

- Can you break sentence (1) into two complete and independent ideas or thoughts? What are they? Underline the subject and verb in each.

- Can you do the same with sentences (2) and (3)? Underline the subjects and verbs.

- In each sentence, circle the word that joins the two parts of the sentence together. What punctuation mark comes before that word?

- *And, but,* and *so* are called *coordinating conjunctions* because they coordinate, or join together, ideas. Other coordinating conjunctions are *for, nor, or,* and *yet.*

To join two complete and independent ideas, use a coordinating conjunction preceded by a comma. To help you remember these words, just think FANBOYS (the first letter of *for*, *and*, *nor*, *but*, *or*, *yet*, **and** *so*).

Now let's see just how coordinating conjunctions connect ideas:

TEACHING TIP

Students often overuse the conjunction *and.* Encourage them to think critically about the exact *relationship* between two independent ideas before they select a conjunction.

Coordinating Conjunctions		
and	*means*	in addition
but, yet	*mean*	in contrast
for	*means*	because
nor	*means*	not either
or	*means*	either, a choice
so	*means*	as a result

BE CAREFUL: *Then, also,* and *plus* are not coordinating conjunctions. By themselves, they cannot join two ideas.

> **Incorrect:** He studied, then he went to work.
>
> **Correct:** He studied, and then he went to work.

Read this paragraph, aloud if possible.

> Lucky found me over the Thanksgiving holiday. She was a gray and white tabby. She looked like a skeleton cat wearing a fur blanket. It was clear that she was starving. Her ribs and rump bone were sticking out. I got to work. I cut up some leftover turkey from the fridge. I popped it into the microwave for thirty seconds. My scrawny visitor ate every bit. I made a second plate and a third. Finally, she curled up on the kitchen mat. That day, Lucky joined our family.

This might have been a good paragraph, but all the short sentences sound monotonous, even childish. Here is the same paragraph, rewritten:

> Lucky found me over the Thanksgiving holiday. She was a gray and white tabby, *but* she looked like a skeleton cat wearing a fur blanket. It was clear that she was starving, *for* her ribs and rump bone were sticking out. I got to work. I cut up some leftover turkey from the fridge, *and* I popped it into the microwave for thirty seconds. My scrawny visitor ate every bit, *so* I made a second plate and a third. Finally, she curled up on the kitchen mat. That day, Lucky joined our family.

- Can you hear the difference? This paragraph sounds smoother and more sophisticated because it uses coordinating conjunctions to connect ideas.

- This writer has joined some of the short sentences into longer ones, using *but*, *for*, *and*, and *so*.

- Because these conjunctions join two complete ideas, a comma precedes the conjunction.

- Three times in this paragraph, *and* is used to join words that are *not* complete ideas. No comma is needed because they are not complete ideas. Find these three *ands*.

  She was a gray *and* white tabby. I made a second plate *and* a third.

REMEMBER: Coordinating conjunctions can join not just two independent ideas but also two words, two phrases, and two dependent clauses. **A comma goes before the conjunction *only* if it links two independent ideas.**

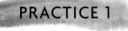

PRACTICE 1

TEACHING TIP

After students complete Practice 1, consider discussing their answers as a class so that they can see which conjunctions work in a sentence and which don't.

Read these sentences for meaning. Then fill in the coordinating conjunction (FANBOY) that best expresses the relationship between the two complete thoughts. REMEMBER: Do you want to *add, contrast, give a reason, show a result,* or *indicate a choice*? Answers will vary.

EXAMPLE: War is no game, _____*yet*_____ games are transforming modern warfare.

1. Young men and women today grew up playing computer games, _____*so*_____ the U.S. Army is using video games to recruit and train soldiers.

Soldiers train for combat on a new simulator that uses video game technology.

2. Since 2002, an online version of "America's Army" has attracted 6.5 million registered players, _____and_____ the game has been used for real combat training.

3. Video games can teach many skills needed in battle, _____and/for_____ they expose players to lifelike war zones such as deserts, jungles, and bombed-out villages.

4. Flashes, explosions, and deadly surprises are part of war, _____so_____ similar computer effects help players adjust to stressful conditions.

5. Some games teach the soldier to load, aim, and fire realistic weapons, _____for_____ he or she must engage in "deadly" combat with other players.

6. Virtual soldiers gain rewards for showing teamwork and bravery, _____and/but_____ they are penalized for sloppy preparation or safety violations.

7. In one scenario, a Humvee driver and gunner must work together, _____or_____ they both will "die."

8. The Army started its own $50 million video game division in 2010, _____so_____ its programmers can create even better and more realistic training games.

9. Critics say that military-themed video games are morally dangerous, _____for_____ they make killing a human enemy less real.

10. Some object to using games to sharpen the skills of shooters and snipers, _____but_____ for now, these games—like war—are here to stay.

EXPLORING ONLINE

<http://www.americasarmy.com/> Explore the America's Army website and perhaps play a video game. Do you think this site would encourage young men and women to enlist in the military? Why or why not? Jot down three reasons for your opinion, and write specifically about why this website would or would not inspire volunteers to enlist.

PRACTICE 2

Punctuate these sentences correctly by adding any missing commas. Write a *C* for "correct" next to a sentence that does not need a comma. To determine if a comma is needed, first locate the coordinating conjunction(s) in each sentence. Any coordinating conjunction that joins *two independent ideas* must be preceded by a comma.

1. Residents of the Greek island of Ikaria live longer, healthier lives than most ~~humans~~ humans, and scientists want to know why.

2. Many Ikarians thrive well into their ~~90s~~ 90s, but the average American lives only to 78.

3. Americans lose years of life to heart disease and ~~cancers~~ cancers, yet these diseases are rare in Ikaria.

4. A key factor in Ikarians' longevity seems to be a diet packed with beans and vegetables but low in meat and sugar. C

5. Ikarians consume wild local greens, herbal teas, and goat's ~~milk~~ milk, so their risk of high blood pressure and heart disease is reduced.

6. This healthy diet is ~~essential~~ essential, but regular exercise is another key factor.

7. Ikaria is a mountainous ~~island~~ island, so its steep terrain gives inhabitants a workout every time they leave home.

8. In addition, Ikarians refuse to rush through life and get lots of rest, including daily naps. C

9. Ikarian natives are lucky to share a strong sense of ~~community~~ community, for close bonds with family and friends promote longevity.

10. Ikarians may be some of the healthiest people on ~~earth~~ earth, but adopting the right habits can help anyone lead a longer, better life.

PRACTICE 3

Each of these thoughts is complete by itself, but you can join them together to make more interesting sentences. Combine pairs of these thoughts, using *and, but, for, nor, or, so,* or *yet,* and write six new sentences on the lines that follow. Punctuate correctly.

babies need constant supervision
Rico overcame his disappointment
in the 1840s, American women began to fight for the right to vote
I will write my essay at home tonight
the ancient Chinese valued peaches
he decided to try again
they are the best Ping-Pong players on the block
you should never leave them by themselves
I will write it tomorrow in the computer lab
they did not win that right until 1920
they can't beat my cousin from Cleveland
they believed that eating peaches made a person immortal

1. 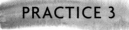 Babies need constant supervision, so you should never leave them by themselves.

2. I will write my essay at home tonight, or I will write it tomorrow in the computer lab.

3. In the 1840s, American women began to fight for the right to vote, yet they did not win that right until 1920.

4. Rico overcame his disappointment, and he decided to try again.

5. They are the best Ping-Pong players on the block, but they can't beat my cousin from Cleveland.

6. The ancient Chinese valued peaches, for they believed that eating peaches made a person immortal.

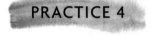

PRACTICE 4

Finish these sentences by adding a second complete idea after the coordinating conjunction. Sample answers

1. She often interrupts me, but _I try not to get upset._

2. Yuri has lived in the United States for ten years, so _his English is quite good._

3. Len has been married three times, and _now he's a widower._

4. I like owning a car, for _it allows me to drive to the country on weekends._

5. I like owning a car, but _I hate the repair bills._

PRACTICE 5

TEACHING TIP

Have each student write his or her best two Practice 5 sentences on the board. Then guide the class as it evaluates each sentence and identifies any needed edits.

On the lines below or on a computer, write seven sentences of your own, using each of the coordinating conjunctions—*and*, *but*, *for*, *nor*, *or*, *so*, and *yet*—to join two independent ideas. Punctuate correctly.

1. _____

2. _____

3. _____

4. _____

5. _____

6. _____

7. _____

Chapter Highlights

- **A comma and a coordinating conjunction join two independent ideas:**

The fans booed, *but* the umpire paid no attention.

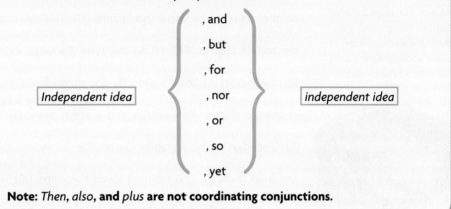

| Independent idea | { , and / , but / , for / , nor / , or / , so / , yet } | independent idea |

- **Note:** *Then, also,* **and** *plus* **are not coordinating conjunctions.**

Proofreading Strategy

Using coordination will improve your writing. Just proofread to make sure that you punctuate correctly.

1. **Search** for the seven coordinating conjunctions, or FANBOYS, and **highlight or underline** each one. If you are using a computer, use the *"Find"* feature to locate these words in your draft.

2. Check to see if each coordinating conjunction joins two complete ideas. Can the words on either side of it stand alone as complete sentences? If so, put a *comma* before the conjunction. Make sure you understand these examples.

CORRECT   CORRECT
The boss and his partner were very supportive but intolerant of those who arrived late for work.

INCORRECT   CORRECT
We paid but later Blanca and I regretted sending that check.

WRITING AND PROOFREADING ASSIGNMENT

Whether you are a teenager, a young adult, middle-aged, elderly, single, or part of a couple, there are characters in TV sitcoms who are supposed to represent you. Do these characters correctly portray the kind of person you are, or are you seeing one or more irritating exaggerations?

Write a letter of praise or complaint to a network that broadcasts one of these sitcoms. Make clear why you think a certain character does or does not correctly portray someone like you. Use examples and specific details. As you revise and proofread, avoid choppy sentences by joining ideas with coordinating conjunctions.

CHAPTER REVIEW

Read this paragraph of short, choppy sentences. Then rewrite it, using different coordinating conjunctions to combine some pairs of sentences. Keep some short sentences for variety. Copy your revised paragraph on a fresh sheet of paper. Punctuate with care. Answers will vary.

(1) Super Bowl parties everywhere owe a debt to Rebecca Webb ~~Carranza.~~ Carranza, yet most (2) ~~Most~~ people don't even know her name. (3) This Mexican-born entrepreneur invented the tortilla chip in 1948. (4) At the time, Carranza and her husband ran the El Zarape Tortilla Factory in Los Angeles. (5) Some tortillas always came off the conveyor belt in strange shapes. (6) Carranza threw them ~~away.~~ away, but she (7) ~~She~~ hated this waste of food. (8) One day before a family party, she cut some discarded tortillas into triangles and fried them. (9) The relatives loved the ~~chips.~~ chips, for they (10) ~~They~~ could easily grab a handful or dip the crunchy morsels in sauce. (11) Carranza began selling her chips for 10 cents a bag in her Mexican delicatessen and factory. (12) By the 1960s, she had named them Tort Chips, and her (13) ~~Her~~ factory now manufactured nothing but this irresistible snack. (14) Demand for the chips took ~~off.~~ off, so Carranza (15) ~~Carranza~~ is now recognized as a snack-food industry pioneer.

(16) She received awards for her work, including, appropriately, two Golden Tortillas.

EXPLORING ONLINE

<http://web2.uvcs.uvic.ca/elc/studyzone/330/grammar/coconj1.htm> Fill in the right coordinating conjunction; the computer checks your answers.

<http://grammar.ccc.commnet.edu/grammar/quizzes/nova/nova1.htm> Interactive quiz: Place commas in sentences with coordinating conjunctions.

CHAPTER 17

Subordination

A: **Defining and Using Subordinating Conjunctions**

B: **Punctuating Subordinating Conjunctions**

A. Defining and Using Subordinating Conjunctions

Another way to join ideas together is with a **subordinating conjunction**. Read this paragraph:

> A great disaster happened in 1857. The SS *Central America* sank. This steamship was carrying six hundred wealthy passengers from California to New York. Many of them had recently struck gold. Battered by a storm, the ship began to flood. Many people on board bailed water. Others prayed and quieted the children. Thirty hours passed. A rescue boat arrived. Almost two hundred people were saved. The rest died. Later, many banks failed. Three tons of gold had gone down with the ship.

This could have been a good paragraph, but notice that all the sentences are short and choppy.

Here is the same paragraph, rewritten to make it more interesting:

> A great disaster happened in 1857 *when* the SS *Central America* sank. This steamship was carrying six hundred wealthy passengers from California to New York. Many of them had recently struck gold. Battered by a storm, the ship began to flood. Many people on board bailed water *while* others prayed and quieted the children. *After* thirty hours passed, a rescue boat arrived. Almost two hundred people were saved *although* the rest died. Later, many banks failed *because* three tons of gold had gone down with the ship.

- Note that the paragraph now reads more smoothly and is more interesting because the following words were used to join some of the choppy sentences: *when, while, after, although,* and *because.*

- *When, while, after, although,* and *because* are part of a large group of words called *subordinating conjunctions.* As you can see from the paragraph, these conjunctions join ideas.

BE CAREFUL: Once you add a *subordinating conjunction* to an idea, that idea can no longer stand alone as a complete and independent sentence. It has become a subordinate or dependent idea; it must rely on an independent idea to complete its meaning.*

ESL TIP

ESL students tend to write dependent clause fragments. In some languages, like Japanese, freestanding dependent clauses are accepted as correct. Further, ESL students often duplicate English oral patterns, in which freestanding dependent clauses are common.

(1) He is tired.
(2) Because he is tired, he will take a nap. _____

(3) I left the room.
(4) As I left the room, the waiter dropped a tray of desserts. _____

(5) You speak Spanish.
(6) If you speak Spanish, you may have some interesting job opportunities. _____

- (1), (3), and (5) are all complete sentences, but once a subordinating conjunction is added, they become dependent ideas. They must be followed by something else—a complete and independent thought.

- (2), for example, could be completed like this: Because he is tired, *he won't go out to eat with us.*

- Add an independent idea to complete each dependent idea on the lines above.

Below is a partial list of subordinating conjunctions.

Common Subordinating Conjunctions		
after	even though	when
although	if	whenever
as	since	where
as if	so that	whereas
as though	though	wherever
because	unless	whether
before	until	while

Each subordinating conjunction expresses a specific *relationship* between two ideas in a sentence. Let's look at some of these relationships:

Subordinating Conjunctions	Meaning	One Example
after, as, before, since, until, when, whenever, while	To show different time relationships	*When* her son was diagnosed with autism, Monique started her research.

_____

* For more work on sentence fragments of this type, see Chapter 10, Part C.

although, even though, though, whereas, while	To show a contrast or contradiction	I love classical music *even though* my parents did not.
as though, as if	To show something *seems* true but is not	He acts *as if* he owned the club.
because, since, so that	To show a reason, a cause, or an effect	He told the truth *because* he respects you.
even if, if, unless, whether	To show a condition for something to happen	*Even if* one has a college degree, good jobs can be hard to find.

PRACTICE 1

Read these sentences for meaning. Then fill in the subordinating conjunction that best expresses the relationship between the two ideas. Answers will vary.

1. _____If_____ you are like most people, you resist admitting mistakes or hurtful actions.

2. _____Although_____ it is commonly thought that apologizing shows weakness, an apology actually requires great strength.

3. A genuine apology is a powerful tool _____because_____ it can repair damaged relationships, heal humiliation, and encourage forgiveness.

4. _____If_____ we learn to apologize sincerely, psychologists say, we can prevent grudges, revenge, and a lot of pain.

5. _____Whenever_____ you apologize to someone, remember the key ingredients of a successful apology.

6. _____Whether_____ you have hurt someone's feelings or betrayed that person, you must first admit your wrongdoing.

7. Specifically describe what you did _____so that_____ you reveal an understanding of your offense and its impact.

8. Say, for example, "I'm sorry for hurting you _____when_____ I criticized you in front of your friends."

9. _____As_____ you apologize, you must communicate remorse with both your words and your body language.

10. The other person will question your sincerity _____unless_____ you seem truly distressed and sorry.

11. _____After_____ you admit your transgression, you should explain your actions.

12. For instance, "My behavior occurred _____while_____ I was feeling stressed (or tired, frustrated, angry)."

13. _____Before_____ you end your apology, reassure the offended person.

14. Explain that you did not intend to wound him or her _____even though_____ you did so.

15. _____Although_____ it is difficult, an apology will be worth the effort.

PRACTICE 2

Now that you understand how subordinating conjunctions join thoughts together, try these sentences. Here you have to supply one idea. Make sure that the ideas you add have subjects and verbs. Sample answers

1. The cafeteria food improved when _the college hired a new food manager._____

   _____

2. Because Damon and Luis both love basketball, _they often attend local games.____

   _____

3. If _the store won't refund his money,_____

   Peyton plans to get legal advice.

4. I was repairing the roof while _Noah was ironing clothes._____

   _____

5. Before _you write that article,_____

   you should get all the facts.

B.   Punctuating Subordinating Conjunctions

As you may have noticed in the preceding exercises, some sentences with subordinating conjunctions use a comma whereas others do not. Here is how it's done.

(1) Because it rained very hard, we had to leave early.

(2) We had to leave early because it rained very hard.

● Sentence (1) has a comma because the dependent idea comes before the independent idea.

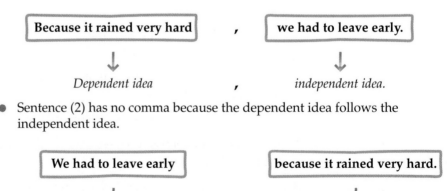

| **Because it rained very hard** | **,** | **we had to leave early.** |

Dependent idea , *independent idea.*

● Sentence (2) has no comma because the dependent idea follows the independent idea.

| **We had to leave early** | **because it rained very hard.** |

Independent idea *dependent idea.*

Use a comma after a dependent idea; do not use a comma before a dependent idea.

PRACTICE 3

If a sentence is punctuated correctly, write C in the blank. If it is not, punctuate it correctly by adding or deleting a comma.

1. Whenever Americans get hungry ~~hungry~~ they want to eat quickly. _____

2. When McDonald's opened in ~~1954~~ 1954, it started a trend that continues today. _____

3. Whether you are talking about pizza or ~~hamburgers~~ hamburgers, fast food is big business—
   earning more than $110 billion a year. _____

4. Fast food is appealing because it is cheap, tasty, and—of course—fast. _C_

5. While it has many ~~advantages~~ advantages, fast food also presents some health hazards. _____

6. Although the industry is ~~booming~~ booming, many people are worried about the amount
   of fat in fast foods. _____

7. Whereas some nutritionists recommend eating only thirty-five grams of fat a
   ~~day~~ day, you often eat more than that in just one fast-food meal. _____

8. If you order a Burger King Double Whopper with ~~cheese~~ cheese, you take in a
   whopping sixty-three grams of fat. _____

9. That goes up to sixty-seven fat grams whenever you devour a McDonald's
   Big Mac, large fries, and chocolate shake. _C_

10. Now some fast-food restaurants are claiming to serve low-fat items so that
    they can attract health-conscious customers. _C_

11. However, you still must pay attention to the ingredients ~~ingredients,~~ if you want to make
    sure that your meal is healthy. _____

12. For example, most grilled or roasted chicken sandwiches are relatively low in

fat before they are slathered with mayonnaise and special sauces. _____C_____

13. Because just one tablespoon of mayonnaise or salad dressing contains eleven

fat ~~grams~~ these tasty toppings add gobs of extra fat and calories. _____
    grams,

14. Although they might taste ~~delicious~~ cheese and cheese sauces also add
    delicious,

surprising quantities of fat to a meal. _____

15. When you next order your favorite fast ~~food~~ don't forget to say,
    food,

"Hold the sauce!" _____

PRACTICE 4

Correctly combine each pair of ideas in two ways: with the subordinating conjunction at the beginning of the sentence and with the subordinating conjunction in the middle. For each pair, write in the subordinating conjunction that expresses the relationship between these ideas. Then make sure you punctuate each sentence correctly. Answers may vary.

EXAMPLE: _____*Although*_____ marriage exists in all societies, every culture has unique wedding customs.

Every culture has unique wedding customs _____*although*_____ marriage exists in all societies.

1. _____*When*_____ young couples in India marry, the ceremony may last for days.
   The ceremony may last for days _____*when*_____ young couples in India marry.

2. _____*After*_____ the wedding takes place at the bride's home, everyone travels to the groom's home for more celebrating.
   Everyone travels to the groom's home for more celebrating _____*after*_____ the wedding takes place at the bride's home.

3. Ducks are often included in Korean wedding processions _____*because*_____ they mate for life.
   _____*Because*_____ they mate for life, ducks are often included in Korean wedding processions.

4. Iroquois brides gave grain to their mothers-in-law _____*whereas*_____ mothers-in-law gave meat to the brides.
   _____*Whereas*_____ Iroquois brides gave grain to their mothers-in-law, mothers-in-law gave meat to the brides.

5. _____*When*_____ the food was exchanged, the bride and groom were considered married.
   The bride and groom were considered married _____*when*_____ the food was exchanged.

6. _____*Until*_____ the tradition went out of style, Finnish brides and grooms used to exchange wreaths.
   Finnish brides and grooms used to exchange wreaths _____*until*_____ the tradition went out of style.

7. A Zulu wedding is not complete _____*unless*_____ the bride, groom, and bridal party dance special dances.
   _____*Unless*_____ the bride, groom, and bridal party dance special dances, a Zulu wedding is not complete.

8. The bride stabs at imaginary enemies with a knife _____ as _____ she dances wildly and gloriously.

   _____ As _____ the bride dances wildly and gloriously, she stabs at imaginary enemies with a knife.

9. _____ Although _____ the wedding ring is a very old symbol, the elaborate wedding cake is even older.

   The wedding ring is a very old symbol _____ although _____ the elaborate wedding cake is even older.

10. _____ Whereas _____ the ring symbolizes the oneness of the new couple, the cake represents fertility.

    The cake represents fertility _____ whereas _____ the ring symbolizes the oneness of the new couple.

PRACTICE 5

Now try writing sentences of your own. Fill in the blanks, being careful to punctuate correctly. Do not use a comma before a dependent idea.

1. _____ because

   _____.

2. Although _____

   _____.

3. _____ whenever

   _____.

4. Unless _____

   _____.

Chapter Highlights

- **A subordinating conjunction joins a dependent idea and an independent idea:**

  When I registered, all the math courses were closed.

  All the math courses were closed *when* I registered.

- **Use a comma after a dependent idea.**

  After
  Because
  Before
  If
  Since
  Unless
  When
  While

  dependent idea, independent idea.

● Do not use a comma before a dependent idea.

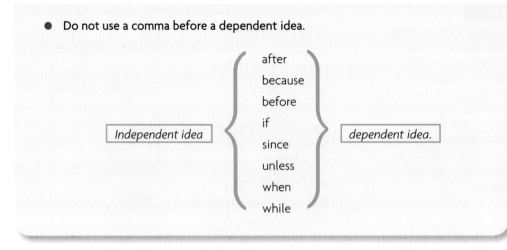

Independent idea

{
after
because
before
if
since
unless
when
while
}

dependent idea.

Proofreading Strategy

Joining ideas with subordinating conjunctions will add sophistication to your writing, but be sure to proofread for correct punctuation.

1. **First, search the document for any subordinating conjunctions** (like *although, because, before, when,* etc.). **Highlight or underline** these words.

2. If a dependent idea comes first in the sentence, **use a comma to separate the dependent from the independent idea.** You know you have the comma in the right spot if there is a complete sentence *after* the comma. Here are two examples:

   Independent idea   dependent idea
   Lia enrolled in classes every semester until she finished her associate degree.

   Dependent idea   independent idea
   When Jorge gets home from work, he takes his dogs for a walk.

WRITING AND PROOFREADING ASSIGNMENT

Imagine that you are a teacher planning a lesson on courtesy for a class of young children. Use a personal experience, either positive or negative, to illustrate your point. Brainstorm, freewrite, or cluster to generate details for the lesson. Then write what—and how—you plan to teach. Keeping in mind that you are trying to reach young children, make sure that the significance of the experience you will describe is clear. When you finish drafting, read over your lesson and look for ideas you can join with subordinating conjunctions. Underline the subordinating conjunctions you use, and check your punctuation.

Form small groups to discuss one another's lessons. Which are most convincing? Why? Would children learn more from examples of good behavior or from examples of bad behavior?

CHAPTER REVIEW

Read this paragraph of short, choppy sentences. Then revise it by making changes above the lines, using different subordinating conjunctions to combine pairs of sentences. Keep some short sentences for variety. Punctuate with care. Answers will vary.

TEACHING TIP

After students try the Chapter Review on their own, consider reading aloud "before" and "after" versions of the paragraph so that students can hear how much smoother the revision sounds. Also, ask them whether the newly combined sentences help them understand the information better.

(1) Jacob Lawrence was a great American painter, a powerful teller of stories on canvas. (2) ~~Young~~ Jacob joined his mother in Harlem in ~~1930.~~ ~~(3) He~~ began to paint the people around him. (4) Luckily, he found excellent art classes in ~~Harlem.~~ ~~(5) The~~ big art academies often excluded blacks then. (6) ~~He~~ was only ~~23.~~ ~~(7) He~~ gained fame for his sixty-picture *Migration Series*. (8) A New York gallery displayed these ~~paintings.~~ ~~(9) No~~ major commercial gallery had showcased an African American artist before. (10) The *Migration Series* depicts southern blacks journeying north to find work after World War I. (11) The paintings show people searching for a better life. (12) Lawrence's work portrays the poverty and prejudice the migrants ~~endured.~~ ~~(13) He~~ also wanted viewers of his work "to experience the beauty of life." (14) During his long career, Lawrence painted many more energetic canvases and series. (15) His work reminds us that we are all ~~migrants.~~ ~~(16) We~~ are always on the move. (17) We are seeking something more.

(handwritten annotations: After young; 1930, he; Harlem because the; When he; 23, he; paintings although no; Although; endured, he; migrants because we)

EXPLORING ONLINE

See Lawrence's paintings at the Whitney Museum of Art online. <http://www.whitney.org/Collection/JacobLawrence/>

Learn about Lawrence's Migration series at the Phillips Collection. <http://www.phillipscollection.org/collection/migration-series/> Describe your favorite painting for someone who has never seen it.

"Street Scene," 1962 by Jacob Lawrence

TEACHING TIP

Students can learn more about this great American painter and view excellent images of Lawrence's work on the Whitney Museum and The Phillips Collection websites.

EXPLORING ONLINE

TEACHING TIP

Instructor tools for *Grassroots* include a computerized Test Bank, PowerPoint slides, an Instructor's Manual with teaching tips, and more, and can be accessed at ‹**login .cengage.com**›.

<http://a4esl.org/q/h/vm/conj02.html> Quiz with answers: Combine sentences with a conjunction.

<http://web2.uvcs.uvic.ca/elc/studyzone/330/grammar/subcon.htm> Explanation of subordination followed by interactive practice sets.

CHAPTER **18**

Avoiding Run-Ons and Comma Splices

N ow that you have had practice in joining ideas together, here are two serious errors to watch out for: the **run-on** and the **comma splice**. If run-ons and comma splices are among your personal error patterns, pay close attention to this chapter.

> **Run-on:** Herb talks too much nobody seems to mind.

- There are two complete ideas here: *Herb talks too much* and *nobody seems to mind.*
- A *run-on* incorrectly runs together two complete ideas without using a conjunction or punctuation.

> **Comma splice:** Herb talks too much, nobody seems to mind.

- A *comma splice* incorrectly joins two complete ideas with a comma but no conjunction.

    BE CAREFUL: Run-ons and comma splices are considered serious mistakes in college and the workplace because they force readers to stop, back up, and try to figure out where one idea ends and another begins.

    Here are three ways to correct a run-on or a comma splice:

1. **Write two separate sentences, making sure each is complete.**

    Herb talks too much. Nobody seems to mind.

2. **Use a comma and a coordinating conjunction or FANBOY** (*for, and, nor, but, or, yet, so*).*

    Herb talks too much, *but* nobody seems to mind.

3. **Use a subordinating conjunction** (for example, *although, because, if,* or *when*).**

    Although Herb talks too much, nobody seems to mind.

---

* For more work on coordinating conjunctions, see Chapter 16.
** For more work on subordinating conjunctions, see Chapter 17.

Try This Try this "run-on" test, which works for some people. Ask **"Is it true that . . ."** followed by the test sentence. If the answer is *yes,* the sentence is correct; if the answer is *no,* it is a run-on or comma splice.

Is it true that _Many drivers in my city don't use their blinkers to warn the driver behind_

them that they are going to turn this reckless behavior really frustrates me ? **NO**

This confusing example gets a *no,* so try breaking it into possible sentences:

Is it true that _Many drivers in my city don't use their blinkers to warn the driver behind_

them that they are going to turn ? **YES**

Is it true that _this reckless behavior really frustrates me_ ? **YES**

PRACTICE 1

Many of these sentences contain run-ons or comma splices. If a sentence is correct, write *C* in the right-hand column. If it contains a run-on or a comma splice, write either *RO* or *CS.* Then correct the error in any way you wish. Use each method at least once. Answers will vary.

EXAMPLE: When a
A talented celebrity like actor Heath Ledger dies of a drug

overdose, we remember the dreadful price of addiction. _CS_

1. Because a   addiction,
A number of celebrities struggle with ~~addiction~~ public awareness of

addiction has increased. _RO_

2. Often politicians, athletes, and actors hide their addiction and their
recovery because
~~recovery;~~ they do not want to risk ruining their careers. _CS_

3. Other celebrities are forced to go public in their battles with alcohol

or drugs. _C_

4. so
A few feel that their struggles may help others, they want to act as positive

role models. _CS_

5. lady. With
One such person was Betty Ford, a former first ~~lady with~~ her family's

help, she became sober at age sixty. _RO_

6. Because her   successful,
~~Her~~ recovery was ~~successful~~ she agreed to help several friends create

a treatment center in Rancho Mirage, California. _RO_

7. At the Betty Ford Center, celebrities like Keith Urban as well as everyday

people receive support for their new way of life. _C_

8. for
Treatment centers now exist around the country, the problem of addiction

seems to be increasing, especially among the young. _CS_

9. For example, Drew Barrymore was famous at age six for her role in the
but
film *E.T.,* by age nine she was addicted to drugs and alcohol. _CS_

10. Forced into rehab at age thirteen, Drew was able to get her acting

career back on track. _C_

11. After Fergie   Ecstasy,
~~Fergie~~ kicked her addiction to crystal methamphetamine and ~~Ecstasy~~

this lead vocalist for the Black Eyed Peas went on to become one of

music's biggest stars. _RO_

Although actress
12. ~~Actress~~ Eva Mendes and actor Robert Downey Jr. likewise developed
addictions,
~~addictions~~ getting treatment helped them stay on top in their profession.   _RO_

13. Legendary athlete and NBA coach John Lucas went through detox, turned
his life around, and now helps athletes recover.   _C_

14. Alcohol and drugs might seem glamorous, especially to the young, ^yet^ they
can destroy relationships, careers, and self-esteem.   _CS_

Although millions
15. ~~Millions~~ of Americans are affected, when someone returns from substance
abuse, his or her triumph can encourage others to seek help.   _CS_

PRACTICE 2

Label each sentence *RO* or *CS*. Then correct each run-on (RO) or comma splice (CS) in two ways. Be sure to punctuate correctly. Answers will vary.

EXAMPLE: "Awesome" is an overused word awe can change us. *RO*

a. _Awesome is an overused word, but awe can change us._

b. _Although awesome is an overused word, awe can change us._

1. A child might feel awe gazing at the Grand Canyon, wonder and reverence fill her. CS

a. A child might feel awe gazing at the Grand Canyon as wonder and reverence fill her.

b. A child might feel awe gazing at the Grand Canyon. Wonder and reverence fill her.

2. Researchers tested 63 students, they wanted to study the effects of awe. CS

a. Researchers tested 63 students because they wanted to study the effects of awe.

b. Researchers tested 63 students, for they wanted to study the effects of awe.

3. They showed different videos to two groups they recorded the reactions. RO

a. They showed different videos to two groups, and they recorded the reactions.

b. As they showed different videos to two groups, they recorded the reactions.

4. Some students watched waterfalls, whales, and astronauts in space this group felt awe. RO

a. Some students watched waterfalls, whales, and astronauts. This group felt awe.

b. Some students watched waterfalls, whales, and astronauts, and this group felt awe.

5. Others watched scenes of people having fun this group felt happiness. RO

   a. Others watched scenes of people having fun. This group felt happiness.

   _____

   b. Others watched scenes of people having fun, and this group felt happiness.

   _____

6. Later, the awe group felt that time slowed down stress lifted. RO

   a. Later, because the awe group felt that time slowed down, stress lifted.

   _____

   b. Later, the awe group felt that time slowed down, so stress lifted.

   _____

7. The other group did not feel this slowing of time their to-do lists still worried them. RO

   a. The other group did not feel this slowing of time, so their to-do lists still worried them.

   _____

   b. The other group did not feel this slowing of time. Their to-do lists still worried them.

   _____

8. People who often feel awe are more creative, they are better problem solvers. CS

   a. People who often feel awe are more creative. They are better problem solvers.

   _____

   b. People who often feel awe are more creative, and they are better problem solvers.

9. Children who experience awe feel more connected to others, they are kinder people. CS

   a. Children who experience awe feel more connected to others, so they are kinder people.

   _____

   b. Because children who experience awe feel more connected to others, they are kinder.

   _____

10. The ocean, a night sky, a thrilling concert, a wild animal all can evoke awe what experiences would bring you more awe? RO

    a. The ocean, a night sky, a concert, a wild animal all can evoke awe. What experiences might bring

    you more awe?

    b. The ocean, a night sky, a concert, a wild animal can all evoke awe, so what experiences might

    bring you more awe?

Chapter Highlights

Avoid run-ons and comma splices:

Error: Her house faces the ocean the view is breathtaking. (*run-on*)

Error: Her house faces the ocean, the view is breathtaking. (*comma splice*)

Use these techniques to avoid run-ons and comma splices:

- Write two complete sentences.

   Her house faces the ocean. The view is breathtaking.

- Use a coordinating conjunction (*for, and, nor, but, or, yet, so*).

   Her house faces the ocean, *so* the view is breathtaking.

- Use a subordinating conjunction (*although, before, because, when,* etc.).

   Because her house faces the ocean, the view is breathtaking.

Proofreading Strategy

Proofread your work very carefully if comma splices are among your error patterns.

1. Go back through your draft and **circle every comma** in every sentence.

2. For each comma, ask yourself, *"Would substituting a period for this comma create a complete sentence that could stand alone?"*

   NO   YES

   Before he joined the Army, he completed his associate's degree, he also married his high-school sweetheart.

3. If the answer is yes, you have written a comma splice and will need to replace the comma with **a period or keep the comma and add a coordinating conjunction after it.**

   Before he joined the Army, he completed his associate's degree, and he married his high-school sweetheart.

WRITING AND PROOFREADING ASSIGNMENT

TEACHING TIP

If some students have never held a job, suggest that they summarize their academic achievements, volunteer work, and interests.

A letter of application, which is a vital job-search tool, always includes a paragraph that summarizes the applicant's qualifications for a particular job. Write a summary of your work experience, beginning with your very first job and moving in chronological order from that job to your current job. Include both paid and volunteer positions. For each job, provide your dates of employment and a brief description of your major responsibilities. A letter of application must be error-free, so proofread it carefully. Exchange papers with a classmate and check each other's work, especially for comma splices and run-ons.

CHAPTER REVIEW

Run-ons and comma splices are most likely to occur in paragraphs or longer pieces of writing. Proofread each of the following paragraphs for run-ons and comma splices. Correct them in any way that makes sense: make two separate sentences, add a coordinating conjunction, or add a subordinating conjunction. Make your corrections above the lines. Punctuate with care. Answers will vary.

A. (1) Sodas and other sugary drinks are hugely popular, earning the beverage companies a whopping $60 billion a year. (2) The average American male 12 to 19 years old drinks

year, so that's

898 cans of soda a ~~year, that's~~ 2½ cans a day. (3) The average young female drinks about

675 cans a year. (4) Every can of Coke, Dr. Pepper, 7UP, or other soda contains at least

sugar. These

10 teaspoons of added ~~sugar, these~~ days, fast-food chains and manufacturers are pushing

sugar while a

larger and larger sodas. (5) A 20-ounce bottle of soda has 20 teaspoons of ~~sugar a~~ 1-liter

bottle has 31 teaspoons. (6) No wonder soda has been called "liquid candy." (7) Except for

water, sugar is the main ingredient in every brand. (8) Soda companies don't want customers

to know that their products are a major factor in America's obesity and diabetes epidemics.

year, and a

(9) Drinking a can of soda a day puts on 15 pounds a ~~year, a~~ daily 20-ounce soda packs on

when

25 pounds. (10) Sarah Bradley was a self-described soda addict, 40 pounds overweight, she

and her two children decided enough was enough. (11) They cut out all soda and fruit juice

and encouraged each other to get more active. (12) Sarah and the kids have lost 35 pounds

among them. (13) "It's up to us to get healthy," Sarah says, "or the soda companies will just

get rich by making us fat and sick."

but

B. (1) Skateboarder Tony Hawk has not only dramatically changed his sport, he also has

contributed to the popularity of all extreme sports. (2) The wholesome Hawk is responsible

hoodlums. Now

for cleaning up skateboarding's early reputation as the pastime of rebels and ~~hoodlums now~~

it's an acceptable, mainstream activity. (3) Hawk is also famous for defying the laws of physics

to create amazing new aerial acrobatics. (4) In 1999, at the age of 31, he was the first skater

900. This

ever to complete a ~~900, this~~ is a 360-degree spin done two-and-a-half times in midair. (5) As

a result, he is called "the Michael Jordan of skateboarding." (6) Today, although he has retired

country, and

from competition, he performs in exhibitions all over the ~~country~~ surveys of young people

reveal that he is more popular than Shaquille O'Neal or Tiger Woods. (7) Hawk's fame has created a huge interest in skateboarding. (8) In 2005, 10.3 million Americans six years old or

older played baseball, 11.4 million skateboarded. (9) Today, these young athletes roll into skate

but

parks that have sprung up all over the country, thanks to Hawk's influence.

C.   (1) What do you do every night before you go to sleep and every morning when you

but

wake up? (2) You probably brush your teeth, most people in the United States did not

start brushing their teeth until after the 1850s. (3) People living in the nineteenth century

toothpaste, so

did not have ~~toothpaste,~~ Dr. Washington Wentworth Sheffield developed a tooth-

cleaning substance, which soon became widely available. (4) With the help of his son, this

toothpaste. It

Connecticut dentist changed our daily habits by making the first ~~toothpaste it~~ was called

Because the

Dr. Sheffield's Creme Dentifrice. (5) ~~The~~ product was not marketed cleverly enough, the

tubes, and

idea of using toothpaste caught on slowly. (6) Then toothpaste was put into tin ~~tubes~~

everyone wanted to try this new product. (7) Think of life without tubes of mint-flavored

toothpaste, and

~~toothpaste~~ then thank Dr. Sheffield for his idea.

because

D.   (1) The first semester of college is difficult for many students they must take on many

new responsibilities. (2) For instance, they must create their own schedules. (3) New students

courses. In

get to select their ~~courses in~~ addition, they have to decide when they will take them.

textbooks. Colleges

(4) Students also must purchase their own ~~textbooks, colleges~~ do not distribute textbooks

end, yet

each term as high schools do. (5) No bells ring to announce when classes begin and ~~end~~

students are supposed to arrive on time. (6) Furthermore, many professors do not call the

roll, for

~~roll~~ they expect students to attend classes regularly and know the assignments. (7) Above

all, new students must be self-disciplined. (8) No one stands over them telling them to do

help. They

their homework or to visit the writing lab for extra ~~help, they~~ must balance the temptation

to have fun and the desire to build a successful future.

Last Words

E.   (1) Every 14 days, a language somewhere in the world dies. (2) For example, the last

Jones. When

fluent speaker of the Alaskan language of Eyak was Chief Marie ~~Jones, when~~ she passed

away in 2008, Eyak died with her. (3) Languages are disappearing on every continent.

A teacher at the Nixyaawii Charter School in Mission, Oregon, gives a lesson in an endangered Native American language.

(4) North America has 200 Native American languages, ~~,~~ only about 50 now have more than *but*

a thousand speakers. (5) ~~The~~ endangered Gaelic language is undergoing a revival in Ireland, *Although the*

the other Celtic languages in northwestern Europe have been declining for generations. (6)

The death of languages is most noticeable in isolated communities in Asia, South America,

and Australia, however. (7) Each tiny community might have its own ~~language~~ only a few *language, so*

people speak it.

(8) In such small communities, a whole language can die if one village perishes. (9) When

Westerners explored a rain forest in Venezuela in the ~~1960s~~ they carried a flu virus into a *1960s,*

tiny community. (10) The virus killed all the villagers, ~~their~~ language disappeared with them. *and*

(11) However, most languages fade out when a smaller community comes into close contact

with a larger, more powerful ~~one, people~~ begin to use the "more important" language. *one. People*

(12) A language that gives better access to education, jobs, and new technology usually

prevails over a native mother tongue.

(13) According to scholars who study languages, almost half of the world's 7,000 languages

are in danger of extinction. (14) That statistic represents more than the loss of specific

~~languages,~~ every language represents a way of looking at the world. (15) Whenever a language *languages because*

disappears, we lose a unique point of view. (16) No other language can really take its place.

PRACTICE 3   Teamwork: Critical Thinking and Writing

In a group with several classmates, reread and discuss Chapter Review, Paragraph A, on sugary drinks. Did you find any of the facts or statistics powerful or surprising? Which ones? How many sodas or fruit juices does each member of your group drink daily? What size of soda or fruit juice does each of you usually drink? A can? A medium bottle? A large bottle? Sarah Bradley changed her family's beverage habits. Can anything be done to encourage other families to cut back on sugar consumption?

EXPLORING ONLINE

TEACHING TIP

Instructor tools for *Grassroots* include a computerized Test Bank, PowerPoint slides, an Instructor's Manual with teaching tips, and more, and can be accessed at ‹**login .cengage.com**›.

<http://depts.dyc.edu/learningcenter/owl/exercises/run-ons_ex1.htm>
Interactive quiz: Correct the run-ons and click for your score.

<http://grammar.ccc.commnet.edu/grammar/quizzes/nova/nova4.htm>
Interactive quiz: Find and fix the comma splices in these sentences.

<http://www.uvu.edu/owl/infor/test_n_games/games/fragments/gameshow/
gameshow/index.html> Game show! Win fake cash and real pride as you identify the worst sentence errors.

CHAPTER 19

Semicolons and Conjunctive Adverbs

A: **Defining and Using Semicolons**

B: **Defining and Using Conjunctive Adverbs**

C: **Punctuating Conjunctive Adverbs**

A. Defining and Using Semicolons

TEACHING TIP

Students may have a tendency to use semicolons inappropriately. You might want to emphasize that there are only *two* uses for the semicolon: (1) to separate two sentences, and (2) to separate items in a series that contains internal commas.

So far you have learned to join ideas together in two ways.

Coordinating conjunctions (*and, but, for, nor, or, so, yet*) can join ideas:

> (1) This is the worst food we have ever tasted, *so* we will never eat in this restaurant again.

Subordinating conjunctions (for example, *although, as, because, if,* and *when*) also can join ideas:

> (2) *Because* this is the worst food we have ever tasted, we will never eat in this restaurant again.

ESL TIP

Few languages use the semicolon as English does. ESL students may be helped by a preliminary discussion of how punctuation is used in their native languages.

Another way to join ideas is with a **semicolon**:

> (3) This is the worst food we have ever tasted; we will never eat in this restaurant again.

A *semicolon* **joins two related independent ideas without a conjunction; do not capitalize the first word after a semicolon unless it is a word that is always capitalized, like someone's name.**

Use the semicolon for variety. In general, use no more than one or two semicolons in a paragraph.

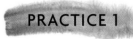
PRACTICE 1

Each independent idea that follows is the first half of a sentence. Add a semicolon and a second complete idea, one that can stand alone. Sample answers

EXAMPLE: Domingo was a cashier at Food City *; now he manages the store.*

1. My cat spotted a mouse *; both of them ran in opposite directions.*

2. The garage became an art studio *; it was filled with canvases and old magazines for collage images.*

3. Beatrice has an unlisted phone number *; I have it programmed into my phone.*

4. I felt sure someone had been in the room *; my coat was not where I had left it.*

5. Roslyn's first car had a stick shift *; her second one has an automatic transmission.*

Semicolons should connect two *related independent ideas*. If two ideas do not have a close relationship—such as a cause and its effect, a comparison of two like things, or a time order relationship—the sentences probably should be separated with a period.

BE CAREFUL: Do not use a semicolon between a dependent idea and an independent idea.

> Although he is never at home, he is not difficult to reach at the office.

- You cannot use a semicolon in this sentence because the first idea (*although he is never at home*) cannot stand alone.

- The word *although* requires that another idea be added in order to make a complete sentence.*

PRACTICE 2

Which of these ideas can be followed by a semicolon and an independent thought? Check them (✔).

1. When Molly peered over the counter _____
2. The library has installed new computers ✔
3. After he finishes cleaning the fish _____
4. She suddenly started to laugh ✔
5. My answer is simple ✔
6. I cannot find my car keys ✔
7. The rain poured down in buckets ✔
8. Before the health fair is over _____
9. Unless you arrive early _____
10. Because you understand, I feel better ✔

* For work on subordinating conjunctions, see Chapter 17.

Now copy the sentences you have checked, add a semicolon, and complete each sentence with a second independent idea. You should have checked sentences 2, 4, 5, 6, 7, and 10. Sample answers

2. The library has installed new computers; we can find information faster now.

   _____

4. She suddenly started to laugh; her dog had switched on the light.

   _____

5. My answer is simple; I will go.

   _____

6. I cannot find my car keys; I have looked everywhere.

   _____

7. The rain poured down in buckets; everyone left the stands.

   _____

10. Because you understand, I feel better; I am ready to try again.

   _____

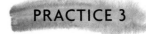

PRACTICE 3

Proofread for incorrect semicolons and capital letters. Make your corrections above the lines.

(1) The Swiss Army knife is carried in the pockets and purses of millions of travelers, campers, and just plain folks. (2) Numerous useful gadgets are folded into its famous red handle; ~~These~~ these include knife blades, tweezers, scissors, toothpick, screwdriver, bottle opener, fish scaler, and magnifying glass. (3) Because the knife contains many ~~tools;~~ tools, it is also carried by explorers, mountain climbers, and astronauts. (4) Lives have been saved by the Swiss Army knife. (5) It once opened the iced-up oxygen system of someone climbing Mount Everest; ~~It~~ it saved the lives of scientists stranded on an island, who used the tiny saw on the knife to cut branches for a fire. (6) The handy Swiss Army knife was created for Swiss soldiers in ~~1891; and~~ 1891 and soon became popular all over the world. (7) It comes in many models and ~~colors many~~ colors; many people prefer the classic original. (8) The Swiss Army knife deserves its reputation for beautiful design and usefulness; a red one is on permanent display in New York's famous Museum of Modern Art.

B. Defining and Using Conjunctive Adverbs

Another excellent method of joining ideas is to use a semicolon and a special kind of adverb. This special adverb is called a **conjunctive adverb** because it is part *conjunction* and part *adverb*.

(1) (a) He received an A on his term paper; *furthermore,*

    (b) the instructor exempted him from the final.

- *Furthermore* adds idea (b) to idea (a).
- The sentence might have been written, "He received an *A* on his term paper, *and* the instructor exempted him from the final."
- However, *furthermore* is stronger and more emphatic.
- Note the punctuation.

(2) (a) Luzette has never studied finance; *however,*

    (b) she plays the stock market like a pro.

- *However* contrasts ideas (a) and (b).
- The sentence might have been written, "Luzette has never studied finance, *but* she plays the stock market like a pro."
- However, the word *however* is stronger and more emphatic.
- Note the punctuation.

(3) (a) The complete dictionary weighs 30 pounds; *therefore,*

    (b) I have a dictionary app on my phone.

- *Therefore* shows that idea (a) is the cause of idea (b).
- The sentence might have been written, "*Because* the complete dictionary weighs 30 pounds, I have a dictionary app on my phone."
- However, *therefore* is stronger and more emphatic.
- Note the punctuation.

A *conjunctive adverb* **may be used with a semicolon only when both ideas are independent and can stand alone.**

Here are some common conjunctive adverbs and their meanings:

Common Conjunctive Adverbs		
consequently	*means*	as a result
for example	*means*	as one example
furthermore	*means*	in addition
however	*means*	in contrast
in fact	*means*	in truth, to emphasize
instead	*means*	in place of
meanwhile	*means*	at the same time
nevertheless	*means*	in contrast
otherwise	*means*	as an alternative
therefore	*means*	for that reason

Conjunctive adverbs are also called **transitional expressions**. They help the reader see the transitions, or changes in meaning, from one idea to the next.

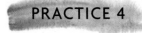
PRACTICE 4

Add an idea after each conjunctive adverb. The idea you add must make sense in terms of the entire sentence, so keep in mind the meaning of each conjunctive adverb. If necessary, refer to the chart. Sample answers

EXAMPLE: Several students had questions about the final; therefore, *they stayed after class to chat with the instructor.*

1. Aunt Bessie did a handstand; meanwhile, Uncle Sid pole-vaulted over the fence.

2. Anna says whatever is on her mind; consequently, she sometimes offends people.

3. I refuse to wear those red cowboy boots again; furthermore, I won't wear the ten-gallon hat.

4. Travis is a good role model; otherwise, his little son might not be so polite.

5. Kim wanted to volunteer at the hospital; however, she couldn't find time to take the training course for volunteers.

6. My mother carried two bulky pieces of luggage off the plane; furthermore, she had her coat and a tennis racket under her arm.

7. I have many chores to do today; nevertheless, I will take time to shoot some baskets.

8. The gas gauge on my car does not work properly; therefore, I record my mileage every time I fill the gas tank.

C. Punctuating Conjunctive Adverbs

Notice the punctuation pattern:

> Complete idea; conjunctive adverb, complete idea.

- The conjunctive adverb is preceded by a semicolon.
- It is followed by a comma.

PRACTICE 5

Highlight or underline the conjunctive adverb in each sentence. Then punctuate each sentence correctly.

1. For centuries, humans have tried to understand why we ~~dream consequently~~ many different theories have been proposed.
   <small>dream; consequently,</small>

2. To the ancients, dreams had divine ~~meaning for example~~ the Greeks thought a god actually entered the sleeper and delivered a message.
   <small>meaning; for example,</small>

3. The ancient Egyptians also looked for divine guidance in ~~dreams furthermore~~, they built dream temples for this purpose.
   <small>dreams; furthermore,</small>

4. In 1899, Sigmund Freud brought attention to dreams ~~again in fact~~ his book *Interpretation of Dreams* helped create modern psychology.
   <small>again; in fact,</small>

5. According to Freud, dreams don't deal with conscious problems at ~~all instead~~ they reveal our *unconscious* thoughts, desires, and fears.
   <small>all; instead,</small>

6. A dream about being fired might reveal a hidden wish for a new ~~career therefore~~ analyzing such a dream might expand one's self-knowledge.
   <small>career; therefore,</small>

7. In the last ten years, brain scientists have proposed many new theories about why we ~~dream furthermore~~ two of these have become widely accepted.
   <small>dream; furthermore,</small>

Fantastic images like this ship appear to us in dreams. Do dreams send messages, solve problems, or just cause brain static?

8. The first idea is that we dream to exercise our ~~brains, consequently~~ our minds will be
   alert in the morning.
   brains; consequently,

9. The second idea is that we dream to solve problems from the day ~~before in fact~~
   college students given a logic problem right before bed often discovered the
   answers in their sleep.
   before; in fact,

10. We may not study or even remember our ~~dreams, however;~~ dreaming seems to play
    an important role in our lives.
    dreams; however,

PRACTICE 6

Writing Assignment

Have you ever had a dream that sparked a new idea or new insights? Has a dream ever
helped you find a solution to a problem you faced? Have you ever gained new awareness
of your hidden thoughts and feelings because of a dream?

   Write a description of an important dream you have had, and then explain the effects,
if any, this dream had on your actions and decisions.

PRACTICE 7

Combine each set of sentences into one, using a conjunctive adverb. Choose a conjunctive
adverb that expresses the relationship between the two ideas. Punctuate with care. Answers
will vary.

1. a. Belkys fell asleep on the train.

   b. She missed her stop.

   Combination: _Belkys fell asleep on the train; therefore, she missed her stop._
   _____

2. a. Last night Channel 20 televised a special about gorillas.

   b. I did not get home in time to see it.

   Combination: _Last night Channel 20 televised a special about gorillas; however, I did not get home_
   in time to see it.

3. a. Roberta writes to her nephew every month.

   b. She sends a gift with every letter.

   Combination: _Roberta writes to her nephew every month; furthermore, she sends a gift with_
   every letter.

4. a. It takes me almost an hour to get to school each morning.

   b. The scenery makes the drive a pleasure.

   Combination: _It takes me almost an hour to get to school each morning; nevertheless, the scenery_
   makes the drive a pleasure.

5. a. Luke missed work on Monday.

   b. He did not proofread the quarterly report.

   Combination: _Luke missed work on Monday; consequently, he did not proofread the quarterly_
   report.

BE CAREFUL: Never use a semicolon and a conjunctive adverb when the conjunctive adverb does not join two independent ideas.

(1) *However,* I don't climb mountains.

(2) I don't, *however,* climb mountains.

(3) I don't climb mountains, *however.*

- Why aren't semicolons used in sentences (1), (2), and (3)?
- These sentences contain only one independent idea; therefore, a semicolon cannot be used.

Never use a semicolon to join two ideas if one of the ideas is subordinate to the other.

(4) If I climbed mountains, *however,* I would hike in the Rockies.

- Are the two ideas in sentence (4) independent?
- *If I climbed mountains* cannot stand alone as an independent idea; therefore, a semicolon cannot be used.

Chapter Highlights

- **A semicolon joins two related independent ideas:**

    I like hiking; she prefers fishing.

- **Do not capitalize the first word after a semicolon unless it is always capitalized.**

    | *Independent idea* | ; | *independent idea.* |

- **A semicolon and a conjunctive adverb join two independent ideas:**

    We can't go rowing now; *however,* we can go on Sunday.

    Lou earned an 83 on the exam; *therefore,* he passed physics.

    Independent idea
    ; consequently,
    ; furthermore,
    ; however,
    ; instead, *independent idea.*
    ; meanwhile,
    ; nevertheless,
    ; therefore,

- **Use a semicolon only when the conjunctive adverb joins two independent ideas:**

    I wasn't sorry; however, I apologized. (*two independent ideas*)

    I apologized, however. (*one independent idea*)

    If you wanted to go, however, you should have said so. (*one dependent idea + one independent idea*)

Proofreading Strategy

Use semicolons and conjunctive adverbs to add style and variety to your writing; just proofread with care, especially for punctuation errors. **Highlight or underline any conjunctive adverbs** (like *however*, *consequently*, and *for example*). Make sure the ideas on both sides of the conjunctive adverb are complete. Add any missing semicolons and commas.

Now **circle the semicolons.** Make sure the ideas on both sides are complete, closely related thoughts. No word after a semicolon should be capitalized unless it is always capitalized, like the pronoun "I" or someone's name. Here are two examples:

My dog Garbo badly needed a bath; ~~She~~ *she* was sprayed by a skunk.

Randy grabbed the dog shampoo and filled the wading pool with water *water; however,* however; Garbo had other ideas.

WRITING AND PROOFREADING ASSIGNMENT

Many people find that certain situations make them nervous or anxious—for example, taking a test or meeting strangers at a social gathering. Have you ever conquered such an anxiety yourself or even learned to cope with it successfully?

Write to someone who has the same fear you have had; encourage him or her with your success story, explaining how you managed the anxiety. Describe the steps you took.

Use one or two semicolons and at least one conjunctive adverb in your paper. Make sure that you are joining two independent ideas. Finally, highlight your conjunctive adverbs and circle your semicolons. Check for correctness.

CHAPTER REVIEW

Proofread this paragraph for semicolon errors, conjunctive adverb errors, and punctuation or capitalization errors. You might use the proofreading strategy above.

(1) Shakira is a more than a gifted Colombian singer and ~~songwriter she~~ *songwriter; she* is also a philanthropist, determined to give children a brighter future. (2) By the age of 8, Shakira had decided she would succeed as a professional ~~musician; In addition~~ *musician; in addition,* she vowed to use her fame and money to help children. (3) In her hometown of Barranquilla, Colombia, she saw countless children struggle in ~~poverty consequently;~~ *poverty; consequently,* at 18 she released *Pies Descalzos* ("Barefoot"), her breakthrough album in Latin America. (4) As her fame grew, Shakira started the Pies Descalzos Foundation to provide education for poor children. (5) Because violence and conflict have long plagued ~~Colombia;~~ *Colombia,* many families have lost their stable communities. (6) Today, Pies Descalzos sponsors six schools throughout that country, offering family services and classes for children. (7) Subjects include reading, writing, and ~~art,~~ *art;* furthermore,

Shakira meets with Israeli and Palestinian children as a UNICEF Goodwill Ambassador.

David Vaaknin/Getty Images

the schools aim to help students grow emotionally and socially. (8) Shakira's work with children extends beyond her foundation; she serves as a UNICEF Goodwill Ambassador and honorary chairperson of the Global Campaign for Education. (9) This exceptional woman wants education and a bright future for every ~~child, meanwhile~~; child; meanwhile, she is writing songs and producing her next album. (10) Once asked what part of her body she likes best, Shakira replied, "My brain."

EXPLORING ONLINE

<http://owl.english.purdue.edu/owl/resource/607/04/> Comma or semicolon? Review the rules.

<http://grammar.ccc.commnet.edu/grammar/cgi-shl/quiz.pl/run-ons_add1 .htm> Interactive quiz: Bring your semicolon style to these frumpy run-ons!

CHAPTER 20

Relative Pronouns

A: Defining and Using Relative Pronouns

B: Punctuating Ideas Introduced by WHO, WHICH, or THAT

A. Defining and Using Relative Pronouns

To add variety to your writing, you sometimes may wish to use **relative pronouns** to combine two sentences.

ESL TIP

For ESL students and *visual learners*, color coding can help show how relative clauses can be embedded in the main sentence or independent clause.

(1) My grandfather is 80 years old.

(2) He collects stamps.

● Sentences (1) and (2) are grammatically correct.

● They are so short, however, that you may wish to combine them.

(3) My grandfather, *who* is 80 years old, collects stamps.

● Sentence (3) is a combination of (1) and (2).

● *Who* has replaced *he*, the subject of sentence (2). *Who* introduces the rest of the idea, *is 80 years old.*

● *Who* is called a *relative pronoun* because it *relates* "is 80 years old" to "my grandfather."*

BE CAREFUL: An idea introduced by a relative pronoun cannot stand alone as a complete and independent sentence. It is dependent; it needs an independent idea (like "My grandfather collects stamps") to complete its meaning.

TEACHING TIP

You may want to take a moment to review with students what they learned about correcting fragments in Chapter 10, Part C. Point out that the sentences they completed in Practice 6 on page 134 are all relative pronoun clause fragments.

Here are some more combinations:

(4) He gives great singing lessons.

(5) All his pupils love them.

(6) He gives great singing lessons, *which* all his pupils love.

* For work on subject-verb agreement with relative pronouns, see Chapter 11, Part E.

ESL TIP

ESL students face formidable challenges with relative clauses. In English and most European languages, the relative clause *follows* the noun being modified, but in several languages (e.g., Japanese, Chinese, and Korean), the relative clause *precedes* the noun being modified.

(7) I have a large dining room.

(8) It can seat 20 people.

(9) I have a large dining room *that* can seat 20 people.

● As you can see, *which* and *that* can also be used as relative pronouns.

● In sentence (6), what does *which* relate or refer to? ___great singing lessons___

● In sentence (9), what does *that* relate or refer to? ___a large dining room___

When *who, which,* and *that* are used as relative pronouns, they usually come directly after the words they relate to.

> *My grandfather, who . . .*
>
> *. . . singing lessons, which . . .*
>
> *. . . dining room that . . .*

TEACHING TIP

Students will need to memorize that the pronoun *that* is not used with a comma and the pronoun *which* is.

Relative Pronouns
BE CAREFUL: *Who, which,* and *that* cannot be used interchangeably.
Who **refers to people.**
Which **refers to things.**
That **refers to things.**

PRACTICE 1

TEACHING TIP

Sentence-combining exercises like Practice 1 are an excellent way for students to practice writing more sophisticated sentences. Students will find more sentence-combining practice in this book, and they can try the interactive, computer-graded exercises at ‹**http://grammar.ccc .commnet.edu/grammar/ combining_skills.htm**›.

Combine each set of sentences into one sentence. Make sure to use *who, which,* and *that* correctly. Answers will vary.

EXAMPLE: a. The garden is beginning to sprout.

b. I planted it last week.

Combination: *The garden that I planted last week is beginning to sprout.*

1. a. My uncle is giving me diving lessons.
    b. He was a state champion.

    Combination: ___My uncle, who was a state champion, is giving me diving lessons.___

    ___

2. a. Our marriage ceremony was quick and sweet.
    b. It made our nervous parents happy.

    Combination: ___Our marriage ceremony, which was quick and sweet, made our nervous parents___ ___happy.___

3. a. The manatee is a sea mammal.
    b. It lives along the Florida coast.

    Combination: ___The manatee is a sea mammal that lives along the Florida coast.___

    ___

4. a. Donna bought a new backpack.

   b. The backpack has thickly padded straps.

   Combination: _Donna bought a new backpack that has thickly padded straps._

   _____

5. a. This walking tour has 32 stops.

   b. It is a challenge to complete.

   Combination: _This walking tour, which has 32 stops, is a challenge to complete._

   _____

ESL TIP

Spanish does not distinguish between personal (*who*) and impersonal (*which, that*) pronouns in the same way that English does. Furthermore, a relative pronoun cannot be omitted in Spanish, as it has been in the English sentence *The girls we saw looked so happy.*

6. a. Hockey is a fast-moving game.

   b. It often becomes violent.

   Combination: _Hockey, which is a fast-moving game, often becomes violent._

   _____

7. a. Andrew Jackson was the seventh U.S. president.

   b. He was born in South Carolina.

   Combination: _Andrew Jackson, who was born in South Carolina, was the seventh U.S. president._

   _____

8. a. At the beach, I always use sunscreen.

   b. It prevents burns and lessens the danger of skin cancer.

   Combination: _At the beach, I always use sunscreen, which prevents burns and lessens the danger of skin cancer._

   _____

B. Punctuating Ideas Introduced by WHO, WHICH, or THAT

Ideas introduced by relative pronouns can be one of two types, **restrictive** or **nonrestrictive**. Punctuating them must be done carefully.

Restrictive

> Never eat peaches *that are green*.

TEACHING TIP

A caution for students: improper punctuation of relative pronoun clauses can create fragments, and wrong placement can create dangling or misplaced modifiers.

- A *relative clause* has (1) a subject that is a relative pronoun and (2) a verb.
- What is the relative clause in the sentence in the box? _that are green_
- Can you leave out *that are green* and still keep the basic meaning of the sentence?
- No! You are not saying *don't eat peaches*; you are saying don't eat *certain kinds* of peaches—*green* ones.
- Therefore, *that are green* is *restrictive*; it restricts the meaning of the sentence.

A *restrictive clause* **is not set off by commas because it is necessary to the meaning of the sentence.**

Nonrestrictive

My guitar, *which is a Martin*, was given to me as a gift.

● In this sentence, the relative clause is ___which is a Martin___.

● Can you leave out *which is a Martin* and still keep the basic meaning of the sentence?

● Yes! *Which is a Martin* merely adds a fact. It does not change the basic idea of the sentence, which is *my guitar was given to me as a gift.*

● Therefore, *which is a Martin* is *nonrestrictive;* it does not restrict or change the meaning of the sentence.

A *nonrestrictive clause* **is set off by commas because it is not necessary to the meaning of the sentence.**

Note: *Which* **is often used as a nonrestrictive relative pronoun.**

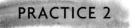

PRACTICE 2

Underline or highlight the relative pronoun in each sentence. Punctuate correctly. Write a *C* next to each correct sentence.

LEARNING STYLES TIP

To assist *visual learners*, write the first few sentences of Practice 2 on the board, circle each relative clause, and draw an arrow from that clause to the word being modified. Students who find this strategy helpful should employ it as they complete Practice 2.

1. People who need help are often embarrassed to ask for it. _____C_____

2. Ovens that clean themselves are the best kind. _____C_____

3. Paint that contains lead can be dangerous to children. _____C_____

         anaconda,   world,
4. The ~~anaconda~~ which is the largest snake in the ~~world~~ can weigh 550 pounds. _____

         watch,   date,
5. Edward's ~~watch~~ which tells the time and the ~~date~~ was a gift from his wife. _____

       Carol,   attendant,
6. ~~Carol~~ who is a flight ~~attendant~~ has just left for Pakistan. _____

       Upton,   students,
7. Joel ~~Upton~~ who is a dean of ~~students~~ usually sings in the yearly talent show. _____

8. Exercise that causes severe dehydration is dangerous. _____C_____

PRACTICE 3

Complete each sentence by completing the relative clause. Sample answers

EXAMPLE: Boxing is a sport that ___upsets me___.

1. My aunt, who ___doesn't even like animals___, rescued a cat last week.

2. A family that ___works as a team___ can solve its problems.

3. I never vote for candidates ___who promise too much___.

4. This T-shirt, which ___lists all of Shakespeare's history plays___, was a gift.

5. Paris, ___which has wonderful restaurants___, is an exciting city to visit.

6. James, who ___wants to be a pilot___, just enlisted in the Air Force.

7. I cannot resist stores that ___have bargain basements___.

8. This company, which ___manufactures sportswear___, provides health benefits and retirement plans for employees.

PRACTICE 4

On paper or on a computer, write four sentences using restrictive relative clauses and four using nonrestrictive relative clauses. Punctuate with care.

Chapter Highlights

- **Relative pronouns (who, which, and that) can join two independent ideas:**

    We met Krizia Stone. She runs an advertising agency.

    We met Krizia Stone, *who* runs an advertising agency.

    My favorite radio station is WQDF. It plays mostly jazz.

    My favorite radio station is WQDF, *which* plays mostly jazz.

    Last night, I had a hamburger. It was too rare.

    Last night, I had a hamburger *that* was too rare.

- **Restrictive relative clauses change the meaning of the sentence. They are not set off by commas:**

    The uncle *who is helping me through college* lives in Texas.

    The car *that we saw Ned driving* was not his.

- **Nonrestrictive relative clauses do not change the meaning of the sentence. They are set off by commas:**

    My uncle, *who lives in Texas*, owns a supermarket.

    Ned's car, *which is a 1992 Mazda*, was at the repair shop.

Proofreading Strategy

If *who, which, that* errors are one of your error patterns, **search your drafts for the words *who, which*, and *that*** and **highlight or underline** them. If you are using a computer, use the *"Find"* feature to locate these words. Whenever *who, which*, or *that* is being used as a relative pronoun, ask yourself, *"Have I selected the correct relative pronoun?"* Who is for people, *which* and *that* for things.

Now check your punctuation. Would omitting the *who, which*, or *that* clause *change* the meaning of the sentence? If the answer is "No," then use commas to set off this *nonrestrictive* clause. Here is an example:

| YES | NO |

The man who caused the accident did not see the stop sign, which was hidden under thick vines.

WRITING AND PROOFREADING ASSIGNMENT

In a small group, discuss a change that would improve life in your neighborhood—a new traffic light or more police patrols, for instance. Your task is to write a flier that will convince neighbors that this change is important; your purpose is to win them over to your side. The flier might note, for instance, that a child was killed at a certain intersection or that several burglaries could have been prevented. Each group member should write his or her own flier, including two sentences with relative pronouns and correct punctuation. Then read the fliers aloud; decide which are effective and why. Finally, exchange papers and check for correct relative pronoun use.

CHAPTER REVIEW

Proofread the following paragraph for relative pronoun errors and punctuation errors. Correct each error above the line.

(1) Charles Anderson is best known as the trainer of the Tuskegee ~~Airmen~~ *Airmen,* who were the first African American combat pilots. (2) During a time when African Americans were prevented from becoming pilots, Anderson was fascinated by planes. (3) He learned about flying from books. (4) At age 22, he bought a used ~~plane which,~~ *plane, which* became his teacher. (5) Eventually he met ~~someone,~~ *someone* who helped him become an expert flyer. (6) Battling against discrimination, Anderson became the first African American to earn an

Seven of the famous African American pilots of World War II, the Tuskegee Airmen

air transport pilot's license. (7) He and another pilot made the first round-trip flight across

America by black Americans. (8) In 1939 Anderson started a civilian pilot training program

at Tuskegee Institute in Alabama. (9) One day Eleanor Roosevelt, ~~which~~ who, was first lady at the

~~time~~ time, insisted on flying with him. (10) Soon afterward, Tuskegee Institute was chosen by the

Army Air Corps for a special program. (11) ~~Anderson~~ Anderson, who was chief flight ~~instructor~~ instructor, gave

America's first African American World War II pilots their initial training. (12) During the war,

the Tuskegee Airmen showed great skill and ~~heroism~~ heroism, which were later recognized by an

extraordinary number of honors and awards.

EXPLORING ONLINE

TEACHING TIP

Instructor tools for *Grassroots* include a computerized Test Bank, PowerPoint slides, an Instructor's Manual with teaching tips, and more, and can be accessed at ‹**login .cengage.com**›.

<http://grammar.ccc.commnet.edu/grammar/quizzes/which_quiz.htm>
Interactive quiz: Choose *who*, *which*, or *that*.

<http://wwwedu.ge.ch/cptic/prospective/projets/anglais/exercises/
whowhich.htm> Test your relatives (*who*, *which*, and *that*, that is).

CHAPTER 21

-*ING* Modifiers

A: Using -*ING* Modifiers

B: Avoiding Confusing Modifiers

A. Using -*ING* Modifiers

Another way to join ideas together is with an **-*ing*** **modifier**, or **present participle**.

(1) Beth was learning to ski. She broke her ankle.

(2) Learning to ski, Beth broke her ankle.

● It seems that *while* Beth was learning to ski, she had an accident. Sentence (2) emphasizes this time relationship and also joins two short sentences in one longer one.

● In sentence (2), *learning* without its helping verb, *was*, is not a verb. Instead, *learning to ski* refers to or modifies *Beth*, the subject of the new sentence.

Learning to ski, Beth broke her ankle.

● Note that a comma follows the introductory -*ing* modifier, setting it off from the independent idea.

PRACTICE 1

Combine the two sentences in each pair, using the -*ing* modifier to connect them. Drop unnecessary words. Draw an arrow from the -*ing* word to the word or words to which it refers.

EXAMPLE: Tom was standing on the deck. He waved good-bye to his family.

Standing on the deck, Tom waved good-bye to his family.

1. Kyla was searching for change. She found her lost earring.

Searching for change, Kyla found her lost earring.

2. The children worked all evening. They completed the jigsaw puzzle.

Working all evening, the children completed the jigsaw puzzle.

3. They were hiking cross-country. They made many new friends.

   Hiking cross-country, they made many new friends. _____

4. She was visiting Santa Fe. She decided to move there.

   Visiting Santa Fe, she decided to move there. _____

5. You are replacing the battery pack in your camera. You spot a grease mark on the lens.

   Replacing the battery pack in your camera, you spot a grease mark on the lens. _____

6. Seth was mumbling to himself. He named the 50 states.

   Mumbling to himself, Seth named the fifty states. _____

7. Judge Smithers was pounding his gavel. He called a recess.

   Pounding his gavel, Judge Smithers called a recess. _____

8. The masons built the wall carefully. They were lifting huge rocks and cementing them in place.

   Lifting huge rocks and cementing them in place, the masons built the wall carefully. _____

B. Avoiding Confusing Modifiers

TEACHING TIP

In addition to creating misplaced or dangling modifiers with *-ing* phrases, students are also likely to create fragments by punctuating these phrases as independent sentences.

Be sure that your *-ing* modifiers say what you mean!

(1) Hanging by the toe from the dresser drawer, Joe found his sock.

- Probably the writer did not mean that Joe spent time hanging by his toe. What, then, was hanging by the toe from the dresser drawer?

- *Hanging* refers to the *sock*, of course, but the order of the sentence does not show this. We can clear up the confusion by turning the ideas around.

Joe found his sock hanging by the toe from the dresser drawer.

Read your sentences in Practice 1 to make sure the order of the ideas is clear, not confusing.

(2) Visiting my cousin, our house was robbed.

- Does the writer mean that *our house* was visiting my cousin? To whom or what, then, does *visiting my cousin* refer?

- *Visiting* seems to refer to *I*, but there is no *I* in the sentence. To clear up the confusion, we would have to add or change words.

> Visiting my cousin, I learned that our house was robbed.

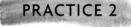

PRACTICE 2

TEACHING TIP

Misplaced and confusing modifiers may be a new notion for many students, and learning to fix them will add clarity to their writing. The unintentional humor in Practice 2 makes it an excellent one to do with the full class.

Rewrite the following sentences to clarify any confusing *-ing* modifiers.

1. Biking and walking daily, Cheryl's commuting costs were cut.

   Rewrite: Biking and walking daily, Cheryl cut her commuting costs.

2. Leaping from tree to tree, Professor Fernandez spotted a monkey.

   Rewrite: Professor Fernandez spotted a monkey leaping from tree to tree.

3. Painting for three hours straight, the bathroom and the hallway were finished by Theresa.

   Rewrite: Painting for three hours straight, Theresa finished the bathroom.

4. My son spotted our dog playing soccer in the schoolyard.

   Rewrite: Playing soccer in the schoolyard, my son spotted our dog.

5. Lying in the driveway, Tonya discovered her calculus textbook.

   Rewrite: Tonya discovered her calculus textbook lying in the driveway.

PRACTICE 3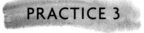

On paper or on a computer, write three sentences of your own, using *-ing* modifiers to join ideas.

Chapter Highlights

- **An *-ing* modifier can join two ideas:**

    (1) Sol was cooking dinner.

    (2) He started a small fire.

    (1) + (2) *Cooking* dinner, Sol started a small fire.

- **Avoid confusing modifiers:**

    I finally found my cat riding my bike. (*incorrect*)

    Riding my bike, I finally found my cat. (*correct*)

Proofreading Strategy

If confusing *-ing* modifiers are one of your error patterns:

1. **Search your draft for -*ing* words or phrases**, and circle them. If you are using a computer, use the "*Find*" feature to locate these words.

2. If an *-ing* word or phrase is used as a modifier, ask yourself, "***What word in the sentence is being modified?***" Draw an arrow to that word.

3. Ask yourself, *"Does the -ing word or phrase come immediately before or after the word it modifies?"* If the answer is no, rewrite to move the modifier to its rightful place. Is the modifier in the sentence below positioned correctly?

INCORRECT

The seal delighted the children performing tricks for fish treats.

CORRECT

Performing tricks for fish treats, the seal delighted the children.

WRITING AND PROOFREADING ASSIGNMENT

Some people feel that much popular music degrades women and encourages drug abuse and violence. Others feel that popular songs expose many of the social ills we suffer from today. What do you think?

Prepare to take part in a debate to defend or criticize popular music. Your job is to convince the other side that your view is correct. Use specific song titles and artists as examples to support your argument. After you write, take a break. Then revise to use one or two *-ing* modifiers to join ideas. Proofread for correct punctuation.

PRACTICE 4

Highlight or underline all the *-ing* modifiers in this paragraph. Then proofread the following paragraph for comma errors and confusing modifiers. Correct each error above the line.

(1) Harming native plants, animals, and human ~~health~~ *invasive species* are plants and [*health,*]

animals brought to the United States from other places. (2) Once here, they take over or

attack native species. (3) The list includes Burmese pythons, killer bees, and saltwater

crocodiles, but the most deadly invasive species of all is a fragrant flowering vine from Japan

called kudzu. (4) Experts urged Americans to plant kudzu as a decorative plant, an erosion [*Admiring this vine at an 1865 show, experts*]

control, or a food for animals, ~~admiring this vine at a 1865 garden show. (5) Climbing trees~~

~~and strangling to death all greenery in its path, people~~ soon saw that kudzu grew too [*People*]

well, climbing trees and strangling to death all greenery in its path.

well. (6) "Mile-a-minute-vine," as it was called, first thrived in the South. (7) Its roots, which

must be destroyed to kill it, run wide and deep. (8) In 1970 the U.S. declared kudzu a weed

and in 1997, a very dangerous weed. (9) Kudzu has become a nightmare for environmental [*Now smothering forests as far north as New England, kudzu*]

scientists, ~~now smothering whole forests as far North as New England.~~ (10) Like a green

tsunami, this monster vine has destroyed 7 million acres with no end in sight.

Kudzu vine destroying a forest

EXPLORING ONLINE

<http://grammar.ccc.commnet.edu/grammar/cgi-shl/quiz.pl/modifier_quiz.htm>
Are your modifiers misplaced? Take this quiz and improve your skills.

UNIT 4
Writing Assignments

As you complete each writing assignment, remember to perform these steps:

● Write a clear, complete topic sentence.

● Use freewriting, brainstorming, or clustering to generate ideas for the body of your paragraph, essay, or letter.

● Arrange your best ideas in a plan.

● Revise for support, unity, coherence, and exact language.

● Proofread for grammar, punctuation, and spelling errors.

Writing Assignment 1 *Post your thoughts online.* Many websites and blogs invite viewers to respond by posting their comments or opinions. Find a blog or website forum that focuses on a topic you find interesting, such as music, sports, health/fitness, politics, the media, art, or technology. Select a site you already know and like, or find one in a list of the best websites (<http://www.100bestwebsites.org/>) or blogs (<http://blogs.botw.org/>). Then, contribute your thoughts or feedback. For example, you could post your thoughts about a favorite television show at <http://www.televisionwithoutpity.com/>, contribute to a spiritual discussion at <http://community.beliefnet.com/>, or comment on current events at <http://ireport .cnn.com/community/assignment>. Use as many techniques for joining ideas as you can, and proofread for run-ons and comma splices.

Writing Assignment 2 *Be a witness.* You have just witnessed a fender-bender involving a car and an ice cream truck. No one was hurt, but the insurance company has asked you to write an eyewitness report. First, visualize the accident and how it occurred. Then jot down as many details as possible to make your description of the accident as vivid as possible. Use subordinating conjunctions that indicate time (*when*, *as*, *before*, *while*, and so on) to show the order of events. Use as many techniques for joining ideas as you can, being careful about punctuation. Proofread for run-ons and comma splices.

Writing Assignment 3 *Evaluate so-called reality TV shows.* A newspaper has asked readers to respond to the question "Has reality television gone too far?" Think about popular reality programs—*Survivor*, *Biggest Loser*, and similar shows in which contestants are often humiliated and forced to do bizarre things. State whether reality TV has, or has not, gone too far. Then explain why you feel this way, using vivid details and examples from programs to support your point. Use a variety of techniques for joining ideas; proofread for run-ons and comma splices.

Writing Assignment 4 *React to a quotation.* From the "Work and Success" section of the Quotation Bank at the end of this book, choose a quotation that you strongly agree or disagree with. For instance, do you think it is true that "most of us are looking for a calling, not a job" or that "money is like manure"? In your first sentence, repeat the entire quotation, explaining whether you do or do not agree with it. Then brainstorm, freewrite, or cluster to generate examples and facts supporting your view. Use your own or other people's experiences to strengthen your argument. Use as many techniques for joining ideas as you can. Proofread for run-ons and comma splices.

UNIT 4

Review

Five Useful Ways to Join Ideas

In this unit, you have combined simple sentences by means of a **coordinating conjunction**, a **subordinating conjunction**, a **semicolon**, and a **semicolon** and **conjunctive adverb**. Here is a review chart of the sentence patterns discussed in this unit.

LEARNING STYLES TIP

To review the concepts in Unit 4, you might reproduce the "Five Useful Ways to Join Ideas" chart with one or more elements in each option removed. Have students fill in the missing information.

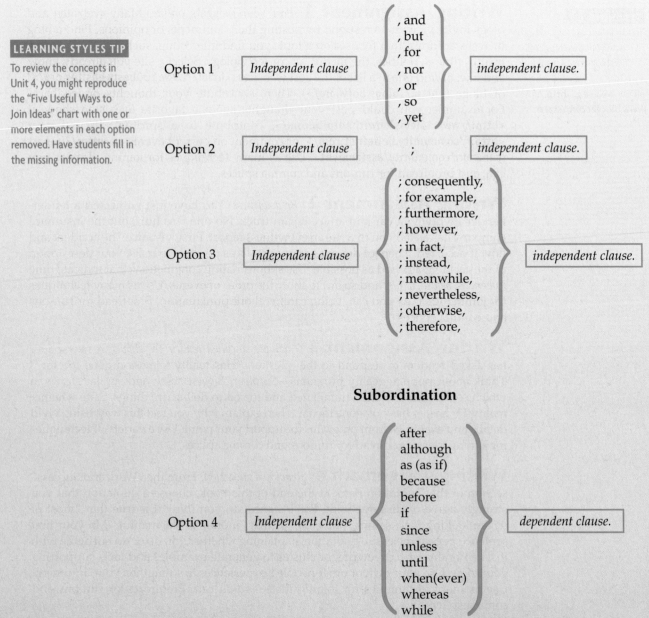

Coordination

Option 1 — *Independent clause* { , and / , but / , for / , nor / , or / , so / , yet } *independent clause.*

Option 2 — *Independent clause* ; *independent clause.*

Option 3 — *Independent clause* { ; consequently, / ; for example, / ; furthermore, / ; however, / ; in fact, / ; instead, / ; meanwhile, / ; nevertheless, / ; otherwise, / ; therefore, } *independent clause.*

Subordination

Option 4 — *Independent clause* { after / although / as (as if) / because / before / if / since / unless / until / when(ever) / whereas / while } *dependent clause.*

	After
Option 5	Although
	As (as if)
	Because
	Before
	If
	Since
	Unless
	Until
	When(ever)
	Whereas
	While

dependent clause, independent clause.

Proofreading

The student composition below has been changed to contain run-ons, comma splices, and misused semicolons. Proofread for these errors. Then correct them above the lines in any way you choose. (You should find eight errors.) Answers will vary.

Managing Time in College

(1) When I started college, time was a problem. (2) I was always desperately reading an assignment just before class or racing to get to work on time. (3) The stress became too much. (4) It took a ~~while~~ *while, but* now I know how to manage my time. (5) The secret of my success is flexible planning.

(6) At the beginning of each semester, I mark a calendar with all the due dates for the ~~term these~~ *term. These* include deadlines for assignments, papers, and tests. (7) I also write in social events and ~~obligations, therefore;~~ *obligations; therefore,* I know at a glance when I need extra time during the next few months.

(8) Next, I make out a model weekly study schedule. (9) First, I block in the hours when I have to sleep, eat, work, go to class, and tend to my ~~family then~~ *family. Then* I decide what time I will devote to study and relaxation. (10) Finally, I fill in the times I will study each subject, making sure I plan at least one hour of study time for each hour of class time. (11) Generally, I plan some time just before or after a ~~class that~~ *class. That* way I can prepare for a class or review my notes right after a lecture.

(12) In reality, I don't follow this schedule ~~rigidly,~~ *rigidly;* I vary it according to the demands of the week and day. (13) In addition, I spend more time on my harder subjects and less time on the easy ones. (14) I also try to study my harder subjects in the ~~morning;~~ *morning* when I am most awake.

273

(15) I find that by setting up a model schedule but keeping it flexible, I can accomplish all I have to do with little worry. (16) This system may not help everyone; however, ~~everyone,~~ it has certainly worked for me.

Jesse Rose, student

Combining

Read each pair of sentences below to determine the relationship between them. Then join each pair in two different ways, using the conjunctions shown. Punctuate correctly. Answers will vary.

1. The tide had not yet come in.
   We went swimming.

   (although) Although the tide had not yet come in, we went swimming.

   (but) The tide had not yet come in, but we went swimming.

2. Michael enjoys drinking coffee.
   He needs to limit his caffeine intake.

   (yet) Michael enjoys drinking coffee, yet he needs to limit his caffeine intake.

   (nevertheless) Michael enjoys drinking coffee; nevertheless, he needs to limit his caffeine intake.

3. Alexis plays the trumpet very well.
   She hopes to have her own band someday.

   (and) Alexis plays the trumpet very well, and she hopes to have her own band someday.

   (furthermore) Alexis plays the trumpet very well; furthermore, she hopes to have her own band someday.

4. The lecture starts in five minutes.
   We had better get to our seats.

   (because) Because the lecture starts in five minutes, we had better get to our seats.

   (so) The lecture starts in five minutes, so we had better get to our seats.

5. He knows how to make money.

   He doesn't want to start another company.

   (although) _Although he knows how to make money, he doesn't want to start another_

   company.

   (however) _He knows how to make money; however, he doesn't want to start another company._

Revising

Read through this essay of short, choppy sentences. Then revise it, combining some sentences. Use one coordinating conjunction, one subordinating conjunction, and any other ways you have learned to join ideas together. Keep some short sentences for variety. Make your corrections above the lines, and punctuate with care. Answers will vary.

Control Your Credit

(1) One-fourth of all Americans want to get out of ~~debt.~~ *debt, and many* (2) ~~Many~~ college students are among them. *When these students graduate, they* (3) ~~These students graduate.~~ (4) ~~They~~ owe more than $2,000 in credit-card debt. (5) Good credit habits can be learned. (6) You may have abused your plastic and gotten into ~~trouble.~~ *trouble, or you* (7) ~~You~~ might be using credit cards for the first ~~time.~~ *time, but you* (8) ~~You~~ can develop three habits to help control your credit-card debt.

(9) First, have and carry just one credit ~~card.~~ *card because using* (10) ~~Using~~ two or more can quickly lead to overspending. (11) Choose your card ~~wisely.~~ *wisely; some* (12) ~~Some~~ cards are better than others. (13) The best card offers the lowest interest ~~rate.~~ *rate; in addition, it* (14) ~~It~~ should not charge an annual fee.

(15) A second good habit is to use a credit card only as a last resort. (16) Whenever possible, use cash, a debit card, or a ~~check.~~ *check, and save* (17) ~~Save~~ your credit cards for true emergencies. (18) When cash is low, don't grab a ~~card.~~ *card; reduce* (19) ~~Reduce~~ spending instead. (20) Experts also offer this rule of thumb: "If you can eat it or drink it, don't charge it!"

(21) Finally, get in the habit of thinking of credit cards as just another form of cash. (22) *If you* ~~You~~ never let your charges exceed your available ~~funds.~~ *funds, you* (23) ~~You~~ will be able to pay your full balance each month. (24) As a result, you'll avoid expensive interest charges that only increase your debt.

(25) *When you* ~~You~~ develop good credit card ~~habits.~~ *habits, you* (26) ~~You~~ will stay in control of ~~debt.~~ *debt, and it* (27) ~~It~~ will not take control of you.

275

UNIT 4

Writers' Workshop

Describe a Detour off the Main Highway

When a writer really cares about a subject, often the reader will care too. In your group or class, read this student's paragraph, aloud if possible. As you read, underline any words or details that strike you as vivid or powerful.

Sometimes detours off the main highway can bring wonderful surprises, and last week this happened to my husband and me. On the Fourth of July weekend, we decided to drive home the long way, taking the old dirt farm road. Pulling over to admire the afternoon light gleaming on a field of wet ~~corn~~ *corn,* we saw a tiny farm stand under a tree. No one was in sight, but a card table covered with a red checkered cloth held pints of tomatoes, jars of jam, and a handwritten price list. Next to these was a vase full of red poppies and tiny American flags. We bought tomatoes, leaving our money in the tin box stuffed with dollar bills. Driving ~~home~~ *home,* we both felt so happy—as if we had been given a great gift.

Kim Lee, student

1. How effective is Kim Lee's paragraph?

   __Y__ Clear topic sentence?   __Y__ Rich supporting details?

   __Y__ Logical organization?   __Y__ Effective conclusion?

2. Discuss your underlinings with one another, explaining as specifically as possible why a particular word or sentence is effective. For instance, the "red poppies and tiny American flags" are so exact that you can see them.

3. This student supports her topic sentence with a single *example*, one brief story told in detail. If you were to support the same topic sentence, what example from your own life might you use?

4. The concluding sentence tells the reader that she and her husband felt they had been given "a great gift." Do you think that the gift was being trusted to be honest?

5. Proofread for grammar and spelling. Do you notice any error patterns (two or more errors of the same type) that this student should watch out for?
   She omits the comma when she begins a sentence with an *-ing* modifier.

276

About her writing process, Kim Lee says:

> I wrote this paper in my usual way—I sort of plan, and then I freewrite on the subject. I like freewriting—I pick through it for certain words or details, but of course it is also a mess. From my freewriting I got "light gleaming on a field of wet corn" and the last sentence, about the gift.

Writing and Revising Ideas

1. Develop the topic sentence "Sometimes detours off the main highway can bring wonderful [disturbing] surprises."

2. Write about a time when you were trusted or distrusted by a stranger. What effect did this have on you?

As you plan your paragraph, try to angle the subject toward something that interests *you*—chances are, it will interest your readers too. Consider using one good example to develop your paragraph. As you revise, make sure that the body of your paragraph perfectly fits the topic sentence.

UNIT 5   Choosing the Right Noun, Pronoun, Adjective, Adverb, or Preposition

Choosing the right form of many words in English can be tricky. This unit will help you avoid some common errors. In this unit, you will

- Learn about singular and plural nouns
- Choose correct pronouns
- Use adjectives and adverbs correctly
- Choose the right prepositions
- Learn proofreading strategies to find and correct your own errors

Spotlight on Reading and Writing

Here two researchers set forth new findings about happiness. If possible, read the paragraph aloud.

In study after study, four traits characterize happy people. First, especially in individualistic Western cultures, they like themselves. They have high self-esteem and usually believe themselves to be more ethical, more intelligent, less prejudiced, better able to get along with others, and healthier than the average person. Second, happy people typically feel personal control. Those with little or no control over their lives—such as prisoners, nursing home patients, severely impoverished groups or individuals, and citizens in totalitarian regimes—suffer lower morale and worse health. Third, happy people are usually optimistic. Fourth, most happy people are extroverted. Although one might expect that introverts would live more happily in the serenity of their less stressed lives, extroverts are happier—whether alone or with others.

David G. Myers and Ed Diener, "The Pursuit of Happiness," *Scientific American*. Reproduced with permission. Copyright © 1996 Scientific American, Inc. All rights reserved.

- This well-organized paragraph tells us the traits of happy people. They see themselves as "more *ethical*, more *intelligent*, less *prejudiced*, better *able . . .*, and *healthier. . . .*" Does this sound true to you?

- All five parts of speech discussed in this unit are used here: nouns, pronouns, adjectives, adverbs, and prepositions. Can you identify one of each?

- If you don't know the meaning of the words *extrovert* and *introvert*, look them up. Which refers to you?

Writing Ideas

- *Analyze how happy you are, based on the four traits mentioned above.*

- *Describe an extrovert or an introvert you have observed.*

279

CHAPTER 22

Nouns

A: **Defining Singular and Plural**

B: **Signal Words: Singular and Plural**

C: **Signal Words with OF**

A. Defining Singular and Plural

A **noun** names a person, a place, or a thing. Nouns may be **singular** or **plural**. *Singular* means one. *Plural* means more than one.

Singular	Plural
a reporter	the reporters (person nouns)
a forest	the forests (place nouns)
a couch	the couches (thing nouns)

● Most nouns in English form the plural by adding *-s* or *-es*.

Other nouns form their plurals in unusual ways. Learning them is easier if they are divided into groups.

Some nouns form their plurals by changing their spelling:

Singular	Plural
child	children
foot	feet
goose	geese
man	men
mouse	mice
person	people
tooth	teeth
woman	women

Many nouns ending in *-f* or *-fe* change their endings to *-ves* in the plural:

Singular	Plural
half	halves
knife	knives
leaf	leaves
life	lives

scarf	scarves
shelf	shelves
wife	wives
wolf	wolves

Most nouns that end in -o add -es in the plural:

echo + *es* = echoes   potato + *es* = potatoes

hero + *es* = heroes   veto + *es* = vetoes

● Here are some exceptions to memorize:

pianos	solos
radios	sopranos

Other nouns do not change at all to form the plural. Here is a partial list:

Singular	**Plural**
deer	deer
fish	fish
moose	moose
sheep	sheep

Hyphenated nouns usually form plurals by adding -s or -es to the first word:

Singular	**Plural**
brother-in-law	brothers-in-law
maid-of-honor	maids-of-honor
mother-to-be	mothers-to-be
runner-up	runners-up

LEARNING STYLES TIP

If your students' preparedness is poor, you might show them the classic *Grammar Rock* cartoon and song. Search online for "Grammar Rock, nouns."

If you are ever unsure about the plural of a noun, check a dictionary. For example, if you look up the noun *woman* in the dictionary, you will find an entry like this:

woman / women

The first word listed, *woman*, is the singular form of the noun; the second word, *women*, is the plural. Some dictionaries list the plural form of a noun only if the plural is unusual. If no plural is listed, the noun probably adds -s or -es.

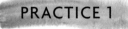

PRACTICE 1

Make the following nouns plural.* If you are not sure of a particular plural, check the charts on this page and the previous page.

	Singular	**Plural**		**Singular**	**Plural**
1.	notebook	notebooks	4.	brother-in-law	brothers-in-law
2.	hero	heroes	5.	technician	technicians
3.	man	men	6.	shelf	shelves

* For help with spelling, see Chapter 34.

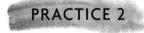

7.	half	halves	14.	potato	potatoes
8.	bridge	bridges	15.	mouse	mice
9.	deer	deer	16.	child	children
10.	runner-up	runners-up	17.	flight	flights
11.	woman	women	18.	wife	wives
12.	radio	radios	19.	place	places
13.	tooth	teeth	20.	maid-of-honor	maids-of-honor

REMEMBER: **Do not add an** -s **to words that form plurals by changing an internal letter or letters. For example, the plural of** man **is** men**, not** mens**; the plural of** woman **is** women**, not** womens**; the plural of** foot **is** feet**, not** feets**.**

PRACTICE 2

Proofread the following paragraph for incorrect plural nouns. Cross out the errors and correct them above the lines.

(1) Many ~~peoples~~ *people* consider Glacier National Park the jewel of the National Park Service. (2) Its many mountains, glaciers, waterfalls, blue-green ~~lake~~ *lakes*, and amazing ~~wildlifes~~ *wildlife* are in the remote Rocky Mountains in the northwest corner of Montana. (3) Several ~~road~~ *roads* take visitors into the park, especially Going-to-the-Sun Road, which clings to the mountainside and offers spectacular, stomach-churning views. (4) At Logan Pass—6,646 ~~foot~~ *feet* high—the road crosses the Continental Divide. (5) From this line along the spine of the ~~Rocky~~ *Rockies*, all ~~river~~ *rivers* flow either west to the Pacific Ocean, south to the Gulf, or east. (6) Because Glacier is truly a wilderness park, it is best seen by hikers, not drivers. (7) Most men, ~~woman~~ *women*, and ~~childs~~ *children* who hike the park's 700 miles of trails come prepared—with hats, long-sleeved shirts, and on their ~~feets~~ *feet*, proper hiking shoes. (8) Their ~~equipments~~ *equipment* includes bottled water and, just in case, bear spray. (9) Glacier has a large population of grizzly bears, which can weigh up to 1,400 pounds, have four-inch claws, and dislike surprises. (10) Besides grizzlies, one might glimpse mountain lions, ~~wolfs~~ *wolves*, black ~~bear~~ *bears*, white mountain goats, moose, bighorn ~~sheeps~~ *sheep*, elk, and many smaller mammals. (11) Salmon, ~~trouts~~ *trout*, and other ~~fishs~~ *fish* swim in the ice-cold rivers and lakes. (12) ~~Scientist~~ *Scientists* worry that the glaciers are melting too quickly, but Glacier Park remains a treasure.

EXPLORING ONLINE

‹http://www.nps.gov/findapark/› Visit the National Park Service website. Use the find-a-park search tool to explore the many parks the public can visit and select one (Glacier National Park or some other) that you might like to learn about. Read, explore, and jot down any writing—or travel—ideas.

B. Signal Words: Singular and Plural

A *signal word* **tells you whether a singular or a plural noun usually follows.**
These **signal words** tell you that a *singular noun* usually follows:

Signal Words

$$
\left.
\begin{array}{l}
\text{a(n)} \\
\text{another} \\
\text{a single} \\
\text{each} \\
\text{every} \\
\text{one}
\end{array}
\right\} \text{motorboat}
$$

These signal words tell you that a *plural noun* usually follows:

$$
\left.
\begin{array}{l}
\text{all} \\
\text{both} \\
\text{few} \\
\text{many} \\
\text{several} \\
\text{some} \\
\text{two (or more)}
\end{array}
\right\} \text{motorboats}
$$

 **PRACTICE 3**

In the blank following each signal word, write either a singular or a plural noun. Use as many different nouns as you can think of. Sample answers

EXAMPLES: a single ___stamp___

most ___fabrics___

1.	a(n)	map	7.	another	tent
2.	some	suitcases	8.	each	moment
3.	few	words	9.	a single	governor
4.	nine	pens	10.	every	family
5.	one	carton	11.	both	situations
6.	all	ticket holders	12.	many	countries

PRACTICE 4

Read the following essay and underline or highlight the signal words. Then check for incorrect singular or plural nouns. Cross out the errors and correct them above the lines.

The Best Medicine

(1) Many ~~researcher~~ researchers believe that laughter is good for people's health. (2) In fact, some ~~doctor~~ doctors have concluded that laughter actually helps patients heal faster. (3) To put this theory into practice, several ~~hospital~~ hospitals have introduced humor routines into their treatment programs. (4) One ~~programs~~ program is a children's clown care unit that operates in seven New York City hospitals. (5) Thirty-five ~~clown~~ clowns from the Big Apple Circus go to the hospitals three times every ~~weeks~~ week. (6) Few ~~child~~ children can keep from laughing at the "rubber chicken soup" and

"red nose transplant" routines. (7) Although the program hasn't been studied scientifically,

~~observers~~
many ~~observer~~ have witnessed its positive effects.

~~specialists~~
(8) However, some ~~specialist~~ are conducting strictly scientific research on health and

laughter. (9) One study, carried out at Loma Linda University in California, has shown the

~~test~~
positive effects of laughter on the immune system. (10) Another ~~tests~~, done at the College

of William and Mary in Virginia, has confirmed the California findings. (11) Other studies

~~systems~~
in progress are suggesting that all physiological ~~system~~ may be affected positively by

~~claim~~
laughter. (12) Finally, research also is backing up a ~~claims~~ made by Norman Cousins, author

~~disease~~
of the book *Anatomy of an Illness*. (13) While he was fighting a life-threatening ~~diseases~~,

~~studies~~
Cousins maintained that hearty laughter took away his pain. (14) Several recent ~~study~~ have

shown that pain does become less intense when the sufferer responds to comedy.

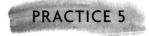
PRACTICE 5   On paper or on a computer, write three sentences using signal words that require singular nouns. Then write three sentences using signal words that require plural nouns.

C. Signal Words with OF

Many signal words are followed by *of . . .* or *of the. . . .* Usually, these signal words are followed by a *plural* noun (or a collective noun) because you are really talking about one or more from a larger group.*

$$
\left.\begin{array}{l}
\text{many of the} \\
\text{a few of the} \\
\text{lots of the}
\end{array}\right\} \quad \text{houses are . . .}
$$

BE CAREFUL: The signal words *one of the* and *each of the* are followed by a *plural* noun, but the verb is *singular* because only the signal word (*one, each*) is the real subject.**

$$
\left.\begin{array}{l}
\text{one of the} \\
\text{each of the}
\end{array}\right\} \quad \text{houses is . . .}
$$

(1) *One* of the apples *is* spoiled.

(2) *Each* of the trees *grows* quickly.

- In sentence (1), *one* is the subject, not *apples.*

- In sentence (2), *each* is the subject, not *trees.*

---

* For more work on collective nouns, see Chapter 23, Part D.

** For more work on this type of construction, see Chapter 11, Part E.

PRACTICE 6

Fill in your own nouns in the following sentences. Use a different noun in each sentence. Sample answers

1. Many of the _____students_____ enrolled in Chemistry 202.

2. Sipho lost one of his _____sandals_____ at the beach.

3. This is one of the _____suggestions_____ that everyone liked.

4. Each of the _____protesters_____ carried a sign.

5. You are one of the few _____parents_____ who can do somersaults.

6. Few of the _____whales_____ produced calves.

PRACTICE 7

Write five sentences, using the signal words with *of* provided in parentheses. Use a different noun in each sentence.

EXAMPLE: (many of those . . .) _____*I planted many of those flowers myself.*_____

1. (one of my . . .) _____

   _____

2. (many of the . . .) _____

   _____

3. (lots of the . . .) _____

   _____

4. (each of these . . .) _____

   _____

5. (a few of your . . .) _____

   _____

PRACTICE 8

Proofread the following paragraph for correct plural nouns. Underline or highlight any signal words. Then cross out the errors and correct them above the lines.

(1) In 1782 the bald eagle became the national symbol of the United States. (2) Sadly, over
                                                          birds
the years, many of these magnificent bird suffered destruction of their habitat, poisoning

of their food sources, and illegal extermination by farmers, ranchers, and hunters. (3) By

the 1960s, these majestic raptors were declared an endangered species. (4) Today, however,
                                                                       methods
eagles are back in American skies, thanks to some of the new recovery method used by
                                                              eggs
wildlife specialists. (5) In one such method, scientists remove each of the egg from a wild

eagle's nest and place it in an incubator. (6) Baby eagles must not attach themselves to

Eagle puppet feeding a three-day-old bald eaglet.

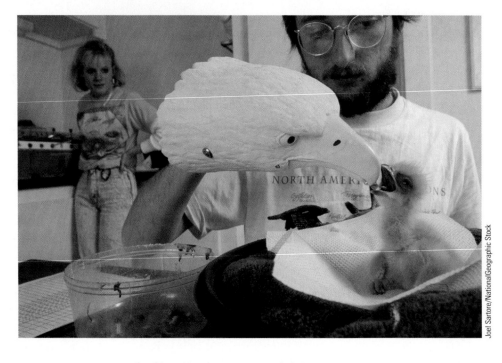

people, so all of the ~~hatchling~~ hatchlings are fed first with tweezers and later with eagle puppets.

(7) In this way, they learn to recognize Mom and Dad. (8) Protected and well fed, lots of the ~~chick~~ chicks grow strong enough to be placed in the nests of adult eagles. (9) Instinct kicks in, and the adults adopt and raise the chicks as their own. (10) Today, many of our wild ~~eagle~~ eagles got their start in eaglet nurseries.

Chapter Highlights

- **Most plural nouns are formed by adding -s or -es to the singular noun:**

    job/jobs   watch/watches

- **Some plurals are formed in other ways:**

    child/children   woman/women   wolf/wolves

- **Some nouns ending in -o add -es; others add -s:**

    echo/echoes   solo/solos

- **Some nouns have identical singular and plural forms:**

    fish/fish   equipment/equipment

- **Hyphenated nouns usually add -s or -es to the first word:**

    father-in-law/fathers-in-law

- **Signal words, with and without _of_, indicate whether a singular or a plural noun usually follows:**

    another musician   _many of the_ musicians

Proofreading Strategy

Incorrect singular and plural nouns are considered serious errors, so proofread with care if these are among your error patterns.

First, **search each sentence for signal words and phrases** (such as *an, each, one, many, several, a few*) that "announce" the need for either a singular or a plural noun. Underline or color code these signal words. Code in a different color all phrases like *one of the . . .* and *a few of the . . .* that are *always* followed by a plural. **Locate the noun** following each signal word and check for correctness.

Notice how the color-coded signal words in this example make it easier to see if the nouns are correct.

                                      ideas   *suggestions*

The teams generated several idea, but only a few of the suggestion seemed like workable solutions.

WRITING AND PROOFREADING ASSIGNMENT

For some families, shopping—whether for food, clothing, or electronics—is a delightful group outing, a time to be together and share. For other families, it is an ordeal, a time of great stress, with arguments about what to purchase and how much to spend.

Describe a particularly enjoyable or awful family shopping experience. Your first sentence might read, "Shopping for _____ was (is) a(n) _____ experience." Explain what made it so good or so bad: Was it what you were shopping for or where you were shopping? Were there arguments? Why?

Proofread your work for the correct use of singular and plural nouns. Be especially careful of nouns that follow signal words.

CHAPTER REVIEW

Proofread the following essay for incorrect singular and plural nouns. First underline or highlight the signal words. Then cross out the errors and correct them above the lines.

The Effects of Alcohol on Pregnancy

               mothers-to-be   *child*
(1) All mother-to-bes who drink alcohol run the risk of harming an innocent children.

                woman
(2) When a pregnant women takes a drink, the alcohol goes straight from her bloodstream

                                              drinks
into the bloodstream of her child. (3) When she has several drink, the blood-alcohol level

of her child rises as high as her own.

                                     ways   *infants*
(4) Newborns can be harmed by alcohol in many way. (5) Some infant are born addicted

                                                 doctors
to alcohol. (6) Other children are born mentally retarded. (7) In fact, most doctor believe

                                        causes
that exposure to alcohol before birth is one of the major cause of mental retardation.

(8) In the worst cases, babies are born with a disease called fetal alcohol syndrome.

(9) These unfortunate children not only are mentally retarded but also can have many

        deformities
physical deformity. (10) In milder cases, the children's problems don't show up until they

TEACHING TIP

If your students have computer access, Exploring Online, link 3, is unusual and fun: a painting and "noun hunt."

go to school. (11) For instance, they may have poor memories and short attention spans.

job
(12) Later, they may have trouble holding a ~~jobs~~.

lives
(13) Too many young ~~life~~ have been ruined before birth because of alcohol consumption.

children   future
(14) All unborn ~~child~~ need and deserve a chance to have a healthy, normal ~~futures~~. (15) If you

woman
are a ~~women~~ who is expecting a baby, stop drinking alcohol now!

EXPLORING ONLINE

TEACHING TIP

Instructor tools for *Grassroots* include a computerized Test Bank, PowerPoint slides, an Instructor's Manual with teaching tips, and more, and can be accessed at ‹**login .cengage.com**›.

<http://a4esl.org/q/h/vf004-bp.html> Interactive quiz: Click on the correct singular or plural.

<http://grammar.ccc.commnet.edu/grammar/quizzes/cross/plurals_gap.htm> Tricky plurals quiz. Drill, baby, drill.

<http://grammar.ccc.commnet.edu/grammar/noun_exercise2.htm> Art Class! Study Bruegel's famous painting and hunt for nouns.

CHAPTER 23

Pronouns

A: **Defining Pronouns and Antecedents**

B: **Referring to Indefinite Pronouns**

C: **Referring to Special Singular Constructions**

D: **Referring to Collective Nouns**

E: **Avoiding Vague and Repetitious Pronouns**

F: **Using Pronouns as Subjects, Objects, and Possessives**

G: **Choosing the Correct Pronoun Case**

H: **Using Pronouns with -*SELF* and -*SELVES***

A. Defining Pronouns and Antecedents

Pronouns take the place of or refer to nouns or other pronouns. The word or words that a pronoun refers to are called the **antecedent** of the pronoun.

(1) *Tory* said that *he* was tired.

(2) *Sonia* left early, but I did not see *her* until later.

(3) *Robert and Tyrone* have been good friends ever since *their* college days.

- In sentence (1), *he* refers to *Tory*.
- *Tory* is the antecedent of *he*.

- In sentence (2), *her* refers to *Sonia*.
- *Sonia* is the antecedent of *her*.

- In sentence (3), *their* refers to *Robert and Tyrone*.
- *Robert and Tyrone* is the antecedent of *their*.

ESL TIP
Pronoun forms do not usually present a learning hardship to ESL students because the English pronoun system is far simpler than that of many other languages.

A pronoun must **agree** with its antecedent. In sentence (1), the antecedent *Tory* requires the singular, masculine pronoun *he*. In sentence (2), the antecedent *Sonia* requires the singular, feminine pronoun *her*. In sentence (3), the antecedent *Robert and Tyrone* requires the plural pronoun *their*.

289

PRACTICE 1

In each of the following sentences, circle the pronoun. In the columns on the right, write the pronoun and its antecedent as shown in the example.

	Pronoun	**Antecedent**
EXAMPLE: Susan B. Anthony promoted women's rights before (they) were popular.	*they*	*rights*
1. Susan B. Anthony deserves praise for (her) accomplishments.	her	Susan B. Anthony
2. Anthony became involved in the antislavery movement because of (her) principles.	her	Anthony
3. She helped President Lincoln develop (his) plans to free the slaves during the Civil War.	his	President Lincoln
4. Eventually, Anthony realized that women wouldn't be fully protected by law until (they) could vote.	they	women
5. When Anthony voted in the presidential election of 1872, (she) was arrested.	she	Anthony
6. She was found guilty and given a $100 fine, but she refused to pay (it).	it	fine
7. The judge did not sentence Anthony to jail because a sentence would have given (her) grounds for an appeal.	her	Anthony
8. If the Supreme Court had heard her appeal, (it) might have ruled that women had the right to vote.	it	Supreme Court
9. Audiences in England and Germany showed (their) appreciation of Anthony's work with standing ovations.	their	audiences
10. Unfortunately, women in the United States had to wait until 1920 before (they) could legally vote.	they	women

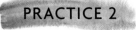

PRACTICE 2

Read this paragraph for meaning; then circle each pronoun you find and write its antecedent above the pronoun.

(1) Driverless cars are already making (their) — *cars* — way along the freeways of Los Angeles. (2) In 2012, the Google company secured a new bill in California, allowing (its) — *Google company* — fleet of driverless cars to bring visitors from the airport to company headquarters. (3) Although much attention has focused on amazing videos of a blind man doing (his) — *man* — errands in a car with no

one at the wheel, the effort is very serious. (4) Because human error accounts for 77 to 90

percent of traffic accidents, Google wants to take drivers out of the equation completely,

drivers

rather than try to improve ⟨their⟩ driving skills. (5) Police officers periodically pull the robotic

police officers

cars over, but usually because ⟨they⟩ want to take a picture. (6) Google engineer Sebastian

Sebastian Thrun

Thrun is in charge of the project. (7) ⟨He⟩ also co-invented Google's Street View. (8) So far,

Florida, Nevada, and California

Florida, Nevada, and California have legalized robotic vehicles on ⟨their⟩ roads. (9) Many

other companies are investing in driverless technology too, so the only certainty is that

driverless cars will exist in everyone's future.

B. Referring to Indefinite Pronouns

Indefinite pronouns do not point to a specific person.

LEARNING STYLES TIP

Challenge students to memorize the list of singular indefinite pronouns. In groups or as a class, invent a mnemonic device to help remember them. *Aural and kinesthetic learners* will benefit.

anybody
anyone
each
everybody
everyone
no one
nobody
somebody
someone

Indefinite pronouns are usually *singular*. A pronoun that refers to an indefinite pronoun should also be singular.

TEACHING TIP

Explain to students that although we might not make our subjects and pronouns agree in casual conversation, we must do so in writing. Students have particular trouble with the special cases covered in Parts B, C, and D in this chapter—and with Part E on vague or repeated pronouns.

(1) *Everyone* should do what *he* or *she* can to help.

(2) *Each* wanted to read *his* or *her* composition aloud.

(3) If *someone* smiles at you, give *him* or *her* a smile in return.

- In sentence (1), *everyone* is a singular antecedent and must be used with the singular pronoun *he* or *she*.

- In sentence (2), *each* is a singular antecedent and must be used with the singular pronoun *his* or *her*.

- In sentence (3), *someone* is a singular antecedent and must be used with the singular pronoun *him* or *her*.

In the past, writers used *he, his,* or *him* to refer to both men and women. Now, however, many writers use *he or she, his or her,* or *him or her*. Of course, if *everyone* is a woman, use *she* or *her*; if *everyone* is a man, use *he, his,* or *him*.*

Someone left *her* purse in the classroom.

Someone left *his* wallet on the bus.

Someone left *his or her* glasses on the back seat.

---

* For more work on pronoun reference, see Chapter 27, "Consistent Person."

It is often best to avoid the repetition of *his or her* and *he or she* by changing the indefinite pronoun to a plural.

> (4) *Everyone* in the club agreed to pay *his or her* dues on time.
>
> *or*
>
> (5) The club *members* agreed to pay *their* dues on time.

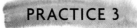

PRACTICE 3

Fill in the blanks with the correct pronouns. Then write the antecedent of each pronoun in the column on the right.

Antecedent

EXAMPLE: Everyone should do ____*his or her*____ best.   *everyone*

1. The average citizen does not take ____*his or her*____ right to vote seriously enough.   *citizen*

2. If a person chooses a career in accounting, ____*he or she*____ must enjoy working with numbers.   *person*

3. Each player gave ____*her*____ best in the women's basketball finals.   *player*

4. Anyone can learn to do research on the Internet if ____*he or she*____ will put the time into it.   *anyone*

5. Amir and Fatima always do ____*their*____ housecleaning on Tuesday.   *Amir and Fatima*

6. Someone left ____*his or her*____ fingerprints on the windshield.   *someone*

7. Everyone should see ____*his or her*____ dentist at least once a year.   *everyone*

8. Nobody wanted to waste ____*his or her*____ money on a singing stapler.   *nobody*

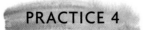

PRACTICE 4

As you read this paragraph, determine which pronoun correctly refers to the antecedent and circle it. If you have trouble, locate the antecedent of the pronoun in question.

(1) Educational expert Dr. Ken Robinson says that to make the right career choice, everyone needs to understand how (his or her, their) passions and talents come together. (2) For example, someone who loves to draw will probably be happiest and most successful if (they pursue, he or she pursues) an artistic profession. (3) Anyone who enjoys interacting with people and has a knack for selling may enjoy a career in which (they, he or she) can express these gifts—entrepreneur or sales manager, for example. (4) Dr. Robinson says that

everyone should first ask (himself or herself, themselves), "What do I love to do?" (5) Then, (they, he or she) should ask, "What am I good at?" (6) This second question is difficult because many people tend to exclude answers that don't seem relevant to (his or her, their) career options (like dribble a soccer ball, play the banjo, or create new recipes). (7) No one should limit (themselves, himself or herself) only to standard academic majors or jobs with society's stamp of approval. (8) Because a career choice is one of the most important decisions a person ever makes, it should arise from who that person is and what (he or she enjoys, they enjoy).

PRACTICE 5

On paper or on a computer, write three sentences using indefinite pronouns as antecedents.

C. Referring to Special Singular Constructions

each of . . .
either of . . .
every one of . . .   Each of these constructions is *singular*.
neither of . . .   Pronouns that refer to them must also
one of . . .   be singular.

(1) *Each* of the women did her work.

(2) *Neither* of the men finished his meal.

(3) *One* of the bottles is missing from its place.

TEACHING TIP

In Chapter 11, "Present Tense (Agreement)," students learned to cross out prepositional phrases between subjects and verbs. Suggest that they continue this practice here to make sure that both verbs and pronouns agree with these special singular constructions.

● In sentence (1), *each* is a singular antecedent and is used with the singular pronoun *her*.

● Do not be confused by the prepositional phrase *of the women*.

● In sentence (2), *neither* is a singular antecedent and is used with the singular pronoun *his*.

● Do not be confused by the prepositional phrase *of the men*.

● In sentence (3), *one* is a singular antecedent and is used with the singular pronoun *its*.

● Do not be confused by the prepositional phrase *of the bottles*.*

PRACTICE 6

Fill in the blanks with the correct pronouns. Then write the antecedent of each pronoun in the column on the right.

Antecedent

EXAMPLE: Each of my nephews did ____*his*____ homework.   ____*each*____

_____

* For more work on these special constructions, see Chapter 11, Part E.

1. One of the hikers filled _____his or her_____ canteen. _____one_____

2. Every one of the women scored high on _____her_____ entrance examination. _____every one_____

3. Each of the puzzles has _____its_____ own solution. _____each_____

4. Either of them should be able to learn _____his or her_____ lines before opening night. _____either_____

5. One of my brothers does not have a radio in _____his_____ car. _____one_____

6. Neither of the dental technicians has had _____his or her_____ lunch yet. _____neither_____

7. Every one of the children sat still when _____his or her_____ photograph was taken. _____every one_____

8. Lin Li and her mother opened _____their_____ boutique in 1998. _____Lin Li and her mother_____

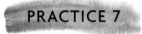

PRACTICE 7

As you read this paragraph, determine which pronoun correctly refers to the antecedent and circle it. If you have trouble, locate the antecedent of the pronoun in question.

(1) Cal Newport is the author of *So Good They Can't Ignore You: Why Skills Trump Passion in the Quest for Work You Love.* (2) On most college campuses, he says, each of the students has been told to follow (his or her, their) passion and this will lead to a great job. (3) This assumes, however, that a student knows what (their, his or her) passion is. (4) If the student doesn't know, Newport claims, (he or she is, they are) better off developing excellent skills and letting the passion follow. (5) Newport was one of those students who didn't know (their, his or her) passion, so he attended Massachusetts Institute of Technology (the famous MIT) and worked very hard to earn degrees in engineering. (6) There wasn't much to love in the exhausting workload and long hours. (7) But today Newport is a computer science professor—and one of the lucky people who loves (his or her, their) job. (8) He advises, "Put in the hard work, make yourself valuable to society, and your passion will follow."

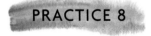

PRACTICE 8

On paper or on a computer, write three sentences that use special singular constructions as antecedents.

D. Referring to Collective Nouns

Collective nouns imply more than one person but are generally considered *singular.* Here is a partial list:

> ### Common Collective Nouns
>
> | | | |
> |---|---|---|
> | board | family | panel |
> | class | flock | school |
> | college | government | society |
> | committee | group | team |
> | company | jury | tribe |

(1) The *jury* meets early today because *it* must decide on a verdict.

(2) *Society* must protect *its* members from violence.

- In sentence (1), *jury* is a singular antecedent and is used with the singular pronoun *it*.

- In sentence (2), *society* is a singular antecedent and is always used with the singular pronoun *it*.

- Use *it* or *its* when referring to collective nouns.

- Use *they* or *their* only when referring to collective nouns in the plural (*schools, companies*, and so forth).

PRACTICE 9

Write the correct pronoun in the blank. Then write the antecedent of the pronoun in the column on the right.

Antecedent

EXAMPLE: The society sent _____*its*_____ latest recommendations for the butterfly exhibit.

_____*committee*_____

1. Wanda's company will have _____*its*_____ annual picnic next week.

_____*company*_____

2. The two teams picked up _____*their*_____ gloves and bats and walked off the field.

_____*teams*_____

3. My high school class will soon have _____*its*_____ tenth reunion.

_____*class*_____

4. The city is doing _____*its*_____ best to build a new stadium.

_____*city*_____

5. Many soap operas thrive on _____*their*_____ viewers' enjoyment of "a good cry."

_____*soap operas*_____

6. Each band has _____*its*_____ guitar player and drummer.

_____*band*_____

7. The panel made _____*its*_____ report public.

_____*panel*_____

8. This college plans to train _____*its*_____ student teachers in classroom management.

_____*college*_____

PRACTICE 10

Proofread this paragraph carefully for errors in pronoun reference. Cross out any errors and write the correct pronouns above the lines.

(1) Last year, the board of directors at Blue Pines College decided ~~they~~ [it] would invest much more money to create a superior learning experience for all students. (2) As a result, Blue Pines is undergoing major changes. (3) Many of ~~their~~ [its] classroom buildings are being updated with the latest technology. (4) With a tap of the finger, an architecture instructor can take his or her students from a tour of an ancient Aztec pyramid to the wildest new building by architect Zaha Hadid. (5) The class will use both ~~their~~ [its] paper books and digital devices, according to the task. (6) In addition, the college encourages ~~their~~ [its] instructors to bring leaders from local businesses into the classroom. (7) For example, the Premier Athletic Equipment Company, based in town, sent ~~their~~ [its] Personnel Director to campus. (8) Students learned just what skills Premier is looking for in ~~their~~ [its] entry-level employees. (9) Other companies have sent ~~its~~ [their] representatives, too, giving students a realistic picture of what it takes to get hired and what it takes to move up. (10) This year, the state panel on higher education gave Blue Pines College ~~their~~ [its] Medal of Excellence.

PRACTICE 11

On paper or on a computer, write three sentences using collective nouns as antecedents.

E. Avoiding Vague and Repetitious Pronouns

Vague Pronouns

Be sure that all pronouns *clearly* refer to their antecedents. Be especially careful of the pronouns *they* and *it*. If *they* or *it* does not refer to a *specific* antecedent, change *they* or *it* to the exact word you have in mind.

> (1) **Vague pronoun:** At registration, they said I should take Math 101.
>
> (2) **Revised:** At registration, an adviser said I should take Math 101.
>
> (3) **Vague pronoun:** On the beach, it says that no swimming is allowed.
>
> (4) **Revised:** On the beach, a sign says that no swimming is allowed.

- In sentence (1), who is *they*? The pronoun *they* does not clearly refer to an antecedent.

- In sentence (2), the vague *they* has been replaced by *an adviser*.

- In sentence (3), what is *it*? The pronoun *it* does not clearly refer to an antecedent.

- In sentence (4), the vague *it* has been replaced by *a sign*.

ESL TIP

Some ESL students tend to double the subject, writing both the subject and a pronoun. Remind them that in English, *either* a noun *or* a pronoun subject is used, not both.

Repetitious Pronouns

Don't repeat a pronoun directly after its antecedent. Use *either* the pronoun *or* the antecedent—not both.

(1) **Repetitious Pronoun:** The doctor, she said that my daughter is in perfect health.

(2) **Revised:** *The doctor* said that my daughter is in perfect health.

or

She said that my daughter is in perfect health.

- In sentence (1), the pronoun *she* unnecessarily repeats the antecedent *doctor*, which is right before it.

- In sentence (2), use either *the doctor* or *she*, not both.

PRACTICE 12

Rewrite the sentences that contain vague or repetitious pronouns. If a sentence is correct, write C.

TEACHING TIP

Doing Practice 12 in class provides an opportunity for students to hone both their critical thinking and their revising skills.

EXAMPLE: Dyslexia, it is a learning disorder that makes reading difficult.

Revised: *Dyslexia is a learning disorder that makes reading difficult.*

1. Many dyslexic persons, they have achieved success in their chosen professions.

   Revised: Many dyslexic persons have achieved success in their chosen professions.

   _____

2. For example, Albert Einstein, he was dyslexic.

   Revised: For example, Albert Einstein was dyslexic.

   _____

3. In his biography, it says that he couldn't interpret written words the way others could.

   Revised: His biography says that he couldn't interpret written words the way others could.

   _____

4. At his elementary school, they claimed that he was a slow learner.

   Revised: His elementary school teachers claimed that he was a slow learner.

   _____

5. However, this slow learner, he changed the way science looked at time and space.

   Revised: However, this slow learner changed the way science looked at time and space.

   _____

6. Even politics has had its share of dyslexic leaders.

   Revised: _C_____

   _____

7. American history, it teaches us that President Woodrow Wilson and Vice President Nelson Rockefeller, they were both dyslexic.

   Revised: _American history teaches us that President Woodrow Wilson and Vice President Nelson_

   Rockefeller were both dyslexic.

8. Authors can have this problem too; the well-known mystery writer Agatha Christie, she had trouble reading.

   Revised: _Authors can have this problem too; the well-known mystery writer Agatha Christie had_

   trouble reading.

9. Finally, in several magazines, they report that both Jay Leno and Cher are dyslexic.

   Revised: _Finally, several magazines report that both Jay Leno and Cher are dyslexic._

   _____

10. Cher, she wasn't able to read until she was 18 years old.

    Revised: _Cher wasn't able to read until she was 18 years old._

    _____

F. Using Pronouns as Subjects, Objects, and Possessives

Pronouns have different forms, depending on how they are used in a sentence. Pronouns can be *subjects*, *objects*, or *possessives*. They can be in the *subjective case*, *objective case*, or *possessive case*.

Pronouns as Subjects

A pronoun can be the *subject* of a sentence:

> (1) *He* loves the summer months.
>
> (2) By noon, *they* had reached the top of the hill.

● In sentences (1) and (2), the pronouns *he* and *they* are subjects.

Pronouns as Objects

A pronoun can be the *object* of a verb:

> (1) Graciela kissed *him*.
>
> (2) Sheila moved *it* to the corner.

- In sentence (1), the pronoun *him* tells whom Graciela kissed.
- In sentence (2), the pronoun *it* tells what Sheila moved.
- These objects answer the questions *kissed whom?* and *moved what?*

A pronoun can also be the *object* of a preposition (a word like *to, for,* or *at*).*

(3) The umpire stood between *us*.

(4) Near *them*, the children played.

- In sentences (3) and (4), the pronouns *us* and *them* are the objects of the prepositions *between* and *near*.

Sometimes the prepositions *to* and *for* are understood, usually after words like *give, send, tell,* and *bring*.

(5) I gave *her* the latest sports magazine.

(6) Carver bought *him* a cowboy hat.

- In sentence (5), the preposition *to* is understood before the pronoun *her*: I gave *to* her . . .
- In sentence (6), the preposition *for* is understood before the pronoun *him*: Carver bought *for* him . . .

Pronouns That Show Possession

A pronoun can show *possession* or ownership.

(1) Bill took *his* report and left.

(2) The climbers spotted *their* gear on the slope.

- In sentences (1) and (2), the pronouns *his* and *their* show that Bill owns *his* report and that the climbers own *their* gear.

The chart below can help you review all the pronouns discussed in this part.

Pronoun Case Chart					
Singular Pronouns			**Plural Pronouns**		
Subjective	Objective	Possessive	Subjective	Objective	Possessive
1st person: I	me	my (mine)	we	us	our (ours)
2nd person: you	you	your (yours)	you	you	your (yours)
3rd person: he	him	his	they	them	their (theirs)
she	her	her (hers)			
it	it	its			

* See the list of prepositions on page 321.

PRACTICE 13

Underline the pronouns in this paragraph. Then, over each pronoun, write an *S* if the pronoun is in the subjective case, an *O* if it is in the objective case, and a *P* if it is in the possessive case.

(1) These days, iReporters all over the world help bring the news to us. (2) My friend Mahit and I have joined the thousands of iReporters, or citizen reporters, who share stories from their communities. (3) We capture important or strange events as they unfold near us before the professional media even knows they are happening. (4) Using the cameras and Internet connections in our mobile phones, we take pictures or videos, add our words, and send them anywhere. (5) News organizations such as CNN and CBS post our reports in special sections of their websites. (6) They don't screen or edit the submissions before posting them. (7) Mahit became a CNN iReporter when he took photographs of a deadly tornado here in Mississippi and posted them online. (8) Sending my video of citizens protesting taxes in Washington, D.C., to YouTube made me proud. (9) Some people claim that our reports are nothing more than gossip and unverified stories. (10) They say that journalism cannot keep its integrity and ethical standards unless it is practiced only by trained professionals. (11) Others praise us as "citizen journalists," but we are hooked on iReporting and wouldn't dream of leaving home without our phones.

G. Choosing the Correct Pronoun Case

Correct Case After AND or OR

When nouns or pronouns are joined by *and* or *or*, be careful to use the correct pronoun case after the *and* or the *or*.

(1) **Incorrect:** *Carlos* and *her* have to leave soon.

(2) **Revised:** *Carlos* and *she* have to leave soon.

- In sentence (1), the pronoun *her* should be in the *subjective case* because it is part of the subject of the sentence.

- In sentence (2), change *her* to *she*.

(3) **Incorrect:** The dean congratulated *Charles* and *I.*

(4) **Revised:** The dean congratulated *Charles* and *me.*

- In sentence (3), the pronoun *I* should be in the *objective case* because it is the object of the verb *congratulated*.

- The dean congratulated *whom*? The dean congratulated *me*.

- In sentence (4), change *I* to *me*.

> (5) **Incorrect:** Is that letter for *them* or *he*?

- In sentence (5), both objects of the preposition *for* must be in the *objective case*. What should *he* be changed to? ____him____

Try This   One simple way to make sure that you have the right pronoun case is to leave out the *and* or the *or* and the word before it. You probably would not write these sentences:

> (6) **Incorrect:** *Her* have to leave soon.
>
> (7) **Incorrect:** The dean congratulated *I*.
>
> (8) **Incorrect:** Is that letter for *he*?

These sentences look and sound strange, and you would know that they have to be corrected.

PRACTICE 14

In the sentences below, circle the correct pronoun in the parentheses. If the pronoun is a *subject*, use the *subjective case*. If the pronoun is the *object* of a verb or a preposition, use the *objective case*.

1. Frieda and (I, me) were born in Bogotá, Colombia.
2. (We, Us) girls are determined to make an A on the next exam.
3. For (we, us), a swim in the ocean on a hot day is one of life's greatest joys.
4. If it were up to Angelo and (he, him), they would spend all their time snow skiing.
5. Our lab instructor expects Dan and (I, me) to hand in our report today.
6. Between you and (I, me), I don't like spinach.
7. Robert and (they, them) have decided to go to Rocky Mountain National Park with Jacinto and (she, her).
8. Either (he, him) or (she, her) must work overtime.

Correct Case in Comparisons

Pronouns in comparisons usually follow *than* or *as*.

> (1) Ferdinand is taller *than* I.
>
> (2) These guidelines help you as much *as* me.

- In sentence (1), the comparison is completed with a pronoun in the subjective case, *I*.

- In sentence (2), the comparison is completed with a pronoun in the objective case, *me*.

---

(3) Ferdinand is taller than I . . . (am tall).

(4) These guidelines help you as much as . . . (they help) . . . me.

- A comparison is really a kind of shorthand that omits repetitious words.

By completing the comparison mentally, you can choose the correct case for the pronoun.

BE CAREFUL: The case of the pronoun you place after *than* or *as* can change the meaning of the sentence.

---

(5) Diana likes Tom more than *I* . . . (more than *I* like him).

or

(6) Diana likes Tom more than *me* . . . (more than she likes *me*).

- Sentence (5) says that Diana likes Tom more than I like Tom.
- Sentence (6) says that Diana likes Tom more than she likes me.*

PRACTICE 15

Circle the correct pronoun in these comparisons.

TEACHING TIP

Students will be able to "hear" the correct pronoun better if they supply the missing words of a comparison [see example sentences (3), (4), (5), and (6) in the preceding box]. Ask them to add these words and then determine the correct pronoun case.

1. You study more often than (I, me).
2. The movie scared us more than it did (he, him).
3. Diego eats dinner earlier than (I, me).
4. She ran a better campaign for the local school board than (he, him).
5. Stan cannot memorize vocabulary words faster than (he, him).
6. I hate doing laundry more than (they, them).
7. Sometimes our children are more mature than (we, us).
8. Remembering birthdays seems easier for me than for (he, him).

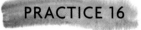

PRACTICE 16

Proofread this paragraph carefully for errors in pronoun case. Cross out any errors and write the correct pronouns above the lines.

(1) My sister Tina and ~~me~~ visited Miami for the first time this year. (2) Our cousin JJ met her and ~~I~~ at their airport and drove us to Wynwood, where he lives. (3) JJ is a graphic designer. (4) He has always been more artistic and trendy than ~~us~~. (5) JJ loves living in

---

* For more work on comparisons, see Chapter 24, Part C.

Shepard Fairey's Wall of
Heroes, Wynwood Walls,
Miami

Photo by Susan Fawcett

Wynwood, which is Miami's design district. (6) Of all the things we saw, my favorite was

the Wynwood Walls, many city blocks of whitewashed warehouse walls painted with

colorful cartoons and graphics by some of the world's best street artists. (7) We saw the

Wall of Heroes by Shepard Fairey, who painted the famous poster portrait of Obama. (8) A

mural about modern life by Liqen from Spain amazed Tina and ~~I~~. ^{me} (9) It shows creatures,

part human, part insect or animal, trapped inside concrete chambers. (10) A Brazilian

artist named Kobra painted huge colorful murals with images from the past, like roller

coasters. (11) Liqen's vision of life was much darker than ~~him~~. ^{his} (12) My sister took pictures of

a giant lobster between JJ and ~~I~~. ^{me} (13) I took one of JJ and ~~she~~ ^{her} pretending to ride a painted

motorcycle. (14) All this inspiring work is art, not graffiti, we decided. (15) On that day, no

one could have been happier than ~~me~~. ^I

EXPLORING ONLINE

<http://thewynwoodwalls.com/> To explore the Wynwood Walls, visit this
site. You might look for the work of Fairey and Liqen. Do you think this
is graffiti or art? What is the difference?

PRACTICE 17

On paper or on a computer, write three sentences using comparisons that are completed with pronouns. Choose each pronoun case carefully.

H. Using Pronouns with -*SELF* and -*SELVES*

Pronouns with -*self* and -*selves* are used in two ways.

> (1) José admired *himself* in the mirror.
>
> (2) The teacher *herself* thought the test was too difficult.

- In sentence (1), José did something to *himself*; he admired *himself*. In this sentence, *himself* is called a **reflexive pronoun**.

- In sentence (2), *herself* emphasizes the fact that the teacher—much to her surprise—found the test too hard. In this sentence, *herself* is called an **intensive pronoun**.

This chart will help you choose the right reflexive or intensive pronoun.

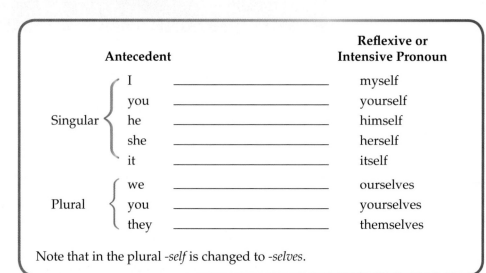

	Antecedent		Reflexive or Intensive Pronoun
Singular	I	_____	myself
	you	_____	yourself
	he	_____	himself
	she	_____	herself
	it	_____	itself
Plural	we	_____	ourselves
	you	_____	yourselves
	they	_____	themselves

Note that in the plural -*self* is changed to -*selves*.

PRACTICE 18

Write the correct reflexive or intensive pronoun in each sentence. Be careful to match the pronoun with the antecedent. Answers will vary.

EXAMPLES: I should have stopped ___*myself*___.

Roberta ___*herself*___ made this bracelet.

1. We built all the cabinets ___*ourselves*___.

2. He ___*himself*___ was surprised to discover that he had a green thumb.

3. Did you give ___*yourselves*___ a party after you graduated?

4. Rick, look at ___*yourself*___ in the mirror!

5. Don't bother; Don and André will hang the pictures ___*themselves*___.

6. These new lamps turn ___themselves___ on and off.

7. The oven cleans ___itself___.

8. Because he snores loudly, he wakes ___himself___ up several times each night.

PRACTICE 19

On paper or on a computer, write three sentences, using either a reflexive or an intensive pronoun in each.

Chapter Highlights

- **A pronoun takes the place of or refers to a noun or another pronoun:**

   Louise said that *she* would leave work early.

- **The word that a pronoun refers to is its antecedent:**

   I have chosen *my* seat for the concert.

   (*I* is the antecedent of *my*.)

- **A pronoun that refers to an indefinite pronoun or a collective noun should be singular:**

   Everyone had cleared the papers off *his* or *her* desk.

   The *committee* will give *its* report Friday.

- **A pronoun after *and* or *or* is usually in the subjective or objective case:**

   Dr. Smythe and *she* always work as a team. (*subjective*)

   The bus driver wouldn't give the map to Ms. Tallon or *me*. (*objective*)

- **Pronouns in comparisons usually follow *than* or *as*:**

   Daisuke likes Sally more than *I*.
   (*subjective*: . . . more than I like Sally)

   Daisuke likes Sally more than *me*.
   (*objective*: . . . more than he likes me)

- **A pronoun ending in -*self* (singular) or -*selves* (plural) may be used as a reflexive or an intensive pronoun. A reflexive pronoun shows that someone did something to himself or to herself; an intensive pronoun is used for emphasis:**

   On his trip, Martin bought nothing for *himself*.

   The musicians *themselves* were almost late for the street fair.

Proofreading Strategy

One of the most common pronoun errors is using the plural pronouns *they*, *them*, or *their* incorrectly to refer to a singular antecedent. If this is one of your error patterns, **search your draft for *they*, *them*, and *their*** and **highlight or underline** them. If you are using a computer, use the *"Find"* feature to locate these words.

Take a moment to **identify the antecedent** for each of these highlighted words by drawing an arrow from the highlighted word to its antecedent. Do the two words agree?

The **people** who work here usually clean up their messes, but

his or her
somebody let their lunch splatter in the microwave and didn't wipe it up.

(*Somebody* means *one*, so *their* must be changed to *his or her*.)

WRITING AND PROOFREADING ASSIGNMENT

In a small group, discuss the factors that seem absolutely necessary for a successful marriage or long-term relationship. As a group, brainstorm to identify four or five key factors.

Now imagine that a friend with very little experience has asked you for written advice about relationships. Each member of the group should choose just one of the factors and write a letter to this person. Explain in detail why this factor—for example, honesty or mutual respect—is so important to a good relationship.

Read the finished letters to one another. Which letters give the best advice or are the most convincing? Why? Exchange letters with a partner, proofreading for the correct use of pronouns.

CHAPTER REVIEW

Proofread the following essay for pronoun errors. Cross out any incorrect, vague, or repetitious pronouns and make your corrections above the lines. Use nouns to replace vague pronouns. Hint: There are 12 errors.

ESL TIP

Many ESL speakers learn English through their ears, so they repeat pronoun errors that they hear. Remind students that written English is more formal than spoken English, so they must follow pronoun rules rather than informal spoken pronoun usage.

© Pete Saloutos/Shutterstock.com

The Devastating Cost of Concussions

(1) Professional football players are America's gladiators. (2) Each of them is a nearly
his
superhuman young man who crashes into ~~their~~ opponents at high speeds. (3) Concussions—

brain injuries caused by a blow—are common in football and other contact sports. (4) Until

recently, a concussion was thought to be a minor injury. (5) One of the players who suffered
his
a concussion might just say ~~their~~ "bell was rung" and be sent back into the game. (6) In the
researchers
last 10 years, however, ~~they~~ have exposed the tragic, long-term effects of concussions on

the human brain.

its
(7) The National Football League has conducted studies of ~~their~~ retired players. (8) Each
his
of these men had ~~their~~ brain and body tested. (9) The rate of depression and nerve damage

was three times that of the average population. (10) Tragically, six retired players have killed

^{themselves}   ^{their}
~~theirself~~ recently and left notes asking that ~~his or her~~ brains be studied. (11) Autopsies

showed that all of them had a serious type of dementia that can cause memory loss,

violent outbursts, depression, and suicidal thoughts. (12) The public is just becoming aware

of the enormity of the problem.

                                                     ^{its}
(13) The NFL is taking steps to make ~~their~~ players safer, with a new policy for handling

concussions, helmet improvements, and stiffer penalties for head hits. (14) But the NFL

                                                     ^{its}
must also walk a fine line in trying to do right by ~~their~~ players without changing the core of

                            ^{Its}
what makes football popular. (15) ~~Their~~ goal, after all, is to make money, and violence sells.

(16) Other sports—including boxing, hockey, and even soccer—will need to make changes,

                                                                            ^{they}
too. (17) All agree that children and teens face more risk than adults if ~~he or she~~ gets a

concussion. (18) This is why every parent should keep a watchful eye on the concussion

                   ^{his or her}
policy at ~~their~~ children's school.

PRACTICE 20 · Teamwork: Critical Thinking and Writing

In a group with several classmates, discuss the issue of concussions in the NFL. Should the rules and nature of football change in order to protect players' brains? Do you agree with some experts who say that professional football can never sufficiently protect players' brains, so the sport should be banned? Be prepared to defend your stand to the class.

EXPLORING ONLINE

<http://grammar.ccc.commnet.edu/grammar/cgi-shl/quiz.pl/pronouns_add2 .htm> Interactive quizzes: Choose the correct pronoun or verb.

<http://aliscot.com/bigdog/agrpa_exercise.htm> Take Big Dog's pronoun quiz to see how well you have mastered pronoun use.

CHAPTER 24

Adjectives and Adverbs

A. Defining and Writing Adjectives and Adverbs

Adjectives and adverbs are two kinds of descriptive words. An **adjective** describes a noun or a pronoun. It tells *which one*, *what kind*, or *how many*.

> (1) The *red* coat belongs to me.
>
> (2) He looks *healthy*.

- In sentence (1), the adjective *red* describes the noun *coat*.

- In sentence (2), the adjective *healthy* describes the pronoun *he*.

    An **adverb** describes a verb, an adjective, or another adverb. Adverbs often end in *-ly*. They tell *how*, *to what extent*, *why*, *when*, or *where*.

> (3) Laura sings *loudly*.
>
> (4) My biology instructor is *extremely* short.
>
> (5) Lift this box *very* carefully.

- In sentence (3), *loudly* describes the verb *sings*. How does Laura sing? She sings *loudly*.

- In sentence (4), *extremely* describes the adjective *short*. How short is the instructor? *Extremely* short.

- In sentence (5), *very* describes the adverb *carefully*. How carefully should you lift the box? *Very* carefully.

PRACTICE 1

Complete each sentence with an appropriate adjective from the list below. Answers will vary.

funny	orange	sarcastic	energetic
old	tired	bitter	little

1. Bella is _____energetic_____.
2. He often wears a(n) _____orange_____ baseball cap.
3. _____Sarcastic_____ remarks will be his downfall.
4. My daughter collects _____old_____ movie posters.
5. This coffee tastes _____bitter_____.

PRACTICE 2

Complete each sentence with an appropriate adverb from the list below. Answers will vary.

quietly	loudly	wildly	convincingly
madly	quickly	constantly	happily

1. The waiter _____quickly_____ cleaned the table.
2. Mr. Huff whistles _____constantly_____.
3. The lawyer spoke _____convincingly_____.
4. They charged _____madly_____ down the long hallway.
5. _____Quietly_____, he entered the rear door of the church.

Many adjectives can be changed into adverbs by adding an *-ly* ending. For example, *glad* becomes *gladly*, *thoughtful* becomes *thoughtfully*, and *wise* becomes *wisely*.

Be especially careful of the adjectives and adverbs in this list; they are easily confused.

Adjective	Adverb	Adjective	Adverb
awful	awfully	quick	quickly
bad	badly	quiet	quietly
easy	easily	real	really
poor	poorly	sure	surely

(6) This chair is a *real* antique.

(7) She has a *really* bad sprain.

- In sentence (6), *real* is an adjective describing the noun *antique*.

- In sentence (7), *really* is an adverb describing the adjective *bad*. How bad is the sprain? The sprain is *really* bad.

PRACTICE 3

Change each adjective in the left-hand column into its adverb form.*

EXAMPLE: You are polite. You answer _____politely_____.

Adjective	Adverb
1. She is honest.	1. She responds _____honestly_____.

_____

* If you have questions about spelling, see Chapter 34, Part E.

2. They are loud.
3. It is easy.
4. We are careful.
5. He is creative.
6. She was quick.
7. It is perfect.
8. It is real.
9. He is eager.
10. We are joyful.

2. They sing ___loudly___.
3. It turns ___easily___.
4. We decide ___carefully___.
5. He thinks ___creatively___.
6. She acted ___quickly___.
7. It fits ___perfectly___.
8. It is ___really___ hot.
9. He waited ___eagerly___.
10. We watch ___joyfully___.

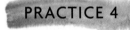

PRACTICE 4

TEACHING TIP

Practice 4 is an engaging full-class activity. It not only sharpens students' skill with adjectives and adverbs but also enhances their cultural literacy by teaching them about an important ecosystem.

Circle the adjective or adverb form of the word in parentheses.

EXAMPLE: Lovers of nature argue (passionate, (passionately)) that we must protect the Galapagos Islands.

1. These ((remote,) remotely) islands lie in the Pacific Ocean six hundred miles off the coast of Ecuador.
2. They are (actual, (actually)) just piles of volcanic lava.
3. Nevertheless, they are home to ((abundant,) abundantly) wildlife.
4. For centuries, the Galapagos Islands remained (complete, (completely)) isolated and undisturbed by humans.
5. As a result, some ((rare,) rarely) animal species developed there.
6. For example, giant tortoises up to six feet long from head to tail lumber (slow, (slowly)) across the hills and beaches.
7. The world's only swimming iguanas (lazy, (lazily)) sun themselves on jet-black rocks.
8. The islands are also home to many ((amazing,) amazingly) birds.
9. Blue-footed boobies waddle (comic, (comically)) over the boulders.

Blue-footed boobies of the Galapagos Islands engage in a courtship dance.

10. Flightless cormorants, which live only in the Galapagos, dive (graceful, gracefully) into the sea, searching for eel and octopus.

11. Tiny Galapagos penguins, the only ones north of the equator, hop (easy, easily) into and out of the ocean.

12. During his voyage of 1831, Charles Darwin visited the Galapagos Islands and gathered evidence to support his (famous, famously) theory of natural selection.

13. Today, the islands are still the (perfect, perfectly) place for scientists to conduct research.

14. Ecotourists, too, are drawn to the (spectacular, spectacularly) scenery and (fabulous, fabulously) animals.

15. If we tread very (gentle, gently) on this fragile ecosystem, we might preserve it for future generations.

EXPLORING ONLINE

Using Google or your favorite search engine, look up "Galapagos, animals, birds" or "Galapagos, Darwin's voyage" to see pictures and learn more about these islands.

PRACTICE 5

On paper or computer, write sentences using the following adjectives and adverbs: *quick/quickly, bad/badly, glad/gladly, real/really, easy/easily.*

LEARNING STYLES TIP

Have students write some or all of their answers to Practice 5 on the board. As a class, discuss any needed edits.

EXAMPLES: (*cheerful*) *You are cheerful this morning.*

(*cheerfully*) *You make breakfast cheerfully.*

B. A Troublesome Pair: GOOD/WELL

Unlike most adjectives, *good* does not add *-ly* to become an adverb; it changes to *well.*

TEACHING TIP

The error most commonly made is using *good* in place of *well* (as in *Julian plays ball very good*). Point out that although we might hear this in casual speech, it is a red-flag error in writing. Before students start Practice 6, you might suggest that they name the missing word's part of speech *before* they choose *good* or *well.*

(1) **Adjective:** Peter is a *good* student.

(2) **Adverb:** He writes *well.*

- In sentence (1), the adjective *good* describes or modifies *student.*

- In sentence (2), the adverb *well* describes or modifies *writes.*

Note, however, that *well* can be used as an adjective to mean *in good health*—for example, *He felt well after his long vacation.*

PRACTICE 6

Write either *good* or *well* in each blank.

EXAMPLE: Charles plays ball very _____well_____.

1. Lorelle is a _____good_____ pilot.

2. She handles a plane _____well_____.

3. How _____well_____ do you understand virtual reality?

4. Tovah knows my bad habits very _____well_____.

5. It is a _____good_____ thing we ran into each other.

6. Brian works _____ well _____ with other people.

7. How _____ well _____ or how badly did you do at the tryouts?

8. Were the cherry tarts _____ good _____ or tasteless?

9. Denzel Washington is not just a _____ good _____ actor; he's a great one.

10. These plants don't grow very _____ well _____ in the sunlight.

11. Carole doesn't look as though she takes _____ good _____ care of herself.

12. He asked _____ good _____ questions at the meeting, and she answered them _____ well _____.

C. Writing Comparatives

> (1) John is *tall*.
>
> (2) John is *taller* than Mike.

● Sentence (1) describes John with the adjective *tall*, but sentence (2) *compares* John and Mike in terms of how tall they are: John is the *taller* of the two.

Taller **is called the** *comparative* **of** *tall*.

Use the comparative when you want to compare two people or things.

To Form Comparatives
Add *-er* to adjectives and adverbs that have *one syllable*:*
short   shorter fast   faster thin   thinner
Place the word *more* before adjectives and adverbs that have *two or more syllables*:
foolish   more foolish rotten   more rotten happily   more happily

Use either *more* **or** *-er* **to show a comparison—never both.**

Example: Your voice is *louder* **than mine. (**not *more louder*)

PRACTICE 7

Write the comparative form of each word. Either add *-er* to the word or write *more* before it. Never add both *-er* and *more*!

EXAMPLES: _____ fresh _er_ _____

_____ more _____ willing _____

1. _____ fast _er_ _____   3. _____ thick _er_ _____

2. _____ more _____ interesting _____   4. _____ more _____ modern _____

* For questions about spelling, see Chapter 34, Part D.

5. ___more___ hopeful _____   7. ___more___ valuable _____

6. _____ sweet _er_____   8. _____ cold _er_____

Here is one important exception to the rule that two-syllable words use *more* to form the comparative:

> To show the comparative of two-syllable adjectives ending in *-y*, change the *y* to *i* and add *-er*.*
>
> | cloudy | cloudier |
> | sunny | sunnier |

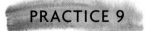

PRACTICE 8   Write the comparative form of each adjective.

EXAMPLE: happy _____ *happier* _____

1. shiny _____ shinier _____   5. fancy _____ fancier _____
2. friendly _____ friendlier _____   6. lucky _____ luckier _____
3. lazy _____ lazier _____   7. lively _____ livelier _____
4. easy _____ easier _____   8. crazy _____ crazier _____

PRACTICE 9   The following incorrect sentences use both *more* and *-er*. Decide which one is correct and write your revised sentences on the lines provided.

REMEMBER: Write comparatives with either *more* or *-er*—not both!

EXAMPLES: Halle is more younger than her brother.

Halle is younger than her brother.

I feel more comfortabler in this chair than on the couch.

I feel more comfortable in this chair than on the couch.

1. Her new boss is more fussier than her previous one.

Her new boss is fussier than her previous one.

2. The trail was more rockier than we expected.

The trail was rockier than we expected.

3. The people in my new neighborhood are more friendlier than those in my old one.

The people in my new neighborhood are friendlier than those in my old one.

4. Magda has a more cheerfuler personality than her sister.

Magda has a more cheerful personality than her sister.

5. I have never seen a more duller TV program than this one.

I have never seen a duller TV program than this one.

---

* For questions about spelling, see Chapter 34, Part G.

6. The audience at this theater is more noisier than usual.

The audience at this theater is noisier than usual.

7. His jacket is more newer than Rudy's.

His jacket is newer than Rudy's.

8. If today is more warmer than yesterday, we'll picnic on the lawn.

If today is warmer than yesterday, we'll picnic on the lawn.

PRACTICE 10   On paper or on a computer, write sentences using the comparative form of the following adjectives or adverbs: _dark, cloudy, fortunate, slowly, wet._

EXAMPLE: (_funny_) _This play is funnier than the one we saw last week._

D. Writing Superlatives

(1) Niko is the _tallest_ player on the team.

(2) Juan was voted the _most useful_ player.

- In sentence (1), Niko is not just _tall_ or _taller than_ someone else; he is the _tallest_ of all the players on the team.

- In sentence (2), Juan was voted the _most useful_ of all the players.

Tallest **and** _most useful_ **are called** _superlatives_.

Use the superlative when you wish to compare more than two people or things.

To Form Superlatives
Add _-est_ to adjectives and adverbs of _one syllable_:
short   shortest
Place the word _most_ before adjectives and adverbs that have _two or more syllables_:
foolish   most foolish
Exception: With two-syllable adjectives ending in _-y_, change the _y_ to _i_ and add _-est._*
happy   happiest

Use either _most_ **or** _-est_ **to compare three or more things—never both.**

Example: Jaden is the most creative web designer. (<u>not</u> _most creativest_**)**

---

* For questions about spelling, see Chapter 34, Part G.

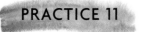

PRACTICE 11   Write the superlative form of each word. Either add -est to the word or write *most* before it; do not do both.

EXAMPLES: _____ tall *est* _____

_____ *most* _____ ridiculous _____

1. _____ loud *est* _____   6. _____ wild *est* _____
2. _____ *most* colorful _____   7. _____ *most* practical _____
3. _____ brave *est* _____   8. _____ *most* frightening _____
4. _____ strong *est* _____   9. _____ green *est* _____
5. _____ *most* brilliant _____   10. _____ hazy *haziest* _____

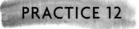

PRACTICE 12   The following incorrect sentences use both *most* and -est. Decide which one is correct and write your revised sentences on the lines provided.

REMEMBER: Write superlatives with either *most* or -est—not both!

EXAMPLES: Emmy is the most youngest of my three children.

Emmy is the youngest of my three children.

He is the most skillfulest guitarist in the band.

He is the most skillful guitarist in the band.

1. My nephew is the most thoughtfulest teenager I know.

My nephew is the most thoughtful teenager I know.

2. Mercury is the most closest planet to the sun.

Mercury is the closest planet to the sun.

3. This baby makes the most oddest gurgling noises we have ever heard.

This baby makes the oddest gurgling noises we have ever heard.

4. Jackie always makes us laugh, but she is most funniest when she hasn't had enough sleep.

Jackie always makes us laugh, but she is funniest when she hasn't had enough sleep.

5. When I finally started college, I was the most eagerest student on campus.

When I finally started college, I was the most eager student on campus.

6. Ms. Dross raises the most strangest reptiles in her basement.

Ms. Dross raises the strangest reptiles in her basement.

7. This peach is the most ripest in the basket.

This peach is the ripest in the basket.

8. He thinks that the most successfulest people are just lucky.

He thinks that the most successful people are just lucky.

E. Troublesome Comparatives and Superlatives

These comparatives and superlatives are some of the trickiest you will learn:

		Comparative	Superlative
Adjective:	good	better	best
Adverb:	well	better	best
Adjective:	bad	worse	worst
Adverb:	badly	worse	worst

PRACTICE 13

Fill in the correct comparative or superlative form of the word in parentheses.

REMEMBER: *Better* and *worse* compare *two* persons or things. *Best* and *worst* compare three or more persons or things.

EXAMPLES: Is this report ___*better*___ (good) than my last one?
(Here two reports are compared.)

It was the ___*worst*___ (bad) movie I have ever seen.
(Of *all* movies, it was the *most* awful.)

1. He likes jogging ___better___ (well) than running.
2. I like country and western music ___best___ (well) of all.
3. Bob's motorcycle rides ___worse___ (bad) now than it did last week.
4. That is the ___worst___ (bad) joke Molly has ever told!
5. The volleyball team played ___worse___ (badly) than it did last year.
6. He plays the piano ___better___ (well) than he plays the guitar.
7. The traffic is ___worse___ (bad) on Fridays than on Mondays.
8. That was the ___worst___ (bad) cold I have had in years.
9. Sales are ___better___ (good) this year than last.
10. Do you take this person for ___better___ (good) or for ___worse___ (bad)?

F. Demonstrative Adjectives: THIS/THAT and THESE/THOSE

This, that, these, and *those* are called **demonstrative adjectives** because they point out, or demonstrate, which noun is meant.

> (1) I don't trust *that* wobbly front wheel.
>
> (2) *Those* toys are not as safe as their makers claim.

- In sentence (1), *that* points to a particular wheel, the wobbly front one.
- In sentence (2), *those* points to a particular group of toys.

Demonstrative adjectives are the only adjectives that change to show singular and plural:

Singular	Plural
this book	these books
that book	those books

This and *that* are used before singular nouns; *these* and *those* are used before plural nouns.

PRACTICE 14

In each sentence, circle the correct form of the demonstrative adjective in parentheses.

1. (This, These) corn flakes taste like cardboard.

2. Mr. Lathorpe is sure (this, these) address is correct.

3. You can find (that, those) maps in the reference room.

4. Can you catch (that, those) waiter's eye?

5. I can't imagine what (that, those) gadgets are for.

6. We prefer (this, these) tennis court to (that, those) one.

7. The learning center is in (that, those) gray building.

8. (These, This) biography tells the story of Charles Curtis, the first Native American elected to the Senate.

Chapter Highlights

- **Most adverbs are formed by adding -ly to an adjective:**

  quick/quickly   bright/brightly   *but* good/well

- **Comparative adjectives and adverbs compare two persons or things:**

  I think that Don is *happier* than his brother.

  Laura can balance a checkbook *more quickly* than I can.

- **Superlative adjectives and adverbs compare more than two persons or things:**

  Last night, Ingrid had the *worst* headache of her life.

  That was the *most carefully* prepared speech I have ever heard.

- **The adjectives *good* and *bad* and the adverbs *well* and *badly* require special care in the comparative and the superlative:**

  good/better/best
  bad/worse/worst

  well/better/best
  badly/worse/worst

- **Demonstrative adjectives can be singular or plural:**

  this/that (chair)
  these/those (chairs)

Proofreading Strategy

To help you proofread for *adjective* and *adverb* errors, use two highlighters to code the text. Read slowly, and **mark every adjective purple and every adverb gray** (or colors of your choice), like these sentences below from one student's paper.

Next check every purple and gray word, one by one. **Ask yourself what word each one describes.** For example, *What word do gold and purple describe?* (*Gold* and *purple* describe *jersey*, a noun. Thus, the adjectives *gold* and *purple* are correct.) *What does the word proudly describe?* (*Proudly* describes *wears*, a verb. Thus, the adverb *proudly* is correct.)

My son wears his gold and purple jersey proudly. He longs to be *really* real tall, like his favorite players. He tells me he will have the *most amazing* most amazingest jump shot in the NBA.

WRITING AND PROOFREADING ASSIGNMENT

Sports figures and entertainers can be excellent role models. Sometimes, though, they teach the wrong lessons. For example, an athlete or entertainer might take drugs, have affairs, or get in trouble with the law; another might set a bad example through lifestyle or even dress.

Assume that you are concerned that your child or young sibling is being negatively influenced by one of these figures. Write a "fan letter" to this person, explaining the bad influence he or she is having on young people—in particular, on your child or sibling. Convince him or her that being in the spotlight is a serious responsibility and that a positive change in behavior could help young fans.

Brainstorm, freewrite, or cluster to generate ideas and examples to support your concern. After you revise your letter, take time to proofread: color code your adjectives and adverbs. Then check the word each one refers to and make sure your choices are correct.

CHAPTER REVIEW

Proofread these paragraphs for adjective and adverb errors. Cross out the errors and correct them above the lines.

A. (1) The Hubble Space Telescope is the world's ~~famousest~~ *most famous* telescope and one of the most important in history. (2) Launched into space in 1990, it orbits ~~regular~~ *regularly* around the Earth and takes ~~incredibly~~ *incredible* photographs. (3) Named for astronomer Dr. Edwin Hubble, it carries ~~real~~ *really* sensitive equipment that captures ~~more better~~ *better* and ~~sharp~~ *sharper* images than Earth-based telescopes do. (4) ~~This extreme~~ *These extremely* detailed pictures of planets, galaxies, nebulas, and black holes have helped scientists solve age-old riddles, such as the age of the universe.

(5) Hubble has helped find new galaxies and the ~~most old~~ *oldest* planet known—3 billion years.

(6) Many people log on to the Hubble website every day just to gaze at beautiful close-ups

The Hubble Telescope
orbiting in space

of Mars or ~~brilliantly~~ _brilliant_ gas towers rising from a nebula. (7) For them, viewing the universe

through Hubble's eyes is inspirational, even ~~spiritually~~ _spiritual_. (8) Soon, NASA plans to let the

Hubble telescope burn up in Earth's atmosphere. (9) Some say that its demise won't be the

~~baddest~~ _worst_ thing that could happen because plans to launch an even ~~more big~~ _bigger_ telescope in

2018 are already under way.

EXPLORING ONLINE

<http://hubblesite.org/> Go to the Hubble website, click on Gallery, and
take notes as you look at the images. Why do you think so many people
log on to gaze? Why do some call the pictures "spiritual"?

B. (1) One of the ~~real~~ _really_ inspirational stories of recent years is that of Malala Yousafzai.

(2) In 2009, when Malala was 12 years old, the terrorist Taliban organization took over her

hometown in Pakistan and demanded that the schools stop educating girls. (3) Putting

herself in grave danger, Malala ~~heroic~~ _heroically_ refused to stop reading and learning. (4) Instead,

she spoke out ~~strong~~ _strongly_ for women's education, criticizing the Taliban's actions on television,

at protests, and in her blog. (5) In revenge, Taliban assassins attempted to silence the

~~courageously~~ _courageous_ girl, but they achieved the opposite.

(6) On October 9, 2012, when Malala was 15, Taliban assassins stormed her school bus,

Critically
shooting her in the head and neck. (7) ~~Critical~~ wounded, she was rushed to a Pakistan

hospital. (8) Later, transferred to a British hospital, she endured months of treatment and

many surgeries. (9) The attack sparked worldwide media coverage, outrage, and admiration

louder   clearer
for this teenager's courage. Malala survived, becoming an even ~~more louder~~ and ~~more clear~~

voice for girls' education around the world.

(10) Pakistan awarded her its first National Youth Peace Prize. (11) CNN.com readers voted

most intriguing
her one of 2012's ~~most intriguingest~~ people. (12) The United Nations named November 10

best
"Malala Day" to honor her work. (13) The ~~most best~~ result, though, has been the "Malala

educational
effect," a new interest in providing ~~educationally~~ opportunities for the 32 million girls who

have never attended school. (14) Despite the Taliban's continued threats against her life,

Malala has vowed to continue her fight for girls' right to learn.

EXPLORING ONLINE

TEACHING TIP

Instructor tools for *Grassroots* include a computerized Test Bank, PowerPoint slides, an Instructor's Manual with teaching tips, and more, and can be accessed at ‹**login .cengage.com**›.

<http://a4esl.org/q/f/z/zz60fck.htm> Interactive quiz: Choose the adjective or the adverb.

<http://www.dailygrammar.com/066to070.shtml> Five tests with answers: Choose the correct form—adjective or adverb.

<http://a4esl.org/q/h/vm/compsup2.html> Interactive quiz: Pick the correct comparatives and superlatives.

CHAPTER 25

Prepositions

A: Defining and Working with Prepositional Phrases

B: Troublesome Prepositions: IN, ON, and LIKE

C: Prepositions in Common Expressions

A. Defining and Working with Prepositional Phrases

A **preposition** is a word like *at*, *beside*, *from*, *of*, or *with* that shows the *relationship* between other words in a sentence. Prepositions usually show *location*, *direction*, or *time*. Here are a few examples:

Prepositions of location	above, against, around, behind, beside, between, beyond, in, under
Prepositions of direction	across, down, through, to, toward, up
Prepositions of time	after, before, during, until

Because there are so many prepositions in English, these words can be confusing, especially to nonnative speakers. Here is a partial list of common prepositions.*

Common Prepositions			
about	beneath	inside	through
above	beside	into	throughout
across	between	like	to
after	beyond	near	toward
against	by	of	under
along	despite	off	underneath
among	down	on	until
around	during	onto	up
at	except	out	upon
before	for	outside	with
behind	from	over	within
below	in	past	without

* For more work on prepositions, see Chapter 9, Part C.

A preposition is usually followed by a noun or pronoun. The noun or pronoun is called the **object** of the preposition. Together, the preposition and its object are called a **prepositional phrase**.

Here are some prepositional phrases:

Prepositional Phrase	=	Preposition	+	Object
after the movie		after		the movie
at Kean College		at		Kean College
beside them		beside		them
between you and me		between		you and me

ESL TIP

Suggest that students try learning prepositions with flashcards, memorizing when necessary. Also refer them to online exercises like the crossword puzzle at ‹**http://grammar.ccc.commnet.edu/grammar/quizzes/cross/cross_prep2.htm**›.

The preposition shows a relationship between the object of the preposition and some other word in the sentence. Below are some sentences with prepositional phrases:

(1) Ms. Kringell arrived *at noon.*

(2) A man *in a gray suit* bought 30 lottery tickets.

(3) The huge moving van sped through the tunnel.

● In sentence (1), the prepositional phrase *at noon* tells when Ms. Kringell arrived. It describes *arrived.*

● In sentence (2), the prepositional phrase *in a gray suit* describes how the man was dressed. It describes *man.*

● What is the prepositional phrase in sentence (3)? _____through the tunnel_____

   Which word does it describe? _____sped_____

PRACTICE 1

Underline the prepositional phrases in the following sentences.

1. Bill collected some interesting facts about human biology.

2. Human eyesight is sharpest at midday.

3. In extreme cold, shivering produces heat, which can save lives.

4. A pound of body weight equals 3,500 calories.

5. Each of us has a distinguishing odor.

6. Fingernails grow fastest in summer.

7. One of every ten people is left-handed.

8. The human body contains approximately ten pints of blood.

9. Beards grow more rapidly than any other hair on the human body.

10. Most people with an extra rib are men.

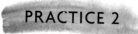

PRACTICE 2

Teamwork: Critical Viewing and Writing

In pairs or small groups, look at this photograph. Describe it by writing at least ten sentences using prepositional phrases.

EXAMPLES: She holds *onto a rope.*
The blue sea lies *beneath her.*

B. Troublesome Prepositions: IN, ON, and LIKE

IN/ON for Time

Use *in* before seasons of the year, before months not followed by specific dates, and before years that do not include specific dates.

(1) *In the summer,* some of us like to lie around in the sun.

(2) No classes will meet *in January.*

(3) Rona was a student at Centerville Business School *in 2004.*

Use *on* before days of the week, before holidays, and before months if a date follows.

---

(4) *On Thursday*, the gym was closed for renovations.

(5) The city looked deserted *on Christmas Eve*.

(6) We hope to arrive in Burlington *on October 3*.

IN/ON for Place

In means *inside of*.

---

(1) My grandmother slept *in the spare bedroom*.

(2) The exchange student spent the summer *in Sweden*.

On means *on top of* or *at a particular place*.

---

(3) The spinach pie *on the table* is for tonight's book discussion group meeting.

(4) Dr. Helfman lives *on Marblehead Road*.

LIKE

Like is a preposition that means *similar to*. Therefore, it is followed by an object (usually a noun or a pronoun).

---

(1) *Like you*, I prefer watching films on demand rather than going to a crowded movie theater.

Do not confuse *like* with *as* or *as if*. *As* and *as if* are subordinating conjunctions.* They are followed by a subject and a verb.

---

(2) *As the instructions explain*, insert flap B into slit B before folding the bottom in half.

(3) Robert sometimes acts *as if he has never made a mistake*.

PRACTICE 3

Fill in the correct prepositions in the following sentences. Be especially careful when using *in*, *on*, and *like*.

1. To celebrate America's one hundredth birthday, _____on_____ July 4, 1876, the French decided to give a special statue _____to_____ their "sister country."

---

* For more work on subordinating conjunctions, see Chapter 17.

2. Sculptor Frédéric-Auguste Bartholdi sailed _____to_____ America, seeking support _____for_____ the ambitious project.

3. Bartholdi was awed _____by_____ America's vastness as he traveled _____through_____ redwood forests, _____across_____ prairies, and _____over_____ mountains.

4. _____In_____ Egypt he had seen huge monuments _____like_____ the pyramids and the Sphinx, and he wanted to honor liberty _____with_____ a structure as majestic as those.

5. His monument would be so big that visitors would be able to walk _____into_____ it and climb _____up_____ a staircase _____to_____ its top.

6. Funded _____by_____ the French, Bartholdi finally built his statue _____of_____ a woman raising her torch _____toward_____ the sky.

7. _____After_____ many delays, a newspaper urged American citizens to help pay for the statue's base; money poured _____in_____ , and the base was erected _____on_____ Bedloe's Island _____in_____ New York Harbor.

8. The Statue of Liberty was not shipped _____from_____ France _____to_____ America _____until_____ 1885, and then it took six months to mount her _____on_____ the foundation.

9. One million people and hundreds of ships gathered _____in_____ the rain and fog to see the statue unveiled _____on_____ October 28, 1886.

10. Today, Lady Liberty still rises 305 feet _____above_____ the harbor, lighting the darkness _____with_____ her torch and symbolizing freedom _____around_____ the globe.

The Statue of Liberty's arm and torch under construction in a Paris studio

AP Photo/Agence Papyrus

EXPLORING ONLINE

To learn more, look up "Statue of Liberty" on your favorite search engine. Can you answer these questions? 1. What famous person designed the metal skeleton, or scaffolding, that holds up Lady Liberty? 2. In how many pieces was the Statue of Liberty shipped from France? 1. Gustave Eiffel, who designed the Eiffel Tower   2. 350 pieces

C. Prepositions in Common Expressions

Prepositions often are combined with other words to form certain expressions—groups of words, or phrases, in common use. These expressions can sometimes be confusing. Below is a list of some troublesome expressions. If you are in doubt about others, consult a dictionary.

Common Expressions with Prepositions	
Expression	**Example**
acquainted with	He became *acquainted with* his duties.
addicted to	I am *addicted to* chocolate.
agree on (a plan)	They finally *agreed on* a sales strategy.
agree to (another's proposal)	Did she *agree to* their demands?
angry about or at (a thing)	The subway riders are *angry about* (or *at*) the delays.
angry with (a person)	The manager seems *angry with* Jake.
apply for (a position)	You should *apply for* this job.
approve of	Does he *approve of* the proposed budget?
consist of	The plot *consisted of* both murder and intrigue.
contrast with	The red lettering *contrasts* nicely *with* the gray stationery.
convenient for	Is Friday *convenient for* you?
correspond with (write)	My daughter *corresponds with* a pen pal in India.
deal with	How do you *deal with* friends who always want to borrow your notes?
depend on	He *depends on* your advice.
differ from (something)	A diesel engine *differs from* a gasoline engine.
differ with (a person)	On that point, I *differ with* the medical technician.
different from	His account of the accident is *different from* hers.
displeased with	She is *displeased with* all the publicity.
fond of	We are all *fond of* Sam's grandmother.
grateful for (something)	Tia was *grateful for* the two test review sessions.
grateful to (someone)	We are *grateful to* the plumber for repairing the leak on Sunday.

identical with or to	This watch is *identical with* (or *to*) hers.
interested in	George is *interested in* modern art.
interfere with	Does the party *interfere with* your study plans?
object to	She *objects to* the increase in the state sales tax.
protect against	This vaccine *protects* people *against* the flu.
reason with	Don't *reason with* a hungry pit bull.
reply to	Did the newspaper editor *reply to* your letter?
responsible for	Omar is *responsible for* marketing.
shocked at	We were *shocked at* the damage to the buildings.
similar to	That popular song is *similar to* another one I know.
specialize in	The shop *specializes in* clothing for large men.
succeed in	Gandhi *succeeded in* freeing India from British rule.
take advantage of	Let's *take advantage of* that two-for-one paperback book sale.
worry about	I no longer *worry about* my manager's moods.

ESL TIP

For lists of other idiomatic expressions containing prepositions, see "The Most Frequently Used Spoken American English Idioms," *TESOL Quarterly*, Vol. 37, No. 4, Winter 2003. Examples from the lists: *in terms of, look for, go ahead, in order to, with respect to,* and *call for*.

PRACTICE 4

Circle the correct expressions in these sentences.

1. Most people need time to adjust to a new environment that (differs with, (differs from)) what is familiar and comfortable.

2. For example, entering a new college or country requires that a person ((deal with,) deal in) strange sights, customs, and values.

3. The difficulty of the adjustment period ((depends on,) depends with) the individual.

4. The process of cultural adjustment (consists in, (consists of)) four predictable stages.

5. During the enjoyable "honeymoon stage," a person is (interested on, (interested in)) the new place.

6. He or she settles in and gets ((acquainted with,) acquainted to) the new surroundings.

7. In the second stage, however, the excitement wears off, and the person might (worry of, (worry about)) not fitting in.

8. In this "conflict stage," people struggle to understand behaviors and expectations ((different from,) different with) those in their native country or hometown.

9. In the third, so-called critical stage, some (take advantage on, (take advantage of)) the opportunity and immerse themselves in the foreign culture.

10. Others feel ((displeased with,) displeased in) their experience and spend more time with people who share their customs.

11. During the final stage, the recovery stage, those who (deal about, (deal with)) their experience as an adventure usually begin to feel more at ease.

12. They (succeed on, (succeed in)) adapting to their new home.

Chapter Highlights

- **Prepositions are words like** *at*, *from*, *in*, **and** *of*. **A prepositional phrase contains a preposition and its object:**

  The tree *beneath my window* has lost its leaves.

- **Be careful of the prepositions** *in*, *on*, **and** *like*:

  I expect to graduate *in* June.
  I expect to graduate *on* June 10.

  The Packards live *in* Tacoma.
  The Packards live *on* Farnsworth Avenue.

  Like my father, I am a Dodgers fan.

- **Prepositions are often combined with other words to form fixed phrases:**

  convenient for, different from, reason with

Proofreading Strategy

If preposition errors are one of your error patterns, try this strategy. Using the feedback you've received from instructors and tutors who know your writing, **record the five prepositions that give you the most trouble** on your Personal Error Patterns Chart.

Carefully scan your writing for each of these five prepositions. If you are using a computer, use the *"Find"* feature to locate these words in your draft. Then **make sure that you have used each of these prepositions correctly.**

In
On the United States, citizens celebrate Independence Day *on* in July 4 with parades, picnics, and fireworks.

WRITING AND PROOFREADING ASSIGNMENT

A friend or relative of yours has come to spend a holiday week in your city. He or she has never been there before and wants advice on sightseeing. In complete sentences, write directions for one day's sightseeing. Make sure to explain why you think this person would enjoy visiting each particular spot.

Organize your directions according to time order—that is, what to do first, second, and so on. Use transitional expressions like *then*, *after*, and *while* to indicate time order. Try to work in a few of the expressions listed in Part C. Proofread for your five most troublesome prepositions.

CHAPTER REVIEW

Proofread the following essay for preposition errors. Cross out the errors and correct them above the lines.

Science Babe: What's in a Name?

(1) Deborah Berebichez grew up ~~at~~ *in* Mexico City in a traditional family. (2) One day she told her parents that she wanted to be a mathematician. (3) They were shocked ~~of~~ *by* this idea and did not approve ~~about~~ *of* their daughter studying math. (4) "Then you will never find a man to marry ~~with~~ you," they declared. (5) Deborah, however, did not worry ~~of~~ *about* being too smart to find a husband. (6) Instead, she searched for colleges with the best math and science programs.

(7) In 2005 Dr. Berebichez became the first Mexican woman to earn a PhD ~~about~~ *in* physics at California's Stanford University. (8) In addition to science, she had always been interested ~~on~~ *in* communication. (9) Knowing that many people are afraid ~~about~~ *of* math and science, she wished they could see these subjects as a fascinating and important part ~~off~~ *of* everyday life. (10) In particular, she dreamed ~~on~~ *of* teaching this view to the next generation of girls.

(11) Now Dr. Berebichez is igniting new interest in science ~~from~~ *through* speaking tours, radio and television appearances, and Web videos ~~of~~ *with* titles like "The Physics of High Heels." (12) Who knew that a 110-pound woman wearing stiletto high heels puts more pressure ~~for~~ *on* the ground than a 6,000-pound elephant? (13) Showing that scientists, as well as science, can be interesting and fun, she goes ~~with~~ *by* the name of Science Babe. (14) Perhaps the Science Babe is telling her parents and others that science and feminine appeal can exist ~~during~~ *in* the same person.

EXPLORING ONLINE

TEACHING TIP

Instructor tools for *Grassroots* include a computerized Test Bank, PowerPoint slides, an Instructor's Resource Manual with teaching tips, and more, and can be accessed at ‹**login .cengage.com**›.

<http://a4esl.org/q/h/vm/prepos01.html> Interactive quiz: Select the right prepositions for each sentence.

<http://a4esl.org/q/j/ck/mc-prepositions.html> Test your preposition intuition with this 52-question quiz.

<http://grammar.ccc.commnet.edu/grammar/quizzes/cross/cross_prep3.htm> Crossword puzzle: Have you mastered prepositions?

UNIT 5
Writing Assignments

As you complete each writing assignment, remember to perform these steps:

- Write a clear, complete topic sentence.

- Use freewriting, brainstorming, or clustering to generate ideas for the body of your paragraph, essay, or speech.

- Arrange your best ideas in a plan.

- Revise for support, unity, coherence, and exact language.

- Proofread for grammar, punctuation, and spelling errors.

Writing Assignment 1 *Imagine yourself going global.* Have you ever imagined leaving your familiar culture in the United States to study, work, or volunteer abroad? If you could live for one year anywhere in the world, where would you go and to what task or cause would you devote yourself? Would you want to focus on doing humanitarian work or on developing your knowledge, career, or language skills? Describe your dream destination and the work you would want to do there. Proofread for the correct use of nouns, pronouns, adjectives, adverbs, and prepositions.

Writing Assignment 2 *Explain your job.* Explain what you do—your duties and responsibilities—to someone who knows nothing about your kind of work but is interested in it. In your first sentence, sum up the work you do. Then name the equipment you use and tell how you spend an average working day. Explain the rewards and drawbacks of your job. Finally, proofread for the correct use of nouns, pronouns, adjectives, adverbs, and prepositions.

Writing Assignment 3 *Give an award.* When we think of awards, we generally think of awards for the most home runs or the highest grade average. However, Cal Ripken Jr. of the Baltimore Orioles became famous because he played in a record number of consecutive games. In other words, his award was for *showing up*, for *being there*, for *constancy*. Write a speech for an awards dinner in honor of someone who deserves recognition for this kind of constancy. Perhaps your parents deserve the award, or your spouse, or the law enforcement officer in your neighborhood. Be specific in explaining why this person deserves the award. You might try a humorous approach. Proofread your speech for the correct use of nouns, pronouns, adjectives, adverbs, and prepositions.

Writing Assignment 4 *Discuss your future.* Imagine yourself 10 years from now; how will your life be different? Pick one major way in which you expect it will have changed. You may want to choose a difference in your income, your marital status, your idea of success, or anything else that is important to you. Your first sentence should state this expected change. Then explain why this change will be important to you. Proofread for the correct use of nouns, pronouns, adjectives, adverbs, and prepositions.

UNIT 5
Review

Proofreading

Proofread the following essay for the incorrect use of nouns, pronouns, adjectives, adverbs, and prepositions. Cross out errors and correct them above the lines. (You should find 28 errors.)

The Last Frontier

(1) When the government of Brazil opened the Amazon rain forest for settlement ~~on~~ in the 1970s, ~~they~~ it created the last frontier on Earth. (2) Many concerned ~~man~~ men and ~~woman~~ women everywhere now fear that the move has been a ~~disasters~~ disaster for the land and for the people.

(3) The ~~most large~~ largest rain forest in the world, the Amazon rain forest has been hit ~~real~~ really hard. (4) The government built highways to make it ~~more easy~~ easier for poor people to get to the land, but the roads also made investors interested ~~to~~ in the forest. (5) Lumber companies chopped down millions of ~~tree~~ trees. (6) Ranchers and settlers ~~theirselves~~ themselves

In a new effort to save the rain forest, school children in the Amazon are given outdoor classes about the value of rain forest trees.

burned the forest to make room for cattle and crops. (7) All ~~this~~ [these] activities have taken their toll: in one area, which is the size of Colorado, three-quarters of the rain forest has already been destroyed. (8) Many kinds of plants and animals have been lost forever.

(9) ~~As~~ [Like] the rain forest itself, the Indians who live there are threatened by ~~these~~ [this] wholesale destruction. (10) Ranchers, miners, loggers, and settlers have moved onto Indian lands. (11) Contact with the outside world has changed the Indians' traditional way of life. (12) A few Indian ~~tribe~~ [tribes] have made economic and political gains; many tribes have totally disappeared, however.

(13) Many of the ~~settler~~ [settlers] are not doing very ~~good~~ [well] either. (14) People have poured into the region too ~~rapid~~ [rapidly], and the government is unable to provide the needed services. (15) Small villages have become crowded cities, diseases (especially malaria) have spread, and lawlessness is common. (16) ~~Worse~~ [Worst] of all, the soil beneath the rain forest is not fertile. (17) After a few years, the settlers' ~~land, it~~ [land] is worthless. (18) As the settlers go into debt, businesses take advantage ~~for~~ [of] the situation by buying land ~~quick~~ [quickly] and exploiting it ~~bad~~ [badly].

(19) Can the situation in the rain forest improve? (20) Although the Brazilian government has been trying to preserve ~~those~~ [that] forest, thousands of fires are still set every year to clear land for cattle grazing, planting, and building. (21) On the more hopeful side, however, scientists have discovered fruits in the rain forest that are ~~extreme~~ [extremely] high in vitamins and proteins. (22) Those fruits would be much better crops for the rain forest than the corn, rice, and beans that farmers are growing there now. (23) In new outdoor ~~course~~ [courses], schools teach children of the Amazon that the rain forest is worth more alive than dead. (24) The world watches ~~nervous~~ [nervously]. (25) Will the Earth's ~~preciousest~~ [most precious] rain forest survive?

Transforming

Change the subject of this paragraph from singular (*the hybrid*) to plural (*hybrids*), changing every *the car* to *cars*, every *it* to *they*, and so forth. Make all necessary verb and other changes. Write your revisions above the lines.

(1) ~~The hybrid automobile is~~ [Hybrid automobiles are] gaining popularity worldwide, especially in the United States, Europe, and Japan. (2) ~~It is~~ [They are] powered by a combination of gasoline and a rechargeable electric battery instead of gasoline alone. (3) Admirers of ~~the hybrid~~ [hybrids] like ~~its~~ [their] excellent gas mileage and the fact that ~~it is~~ [they are] less polluting than conventional cars. (4) Although ~~a hybrid car, truck, or SUV~~ [hybrid cars, trucks, or SUVs] will not solve our global warming problem, ~~it will~~ [they will] help reduce the emission of gases harmful to our environment. (5) In the future, ~~this vehicle~~ [these vehicles] may be supplanted by ~~a car~~ [cars] powered by hydrogen fuel cells or other technologies. (6) But for now, ~~it is~~ [they are] probably the most environmentally friendly ~~car~~ [cars] on the road.

A whole new world: parking spots for electric vehicles in Texas

UNIT 5

Writers' Workshop

Tell How Someone Changed Your Life

Strong writing flows clearly from point to point so that a reader can follow easily. In your class or group, read this essay, aloud if possible. As you read, pay special attention to organization.

Stephanie

(1) There are many people who are important to me. However, the most important person is Stephanie. Stephanie is my daughter. She has changed my life completely. She has changed my life in a positive way.

(2) Stephanie is only five years old, but she has taught me the value of education. ~~When I found out that I was pregnant, my life changed in a positive way.~~ Before I got pregnant, I didn't like school. I went to school just to please my mom, but I wasn't learning anything. When I found out that I was pregnant, I changed my mind about education. I wanted to give my baby the best of this world. I knew that without a good education, I wasn't going anywhere, so I decided to get my life together.

(3) Stephanie taught me not to give up. I remember when she was trying to walk, and she fell down. She didn't stop but kept on going until she learned how to walk. Add 2-3 more supporting sentences.

(4) In conclusion, you can learn a lot from babies. ~~I learned not to give up.~~ Stephanie is the most important person in the whole world to me. She has changed me in the past, and she will continue to change me in the future.

Claudia Huezo, student

1. How effective is this essay?

_Y_ Clear thesis statement?   _N_ Good support?

_Y_ Logical organization?   _Y_ Effective conclusion?

2. Claudia Huezo has organized her essay very well: introduction and thesis statement, two supporting paragraphs, conclusion. Is the main idea of each supporting paragraph clear? Does each have a good topic sentence?

3. Is each supporting paragraph developed with enough facts and details? If not, what advice would you give the writer for revising, especially for reworking paragraph (3)? No. Avoid repetition (see crossouts); add more fresh facts and details.

4. This student has picked a wonderful subject and writes clearly—two excellent qualities. However, did you find any places where short, choppy, or repetitious sentences could be improved?

    If so, point out one or two places where Huezo might cross out or rewrite repetitious language (where she says the same thing twice in the same words). Point out one or two places where she might combine short sentences for variety.

5. Proofread for grammar and spelling. Do you spot any error patterns this student should watch out for? No grammar errors

Writing and Revising Ideas

1. Tell how someone changed your life.

2. Discuss two reasons why education is (is not) important.

Before you write, plan or outline your paragraph or essay so that it will be clearly organized (see Chapter 3, Part E, and Chapter 4, Part A). As you revise, pay special attention to the order of ideas and to clear, concise writing without needless repetition (see Chapter 4, Part B).

UNIT 6   Revising for Consistency and Parallelism

This unit will teach you some easy but effective ways to add style to your writing. In this unit, you will

- Make sure your verbs and pronouns are consistent
- Use a secret weapon of many writers—parallel structure
- Vary the lengths and types of your sentences
- Learn proofreading strategies to find and correct your own errors

Spotlight on Reading and Writing

This writer uses balanced words and phrases to describe a popular celebration in her culture. If possible, read the paragraph aloud.

Quinceañeras are coming-of-age ceremonies for Latina girls when they turn fifteen (*quince años*, thus, "quinceañera"). They can be highly <u>elaborate</u> and <u>ritualized</u>. Many start with a mass that is kind of like a wedding without the groom. The girl is traditionally dressed in a pink gown, white being reserved for brides. She is blessed by the priest, who also blesses certain symbolic objects: the quinceañera's first <u>set of heels</u>, her <u>crown</u>, her "<u>last doll</u>." These symbolic objects open the party part of the celebration in which <u>her father changes her shoes from flats to heels</u>, <u>her mother crowns her</u>, <u>she receives a last doll from a *madrina*</u> (godmother), and sometimes, like the bride with her bouquet, <u>she tosses this "last doll" into a crowd of screaming little girls</u> who will some day be quinceañeras, too. Now, as a woman, she dances her first public dance as an adult with her *papi*—traditionally, the dance is a waltz—and then a dance that is more specific to the country of origin: a <u>*merengue*</u> for Dominicans, a <u>*danzón*</u> for Cubans. Throughout this ritual she is accompanied by a "court" of 14 couples, representing her 14 years, as well as her escort, who will be handed the young lady after the men in her family (<u>father</u>, <u>grandfather</u>, <u>brothers</u>, sometimes a dozen <u>uncles</u>!) have danced with her.

Julia Alvarez, excerpted from an interview found at
<http://us.penguingroup.com/static/html/features/alvarez.html>

- Describing the *quinceañera*, this writer employs two techniques you will learn in this unit. First, she uses *one verb tense consistently* all the way through.

- She also uses *balanced pairs or series of words*: *elaborate* and *ritualized* (underlined) are both adjectives. The next underlined words are all nouns: *set* of heels, *crown*, *doll*.

- Can you find any other balanced pairs or series of words?

Writing Ideas

- *A ritual or custom you know well*
- *An aspect of your cultural heritage that you value (or that your parents valued)*

CHAPTER 26

Consistent Tense

Consistent tense means using the same verb tense whenever possible within a sentence or paragraph. As you write and revise, avoid shifting from one tense to another—for example, from present to past—without a good reason for doing so.

(1) **Inconsistent tense:**	We *were* seven miles from shore. Suddenly, the sky *turns* dark.
(2) **Consistent tense:**	We *were* seven miles from shore. Suddenly, the sky *turned* dark.
(3) **Consistent tense:**	We *are* seven miles from shore. Suddenly, the sky *turns* dark.

- The sentences in (1) begin in the past tense with the verb *were* but then shift into the present tense with the verb *turns*. The tenses are inconsistent because both actions are occurring at the same time.

- The sentences in (2) are consistent. Both verbs, *were* and *turned*, are in the past tense.

- The sentences in (3) are also consistent. Both verbs, *are* and *turns*, are in the present tense.

Of course, you should use different verb tenses in a sentence or paragraph if they convey the meaning you want to express.

(4) Two years ago, I *wanted* to be a chef, but now I *am studying* forestry.

- The verbs in sentence (4) accurately show the time relationship: In the past, I *wanted* to be a chef, but now I *am studying* forestry.

As you proofread your papers for tense consistency, ask yourself: Have I unthinkingly moved from one tense to another, from past to present, or from present to past?

PRACTICE 1

Underline the verbs in these sentences. Then correct any tense inconsistencies above the line. Answers will vary.

                                    got

EXAMPLE: As soon as I <u>get</u> out of bed, I <u>did</u> 50 push-ups.

or   *do*

As soon as I <u>get</u> out of bed, I <u>did</u> 50 push-ups.

                                                      appeared

1. We <u>were walking</u> near the lake when a large moose <u>appears</u> just ahead.

                  asked

2. When Bill <u>asks</u> the time, the cab driver <u>told</u> him it <u>was</u> after six.

                                                                was

3. The woman on the red bicycle <u>was delivering</u> newspapers while she <u>is enjoying</u> the morning sunshine.

                        welcomed

4. Dr. Choi <u>smiled</u> and <u>welcomes</u> the next patient.

5. The Oklahoma prairie <u>stretches</u> for miles, flat and rusty red. Here and there, an oil rig

  breaks

<u>broke</u> the monotony.

                                            went

6. They <u>were strolling</u> down Main Street when the lights <u>go</u> out.

                                            described

7. My cousins <u>questioned</u> me for hours about my trip. I <u>describe</u> the flight, my impressions of Paris, and every meal I <u>ate</u>.

                                approached

8. We <u>started</u> cheering as he <u>approaches</u> the finish line.

                                            doesn't

9. If Zahra <u>takes</u> short naps during the day, she <u>didn't</u> feel tired in the evening.

                  found   *needed*

10. Yesterday, we <u>find</u> the book we <u>need</u> online. We <u>ordered</u> it immediately.

                                          look

11. Whenever I <u>attempt</u> the tango, I <u>am looking</u> goofy, not sexy.

                        saved

12. My roommate <u>saves</u> money for three years and then <u>took</u> the trip of a lifetime to Vietnam and Cambodia.

                                                keep

13. An afternoon protein shake <u>can provide</u> an energy boost and <u>kept</u> a person from overeating later in the day.

                  opened

14. As Cal <u>opens</u> the door, we all <u>broke</u> into song.

Chapter Highlights

- **In general, use the same verb tense within a sentence or a paragraph:**

  She *sings* beautifully, and the audience *listens* intently.

  or

  She *sang* beautifully, and the audience *listened* intently.

- **However, at times different verb tenses are required because of meaning:**

  He *is* not *working* now, but he *spent* 60 hours behind the counter last week.

Proofreading Strategy

To proofread for inconsistent tense (confusing tense changes), go through your draft and **underline or highlight every verb**.

Identify the tense of every verb. Whenever the tense *changes*, is there a good reason for the change? Here is an example:

PAST-CORRECT

In 2008, Sophia completed her two-year degree in culinary arts. After graduating,

PAST-CORRECT   PRESENT-WRONG

she got a job as a chef in a Jacksonville restaurant. She decides to open her own

PRESENT-CORRECT

restaurant in 2009 and now owns two popular downtown eateries.

In this example, the past tense works well because the writer is describing past events. The last sentence, however, should shift from past tense (*decided* in 2009) to present tense (now *owns* two restaurants).

WRITING AND PROOFREADING ASSIGNMENT

Suppose that you have been asked for written advice on what makes a successful family. Your adult child, an inexperienced friend, or a sibling has asked you to write down some words of wisdom on what makes a family work. Using your own family as an example, write your suggestions for making family life as nurturing, cooperative, and joyful as possible. You may draw on your family's experience to give examples of pitfalls to avoid or of positive behaviors and attitudes. Revise for consistent tense.

CHAPTER REVIEW

Read each of these paragraphs for consistent tense. Correct any inconsistencies by changing the tense of the verbs. Write your corrections above the lines.

A.   (1) It was 1954. (2) Eight-year-old Jack Horner discovered his first dinosaur fossil as

roamed

he ~~roams~~ the dry hills near Shelby, Montana. (3) His discovery ~~sparks~~ a lifelong passion for

sparked

learned

dinosaurs and science. (4) Horner struggled with school work and only later ~~learns~~ that he

earned

had dyslexia, yet he ~~earns~~ a degree in paleontology, the study of prehistoric life forms.

found

(5) Horner and his team overturned many theories about dinosaurs. (6) For instance, he ~~finds~~

realized

clusters of dinosaur nests and ~~realizes~~ that dinosaur mothers were fierce protectors of

their young. (7) He located the largest *Tyrannosaurus Rex* on record. (8) When his team dug

concluded   wasn't

up a whole group of *T. rex* skeletons, he ~~concludes~~ that the *T. rex* ~~isn't~~ the dreaded solitary

killer of popular imagination but rather a scavenger roaming in packs. (9) Dr. Horner's fame

advised

grew. (10) He ~~advises~~ director Steven Spielberg on all three *Jurassic Park* films. (11) In 2009,

announced

Horner ~~announces~~ plans to grow a live dinosaur from DNA, a real-life Jurassic Park idea that critics called dangerous and unethical. (12) Today, by visiting schools and hosting a

television science show, Horner ~~hoped~~ *hopes* to inspire other children to question, explore, and

love science.

B.   (1) Self-confidence is vital to success both in childhood and in adulthood. (2) With

self-confidence, children ~~knew~~ *know* that they are worthwhile and that they have important

goals. (3) Parents can teach their children self-confidence in several ways. (4) First, children

~~needed~~ *need* praise. (5) When they ~~drew~~ *draw*, for example, parents can tell them how beautiful their

drawings are. (6) The praise lets them know they ~~had~~ *have* talents that other people admire.

(7) Second, children ~~required~~ *require* exposure to many different experiences. (8) They soon ~~found~~ *find*

that they need not be afraid to try new things. (9) They ~~realized~~ *realize* that they can succeed

as well at chess as they do at basketball. (10) They ~~discovered~~ *discover* that a trip to a museum to

examine medieval armor is fascinating or that they enjoy taking a class in pottery. (11) Finally,

it ~~was~~ *is* very important to treat children individually. (12) Sensitive parents ~~did~~ *do* not compare

their children's successes or failures with those of their brothers or sisters, relatives, or

friends. (13) Of course, parents should inform children if their behavior or performance in

school needs improvement. (14) Parents ~~helped~~ *help* children do better, however, by showing

them how much they have accomplished so far and by suggesting how much they can and

will accomplish in the future.

C.   (1) Like many ancient Greek myths, the story of Narcissus provided psychological

insight and vocabulary still relevant today. (2) Although Narcissus was a mere mortal, this

conceited young man ~~believes~~ *believed* himself to be as handsome as the gods. (3) Many young

women ~~fall~~ *fell* in love with him, including a pretty nymph[1] named Echo. (4) When Narcissus

rejected her affections, Echo ~~sinks~~ *sank* into heartbreak. (5) She faded into the landscape until

the only thing left ~~is~~ *was* the echo of her voice. (6) The youth's outrageous vanity infuriated the

goddess Nemesis.[2] (7) She ~~decides~~ *decided* to teach Narcissus a lesson and ~~dooms~~ *doomed* him to fall in love

---

1. nymph: a minor nature goddess
2. Nemesis: goddess of divine vengeance and retribution

TEACHING TIP

You might ask your students to discuss and/or write a journal entry about the question "Do I know a narcissist?" Alternatively, as the class studies the painting, ask: "Does this painting capture your image of Narcissus? What would a twenty-first-century Narcissus look like?"

Narcissus, 1597–1599, as imagined by the painter Caravaggio. Oil on canvas, 110 × 92 cm.

What would a twenty-first-century Narcissus look like?

TEACHING TIP

You might want to point out that three English terms derive from this ancient story: *narcissist, echo,* and *nemesis.*

    with his own image. (8) As he passed by Echo's pond, he ~~glimpses~~ [glimpsed] himself in the water and ~~falls~~ [fell] in love with his own reflection. (9) For days, Narcissus lay lovesick on the bank, pining hopelessly for his own eyes, lips, and curls, until he ~~dies~~ [died]. (10) From the ashes of his funeral pyre ~~growns~~ [grew] a white flower now known as the narcissus. (11) The story of this arrogant young man also gave modern psychology the term *narcissist*, a person so admiring of himself that he cannot love others.

EXPLORING ONLINE

TEACHING TIP

Instructor tools for *Grassroots* include a computerized Test Bank, PowerPoint slides, an Instructor's Resource Manual with teaching tips, and more, and can be accessed at ‹**login .cengage.com**›.

<http://owl.english.purdue.edu/owl/resource/601/04/> Good review of tense consistency.

<http://aliscot.com/bigdog/consist_exercise.htm> Big Dog's self-test on the verbs.

<http://www.towson.edu/ows/exercisetenseconsistency3.htm> Interactive quiz. This one is difficult. Test yourself.

Consistent Person

Consistent person means using the same person or personal pronoun throughout a sentence or a paragraph. As you write and revise, avoid confusing shifts from one person to another. For example, don't shift from *first person* (*I, we*) or *third person* (*he, she, it, they*) to *second person* (*you*).*

(1)	**Inconsistent person:**	College *students* soon see that *you* are on *your* own.
(2)	**Consistent person:**	College *students* soon see that *they* are on *their* own.
(3)	**Consistent person:**	In college, *you* soon see that *you* are on *your* own.

- Sentence (1) shifts from the third person plural *students* to the second person *you* and *your*.

- Sentence (2) uses the third person plural consistently. *They* and *their* now clearly refer to *students*.

- Sentence (3) is also consistent, using the second person *you* and *your* throughout.

PRACTICE 1

Correct any inconsistencies of person in these sentences. If necessary, change the verbs to make them agree with any new subjects. Make your corrections above the lines.

                his or her
EXAMPLE: Each hiker should bring ~~your~~ own lunch.

                                            me
1. Touria treats me like family when I visit her. She always makes ~~you~~ feel at home.

                         I
2. I love to go dancing. ~~You~~ can exercise, work off tension, and have fun, all at the same time.

                                      he or she
3. If a person has gone to a large high school, ~~you~~ may find a small college a welcome change.

                                           we
4. When Lee and I drive to work at 6 A.M., ~~you~~ see the city waking up.

                                      he or she has
5. Every mechanic should make sure ~~they have~~ a good set of tools.

---

* For more work on pronouns, see Chapter 23.

343

6. People who want to buy cars today are often stopped by high prices. ~~You~~ aren't sure *They*
   how to get the most for ~~your~~ money. *their*

7. ~~Do~~ each of you have ~~his or her~~ own e-mail address? *Does* *your*

8. Many people mistakenly think that ~~your~~ vote doesn't really count. *their*

9. A teacher's attitude affects the performance of ~~their~~ students. *his or her*

10. It took me three years to decide to enroll in college; in many ways, ~~you~~ really didn't *I*
    know what ~~you~~ wanted to do when ~~you~~ finished high school. *I* *I*

11. Each person should seek a type of exercise that ~~you enjoy~~. *he or she enjoys*

12. The students in my CSI class were problem solvers; ~~he~~ loved a challenge. *they*

13. If that is your heart's desire, ~~she~~ should pursue it. *you*

Chapter Highlights

- **Use the same personal pronoun throughout a sentence or a paragraph:**

    When *you* apply for a driver's license, *you* may have to take a written test and a driving test.

    When a *person* applies for a driver's license, *he or she* may have to take a written test and a driving test.

Proofreading Strategy

You, your, they, and *their* are probably the most misused personal pronouns. If pronoun agreement is one of your error patterns, **color code *you, your, they,* and *their* in your draft**. If you are using a computer, use the *"Find"* feature to locate these words.

Every time you spot one of these pronouns in your writing, **draw an arrow to its antecedent**. If the **antecedent is plural**, make sure the **pronoun is plural**. If the **antecedent is singular**, make sure the **pronoun is singular**. Here is an example:

they
Job seekers must create an excellent resume if you want a potential employer to

them   *his or her*
call you for an interview. Each candidate must highlight their special strengths.

WRITING AND PROOFREADING ASSIGNMENT

In small groups, write as many endings as you can think of for this sentence: "You can (cannot) tell much about a person by . . ." You might write, "the way he or she dresses," "the way he or she styles his or her hair," or "the place he or she is from." Each group member should write down every sentence.

Then let each group member choose one sentence and write a short paragraph supporting it. Use people in the news or friends as examples to prove your point. When you finish drafting, proofread to make sure you have used the first, second, or third person correctly. When everyone is finished, exchange papers, locate all *you* and *they* pronouns, and check each other's work for consistent person.

CHAPTER REVIEW

Correct the inconsistencies of person in these paragraphs. Then make any other necessary changes. Write your corrections above the lines.

A.   (1) When exam time comes, do you become anxious because you aren't sure how to study for tests? (2) ~~They~~ *(You)* may have done all the work for ~~their~~ *(your)* courses, but you still don't feel prepared. (3) Fortunately, ~~he~~ *(you)* can do some things to make taking tests easier. (4) ~~They~~ *(You)* can look through the textbook and review the material ~~one has~~ *(you have)* underlined. (5) You might read the notes you have taken in class and highlight or underline the main points. (6) ~~A person~~ *(You)* can think about some questions the professor may ask and then try writing answers. (7) Sometimes, ~~they~~ *(you)* can find other people from your class and form a study group to compare class notes. (8) The night before a test, ~~they~~ *(you)* shouldn't drink too much coffee. (9) ~~They~~ *(You)* should get a good night's sleep so that your mind will be as sharp for the exam as your pencil.

B.   (1) The sport of mountain biking began in northern California in the 1970s. (2) Some experienced cyclists began using ~~his or her~~ *(their)* old, one-speed, fat-tire bikes to explore dirt roads and trails. (3) ~~You~~ *(They)* began by getting car rides up one of the mountains and pedaling their bikes down. (4) Then they began cycling farther up the mountain until ~~he and she~~ *(they)* were pedaling to the top. (5) Those cyclists eventually started designing bikes to fit ~~our~~ *(their)* sport. (6) By the end of the 1970s, road bike manufacturers decided ~~you~~ *(they)* would join the action. (7) By the mid-1980s, mountain biking had become a national craze, and sales of mountain bikes were exceeding sales of road bikes.

   (8) Today, mountain bikers pay about $1,000 for bikes that have everything ~~we~~ *(they)* need for riding on rough trails: front-wheel shock absorbers, 24 gears that shift easily, a lightweight

chassis, flexible wheels, and even a full-suspension frame. (9) Cyclists ride ~~your~~ *their* bikes

everywhere; some of their favorite places are South Dakota's Badlands, Colorado's ski resorts,

and Utah's Canyonlands National Park. (10) ~~You~~ *They* compete in mountain bike races all over the

world. (11) To top this off, in 1996 some of ~~you~~ *them* competed in the first Olympic mountain bike

race, outside Atlanta, Georgia. (12) The course, which had tightly spaced trees and large rocks,

included steep climbs and sharp descents with surprise jumps. (13) What were those early

"inventors" thinking as ~~he and she~~ *they* watched that first Olympic race?

EXPLORING ONLINE

TEACHING TIP

Instructor tools for *Grassroots* include a computerized Test Bank, PowerPoint slides, an Instructor's Resource Manual with teaching tips, and more, and can be accessed at ‹**login .cengage.com**›.

<http://www.powa.org/edit/six-problem-areas?showall=&start=5> Review and then complete Activity 4.16: Rewrite the paragraph in consistent first person (*I* or *we*) and then in third person (*he/she* or *they*).

<http://grammar.ccc.commnet.edu/grammar/cgi-shl/quiz.pl/consistency _quiz.htm> Interactive quiz: Test your pronoun IQ.

28

Parallelism

A: Writing Parallel Constructions

B: Using Parallelism for Special Effects

A. Writing Parallel Constructions

This chapter will show you an excellent way to add clarity and smoothness to your writing. Which sentence in each pair sounds better to you?

(1) Jennie is an artist and flies planes also.

(2) Jennie is *an artist* and *a pilot*.

(3) He slowed down and came sliding. The winning run was scored.

(4) He *slowed* down, *slid*, and *scored* the winning run.

- Do sentences (2) and (4) sound smoother and clearer than sentences (1) and (3)?

- Sentences (2) and (4) balance similar words or phrases to show similar ideas.

This technique is called *parallelism* **or** *parallel structure*. **The italicized parts of (2) and (4) are** *parallel*. **When you use** *parallelism*, **you repeat similar parts of speech or phrases to express similar ideas.**

Jennie is	an artist . . . a pilot
He	slowed . . . slid . . . scored

- Can you see how *an artist* and *a pilot* are parallel? Both words in the pair are singular nouns.

- Can you see how *slowed, slid,* and *scored* are parallel? All three words in the series are verbs in the past tense.

Now let's look at two more pairs of sentences. Note which sentence in each pair contains parallelism.

ESL TIP

Although the regularity of parallel structures makes the *concept* easy to learn, ESL students who struggle with word endings have trouble with parallelism. Typically, ESL learners confuse adjective and noun endings. Try coupling the practices in this chapter with a review of word-ending choices and common endings. Refer students to Appendix 1, Parts of Speech Review, to begin their study of suffixes.

(5) The car was big, had beauty, and it cost a lot.

(6) The car was *big, beautiful,* and *expensive.*

(7) They raced across the roof, and the fire escape is where they came down.

(8) They raced *across the roof* and *down the fire escape.*

● In sentence (6), how are *big, beautiful,* and *expensive* parallel words?

All three words are adjectives.

● In sentence (8), how are *across the roof* and *down the fire escape* parallel phrases?

Both are prepositional phrases.

Try This   Try this parallelism test: Does each word or phrase complete the sentence in the same balanced way, with the same part of speech? If so, it is parallel. Test sentence: *The car was big, beautiful, and a Chevy Tahoe.*

The car was *big.*   YES (adjective)

The car was *beautiful.*   YES (adjective)

The car was *a Chevy Tahoe.*   NO (noun—replace with an adjective)

Certain special constructions require parallel structure:

 (9) The room is *both* light *and* cheery.

(10) You *either* love geometry *or* hate it.

(11) Aricelli *not only* plays the guitar *but also* sings.

(12) Richard would *rather* fight *than* quit.

● Each of these constructions has two parts:

both . . . and   not only . . . but also

(n)either . . . (n)or   rather . . . than

● The words, phrases, or clauses following each part must be parallel:

light . . . cheery   plays . . . sings

love . . . hate   fight . . . quit

Parallelism is an excellent way to add smoothness and power to your writing. Use it in pairs or in a series of ideas, balancing a noun with a noun, an *-ing* verb with an *-ing* verb, a prepositional phrase with a prepositional phrase, and so on.

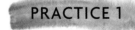

PRACTICE 1

TEACHING TIP

Suggest that students read this chapter's examples and exercise items aloud so that they can "hear" the parallel and nonparallel structures.

Circle the element that is *not* parallel in each list.

EXAMPLE: blue

red

(colored like rust)

purple

1. rowing
    jogging
    (runner)
    lifting weights

2. (my four dogs)
    out the door
    across the yard
    under the fence

3. (painting the kitchen)
    cans of paint
    several brushes
    one roller

4. persistent
    strong-willed
    (work)
    optimistic

5. opening his mouth to speak
    (toward the audience)
    smiling with anticipation
    leaning against the table

6. music shops
    clothing stores
    (buying a birthday present)
    electronics shops

7. (dressed for the office)
    laptop computer
    leather briefcase
    cellular phone

8. We shop for fruits at the market.
    We buy enough food to last a week.
    (We are baking a cake tonight.)
    We cook healthy meals often.

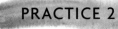

PRACTICE 2

Rewrite each sentence, using parallelism to accent the similar ideas.

EXAMPLE: Do you believe that gratitude and feeling happy are related?

Rewrite: *Do you believe that gratitude and happiness are related?*

1. Many people believe that they will be happy once they have money, they are famous, married to a spouse, or working at a good job.

    Rewrite: Many people believe that they will be happy once they have money, fame, a spouse, or a good job.

2. Psychologist Martin Seligman found that gratitude is a key ingredient of happiness, and the "gratitude visit" was his invention.

    Rewrite: Psychologist Martin Seligman found that gratitude is a key ingredient of happiness and invented the "gratitude visit."

3. First, you think of a person who was truly helpful to you, and then a "gratitude letter" is written by you to that person.

    Rewrite: First, you think of a person who was truly helpful to you, and then you write a "gratitude letter" to that person.

4. In this letter, explain sincerely and with specifics why you are grateful.

    Rewrite: In this letter, explain sincerely and specifically why you are grateful.

5. Then visit this person and reading your letter aloud.

   Rewrite: Then visit this person and read your letter aloud.

   _____

6. According to Seligman, the ritual is moving, powerful, and there is a lot of emotion.

   Rewrite: According to Seligman, the ritual is moving, powerful, and emotional.

   _____

7. Seligman says people feel happier if they focus on the positive aspects of the past rather than being negative.

   Rewrite: Seligman says people feel happier if they focus on the positive aspects of the past rather

   than on the negative.

8. Gratitude visits, he believes, increase how intense, length, and frequency of positive memories.

   Rewrite: Gratitude visits, he believes, increase the intensity, length, and frequency of

   positive memories.

9. In addition, they tend to inspire the receivers of thanks to become giving of thanks.

   Rewrite: In addition, they tend to inspire the receivers of thanks to become givers of thanks.

   _____

10. One gratitude visit leads to another, creating a chain of appreciation and also to make everyone feel more content.

    Rewrite: One gratitude visit leads to another, creating a chain of appreciation and contentment for

    everyone.

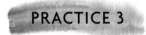

PRACTICE 3

Fill in the blanks in each sentence with parallel words or phrases of your own. Be creative. Take care that your sentences make sense and that your parallels are truly parallel. Sample answers

EXAMPLE: I feel _____ rested _____ and _____ happy _____.

1. Ethan's favorite colors are _____ yellow _____ and _____ green _____.

2. The day of the storm, we _____ sat by the window _____, and they _____ played cards _____.

3. Her attitude was strange. She acted as if _____ she were always right _____ and as if _____ everyone else were always wrong _____.

4. I like people who _____ love to hike _____ and who
_____ love to sing _____.

5. Some married couples _____ spend most of their time together _____, whereas others
_____ pursue separate interests _____.

6. Harold _____ flies a plane _____, but I just
_____ fly my kite _____.

7. To finish this project, work _____ through the day _____ and
_____ into the night _____.

8. _____ Playing the piano _____ and _____ lying on the beach _____
relax me.

9. We found _____ delicate shells _____, _____ smooth stones _____,
and _____ broken glass _____ on the beach.

10. They might want to _____ paint the walls _____ or to
_____ wallpaper the room _____.

B. Using Parallelism for Special Effects

By rearranging the order of a parallel series, you can sometimes add a little drama or humor to your sentences. Which of these two sentences is more dramatic?

(1) Bharati is a wife, a mother, and a black belt in karate.

(2) Bharati is a wife, a black belt in karate, and a mother.

● If you chose sentence (1), you are right. Sentence (1) saves the most surprising item—*a black belt in karate*—for last.

● Sentence (2), on the other hand, does not build suspense but gives away the surprise in the middle.

You can also use parallelism to set up your readers' expectations and then surprise them with humor.

(3) Mike Hardware was the kind of private eye who didn't know the meaning of the word *fear,* who could laugh in the face of danger and spit in the eye of death—in short, a moron with suicidal tendencies.

● Clever use of parallelism made this sentence a winner in the Bulwer-Lytton Contest. Every year, contestants make each other laugh by inventing the first sentence of a bad novel.

PRACTICE 4

On paper or on a computer, write five sentences of your own, using parallel structure. In one or two of your sentences, arrange the parallel elements to build toward a dramatic or humorous conclusion. For ideas, look at Practice 3, but create your own sentences.

Chapter Highlights

- Parallelism balances similar words or phrases to express similar ideas:

  He left the gym *tired*, *sweaty*, and *satisfied*.

  Tami not only *finished the exam in record time* but also *answered the question for extra credit*.

  To celebrate his success, Alejandro *took in a show*, *went dancing*, and *ate a late dinner*.

Proofreading Strategy

To proofread for parallelism problems, read through your draft and **find pairs, lists, or series of words, phrases, or clauses.**

Circle or highlight the items in each pair, list, or series. **Test for parallelism** by rewriting to see whether each item could complete the sentence. Here is one example:

teamwork

Being successful in this position requires attention to detail, to work on a team, and the ability to prioritize.

TEST: Being successful in this position requires *attention to detail*	YES (noun)
requires *to work on a team*	NO (infinitive)
requires *the ability to prioritize*	YES (noun)

WRITING AND PROOFREADING ASSIGNMENT

Write a one-paragraph newspaper advertisement to rent or sell your house or apartment. Using complete sentences, let the reader know the number of rooms, their size, and their appearance, and explain why someone would be happy there. Emphasize your home's good points, such as "lots of light" or "closet space galore," but don't hide the flaws. If possible, minimize them while still being honest.

You may want to begin with a general description such as "This apartment is a plant lover's dream." Be careful, though: if you describe only the good features or exaggerate, readers may think, "It's too good to be true." Use parallel structure to help your sentences read more smoothly. As you proofread, test for correct parallelism.

CHAPTER REVIEW

TEACHING TIP

Read "before" and "after" versions of this Chapter Review passage aloud so that students can hear both the faulty and the correct parallelism.

This essay contains both correct and faulty parallel constructions. Revise the faulty parallelism. Write your corrections above the lines. You should make 11 corrections.

Chinese Medicine in the United States

(1) When diplomatic relations between the United States and mainland China were restored in 1972, acupuncture was one import that sparked America's imagination and
interest
~~made people interested~~. (2) In the United States today, the most popular form of Chinese medicine is acupuncture.

© Charles Taylor/Shutterstock.com

(3) Acupuncture involves the insertion of thin, sterile, ~~made of~~ stainless-steel needles at specific points on the body. (4) Chinese medical science believes that the *chi*, or life
manipulating
force, can be redirected by inserting and ~~by the manipulation of~~ these needles. (5) They are
left
inserted to just below the skin and are either removed quickly or ~~leave them~~ in for up to
charge
40 minutes. (6) In addition, the acupuncturist can twirl them, heat them, or ~~charging~~ them with a mild electrical current. (7) Acupuncture can reduce pain for those suffering from allergies, arthritis, backache, or ~~with a~~ toothache. (8) It also has helped in cases of chronic
depression
substance abuse, anxiety, and ~~for depressed people~~.

importance
(9) Chinese medicine has grown in popularity and ~~become important~~ in America. (10) Thirty-five schools in the United States teach Chinese acupuncture. (11) Forty-four
license
states have passed laws that regulate or ~~for licensing~~ the practice of acupuncture. (12) Since 1974, the federal government has authorized several studies of acupuncture's effectiveness
reliability
and ~~how reliable it is~~. (13) Although research has failed to explain how acupuncture works, it has confirmed that it does work. (14) The studies also suggest that acupuncture should
used
continue to be tested and ~~using it~~.

EXPLORING ONLINE

TEACHING TIP

Instructor tools for *Grassroots* include a computerized Test Bank, PowerPoint slides, an Instructor's Manual with teaching tips, and more, and can be accessed at ‹login .cengage.com›.

<http://aliscot.com/bigdog/parallel_exercise.htm> Take Big Dog's parallelism test.

<http://grammar.ccc.commnet.edu/grammar/cgi-shl/quiz.pl/parallelism_quiz .htm> Interactive quiz: Click on the sentence that uses parallelism correctly.

<http://grammar.ccc.commnet.edu/grammar/quizzes/niu/niu10.htm> Interactive quiz: Which sentence in each group has parallelism errors?

UNIT 6
Writing Assignments

As you complete each writing assignment, remember to perform these steps:

- Write a clear, complete topic sentence.

- Use freewriting, brainstorming, or clustering to generate ideas for the body of your paragraph, essay, or speech.

- Arrange your best ideas in a plan.

- Revise for support, unity, coherence, and exact language.

- Proofread for grammar, punctuation, and spelling errors.

Writing Assignment 1 *Pay a gratitude visit.* Experts like psychologist Martin Seligman claim that people who let themselves feel and express gratitude are happier than people who do not. Do your own research. 1. Pick a person who has been kind or helpful to you but whom you have never properly thanked. 2. Write a letter to this person, discussing specifically, in concrete terms, why you feel grateful to him or her. 3. Arrange a visit to the object of your gratitude and—in person—read your letter aloud. 4. Then write a one-paragraph report on how the two of you felt about the experience. Are the experts right? Revise for consistent tense and person; use parallelism to make your sentences read smoothly.

Writing Assignment 2 *Send an e-mail of praise or complaint to a company.* What recent purchase either pleased or disappointed you? Use a search engine to find the website of this product's manufacturer. Locate the Contact Us or Customer Support page of the website, and write an e-mail that explains specifically what you like or dislike about the product. Before you click Send, proofread for the correct use of nouns, pronouns, adjectives, adverbs, and prepositions. Be sure to print a copy or send one to your instructor.

Writing Assignment 3 *Write about a celebration.* Reread Julia Alvarez's paragraph about the quinceañera, page 337 at the beginning of this unit. Notice how the author uses parallelism as she describes the steps in this ceremony and their meaning. Plan and write a paragraph or short essay about a ceremony or celebration from your cultural tradition. Brainstorm for rich details so that your reader can visualize the steps in this ceremony. Select the best details, arrange them, and write for a diverse audience. Take a break before you revise, looking for opportunities to use parallelism to underscore pairs or series of actions or steps. Be sure you use one consistent verb tense, either past or present.

Writing Assignment 4 *Review a restaurant.* You have been asked to review the food, service, and atmosphere at a local restaurant. Your review will appear in a local newspaper and will have an impact on the success or failure of this eating establishment. Tell what you ordered, how it tasted, and why you would or would not recommend this dish. Note the service: was it slow, efficient, courteous, rude, or generally satisfactory? Is the restaurant one in which customers can easily carry on a conversation, or is there too much noise? Is the lighting good or poor? Include as much specific detail as you can. Revise for consistent tense and person.

UNIT 6

Review

Proofreading

A. This composition contains inconsistent tense errors and faulty parallelism. Proofread for these errors, and correct them above the lines. (You should find 13 errors.)

A New Beginning

(1) Martha Andrews was a good student in high school. (2) After graduation, she
found
~~finds~~ a job as a bank teller to save money for college. (3) At the bank, she enjoyed
handling
knowing her regular customers and ~~to handle~~ their business. (4) When she was 19,
fell
she ~~falls~~ in love and married Patrick Kelvin, another teller. (5) By the time she was 22,
was
she ~~is~~ the mother of three children. (6) Martha's plans for college faded.

began
(7) As her fortieth birthday approached, Martha ~~begins~~ thinking about going to
had
college to study accounting; however, she ~~has~~ many fears. (8) Would she remember

how to study after so many years? (9) Would she be as smart as the younger students?

(10) Would she feel out of place among them? (11) Worst of all, her husband worried
feared
that Martha would neglect him. (12) He also ~~fears~~ that Martha would be more

successful than he.

(13) Martha's son Lucas, who was in college himself, gave her both advice and
encouragement   got
~~he encouraged her~~. (14) With his help, Martha ~~gets~~ the courage to visit Middleton
told
College. (15) An advisor in the admissions office ~~tells~~ her that older students were

valued at Middleton. (16) Older students often enriched classes because they brought
learned
a wealth of experiences with them. (17) Martha also ~~learns~~ that the college had a

special program to help older students adjust to school.
enrolled
(18) Martha ~~enrolls~~ in college the next fall. (19) To their credit, she and her husband
realized
soon ~~realize~~ that they had made the right decision.

B. Proofread the following essay for inconsistent person and faulty parallelism. Correct the errors above the lines. (You should find 13 errors.)

True Colors

(1) One day in 1992, the life of Californian John Box changed radically for the second time. (2) That day John drove four hours to buy a new wheelchair that would allow ~~you~~ ^{him} to play tennis. (3) Years before, a motorcycle accident had left both his legs paralyzed, but John refused to surrender his love of sports. (4) Instead, he turned anger into ~~being determined~~ ^{determination}. (5) Now a weekend wheelchair athlete, John wanted a better, ~~lighter chair, and one that was faster~~ ^{lighter, faster chair}. (6) When he arrived at the wheelchair manufacturer, however, the salespeople ignored him as if his disability made him invisible.

(7) Back home, furious and ~~feeling frustration~~ ^{frustrated}, John and his brother Mike decided to design ~~one's~~ ^{their} own sports wheelchair. (8) The result inspired them to start

Wheelchair athletes Zach Tapec and Bobby Rohan play Quad Rugby, an extremely competitive contact sport.

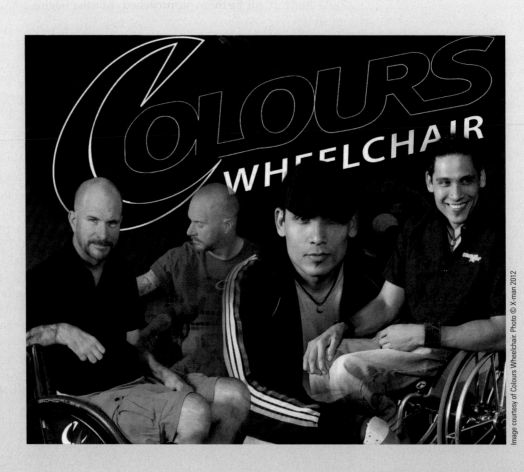

                                                                    it
a company and name ~~her~~ Colours. (9) Colours Wheelchair sells high-performance

chairs with edgy names like Hammer, Avenger, Swoosh, and ~~one is called~~ Boing.
                                                                        they
(10) John Box, the company's president, hires other "wheelers," and ~~he or she~~ often

contribute new product ideas. (11) The company also sponsors 75 wheelchair athletes.

(12) In fact, Aaron Fotheringham, a wheelchair skateboarder, became the first human

to perform a somersault flip in a wheelchair when he was just 14 years old.
                                                                      their
    (13) Today John Box and his brother not only want to expand ~~his or her~~ successful
                            educate
company but also ~~in educating~~ the public about disability. (14) "A person doesn't lose
his or her
~~their~~ personality by becoming disabled," declares John. (15) The disabled, he says,
                    brilliant   *competitive*
can be funny, ~~brilliance,~~ pregnant, ~~competing,~~ sexy, or none of the above, just like

everyone else.

TEAMWORK: CRITICAL VIEWING AND WRITING

In a group with several classmates, study the photograph on page 356, which
appears on the Colours Wheelchair website, <www.colourswheelchair.com/>.
Note that each man is shown twice, collage style. List at least three important
details about each man. What message do you think this picture sends about
disability? Does that message change or intensify when you learn that both
men represent Team Colours and play wheelchair rugby, a contact sport
so competitive that insiders call it "murderball"? Take notes as your group
discusses these questions, and be prepared to report your thoughts.

Journal Assignment: Imagine that a newly disabled person has just
discovered the Colours Wheelchair website. What effects might the photos and
information have on this person's state of mind and view of the future?

357

UNIT 6

Writers' Workshop

Shift Your Audience and Purpose

Playing with the idea of audience and purpose can produce some interesting writing—such as writing to your car to persuade it to keep running until finals are over. Likewise, writing as if you are someone else can be a learning experience.

In your class or group, read this unusual essay, aloud if possible.

A Fly's-Eye View of My Apartment

(1) Hey, are you guys ready? Today is Armageddon!* When you enter this door, remember, you're not getting out alive. She's a pretty tough lady. Oh, and don't forget to eat all you can. The kids are always dropping crumbs. You can make it through the night if you stay on the ceilings. Whatever you do, stay out of the peach room that is always humid. Once the door is shut, you're trapped. Try not to be noticed on the cabinets in the room where the smells come from. There is nothing interesting in the room with the big screen, but the room with the large bed can be rather stimulating if you stay on the walls.

(2) She won't get tired of us until about 6 P.M.; that is usually around dinnertime. She switches around, using different swatters, so you never really know what to look for. When you hear the gospel music, start looking out. She gets an enormous amount of energy from this music, and her swats are accurate, which means they're deadly. It kills me how she becomes so baffled about how we get in since she has screens on the windows. Little does she know that it's every time she opens the front door.

(3) Well, I think she's ready to leave for work. I hear the lock. To a good life, fellows. See you in heaven—and remember to give her hell!

Tanya Peck, student

_____

* Armageddon: a final battle between forces of good and evil

1. How effective is Tanya Peck's essay?

   __Y__ Interesting subject?   __Y__ Good supporting details?

   __Y__ Logical organization?   __Y__ Effective conclusion?

2. This writer cleverly plays with the notions of speaker, audience, and purpose. Who is Peck pretending to be as she writes? Whom is she addressing and for what purpose?   She is a fly addressing flies about to enter Peck's apartment.

3. The writer/speaker refers to the "pretty tough lady" of the house. Who is that lady? How do you know?   The lady is Tanya. We know because of the story's title.

4. Peck divides her essay into two main paragraphs and a brief conclusion. Because of her unusual subject, the paragraphs do not have topic sentences. However, does each paragraph have a clear main idea? What is the main idea of paragraph (1)? Of paragraph (2)?   (1) a guide to the rooms
   (2) advice about the homeowner

5. Underline any details or sentences that you especially liked—for example, in paragraph (2), the clever idea that the fly realizes that gospel music (for some mysterious reason) energizes the woman with the swatter. Can you identify the rooms described in paragraph (1)?

6. The essay concludes by playing with the terms *heaven* and *hell.* Do you find this effective—or offensive? Are these words connected to *Armageddon* in the introduction? How?

7. Proofread for any grammar or spelling errors. No errors

Writing and Revising Ideas

1. Write a _____'s-eye view (dog, cat, flea, canary, goldfish, ant, roach) of your home.

2. Describe an important moment in history as if you were there.

Before you write, read about audience and purpose in Chapter 1, Part B. Prewrite and plan to get an engaging subject. As you revise, pay special attention to keeping a consistent point of view; really try to imagine what that person (or other creature) would say in those circumstances.

UNIT 7

Mastering Mechanics

Even the best ideas may lose their impact if the writer doesn't know how to capitalize and punctuate correctly. In this unit, you will

- Learn when—and when not—to capitalize
- Recognize when—and when not—to use commas
- Find out how to use apostrophes
- Learn how to quote the words of others in your writing
- Learn proofreading strategies to find and correct your own errors

Spotlight on Reading and Writing

In this humorous paragraph on a serious subject, the writer correctly uses capital letters, commas, apostrophes, and quotation marks. As you will learn in this unit, knowing these rules will add clarity to your writing and improve your grades. Read this paragraph aloud.

My daughter, Olivia, who just turned three, has an imaginary friend whose name is Charlie Ravioli. Olivia is growing up in Manhattan, and so Charlie Ravioli has a lot of local traits: he lives in an apartment "on Madison and Lexington," he dines on grilled chicken, fruit, and water, and having reached the age of seven and a half, he feels, or is thought, "old." But the most peculiarly local thing about Olivia's imaginary playmate is this: he is always too busy to play with her. She holds her toy cell phone up to her ear, and we hear her talk into it. "Ravioli? It's Olivia . . . It's Olivia. Come and play? OK. Call me. Bye." Then she snaps it shut and shakes her head. "I always get his machine," she says. Or she will say, "I spoke to Ravioli today." "Did you have fun?" my wife and I ask. "No. He was busy working. On a television" (leaving it up in the air if he repairs electronic devices or has his own talk show).

Adam Gopnik, "Bumping into Mr. Ravioli," *The New Yorker*

- This writer describes his daughter's imaginary playmate as someone too busy to play! Why do you think Olivia has invented a playmate like Ravioli? Where did she learn about cell conversations, phone machines, and busyness?

- Does this paragraph point out a modern problem? If so, is it a big-city problem or a problem that exists in many places? What is the solution?

Writing Ideas

- *Taking time to play*

- *A time when "child's play" taught you something important*

CHAPTER 29

Capitalization

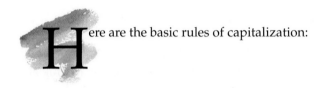 **H** ere are the basic rules of capitalization:

1. nationality, race, language, religion → *Capitalize* → American, African American, French, Latino, Protestant, Jewish, Catholic, Muslim, Buddhist, and so forth

- This group is *always capitalized*.

2. names of persons, countries, states, cities, places, streets, bodies of water, and so forth → *Capitalize* → Bill Morse, New Zealand, Texas, Denver, Golden Gate Bridge, Jones Street, Pacific Ocean, and so forth

but → a person, a country, a large state, a city, a bridge, an ocean, and so forth

- If you name a specific person, state, city, street, or body of water, *capitalize*; if you don't, use small letters.

3. buildings, organizations, institutions → *Capitalize* → Art Institute of Chicago, Apollo Theater, National Council of La Raza, Johnson City Library, Smithson University, and so forth

but → a museum, a famous theater, an activist group, a library, an old school, and so forth

- If you name a specific building, group, or institution, *capitalize*; if you don't, use small letters.

4. historic events, periods, documents → *Capitalize* → the Spanish-American War, the Renaissance, the Constitution, and so forth

but → a terrible war, a new charter, and so forth

- If you name a specific historical event, period, or document, *capitalize;* if you don't, use small letters.

5. months, days, holidays → *Capitalize* → June, Monday, the Fourth of July, and so forth

but → summer, fall, winter, spring

- *Always capitalize* months, days, and holidays; use small letters for the seasons.

6. professional and civil titles → *Capitalize* → Dr. Smith, Professor Greenstein, Judge Alvarez, and so forth

but → the doctor, the professor, the judge, and so forth

- If you name the doctor, judge, and so forth, *capitalize;* if you don't, use small letters.

7. family names → *Capitalize* → Uncle Xavier, Grandmother Stein, Cousin Emma, Mother, Grandfather, and so forth

but → an uncle, the grandmother, our cousin, my mother, and so forth

- If you name a relative or use *Mother, Father, Grandmother,* or *Grandfather* as a name, *capitalize;* however, if one of these words is preceded by the word *a, an,* or *the,* a possessive pronoun, or an adjective, use a small letter.

8. brand names → *Capitalize* → Greaso hair oil, Quick drafting ink, and so forth

- *Capitalize* the brand name but not the type of product.

9. geographic locations

Capitalize → the East, the Northwest, the South, and so forth

but → east on the boulevard

● If you mean a geographic location, *capitalize*; if you mean a direction, use small letters.

10. academic subjects

Capitalize → Mathematics 51, Sociology 11, English Literature 210, and so forth

but → a tough mathematics course, an A in sociology, a course in English literature, and so forth

● If you use the course number, *capitalize*; if you don't, use small letters. Remember to capitalize languages and countries, however.

TEACHING TIP

Urge students to use uppercase and lowercase letters (rather than all capitals) in *all* written work, including e-mail messages. Text written in all caps not only is hard to read but also seems to shout at the reader. Using good writing and well-chosen words is the best way to hold the reader's attention.

11. titles of books, poems, plays, films

Capitalize → *Pride and Prejudice*, "Ode to a Bat," *Fences*, *Women on the Verge of a Nervous Breakdown*, and so forth

● *Capitalize* the first letter of words in titles except for *a*, *an*, and *the*; prepositions; and coordinating conjunctions. However, always capitalize the first letter of the *first* and *last* words of the title.

 **PRACTICE 1**

Capitalize where necessary.

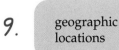 **EXAMPLE:** Dr. ^R richard ^C carmona went from high school dropout to Surgeon General of the ^U united ^S states.

1. Richard ^C carmona grew up in a poor ^P puerto ^R rican family in ^H harlem, ^N new ^Y york.

2. He started skipping classes in middle school and dropped out of ^D dewitt ^C clinton ^H high ^S school at age 17.

3. Carmona worked at dull, low-paying jobs until a conversation with a young man on leave from the ^{U.S. A} u.s. army changed his life.

4. This soldier inspired him to join the military in 1967, and Carmona soon found himself working as a medic in ^V vietnam.

5. He joined the ^G green ^B berets, earning two ^P purple ^H hearts for his brave service.

Dr. Richard Carmona speaks with children about health and wellness.

6. Carmona returned to america determined to become a doctor, so he enrolled at
   bronx community college.

7. He says that he owes his career to that college and to several of its professors—
   including michael steuerman and richard kor, who inspired him to succeed.

8. Carmona went on to earn degrees in biology and chemistry; he attended medical
   school at the university of california, graduating first in his class in three years instead of
   four.

9. Even after becoming a trauma surgeon and professor at the university of arizona, he
   continued to use his military training and knowledge of special operations.

10. This crime-fighting doctor joined the SWAT team for the pima county sheriff's
    department in 1986.

11. Carmona made headlines in 1992 when he dangled out of a helicopter to rescue a
    person stranded on the side of a cliff, an event that inspired a television movie.

12. In 1999 he stopped at a traffic accident in tucson, arizona; saw a hostage taker
    holding a woman at gunpoint; and shot the suspect.

13. Less than a year after the terrorist attacks of september 11, 2001, president george w.
    bush selected dr. carmona for the country's top medical post, noting his knowledge
    of law enforcement, bioterrorism, and emergency preparedness.

14. The second latino to be named to the u.s. post, surgeon general Carmona thanked
    the president in both spanish and english.

15. Senator john mccain said in the u.s. congress that carmona is "the embodiment of
    the american dream."

Chapter Highlights

- **Capitalize nationalities, languages, races, and religions:**

  Asian, French, Caucasian, Baptist

- **Capitalize specific countries, states, cities, organizations, and buildings:**

  Belgium, Utah, Akron, United Nations, the White House

- **Capitalize months, days, and holidays, but not seasons:**

  November, Friday, Labor Day, summer

- **Capitalize professional titles only when a person is named:**

  Mayor Gomez, the mayor, Superintendent Alicia Morgan

- **Capitalize brand names, but not the type of product:**

  Dawn dishwashing detergent

- **Capitalize geographic locations, but not directions:**

  the West, west of the city

- **Capitalize academic subjects only when they are followed by a course number:**

  History 583, psychology

- **Capitalize titles of books, poems, plays, and films:**

  The House on Mango Street, "The Raven," *Rent, The Perfect Storm*

Proofreading Strategy

Incorrect use of capital and lowercase letters can confuse your readers. If capitalization is one of your error patterns, try this:

1. Proofread your entire draft once, **searching for any proper nouns** (names of specific people, places, and things). Circle or color code every proper noun and capitalized word.

2. Now check to **make sure that you have correctly capitalized** each one. This student coded his proper nouns blue:

   Community College
   In August, I will begin attending Northern Virginia community college, where I will

   math,
   take classes in Math, English, and psychology.

"Community College" is part of the college's name and must be capitalized whereas "math" is not a *specific* math course, so it needs no capital.

WRITING AND PROOFREADING ASSIGNMENT

Is your vacation usually a disaster or a success? Describe a particularly memorable vacation—either bad or good—in which you learned something about how to plan or enjoy a vacation.

In your first sentence, tell what you learned. Explain what went right and what went wrong. Be sure to name the places you visited and the sights you saw. You will probably want to arrange events in time order. Proofread for correct capitalization.

CHAPTER REVIEW

Proofread the following essay for errors in capitalization; correct the errors above the lines.

The Strange Career of Deborah Sampson

(1) Few ^sSoldiers have had a stranger army career than Deborah Sampson. (2) Sampson disguised herself as a man so that she could fight in the ^Rrevolutionary ^Wwar. (3) Born on ^Ddecember 17, 1760, she spent her early years in a ^tTown near ^Pplymouth, ^Mmassachusetts. (4) Her ^fFather left his large family, however, and went to sea when Sampson was seven years old. (5) After living with a ^cCousin and then with the widow of a ^mMinister, ^Ssampson became a servant in a wealthy family.

(6) Household tasks and hard outdoor work built up her physical strength. (7) She was taller than the average ^mMan and more muscular than the average ^wWoman. (8) Therefore, she was able to disguise herself successfully. (9) Sampson enlisted in the ^Ccontinental ^Aarmy on ^Mmay 20, 1782, under the name of ^Rrobert ^Sshurtleff.

(10) Sampson fought in several ^bBattles and was wounded at least twice. (11) One story says that she took a bullet out of her own leg with a penknife to avoid seeing a ^dDoctor. (12) However, after the surrender of the ^Bbritish, Sampson's regiment was sent to ^pphiladelphia, where she was hospitalized with a high fever and lost consciousness. (13) At the ^hHospital, ^Ddr. Barnabas Binney made the discovery that ended Sampson's army life. (14) She was honorably discharged by ^Ggeneral ^Hhenry ^Kknox at ^Wwest ^Ppoint on ^Ooctober 28, 1783.

(15) Officially female again, Sampson returned to Massachusetts and eventually married a ^fFarmer named ^Bbenjamin ^Ggannett. (16) The story of Sampson's adventures spread; in 1797 a book titled *^Tthe ^Ffemale ^Rreview* was published about her. (17) When Sampson decided to earn money by telling her own story, she became the first ^Aamerican woman to be paid as a ^pPublic ^sSpeaker. (18) She gave her first talk at the ^Ffederal ^Sstreet ^Ttheatre in ^Bboston in ^Mmarch

North Wind Picture Archives via AP Images

                                         S
1802 and toured until september. (19) Her health was poor, however, and she could not continue her appearances.

             P R   G
(20) In 1804, paul revere, who was a neighbor of the gannetts, wrote to a member of

U   S   C   S
the united states congress. (21) He asked for a pension for this Soldier who had never been paid and was still suffering from her war wounds.

                                              D   S
(22) Congress granted deborah sampson

G
gannett a pension of four dollars a month.

                              S   A
(23) Deborah Sampson died in sharon, Massachusetts, in april 1827. (24) Her story inspired

p   p
the People of her own time and continues to inspire People today. (25) Two plays have

                      S W   T   P   D   V   D
been written about her: *she was there* and *portrait of deborah.* (26) On veterans day in 1989,

                                                S   P   L
a life-size bronze statue was dedicated in front of the sharon public library to honor her.

EXPLORING ONLINE

<http://grammar.ccc.commnet.edu/grammar/cgi-shl/par_numberless_quiz.pl/caps_quiz.htm> Interactive quiz: Capitalize as needed.

<http://a4esl.org/q/j/ck/ed-caps.html> Proofread for "caps" errors and correct them; then electronically check your work.

Commas

The comma is a pause. It gives your reader a chance to stop for a moment to think about where your sentence has been and where it is going, and to prepare to read on.

Although this chapter covers basic uses of the comma, always keep this generalization in mind: If there is no reason for a comma, leave it out!

A. Commas after Items in a Series

(1) I like apples, oranges, and pears.

- What three things do I like? _____apples_____, _____oranges_____, and _____pears_____

Use commas to separate three or more items in a series.

(2) We will walk through the park, take in a film, and visit a friend.

- What three things will we do? _____walk through the park_____, _____take in a film_____, and _____visit a friend_____

(3) She loves to explore new ~~cultures~~ ^{cultures,} sample different ~~foods~~ ^{foods,} and learn foreign languages.

- In sentence (3), what are the items in the series? ___explore new cultures___,
  ___sample different foods___, and ___learn foreign languages___
- Punctuate sentence (3).

However, if you want to join three or more items with *and* or *or* between the items, do not use commas.

(4) She plays tennis *and* golf *and* softball.

- Note that commas are not used in sentence (4).

Punctuate these sentences correctly.

1. I can't find my ~~shoes~~ ^{shoes,} my ~~socks~~ ^{socks,} or my hat!
2. ~~Sylvia Eric~~ ^{Sylvia, Eric,} and Jagger have just completed a course in welding.
3. Over lunch, they discussed new ~~accounts~~ ^{accounts,} marketing ~~strategy~~ ^{strategy,} and motherhood.
4. Frank is in ~~Florida~~ ^{Florida,} Bob is in ~~Brazil~~ ^{Brazil,} and I am in the bathtub.
5. On Sunday, we repaired the ~~porch~~ ^{porch,} cleaned the ~~basement~~ ^{basement,} and shingled the roof.
6. The exhibit will include ~~photographs diaries~~ ^{photographs, diaries,} and love letters.
7. ~~Spinning kickboxing~~ ^{Spinning, kickboxing,} and tai chi have become very popular recently.
8. Katya hung her coat on the ~~hook~~ ^{hook,} Oscar draped his jacket over her ~~coat~~ ^{coat,} and Ruby threw her scarf on top of the pile.

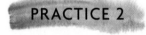

On paper or on a computer, write three sentences, each containing three or more items in a series. Punctuate them correctly.

B. Commas after Introductory Phrases

(1) By the end of the season, our local basketball team will have won 30 games straight.

- *By the end of the season* introduces the sentence.

An introductory phrase is usually followed by a comma.

(2) On Thursday we left for Hawaii.

However, a very short introductory phrase, like the one in sentence (2), need not be followed by a comma.

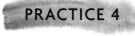

PRACTICE 3

Punctuate these sentences correctly. One sentence is already punctuated correctly.

1. During the ~~rainstorm~~ rainstorm, we huddled in a doorway.
2. Every Saturday at 9 ~~P.M.~~ P.M., she carries her telescope to the roof.
3. After their last ~~trip~~ trip, Fred and Nita decided on separate vacations.
4. The first woman was appointed to the U.S. Supreme Court in 1981.
5. By the light of the ~~moon~~ moon, we could make out a dim figure.
6. During the coffee ~~break~~ break, George reviewed his psychology homework.
7. In the deep end of the ~~pool~~ pool, he found three silver dollars.
8. In almost no ~~time~~ time, they had changed the tire.

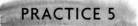

PRACTICE 4

On paper or on a computer, write three sentences using introductory phrases. Punctuate them correctly.

C. Commas for Direct Address

> (1) Bob, you must leave now.
>
> (2) You must, Bob, leave now.
>
> (3) You must leave now, Bob.
>
> (4) Don't be surprised, old buddy, if I pay you a visit very soon.

- In sentences (1), (2), and (3), *Bob* is the person spoken to; he is being *addressed directly*.
- In sentence (4), *old buddy* is being *addressed directly*.

The person addressed directly is set off by commas wherever the direct address appears in the sentence.

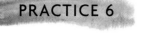

PRACTICE 5

Circle the person or persons directly addressed, and punctuate the sentences correctly.

1. I am happy to inform you, (Mr. Forbes,) that you are the father of twins.
2. We expect to return on Monday, (Miguel.)
3. It appears, (my friend,) that you have won two tickets to the opera.
4. Get out of my roast, (you mangy old dog.)
5. (Tom,) it's probably best that you sell the old car at a loss.
6. If I were you, (Hilda,) I would wait to make the phone call until we are off the highway.
7. (Max,) it's time you learned to operate the lawn mower!
8. I am pleased to announce, (ladies and gentlemen,) that Beyoncé is our surprise guest tonight.

PRACTICE 6

On paper or on a computer, write three sentences using direct address. Punctuate them correctly.

D. Commas to Set Off Appositives

> **(1) The Rialto, a new theater, is on Tenth Street.**

- *A new theater* describes *the Rialto*.

> **(2) An elderly man, my grandfather walks a mile every day.**

- What group of words describes *my grandfather*?
  an elderly man

> **(3) They bought a new painting, a rather beautiful landscape.**

- What group of words describes *a new painting*?
  a rather beautiful landscape

- *A new theater*, *an elderly man*, and *a rather beautiful landscape* are called *appositives*.

An *appositive* **is a group of words that renames a noun or pronoun and gives more information about it. The appositive can appear at the beginning, middle, or end of a sentence. An appositive is usually set off by commas.**

PRACTICE 7

Circle the appositive, and punctuate the sentences correctly.

1. That door, the one with the X on it, leads backstage.
2. A short man, he decided not to pick a fight with the basketball player.
3. Hassim, my friend from Morocco, will be staying with me this week.
4. My nephew wants to go to Mama's Indoor Arcade, a very noisy place.
5. George Eliot, a nineteenth-century novelist, was a woman named Mary Ann Evans.
6. A very close race, the election for mayor wasn't decided until 2 A.M.
7. On the Fourth of July, my favorite holiday, my high school friends get together for an all-day barbecue.
8. Dr. Bawa, a specialist in tribal music, always travels with a digital recorder.

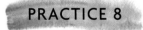**PRACTICE 8**

On paper or on a computer, write three sentences using appositives. Punctuate them correctly.

E.   Commas for Parenthetical Expressions

> (1) By the way, I think that you're beautiful.
>
> (2) I think, by the way, that you're beautiful.
>
> (3) I think that you're beautiful, by the way.

TEACHING TIP

You may want to remind students that nonrestrictive relative clauses, covered in Part B of Chapter 20, are a type of parenthetical expression that requires commas.

● *By the way* modifies or qualifies the entire sentence or idea.

● It is called a **parenthetical expression** because it is a side remark, something that could be placed in parentheses: *(By the way) I think that you're beautiful.*

Set off a parenthetical expression with commas.

Here is a partial list of parenthetical expressions:

as a matter of fact	in fact
believe me	it seems to me
I am sure	it would seem
I assure you	to tell the truth

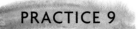
PRACTICE 9

Circle the parenthetical expressions in the sentences below; then punctuate them correctly.

TEACHING TIP

Commas in direct quotations are covered in Chapter 32.

1. (Believe me) Felice has studied hard for her law boards.

2. He possesses (it would seem) an uncanny gift for gab.

3. It was (I assure you) an accident.

4. (To tell the truth) I just put a treadmill in your basement.

5. Her supervisor (by the way) will never admit when he is wrong.

6. A well-prepared résumé (as a matter of fact) can help you get a job.

7. He is (in fact) a black belt.

8. (To begin with) you need a new carburetor.

PRACTICE 10

On paper or on a computer, write three sentences using parenthetical expressions. Punctuate them correctly.

F.   Commas for Dates

> (1) I arrived on Monday, March 20, 2009, and found that I was in the wrong city.

● Note that commas separate the different parts of the date.

● Note that a comma follows the last item in the date.

(2) She saw him on Wednesday and spoke with him.

However, a one-word date (*Wednesday* or *1995*) preceded by a preposition (*in*, *on*, *near*, or *from*, for example) is not followed by a comma unless there is some other reason for it.

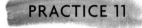
PRACTICE 11

Punctuate these sentences correctly. Not every sentence requires additional punctuation.

1. By ~~Tuesday~~ *Tuesday,* October 6 *6,* he had outlined the whole history text.
2. ~~Thursday~~ *Thursday,* May 8 *8,* is Hereford's birthday.
3. She was born on January 9, ~~1985~~ *1985,* in a small Iowa town.
4. He was born on July ~~4 1976~~ *4, 1976,* the two-hundredth anniversary of the Declaration of Independence.
5. Do you think we will have finished the yearbook by May?
6. On January ~~24 1848~~ *24, 1848,* James Wilson Marshall found gold in California.
7. My aunt is staying with us from Tuesday to Friday.
8. Charles Schulz's final *Peanuts* comic strip was scheduled for February ~~13 2000~~ *13, 2000,* the day on which he died.

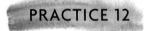
PRACTICE 12

On paper or on a computer, write three sentences using dates. Punctuate them correctly.

G. Commas for Addresses

(1) We just moved from 11 Landow Street, Wilton, Connecticut, to 73 James Street, Charleston, West Virginia.

- Commas separate different parts of an address.
- A comma generally follows the last item in an address, usually a state (*Connecticut*).

(2) Julio Perez *from* Queens was made district sales manager.

However, a one-word address preceded by a preposition (*in*, *on*, *at*, *near*, or *from*, for example) is not followed by a comma unless there is another reason for it.

(3) Julio Perez, Queens, was made district sales manager.

Commas are required to set off a one-word address if the preposition before the address is omitted.

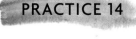

PRACTICE 13   Punctuate these sentences correctly. Not every sentence requires additional punctuation.

1. Their address is 6 Great Ormond ~~Street London~~ England.
   Street, London,
2. ~~Seattle Washington~~ faces the Cascade Mountains.
   Seattle, Washington,
3. That package must be sent to 30 West Overland ~~Street Phoenix~~ Arizona.
   Street, Phoenix,
4. We parked on Marble Lane, across the street from the bowling alley.
5. His father now lives in ~~Waco Texas~~ but his sister has never left Vermont.
   Waco, Texas,
6. How far is ~~Kansas City Kansas~~ from ~~Independence~~ Missouri?
   Kansas City, Kansas,   *Independence,*
7. The old watch factory at 43 North Oak ~~Street Scranton Pennsylvania~~ has been condemned by the building inspector.
   Street, Scranton, Pennsylvania,
8. Foster's ~~Stationery~~ 483 Heebers ~~Street Plainview~~ sells special calligraphy pens.
   Stationery,   *Street, Plainview,*

PRACTICE 14   On paper or on a computer, write three sentences using addresses. Punctuate them correctly.

H. Commas for Coordination and Subordination

Chapters 16 and 17 cover the use of commas with coordinating and subordinating conjunctions. This is a brief review.

LEARNING STYLES TIP

Engage *all types of learners* and have some fun: have students create mnemonics, skits, drawings, songs, or rhymes to help them remember the eight comma rules (for example *AD SAID PJ*, for **A**ppositives, **D**irect address, **S**eries, **A**ddresses, **I**ntroductory phrases, **D**ates, **P**arentheticals, **J**oining with coordination and subordination).

(1) Enzio enjoys most kinds of music, but heavy metal gives him a headache.

(2) Although the weather bureau had predicted rain, the day turned out bright and sunny.

(3) The day turned out bright and sunny although the weather bureau had predicted rain.

- In sentence (1), a comma precedes the coordinating conjunction *but*, which joins two independent ideas.

- In sentence (2), a comma follows the dependent idea because it precedes the independent idea.

- Sentence (3) does not require a comma because the independent idea precedes the subordinate one.

Use a comma before coordinating conjunctions—*and*, *but*, *for*, *nor*, *or*, *so*, *or yet*— that join two independent ideas.

Use a comma after a dependent idea only when the dependent idea precedes the independent one; do not use a comma if the dependent idea follows the independent one.

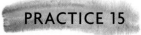

PRACTICE 15   Punctuate correctly. Not every sentence requires additional punctuation.

EXAMPLE: Because scrapped cars create millions of tons of ~~waste~~ recycling auto parts has become an important issue.
   waste,

1. Today new cars are made from many old ~~parts~~ and manufacturers are trying to increase the use of recycled materials from old cars.
   parts,

2. Scrapped cars can be easily recycled because they consist mostly of metals.

3. After these cars are ~~crushed~~ ^{crushed,} magnets draw the metals out of them.

4. However, the big problem in recycling cars is the plastic they contain.

5. Although plastic can be ~~recycled~~ ^{recycled,} the average car contains about 20 kinds of plastic.

6. Separating the different types of plastic takes much ~~time~~ ^{time,} but companies are developing ways to speed up the process.

7. Still, new cars need to be made differently before recycling can truly succeed.

8. Their parts should detach ~~easily~~ ^{easily,} and they should be made of plastics and metals that can be separated from each other.

9. As we develop more markets for the recycled auto ~~parts~~ ^{parts,} new cars may soon be 90 percent recycled and recyclable.

10. Our environment will ~~benefit~~ ^{benefit,} and brand-new cars will really be more than 50 years old!

TEACHING TIP

Consider illustrating the importance of commas by bringing in a passage *without* any. (Exploring Online at the end of this chapter provides one such essay about basketball.) Have your students find sentences that are confusing or changed in meaning because of the absence of commas.

PRACTICE 16

On paper or on a computer, write three sentences, one with a coordinating conjunction, one beginning with a subordinating conjunction, and one with the subordinating conjunction in the middle.

Chapter Highlights

- **Commas separate three or more items in a series:**

  He bought a ball, a bat, and a fielder's glove.

- **Unless it is very short, an introductory phrase is followed by a comma:**

  By the end of January, I'll be in Australia.

- **Commas set off the name of a person directly addressed:**

  I think, Aunt Betty, that your latest novel is a winner.

- **Commas set off appositives:**

  My boss, the last person in line in the cafeteria, often forgets to eat lunch.

- **Commas set off parenthetical expressions:**

  My wife, by the way, went to school with your sister.

- **Commas separate the parts of a date or an address, except for a one-word date or an address preceded by a preposition:**

  On April 1, 1997, I was in a terrible blizzard.

  I live at 48 Trent Street, Randolph, Michigan.

  She works in Tucson as a plumber.

- **A comma precedes a coordinating conjunction that joins two independent ideas:**

  We had planned to see a movie together, but we couldn't agree on one.

- **If a dependent idea precedes the independent idea, it is followed by a comma; if the independent idea comes first, it is not followed by a comma:**

  Although I still have work to do, my project will be ready on time.

  My project will be ready on time although I still have work to do.

Proofreading Strategy

Armed with the eight comma rules, you can proofread effectively for comma errors.

1. **Circle or highlight every comma** in your draft. This forces your eye and brain to focus on every one of them. If you are writing on a computer, use the *"Find"* feature to locate all your commas.

2. For every comma, ask, ***Does one of the eight comma rules explain why this comma needs to be here?*** If you aren't sure, review the rules in the Chapter Highlights. Make any needed corrections, like this:

C (introductory phrase)
Unlike our planet's Northern Hemisphere, the Southern Hemisphere contains fewer
X (*not* a series—remove comma)   C (series)   C (series)
land masses, and more water. The South Pacific Ocean, South Atlantic Ocean,
C (series)
Indian Ocean, and various seas cover almost 81 percent of Earth's southern half.

WRITING AND PROOFREADING ASSIGNMENT

We live in what is often called "the age of invention" because of rapid advances in technology, communication, and medicine. Which modern invention has meant the most to *you*, and why? You might choose something as common as disposable diapers or as sophisticated as a special feature of a personal computer.

In the first sentence, name the invention. Then, as specifically as possible, discuss why it means so much to you. Proofread for the correct use of commas.

CHAPTER REVIEW

Proofread the following essay for comma errors—either missing commas or commas used incorrectly. Correct the errors above the lines.

Treetop Crusader

1999,
(1) On December 18, 1999 Julia Butterfly Hill's feet touched ground for the first time in

top
more than two years. (2) She had just climbed down from the top, of an ancient tree in

County,   tree,   redwood,
Humboldt County California. (3) The tree a thousand-year-old redwood was named Luna.

10, 1997,
(4) Hill had climbed 180 feet up Luna on December 10 1997 for what she thought would be

a protest of two or three weeks.

Lumber,
(5) Hill's action was intended to stop Pacific Lumber a division of the Maxxam

Corporation,   Luna had
Corporation from cutting down old-growth forests. (6) The area immediately next to Luna,

had already been stripped of trees. (7) Because nothing was left to hold the soil to the

mountain,   Stafford,
mountain a huge part of the hill had slid into the town of Stafford California. (8) Many

homes had been destroyed.

TEACHING TIP

This Chapter Review makes an interesting in-class activity likely to spark discussion about the power of one person to make a difference. Ask the class why Julia gave up so much for a single tree. Is there a cause or value for which any of them would sacrifice so much?

Julia Hill and Luna

© Shaun Walker

(9) During her long tree-sit, Hill endured incredible hardships. (10) For more than two

years,
years she lived on a tiny platform 18 stories off the ground. (11) El Niño storms almost

winds,   rain,
destroyed her with ferocious winds razor-sharp rain and numbing cold. (12) She once wore

socks, booties,   pants,   shirts,   sweater,
two pairs of socks booties two pairs of thermal ski pants two thermal shirts a wool sweater

windbreakers,   raincoat, gloves,
two windbreakers a raincoat gloves and two hats to keep from freezing to death during

hardships,
a storm. (13) In addition to enduring nature's hardships Hill withstood life-threatening

helicopters,   sieges,
torment from the logging company. (14) She was harassed by helicopters various sieges and

course,   loneliness,
interference with receiving supplies. (15) Of course she also endured loneliness sometimes

fear,
paralyzing fear and always deep sorrow for the destruction around her.

(16) Only 23 at the beginning of her ~~tree-sit~~ ^{tree-sit,} Hill eventually became both world famous and very knowledgeable about ancient forests. (17) At the top of ~~Luna~~ ^{Luna,} she used a cell ~~phone~~ ^{phone,} a ~~pager~~ ^{pager,} and a daily engagement planner. (18) She was trying to protect the tree ~~itself~~ ^{itself,} to slow down all logging in the ~~area~~ ^{area,} and to raise public awareness. (19) She gave hundreds of phone interviews and answered hundreds of letters.

(20) Hill's action was dramatically successful; Luna was eventually saved from destruction. (21) When Hill returned to normal ~~life~~ ^{life,} she wrote a ~~book~~ ^{book,} *The Legacy of Luna: The Story of a Tree, a Woman, and the Struggle to Save the Redwoods.* (22) Julia Butterfly Hill is now a ~~writer~~ ^{writer,} a ~~poet~~ ^{poet,} and an activist. (23) She is a frequent speaker at environmental ~~conferences~~ ^{conferences,} she helped found the Circle of Life Foundation for preserving all ~~life~~ ^{life,} and she has received many honors and awards.

EXPLORING ONLINE

TEACHING TIP

Instructor tools for *Grassroots* include a computerized Test Bank, PowerPoint slides, an Instructor's Manual with teaching tips, and more, and can be accessed at ‹**login .cengage.com**›.

<http://owl.english.purdue.edu/exercises/3/5/15> Quiz with answers: Where have all the commas gone?

<http://chompchomp.com/hotpotatoes/commas01.htm> Interactive quiz: Put those comma rules into action at Grammar Bytes.

<http://grammar.ccc.commnet.edu/grammar/quizzes/comma_quiz.htm> Interactive quiz: Add commas to this essay about basektball and score!

CHAPTER 31

Apostrophes

A: **Using the Apostrophe for Contractions**

B: **Defining the Possessive**

C: **Using the Apostrophe to Show Possession (in Words That Do Not Already End in -S)**

D: **Using the Apostrophe to Show Possession (in Words That Already End in -S)**

The apostrophe is a small mark that greatly confuses many people. The apostrophe has just two important uses, and this chapter will help you master both of them.

A. Using the Apostrophe for Contractions

A contraction combines two words into one.

TEACHING TIP

Students should understand that the apostrophe has just two uses: (1) to form a contraction and (2) to indicate possession. A writer should be able to justify every apostrophe with one of these two rules.

> do + not = don't
> should + not = shouldn't
> I + have = I've

● Note that an apostrophe (') replaces the omitted letters: "o" in *don't* and *shouldn't* and "ha" in *I've*.

BE CAREFUL: *Won't* is an odd contraction because it cannot be broken into parts in the same way the previous contractions can.

> will + not = won't

PRACTICE 1

TEACHING TIP

Have students think critically about the effect of contractions in writing. (They create an informal tone often inappropriate for formal academic assignments and workplace documents.)

Write these words as contractions.

1. you + are = _____you're_____

2. who + is = _____who's_____

3. was + not = _____wasn't_____

4. she + will = _____she'll_____

5. can + not = _____can't_____

6. it + is = _____it's_____

7. I + am = _____I'm_____

8. will + not = _____won't_____

380

PRACTICE 2

Proofread this paragraph for incorrect or missing apostrophes in contractions. Write each corrected contraction above the lines.

(1) For musicians and music lovers in the twenty-first century, ~~its~~ *it's* a small world. (2) Musicians ~~whove~~ *who've* grown up in Asia, for instance, ~~arent~~ *aren't* influenced by just Asian musical traditions anymore. (3) Hip-~~hops~~ *hop's* a perfect example of musical globalization. (4) ~~Its~~ *It's* inspired musicians all over the world, something the first American rappers ~~couldnt~~ *couldn't* have foreseen. (5) Many hip-hop artists in other countries, however, ~~dont~~ *don't* like the focus on money and sex in much of American hip-hop. (6) For example, Korean performers like Jo PD and Drunken Tiger are proud that ~~theyre~~ *they're* forces for social justice. (7) Many hip-hop stars from New Zealand are Pacific Islanders or Maori tribal people ~~whove~~ *who've* developed world-class skills and fight oppression with music. (8) In Senegal, politically active rappers claim that ~~theyre~~ *they're* responsible for toppling an oppressive government in the 2000 elections. (9) Sister Fa, ~~whose~~ *who's* Senegalese, raps in French about arranged marriages and the oppression of women. (10) Some South American hip-hop stars also have embraced a lifestyle ~~thats~~ *that's* committed to social justice. (11) Brazilian rappers, for example, ~~do'nt~~ *don't* perform just music; they also perform community service, teaching youth ~~wholl~~ *who'll* spread the word about social change, music, and art.

Members of this all-girl Iraqi rap group, Rap Curse, learned their moves from satellite TV.

EXPLORING ONLINE

<http://www.hiphoparchive.org/> Explore The Hiphop Archive. Click "Hiphop University" to tap the research on this musical form. Topics on the site include global hip-hop, conferences and events, information on particular artists and groups, and women in hip-hop (watch the trailer for *Say My Name*, a film on this subject).

PRACTICE 3

On paper or a computer, write five sentences using an apostrophe in a contraction.

B. Defining the Possessive

A *possessive* is a word that shows that someone or something owns someone or something else.

PRACTICE 4

In the following phrases, who owns what?

EXAMPLE: "The hat of the man" means _the man owns the hat_.

1. "The camera of Judson" means _Judson owns the camera_.

2. "The hopes of the people" means _the people have hopes_.

3. "The thought of the woman" means _the woman has the thought_.

4. "The trophies of the home team" means _the home team owns trophies_.

5. "The ideas of that man" means _that man has ideas_.

C. Using the Apostrophe to Show Possession (in Words That Do Not Already End in -*S*)

| (1) the hands of my father | becomes | (2) my father's hands |

- In phrase (1), who owns what? _My father owns the hands._

- In phrase (1), what is the *owner word*? _father_

- How does the owner word show possession in phrase (2)?
  Father ends in 's.

- Note that what is owned, *hands*, follows the owner word.

  If the *owner word* (possessive) does not end in -*s*, add an apostrophe and an -*s* to show possession.

PRACTICE 5

Change these phrases into possessives with an apostrophe and an -*s*. (Note that the owner words do not already end in -*s*.)

EXAMPLE: the friend of my cousin = _my cousin's friend_

1. the eyes of Rona = _Rona's eyes_

2. the voice of the coach = _the coach's voice_

3. the ark of Noah = _____Noah's ark_____

4. the technology of tomorrow = _____tomorrow's technology_____

5. the jacket of someone = _____someone's jacket_____

PRACTICE 6

Add an apostrophe and an -*s* to show possession in these phrases.

1. ~~Judy~~ briefcase (Judy's)
2. the ~~diver~~ tanks (diver's)
3. ~~Murphy~~ Law (Murphy's)
4. ~~Brock~~ decision (Brock's)
5. ~~somebody~~ umbrella (somebody's)

6. ~~everyone~~ dreams (everyone's)
7. your ~~daughter~~ sandwich (daughter's)
8. last ~~month~~ prices (month's)
9. that ~~woman~~ talent (woman's)
10. ~~anyone~~ guess (anyone's)

PRACTICE 7

On paper or on a computer, write five sentences. In each, use an apostrophe and an -*s* to show ownership. Use owner words that do not already end in -*s*.

D. Using the Apostrophe to Show Possession (in Words That Already End in -*S*)

(1) the uniforms of the pilots	becomes	(2) the pilots' uniforms

- In phrase (1), who owns what? _The pilots own the uniforms._
- In phrase (1), what is the *owner word*? _pilots_
- How does the owner word show possession in phrase (2)?
  Pilots ends in '.
- Note that what is owned, *uniforms*, follows the owner word.

   If the *owner word* (possessive) ends in -*s*, add an apostrophe after the -*s* to show possession.*

PRACTICE 8

Change these phrases into possessives with an apostrophe. (Note that the owner words already end in -*s*.)

EXAMPLE: the helmets of the players = _the players' helmets_

1. the farm of my grandparents = _my grandparents' farm_

2. the kindness of my neighbors = _my neighbors' kindness_

3. the dunk shots of the basketball players = _the basketball players' dunk shots_

4. the music of Alicia Keys = _Alicia Keys' music_

5. the trainer of the horses = _the horses' trainer_

_____

* Some writers add an '*s* to one-syllable proper names that end in -*s*: *James's book.*

PRACTICE 9

Add either *'s* or *'* to show possession in these phrases. BE CAREFUL: Some of the owner words end in *-s* and some do not.

models'
1. the ~~models~~ faces

model's
2. the ~~model~~ face

captain's
3. the ~~captain~~ safety record

children's
4. the ~~children~~ room

runner's
5. the ~~runner~~ time

Boris'/Boris's
6. ~~Boris~~ radio

niece's
7. my ~~niece~~ two iPads

parents'
8. your ~~parents~~ anniversary

men's
9. the ~~men~~ locker room

students'
10. three ~~students~~ exams

contestants'
11. several ~~contestants~~ answers

Jones'/Jones's
12. Mr. ~~Jones~~ band

PRACTICE 10

Rewrite each of the following pairs of short sentences as *one* sentence by using a possessive.

TEACHING TIP

You might enjoy telling students about a British society formed to protect the "much-abused" apostrophe from misuse: ‹**http://www.apostrophe.org.uk**›.

EXAMPLE: Joan has a friend. The friend comes from Chile.

Joan's friend comes from Chile.

1. Rusty has a motorcycle. The motorcycle needs new brakes.

   Rusty's motorcycle needs new brakes.

2. The nurses had evidence. The evidence proved that the doctor was not careless.

   The nurses' evidence proved that the doctor was not careless.

3. Ahmad has a salary. The salary barely keeps him in peanut butter.

   Ahmad's salary barely keeps him in peanut butter.

4. Lee has a job. His job in the Complaint Department keeps him on his toes.

   Lee's job in the Complaint Department keeps him on his toes.

5. Bruno has a bad cold. It makes it hard for him to sleep.

   Bruno's bad cold makes it hard for him to sleep.

6. Jessie told a joke. The joke did not make us laugh.

   Jessie's joke did not make us laugh.

7. John Adams had a son. His son was the first president's son to also become president of the United States.

   John Adams' (Adams's) son was the first president's son to also become president

   of the United States.

8. My sisters have a daycare center. The daycare center is open seven days a week.

   My sisters' daycare center is open seven days a week.

9. The twins have a goal. Their goal is to learn synchronized swimming.

   The twins' goal is to learn synchronized swimming.

10. Darren has a thank-you note. The thank-you note says it all.

    Darren's thank-you note says it all.

PRACTICE 11

Proofread this paragraph. Above the lines, correct any missing or incorrectly used apostrophes in possessives. BE CAREFUL: some owner words end in -s and some do not.

(1) Apple ~~Computers'~~ *Computer's* founder, Steven Jobs, was one of the ~~industrys~~ *industry's* greatest innovators— and survivors. (2) ~~Jobs~~ *Jobs'/Jobs's* first position, in the 1970s, was designing computer games for Atari. (3) Then he saw a ~~friends~~ *friend's* home-built computer. (4) Jobs convinced this friend, Steve Wozniak, to go into business with him. (5) At first, the partners built computers in the Jobs ~~familys~~ *family's* garage. (6) Their ~~companys~~ *company's* name came from the story of Isaac Newton, who supposedly formulated his great theory of gravity when he watched an apple fall from a tree. (7) The ~~mens'~~ *men's* small computers were a huge success. (8) In 1984, they launched the Macintosh, which simplified ~~peoples~~ *people's* interactions with their computers by replacing typed commands with clicks. (9) But then, ~~Job's~~ *Jobs'/Jobs's* luck changed. (10) After some poor management decisions, he was fired by ~~Apples'~~ *Apple's* board of directors. (11) Despite public failure, he started over. (12) Ironically, his new company was bought by Apple ten years later. (13) As Apple's leader once again, Jobs soon captured ~~consumer's~~ *consumers'* attention with his revolutionary iPod, iTunes software, iPhone, and iPad. (14) When he died in 2011, Apple was one of the ~~worlds'~~ *world's* strongest brands. (15) This ~~mans'~~ *man's* success flowed not just from farsighted ideas but also from a willingness to learn ~~failures~~ *failures'* lessons and begin again.

PRACTICE 12

On paper or on a computer, write six sentences that use an apostrophe to show ownership—three using owner words that do not end in -s and three using owner words that do end in -s.

BE CAREFUL: Apostrophes show possession by nouns. As the following chart indicates, possessive pronouns do not have apostrophes.

TEACHING TIP

Many students confuse plurals and possessives—e.g., incorrectly adding 's at the end of a noun to form a plural. Take a few minutes to underscore the difference. Have students find online plural and possessive exercises like this one: ‹http://a4esl. org/q/j/ck/ mc-plurals.html›.

Possessive Pronouns	
Singular	**Plural**
<u>my</u> book, <u>mine</u>	<u>our</u> book, <u>ours</u>
<u>your</u> book, <u>yours</u>	<u>your</u> book, <u>yours</u>
<u>his</u> book, <u>his</u>	<u>their</u> book, <u>theirs</u>
<u>her</u> book, <u>hers</u>	
<u>its</u> book, <u>its</u>	

Do not confuse *its* (possessive pronoun) with *it's* (contraction for *it is* or *it has*) or *your* (possessive pronoun) with *you're* (contraction for *you are*).*

---

* See Chapter 35 for work on words that look and sound alike.

LEARNING STYLES TIP

Give students extra credit for bringing in apostrophe errors they spot on signs, billboards, flyers, and so on. Errors like "Hanks Jet Ski Rental" and "Whole Grains and Wild Berry's Café" abound in the real world. Students might use their cell phone cameras to capture photographic evidence.

REMEMBER: Use apostrophes for contractions and possessive nouns only. Do not use apostrophes for plural nouns (*four marbles*), verbs (*he hopes*), or possessive pronouns (*his, hers, yours, its*).

Chapter Highlights

● **An apostrophe can indicate a contraction:**

We're glad you could come.

They *won't* be back until tomorrow.

● **A word that does not end in -s takes an 's to show possession:**

Is that *Barbara's* coat on the sofa?

I like *Clint Eastwood's* movies.

● **A word that ends in -s takes just an ' to show possession:**

That store sells *ladies'* hats with feathers.

I depend on my *friends'* advice.

Proofreading Strategy

Knowing the two main uses of apostrophes—contractions and possessives—will help you avoid the mistake of sticking apostrophes where they don't belong, for instance, into plural nouns or possessive pronouns like *hers* or *its*.

Go through your draft and **highlight every word that contains an apostrophe**. If you are using a computer, use the *"Find"* feature to locate all apostrophes in your draft.

For every apostrophe, you should be able to answer YES to one of two questions:

Is this apostrophe used to form a contraction?

Is this apostrophe used to indicate possession?

YES   YES   NO   YES

Example: Ronald didn't realize that the children's toy's weren't in the box.

         toys

To find **missing apostrophes**, highlight all words ending in -s. If the word is a plural, leave it alone. If the word is a possessive noun, add an apostrophe.

coach's   OK—plural

Example: When the coachs whistle blew, the swimmers dove into the pool.

WRITING AND PROOFREADING ASSIGNMENT

Assume that you are writing to apply for a position as a teacher's aide. You want to convince the school principal that you would be a good teacher, and you decide to do this by describing a time when you taught a young child—your own child, a younger sibling, or a friend's child—to do something new.

In your topic sentence, briefly state who the child was and what you taught him or her. What made you want to teach this child? Was the experience easier or harder than you expected? How did you feel afterward? Proofread for the correct use of apostrophes.

CHAPTER REVIEW

Proofread this paragraph for apostrophe errors—missing apostrophes and apostrophes used incorrectly. Correct the errors above the lines.

The Magic Fastener

(1) ~~Its~~ *It's* hard to remember the world without Velcro. (2) Shoelaces had to be tied; ~~jackets'~~ *jackets* had to be zipped and ~~did'nt~~ *didn't* make so much noise when they were loosened. (3) We have a Swiss ~~engineers'~~ *engineer's* curiosity to thank for ~~todays~~ *today's* changes. (4) On a hunting trip in 1948, Georges de Mestral became intrigued by the seedpods that clung to his clothing. (5) He knew that they ~~we're~~ *were* hitching rides to new territory by fastening onto him, but he ~~could'nt~~ *couldn't* tell how they were doing it. (6) He examined the seedpods to find that their tiny hooks were catching onto the threads of his jacket. (7) The idea of Velcro was born, but the actual product ~~wasnt~~ *wasn't* developed overnight. (8) It took eight more ~~years'~~ *years* before Georges de ~~Mestrals~~ *Mestral's* invention was ready for the market. (9) Today, Velcro is used on clothing, on space suits, and even in artificial hearts. (10) Velcro not only can help keep a skier warm but can also save a ~~persons'~~ *person's* life.

EXPLORING ONLINE

<http://grammar.ccc.commnet.edu/GRAMMAR/quizzes/apostrophe_quiz2.htm>
Test your expertise with this "Catastrophes of Apostrophic Proportions" Quiz.

<http://grammar.ccc.commnet.edu/grammar/cgi-shl/par_numberless_quiz.pl/plurals_quiz.htm> Review plurals and possessives in this challenging interactive quiz.

CHAPTER 32

Direct and Indirect Quotations

A: **Defining Direct and Indirect Quotations**

B: **Punctuating Simple Direct Quotations**

C: **Punctuating Split Quotations**

D: **Ending Direct Quotations**

A. Defining Direct and Indirect Quotations

ESL TIP

Direct and indirect quotations challenge ESL students of all levels because presenting the words or ideas of others is not as strictly controlled in some languages as it is in English. Further, the shifting of verb tenses in reported speech is problematic, and paraphrasing can lead to wordiness or awkward meaning. Reinforcement may be needed throughout the term.

(1) John said that he was going.

(2) John said, "I am going."

- Which sentence gives the *exact words* of the speaker, John?

  sentence (2)

- Why is sentence (2) called a *direct quotation*?

  It gives the speaker's exact words.

- Why is sentence (1) called an *indirect quotation*?

  It reports the speaker's words without giving his exact words.

- Note that the word *that* introduces the *indirect quotation*.

PRACTICE 1

Write *D* in the blank at the right if the sentence uses a *direct quotation*. Write *I* in the blank at the right if the sentence uses an *indirect quotation*.

1. She said that she was thirsty. _____ I

2. Malcolm asked, "Which is my laptop?" _____ D

3. Ellah insisted that one turkey would feed the whole family. _____ I

4. The students shouted, "Get out of the building! It's on fire!" _____ D

5. "This is silly," she said, sighing. _____ D

6. I suggested that Rod's future was in the catering business. _____ I

B. Punctuating Simple Direct Quotations

Note the punctuation:

> (1) Rafael whispered, "I'll always love you."

- Put a comma before the direct quotation.
- Put quotation marks around the speaker's exact words.
- Capitalize the first word of the direct quotation.
- Put the period *inside* the end quotation marks.

   Of course, the direct quotation may come first in the sentence:

> (2) "I'll always love you," Rafael whispered.

- List the rules for a direct quotation written like the sentence above:

   Put quotation marks around the speaker's exact words.

   Capitalize the first word of the direct quotation.

   Put the comma inside the end quotation marks.

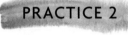

PRACTICE 2

Rewrite these simple direct quotations, punctuating them correctly.

1. He yelled answer the phone!

   Rewrite: He yelled, "Answer the phone!"

2. The usher called no more seats in front.

   Rewrite: The usher called, "No more seats in front."

3. My back aches she repeated dejectedly.

   Rewrite: "My back aches," she repeated dejectedly.

4. Examining the inside cover, Pierre said this book was printed in 1879.

   Rewrite: Examining the inside cover, Pierre said, "This book was printed in 1879."

5. A bug is doing the backstroke in my soup the man said.

   Rewrite: "A bug is doing the backstroke in my soup," the man said.

C. Punctuating Split Quotations

Sometimes one sentence of direct quotation is split into two parts:

> (1) "Because it is 2 A.M.," he said, "you had better go."

- *He said* is set off by commas.

- The second part of the quotation—*you had better go*—begins with a small letter because it is part of one directly quoted sentence.

(2) "Because it is 2 A.M. . . . you had better go."

A direct quotation can also be broken into separate sentences:

(3) "It is a long ride to San Francisco," he said. "We should leave early."

- Because the second part of the quotation is a separate sentence, it begins with a capital letter.
- Note the period after *said*.

    BE CAREFUL: If you break a direct quotation into separate sentences, be sure that both parts of the quotation are complete sentences.

PRACTICE 3   Rewrite these split direct quotations, punctuating them correctly.

1. Before the guests arrive she said let's relax.

   Rewrite: "Before the guests arrive," she said, "let's relax."

2. Don't drive so fast he begged I get nervous.

   Rewrite: "Don't drive so fast," he begged. "I get nervous."

3. Although Mort is out shellfishing Fran said his hip boots are on the porch.

   Rewrite: "Although Mort is out shellfishing," Fran said, "his hip boots are on the porch."

4. Being the youngest in the family she said has its advantages.

   Rewrite: "Being the youngest in the family," she said, "has its advantages."

5. This catalog is fantastic the clerk said and you can have it for free.

   Rewrite: "This catalog is fantastic," the clerk said, "and you can have it for free."

PRACTICE 4   On paper or on a computer, write three sentences using split quotations.

D. Ending Direct Quotations

A sentence can end in any of three ways:

- with a period (.)
- with a question mark (?)
- with an exclamation point (!)

The period is *always* placed inside the end quotation marks:

(1) He said, "My car cost five thousand dollars."

The question mark and the exclamation point go before or after the quotation marks—depending on the sense of the sentence.

(2) He asked, "Where are you?"

(3) Did he say, "I am 32 years old"?

(4) She yelled, "Help!"

- The question mark in sentence (2) is placed before the end quotation marks because the direct quotation is a question.

- The question mark in sentence (3) is placed after the end quotation marks because the direct quotation itself *is not a question*.

Note that sentence (2) can be reversed:

(5) "Where are you?" he asked.

- Can you list the rules for the exclamation point used in sentence (4)?

  Place the exclamation point inside the end quotation marks.

  Place the quotation marks around the speaker's exact words.

Note that sentence (4) can be reversed:

(6) "Help!" she yelled.

PRACTICE 5

Rewrite these direct quotations, punctuating them correctly.

1. Marlena asked is that your Humvee.

   Rewrite: Marlena asked, "Is that your Humvee?"

2. Did Shenoya make the team he inquired.

   Rewrite: "Did Shenoya make the team?" he inquired.

3. Be careful with that mirror she begged the movers.

   Rewrite: "Be careful with that mirror!" she begged the movers.

4. The truck driver shouted give me a break.

   Rewrite: The truck driver shouted, "Give me a break!"

5. Did she say I wouldn't give my social security number to that telemarketer?

   Rewrite: Did she say, "I wouldn't give my social security number to that telemarketer"?

Chapter Highlights

- **A direct quotation requires quotation marks:**

  Benjamin Franklin said, "There never was a good war or a bad peace."

- **Both parts of a split quotation require quotation marks:**

  "It isn't fair," she argued, "for us to lose the money for the after-school programs."

- **When a direct quotation is split into separate sentences, begin the second sentence with a capital letter:**

  "It's late," he said. "Let's leave in the morning."

- **Always place the period inside the end quotation marks:**

  He said, "Sometimes I talk too much."

- **A question mark or an exclamation point can be placed before or after the end quotation marks, depending on the meaning of the sentence:**

  She asked, "Where were you when we needed you?"

  Did she say, "Joe looks younger without his beard"?

Proofreading Strategy

If quotation marks give you trouble, use this strategy.

1. **Scan your draft** for sentences in which you give **someone's exact words**.

2. **Check these sentences** for correct use of commas, quotation marks, and capitalization.

3. For every quotation mark before the quoted words start, **make sure that you have provided the end quotation mark.**

   "Can
   Gwendolyn just texted, ~~can~~ you meet me for coffee?"

WRITING AND PROOFREADING ASSIGNMENT

Write a note to someone with whom you have had an argument. Your goal is to get back on friendly terms with this person. In your first sentence, state this goal, asking for his or her open-minded attention. Then tell him or her why you think a misunderstanding occurred and explain how you think conflict might be avoided in the future. Refer to the original argument by using both direct and indirect quotations. When you are finished drafting, proofread for the correct use of quotation marks; be careful with *all* punctuation.

CHAPTER REVIEW

Proofread this essay for direct and indirect quotations. Punctuate the quotations correctly and make any other necessary changes above the lines.

Satchel Paige

(1) Some people say that the great pitcher Leroy Paige was called Satchel because of his big feet. (2) Paige himself ~~said I~~ *said, "I* got the nickname as a boy in Mobile before my feet ~~grew.~~ *grew."*

(3) He earned money by carrying bags, called satchels, at the railroad station. (4) ~~I~~ *"I* figured out a way to make more money by carrying several bags at a time on a ~~pole~~ *pole,"* he said. (5) Other boys began shouting at him that he looked like a satchel tree. (6) The name stuck.

(7) Unfortunately, for most of Paige's long pitching career, major league baseball excluded African American players. (8) However, Satchel Paige pitched impressively in the black leagues and in tours against white teams. (9) In 1934 he won a thirteen-inning, one-to-nothing pitching duel against the white pitcher Dizzy Dean and a team of major league all-stars. (10) ~~My~~ *"My* fast ~~ball~~ *ball,"* admitted ~~Dean looks~~ *Dean, "looks* like a change of pace alongside of that little bullet old Satchel shoots up to the ~~plate!~~ *plate!"*

(11) After Jackie Robinson broke the major league color barrier in 1948, Satchel Paige took his windmill windup to the Cleveland Indians. (12) He became the oldest rookie in major league history. (13) Some people said that he was too old, but his record proved them wrong. (14) His plaque in the Baseball Hall of Fame ~~reads he~~ *reads, "He* helped pitch the Cleveland Indians to the 1948 ~~pennant.~~ *pennant."*

(15) Satchel Paige pitched off and on until he was 60 years old. (16) When people asked how he stayed young, he gave them his famous rules. (17) Everyone remembers the last one. (18) ~~Don't~~ *"Don't* look ~~back~~ *back,"* he said. (19) ~~Something~~ *"Something* might be gaining on ~~you.~~ *you."*

EXPLORING ONLINE

TEACHING TIP

Instructor tools for *Grassroots* include a computerized Test Bank, PowerPoint slides, an Instructor's Manual with teaching tips, and more, and can be accessed at ‹**login .cengage.com**›.

<http://www.dailygrammar.com/371to375.shtml> Practice with answers:
  Place quotation marks and capitalize correctly.

<http://grammar.ccc.commnet.edu/grammar/quizzes/quotes_quiz.htm>
  Challenging interactive quiz: Think hard and punctuate.

CHAPTER 33

Putting Your Proofreading Skills to Work

Proofreading is the important final step in the writing process. After you have planned and written a paragraph or an essay, you must **proofread**, carefully checking each sentence for correct grammar, punctuation, and capitalization. Proofreading means applying everything you have learned in Units 2 through 7. Is every sentence complete? Do all your verbs agree with their subjects? Have you mistakenly written any comma splices or sentence fragments?

This chapter gives you the opportunity to practice proofreading skills in real-world situations. As you proofread the paragraphs and essays that follow, you must look for any—and every—kind of error, just as you would in the real world of college or work. The first five practices tell you what kinds of errors to look for. If you have trouble, go back to the chapters listed and review the material. The final practices, however, give you no clues at all, so you must put your proofreading skills to the real-world test.

- Before you proofread, review your **Personal Error Patterns Chart** that you learned to keep in Chapter 8. Take special care to proofread for the errors you tend to make.

- Use the **proofreading strategies** that work best for you. In this book, you have practiced strategies like reading out loud as you look for errors, reading from the bottom up, and color highlighting. Apply your favorite strategies here!

- Examine the **proofreading checklist** at the end of this chapter for a quick reminder of what to look for.

- Keep a **dictionary** handy. If you are not sure of the spelling of a word, look it up.

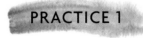

PRACTICE 1

Proofread this paragraph, correcting any errors above the lines. (You should find 12 individual errors.) To review, see these chapters:

Chapter 10   sentence fragments

Chapter 12   past tense errors

Chapter 24   adjective and adverb errors

Chapter 28   parallelism

(1) Can exercise make us smarter? (2) Vigorous exercise tones muscles, aids weight loss, and ~~the heart is strengthened~~ [strengthens the heart]. (3) But, according to recent studies, aerobic workouts also increase brainpower. (4) In one experiment, students at the University of Illinois memorized ~~letters.~~ [letters and then] (5) ~~Then~~ picked those letters from a list. (6) Next, the students were divided into three groups. (7) For 30 minutes, some sat ~~quiet,~~ [quietly] some ~~run~~ [ran] on a treadmill, and ~~weight lifting was done by some~~ [some lifted weights]. (8) After a 30-minute rest ~~period.~~ [period, the] (9) ~~The~~ students ~~taked~~ [took] the letter test again. (10) Every time, the group who ~~runned~~ [ran] on the treadmill was ~~more~~ quicker and more accurate than the other two groups. (11) Studies of laboratory mice in Taiwan reinforced these results. (12) The rodents who worked out strenuously on tiny treadmills performed complex mental tasks more ~~effective~~ [effectively] than mice who raced at their own pace. (13) Examining the animals' brains under a ~~microscope~~ [microscope, scientists] (14) ~~Scientists~~ found positive changes in the brain cells of those who had exercised harder. (15) They concluded that the greatly increased blood flow during aerobic exercise carries growth-promoting chemicals to the brain. (16) Hard, aerobic exercise, it ~~seems.~~ [seems, benefits] (17) ~~Benefits~~ both body *and* mind.

PRACTICE 2

Proofread this paragraph, correcting any errors above the lines. (You should find 16 individual errors.) To review, see these chapters:

Chapter 10	sentence fragments
Chapter 13	past participle verb errors
Chapter 18	run-ons and comma splices
Chapters 22 and 31	plural and possessive errors

(1) Christiane Amanpour is one of the most respected foreign correspondents in the world, but she calls herself an "accidental ~~journalist.~~ [journalist"] (2) ~~Because~~ [because] she never intended to become one. (3) Her native Iran had no freedom of the ~~press, journalism~~ [press, so journalism] did not interest her. (4) Christiane attended high school in England. (5) Then the revolution in Iran brought chaos to her family, her ~~fathers~~ [father's] money was ~~froze,~~ [frozen, and] the ~~families fund~~ [family's funds] were very tight. (6) ~~Christianes'~~ [Christiane's] sister dropped out of journalism college in ~~London, Christiane~~ [London, and Christiane] took her place for the sole reason of saving the tuition money. (7) Soon she was ~~hook~~ [hooked] on reporting.

(8) After graduating from the University of Rhode Island, she applied for a job at a new cable ~~station.~~ [station called] (9) ~~Called~~ CNN. (10) She longed to write news ~~story's~~ [stories] and go overseas but was

CNN news anchor Christiane Amanpour on assignment in the Middle East

Courtesy CNN

mocked
~~mock~~ by her boss, who said she didn't have the right looks and that her name was difficult

to pronounce. (11) Amanpour worked hard and hid her frustration with doing routine
tasks, like
~~task.~~ (12) ~~Like~~ bringing people coffee. (13) Every time a new job opened at CNN, she applied
                                            sent   gunfire
for it. (14) Her big break was being ~~send~~ to Germany and the Gulf War. (15) With ~~gunfires~~ and

rockets around her, she reported the news with intelligence and heart. (16) Today Amanpour

says it is not so bad that some people "always try to knock your dreams." (17) This gives you

the chance, she believes, to prove that you are strong enough to keep going.

TEACHING TIP

Remind students that although programs like Microsoft Word can help them identify spelling and some grammatical errors in their papers, computers are far from foolproof. Proofreading is still the job of every writer.

PRACTICE 3

Proofread this paragraph, correcting any errors above the lines. (You should find 20 individual errors.) To review, see these chapters:

Chapter 10   sentence fragments

Chapter 11   subject/verb agreement errors

Chapter 30   comma errors

Chapter 31   apostrophe errors

ESL TIP

Another technique for self-correction is to have students read their writing aloud—first at home, to themselves, and later, to a partner. Have students listen for errors and edit their writing.

                                                    chasers spread
(1) Every spring and summer, storm ~~chaser's spreads~~ out across the Midwestern part of
                                                    cameras, maps,   radios,
the United States known as Tornado Alley. (2) Armed with video ~~cameras maps~~ and ~~radios.~~
these   follow
(3) ~~These~~ lovers of violent weather ~~follows~~ huge weather systems called supercells, which

               produce   supercell and
sometimes ~~produces~~ tornadoes. (4) On a good day, a storm chaser may find a ~~supercell.~~ (5) ~~And~~

join
get close enough to film the brief, destructive life of a tornado. (6) Some ~~joins~~ the storm-

chasing tours offered every summer by universities or private companies. (7) Others

set
learn what they can from Internet websites and ~~sets~~ off on their own to hunt tornadoes.

(8) Storm chasing can be very dangerous. (9) A large tornado spins winds between 125 and

houses,
175 mph, tearing roofs off ~~houses~~ ripping limbs from trees, and overturning cars. (10) The

branches, boards, shingles,
greatest danger comes from airborne ~~branches boards shingles~~ and glass hurtling through

doesn't   tornadoes, it
the air like deadly weapons. (11) Even if a supercell ~~don't~~ spawn ~~tornadoes.~~ (12) ~~It~~ often

produces winds over 50 mph, heavy rain, large hail, and intense lightning. (13) Most storm

avoid   tornado's
chasers ~~avoids~~ these risks by racing out of a ~~tornados'~~ path before it gets too close.

Twister, storm
(14) Despite or perhaps because of these dangers, dramatized in the 1996 movie ~~Twister.~~

match
(15) ~~Storm~~ chasing remains popular. (16) Fans claim that few things in life ~~matches~~ the thrill

of discovering a tornado and witnessing the power of nature.

PRACTICE 4

Proofread this paragraph, correcting any errors above the lines. (You should find 17 individual errors.) To review, see these chapters:

Chapter 13   past participle verb errors
Chapter 18   run-ons and comma splices
Chapter 22   errors in forming plural nouns
Chapter 25   preposition errors

on   sprees
(1) Bono is an unusual superstar. (2) Instead of going ~~in~~ shopping ~~spree~~ and polishing

his ego, he travels the world, using his fame to empower others. (3) Bono was born Paul

in
Hewson ~~at~~ Ireland. (4) Young friends there nicknamed him *Bonovox*, which means "good

dropped, but
voice" in Latin. (5) The *vox* was ~~dropped,~~ *Bono* stuck. (6) Bono became the lead singer of

sold
the Irish rock band U2. (7) Using music to send a message of love and peace, U2 has ~~sell~~

albums
more than 100 million ~~album~~ worldwide and has won 22 Grammy Awards. (8) Yet perhaps

inside
Bono's greatest influence is not the sound of his voice crooning U2 songs ~~under~~ the heads

in   used
of fans. (9) Rather, it is his work for human beings ~~on~~ need. (10) Bono has ~~use~~ his celebrity

destroyed
to turn the media's attention to Africa, where the lives of millions are being ~~destroy~~ by

AIDS and starvation. (11) Frightening numbers of African ~~child~~ children are already AIDS ~~orphans,~~ orphans;

social structures in Africa are breaking down. (12) Bono urges the United States and

other nations to relieve the crippling debt of African nations, one of the ~~factor~~ factors that keeps

them unable to afford AIDS drugs and prevention programs. (13) He has ~~work~~ worked with for-

mer President Clinton, Oprah, and others to make the love he sings about become reality.

(14) Bono has received many ~~award~~ awards for this humanitarian ~~work he~~ work; he was even ~~nominate~~ nominated for

the Nobel Peace Prize.

PRACTICE 5

Proofread this paragraph, correcting any errors above the lines. (You should find 14 individual errors.) To review, see these chapters:

Chapter 20	relative pronoun errors
Chapter 24	adjective and adverb errors
Chapter 29	capitalization errors
Chapter 30	comma errors

TEACHING TIP

Urge students to review the errors they fail to identify in this chapter's practices. Suggest that they either return to relevant chapters or complete additional online exercises such as those in the Guide to Grammar and Writing website at ‹http://grammar.ccc.commnet.edu/grammar/›.

(1) A courageous child ~~whom~~ who lost his life to cancer lives on in thousands of random acts

of kindness. (2) Jayden Lamb was a ~~happy~~ happy, generous first grader in ~~michigan~~ Michigan when he was

diagnosed with a rare form of cancer. (3) During his three-year battle with the disease, he

remained ~~brave uncomplaining~~ brave, uncomplaining, and upbeat. (4) Just after his death in 2012, Jayden's grieving

parents were getting coffee from a ~~Drive-through~~ drive-through when, on a whim, they paid the tab of

the driver behind them. (5) Several days later, they ~~anonymous~~ anonymously paid off a stranger's layaway

bill at ~~walmart~~ Walmart. (6) These acts of giving eased their grief. (7) When they wrote about these

experiences on their Facebook page, "Keep on Truckin' Team Jayden," they set off a chain

reaction. (8) Inspired by Jayden's ~~story~~ story, strangers began committing random acts of kindness.

(9) One waitress received a $50 tip with a note ~~which~~ that read, "In memory of Jayden Lamb."

(10) An unemployed man was told that the bicycle his son wanted for ~~christmas~~ Christmas had been

paid for in Jayden's honor. (11) A nameless donor even dropped a $2,000 diamond ring in a

red ~~salvation army~~ Salvation Army kettle, along with the words, "Paying it forward, Jayden style." (12) Tens of

thousands of people have bought others' meals and gas, shoveled snow from a neighbor's

drive, given to charities, and sometimes shared descriptions of their ~~well~~ good deeds on the

Lambs' Facebook page.

PRACTICE 6

Proofread this essay, correcting any errors above the lines.

Crime-Fighting Artist

(1) Jeanne Boylan helps capture ~~Americas~~ [America's] most wanted ~~criminals~~ [criminals,] but she's not a police officer or a detective. (2) Instead, she is an artist who draws the faces of suspects, ~~base~~ [based] only on her gentle conversations with ~~victim's~~ [victims] and eyewitnesses. (3) Her portraits are so lifelike and accurate that she has ~~became~~ [become] famous for drawing nearly mirror images of criminals. (4) Boylan's sketches often ~~leads~~ [lead] to arrests. (5) She drew the Unabomber in his sunglasses and hooded sweatshirt, the kidnapper-murderer of 12-year-old Polly Klaas, and Timothy ~~McVeigh.~~ [McVeigh, who] (6) ~~Who~~ bombed the Murrah Federal Building in Oklahoma City. (7) Once doubtful, FBI officials and police now ~~calls~~ [call] on Boylan in almost every major case.

(8) Boylan decided to become a sketch artist after she was the victim of a crime. (9) The police, following standard procedure, asked her to describe her attackers' ~~faces,~~ [faces;] then they showed her mug shots of ~~criminals.~~ [criminals, hoping] (10) ~~Hoping~~ that she would recognize the suspects. (11) Boylan sensed that this was the wrong approach to help her mind remember. (12) She realized that the ~~authorities~~ [authorities'] leading questions—questions like "Did he have a moustache? Was he wearing glasses?"—clutter the victim's mind with details that might not be true. (13) At the same time, the subconscious mind is trying to avoid reliving a traumatic ~~experience~~ [experience;] consequently, memories easily become distorted.

Boylan's sketch (left) and a photo of the Unabomber, Ted Kaczynski

AP Photo/ho

AP Photo/Elaine Thompson, File

(14) Boylan developed a very different method for coaxing images from victims and

witnesses. (15) What distinguishes her method from others, she says, is that she *listens.*

time, talking
(16) She takes her ~~time.~~ (17) ~~Talking~~ for hours with eyewitnesses to a crime. (18) She does

not pressure them to recall the color of a suspect's eyes or ~~what~~ the shape of his nose

~~was.~~ (19) Instead, she asks about their daily lives and interests, here and there asking

carefully,
nonleading questions about what they saw. (20) Slowly and ~~careful,~~ she guides people

saw
back through their confusion and pain to the moment when they ~~seen~~ or felt something

that they desperately want to forget. (21) She asks them to describe whole shapes, forms,

and textures rather than specific details. (22) She sometimes gives children Play-Doh to

mold as they explore their memories. (23) As they draw closer and closer to the terrifying

minds,   sketches
images seared into their ~~minds.~~ (24) Boylan watches, listens, and ~~sketching.~~ (25) "What

people see," she says, "is evidence as fragile and valuable as a fingerprint. (26) And it should

be protected with as much care."

(27) Many have claimed that Boylan's method, a blend of art, psychology, and human

is   taught
compassion, ~~are~~ a unique gift. (28) Boylan insists, though, that her technique can be ~~teach.~~

mystery,"
(29) "What I do is no great ~~mystery~~ she says. (30) "It has to do with allowing someone the

freedom and the time to remember. (31) It has to do with the human heart."

PRACTICE 7

Proofread this essay, correcting any errors above the lines.

Quiet, Please!

pierce   air; car
(1) America is loud. (2) Horns and sirens ~~pierces~~ the ~~air, car~~ stereos pump out loud music.

ring   trumpet
(3) Cell phones ~~rings,~~ shriek, or ~~trumpets~~ the owner's noise of choice. (4) Construction

equipment
~~equipments,~~ lawnmowers, and leaf blowers buzz and roar into the public space.

managers
(5) Restaurant and movie theater ~~manager's~~ often seem to link loudness with cultural cool.

decibels;
(6) Sounds are measured in decibels, with the human voice measuring about 60 ~~decibels,~~

the sound of a car is about 80 decibels. (7) According to the U.S. Environmental Protection

Agency, 70 decibels is a safe daily average. (8) Here is the problem: the level of noise that

is
many of us hear every day ~~are~~ far above this.

(9) The sound of a food blender, for example, measures 90 decibels. (10) Many leaf

blowers
~~blower~~ exceed 115 decibels, and a jet taking off is 120 decibels of ear-blasting noise.

is   its   psychologically
(11) All of this racket ~~are~~ taking ~~it's~~ toll on us both physically and ~~in psychological ways~~.

(12) According to the American Speech-Language-Hearing Association (ASHA), 28 million

suffered
U.S. citizens have already ~~suffer~~ hearing loss from too much noise. (13) Furthermore, loud

pressure,
noise raises blood ~~pressure~~ increases stress hormone levels, and deprives us of sleep.

(14) Noise pollution also increases aggression and even violence and harms concentration

York
and learning. (15) One study found that New ~~york~~ children in classrooms that faced the

quieter
train tracks were almost a year behind children taught in ~~more quieter~~ parts of the same

school.

seriously
(16) In Europe, noise pollution has been taken ~~serious~~ for years. (17) Now in the United

are
States, organizations like the Noise Pollution Clearinghouse ~~is~~ trying to raise awareness of

believe
the problem and promote solutions. (18) Members of this organization ~~believes~~ that just as

smoke or toxins in the air are not acceptable, neither is loud noise. (19) They are working

laws to
for new ~~laws.~~ (20) ~~To~~ enforce our right to peace and quiet.

Chapter Highlights

- **Know your error patterns.** In Chapter 8, you learned how to recognize and chart your **personal error patterns**, the mistakes—such as sentence fragments or apostrophes—you tend to make. Before you proofread, review your **Personal Error Patterns Chart**. Take special care to proofread for these errors.

- **Use the proofreading strategies that work best *for you*.** In Chapter 8 and throughout the book, you have learned and practiced many strategies—like reading out loud, reading from the bottom up, and color highlighting. Put your favorite strategies to work.

- **Know where to find help.** If you need more help with recognizing and eliminating your personal error patterns, consult print sources, such as this book; online resources, such as the *Grassroots* student website, the Exploring Online websites listed at the end of each chapter, or the OWLs you have bookmarked; and expert people, such as the staff of your college's writing lab.

Proofreading Strategy

A proofreading checklist like the one below can be an effective tool for remembering what to look for when reviewing your writing.

Proofreading Checklist

☐ Check for sentence fragments, comma splices, and run-on sentences.

☐ Check for verb errors: present tense -*s* endings (verb agreement), past tense -*ed* endings, past participles, and tense consistency.

☐ Check for incorrect singular and plural nouns, incorrect pronouns, confused adjectives and adverbs, and incorrect prepositions.

☐ Check all punctuation: commas, apostrophes, semicolons, quotations marks.

☐ Check all capitalization.

☐ Check spelling and look-alikes/sound-alikes.

☐ Check for omitted words and typos.

☐ Check layout, format, titles, dates, and spacing.

☐ Check for all personal error patterns.

WRITING AND PROOFREADING ASSIGNMENT

How have you strengthened your writing skills by taking this course? If possible, look back at a paper you wrote early in the term, and reflect on how you have developed as a writer. Write one or more paragraphs in which you describe the concepts and skills you have learned that have improved your writing the most.

Apply what you have learned throughout this course to produce an error-free paper. Use this opportunity to practice consulting your Personal Error Patterns Chart, applying your favorite proofreading strategies, and using a proofreading checklist to find and rid your writing of mistakes.

EXPLORING ONLINE

TEACHING TIP

Instructor tools for *Grassroots* include a computerized Test Bank, PowerPoint slides, an Instructor's Resource Manual with teaching tips, and more, and can be accessed at ‹**login .cengage.com**›.

<http://owl.english.purdue.edu/owl/resource/561/01/> Proofreading guide.

<http://a4esl.org/q/j/vm/mc-stockmarket.html> Interactive quiz: Correct a mix of errors and learn about the stock exchange.

<http://jcomm.uoregon.edu/~russial/grammar/grambo.html> Test of the Emergency Grammar System. Challenge yourself and have fun.

UNIT 7
Writing Assignments

As you complete each writing assignment, remember to perform these steps:

● Write a clear, complete topic sentence.

● Use freewriting, brainstorming, or clustering to generate ideas for the body of your paragraph, essay, letter, or commercial.

● Arrange your best ideas in a plan.

● Revise for support, unity, coherence, and exact language.

● Proofread for grammar, punctuation, and spelling errors.

Writing Assignment 1 *Discuss an unusual friendship.* Have you ever had or witnessed a truly unusual friendship—for instance, between two people many years apart in age, between people from different social worlds who bonded because of a shared hobby or problem, or between a human being and an animal? Select one such unusual friendship and capture its essence in writing. How did the friendship start? What do you think bonded the two friends? Be as specific as possible so that the reader will understand this special relationship. Proofread carefully for correct use of capitals, commas, apostrophes, and quotation marks.

Writing Assignment 2 *Write a letter to compliment or to complain.* Write a letter to a store manager or a dean to praise an especially helpful salesperson or a particularly good teacher. If you are not feeling complimentary, write the opposite: a letter of complaint about a salesperson or an instructor. State your compliment or complaint, describing what occurred and explaining why you are pleased or displeased. Remember, how well your letter is written will contribute to the impression you make. Proofread carefully for the correct use of capitals, commas, apostrophes, and quotation marks.

Writing Assignment 3 *Create a print ad.* You and several classmates considering careers in advertising have been asked to create a print ad for a magazine, newspaper, or billboard. You must sell one product or idea of your choice—anything from a brand of jeans to a cell phone to a good cause, like recycling or becoming a foster parent. Your goal is to capture people's attention with a strong picture and then persuade them with a few well-chosen words. Sketch and draft your ad; don't let punctuation errors get in the way of your message. For online help step by step, visit this website: <http://adbusters.org/spoofads/printad/>.

Writing Assignment 4 *Revise a quotation.* Pick a quotation from the Quotation Bank at the end of this book, and alter it to express something new. For example, you might want to change "Insanity is hereditary—you get it from your children" to "Insanity is learned—you get it from going to school." Be as serious or as humorous as you would like. Prove that your quotation is valid, arguing from your own or others' experience. Proofread carefully for the correct use of capitals, commas, apostrophes, and quotation marks.

UNIT 7

Review

Proofreading

A. Proofread the following application letter for incorrect or missing capitals, commas, apostrophes, and quotation marks. Correct all errors above the lines. (You should find 28 individual errors.)

99 ~~somers street~~ Somers Street

~~hickory, nc~~ Hickory NC 28601

~~january 11~~ January 11, 2014

Ms. Teresa Willingham

Valley ~~medical center~~ Medical Center

6500 ~~tate boulevard~~ Tate Boulevard

~~lincolnton~~ Lincolnton, NC 28092

Dear Ms. Willingham:

I saw your advertisement for a Certified Nursing Assistant position in ~~Sundays~~ Sunday's newspaper, and I would like to apply for the job. I have all of the qualifications ~~youre~~ you're seeking.

For the past year and a half I have worked as a part-time CNA I for Baxter ~~home health care~~ Home Health Care. My duties have included assisting clients with personal care (bathing, dressing, and grooming), monitoring and assisting with medications, checking vital signs, making and serving meals, and documenting all of my actions and observations. I graduated from Valley View ~~high school~~ High School in 2012. On ~~may 11 2013~~ May 11, 2013, I earned my CNA certification at ~~eastland community college~~ Eastland Community College. Since then, I have continued to attend classes as a pre-nursing major. ~~Im~~ I'm dependable, punctual, and detail-oriented. In my last evaluation, my supervisor wrote, ~~Kayla~~ "Kayla is one of our most caring and conscientious ~~employees.~~ employees."

I would like the opportunity to tell you more about myself. I hope that you will call me at (801) 555-1616 to schedule an interview.

Sincerely ~~your's~~ yours,

Kayla Johnston

B. Proofread the following essay for incorrect or missing capitals, commas, apostrophes, and quotation marks. Correct the errors above the lines. (You should find 32 individual errors.)

Most Valuable

(1) One of ~~baseballs~~ baseball's most feared sluggers, José ~~albert~~ Albert Pujols was ~~name~~ named greatest player of the decade by ESPN in 2010. (2) Talent, luck, and hard work helped him realize his dreams. (3) Pujols was born on January ~~16 1980~~ 16, 1980, in Santo ~~domingo~~ Domingo.

(4) The son of a well-known Dominican pitcher, he was raised by his grandmother. (5) Although they were poor, ~~Pujols'~~ Pujols was ~~Happy~~ happy. (6) Playing ball in the dusty fields of the ~~dominican republic~~ Dominican Republic, he dreamed of a career in the majors. (7) When he was ~~16~~ 16, the family moved to the ~~united states~~ United States and settled in ~~Independence~~ Independence, Missouri. (8) ~~Alberts'~~ Albert's obsessions were learning ~~english~~ English and playing amazing baseball on the Fort Osage ~~high school~~ High School team.

(9) His work ethic and skills attracted scouts, and in 1999 he was drafted by the St. Louis ~~cardinals~~ Cardinals. (10) In 2001 Pujols was voted the National ~~Leagues~~ League's top rookie player, with a .329 batting ~~average~~ average, 194 ~~hits~~ hits, and 130 runs batted in. (11) He helped carry the Cardinals to a ~~world series~~ World Series title in 2006.

(12) According to Sparky Anderson, ~~whos~~ who's managed many elite players, ~~Before~~ "Before he's done, we might be saying ~~hes~~ he's the best of them all." (13) A strong faith in God spurs Pujols to give back through the Pujols ~~family~~ Family Foundation. (14) Because his ~~wifes~~ wife's child has Down syndrome, they support this cause. (15) In addition, Pujol's foundation helps underprivileged children in his beloved ~~dominican republic~~ Dominican Republic.

(16) More than all his baseball awards, Pujols treasures a 2008 Roberto Clemente Award for his ~~foundations~~ foundation's work.

405

UNIT 7

Writers' Workshop

Explain a Cause or an Effect

Examining causes and effects is a useful skill, both in college and at work. This student's thoughtful essay looks at the effects of school pressure to "speak like an American." In your group or class, read it aloud if possible. As you read, pay attention to the causes and effects he describes.

In America, Speak Like an American

(1) Many teachers tell immigrant students to lose their accents and "speak like an American." They mean well. They want the children to succeed. However, this can also encourage children to be ashamed of who they are and give up their heritage.

(2) When I was in fourth grade, I was sent to a class for "speech imperfections." Apparently, I had a Spanish accent. The class wasn't so ~~bad, it~~ bad. It taught us to say "chair" instead of "shair" and "school" instead of "eschool." It was so important for me to please the teacher, I did practically everything she asked. She told us things like "The bums on the street have ~~accents, that's~~ accents. That's why they're not working." I abandoned my roots and my culture and embraced "America." I learned about Stonewall Jackson and William Shakespeare. Soon Ponce de León and Pedro Calderón de la Barca were just memories at the back of my mind. I listened to country music and rock because this was "American."

(3) I can't remember when it happened, but suddenly I found myself listening to Spanish love songs. They were great! They were so sincere, and the lyrics were beautiful. While turning the radio dial one day, I stopped at a Hispanic radio station. It was playing salsa. "Holy smokes," I thought to myself. All the instruments were synchronized so tightly. The horn section kept accenting the singer's lines. All of a sudden, my hips started swaying, my feet started tapping,

TEACHING TIP

This well-crafted and beautifully detailed student essay (to which five comma splices were added for instructional purposes) usually inspires students and elicits their own sharing of experiences. The essay models cause and effect.

406

and I stood up. And then the horror. I couldn't dance to this ~~music, I~~ had never

^{music. I}

learned how. There I was, a Puerto Rican boy, listening to Puerto Rican music

but unable to dance the typical Puerto Rican way.

(4) Anger flared through me as I remembered my fourth-grade teacher. I was

also upset with my ~~parents, in~~ their zeal to have me excel, they kept me from

^{parents. In}

my roots as a first-generation Hispanic American. But that was years ago. I

have searched for my Latin heritage. I've found beautiful music, wonderful

literature, and great foods. I now associate with "my people" as well as with

everyone else, and I am learning the joys of being Sam Rodriguez, Puerto Rican.

Sam Rodriguez, student

1. How effective is Sam Rodriguez's essay?

   _Y_ Clear main idea?   _Y_ Good supporting details?

   _Y_ Logical organization?   _Y_ Effective conclusion?

2. Does the essay have a *thesis statement*, one sentence that states the main idea of the entire essay? Which sentence is it? Paragraph 1, sentence 4

3. In paragraph (2), the writer says that he "abandoned [his] roots." In his view, what caused him to do this?

4. Underline the lines and ideas you find especially effective and share them with your group or class. Try to understand exactly why you like a word or sentence. For example, in paragraph (3), we can almost experience the first time the writer really *hears* salsa—the instruments, the horns accenting the singer's lines, his tapping feet and swaying hips.

5. As the writer gets older, he realizes he has lost too much of his heritage. At first he is angry (short-term effect), but what long-term effect does this new understanding have on him?

6. What order does this writer follow throughout the essay? Time order

7. This fine essay is finished and ready to go, but the student makes the same punctuation error five times. Can you spot and correct the error pattern that he needs to watch out for? Five comma splices

Writing and Revising Ideas

1. What does it mean to "become American"?

2. Write about something important that you gave up and explain why you did so.

Plan carefully, outlining your paragraph or essay before you write. State your main idea clearly and plan your supporting ideas or paragraphs. As you revise, pay special attention to clear organization and convincing, detailed support.

407

UNIT 8

Improving Your Spelling

Some people are naturally better spellers than others, but anyone can become a better speller. In this unit, you will

- Master six basic spelling rules
- Learn to avoid common look-alike/sound-alike errors
- Learn proofreading strategies to find and correct your own errors

Spotlight on Reading and Writing

Read this paragraph aloud if possible. Do you know why each underlined word is spelled correctly?

The current trend to sexualize female news anchors may help some networks <u>seize</u> higher ratings, but it has negative <u>effects</u> as well. According to a recent study from Indiana University, male viewers have more trouble understanding the news when it is delivered by a sexy TV anchor. In the study, researchers Maria Elizabeth Grabe and Lelia Samson showed two news clips to 400 test subjects. In both clips, the same journalist reported the same <u>stories</u>, but in one she wore a tightly <u>fitting</u> suit that accentuated her waist, red lipstick, and jewelry. In the other clip, she wore a shapeless suit, no make-up, and no jewelry. The ability of male <u>viewers</u> to recall the information in her report dropped when they watched the more sexualized anchor. Even more <u>surprising</u> was <u>their</u> assessment that the sexy anchor was less competent to report on serious topics like war and politics though the quality of reporting was identical in both clips. <u>Interestingly</u>, the anchor's appearance had no effect on whether female viewers thought she was a competent professional. Because TV executives are still <u>largely</u> male, the researchers warn that sexualizing female anchors may increase network ratings, but it <u>professionally</u> damages the <u>women</u> themselves.

Dr. Karen Cox, "Sexy Anchors Distract Men from the News" (unpublished article)

- Through her choice and arrangement of words, this writer exposes a worrisome trend in TV news. She also avoids common spelling errors that many college students make. If you can't explain why every underlined word is correct, this unit is for you.

Writing Ideas

- *Examples of anchors' clothing from one network and the message that these looks send*

- *The message sent by someone's style of dress: a rapper, athlete, Goth, nerd, banker, hipster, and so on*

CHAPTER 34

Spelling

A. Suggestions for Improving Your Spelling

One important ingredient of good writing is accurate spelling. No matter how interesting your ideas are, your writing will not be effective if your spelling is incorrect.

Tips for Improving Your Spelling

1. **Look closely at the words on the page.** Use any tricks you can to remember the right spelling. For example, "Argument has no _e_ because I lost the _e_ during an argument" or "_Believe_ has a _lie_ in it."

2. **Use a dictionary.** Even professional writers frequently check spelling in a dictionary. As you write, underline the words you are not sure of and look them up when you write your final draft. If locating words in the dictionary is a real problem for you, consider a "poor speller's dictionary." Ask your professor to recommend one.

3. **Use a spell checker.** If you write on a computer, make a habit of using the spell checker. See Part B for tips and cautions about spell checkers.

4. **Keep a list of the words you misspell.** Look over your list whenever you can and keep it handy as you write.

5. **Look over corrected papers for misspelled words** (often marked _sp_). Add these words to your list. Practice writing each word three or four times.

6. **Test yourself.** Have a friend dictate words from your list or from this chapter or use flashcards; computerized flashcards can be helpful.

7. **Review the basic spelling rules explained in this chapter.** Take time to learn the material; don't rush through the entire chapter all at once.

8. **Study the spelling list on pages 418–419,** and test yourself on those words.

9. **Read through Chapter 35, "Look-Alikes/Sound-Alikes,"** for commonly con-fused words (*their*, *there*, and *they're*, for instance). The practices in that chapter will help you eliminate some common spelling errors from your writing.

B. Computer Spell Checkers

If you write on a computer, always run the spell checker as part of your proofreading process. A spell checker picks up certain spelling errors and gives you alternatives for correcting them. Your program might also highlight misspelled words as you write.

What a spell checker cannot do is *think*. If you have written one correctly spelled word instead of another—*if* for *it*, for example—the spell checker cannot bring that error to your attention. If you have written *then* for *than*, the spell checker cannot help.* To find such errors, you must always proofread your paper *after* running the spell checker.

PRACTICE 1

In a small group, read this poem, which "passed" spell check. Above the lines, correct the errors that the spell checker missed.

    writing   superior
My ~~righting~~ is ~~soup eerier~~
To your paper   time
~~Too yore pay purr~~ this ~~thyme~~.
I ran   essay through
~~Iran~~ my ~~SA threw~~ spell check,
     syllable and rhyme
Each ~~sill able an rime~~.
 Too   you awful writers
~~Two~~ bad, ~~ewe awe full righters~~,
For you probably envy
~~Fore ewe probe lee en vee~~ me.
    verbal sense must be
My ~~verb all cents muss bee~~ immense,
for I write so quickly
~~four aye right sew quick lee~~.
I do not need
~~Eye donut kneed~~ a textbook.
  threw   in
I ~~through~~ it ~~inn~~ the lake.
   professor wrote   red marks
The ~~pro fey sore rote~~ big ~~read Marx~~.
There must be some mistake
~~Their muss bee sum miss take~~!

C. Spotting Vowels and Consonants

To learn some basic spelling rules, you must know the difference between vowels and consonants. Refer to the following chart.

> The **vowels** are *a, e, i, o,* and *u.*
>
> The **consonants** are *b, c, d, f, g, h, j, k, l, m, n, p, q, r, s, t, v, w, x,* and *z.*
>
> **The letter *y* can be either a vowel or a consonant, depending on its sound:**
>
>   happy   shy
>   young   yawn

---

* For questions about words that sound the same but are spelled differently, check Chapter 35, "Look-Alikes/Sound-Alikes."

● In both *happy* and *shy*, *y* is a vowel because it has a vowel sound: an *ee* sound in *happy* and an *i* sound in *shy*.

● In both *young* and *yawn*, *y* is a consonant because it has the consonant sound of *y*.

PRACTICE 2

Write *V* for vowel or *C* for consonant in the space over each letter. Be careful of the *y*.

EXAMPLE: $\underline{\overset{C}{\ }}\ \underline{\overset{C}{\ }}\ \underline{\overset{V}{\ }}\ \underline{\overset{C}{\ }}\ \underline{\overset{C}{\ }}\ \underline{\overset{V}{\ }}$
s   t   a   r   r   y

1. $\underline{\overset{C}{\ }}\ \underline{\overset{C}{\ }}\ \underline{\overset{V}{\ }}\ \underline{\overset{C}{\ }}\ \underline{\overset{V}{\ }}$ 3. $\underline{\overset{C}{\ }}\ \underline{\overset{V}{\ }}\ \underline{\overset{C}{\ }}\ \underline{\overset{V}{\ }}$ 5. $\underline{\overset{C}{\ }}\ \underline{\overset{V}{\ }}\ \underline{\overset{C}{\ }}\ \underline{\overset{C}{\ }}\ \underline{\overset{V}{\ }}\ \underline{\overset{C}{\ }}$
   t   h   e   r   e   r   e   l   y   h   i   d   d   e   n

2. $\underline{\overset{C}{\ }}\ \underline{\overset{V}{\ }}\ \underline{\overset{C}{\ }}\ \underline{\overset{C}{\ }}$ 4. $\underline{\overset{C}{\ }}\ \underline{\overset{V}{\ }}\ \underline{\overset{C}{\ }}\ \underline{\overset{C}{\ }}$ 6. $\underline{\overset{C}{\ }}\ \underline{\overset{V}{\ }}\ \underline{\overset{C}{\ }}\ \underline{\overset{C}{\ }}\ \underline{\overset{V}{\ }}\ \underline{\overset{C}{\ }}$
   j   u   m   p   y   a   m   s   s   i   l   v   e   r

D. Doubling the Final Consonant (in Words of One Syllable)

When you add a suffix, or ending, that begins with a vowel (like *-ed*, *-ing*, *-er*, *-est*) to a word of one syllable, double the final consonant *if* the last three letters of the word are consonant-vowel-consonant, or *cvc*.

mop + ed = mopped	swim + ing = swimming
burn + er = burner	thin + est = thinnest

● *Mop*, *swim*, and *thin* all end in *cvc*; therefore, the final consonants are doubled.

● *Burn* does not end in *cvc*; therefore, the final consonant is not doubled.

PRACTICE 3

Which of the following words double the final consonant? Check to see whether the word ends in *cvc*. Double the final consonant if necessary; then add the suffixes *-ed* and *-ing*.

	Word	Last Three Letters	-ed	-ing
EXAMPLES:	drop	cvc	dropped	dropping
	boil	vvc	boiled	boiling
1.	plan	cvc	planned	planning
2.	brag	cvc	bragged	bragging
3.	dip	cvc	dipped	dipping
4.	sail	vvc	sailed	sailing
5.	stop	cvc	stopped	stopping

PRACTICE 4

Which of the following words double the final consonant? Check for *cvc*. Then add the suffixes *-er* or *-est*.

	Word	Last Three Letters	-er	-est
EXAMPLES:	hot	cvc	hotter	hottest
	cool	vvc	cooler	coolest

1. tall	vcc	taller	tallest
2. short	vcc	shorter	shortest
3. fat	cvc	fatter	fattest
4. slim	cvc	slimmer	slimmest
5. wet	cvc	wetter	wettest
6. quick	vcc	quicker	quickest

E. Doubling the Final Consonant (in Words of More Than One Syllable)

When you add a suffix that begins with a vowel to a word of more than one syllable, double the final consonant *if*

(1) the last three letters of the word are *cvc*, *and*

(2) the accent or stress is on the *last* syllable.

> begin + ing = beginning
> patrol + ed = patrolled

● *Begin* and *patrol* both end in *cvc*.

● In both words, the stress is on the last syllable: *be-gin´, pa-trol´*. (Pronounce the words aloud and listen for the correct stress.)

● Therefore, *beginning* and *patrolled* double the final consonant.

> gossip + ing = gossiping
> visit + ed = visited

● *Gossip* and *visit* both end in *cvc*.

● However, the stress is **not** on the last syllable: *gos´-sip, vis´-it*.

● Therefore, *gossiping* and *visited* do not double the final consonant.

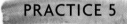

PRACTICE 5

Which of the following words double the final consonant? First, check for *cvc*. Then check for the final stress and add the suffixes *-ed* and *-ing*.

Word	Last Three Letters	-ed	-ing
EXAMPLES: repel	cvc	repelled	repelling
enlist	vcc	enlisted	enlisting
1. occur	cvc	occurred	occurring
2. happen	cvc	happened	happening
3. polish	vcc	polished	polishing
4. commit	cvc	committed	committing
5. offer	cvc	offered	offering
6. prefer	cvc	preferred	preferring

7.	exit	cvc	exited	exiting
8.	travel	cvc	traveled	traveling
9.	wonder	cvc	wondered	wondering
10.	omit	cvc	omitted	omitting

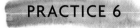

PRACTICE 6

Which words in parentheses double the final consonant? First, check for *cvc*. Then add the suffixes *-ed* and *-ing*. In words of two or more syllables, check for the final stress.

Hayao Miyazaki, Movie Magician

(1) Many Americans are just _____beginning_____ to learn about Hayao Miyazaki,
(begin + ing)

one of the world's greatest animators. (2) Born in Tokyo in 1941, Miyazaki

_____attended_____ college just as the arts of *manga* (Japanese comics) and *anime* (animated
(attend + ed)

movies) were _____budding_____ in Japan. (3) After _____getting_____ his degree, he was
(bud + ing)   (get + ing)

_____offered_____ a job in an animation studio. (4) With his _____stunning_____ ability to
(offer + ed)   (stun + ing)

draw and his creative mind, Miyazaki _____enjoyed_____ the work.
(enjoy + ed)

(5) Soon he was not only _____drawing_____ animes but also _____inventing_____,
(draw + ing)   (invent + ing)

_____planning_____, and _____directing_____ them. (6) With director Isao Takahata, he
(plan + ing)   (direct + ing)

Princess Mononoke, raised by wolves, is one of Miyazaki's strong girl heroines.

_____opened_____ a new film studio, Studio Ghibli. (7) By _____running_____ his own
(open + ed)   (run + ing)

company, he could realize his vision, _____shifting_____ the anime in new directions.
(shift + ing)

(8) Above all, Miyazaki is _____committed_____ to _____filming_____ with children in
(commit + ed)   (film + ing)

mind. (9) With clear colors and imaginative plots, his movies are _____rooted_____ in
(root + ed)

_____feeling_____, not logic. (10) Films like _My Neighbor Totoro_, _Princess Mononoke_, and
(feel + ing)

Ponyo have _____explored_____ themes such as courage, environmental awareness, and the
(explore + ed)

bonds of love. (11) The idea for his film _Spirited Away_ _____occurred_____ to Miyazaki when
(occur + ed)

he had _____stopped_____ _____working_____ for a while and _____stayed_____ with a
(stop + ed)   (work + ing)   (stay + ed)

friend who had a 10-year-old daughter. (12) The filmmaker _____vowed_____ to make a
(vow + ed)

movie that _____appealed_____ to little girls. (13) In fact, his heroines are often strong girls,
(appeal + ed)

some _____possessing_____ superpowers and some not.
(possess + ing)

(14) To make a film, Miyazaki begins without even _____knowing_____ the story, which
(know + ing)

then develops through the drawings. (15) The results have _____propelled_____ him to the
(propel + ed)

top ranks of animated filmmakers, _____winning_____ him many awards and millions of fans,
(win + ing)

first in Japan and then the world over.

F. Dropping or Keeping the Final _E_

TEACHING TIP

The rules for keeping or dropping the final _e_ should be memorized.

When you add a suffix that begins with a vowel (like _-able_, _-ence_, and _-ing_), drop the final _e_.

When you add a suffix that begins with a consonant (like _-less_, _-ment_, and _-ly_), keep the final _e_.

> write + ing = writing   pure + ity = purity

● _Writing_ and _purity_ both drop the final _e_ because the suffixes _-ing_ and _-ity_ begin with vowels.

> hope + less = hopeless   advertise + ment = advertisement

● _Hopeless_ and _advertisement_ keep the final _e_ because the suffixes _-less_ and _-ment_ begin with consonants.

Here are some exceptions to memorize:

TEACHING TIP

Ask students to explain how each of the exceptions deviates from the rules.

argument	courageous	knowledgeable	simply
awful	judgment	manageable	truly

PRACTICE 7   Add the suffix shown to each word.

EXAMPLES: come + ing = _____*coming*_____

rude + ness = _____*rudeness*_____

1. blame + less =	*blameless*	9. response + ible =	*responsible*
2. guide + ance =	*guidance*	10. rejoice + ing =	*rejoicing*
3. debate + ing =	*debating*	11. awe + ful =	*awful*
4. motive + ation =	*motivation*	12. manage + er =	*manager*
5. sincere + ly =	*sincerely*	13. judge + ment =	*judgment*
6. desire + able =	*desirable*	14. fame + ous =	*famous*
7. argue + ment =	*argument*	15. grieve + ance =	*grievance*
8. home + less =	*homeless*	16. arrange + ing =	*arranging*

G. Changing or Keeping the Final Y

When you add a suffix to a word that ends in -*y*, change the *y* to *i* if the letter before the *y* is a consonant.

Keep the final *y* if the letter before the *y* is a vowel.

happy + ness = happiness	delay + ed = delayed

- The *y* in *happiness* is changed to *i* because the letter before the *y* is a consonant, *p*.
- However, the *y* in *delayed* is not changed to *i* because the letter before it is a vowel, *a*.

When you add -*ing* to words ending in *y*, always keep the *y*.

copy + ing = copying	delay + ing = delaying

Here are some exceptions to memorize:

day + ly = daily   pay + ed = paid

lay + ed = laid   say + ed = said

When the final *y* is changed to *i*, add -*es* instead of -*s*.

fly + es = flies	candy + es = candies
marry + es = marries	story + es = stories

TEACHING TIP

Practicing with flashcards may help students learn to apply the rules more consistently.

PRACTICE 8   Add the suffix shown to each of the following words.

EXAMPLES: vary + ed = _____*varied*_____

buy + er = _____*buyer*_____

1. cry + ed = _____cried_____
2. mercy + ful = _____merciful_____
3. worry + ing = _____worrying_____
4. say + ed = _____said_____
5. juicy + er = _____juicier_____

6. enjoy + able = _____enjoyable_____
7. clumsy + ness = _____clumsiness_____
8. wealthy + est = _____wealthiest_____
9. day + ly = _____daily_____
10. merry + ly = _____merrily_____

PRACTICE 9

Add the suffixes in parentheses to each word.

1. lively (er) _____livelier_____
   (est) _____liveliest_____
   (ness) _____liveliness_____
2. beauty (fy) _____beautify_____
   (ful) _____beautiful_____
   (es) _____beauties_____
3. healthy (er) _____healthier_____
   (est) _____healthiest_____
   (ly) _____healthily_____

4. study (es) _____studies_____
   (ous) _____studious_____
   (ing) _____studying_____
5. busy (ness) _____business_____
   (er) _____busier_____
   (est) _____busiest_____
6. try (es) _____tries_____
   (ed) _____tried_____
   (al) _____trial_____

PRACTICE 10

Add the suffix shown to each word in parentheses. Write the correctly spelled word in each blank.

Winter Blues

(1) Although Kim _____tried_____ (try + ed) to ignore her feelings, she always felt _____hungrier_____ (hungry + er), _____sleepier_____ (sleepy + er), _____angrier_____ (angry + er), and _____lonelier_____ (lonely + er) during the winter months. (2) As part of her _____denial_____ (deny + al), she went about her _____business_____ (busy + ness) as usual, but she knew that she no longer found life as _____pleasurable_____ (pleasure + able) as before.

(3) Then one day she read a _____fascinating_____ (fascinate + ing) magazine article about a medical condition called *seasonal affective disorder*, or *SAD*. (4) Kim _____immediately_____ (immediate + ly) saw the _____similarities_____ (similarity + es) between her yearly mood changes and the symptoms that people with SAD _____displayed_____ (display + ed). (5) She learned that winter SAD is a kind of depression triggered _____primarily_____ (primary + ly) by lack of _____exposure_____ (expose + ure) to light—by insufficient sunshine, inadequate indoor light at home or work, or even by _____mercilessly_____ (mercy + lessly) cloudy weather.

(6) _____Happily_____ (Happy + ly), Kim discovered that three or four kinds of treatment are available.

(7) The most severe cases—people who sleep more than fourteen hours a day and still feel _____fatigued_____ (fatigue + ed), for example—are usually cured by light therapy given in a clinic

or at home under a doctor's care. (8) Taking medication, ___exercising___ , or
(exercise + ing)

___changing___ one's diet often brings ___noticeable___ relief. (9) Kim did some
(change + ing)   (notice + able)

research on the Web and found a list of SAD clinics, ___guidance___ , and support.
(guide + ance)

(10) Attending a light-therapy clinic near her home, she soon experienced her

___healthiest___ winter in years.
(healthy + est)

H. Choosing *IE* or *EI*

Write *i* before *e*, except after *c*, or in any *ay* sound like *neighbor*:

> niece, believe, conceive, weigh

- *Niece* and *believe* are spelled *ie*.
- *Conceive* is spelled *ei* because of the preceding *c*.
- *Weigh* is spelled *ei* because of its *ay* sound.

   However, words with a *shen* sound are spelled with an *ie* after the *c*: *ancient, conscience, efficient, sufficient.*

   Here are some exceptions to memorize:

either	height	seize	their
foreign	neither	society	weird

PRACTICE 11 Pronounce each word out loud. Then fill in the blanks with either *ie* or *ei*.

1. f __i__ __e__ ld
2. w __e__ __i__ ght
3. n __e__ __i__ ther
4. w __e__ __i__ rd
5. ch __i__ __e__ f

6. s __e__ __i__ ze
7. rec __e__ __i__ ve
8. br __i__ __e__ f
9. h __e__ __i__ ght
10. ach __i__ __e__ ve

11. effic __i__ __e__ nt
12. v __e__ __i__ n
13. th __e__ __i__ r
14. for __e__ __i__ gn
15. cash __i__ __e__ r

I. Commonly Misspelled Words

Below is a list of commonly misspelled words. They are words that you probably use daily in speaking and writing. Each word has a trouble spot, the part of the word that is often spelled incorrectly. The trouble spot is in bold type.

   Two tricks to help you learn these words are (1) to copy each word twice, underlining the trouble spot, and (2) to copy the words on flashcards and have someone else test you. If possible, consult this list while or after you write.

1. a**c**ross
2. add**r**ess
3. ans**w**er
4. argu**m**ent
5. ath**l**ete
6. begin**n**ing

7. beha**v**ior
8. calen**d**ar
9. car**ee**r
10. cons**c**ience
11. crow**ded**
12. defin**i**te

13. d**e**scribe
14. desp**e**rate
15. diff**e**rent
16. disa**pp**oint
17. disa**pp**rove
18. doesn'**t**

19. eig**h**th
20. embarra**ss**
21. environ**m**ent
22. exa**gg**erate
23. famili**a**r
24. final**ly**

25. government
26. grammar
27. hei**gh**t
28. i**ll**egal
29. immed**iate**ly
30. import**ant**
31. inte**gr**ation
32. inte**ll**igent
33. inte**re**st
34. interfere
35. jew**el**ry
36. ju**dgm**ent
37. knowle**dge**

38. maint**ain**
39. mathematics
40. meant
41. nec**ess**ary
42. nerv**ous**
43. occasion
44. opin**ion**
45. optimist
46. particular
47. **per**form
48. **per**haps
49. perso**nn**el
50. poss**ess**

51. poss**ible**
52. **prefer**
53. pre**jud**ice
54. privil**ege**
55. pro**bably**
56. **psychology**
57. pursue
58. re**fer**ence
59. **rhythm**
60. ridiculous
61. separate
62. sim**ilar**
63. **since**

64. speech
65. stren**gth**
66. success
67. **sur**prise
68. ta**ugh**t
69. tempera**t**ure
70. **thorough**
71. thou**ght**
72. tire**d**
73. until
74. wei**gh**t
75. wri**tt**en

Personal Spelling List

In your notebook, keep a list of words that *you* misspell. Add words to your list from corrected papers and from the exercises in this chapter. First, copy each word as you misspelled it, underlining the trouble spot; then write the word correctly. Use the following form. Study your list often.

As I Wrote It	Correct Spelling
1. *dissappointed*	*disappointed*
2.	
3.	

Chapter Highlights

- **Double the final consonant in one-syllable words that end in *cvc*:**
  hop/hopped   tan/tanning

- **Double the final consonant in words of more than one syllable if they end in *cvc* and if the stress is on the last syllable:**
  begin/beginning   prefer/preferred

- **Drop the final *e* when adding a suffix that begins with a vowel:**
  hope/hoping   time/timer

- **Keep the final *e* when adding a suffix that begins with a consonant:**
  hope/hopeful   time/timely

- **Change the *y* to *i* when adding a suffix if the letter before the *y* is a consonant:**
  snappy/snappiest   pity/pitiful

- **Keep the final *y* when adding a suffix if the letter before the *y* is a vowel:**
  buy/buying   delay/delayed

- **Write *i* before *e*, except after *c*, or in any *ay* sound like *neighbor*:**
  believe, niece, *but* receive, weigh

- **Remember that there are exceptions to all of these rules. Check a dictionary whenever you are uncertain.**

Proofreading Strategy

If poor spelling is one of your error patterns, keep your Personal Spelling List of errors and a dictionary beside you as you write.

1. Use the **bottom-up proofreading technique**. Read your draft sentence by sentence from the last sentence to the first. This will help you see possible misspellings and typos more easily.

2. Ask **someone who is a good speller** to read your draft and help you spot any misspellings and typos. Then correct these yourself; this will help you learn correct spellings. Tutors in your college's writing lab or class-mates who have a good eye for errors can be excellent sources of help.

WRITING AND PROOFREADING ASSIGNMENT

Success can be defined in many ways. In a small group, discuss what the term *success* means to you. Is it a rewarding career, a happy family life, lots of money?

Now pick the definition that most appeals to you and write a paragraph explaining what success is. You may wish to mention people in the news or friends to support your main idea. Proofread your work for accurate spelling, especially the words covered in this chapter. Finally, exchange papers and read each other's work. Did your partner catch any spelling errors that you missed?

CHAPTER REVIEW

Proofread this essay for spelling errors. Correct the errors above the lines.

A Precious Resource

(1) Many people have pleasant ~~memorys~~ memories of ~~recieving~~ receiving their first library card or ~~chooseing~~ choosing

books for the first time at a local public library. (2) Widely recognized as a priceless

resource, the public library is defined just as you might expect: a collection of books and

other materials supported by the public for public use.

(3) Several New England towns claim the honor of ~~contributeing~~ contributing the first public money

for a library. (4) However, the first such library of meaningful size and influence—the first

~~fameous~~ famous public library—originated in Boston, Massachusetts, in 1854. (5) The Boston Public

Library, with its useful ~~refrence~~ reference collection and its policy of ~~circulateing~~ circulating popular books, set

the pattern for all public ~~librarys~~ libraries subsequently created in the United States and Canada.

(6) By the end of the nineteenth century, many state ~~goverments~~ governments were ~~begining~~ beginning to raise

taxes to support libraries. (7) They ~~beleived~~ believed that public libraries had an extremely ~~importent~~ important

role to play in helping people pursue ~~knowlege~~ knowledge and continue ~~thier~~ their education. (8) Although

public ~~libaries~~ libraries today have much the same goal, they now offer a ~~truely~~ truly ~~admireable~~ admirable number

The beautiful Library of Congress in Washington, D.C., offers the public an array of services and resources. Explore online at ‹**http://www.loc.gov/index.html**›.

© PictureNet/CORBIS

of resources and services. (9) These include story hours for children, book discussion clubs for adults, ~~intresting~~ ^{interesting} lectures, art exhibits, literacy classes, and most recently, computer training and ~~guideance~~ ^{guidance}.

(10) Technology, of course, has transformed the management of the public library as well as the way the library is used. (11) The ~~bigest~~ ^{biggest} changes—today's computerized catalogs, searchable databases, and Internet access—would ~~definately~~ ^{definitely} have gone beyond the wildest dreams of even the most ~~commited~~ ^{committed} early public ~~libary~~ ^{library} supporters.

TEACHING TIP

Tell your students about the interactive spelling quizzes at ‹**http://grammar.ccc.commnet.edu/grammar/spelling.htm**›. Scroll down for the quiz list.

EXPLORING ONLINE

TEACHING TIP

Instructor tools for *Grassroots* include a computerized Test Bank, PowerPoint slides, an Instructor's Resource Manual with teaching tips, and more, and can be accessed at ‹**login.cengage.com**›.

<http://grammar.ccc.commnet.edu/grammar/cgi-shl/quiz20.pl/spelling_quiz3.htm> Interactive quiz: Add endings to these words.

<http://owl.english.purdue.edu/exercises/4/20/43> Is that *ei* or *ie*? Take the test and check your answers.

CHAPTER 35

Look-Alikes/ Sound-Alikes

ESL TIP

Look-alikes and sound-alikes present ongoing problems for ESL students, especially when incorrect pronunciation interferes with their spelling. Remind students that, when in doubt, all writers consult reference materials.

The pairs or sets of words in this chapter might look or sound like, but they have different meanings. Review this chart, studying any words that confuse you (for instance *your* and *you're* or *their* and *there*). Add these to your Personal Error Patterns Chart and be sure to do the practice exercises in this chapter.

Commonly Confused Words

Word	Meaning	Examples
a	Used before a word beginning with a consonant or a consonant sound	*a* story *a* lake *a* user (here *u* sounds like the consonant *y*)
an	Used before a word beginning with a vowel (*a, e, i, o, u*) or silent *h*	*an* address *an* onion *an* honor (*h* in *honor* is silent)
and	Joins words or ideas	He owns a car *and* a motorcycle.
accept	To receive	Chris *accepted* the job offer.
except	Other than; excluding	The library is open every day *except* Sunday.
affect	To have an influence on; to change	Her love of cooking *affected* her decision to become a chef.
effect	(noun) The result of a cause or an influence	Forming a study group had a positive *effect* on Anna's grades.
	(verb) To cause	The new law will *effect* tax rate increases.
been	Past participle form of *to be*; usually used after the helping verb *have, has,* or *had*	Mario has never *been* to Portugal.
being	The *-ing* form of *to be*; usually used after the helping verb *is, are, am, was,* or *were*	She was *being* honest.

buy	To purchase	I *buy* my books online.
by	Near; by means of; before	The time flew *by*.
fine	Good or well; a penalty	On a *fine* day like today, we like to be outside.
		The *fine* for the overdue book was $1.50.
find	To locate	We must *find* another apartment.
it's	Contraction of *it is* or *it has*	*It's* still snowing.
its	A possessive that shows ownership	The company just redesigned *its* website.
know	To have knowledge or understanding	Do you *know* Judge Meriwether?
knew	Past tense of the verb *know*	She *knew* the correct answer.
no	A negative	*No*, I don't speak French.
new	Recent, fresh, unused	The *new* manager has made many changes.
lose	To misplace; not to win	You will *lose* weight if you diet and exercise.
loose	Too large; not tightly fitting	The dog was running *loose* in the neighborhood.
mine	A possessive that shows ownership	He gave me his e-mail address, and I gave him *mine*.
mind	Intelligence; to object; to pay attention to	Have you changed your *mind*?
		I didn't *mind* waiting.
past	That which has already occurred; it is over with	We can't change the *past*, but we can learn from it.
passed	The past tense of the verb *to pass*	I *passed* the test.
quiet	Silent, still	He is usually very *quiet* and shy.
quit	To give up; to stop doing something	Donna *quit* smoking three months ago.
quite	Very; exactly	Her new hairstyle made *quite* a change to her appearance.
rise	To get up by one's own power	My grandfather always *rises* at dawn.
raise	To lift an object; to grow or increase	Emil *raises* horses.
sit	To seat oneself	Let's *sit* on the porch.
set	To place or put something down	Please *set* the bucket down.
suppose	To assume or guess	I *suppose* they broke up.
supposed	Ought to or should (it is followed by *to*)	That film is *supposed* to be excellent.
their	A possessive that shows ownership	The children have washed *their* hands.
there	Indicates a direction or a place; also a way of introducing a thought	He left *there* in a hurry.
		There is a solution to this problem.
they're	A contraction: *they* + *are* = *they're*	*They're* too busy to break for lunch.

then	Afterward; at that time	She stretched for ten minutes *then* set off on her run.
than	Used in a comparison	Ken is taller *than* Jorge.
through	In one side and out the other; finished; by means of	If you look *through* this telescope, you'll see Jupiter. *Through* hard work and dedication, she became #1.
though	Although (used with *as*, *though* means as if)	*Though* she's not wealthy, she's happy. You look *as though* you've seen a ghost.
to	Toward *To* can also be combined with a verb to form an infinitive	They love going *to* the beach. We plan *to* practice every day.
too	Also; very	Amir is handsome and smart, *too*.
two	The number 2	The new semester begins in *two* weeks.
use	To make use of	*Use* your time wisely.
used	In the habit of; accustomed to (it is followed by *to*)	I *used* to jog two miles a day.
weather	Refers to atmospheric conditions	Bad *weather* forced the party indoors.
whether	Indicates a question	He's not sure *whether* he can be there.
where	Indicates place or location	*Where* did you go on vacation?
were	The past tense of *are*	The dogs *were* wet and muddy.
we're	A contraction: *we* + *are* = *we're*	*We're* going to be late for our appointment.
whose	Indicates ownership and possession	*Whose* cell phone is ringing?
who's	A contraction of *who is* or *who has*	*Who's* winning?
your	A possessive that shows ownership	*Your* speech was very interesting.
you're	A contraction: *you* + *are* = *you're*	*You're* so lucky!

TEACHING TIP

Alert students to the exhaustive "Notorious Confusables" bank of explanations, examples, and interactive quizzes: ‹http://grammar.ccc .commnet.edu/grammar/ notorious.htm›.

TEACHING TIP

To give students more practice with look-alikes/sound-alikes, you might ask them to write sentences using the words they confuse.

Personal Look-Alikes/Sound-Alikes List

In your Personal Error Patterns Chart or your notebook, keep a list of look-alikes and sound-alikes that you have trouble with. Add words to your list from corrected papers and from the exercises in this chapter; consider also such pairs as *advice/ advise*, *break/brake*, *principle/principal*, *patience/patients*, and so forth.

First, write the word you used incorrectly; then write its meaning or use it correctly in a sentence, whichever best helps you remember. Now do the same with the word you meant to use.

Word	**Meaning**
1. *you're*	*contraction of you are*
your	*You left your key in the lock.*

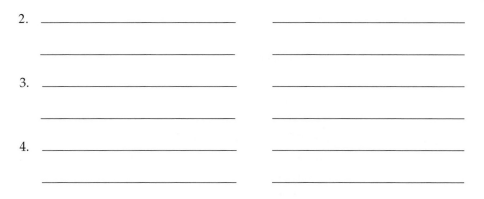

2. _____   _____

    _____   _____

3. _____   _____

    _____   _____

4. _____   _____

    _____   _____

PRACTICE 1

Three sets of these words are confused and misused more than any others: their/they're/there, your/you're, and its/it's. To check your mastery, circle each correct word in parenthesis. If you have trouble, refer to the chart.

1. If (your, **you're**) a parent, what happens at an amazing middle school in Brooklyn, NY, just might change (**your**, you're) child's life.

2. IS 318 in Brooklyn has become famous for (it's, **its**) chess program, but unlike most schools with top chess teams, (its, **it's**) in a high-poverty, high crime area.

3. The school and (**its**, it's) brilliant young players shatter stereotypes; (**their**, they're, there) chess team has won 26 national championships in the last 10 years.

4. "(Your, **You're**) not good at chess because of the color of your skin or how much money your parents make," says one student. "(Your, **You're**) good because of mental discipline, passion, and hard work."

5. A documentary film about the school's chess students and (**their**, they're, there) teachers, *Brooklyn Castle*, takes (**its**, it's) name from the royal names of chess pieces, like queen, king, knight, rook.

6. For the young men and one young woman in the movie, IS 318 is (**their**, they're, there) castle, and (their, **they're**, there) building successful lives along with learning chess.

7. If (**your**, you're) child has ADD, you might be interested in Patrick Johnston, one student in the film who struggles with this problem.

8. (Your, **You're**) going to see Patrick's concentration and self-esteem rise as he struggles to learn chess and win his first tournament games.

9. (Their, They're, **There**) is evidence that students who study and play chess for just four months will see (**their**, they're, there) IQ test scores rise.

10. If you meet the kids and teachers in *Brooklyn Castle*, (your, **you're**) going to see why.

PRACTICE 2

Read each sentence carefully and then circle the correct word or words. If you aren't sure, refer to the chart.

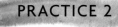
TEACHING TIP

Students who speak certain regional or ethnic dialects may confuse words that they pronounce incorrectly (e.g., in the South, *sit* may be pronounced "set").

1. In the (passed, **past**) books on *etiquette*—polite and respectful behavior in social situations—(**were**, where) best-sellers.

2. (Its, **It's**) different today, when rudeness and even bullying are common, (weather, **whether**) one is at school, in traffic, or online.

3. In "wired" countries around the world, one negative (affect, **effect**) of social media seems (too, **to**) be a lack of concern for the feelings of others.

TEACHING TIP

You might ask students whether they think the United States should begin a similar, massive netiquette program.

4. South Korea is one of the first countries that has (passed, past) laws to make sure (its, it's) children practice netiquette.

5. *Netiquette* refers (to, two) the rules of polite and respectful behavior on the Internet.

6. South Korean second graders study textbooks (who's, whose) lessons include netiquette.

7. They (set, sit) at (their, there) desks and learn not to be cyber bullies; they are taught the signs of computer addiction.

8. As they go (through, though) school, 15 of (they're, their) textbooks will discuss netiquette.

9. As the result of (a, an) 2007 law, any South Korean who posts online is (supposed, suppose) to submit his or her real name and address.

10. Although some argue this hurts free speech, most people say it effectively reduces cruel (an, and) anonymous comments.

PRACTICE 3

The following paragraphs contain 13 look-alike/sound-alike errors. Proofread for these errors, writing the correct word choice above the line.

What Happened to the Honeybees?

(1) Since the 1980s, 30 to 40 percent of the honeybees in the United States have disappeared. (2) Beehives that ~~use~~ *used* to be healthy and buzzing have become ~~quite~~ *quiet*. (3) In 2010 alone, 34 percent of commercial honeybee colonies died out, according to the United States Department of Agriculture. (4) ~~Its~~ *It's* a mystery that urgently needs to be solved because honeybees play a critical role in natural cycles. (5) Bees pollinate many of the fruits, vegetables, and other crops that we eat or feed to farm animals. (6) Without bees, the price of many foods would ~~raise~~ *rise* so much that only the very wealthy could afford ~~too by~~ *to buy* them.

(7) So far, scientists have ~~being~~ *been* unable to pinpoint the cause. (8) Some claim that toxic pesticides sprayed on plants are ~~effecting~~ *affecting* the honeybees. (9) Others believe that parasitic mites, viruses, fungi, or bacteria may be killing them. (10) Still others wonder if the microwave radiation from so many cell phones and cell towers is interfering with bees' ability to navigate and ~~fine there~~ *find their* way back to their hives with the pollen and nectar they collect. (11) Scientists hope that Americans will try to make ~~they're~~ *their* yards and gardens bee-friendly. (12) Remember, ~~your~~ *you're* helping bees whenever you do not ~~used~~ *use* pesticides and when you plant bee balm, foxglove, red clover, and other plants that bees like.

© kesipun/Shutterstock.com

ESL TIP

Many ESL students need vocabulary-development work; consider independent study assignments focusing on prefixes, roots, and suffixes. Alert them to sites like ‹http://a4esl.org/›, where they will find interactive vocabulary quizzes.

Chapter Highlights

Some words look and sound alike. Below are a few of them:

- **it's/its**

    It's the neatest room I ever saw.

    Everything is in *its* place.

- **their/they're/there**

    They found *their* work easy.

    They're the best actors I have ever seen.

    Put the lumber down *there*.

- **then/than**

    I was a heavyweight boxer *then*.

    He is a better cook *than* I.

- **to/too/two**

    We are going *to* the stadium.

    No one is *too* old to learn.

    I bought *two* hats yesterday.

- **whose/who's**

    Whose Italian dictionary is this?

    I'm not sure *who's* leaving early.

- **your/you're**

    Is *your* aunt the famous mystery writer?

    You're due for a promotion and a big raise.

Proofreading Strategy

If you tend to confuse the *look-alikes/sound-alikes*, **keep your Personal Error Patterns Chart updated** with the specific words you misuse, such as *their* and *there*, *affect* and *effect*, and *your* and *you're*.

Every time you proofread, **search your draft for every one of these words**. If you are using a computer, use the *"Find"* feature to locate them. Then double-check the meaning of the sentence to make sure that you've used and spelled the word correctly.

WRITING AND PROOFREADING ASSIGNMENT

Look back through this chapter and make a list of the look-alikes that most confuse you. List at least five pairs or clusters of words. Then use them all correctly in a paper about a problem on your campus or in your neighborhood (such as a lack of public parks or playgrounds, too much drug or alcohol use, or a gulf between computer haves and have-nots). Try to use every word on your look-alikes list and proofread to make sure you have spelled everything correctly.

CHAPTER REVIEW

Proofread this essay for look-alike/sound-alike errors. Write your corrections above the lines.

D'Wayne Edwards: Just for Kicks

(1) If ~~your~~ [you're] a fan of stylish shoes, you might ~~no~~ [know] the work of D'Wayne Edwards. (2) He not only designs the world's top athletic shoes, but he created Pensole Academy, ~~were~~ [where] talented young designers can break into the elite world of shoe design for companies like Nike and Adidas. (3) Edwards's rapid ~~raise~~ [rise] from a talented kid who loved "kicks"* ~~too~~ [to] a creative force is inspiring.

(4) At age 11, Edwards drew his first shoe and ~~new~~ [knew] he wanted to be a footwear designer.

(5) Later, he shared his career goal with a high school guidance counselor in Inglewood, California, but she said he was ~~been~~ [being] unrealistic and should join the military. (6) The ~~affect~~ [effect] of her negativity, he now says, was strong motivation to prove her wrong. (7) At age 17, Edwards won the national Reebok design contest and knew he would never ~~quiet~~ [quit] designing.

(8) After he graduated from high school, Edwards's mother couldn't ~~fine~~ [find] the money for design school, so he worked as ~~an~~ [a] file clerk for footwear company L.A. Gear. (9) Each department had a suggestion box. (10) Every day, D'Wayne dropped a sketch of a new shoe into that box, along with the suggestion that the company hire him as a shoe designer.

(11) Six months and 180 sketches later, L.A. Gear offered him a design job. (12) He poured his

*urban term for shoes

Shoe designer D'Wayne Edwards at
the launch of his Air Jordan XX2

heart and ~~mine~~ ^mind^ into the work. (13) By age 23, he was Head Designer. (14) By 28, he had his

own brand. (15) In 2000, he got a job at Nike, where his Goadome 2 became the best-selling

boot in Nike history. (16) ~~Than~~ ^Then^ he got the chance to design the Air Jordan 2.

(17) Yet Edwards's crowning achievement might be Pensole Academy, ~~we're~~ ^where^ lucky

students learn by doing, creating shoe designs and prototypes all by hand. (18) His academy

welcomes minorities, women, and working-class artists—groups often missing from the

world of shoe design. (19) "~~Its~~ ^It's^ the education you wish you'd had in school," says one student.

(20) The academy is abuzz with energy, colorful materials, and futuristic shoes by designers

~~who's~~ ^whose^ stylish kicks you just might be wearing next year.

PRACTICE 4   **Teamwork: Critical Thinking and Writing**

In a group with four or five classmates, discuss the personal qualities or actions that helped D'Wayne Edwards get his first design job and, later, many promotions. Are there any lessons you can learn for yourself from the story of Edwards's career? Take notes for a composition.

EXPLORING ONLINE

TEACHING TIP

Instructor tools for *Grassroots* include a computerized Test Bank, PowerPoint slides, an Instructor's Resource Manual with teaching tips, and more, and can be accessed at ‹**login .cengage.com**›.

<http://grammar.ccc.commnet.edu/grammar/cgi-shl/quiz.pl/spelling_add1.htm>
Interactive quiz: Choose the correctly spelled words.

<http://grammar.ccc.commnet.edu/grammar/cgi-shl/quiz.pl/lie_lay_quiz.htm>
Interactive quiz: Practice *lie/lay*, *sit/set*.

<http://a4esl.org/q/h/homonyms.html> Practice sound-alikes, like *night / knight*, that may confuse ESL students. Pick easy, medium, or difficult, and test yourself.

UNIT 8

Writing Assignments

As you complete each writing assignment, remember to perform these steps:

- Write a clear, complete topic sentence.
- Use freewriting, brainstorming, or clustering to generate ideas for the body of your paragraph, essay, letter, or review.
- Arrange your best ideas in a plan.
- Revise for support, unity, coherence, and exact language.
- Proofread for grammar, punctuation, and spelling errors.

Writing Assignment 1 *Express your opinion.* Write a letter to either a newspaper editor or an elected official (a mayor, governor, or senator, for example) in which you suggest one solution to a particular problem, such as illegal immigration or gun control. For topic ideas and information, visit Yahoo's directory of websites on current issues and causes at <http://dir.yahoo.com/Society_and_Culture/Issues_and_Causes/> or SpeakOut at <http://www.truth-out.org/speakout/>. State your opinion in your topic sentence or thesis statement, and present at least three reasons in support of your opinion. Consider actually mailing your letter to the recipient, but not before you proofread for spelling errors that would weaken your writing.

Writing Assignment 2 *Solve a problem.* You have identified what you consider to be a problem in your place of employment. When you go to your supervisor, you are asked to write up your concerns and to suggest a solution. Begin first by describing the problem, and then give background information, including what you suspect are the causes of the problem. Then offer suggestions for solving it. End with some guidelines for evaluating the success of the changes. In your concluding sentence, thank your supervisor for his or her consideration of your letter. Don't let typos or mistaken look-alikes/sound-alikes detract from your ideas. Proofread for accurate spelling!

Writing Assignment 3 *Review a movie.* Your college newspaper has asked you to review a movie. Pick a popular film that you especially liked or disliked. In your first sentence, name the film and state whether you recommend it. Explain your evaluation by discussing two or three specific reasons for your reactions to the picture. Describe as much of the film as is necessary to make your point, but do not retell the plot. Proofread for accurate spelling. Consider posting your review at <http://www.movievine.com/> or <http://www.franksreelreviews.com>.

Writing Assignment 4 *Describe a family custom.* Most families have customs that they perform together. These customs often help strengthen the bond that the members of the family feel toward each other. A custom might be eating Sunday dinner together, going to religious services, celebrating holidays in a special way, or even holding a family council to discuss difficulties and concerns. Write about a custom in your family that is especially meaningful. Of what value has this custom been to you or other members of the family? Proofread for accurate spelling.

UNIT 8

Review

Proofreading

The following essay contains a number of spelling and look-alike/sound-alike errors. First, underline the misspelled or misused words. Then write each correctly spelled word above the line. (You should find 38 errors.)

Everyday Angel

(1) On January 2, 2007, construction worker Wesley Autry and his ~~too~~ [two] young ~~daugters~~ [daughters] were standing on a New York City subway platform waiting for the train. (2) Suddenly, a 20-year-old student standing nearby suffered a ~~siezure~~ [seizure] and tumbled onto the subway tracks. (3) Autry saw the headlights of an approaching train and realized that the young ~~men~~ [man] was about to be run over right in front of the children. (4) ~~Leapping~~ [Leaping] onto the rails, Autry pulled the ~~struling~~ [struggling] student down into the shallow drainage ditch between the tracks and ~~pined~~ [pinned] him ~~their~~ [there] while one train and ~~than~~ [then] another rumbled over them with about two ~~inchs~~ [inches] to spare. (5) The next day, national and international headlines proclaimed Autry to be an "~~angle~~ [angel]," a "superman," a "hero," and "one in a million." (6) Autry explained ~~simpley~~ [simply], "I just ~~tryed~~ [tried] to do the right thing."

(7) But his action began a ~~nationel~~ [national] ~~arguement~~ [argument] about how far one should go to help others. (8) People couldn't help wondering if they ~~themselfs~~ [themselves] would make a ~~similer~~ [similar] split-second decision to risk ~~they're~~ [their] own lives for a total stranger. (9) Was Autry's act ~~truely~~ [truly] a one-in-a-million ~~occurence~~ [occurrence]? (10) After all, ~~pychologists~~ [psychologists] and sociologists point out that people ~~quiet~~ [quite] often fail to act in ~~a emergancy~~ [an emergency] because of the "bystander effect." (11) Bystander effect is the tendency to do nothing in a crisis because one assumes that someone else will take any ~~nesessary~~ [necessary] action.

(12) On the other hand, Autry's bravery ~~inspirred~~ [inspired] people worldwide. (13) CNN ~~reconized~~ [recognized] him as an "everyday hero," and in 2007, *Time* magazine

named him one of 100 ~~poeple~~ people "whose power, talent or moral example is transforming the world." (14) Some went so far as to honor his selfless ~~behavor~~ behavior by ~~buy~~ giving him awards, scholarships for his children, cash, and free trips. (15) Others gained new confidence in ~~they're~~ their own ability to ~~peform~~ perform a ~~dareing~~ daring rescue. (16) In one poll, most New Yorkers ~~beleived~~ believed that they would ~~probly~~ probably jump off a ferry boat to save a child who had fallen overboard, try to stop a mugger from ~~steeling~~ stealing an elderly ~~women's~~ woman's money, and even run into a burning building to save someone ~~traped~~ trapped inside.

EXPLORING ONLINE

<http://www.cnn.com/SPECIALS/cnn.heroes/index.html> Visit the CNN Heroes website and read about the difference everyday individuals have made around the world. Whom would you nominate to be a hero in your community? Write down three reasons to support your choice.

UNIT 8

Writers' Workshop

Examine Positive (or Negative) Values

One good way to develop a paragraph or essay is by supporting the topic sentence or the thesis statement with three points. A student uses this approach in the following essay. In your group or class, read her work, aloud if possible.

Villa Avenue

(1) The values I learned growing up on Villa Avenue in the Bronx have guided me through 35 years and three children. Villa Avenue taught me the importance of having a friendly environment, playing together, and helping people.

(2) Villa Avenue was a three-block, friendly environment. I grew up on the middle block. The other ones were called "up the block" and "down the block." Mary's Candy Store was up the block. It had a candy counter and soda fountain on the left and on the right a jukebox that played three songs for 25 cents. My friends and I would buy candy, hang out, and listen to the Beatles and other music of the sixties. A little down from Mary's on the corner was Joey's Deli. When you walked into Joey's, different aromas would welcome you to a world of Italian delicacies. Fresh mozzarella in water always sat on the counter, with salami, pepperoni, and imported provolone cheese hanging above. On Sundays at Joey's, my father would buy us a black-and-white cookie for a weekly treat.

(3) On Villa Avenue, everyone helped everyone else. Everybody's doors were open, so if I had to go to the bathroom or needed a drink of water, I could go to a dozen different apartments. If my parents had to go somewhere, they would leave me with a friend. When people on the block got sick, others went to the store for them, cleaned for them, watched their kids, and made sure they had food to eat. If someone died, everyone mourned and pitched in

to help with arrangements. When I reflect on those days, I realize that the way the mothers looked out for each other's children is like your modern-day play group. The difference is that our play area was "the block."

(4) The whole street was our playground. We would play curb ball at the intersection. One corner was home plate, and the other ones were the bases. Down the block where the street was wide, we would play Johnny on the Pony with 10 to 15 kids. On summer nights, it was kick the can or hide and seek. Summer days we spent under an open fire hydrant. Everyone would be in the water, including moms and dads. Sometimes the teenagers would go to my Uncle Angelo's house and get a wine barrel to put over the hydrant. With the top and bottom of the barrel off, the water would shoot 20 to 30 feet in the air and come down on us like a waterfall.

Loretta M. Carney, student

1. How effective is Loretta Carney's essay?

    __Y__ Clear main idea?   __Y__ Good supporting details?

    __Y/N__ Logical organization? (See #3 below)   __N__ Effective conclusion?

2. What is the main idea of the essay? Can you find the thesis statement, one sentence that states this main idea? Sentence 2

3. The writer states that Villa Avenue taught her three values. What are they? Are these clearly explained in paragraphs 2, 3, and 4? Are they discussed in the same order in which the thesis statement presents them? If not, what change would you suggest? No. Change thesis to match body or vice versa: friendliness, playfulness, helpfulness.

4. Does this essay *conclude* or just stop? What suggestions would you make to the writer for a more effective conclusion? Add a conclusion.

5. Proofread Carney's essay. Do you see any error patterns that she should watch out for? No

Writing and Revising Ideas

1. Describe a place or person that taught you positive (or negative) values.

2. Do places like Villa Avenue exist anymore? Explain why you do or do not think so.

See Chapters 5 and 6 for help with planning and writing. You might wish to present your topic with three supporting points, the way Loretta Carney does. As you revise, pay close attention to writing a good thesis sentence and supporting paragraphs that contain clear, detailed explanations.

UNIT 9   Reading Selections and Quotation Bank

Reading Strategies for the Writer

Reading Selections

Reading Strategies for the Writer

The reading selections that follow were chosen to interest you, inspire you, and make you think. Many deal with issues you face at college, at work, or at home. Your instructor may ask you to read a selection and be prepared to discuss it in class or to write a composition or journal entry about it. The more carefully you read these selections, the better you will be able to think, talk, and write about them. Below are eight strategies that can help you become a more active and effective reader.

1. **Preview the reading selection.** Before you begin to read, scan the whole article to get a sense of the author's main idea and supporting points. First read the title, headnote, and any subtitles; next, quickly read the first and last paragraphs. This should give you a fairly clear idea of the author's subject and point of view. Finally, skim the whole selection, looking for the main supporting ideas. Previewing will increase your enjoyment and understanding as you read.

2. **Underline important ideas.** It is easy to forget what you have read, even though you have recently read it. Underlining or highlighting what you consider the main ideas will help you later to remember and discuss what you have read. Some students number the main points in order to understand the development of the author's ideas.

3. **Write your reactions in the margins.** If you strongly agree or disagree with an idea, write *yes* or *no* next to it. Record other questions and comments also, as if you were having a conversation with the author. Writing assignments will often ask you to respond to a particular idea or situation in a selection. Having already noted your reactions in the margins will help you focus your thinking and your writing.

4. **Prepare questions.** You will occasionally come across material that you cannot follow. Reread the passage. If you still have questions, place a question mark in the margin to remind you to ask a classmate or the instructor for an explanation.

5. **Circle unfamiliar words.** If you come across a new word that makes it difficult to follow what the author is saying, look it up immediately, jot the definition in the margin, and go back to reading. If, however, you can sense the meaning from the context—how the word fits the sentence—just circle it and, when you have finished the selection, consult a dictionary.

6. **Note effective or powerful writing.** If a particular line strikes you as especially important or moving, underline or highlight it. You may wish later to quote it in your written assignment. Be selective, however, in what you mark. *Too much* annotation can make it hard to focus on what is important when you discuss the selection in class or write about it.

7. **Vary your pace.** Some selections can be read quickly because you already know a great deal about the subject or because you find the material simple and direct. Other selections may require you to read slowly, pausing between

sentences. Guard against the tendency to skim when the going gets tough: more difficult material will usually reward your extra time and attention.

8. Reread. If you expect to discuss or write about a selection, one reading is usually not enough. Budget your time so you will be able to give the selection a second or third reading. You will be amazed at how much more you can get from the selection as you reread. You may understand ideas that were unclear the first time around. In addition, you may notice significant new points and details: perhaps you will change your mind about ideas you originally agreed or disagreed with. Rereading will help you discuss and write more intelligently and will increase your reading enjoyment.

The following essay has been marked by a student. Your own responses to this essay would, of course, be different. Examining how this essay was annotated may help you annotate other selections in this book and read more effectively in your other courses.

Daring to Dream Big
Diane Sawyer

I see her on TV—she's a top journalist.

A beauty contest?

I like this comparison—my dad is my island.

I was seventeen years old, a high school senior in Louisville, Kentucky, representing my state in the 1963 America's Junior Miss competition in Mobile, Alabama. In the midst of it all, there was one person who stood at the center—at least my psychological center—someone I viewed as an island in an ocean of anxiety. She was one of the judges, a well-known writer, a woman whose sea-gray eyes fixed on you with laser penetration. Her name was Catherine Marshall.

During the rehearsal on the last day of the pageant, the afternoon before it would all end, several of us were waiting backstage when a pageant official said Catherine Marshall wanted to speak with us. We gathered around. Most of us were expecting a last-minute pep talk, but we were surprised.

Wow, this is interesting. Being a beauty queen is not enough.

Main idea? DREAM BIG.

Many of my friends don't set high goals for themselves. Do I?

Aspired = aimed

She fixed her eyes upon us. "You have set goals for yourselves. I have heard some of them. But I don't think you have set them high enough. You have talent and intelligence and a chance. I think you should take those goals and expand them. Think of the most you could do with your lives. Make what you do matter. Above all, dream big."

It was not so much an instruction as a dare. I felt stunned. This woman I admired so much was disappointed in us—not by what we were but by how little we aspired to be.

I won the America's Junior Miss contest that year. I graduated in 1967 with a BA degree in English and a complete lack of inspiration about what I should do with it. I went to my father. "What is it that you enjoy doing most?" he asked.

Good question: How would I answer it? Should I dream bigger?

"Writing," I replied slowly. "And working with people. And being in touch with what's happening in the world."

He thought for a moment. "Did you ever consider television?"

Marshall's speech really motivated Sawyer to act.

At that time there were few if any women journalists on television. The idea of being a pioneer in the field sounded like dreaming big. That's how I came to get up my nerve and go out to convince the news director at Louisville's WLKY-TV to let me have a chance.

He gave it to me. For the next two and a half years I worked as a combination weather and news reporter. Eventually, though, I began to feel restless. I'd wait for

revelation = discovery

the revelation, the sign pointing in the direction of the Big Dream. What I didn't realize is what Catherine Marshall undoubtedly knew all along—that the dream is not the destination but the journey.

I never thought of it this way.

Today I'm coeditor of CBS's *Sixty Minutes*. I keep a suitcase packed at all times so that I can fly out on assignment at a moment's notice. When I go out into the world, I can almost hear a wonderful woman prodding me with her fiery challenge to stretch farther and, no matter how big the dream, to dream a little bigger still. God, she seems to be saying, can forgive failure, but not failing to try.

This story makes me think of the importance of good role models—a good writing topic?

I'm inspired! Should I go for it and be a dentist instead of a dental assistant?

Put the Brakes on Driving while Texting

Leonard Pitts

Have you ever texted while driving even though you know it's dangerous? Made a phone call? Eaten a burger? In this column for the *Miami Herald*, nationally syndicated columnist Leonard Pitts examines the national problem of otherwise sensible people taking tremendous risks while driving. Pitts won the Pulitzer Prize for insightful commentary on American society in 2004.

1 The amazing thing about the debate over the need for laws to ban texting while driving is that there is a debate over the need for laws to ban texting while driving.

2 In the first place, you'd think you wouldn't need a law, that simple common sense would be enough to tell us it's unsafe to divert attention to a tiny keyboard and screen while simultaneously piloting two tons of metal, rubber, glass and, let us not forget, flesh, at freeway speeds—or even street speeds. In the second place, if common sense were insufficient, you'd think lawmakers would have rushed to back it up with tough laws.

3 Think again.

4 The issue has been moved to the front burner recently by a confluence[1] of events. In late July, a study by the Virginia Tech Transportation Institute quantified[2] the blatantly[3] obvious: Texting while driving is dangerous. Researchers found that the person who does so is the functional equivalent of a drunken driver, a whopping 23 times more likely to be involved in an accident or near-collision. Actually, according to a study in *Car and Driver* magazine, the texter is a significantly greater threat than a mere drunk.

5 About the same time the VTTI study was released, four senators introduced legislation that would require states to pass laws banning drivers from texting or risk losing federal highway funds. According to the *Los Angeles Times*, only 16 states and Washington, D.C., already have such laws on the books.[4]

6 And last week, Transportation Secretary Ray LaHood announced a summit in which lawmakers, law enforcement, academics, safety experts, and other stakeholders will study texting and other driving distractions. You want my response to this flurry of attention and activity? I can give it to you in a syllable: Duh.

---

1. confluence: coming together
2. quantified: expressed in a number or quantity
3. blatantly: glaringly, extremely
4. As of December 2012, 38 states and the District of Columbia had banned texting while driving.

7   What else is there to study? What more is there to say? The danger is all too self-evident. And if it were not, it has been quite aptly[5] illustrated in episodes like last year's commuter train crash in California in which the operator was texting and 25 people died.

"The texter is a significantly greater threat than a mere drunk."

8   Enough. Ban texting while driving. And cell phone use, too. Because what researchers tell us is that it's not the physical difficulty of juggling the devices that endangers us. It is the distraction: a driver so wrapped up in communicating with a person who isn't there that he is drawn away from his primary duty of keeping the car between the lines. The brain doesn't have sufficient bandwidth for both.

9   So yeah, there ought to be a law. And it ought to have some teeth in it. On the second offense, maybe a hefty fine, or brief loss of driving privileges. On the third, maybe you earn a free stay of a couple days and nights at the lovely graybar hotel.

10   If you sense here the zeal of the newly converted, congratulations on your perception. I stopped using my cell behind the wheel (I was never dumb enough to text) two weeks ago. Had myself an epiphany,[6] I did: Was reviewing last night's game with my son really worth dying for? I decided it was not. So I no longer make or take calls while driving.

11   If it's an emergency, I told my family, dial me again and I'll call you back. But the calls are hardly ever urgent, are they? That's not what this epidemic is about. Rather, it's about this idea—new within the last 15 years or so of our hyper-connected, hyper-productive culture—that it's never OK to be out of touch or unreachable.

12   Whither[7] solitude? Whither the moment just spent communing with your own thoughts? Do you really have that much to say? I'll save you the trouble: You don't.

13   Phoning while driving, texting while driving . . . here's a novel idea. How about driving while driving? And for those truly urgent messages that just can't wait, I propose a simple solution:

14   Pull over.

DISCUSSION AND WRITING QUESTIONS

1. Do Pitts's first two paragraphs capture your attention and make you want to read on? What words and sentences did you find especially effective? Do the words convey the author's feelings about the subject? What are those feelings?
2. Pitts argues that common sense alone should keep drivers from texting while driving, but it seems not to (paragraph 2). Why do you think some drivers text anyway? What beliefs might keep them from using common sense?
3. Studies prove that driving while texting is even more dangerous than driving while drunk. Do the statistics that the author cites in paragraph 4 surprise you? Why is "distracted driving" so dangerous? Should states also ban eating in the car?
4. Although texting is banned in 38 states, it is only a primary offense in four. That means that in most states a driver can only be cited for texting if pulled over for another offense. In contrast, not wearing a seat belt is a primary offense in 32 states. Is failing to wear a seat belt more dangerous than texting while driving?

TEACHING TIP

You might ask students to evaluate some antitexting campaigns, such as ‹**http:// www.stoptextsstopwrecks .org/**› campaign or AT&T's "It Can Wait" commercials at ‹**http://itcanwait.com/**›. Do they think these are effective?

---

5. aptly: appropriately, perfectly
6. epiphany: sudden realization or understanding
7. Whither: old-fashioned word for "Where?" "What happened to . . . ?"

WRITING ASSIGNMENTS

1. Pitts wonders if the real reason we spend so much time talking and texting on our cell phones is that we no longer know how to be alone, in solitude (paragraphs 11 and 12). Do you agree or disagree? Do you and your friends take time to do things alone, or must you feel constantly connected?

2. Because research shows that distracted driving is as dangerous as drunk driving, some states are considering a ban on all cell phone use while driving, even if the driver uses a hands-free device. Would you support such a law? Discuss why or why not.

3. The police and a school district in Wales together made a disturbing video that they claim will stop young people from texting and driving. Watch the video and discuss why you do or do not think it will achieve its purpose. *Warning: contains graphic violence.* <http://www.youtube.com/watch?v=ROLCmStIw9E>

Superman and Me

Sherman Alexie

Growing up on the Spokane Indian Reservation, Sherman Alexie and his classmates were "expected to fail." This essay tells the story of how the author refused to fail and instead found his true calling as a writer and poet. In 2010, Alexie's *War Dances* won the Pen/Faulkner Fiction Award, and his movie *Smoke Signals* has become a classic.

I learned to read with a Superman comic book. Simple enough, I suppose. I cannot recall which particular Superman comic book I read, nor can I remember which villain he fought in that issue. I cannot remember the plot, nor the means by which I obtained the comic book. What I can remember is this: I was three years old, a Spokane Indian boy living with his family on the Spokane Indian Reservation in eastern Washington State. We were poor by most standards, but one of my parents usually managed to find some minimum-wage job or another, which made us middle-class by reservation standards. I had a brother and three sisters. We lived on a combination of irregular paychecks, hope, fear and government surplus food.

My father, who is one of the few Indians who went to Catholic school on purpose, was an avid[1] reader of westerns, spy thrillers, murder mysteries, gangster epics, basketball player biographies and anything else he could find. He bought his books by the pound at Dutch's Pawn Shop, Goodwill, Salvation Army, and Value Village. When he had extra money, he bought new novels at supermarkets, convenience stores and hospital gift shops. Our house was filled with books. They were stacked in crazy piles in the bathroom, bedrooms and living room. In a fit of unemployment-inspired creative energy, my father built a set of bookshelves and soon filled them with a random assortment of books about the Kennedy assassination, Watergate, the Vietnam War and the entire twenty-three-book series of the Apache westerns. My father loved books, and since I loved my father with an aching devotion, I decided to love books as well.

I can remember picking up my father's books before I could read. The words themselves were mostly foreign, but I still remember the exact moment when I first understood, with a sudden clarity,[2] the purpose of a paragraph. I didn't have the vocabulary to say "paragraph," but I realized that a paragraph was a fence that

1. avid: enthusiastic and eager
2. clarity: clear understanding

Author Sherman Alexie
taught himself to read
with Superman comics.

held words. The words inside a paragraph worked together for a common purpose. They had some specific reason for being inside the same fence. This knowledge delighted me. I began to think of everything in terms of paragraphs. Our
reservation was a small paragraph within the United States. My family's house
was a paragraph, distinct from the other paragraphs of the LeBrets to the north,
the Fords to our south and the Tribal School to the west. Inside our house, each
family member existed as a separate paragraph but still had genetics[3] and common experiences to link us. Now, using this logic, I can see my changed family as
an essay of seven paragraphs: mother, father, older brother, the deceased sister, my
younger twin sisters and our adopted little brother.

4   At the same time I was seeing the world in paragraphs, I also picked up that
Superman comic book. Each panel, complete with picture, dialogue and narrative was a three-dimensional paragraph. In one panel, Superman breaks through
a door. His suit is red, blue and yellow. The brown door shatters into many pieces.
I look at the narrative above the picture. I cannot read the words, but I assume it
tells me that "Superman is breaking down the door." Aloud, I pretend to read the
words and say, "Superman is breaking down the door." Words, dialogue, also float
out of Superman's mouth. Because he is breaking down the door, I assume he says,
"I am breaking down the door." Once again, I pretend to read the words and say
aloud, "I am breaking down the door." In this way, I learned to read.

5   This might be an interesting story all by itself. A little Indian boy teaches himself to read at an early age and advances quickly. He reads "Grapes of Wrath" in
kindergarten when other children are struggling through "Dick and Jane." If he'd
been anything but an Indian boy living on the reservation, he might have been
called a prodigy.[4] But he is an Indian boy living on the reservation and is simply
an oddity.[5] He grows into a man who often speaks of his childhood in the third-
person, as if it will somehow dull the pain and make him sound more modest
about his talents.

---

3. genetics: characteristics and traits passed from parents to their children
4. prodigy: a child with exceptional talents
5. oddity: an unusual person or thing

"A smart Indian is a dangerous person."

A smart Indian is a dangerous person, widely feared and ridiculed by Indians   6
and non-Indians alike. I fought with my classmates on a daily basis. They wanted
me to stay quiet when the non-Indian teacher asked for answers, for volunteers,
for help. We were Indian children who were expected to be stupid. Most lived up
to those expectations inside the classroom but subverted[6] them on the outside.
They struggled with basic reading in school but could remember how to sing a
few dozen powwow[7] songs. They were monosyllabic[8] in front of their non-Indian
teachers but could tell complicated stories and jokes at the dinner table. They submissively[9] ducked their heads when confronted by a non-Indian adult but would
slug it out with the Indian bully who was ten years older. As Indian children, we
were expected to fail in the non-Indian world. Those who failed were ceremonially
accepted by other Indians and appropriately pitied by non-Indians.

I refused to fail. I was smart. I was arrogant. I was lucky. I read books late   7
into the night, until I could barely keep my eyes open. I read books at recess, then
during lunch, and in the few minutes left after I had finished my classroom assignments. I read books in the car when my family traveled to powwows or basketball games. In shopping malls, I ran to the bookstores and read bits and pieces
of as many books as I could. I read the books my father brought home from the
pawnshops and secondhand. I read the books I borrowed from the library. I read
the backs of cereal boxes. I read the newspaper. I read the bulletins posted on the
walls of the school, the clinic, the tribal offices, the post office. I read junk mail. I
read auto-repair manuals. I read magazines. I read anything that had words and
paragraphs. I read with equal parts joy and desperation. I loved those books, but I
also knew that love had only one purpose. I was trying to save my life.

Despite all the books I read, I am still surprised I became a writer. I was going   8
to be a pediatrician.[10] These days, I write novels, short stories and poems. I visit
schools and teach creative writing to Indian kids. In all my years in the reservation school system, I was never taught how to write poetry, short stories or novels.
I was certainly never taught that Indians wrote poetry, short stories and novels.
Writing was something beyond Indians. I cannot recall a single time that a guest
teacher visited the reservation. There must have been visiting teachers. Who were
they? Where are they now? Do they exist? I visit the schools as often as possible.
The Indian kids crowd the classroom. Many are writing their own poems, short
stories and novels. They have read my books. They have read many other books.
They look at me with bright eyes and arrogant wonder. They are trying to save
their lives. Then there are the sullen[11] and already defeated Indian kids who sit
in the back rows and ignore me with theatrical precision. The pages of their notebooks are empty. They carry neither pencil nor pen. They stare out the window.
They refuse and resist. "Books," I say to them. "Books," I say. I throw my weight
against their locked doors. The door holds. I am smart. I am arrogant. I am lucky.
I am trying to save our lives.

DISCUSSION AND WRITING QUESTIONS

1. Why would a smart Indian be a "dangerous person, widely feared and ridiculed" (paragraph 6)? Why would non-Indians adopt this opinion? Why would
   Indian children adopt this self-defeating idea?
2. What does the author mean when he writes in paragraph 7, "I was trying to save
   my life"? What point is he making about reading books and educating oneself?

---

6. subverted: undercut, defied
7. powwow: an Indian social gathering
8. monosyllabic: speaking only in one-syllable words
9. submissively: without resistance; obediently
10. pediatrician: a doctor who treats children
11. sullen: in a bad mood and silent

3. Based on Alexie's story, what inner characteristics or outward support does a person need to break free of stereotypes and dead ends and forge a path to success?

4. In paragraph 3, the author uses the metaphor that "a paragraph was a fence that held words." Does this metaphor help you understand what a paragraph does? How would you explain a paragraph?

WRITING ASSIGNMENTS

1. Sherman Alexie writes about an activity—reading—that gave him strength and hope during a very painful time in his life. Write a composition describing an activity, tool, or person that gives you strength and hope for your future.

2. Has there ever been a time in your life when someone *expected* you to fail? If so, who was it, what happened, and how did you react?

3. Have you ever been rejected or even ridiculed by your peers for making an unpopular decision or taking an unpopular action? Why did you defy the group's wishes and choose to go your own way?

Heroes Everywhere

John Quiñones

Excerpt from HEROES AMONG US by JOHN QUIÑONES. COPYRIGHT © BY JOHN QUIÑONES. Reprinted by permission of HarperCollins Publishers.

If you saw someone being treated unfairly, would you speak up? ABC News anchor John Quiñones has been filming bullies and bystanders[1] for his TV show *What Would You Do?* He believes that if just one person dares to speak, others will follow. In this powerful chapter from his book *Heroes Among Us: Ordinary People, Extraordinary Choices*, Quiñones describes everyday heroes captured in action by his hidden cameras.

TEACHING TIP

Before your students read Quiñones, you might wish to have them read the paragraph-length boxed definition of "bystander effect" in Chapter 6, Part C.

1   On a Saturday morning, at a bakery near Waco, Texas, I found a display of bigotry[2] as fresh as the coffee and pastries people stopped in to buy. A young Muslim woman dressed in a traditional headscarf ordered a pastry from the man behind the counter.

2   "You'll have to leave," he told her.

3   "What do you mean?" the woman asked politely.

4   "We don't serve camel jockeys in here," he said.

5   Several customers milled about the store, looking uncomfortable, trying not to pay attention. I was watching all this on TV monitors in a room in the back of the bakery. Both the Muslim woman and the man behind the counter were actors and hidden cameras were rolling. It was all part of the TV show I host for ABC News called *What Would You Do?*

6   "You won't serve me?" asked the woman, seemingly dumbfounded.

7   "How do I know you don't have a bomb in that bag?" the man behind the counter retorted.

8   "This is outrageous," said the woman playing the part of a Muslim.

9   I watched in astonishment what happened next. An older man approached and gave our man behind the counter an emphatic thumbs-up. "Good job," he said. "I like the way you dealt with her." Then he took his bag of donuts and left.

10   It was a scene I was ashamed to have witnessed.

---

1. bystanders: those who watch an event but don't get involved
2. bigotry: prejudice, intolerance

Author John Quiñones
on the set of his TV show
What Would You Do?

Moments later, in the parking lot with a camera crew in tow, I caught up with   11
this man as he climbed into his pickup truck.

"Excuse me, sir," I said. "My name is John Quiñones."   12

But before I could ask him a single question, he jumped out of his truck, jabbed   13
his finger in my face and snapped: "You're not an American."

That hit me hard.   14

I'm a native, sixth-generation American. But it's true I grew up in segregation,   15
in the barrio. I'd known where "my place" was, and that was on the west side of
San Antonio. The north side of the city, which was mostly white, was pretty much
forbidden to someone who looked like me. These were the unspoken rules of my
childhood, and now I was hearing them loud and clear.

After a short break, we reset the scene.   16

On cue, our Muslim actress approached the counter and asked to buy a sweet   17
roll. Again, the actor playing the bigoted man behind the counter refused to serve
her.

"How do I know you're not a terrorist?" he taunted her. "You're dressed like   18
one."

"Excuse me?" said the actress playing our Muslim.   19

"Look, take your jihad[3] back out to the parking lot. I've got to protect my cus-   20
tomers," the clerk said.

This time we noticed two young women customers—one of whom later   21
turned out to be Muslim, although her typical Texas clothing gave no indication
of this—who stopped in their tracks. They were staring, their mouths wide open,
incredulous.[4] Finally, one of them mustered the courage to speak up.

"You're really offensive," she practically shouted at the clerk.   22

---

3. jihad: Muslim war or holy war
4. incredulous: disbelieving

23   Her friend joined in: "You're disgusting."

24   They stood their ground and demanded to speak to the clerk's manager. Even though they'd never met the woman who was being abused, her cause was theirs.

25   Watching these women stand up for what they believed in made me proud to live in a country where people are willing to risk getting into a fight, or worse, to defend a stranger being bullied. The millions of viewers who tune in to watch *What Would You Do?* each week get a thrill from seeing everyday heroes like these women in action. And, as the anchor of the show, I get the same thrill.

"I found a display of bigotry as fresh as the coffee and pastries."

26   The confrontation in Waco wouldn't be my last encounter with intolerance and bigotry.

27   A year later, at a delicatessen in New Jersey, I myself jumped into the fray. As customers looked on I pretended to be a Mexican day laborer and, speaking in broken English, tried to order a sandwich. Again, the man behind the counter was an actor.

28   "Speak English or take your pesos down the road," he snapped.

29   "Por favor," I pleaded. "Café con un sandwich."

30   "We're building a wall to keep you people out," he shouted. "We don't serve illegals here."

31   Even though I knew it was all an act, the words cut through me like a knife. I asked the other customers for help. But each one turned away, giving me the cold shoulder.

32   "I don't speak Mexican," they said time and again. One customer not only agreed with our racist man behind the counter, but also told me if I didn't leave, he would throw me out of the deli himself or call the cops.

33   But then, just when I thought no one would step up against racism, the tide turned. All it took were the words of one compassionate customer: "He's a human being just like you and me," she said.

34   Immediately, the crowd joined in, angrily berating the racist proprietor. "This is America! We're a melting pot. Maybe you're the one who should leave!"

35   Finally, people with the courage to face down bigotry. It was as though someone had pulled the knife out.

36   If you ask me, that's what heroism is all about. Most people think it involves dramatic events and near superhuman feats of courage. I have found that this is not the case at all. There are so many problems and challenges in the world today and, as a TV journalist, I see more than my share. But lately, I find myself seeking out everyday heroes, people looking to make the world a better place. I think we're all searching for them, in some way or another.

37   And I find them wherever I go.

DISCUSSION AND WRITING QUESTIONS

1. Quiñones narrates the story of the Muslim woman being verbally abused before he reveals that the scene is a set-up for his TV program *What Would You Do?* (paragraphs 1–5). How does delaying this information make the introduction more powerful?

2. When Quiñones poses as a Mexican day laborer in a deli, he says the actor's racist words "cut through me like a knife" (paragraph 31). Why do these words hurt so much even though Quiñones knows this is an act? Does his experience reveal something about the power of hateful words?

3. In that scene, most customers first remain silent, but the "tide turned" after one customer spoke up (paragraph 33). Read about the definition of "bystander effect" (page 88 of this book). How does the bystander effect relate to this scene and others Quiñones describes? What is the antidote[5] for bystander effect?

TEACHING TIP

You might ask the class whether having experienced prejudice, abuse, or bullying makes a person more likely to become a "hero" later? Some students might wish to share personal experiences.

---

5. antidote: remedy or cure

4. In the last two paragraphs, the author defines heroism and heroes. What is his definition? How does the essay's title and last line relate to this idea? Does your definition of "hero" differ from Quiñones'?

WRITING ASSIGNMENTS

1. If you have watched the program *What Would You Do?*, describe your most memorable episode and what made it stand out. If you haven't seen the program, write about an episode that you think Quiñones should produce and explain why.
2. Write about an everyday hero you know. Is it a specific act of courage that makes this person stand out? Or does this person model a lifestyle that you find heroic? Support your main idea with details and specifics.
3. Experts say that prejudice is often rooted in ignorance or fear of a particular group of people. What is the best way to promote tolerance and respect for people who are different from ourselves? For ideas, you might explore <http://antibullyingprograms.org/> or <http://www.ncpc.org/topics/bullying/strategies/strategy-diversity-and-tolerance-education-in-schools>.

Mrs. Flowers

Maya Angelou

Maya Angelou (born Marguerite Johnson) is one of America's best-loved poets and the author of *I Know Why the Caged Bird Sings*. In this book, her life story, she tells of being raped when she was eight years old. Her response to the traumatic experience was to stop speaking. In this selection, Angelou describes the woman who eventually threw her a "life line."

For nearly a year, I sopped around the house, the Store, the school and the church, like an old biscuit, dirty and inedible. Then I met, or rather got to know, the lady who threw me my first life line. 1

Mrs. Bertha Flowers was the aristocrat of Black Stamps. She had the grace of control to appear warm in the coldest weather, and on the Arkansas summer days it seemed she had a private breeze which swirled around, cooling her. She was thin without the taut[1] look of wiry people, and her printed voile[2] dresses and flowered hats were as right for her as denim overalls for a farmer. She was our side's answer to the richest white woman in town. 2

Her skin was a rich black that would have peeled like a plum if snagged, but then no one would have thought of getting close enough to Mrs. Flowers to ruffle her dress, let alone snag her skin. She didn't encourage familiarity. She wore gloves too. 3

I don't think I ever saw Mrs. Flowers laugh, but she smiled often. A slow widening of her thin black lips to show even, small white teeth, then the slow effortless closing. When she chose to smile on me, I always wanted to thank her. The action was so graceful and inclusively benign.[3] 4

She was one of the few gentlewomen I have ever known and has remained throughout my life the measure of what a human being can be . . . 5

---

1. taut: tight, tense
2. voile: a light, semi-sheer fabric
3. benign: kind, gentle

6 One summer afternoon, sweet-milk fresh in my memory, she stopped at the Store to buy provisions. Another Negro woman of her health and age would have been expected to carry the paper sacks home in one hand, but Momma said, "Sister Flowers, I'll send Bailey up to your house with these things."

7 She smiled that slow dragging smile. "Thank you, Mrs. Henderson. I'd prefer Marguerite though." My name was beautiful when she said it. "I've been meaning to talk to her, anyway." They gave each other age-group looks.

8 Momma said, "Well, that's all right then. Sister, go and change your dress. You going to Sister Flowers's." . . .

9 There was a little path beside the rocky road, and Mrs. Flowers walked in front swinging her arms and picking her way over the stones.

10 She said, without turning her head, to me, "I hear you're doing very good school work, Marguerite, but that it's all written. The teachers report that they have trouble getting you to talk in class." We passed the triangular farm on our left, and the path widened to allow us to walk together. I hung back in the separate unasked and unanswerable questions.

11 "Come and walk along with me, Marguerite." I couldn't have refused even if I wanted to. She pronounced my name so nicely. Or more correctly, she spoke each word with such clarity that I was certain a foreigner who didn't understand English could have understood her.

12 "Now no one is going to make you talk—possibly no one can. But bear in mind, language is man's way of communicating with his fellow man and it is language alone which separates him from the lower animals." That was a totally new idea to me, and I would need time to think about it.

13 "Your grandmother says you read a lot. Every chance you get. That's good, but not good enough. Words mean more than what is set down on paper. It takes the human voice to infuse[4] them with the shades of deeper meaning."

14 I memorized the part about the human voice infusing words. It seemed so valid and poetic.

15 She said she was going to give me some books and that I not only must read them. I must read them aloud. She suggested that I try to make a sentence sound in as many different ways as possible.

16 "I'll accept no excuse if you return a book to me that has been badly handled." My imagination boggled at the punishment I would deserve if in fact I did abuse a book of Mrs. Flowers's. Death would be too kind and brief.

17 The odors in the house surprised me. Somehow I had never connected Mrs. Flowers with food or eating or any other common experience of common people. There must have been an outhouse, too, but my mind never recorded it.

18 The sweet scent of vanilla met us as she opened the door.

19 "I made tea cookies this morning. You see, I had planned to invite you for cookies and lemonade so we could have this little chat. The lemonade is in the icebox."

20 It followed that Mrs. Flowers would have ice on an ordinary day, when most families in our town bought ice late on Saturdays only a few times during the summer to be used in the wooden ice-cream freezers.

21 She took the bags from me and disappeared through the kitchen door. I looked around the room that I had never in my wildest fantasies imagined I would see. Browned photographs leered or threatened from the walls and the white, freshly done curtains pushed against themselves and against the wind. I wanted to gobble up the room entire and take it to Bailey, who would help me analyze and enjoy it.

22 "Have a seat, Marguerite. Over there by the table." She carried a platter covered with a tea towel. Although she warned that she hadn't tried her hand at bak-

---

4. infuse: to fill or penetrate

ing sweets for some time, I was certain that like everything else about her the cookies would be perfect.

They were flat round wafers, slightly browned on the edges and butter-yellow 23 in the center. With the cold lemonade they were sufficient for childhood's lifelong diet. Remembering my manners, I took nice little lady-like bites off the edges. She said she had made them expressly for me and that she had a few in the kitchen that I could take home to my brother. So I jammed one whole cake in my mouth and the rough crumbs scratched the insides of my jaws, and if I hadn't had to swallow, it would have been a dream come true.

As I ate she began the first of what we later called "my lessons in living." She 24 said that I must always be intolerant of ignorance but understanding of illiteracy. That some people, unable to go to school, were more educated and even more intelligent than college professors. She encouraged me to listen carefully to what country people called mother wit. That in those homely sayings was couched the collective[5] wisdom of generations.

"I was liked, and what a difference it made. I was respected not as Mrs. Henderson's grandchild or Bailey's sister but for just being Marguerite Johnson."

When I finished the cookies she brushed off the table and brought a thick, 25 small book from the bookcase. I had read *A Tale of Two Cities* and found it up to my standards as a romantic novel. She opened the first page and I heard poetry for the first time in my life.

"It was the best of times and the worst of times . . ." Her voice slid in and 26 curved down through and over the words. She was nearly singing. I wanted to look at the pages. Were they the same that I had read? Or were there notes, music, lined on the pages, as in a hymn book? Her sounds began cascading[6] gently. I knew from listening to a thousand preachers that she was nearing the end of her reading, and I hadn't really heard, heard to understand, a single word.

"How do you like that?" 27

It occurred to me that she expected a response. The sweet vanilla flavor was 28 still on my tongue and her reading was a wonder in my ears. I had to speak.

I said, "Yes ma'am." It was the least I could do, but it was the most also. 29

"There's one more thing. Take this book of poems and memorize one for me. 30 Next time you pay me a visit, I want you to recite."

I have tried often to search behind the sophistication of years for the enchant- 31 ment I so easily found in those gifts. The essence escapes but its aura[7] remains. To be allowed, no, invited, into the private lives of strangers, and to share their joys and fears, was a chance to exchange the Southern bitter wormwood[8] for . . . a hot cup of tea and milk with Oliver Twist.[9]

I was liked, and what a difference it made. I was respected not as Mrs. Hender- 32 son's grandchild or Bailey's sister but for just being Marguerite Johnson.

Childhood's logic never asks to be proved (all conclusions are absolute). I 33 didn't question why Mrs. Flowers had singled me out for attention, nor did it occur to me that Momma might have asked her to give me a little talking to. All I cared about was that she had made tea cookies for *me* and read to *me* from her favorite book. It was enough to prove that she liked me.

---

5. collective: gathered from a group
6. cascading: falling like a waterfall
7. aura: a special quality or air around something or someone
8. wormwood: something harsh or embittering
9. Oliver Twist: a character from a novel by Charles Dickens

DISCUSSION AND WRITING QUESTIONS

1. Angelou vividly describes Mrs. Flowers's appearance and style (paragraphs 2–5). What kind of woman is Mrs. Flowers? What words and details convey this impression?
2. What strategies does Mrs. Flowers use to reach out to Marguerite?
3. What does Marguerite's first "lesson in living" include (paragraph 24)? Do you think such a lesson could really help a young person live better or differently?
4. In paragraph 31, the author speaks of her enchantment at receiving gifts from Mrs. Flowers. Just what gifts did Mrs. Flowers give her? Which do you consider the most important gift?

WRITING ASSIGNMENTS

1. Has anyone ever thrown you a lifeline when you were in trouble? Describe the problem or hurt facing you and just what this person did to reach out. What "gifts" did he or she offer you (attention, advice, and so forth)? Were you able to receive them?

   If you prefer, write about a time when you helped someone else. What seemed to be weighing this person down? How were you able to help?
2. Mrs. Flowers read aloud so musically that Marguerite "heard poetry for the first time in [her] life." Has someone ever shared a love—of a sport, gardening, or history, for example—so strongly that you were changed? What happened and how were you changed?
3. Many people have trouble speaking up—in class, at social gatherings, even to one other person. Can you express your thoughts and feelings as freely as you would like in most situations? What opens you up, and what shuts you up?

A Day without Media: Heaven or Hell?

Scott Smith

Smith, Scott "An entire day without media: Heaven or hell?" Copyright © The Pueblo Chieftain, Colo. Adapted by permission of the author.

Could you survive 24 hours with no media at all? At the University of Maryland, 200 horrified college students were given this challenge. Newsman Scott Smith of the *Pueblo Chieftain* in Colorado reports in this article on the Maryland challenge, the results, and what our dependency on social media might mean about how we live and how we relate to each another.

1   Imagine a media-free day. No computer. No television. No cell phone. No car radio. No iPod. No newspapers or magazines. No texting. No Facebook. No e-mails. No instant messaging. No tweeting. Nada. Could you do it? Could you spend an entire day pondering your own thoughts, creating your own diversions[1] and interacting only with real people, face to face?

2   That was the recent challenge posed by the International Center for Media and the Public Agenda, which asked 200 journalism students at the University of Maryland to abstain[2] from using all media for 24 hours. After their unplugged day, the students blogged about their experiences, and the center compiled the results. The findings: No surprise. Most college students are flat-out hooked on their social-media security blankets. Wrote one student: "I clearly am addicted, and the dependency is sickening."

---

1. diversions: distractions, entertainments
2. abstain: *not* do something

"Most college students are flat-out hooked on their social media security blankets."

Wrote another: "Although I started the day feeling good, I noticed my mood started to change around noon. I started to feel isolated and lonely. . . . I felt like a person on a deserted island." And another: "Texting and IM-ing my friends gives me a constant feeling of comfort. When I did not have those two luxuries, I felt quite alone and secluded from my life." 3

Welcome to Generation Text (so christened by one of my creative co-workers, Jeff Tucker), a wave of young adults who go beyond tech-savvy. They're obsessed and enmeshed[3] and wired, plugged into an everyday life predicated on[4] a dizzying exchange of information (and misinformation, depending on the source) that ranges from mind-numbingly mundane[5] to truly profound. 4

The truth is that we live in a world ruled by speed, technology, and an insatiable quest for info. The faster you can text, the better. The quicker you can post your Facebook photos, the better. The sooner you can foist[6] your opinions upon the rest of the world, the better. 5

There are natural casualties to this lifestyle, however: An overemphasis on speed in the name of info-sharing makes it harder to assure accuracy, depth, and discernment.[7] I also think it makes it more difficult to stay grounded in reality and, ironically, actually makes us less connected with our fellow humans. 6

Personally, I mourn the continued erosion of genuine human interaction. The fact is, we have an entire generation that is more comfortable communicating via social-site gadgets than they are with flesh-and-blood people. You can call that "connecting" if you want, but in my universe, Facebook and texting and incessant[8] cell-phone chatter are not the same as authentic conversation. I mean, I love my iPod as much as the next guy, and I rely heavily on e-mail to connect with some friends, but I'd much rather hear live music or sit next to someone and gaze into their eyes—and experience their humanity—as we converse. 7

Ah, but I'm a tactile[9] creature. I'd also rather read a book while holding it in my hands than read it on a computer screen or e-reader; I'd rather give someone a kiss and a hug and a smile instead of typing in Xs and Os and :)s. And as far as an unplugged day goes, count me in. It sounds peaceful, alluring, and blissful. 8

DISCUSSION AND WRITING QUESTIONS

1. Why did the University of Maryland students have so much trouble giving up their devices for 24 hours (paragraphs 2 and 3)? Look up the definition of *addiction*. Are they really digital addicts? Would you say that you or your friends are addicted to your devices?

2. Do you agree with Smith that we are now "less connected with our fellow humans" (paragraph 6)? How would you define "authentic conversation" (paragraph 7)? Contrast what the author calls "chatter" with the authentic conversations you have with others. Can authentic conversations occur via Facebook, text, e-mail, or cell phone?

3. Many people who try to unplug seem to feel discomfort and even fear. What are they afraid of? If it's being alone, why is that frightening?

4. Reread the two concluding paragraphs. Does the author make important points here, or does he just *not* get it because he isn't a member of Generation Text? What are the benefits of being constantly plugged in?

TEACHING TIP

A stunning *Frontline* episode called "Digital Nation" examines the wired, distracted, multitasking lives of today's students and gaming-addicted Korean youth who attend deprogramming camp. This video prompts energetic discussion and writing.

---

3. enmeshed: caught
4. predicated on: based on
5. mundane: ordinary
6. foist: force, pass off as worthwhile
7. discernment: the use of careful judgment
8. incessant: nonstop
9. tactile: physical, using touch

WRITING ASSIGNMENTS

1. Take the challenge Smith describes in the first paragraph. Give up *all* your media and devices, completely, for 24 hours. Take detailed notes about your feelings, reactions, and any surprises. Then write a paper describing the experience and what you learned.

2. With a group, create a brief questionnaire and survey your classmates. How many devices does each one have and use regularly? Which one device is the most widely owned and used by your class? What do you think makes it so popular? Go over the results and then write a report summarizing your findings.

3. Plan a perfect, no-work weekend for yourself and your family or partner; the catch is that no one can use any tech devices (except transportation) for two days. You will sleep at home, but be creative in planning your days. Describe the weekend in detail—the short trips or rides, activities, restful times, games (but not video), meals. What might your family gain from this time together?

Another Road Hog with Too Much Oink

Dave Barry

"Another Road Hog with Too Much Oink", copyright © by Dave Barry, from *Dave Barry Is Not Taking This Sitting Down* by Dave Barry. Used by permission of Crown Publishers, a division of Random House, Inc., and the author.

Humorist Dave Barry is the author of more than two dozen books, but he admits that not one of them contains useful information. Until 2005, his Pulitzer–Prize winning humor column appeared in over 500 newspapers. In his spare time, Barry is a candidate for President of the United States. If elected, he promises to seek the death penalty for whoever made Americans install low-flow toilets. In the following essay, he takes on America's love of gigantic sport utility vehicles (SUVs).

1   If there's one thing this nation needs, it's bigger cars. That's why I'm excited that Ford is coming out with a new mound o' metal that will offer consumers even more total road-squatting mass than the current leader in the humongous[1]-car category, the popular Chevrolet Suburban Subdivision—the first passenger automobile designed to be, right off the assembly line, visible from the Moon.

2   I don't know what the new Ford will be called. Probably something like the "Ford Untamed Wilderness Adventure." In the TV commercials, it will be shown splashing through rivers, charging up rocky mountainsides, swinging on vines, diving off cliffs, racing through the surf, and fighting giant sharks hundreds of feet beneath the ocean surface—all the daredevil things that cars do in Sport Utility Vehicle Commercial World, where nobody ever drives on an actual road. In fact, the interstate highways in Sport Utility Vehicle Commercial World, having been abandoned by humans, are teeming[2] with deer, squirrels, birds, and other wildlife species that have fled from the forest to avoid being run over by nature seekers in multi-ton vehicles barreling through the underbrush at 50 miles per hour.

"In the real world, of course, nobody drives a sport utility vehicle in the forest, because the last thing you want is squirrels pooping on it."

3   In the real world, of course, nobody drives sport utility vehicles in the forest, because when you have paid upward of $40,000 for a transportation investment, the last thing you want is squirrels pooping on it. No, if you want a practical "off-road" vehicle, you get yourself a 1973 American Motors Gremlin, which combines the advantage of not being worth worrying about with the advantage of being so ugly that poisonous snakes flee from it in terror.

---

1. humongous: huge
2. teeming: filled

*"We're not certain why they disappeared, but archeologists speculate
that it may have had something to do with their size."*

In the real world, what people mainly do with their sport utility vehicles, as far as I can tell, is try to maneuver[3] them into and out of parking spaces. I base this statement on my local supermarket, where many of the upscale patrons drive Chevrolet Subdivisions. I've noticed that these people often purchase just a couple of items—maybe a bottle of diet water and a two-ounce package of low-fat dried carrot shreds—which they put into the back of their Subdivisions, which have approximately the same cargo capacity, in cubic feet, as Finland. This means there is plenty of room left over back there in case, on the way home, these people decide to pick up something else, such as a herd of bison.   4

Then comes the scary part: getting the Subdivision out of the parking space. This is a challenge, because the driver apparently cannot, while sitting in the driver's seat, see all the way to either end of the vehicle. I drive a compact car, and on a number of occasions I have found myself trapped behind a Subdivision backing directly toward me, its massive metal butt looming[4] high over my head, making me feel like a Tokyo pedestrian looking up at Godzilla.[5]   5

I've tried honking my horn, but the Subdivision drivers can't hear me, because they're always talking on cellular phones the size of Chiclets ("The Bigger Your Car, the Smaller Your Phone," that is their motto). I don't know who they're talking to. Maybe they're negotiating with their bison suppliers. Or maybe they're trying to contact somebody in the same area code as the rear ends of their cars, so they can find out what's going on back there. All I know is, I'm thinking of carrying marine flares, so I can fire them into the air as a warning to Subdivision drivers that they're about to run me over. Although frankly I'm not sure they'd care if they did. A big reason why they bought a sport utility vehicle is "safety," in the sense of, "you, personally, will be safe, although every now and then you may have to clean the remains of other motorists out of your wheel wells."   6

---

3. maneuver: move skillfully
4. looming: appearing to be huge and towering
5. Godzilla: a fictional monster that menaced cities in Japanese films

7   Anyway, now we have the new Ford, which will be *even larger* than the Subdivision, which I imagine means it will have separate decks for the various classes of passengers, and possibly, way up in front by the hood ornament, Leonardo DiCaprio showing Kate Winslet[6] how to fly. I can't wait until one of these babies wheels into my supermarket parking lot. Other motorists and pedestrians will try to flee in terror, but they'll be sucked in by the Ford's powerful gravitational field and become stuck to its massive sides like so many refrigerator magnets. They won't be noticed, however, by the Ford's driver, who will be busy whacking at the side of his or her head, trying to dislodge[7] his or her new cell phone, which is the size of a single grain of rice and has fallen deep into his or her ear canal.

8   And it will not stop there. This is America, darn it, and Chevrolet is not about to just sit by and watch Ford walk away with the coveted title of Least Sane Motor Vehicle. No, cars will keep getting bigger: I see a time, not too far from now, when upscale suburbanites will haul their overdue movies back to the video-rental store in full-size, 18-wheel tractor-trailers with names like The Vagabond.[8] It will be a proud time for all Americans, a time for us to cheer for our country. We should cheer loud, because we'll be hard to hear, inside the wheel wells.

DISCUSSION AND WRITING QUESTIONS

1. What is Barry's point of view about huge sport utility vehicles (paragraph 1)? What lines tell you this? Barry often exaggerates to get a laugh and to make a point. Can you point to examples of this technique?
2. What passages or details in the essay do you find particularly funny? Look for experiences to which you relate, vivid word use, exaggerations, or lines that create humorous mental pictures.
3. In paragraph 6, Barry says that safety is a big reason why people claim to buy SUVs. Do you agree with their reasoning? What are some other reasons why so many Americans choose to drive giant vehicles?
4. Barry ends his essay with a prediction. What does he predict will soon happen as a consequence, or result, of the trend toward larger vehicles? Although the essay is humorous, it makes a serious point. Does the last line underscore this point?

WRITING ASSIGNMENTS

1. Fill in the blank in this sentence: "If there's one thing this nation needs, it's _____ ." Then take a stand, perhaps humorous, as Barry has, about something else Americans crave: fancy cell phones, brand-name clothing, even plastic surgery. Or try a serious approach, arguing for more youth centers, "hybrid" automobiles, or some other goal.
2. Write a response to Dave Barry's criticisms of SUVs and their owners. Defend these vehicles by giving reasons why people *should* drive them. Take a humorous or serious approach, as you wish.
3. Barry suggests that we Americans like our possessions big. What are some other things, besides vehicles, that we continue to super-size? What do you think this trend reveals about Americans?

---

6. Leonardo DiCaprio, Kate Winslet: stars of the film *Titanic*
7. dislodge: remove something stuck
8. vagabond: a wandering person

Buy Yourself Less Stuff

MP Dunleavey

From Dunleavey, MP, Money Can Buy Happiness: How to Spend to Get the Life You Want. Reprinted by permission of the author.

The secret to happiness may not be having more money but knowing how to spend the money you've got. According to personal finance expert and author MP Dunleavey, we can learn to better manage our money and our happiness. But first we need to understand what forces influence our spending decisions and what we really want.

"No wonder Americans are experiencing an epidemic of debt and bankruptcy."

1   Nearly forty years ago, Richard Easterlin, now an economist at the University of Southern California, began examining people's material desires and how they felt once they achieved those goals. Easterlin reviewed surveys of thousands of Americans, who said they believed the good life consisted of owning certain things—like having a nice car, pool, vacation home, and so on. While they themselves had only 1.7 of the desired items, they felt that owning 4.4. (on average) would constitute a satisfactory life.

2   That seems reasonable. You don't quite have all the things you want, but you're sure that when you acquire them, you'll be satisfied. But when Easterlin then studied people's responses to the same questions many years later, he found that although on average people now owned 3.1 of the desired goods, now they believed they wouldn't achieve the so-called good life until they owned 5.6 of them.

3   You can see how the underlying itch to acquire more (and more) turns into a never-ending treadmill of consumption—not because the things we want are bad, but because we attach to them an impossible outcome: that certain possessions can and will increase our happiness.

4   The confounding[1] factor is that owning and buying stuff actually is fun. It's a normal, natural part of life—one of the perks of having to spend your allotted time on planet earth. But a problem unfolds when the momentary kick fades, and your natural instinct is to want to achieve that feel-good state again somehow.

5   So you strive for the next thing, in the belief that maybe if you get more bang for your buck, this time it will last. Unfortunately, a buck can buy only so much bang, and very quickly you're caught on what researchers have dubbed the "hedonic[2] treadmill," the ceaseless quest for *moremoremore* that drives our lives, dominates our thoughts, and erodes our quality of life.

The Grass Is Always Greener

6   Why? Because people have an astonishing ability to adapt to almost any circumstance, positive or negative, with little change in our overall sense of well-being. Even studies of cancer patients and paraplegics[3] have shown that people whom most of us would imagine to be depressed or suffering actually report being about as happy as healthy folks—because they've adapted to their lives. To be sure, a calamity like a sudden death, divorce, or job loss can be traumatic and isn't something you adjust to quickly at all. But the bulk of human experiences, *especially when it comes to most monetary or material gains*, have a surprisingly short-lived effect on how happy you are.

---

1. confounding: confusing
2. hedonic: pleasure-seeking
3. paraplegics: people paralyzed from the waist down

Materialism and Your Neighbor

7　We are all vulnerable to the financial and material influences of the environment in which we live—never mind the pervasive power of media and advertising. But as much as you want to believe you're in charge of your own behavior, it pays to be aware of the impact that others' behavior may have on your own "investment" decisions, whether you know it or not.

8　　This was captured in an article I read about the phenomenon of automaticity[4]—the fascinating and depressing human tendency to imitate what's going on around us. One study found that when people were told to complete a task next to an experimenter who, for example, often rubbed her face, subjects likewise tended to rub their faces, even though afterward they had no idea that the experimenter's fidgeting had been "contagious." Another study found that when people were merely shown a series of words associated with being elderly, they behaved in a more elderly manner (i.e., walked slower, were more forgetful), again, without realizing they had succumbed to a series of covert directions, if you will.

9　　It's not hard to imagine, then, the impact on your own financial desires when a friend spends twenty minutes relating her latest shopping extravaganza, describing her new Bose stereo, or has you take a spin in her cute new customized, fully loaded Mini Cooper.

Inflation of Our Expectations

10　So although it may seem obvious that buying less stuff will provide you with extra resources to invest in a happier way of life, every day you have to fend off a series of stealth[5] assaults on your financial sanity—including the steady inflation of your own expectations for what a so-called "normal" or "average" life consists of.

11　　Witness the average size of a new single-family home. In the early 1970s, it was 1,500 square feet. As of early 2005 the average home size had grown to 2,400 square feet—and with it, people's expectations of how big an "average" home should be as well as which amenities should come with it, says Gopal Ahluwalia, vice president of research for the National Association of Home Builders.

12　　What was once considered upscale is now the "new normal" for homeowners today, Ahluwalia says, from his and hers walk-in closets in the master bedroom to kitchen islands with cooktops to three-car garages. (People don't want a three-car garage because they have three cars, he added, but because they want to make sure they have enough storage for all their excess stuff.)

13　　Nor have home sizes increased because people have bigger families. In the last thirty-five years, Ahluwalia says, the average family size declined to 2.11 people from 3.58.

14　　That hasn't stopped people from spending a lot more money for an expanded way of life—whether or not they can afford it. No wonder Americans are experiencing an epidemic of debt and bankruptcy, the likes of which has never been seen before.

If Only Bigger Was Always Better

15　How do you combat the multitude of forces that influence how you spend your money and live your life? The first step is to become better acquainted with the joys of "inconspicuous consumption."

---

4. automaticity: the unconscious impulse to copy the behavior of those near us
5. stealth: secret, hidden

Inconspicuous consumption[6] doesn't get a lot of airtime. You can't get it on 16
sale at Kmart: Walmart doesn't carry big tubs of it at a discount. The less-tangible[7]
pleasures in life rarely have the same wow power as things, even though they are
more deeply satisfying. The core assets [of happiness][8] are all based on inconspicuous consumption—spending less on stuff and more on life.

Exercise: Your Money and/or Your Life

To illustrate the contrast between conspicuous material desires and inconspicu- 17
ous ones, Cornell economist Robert Frank created a series of thought experiments
(below). The questions are based on his model, which you can find in his excellent
book about the escalating insanity of materialism, *Luxury Fever.* There are no right
answers—just read each one and think about it.

1. If you could live in a 4,000-square-foot home and have one week of vacation a 18
   year, or live in a 2,000-square-foot home and have three weeks' vacation, which
   would you choose?
2. If you could have a job that paid $200,000 a year, but you could only see your
   friends once a month, vs. a job that paid $100,000 and you could see your friends
   every week—which would you choose?
3. If you could buy a new 3,000-square-foot house for $400,000 (incurring a hefty
   mortgage) or an older home of the same size that would require some work for
   $200,000 (and more affordable monthly payments), which would you choose?
4. If you could land a job at the top of your profession, but you got to see your
   children for only a handful of hours a week, vs. keeping a job with less prestige,
   but which gave you a flexible schedule—which would you choose?

   I love these brain twisters because they're a potent reminder that many of 19
the assumptions we all live with—that the bigger house or better job is always
the more desirable choice—may not be deep down what we want at all. In fact,
it would be wise to consider whether choosing the alternatives might be the high
road to a much more satisfying quality of life.

DISCUSSION AND WRITING QUESTIONS

1. Dunleavey says that the problem with the things we want is not the things
   themselves but our belief that they will bring us happiness (paragraph 3). Is she
   right? Have you ever wanted something badly and then gotten it? Did it make
   you happy? For how long?
2. In paragraphs 8 and 9, Dunleavey describes "automaticity," the human impulse
   to copy what we see around us. Does this explain why people buy fad products
   or follow the crowd? Do you see examples of such copying behavior in the lives
   of your peers, friends, or relatives? In your own life?
3. What does Dunleavey mean by "spending less on stuff and more on life" and by
   "core assets of happiness" (paragraph 16 and footnote)? List as many examples
   as you can of your and your loved ones' core assets of happiness.
4. In a small group, choose one of the four thought experiments at the end of
   the article and discuss that choice. Which alternative would you choose (for
   instance, the 4,000-square-foot or 2,000-square-foot home) and why? Weigh and
   explore the plusses and minuses of each choice.

---

6. Inconspicuous consumption: ways of spending our time and money that increase
   happiness, as opposed to conspicuous or "show-off" spending
7. tangible: touchable, material
8. "core assets of happiness:" things that bring more lasting happiness like friends,
   health, fun, spending time wisely, and giving to others

WRITING ASSIGNMENTS

1. Choose one of the four thought experiments at the end of the article, under "Exercise: Your Money and/or Your Life." What choice would you make and why? Give specific examples and details to support your answer.
2. In her books and blogs about the "Not So Big House," Sarah Susanka argues we should downsize American homes. Families are happier living in smaller spaces, she says, because small rooms feel cozier, children learn to share, and adults and children communicate more often. Consider your living situation now or growing up. Do you agree or disagree with her ideas?
3. Define happiness for you and/or your family. Give detailed examples. Do you think your idea of happiness is too connected to the "never-ending treadmill" of buying or wanting stuff? Or do other kinds of low-cost or no-cost experiences bring you happiness?

Stuff

Richard Rodriguez

Do you—like many Americans—own a lot of stuff? Do the things you buy bring brief or lasting pleasure? San Francisco writer Richard Rodriguez wonders whether our relationship to material possessions sets us up for disappointment. Rodriguez is an editor at the *Pacific News* service; he has authored three books and numerous essays and articles.

1   I come often to this huge building to do much of my shopping. It's called Costco. There are warehouse stores like this all over the country where you can buy most anything you need and you buy it in bulk, cheap.

2   A revolution is going on in American shopping habits. Two generations ago Americans went to their corner store where everyone knew the name of the man behind the counter and where toward the end of the month our grandmothers would ask to charge the milk and the bread. And then the suburbs created the supermarket with its Muzak[1] and its wide aisles and its 20 varieties of breakfast cereal. Now we don't go to the corner drugstore. Nor do we shop at a small nursery run by the lady who knows all about roses. We shop at places with names like Drug Barn and Plant World and Shoe Universe.

3   Every choice is available to us, and the prices are low, but no one knows your name and there isn't even Muzak. It's wonderful coming here to Costco. The well-to-do shop here along with immigrant families. Everyone's basket is full. You don't get a bottle of mineral water; you buy a case. You don't get a roll of toilet paper; you get a gigantic package that will last most families several months. You can buy tires at Costco, as well as Pampers and bananas. So people buy and buy and buy. And, yet, despite all the buying there is something oddly unmaterialistic about shopping in places plain as a warehouse.

4   We Americans often criticize ourselves for being materialistic. In fact, we take little pleasure in things, preferring to fill our lives with stuff. Only rarely do we dare a materialism that delights in the sensuality of the material world. In the 1950s, for example, we gave the world wonderful, wide-bodied cars with lots of

---

1. Muzak: the name for easy-listening or "elevator" music played in retail stores and other companies

A family from Bhutan and
all its possessions

*"We end up
surrounded by
stuff and regret."*

chrome and fins like angels—the rare American instance of the materialism of the senses. We leave it, normally, to other cultures to teach us about materialism.

I remember years ago in London a friend of mine urging me to go into Fort- 5
num and Mason's, the fancy food store, go in and buy just one piece of chocolate, he said, and think about that chocolate all day, and when you eat it tonight, eat it slowly, very slowly.

Americans don't eat slowly. We taught the world how to eat on the run, and 6
we treasure food, convenience food, that doesn't take much thinking about, which is why in the end we don't have very much to say about the smell of a piece of chocolate.

To this day I remember the weight and the smells of the first books I ever 7
owned. I can still remember the texture of paper in the first novel I ever got from the library. Now we can order our books on the Internet without first holding them in our hands or fingering the paper. Now Americans watch TV and order jewelry or dolls or whatever on the 24-hour shopping channels. People buy from catalogs without first trying the sweater on and testing its color against their skin.

There are no windows at Costco. 8

In an earlier, more sweetly materialistic America, our parents used to win- 9
dow shop. People would stop on a busy street, peer at the mannequins in the shop windows. Here in San Francisco there are still downtown department stores where one can see elaborate window displays, but who has the time to window shop?

Despite the many dollars we spend, I think we are less materialistic now than 10
at any time in our history. We are not much interested in the shape of an orange or the weight of a book, or the dark scent of a chocolate. We buy appliances online, and we throw them away when they no longer work. Nothing gets repaired in America. Nothing we own grows old. We buy in bulk. We are surrounded by choices. There is little we desire. We end up surrounded by stuff and regret. We take the huge bag of chocolates home, and we end up eating too many.

DISCUSSION AND WRITING QUESTIONS

1. Why does Rodriguez begin his essay with the example about shopping at Costco? How do stores like Costco help prove his point about Americans and material things?
2. Do you agree with Rodriguez that other cultures can teach Americans about healthy materialism? What example does he provide as evidence? Can you think of other examples?
3. In your opinion, is it good or bad to be surrounded by too many choices? What are the advantages of having many choices? What are the advantages of having few choices?
4. In his famous poem "The World Is Too Much with Us," English poet William Wordsworth wrote that "getting and spending, we lay waste our powers." In other words, we squander our energy on making money and spending it. Do you agree? If so, what might humans be able to accomplish if we weren't spending so much time and effort on working and buying?

WRITING ASSIGNMENTS

1. Describe a time when you immersed yourself in and truly savored a specific sensual experience—a moonlit swim, a delicious meal, a slow stroll down your favorite street, or the like. Describe this experience, including details about what you saw, smelled, tasted, touched, and heard.
2. Which of your possessions are crucial to your happiness? What things do you own now that you could live without? What possessions do you lack that you believe will make you happier?
3. In 1993, photographer Peter Menzel asked "statistically average" families in different countries to pose in front of their houses with every possession they owned. In a group with four of five classmates, carefully observe and discuss the photo on page 459 of a family and all its possessions. From this family's home, location, and possessions, can you make any guesses about its values, daily life, or priorities? Is this family like or different from families you know?

The Gift

Courtland Milloy

Help sometimes comes from unexpected places. This newspaper story describes the generosity of a friend whose gift saved someone's life—and baffled most people who knew him. As you read, ask yourself how you would have acted in his place.

1   When Jermaine Washington entered the barbershop, heads turned and clippers fell silent. Customers waved and nodded, out of sheer respect. With his hands in the pockets of his knee-length, black leather coat, Washington acknowledged them with a faint smile and quietly took a seat.

2   "You know who that is?" barber Anthony Clyburn asked in a tone reserved for the most awesome neighborhood characters, such as ball players and ex-cons.

3   A year and a half ago, Washington did something that still amazes those who know him. He became a kidney donor, giving a vital organ to a woman he described as "just a friend."

"They had a platonic[1] relationship," said Clyburn, who works at Jake's Barber Shop in Northeast Washington. "I could see maybe giving one to my mother, but just a girl I know? I don't think so." 4

Washington, who is 25, met Michelle Stevens six years ago when they worked for the D.C. Department of Employment Services. They used to have lunch together in the department cafeteria and chitchat on the telephone during their breaks. 5

> *"I had been on the kidney donor waiting list for 12 months and I had lost all hope. One day, I just called to cry on his shoulder."*

"It was nothing serious, romance-wise," said Stevens, who is 23. "He was somebody I could talk to. I had been on the kidney donor waiting list for 12 months and I had lost all hope. One day, I just called to cry on his shoulder." 6

Stevens told Washington how depressing it was to spend three days a week, three hours a day, on a kidney dialysis machine.[2] She said she suffered from chronic fatigue and blackouts and was losing her balance and her sight. He could already see that she had lost her smile. 7

"I saw my friend dying before my eyes," Washington recalled. "What was I supposed to do? Sit back and watch her die?" 8

Stevens's mother was found to be suffering from hypertension[3] and was ineligible to donate a kidney. Her 14-year-old sister offered to become a donor, but doctors concluded that she was too young. 9

Stevens's two brothers, 25 and 31, would most likely have made ideal donors because of their relatively young ages and status as family members. But both of them said no. 10

So did Stevens's boyfriend, who gave her two diamond rings with his apology. 11

"I understood," Stevens said. "They said they loved me very much, but they were just too afraid." 12

Joyce Washington, Jermaine's mother, was not exactly in favor of the idea, either. But after being convinced that her son was not being coerced,[4] she supported his decision. 13

The transplant operation took four hours. It occurred in April 1991, and began with a painful X-ray procedure in which doctors inserted a metal rod into Washington's kidney and shot it with red dye. An incision nearly 20 inches long was made from his groin to the back of his shoulder. After the surgery he remained hospitalized for five days. 14

Today, both Stevens and Washington are fully recovered. Stevens, a graduate of Eastern High School, is studying medicine at the National Educational Center. Washington still works for D.C. Employment Services as a job counselor. 15

"I jog and work out with weights," Washington said. "Boxing and football are out, but I never played those anyway." 16

A spokesman for Washington Hospital Center said the Washington-to-Stevens gift was the hospital's first "friend-to-friend" transplant. Usually, it's wife to husband, or parent to child. But there is a shortage of even those kinds of transplants. Today, more than 300 patients are in need of kidneys in the Washington area. 17

"A woman came up to me in a movie line not long ago and hugged me," Washington said. "She thanked me for doing what I did because no one had come forth when her daughter needed a kidney, and the child died." 18

About twice a month, Stevens and Washington get together for what they call a gratitude lunch. Since the operation, she has broken up with her boyfriend. Seven months ago, Washington got a girlfriend. Despite occasional pressure by friends, a romantic relationship is not what they want. 19

---

1. platonic: nonromantic
2. kidney dialysis machine: a machine that filters waste material from the blood when the kidneys fail
3. hypertension: high blood pressure
4. coerced: pressured

20   "We are thankful for the beautiful relationship that we have," Stevens said. "We don't want to mess up a good thing."

21   To this day, people wonder why Washington did it. To some of the men gathered at Jake's Barber Shop not long ago, Washington's heroics were cause for questions about his sanity. Surely he could not have been in his right mind, they said.

22   One customer asked Washington where he had found the courage to give away a kidney. His answer quelled[5] most skeptics[6] and inspired even more awe.

23   "I prayed for it," Washington replied. "I asked God for guidance and that's what I got."

DISCUSSION AND WRITING QUESTIONS

1. Long after Jermaine Washington donated a kidney to Michelle Stevens, his friends were still amazed by what he did. Why did they find his action so surprising?

2. Washington says, "What was I supposed to do? Sit back and watch her die?" (paragraph 8). Yet Stevens's brothers and her boyfriend did not offer to donate a kidney. Do you blame them? Do you understand them?

3. In what ways has Stevens's life changed because of Washington's gift? Consider her physical status, her social life, her choice of profession, her "gratitude lunches" with Washington, and so on.

4. According to Washington, where did he find the courage to donate a kidney? How did his action affect his standing in the community? How did it affect other aspects of his life?

WRITING ASSIGNMENTS

1. Have you ever been unusually generous—or do you know someone who was? Describe that act of generosity. Why did you—or the other person—do it? How did your friends or family react?

2. Do you have or does anyone you know have a serious medical condition? Describe the situation. How do or how can friends help? Can strangers help in any way?

3. Stevens and Washington do not have or want a romantic relationship. "We don't want to mess up a good thing," Stevens says (paragraph 20). Does romance "mess things up"? Write about a time when a relationship changed—either for better or for worse—because romance entered the picture.

Why Chinese Mothers Are Superior

Amy Chua

Amy Chua, a professor at Yale Law School, caused a national uproar when she published this *Wall Street Journal* article in 2011, describing how she raised two daughters to be successful adults. Her parenting methods were strict, punishing, and, she claimed, traditionally Chinese. Many American parents were outraged at her methods, and many Chinese accused her of selling cartoon stereotypes. Chua's "experiment" raises many questions about parenting, childhood, and "success" itself.

---

5. quelled: quieted
6. skeptics: people who doubt or question

A lot of people wonder how Chinese parents raise such stereotypically successful kids. They wonder what these parents do to produce so many math whizzes and music prodigies,[1] what it's like inside the family, and whether they could do it too. Well, I can tell them, because I've done it. Here are some things my daughters, Sophia and Louisa, were never allowed to do:

- attend a sleepover
- have a playdate
- be in a school play
- complain about not being in a school play
- watch TV or play computer games
- choose their own extracurricular activities
- get any grade less than an A
- not be the No. 1 student in every subject except gym and drama
- play any instrument other than the piano or violin
- not play the piano or violin.

I'm using the term "Chinese mother" loosely. I know some Korean, Indian, Jamaican, Irish, and Ghanaian parents who qualify too. Conversely, I know some mothers of Chinese heritage, almost always born in the West, who are not Chinese mothers, by choice or otherwise. I'm also using the term "Western parents" loosely. Western parents come in all varieties.

All the same, even when Western parents think they're being strict, they usually don't come close to being Chinese mothers. For example, my Western friends who consider themselves strict make their children practice their instruments 30 minutes every day. An hour at most. For a Chinese mother, the first hour is the easy part. It's hours two and three that get tough.

Despite our squeamishness[2] about cultural stereotypes, there are tons of studies out there showing marked and quantifiable[3] differences between Chinese and Westerners when it comes to parenting. In one study of 50 Western American mothers and 48 Chinese immigrant mothers, almost 70% of the Western mothers said either that "stressing academic success is not good for children" or that "parents need to foster the idea that learning is fun." By contrast, roughly 0% of the Chinese mothers felt the same way. Instead, the vast majority of the Chinese mothers said that they believe their children can be "the best" students, that "academic achievement reflects successful parenting," and that if children did not excel at school then there was "a problem" and parents "were not doing their job." Other studies indicate that compared to Western parents, Chinese parents spend approximately 10 times as long every day drilling academic activities with their children. By contrast, Western kids are more likely to participate in sports teams.

What Chinese parents understand is that nothing is fun until you're good at it. To get good at anything you have to work, and children on their own never want to work, which is why it is crucial to override their preferences. This often requires fortitude[4] on the part of the parents because the child will resist; things are always hardest at the beginning, which is where Western parents tend to give up. But if done properly, the Chinese strategy produces a virtuous circle.[5] Tenacious[6] practice, practice, practice is crucial for excellence; rote repetition is underrated in America. Once a child starts to excel at something—whether it's math, piano, pitching, or ballet—he or she gets praise, admiration, and satisfaction. This builds confidence and makes the once not-fun activity fun. This in turn makes it easier for the parent to get the child to work even more.

---

1. prodigies: people with exceptional skills or talents
2. squeamishness: tendency to be easily disgusted
3. quantifiable: able to be converted into numbers
4. fortitude: strength of mind
5. virtuous circle: good results create more practice
6. tenacious: stubborn

***

7   The fact is that Chinese parents can do things that would seem unimaginable—even legally actionable—to Westerners. Chinese mothers can say to their daughters, "Hey fatty—lose some weight." By contrast, Western parents have to tiptoe around the issue, talking in terms of "health" and never ever mentioning the f-word, and their kids still end up in therapy for eating disorders and negative self-image.

8   I've thought long and hard about how Chinese parents can get away with what they do. I think there are three big differences between the Chinese and Western parental mind-sets.

> *"If a child comes home with an A-minus, the Chinese mother will gasp in horror and ask what went wrong."*

9   First, I've noticed that Western parents are extremely anxious about their children's self-esteem. They worry about how their children will feel if they fail at something, and they constantly try to reassure their children about how good they are notwithstanding[7] a mediocre performance on a test or at a recital. In other words, Western parents are concerned about their children's psyches.[8] Chinese parents aren't. They assume strength, not fragility, and as a result they behave very differently.

10.   For example, if a child comes home with an A-minus on a test, a Western parent will most likely praise the child. The Chinese mother will gasp in horror and ask what went wrong. If the child comes home with a B on the test, some Western parents will still praise the child. Other Western parents will sit their child down and express disapproval, but they will be careful not to make their child feel inadequate or insecure, and they will not call their child "stupid," "worthless," or "a disgrace." Privately, the Western parents may worry that their child does not test well or have aptitude[9] in the subject or that there is something wrong with the curriculum and possibly the whole school. If the child's grades do not improve, they may eventually schedule a meeting with the school principal to challenge the way the subject is being taught or to call into question the teacher's credentials.

11   If a Chinese child gets a B—which would never happen—there would first be a screaming, hair-tearing explosion. The devastated Chinese mother would then get dozens, maybe hundreds of practice tests and work through them with her child for as long as it takes to get the grade up to an A.

12   Chinese parents demand perfect grades because they believe that their child can get them. If their child doesn't get them, the Chinese parent assumes it's because the child didn't work hard enough. That's why the solution to substandard performance is always to excoriate,[10] punish, and shame the child. The Chinese parent believes that their child will be strong enough to take the shaming and to improve from it. (And when Chinese kids do excel, there is plenty of ego-inflating parental praise lavished in the privacy of the home.)

13   Second, Chinese parents believe that their kids owe them everything. The reason for this is a little unclear, but it's probably a combination of Confucian filial piety[11] and the fact that the parents have sacrificed and done so much for their children. (And it's true that Chinese mothers get in the trenches, putting in long grueling hours personally tutoring, training, interrogating, and spying on their kids.) Anyway, the understanding is that Chinese children must spend their lives repaying their parents by obeying them and making them proud.

14   By contrast, I don't think most Westerners have the same view of children being permanently indebted to their parents. My husband, Jed, actually has the

---

7. notwithstanding: in spite of
8. psyches: inner lives and feelings
9. aptitude: natural ability
10. excoriate: to berate viciously, to remove the skin of
11. Confucian filial piety: extreme loyalty children owe their parents, according to Chinese philosopher Confucius

opposite view. "Children don't choose their parents," he once said to me. "They don't even choose to be born. It's parents who foist[12] life on their kids, so it's the parents' responsibility to provide for them. Kids don't owe their parents anything. Their duty will be to their own kids." This strikes me as a terrible deal for the Western parent.

Third, Chinese parents believe that they know what is best for their children and therefore override all of their children's own desires and preferences. That's why Chinese daughters can't have boyfriends in high school and why Chinese kids can't go to sleepaway camp. It's also why no Chinese kid would ever dare say to their mother, "I got a part in the school play! I'm Villager Number Six. I'll have to stay after school for rehearsal every day from 3:00 to 7:00, and I'll also need a ride on weekends." God help any Chinese kid who tried that one.

15

Don't get me wrong: It's not that Chinese parents don't care about their children. Just the opposite. They would give up anything for their children. It's just an entirely different parenting model.

16

Here's a story in favor of coercion,[13] Chinese-style. Lulu was about 7, still playing two instruments, and working on a piano piece called "The Little White Donkey" by the French composer Jacques Ibert. The piece is really cute—you can just imagine a little donkey ambling along a country road with its master—but it's also incredibly difficult for young players because the two hands have to keep schizophrenically[14] different rhythms.

17

Lulu couldn't do it. We worked on it nonstop for a week, drilling each of her hands separately, over and over. But whenever we tried putting the hands together, one always morphed[15] into the other, and everything fell apart. Finally, the day before her lesson, Lulu announced in exasperation that she was giving up and stomped off.

18

"Get back to the piano now," I ordered.

19

"You can't make me."

20

"Oh yes, I can."

21

Back at the piano, Lulu made me pay. She punched, thrashed, and kicked. She grabbed the music score and tore it to shreds. I taped the score back together and encased it in a plastic shield so that it could never be destroyed again. Then I hauled Lulu's dollhouse to the car and told her I'd donate it to the Salvation Army piece by piece if she didn't have "The Little White Donkey" perfect by the next day. When Lulu said, "I thought you were going to the Salvation Army, why are you still here?" I threatened her with no lunch, no dinner, no Christmas or Hanukkah presents, no birthday parties for two, three, four years. When she still kept playing it wrong, I told her she was purposely working herself into a frenzy because she was secretly afraid she couldn't do it. I told her to stop being lazy, cowardly, self-indulgent,[16] and pathetic.

22

Jed took me aside. He told me to stop insulting Lulu—which I wasn't even doing, I was just motivating her—and that he didn't think threatening Lulu was helpful. Also, he said, maybe Lulu really just couldn't do the technique—perhaps she didn't have the coordination yet—had I considered that possibility?

23

"You just don't believe in her," I accused.

24

"That's ridiculous," Jed said scornfully. "Of course I do."

25

"Sophia could play the piece when she was this age."

26

"But Lulu and Sophia are different people," Jed pointed out.

27

---

12. foist: force upon
13. coercion: forcing with pressure or threats
14. schizophrenically: pulled in different directions
15. morphed: changed
16. self-indulgent: too easily giving into one's desires

28   "Oh no, not this," I said, rolling my eyes. "Everyone is special in their special own way," I mimicked sarcastically. "Even losers are special in their own special way. Well don't worry, you don't have to lift a finger. I'm willing to put in as long as it takes, and I'm happy to be the one hated. And you can be the one they adore because you make them pancakes and take them to Yankees games."

29   I rolled up my sleeves and went back to Lulu. I used every weapon and tactic I could think of. We worked right through dinner into the night, and I wouldn't let Lulu get up, not for water, not even to go to the bathroom. The house became a war zone, and I lost my voice yelling, but still there seemed to be only negative progress, and even I began to have doubts.

30   Then, out of the blue, Lulu did it. Her hands suddenly came together—her right and left hands each doing their own imperturbable[17] thing—just like that.

31   Lulu realized it the same time I did. I held my breath. She tried it tentatively again. Then she played it more confidently and faster, and still the rhythm held. A moment later, she was beaming.

32   "Mommy, look—it's easy!" After that, she wanted to play the piece over and over and wouldn't leave the piano. That night, she came to sleep in my bed, and we snuggled and hugged, cracking each other up. When she performed "The Little White Donkey" at a recital a few weeks later, parents came up to me and said, "What a perfect piece for Lulu—it's so spunky and so *her*."

33   Even Jed gave me credit for that one. Western parents worry a lot about their children's self-esteem. But as a parent, one of the worst things you can do for your child's self-esteem is to let them give up. On the flip side, there's nothing better for building confidence than learning you can do something you thought you couldn't.

***

34   Western parents try to respect their children's individuality, encouraging them to pursue their true passions, supporting their choices, and providing positive reinforcement and a nurturing environment. By contrast, the Chinese believe that the best way to protect their children is by preparing them for the future, letting them see what they're capable of, and arming them with skills, work habits, and inner confidence that no one can ever take away.

DISCUSSION AND WRITING QUESTIONS

TEACHING TIP

Especially if some of your students are Chinese, ask the class whether Chua's narrow definitions of Chinese and Western parenting styles are mere cartoon stereotypes. If yes, are these potentially damaging to parents on both sides?

1. How did you react to Chua's list of "nevers" at the beginning of her essay? Do any of her parenting methods upset you? Which ones and why? Do any spark your interest or admiration?

2. Chua says an important difference between Chinese and Western parents is that the latter worry too much about their children's self-esteem (paragraph 9). Chua is not the first to criticize the rise of the "everyone gets a trophy" culture. What might be some problems with raising children to believe that everything they do is excellent?

3. "Nothing is fun until you're good at it," the author writes (paragraph 6). Do you agree? Have you ever tried over and over to learn something, despairing, raging, and then finally learned it? What did you learn? What effect did this experience have on you? When is the right time to give up on an activity and to try something new?

4. When a child gets a bad grade, American parents often blame the school, claims the author, while Chinese parents blame (and berate) the child and their own parenting. Do American parents over-rely on the schools to make their kids successful? How much should a parent be involved in a child's education?

---

17. imperturbable: calm, unexcited

WRITING ASSIGNMENTS

1. Chua opens her article with a list of activities her daughters were never allowed to do in childhood. Do you agree with any of her choices? Choose one item from this list and explain why you would (or would not) let your child engage in this activity. Use details to support your view.
2. Chinese mothers are "superior," Chua's title announces. She believes a good parent is one who will do anything to create a high-achieving child. In your view, what goals, attitudes, and actions define a "good parent"?
3. Scientists who study elite performers, such as world-class pianists and ball players, have discovered that it takes about 10,000 hours of practice to reach the top of one's field. That is about two hours of daily practice for ten years. Does this research justify Chua's rules around long piano practice and her daughter's temporary unhappiness?

A Day in the Life of an Emergency Room Nurse

Beve Stevenson, RN, BN

Beve Stevenson, "A Day in the Life of an ER Nurse," Alberta RN. Adapted by permission of the author. http://www.beeproductions.ca/articles/Dayinthelife.pdf; Other writings: http://beeproductions.ca/index.html

Beve Stevenson is a veteran emergency nurse who has worked emergency rooms in Calgary, Alberta, Canada, and in a trauma helicopter. She is also a stand-up comedian, writer, and motivational speaker who believes that comedy is the perfect antidote to a high-stress job. Here she describes her workday in a busy urban hospital.

TEACHING TIP

You might wish to combine this selection with a study of present tense verbs and verb agreement. Writing Assignment 1 provides an excellent review and application of writing in the present tense.

"What brings you to hospital?"
"A cab."

1. As I enter the hospital through the ER entrance, I assess the overall mood of the waiting room. Is everyone patient and quiet, or is the frustration palpable?[1] I change into my comfy scrubs and secure my stethoscope around my neck as I mentally prepare for my day.

2. I survey the work environment that only an ER nurse could consider normal: patients of all shapes, sizes, and colors in various states of undress, illness, and lucidity.[2] There is a cacophony[3] of loud voices, crying children, gurneys[4] and people darting about in a frantic dance. Continuing through the ER hallway, I can easily hear conversations of physicians behind the curtains with their patients. "You did this . . . how?" "How long have your teeth been itchy?" "With a fork?"

3. "What brings you to hospital?"

4. "A cab."

5. I am relieved not to be assigned to triage[5] today. Increased patient volumes and acuity,[6] bed and nursing shortages, not to mention agonizingly long waiting times, have made triage the bane[7] of the ER nurse's existence. The triage nurse, otherwise known as "The Bag in the Bubble," assumes the brunt[8] of waiting room abuse and acts as detective, counselor, organizer, diplomat, gatekeeper, interpreter, and sometimes magician too. No one taught us any of this in nursing school.

6. "Why do you want to see the doctor today?"

---

1. palpable: obvious
2. lucidity: state of mental clarity
3. cacophony: harsh mixture of sounds
4. gurneys: rolling carts for patient transport
5. triage: process of determining and prioritizing patients' medical needs
6. acuity: the level of severity of illness
7. bane: something that brings misery or difficulty
8. brunt: the main impact

Emergency room staff at a city hospital tend a critically ill patient.

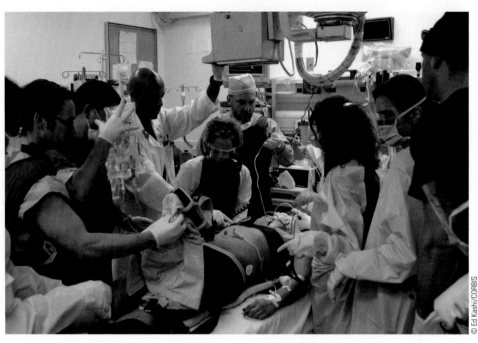

7   "None of your *?&% business!"

8   For twelve hours, I will be responsible for everything that happens in my six-bed area. I will assess and treat twenty-five patients with seemingly every kind of illness or trauma. Two will go to the OR, one will lose her baby, and another will go to heaven. I will witness the effects of domestic abuse. I will calm a frightened child and his parents, then dodge a few punches and the occasional poorly aimed spitball. I will peel off socks that haven't been removed for a year and not be surprised by what is beneath. I will start dozens of IVs, produce mounds of paperwork, and fix at least one computer problem. I will give multiple medications, initiate a blood transfusion, assist with a fracture reduction, then arrange for Home Care. For thirty minutes, a man will insist, with almost religious fervor,[9] that he is unconscious. I will tidy up after a herd of messy medical students. I will print labels, wipe brows and bums, collect blood samples, and educate new immigrants on the proper use of Tylenol. I will convince a teenager that her horoscope is not an effective method of birth control. I will constantly reassess my patients' conditions, making sure to alert the physician if someone deteriorates. Somehow, I will find time to ease my patients' fears by telling a few jokes. I will encourage the use of helmets, teach crutch walking and proper wound care. And that is just *today*.

9   Having *ER*[10] on television has helped in one way; I can now communicate great thirst after work by ordering a STAT[11] margarita. But often patients confuse TV for reality. Haven't they noticed that there aren't any wildly good-looking doctors like George Clooney or Noah Wyle working here? No physicians smooch with gorgeous nurses in the bedpan room. I've never seen a doctor rush out to the ambulance bay—that is, except to get a Coke out of the machine. And no patient's problem can be fixed in just one hour, ever.

10   On a short break, several nurses meet in the staff room for some "Vitamin C." I take mine black. Here we are free to discuss typical ER subjects like festering[12] wounds while we eat. There's almost always a plate of old, greasy "share food"

---

9. fervor: emotional intensity
10. *ER*: a television drama about an emergency room
11. STAT: medical expression meaning "immediately, without delay"
12. festering: infected

that could easily double as a food-poisoning lab. Why do health-care professionals eat this stuff?

Often the shift's most difficult skill is not the tough IV start, but plain old com- 11 munication. Blend several languages, cultural and generational differences; mix in anxiety, fear, missing teeth, intoxication, speech impediments,[13] dementia, igno- rance, and embarrassment. Add a dash of medical jargon,[14] and soon everyone is confused beyond belief. Imagine the loud assessment of the severely hearing- impaired patient; everyone within earshot cannot help but learn much more than they wanted to, including the play-by-play of a rectal examination.

By shift's end, I'm totally exhausted, my hands raw from washing, my voice 12 hoarse, and my feet screaming in agony. When I stop at the grocery store on my way home, I notice how a woman's ankles literally *flow* over the sides of her shoes. I know that her Lasix[15] dose is sub-therapeutic, just as I know the man behind me is an asthmatic who still smokes. I cannot seem to turn off this constant assessment of everyone around me.

At a party in the evening, gore-curious guests who work "normal" jobs and 13 whose trauma experience is likely limited to occasional mishaps with the office stapler, interrogate me about my work. I cannot divulge[16] what truly transpired, nor do they really want to know even if they think they do. One guest launches into the gory details of her recent surgical procedure, even offering to show me her abscess.[17] I decline.

Despite all of this, I am proud to be an Emergency Nurse. Now, where is my 14 STAT margarita?

DISCUSSION AND WRITING QUESTIONS

1. Did any specifics about this nurse's day surprise you? What details did you find most effective?
2. If you went to the emergency room where the author works, would you want her to be your nurse? Why or why not? In your opinion, what are the qualities of a good nurse?
3. Do you think that a sense of humor is important in most workplaces today? Give specific examples that support your opinion.
4. Reread paragraph 8, aloud if possible, underlining examples of *parallelism*. What effect does the author's use of parallel words have on her description of her many daily tasks?

WRITING ASSIGNMENTS

1. Write your own *Day in the Life . . .* composition. Complete the title as you wish (for example, *of a Single Mother, a Soldier in Afghanistan, a Fast-Food Worker, a Video Gamer,* and so on). Use time order, present tense verbs, and many specific details to show the reader exactly what that day is like.
2. What are your main sources of stress at work, at home, or at school? How do you cope with these stresses? Use humor if you wish.
3. The author writes in paragraph 9 that "patients often confuse TV for reality." Give examples of television shows that lead viewers to form misconceptions about certain professions, such as law enforcement, medicine, or teaching. How do the characters in the show differ from the real professionals?

---

13. impediments: difficulties
14. jargon: words used in a specific profession
15. Lasix: medication for water retention
16. divulge: reveal
17. abscess: area of infected tissue and pus

You Can Take This Job and . . . Well, It Might Surprise You

Ana Veciana-Suarez

If you won a lottery jackpot, what would you do? Buy a house? Take a trip? Quit your job? Not so fast, cautions Ana Veciana-Suarez. According to this *Miami Herald* columnist, there are some very good reasons to keep right on working.

1   Have you heard about the part-time letter carrier who won the $183 million jackpot in Maryland? She will collect more than $76 million after state and federal taxes, making her one of the largest individual winners in U.S. lottery history.

2   And she bought the ticket on a *whim*.[1]

3   I read about Bernadette Gietka's good fortune just as I was about to begin a grueling[2] workday that consisted of catching up from vacation while juggling new assignments. She reminded me of all the other lottery winners I had heard about, lucky people made suddenly wealthy (and confused) by happenstance.[3] There was the California software consultant who had a $7 million winning ticket stuffed in her purse for two months. And one Nebraska couple who ended up buying the jackpot after the wife had had a bad day at work.

4   As my mother used to say, "*La suerte es loca y a cualquiera le toca.*" Luck is crazy and it can touch anybody. (Believe me, it sounds better in Spanish.)

5   I'm not much of a player, and gambling, in one form or another, holds little attraction. Life itself, with its tribulations[4] and surprises, is risky enough for me. But belief in steady nose-to-the-grindstone economic growth has never stopped me from daydreaming. So in a biting moment of anxiety, I schlepped[5] on over to the grocery store to buy a lottery ticket for the next drawing. You never know; you just never know.

6   Like most people, my friends and I entertain ourselves by coming up with ways to spend money we don't have. (And money we do have.) It is one of those futile[6] exercises that, done right and not too flippantly,[7] can help you focus on priorities, what truly matters to you when money is taken out of the equation.

7   What would I do with a sudden windfall?[8] Take a trip. Buy a house on the beach. Make sure my family is well taken care of. You know, the usual. I don't know if I would quit my job, however.

8   You would? Well, don't be so sure. Gietka, for one, plans to continue making her rounds.

9   We complain about work, curse our bosses, practice Oscar-winning monologues[9] to deliver when we finally walk out of the sweatshop, but most of us would keep punching that time clock. According to a recent Opinion Research Corporation poll, 70 percent of us would go right on working even if the fiscal gods smiled on us. In fact, we're so wedded to our jobs that only 5 percent would go on a vacation and 3 percent would actually splurge on shopping. I think I know why.

> "*For better or for worse, work provides structure, imposes routine. It gives us an identity.*"

---

1. whim: sudden impulse
2. grueling: difficult, exhausting
3. happenstance: accident or twist of fate
4. tribulations: troubles
5. schlepped: dragged or moved clumsily
6. futile: useless
7. flippantly: without much thought or care
8. windfall: unexpected good fortune
9. monologues: long speeches made by one person

For better or for worse, work provides structure, imposes routine. It gives us 10 an identity. How many party conversations, after all, start with: "What do you do for a living?" Work is often social, the place we share stories about spouses and children and each other. Boardroom, factory, or cubicle, it is the prime venue[10] and source of juicy gossip.

But there's something more, too. Though we think we never have enough of 11 it, we also suspect, somewhere in the deep recesses[11] of our conniving,[12] greedy little hearts, that money, lots and lots of it, isn't all that it's cracked up to be. We nod knowingly when we hear about co-workers who sue each other over lottery winnings. We tsk-tsk when news reports tell us about a couple splitting up over the winning numbers. And we recognize, if only momentarily, that a weekly paycheck is paradoxically[13] both enslaving and liberating. Just ask your unemployed neighbor.

My mother was right: crazy, fickle luck. It arrives in many guises[14] and some- 12 times in the shape of a pay stub.

DISCUSSION AND WRITING QUESTIONS

1. Veciana-Suarez begins this article with three examples of recent lottery winners (paragraphs 1–3). Who are they? Do you think these winners' stories sum up the statement "Luck is crazy and it can touch anybody"?
2. Have you ever dreamed of winning the lottery? What would you do if you won $10 million? Explain why you would—or would not—quit your job.
3. What benefits of working, besides a paycheck, does the author discuss (paragraph 10)? Can you think of other benefits that a job provides? Do all jobs offer such benefits, or do only some jobs?
4. In paragraph 6, Veciana-Suarez says that daydreaming about how to spend lottery winnings "can help you focus on priorities, what truly matters to you when money is taken out of the equation." Is this true? List the three most important things you would do if you won $10 million. Does this list help you understand what truly matters to you?

WRITING ASSIGNMENTS

1. The odds of winning a multimillion-dollar lottery are about one in 13.98 million, yet millions of people exchange their hard-earned cash for lottery tickets every week. Discuss the reasons why so many people play when the odds are so much against them. Use examples from your own or a friend's experience.
2. The author writes that "we suspect, somewhere in the deep recesses of our conniving, greedy little hearts, that money, lots and lots of it, isn't all that it's cracked up to be" (paragraph 11). What is more important than money? Write a composition in which you answer this question.
3. Describe three or four of the most important *benefits* of being employed. Draw on your own experiences or the experiences of people you know for examples or stories that support your points.

---

10. venue: setting
11. recesses: interior spaces
12. conniving: scheming
13. paradoxically: seeming to go against common sense, yet true
14. guises: forms

Introverts Run the World—Quietly

Susan Cain

When you come home from a large party, do you feel energized or exhausted? Do you prefer one-on-one conversations or group activities? Would you rather work alone or on a team? The answers to such questions reveal where you fall on an important personality scale. Susan Cain explores fascinating differences between introverts and extroverts; she is the author of Quiet: The Power of Introverts in a World That Can't Stop Talking.

1   The theory of evolution.[1] The theory of relativity.[2] The *Cat in the Hat*. All were brought to you by introverts.[3] Our culture is biased against quiet and reserved people, but introverts are responsible for some of humanity's greatest achievements—from Steve Wozniak's invention of the Apple computer to J. K. Rowling's Harry Potter. And these introverts did what they did not in spite of their temperaments[4]—but because of them.

2   Introverts make up a third to a half of the population. That's one out of every two or three people you know. Yet our most important institutions—our schools and our workplaces—are designed for extroverts. And we're living with a value system that I call the New Groupthink, where we believe that all creativity and productivity comes from an oddly gregarious[5] place.

3   Picture the typical classroom. When I was a kid, we sat in rows of desks, and we did most of our work autonomously.[6] But nowadays many students sit in "pods" of desks with four or five students facing each other, and they work on countless group projects—even in subjects like math and creative writing. Kids who prefer to work by themselves don't fit, and research by educational psychology professor Charles Meisgeier found that the majority of teachers believe the ideal student is an extrovert[7]—even though introverts tend to get higher grades, according to psychologist Adrian Furnham.

4   The same thing happens at work. Many of us now work in offices without walls, with no respite from the noise and gaze of co-workers. And introverts are routinely passed over for leadership positions, even though the latest research by the management professor Adam Grant at Wharton shows that introverted leaders often deliver better results. They're better at letting proactive[8] employees run with their creative ideas, while extroverts can unwittingly put their own stamp on things and not realize that other people's ideas aren't being heard.

5   Of course, we all fall at different points along the introvert-extrovert spectrum. Even Carl Jung,[9] who popularized these terms in the first place, said there was no such thing as a pure introvert or a pure extrovert—that "such a man would be in a lunatic asylum." There's also a term, ambivert, for people who fall smack in the middle of the spectrum.

---

1. evolution: the process by which all living things gradually develop
2. theory of relativity: Albert Einstein's revolutionary theory of space and time
3. introverts: people who are energized by solitude or one-on-one conversation, not large groups
4. temperaments: personalities, ways of acting and reacting
5. gregarious: sociable
6. autonomously: independently
7. extrovert: person who is outgoing, social, energized by large groups
8. proactive: likely to jump in and take action
9. Carl Jung: influential psychologist of the twentieth century

But many of us recognize ourselves as one or the other. And culturally we 6 need a better balance between the two types. In fact, we often seek out this balance instinctively. That's why we see so many introvert-extrovert couples (I'm an introvert happily married to an extrovert) and the most effective work teams have been found to be a mix of the two types.

The need for balance is especially important when it comes to creativity and 7 productivity. When psychologists look at the lives of the most creative people, they almost always find a serious streak of introversion because solitude is a crucial ingredient for creativity.

Charles Darwin[10] took long walks alone in the woods and emphatically 8 turned down dinner party invitations. Theodore Geisel, better known as Dr. Seuss, dreamed up his creations in a private bell tower in the back of his house in La Jolla. Steve Wozniak invented the first Apple computer alone in his cubicle at Hewlett Packard.

Of course, this doesn't mean that we should stop collaborating with each 9 other—witness Wozniak teaming up with Steve Jobs to form Apple. But it does mean that solitude matters. And for some people it's the air they breathe. In fact, we've known about the transcendent[11] power of solitude for centuries; it's only recently that we've forgotten it. Our major religions all tell the story of seekers— Moses, Jesus, Mohammed, Buddha—who go off alone, to the wilderness, and bring profound revelations back to the community. No wilderness, no revelations.

This is no surprise, if you listen to the insights of contemporary psychology. 10 It turns out that you can't be in a group without instinctively mimicking others' opinions—even about personal, visceral[12] things like who you're physically attracted to. We ape other people's beliefs without even realizing we're doing it.

Groups also tend to follow the most dominant person in the room even though 11 there's zero correlation between good ideas and being a good talker. The best talker might have the best ideas, but she might not. So it's much better to send people off to generate ideas by themselves, freed from the distortion of group dynamics, and only then come together as a team.

I'm not saying that social skills are unimportant, or that we should abolish[13] 12 teamwork. The same religions that send their sages off to lonely mountaintops also teach us love and trust. And the problems we face today in fields like economics and science are more complex than ever, and need armies of people to solve them. But I am saying that we all need alone time. And that the more freedom we give introverts to be themselves, the more they'll dream up their own unique solutions to the problems that bedevil us.

"There's zero correlation between good ideas and being a good talker."

DISCUSSION AND WRITING QUESTIONS

1. After reading this article, do you consider yourself an introvert or an extrovert? Share some specifics or an incident that reveals your personality. To take Cain's 20-question quiz, go here and scroll down: <http://www.npr .org/2012/01/30/145930229/quiet-please-unleashing-the-power-of-introverts>.

2. Do you agree that our society favors extroverts? Was your grade school set up for introverts or extroverts (paragraph 3)? How about the physical arrangement of your present college classes or your workplace (paragraph 4)? Explain.

3. Why might an introvert-extrovert pair make the most effective marriage or work partners (paragraph 6)? Can you think of a pair you've observed who illustrate this claim?

TEACHING TIP

You might ask whether students think that in her zeal to support overlooked introverts, Cain might offend sociable, productive extroverts.

---

10. Charles Darwin: man who proposed the theory of evolution
11. transcendent: beyond ordinary experience, spiritual
12. visceral: gut-level
13. abolish: do away with

4. Cain explains that "solitude is a crucial ingredient for creativity" (paragraph 7). Think about something creative you or another has done (made a photo album, rebuilt a car, redecorated a room, written a fine paper). Was spending time alone an essential part of completing the project successfully? Why or why not?

WRITING ASSIGNMENTS

1. When people brainstorm in groups, says Cain, they tend to follow the most dominant talker in the room rather than the one with the best ideas (paragraph 11). Plan a creative way to manage a classroom or workplace discussion so that everyone gets a chance to speak. How would it work?

2. State one career goal you are considering, and explain two to three ways in which this job will be a good match for your personality. First, state whether you are an introvert, extrovert, or a bit of both. Then show how two or three of your traits are suited to this job. For example, "As an extrovert, I love to keep moving. As a drug company representative, traveling and meeting new people constantly will be good for me."

3. Researchers report in *Time* magazine that the new "open office" design (with glass or no walls between desks) is a source of stress and lowered productivity for everyone, regardless of personality type (<http://ideas.time.com/2012/08/15/why-the-open-office-is-a-hotbed-of-stress/>). The photo shows a typical open office design. Plan an ideal work environment for introverts and extroverts. How could it draw out the best work habits of each?

New open office designs might stimulate anxiety, not productivity (see Writing Assignment 3).

Hot Dogs and Wild Geese

Firoozeh Dumas

More than 31 million people who live in the United States were born in other countries, and most of them did not speak English very well—or at all—when they first came here. As Iranian-born writer Firoozeh Dumas illustrates with her family's story, learning English is not only confusing but often downright hilarious. This essay appears in her book, *Funny in Farsi*.

1 Moving to America was both exciting and frightening, but we found great comfort in knowing that my father spoke English. Having spent years regaling[1] us with stories about his graduate years in America, he had left us with the distinct impression that America was his second home. My mother and I planned to stick close to him, letting him guide us through the exotic American landscape that he knew so well. We counted on him not only to translate the language but also to translate the culture, to be a link to this most foreign of lands. He was to be our own private Rosetta stone.[2]

2 Once we reached America, we wondered whether perhaps my father had confused his life in America with someone else's. Judging from the bewildered looks of store cashiers, gas station attendants, and waiters, my father spoke a version of English not yet shared with the rest of America. His attempts to find a "vater closet"[3] in a department store would usually lead us to the drinking fountain or the home furnishings section. Asking my father to ask the waitress the definition of "sloppy Joe" or "Tater Tots" was no problem. His translations, however, were highly suspect. Waitresses would spend several minutes responding to my father's questions, and these responses, in turn, would be translated as "She doesn't know." Thanks to my father's translations, we stayed away from hot dogs, catfish, and hush puppies, and no amount of caviar[4] in the sea would have convinced us to try mud pie.

3 We wondered how my father had managed to spend several years attending school in America yet remain so utterly befuddled[5] by Americans. We soon discovered that his college years had been spent mainly in the library, where he had managed to avoid contact with all Americans except his engineering professors. As long as the conversation was limited to vectors,[6] surface tension, and fluid mechanics, my father was Fred Astaire[7] with words. But one step outside the scintillating[8] world of petroleum engineering and he had two left tongues.

4 My father's only other regular contact in college had been his roommate, a Pakistani who spent his days preparing curry. Since neither spoke English but both liked curries, they got along splendidly. The person who had assigned them together had probably hoped they would either learn English or invent a common language for the occasion. Neither happened.

5 My father's inability to understand spoken English was matched only by his efforts to deny the problem. His constant attempts at communicating with

"After searching fruitlessly for elbow grease, I asked the salesclerk for help."

---

1. regaling: entertaining
2. Rosetta stone: carved stone tablet, the key to translating ancient Egyptian writing
3. "vater closet": *water closet,* the British term for *bathroom*
4. caviar: fancy fish eggs
5. befuddled: confused
6. vectors: mathematical quantities
7. Fred Astaire: American dancer and film star of the 1930s, 1940s, and 1950s
8. scintillating: sparkling, brilliant

Americans seemed at first noble and adventurous, then annoying. Somewhere between his thick Persian accent and his use of vocabulary found in pre–World War II British textbooks, my father spoke a private language. That nobody understood him hurt his pride, so what he lacked in speaking ability, he made up for by reading. He was the only person who actually read each and every document before he signed it. Buying a washing machine from Sears might take the average American thirty minutes, but by the time my father had finished reading the warranties, terms of contracts, and credit information, the store was closing and the janitor was asking us to please step aside so he could finish mopping the floor.

6   My mother's approach to learning English consisted of daily lessons with Monty Hall and Bob Barker.[9] Her devotion to *Let's Make a Deal* and *The Price Is Right*[10] was evident in her newfound ability to recite useless information. After a few months of television viewing, she could correctly tell us whether a coffeemaker cost more or less than $19.99. How many boxes of Hamburger Helper, Swanson's TV dinners, or Turtle Wax could one buy without spending a penny more than twenty dollars? She knew that, too. Strolling down the grocery aisle, she rejoiced in her celebrity sightings—Lipton tea! Campbell's tomato soup! Betty Crocker Rich & Creamy Frosting! Every day, she would tell us the day's wins and losses on the game shows. "He almost won the boat, but the wife picked curtain number two and they ended up with a six-foot chicken statue." The bad prizes on *Let's Make a Deal* sounded far more intriguing than the good ones. Who would want the matching La-Z-Boy recliners when they could have the adult-size crib and high-chair set?

7   My mother soon decided that the easiest way for her to communicate with Americans was to use me as an interpreter. My brother Farshid, with his schedule full of soccer, wrestling, and karate, was too busy to be recruited for this dubious[11] honor. At an age when most parents are guiding their kids toward independence, my mother was hanging on to me for dear life. I had to accompany her to the grocery store, the hairdresser, the doctor, and every place else that a kid wouldn't want to go. My reward for doing this was the constant praise of every American we encountered. Hearing a seven-year-old translate Persian into English and vice versa made quite an impression on everyone. People lavished[12] compliments on me. "You must be very, very smart, a genius maybe." I always responded by assuring them that if they ever moved to another country, they, too, would learn the language. (What I wanted to say was that I wished I could be at home watching *The Brady Bunch*[13] instead of translating the qualities of various facial moisturizers.) My mother had her own response to the compliments: "Americans are easily impressed."

8   I always encouraged my mother to learn English, but her talents lay elsewhere. Since she had never learned English in school, she had no idea of its grammar. She would speak entire paragraphs without using any verbs. She referred to everyone and everything as "it," leaving the listener wondering whether she was talking about her husband or the kitchen table. Even if she did speak a sentence more or less correctly, her accent made it incomprehensible. "W" and "th" gave her the most difficulty. As if God were playing a linguistic[14] joke on us, we lived in "Veetee-er" (Whittier), we shopped at "Veetvood" (Whitwood) Plaza, I attended "Leffingvell" School, and our neighbor was none other than "Valter Villiams."

---

9. Monty Hall and Bob Barker: early television game show hosts
10. *Let's Make a Deal* and *The Price Is Right*: television game shows that began in the 1960s and 1970s
11. dubious: doubtful, questionable
12. lavished: heaped or poured
13. *The Brady Bunch*: an early 1970s television sitcom
14. linguistic: relating to language

Despite little progress on my mother's part, I continually encouraged her. 9
Rather than teach her English vocabulary and grammar, I eventually decided to
teach her entire sentences to repeat. I assumed that once she got used to speaking
correctly, I could be removed, like training wheels, and she would continue coast-
ing. I was wrong.

Noticing some insects in our house one day, my mother asked me to call the 10
exterminator. I looked up the number, then told my mother to call and say, "We
have silverfish in our house." My mother grumbled, dialed the number, and said,
"Please come rrright a-vay. Goldfeeesh all over dee house." The exterminator told
her he'd be over as soon as he found his fishing pole.

A few weeks later, our washing machine broke. A repairman was summoned 11
and the leaky pipe was quickly replaced. My mother wanted to know how to
remove the black stain left by the leak. "Y'all are gonna hafta use some elbow
grease," he said. I thanked him and paid him and walked with my mother to the
hardware store. After searching fruitlessly[15] for elbow grease, I asked the salesclerk
for help. "It removes stains," I added. The manager was called.

Once the manager finished laughing, he gave us the disappointing explana- 12
tion. My mother and I walked home empty-handed. That, I later learned, is what
Americans call a wild-goose chase.

Now that my parents have lived in America for thirty years, their English has 13
improved somewhat, but not as much as one would hope. It's not entirely their
fault; English is a confusing language. When my father paid his friend's daughter
the compliment of calling her homely, he meant she would be a great housewife.
When he complained about horny drivers, he was referring to their tendency to
honk. And my parents still don't understand why teenagers want to be cool so
they can be hot.

I no longer encourage my parents to learn English. I've given up. Instead, I'm 14
grateful for the wave of immigration that has brought Iranian television, newspapers, and supermarkets to America. Now, when my mother wants to ask the
grocer whether he has any more eggplants in the back that are a little darker and
more firm, because the ones he has out aren't right for *khoresht bademjun,* she can
do so in Persian, all by herself. And for that, I say hallelujah, a word that needs no
translation.

DISCUSSION AND WRITING QUESTIONS

1. Why was Dumas so sure that her father would guide the family easily through
   the mysteries of American life (paragraph 1)? Why was he, in fact, so little help
   (paragraph 2)? How do you guess that he translated the words *hot dogs, catfish,
   hush puppies,* and *mud pie* so that his family refused to eat these foods?
2. The author humorously describes the weird skills her mother learned by
   watching so much American television. What did the mother learn?
3. In paragraph 7, Dumas writes, "At an age when most parents are guiding their
   kids toward independence, my mother was hanging on to me for dear life." If
   a child of immigrants must serve as a translator for his or her parents, parent-
   child roles sometimes can be reversed. Is this a problem?
4. Dumas uses funny examples to show how confusing English can be. If English
   was not your first language, what words or aspects of American culture
   especially confused you? What was funniest (or most frustrating)?

---

15. fruitlessly: without success

WRITING ASSIGNMENTS

1. The United States, with its many races and ethnic groups, has been called a "melting pot." In a group with several classmates, decide whether the United States is more like a *melting pot* (where various ingredients melt together into one soup or goo), a *salad* (where different ingredients are tossed together but keep their separate flavors), or a *grocery store shelf* (where many foods in sealed containers do not mix). Write a paper presenting your own ideas.

2. Have you ever found yourself in a place where you did not understand the "rules"? This place might be a new country, a new school, a new job, or the dinner table of your future in-laws. Describe the challenges you faced in this strange new world and tell how you dealt with them. Use humor if you wish.

3. Does your town have ethnic shops, markets, restaurants, or neighborhoods that you have never explored? Choose one place that you would like to learn more about and visit there, chat with people, and perhaps have something to eat. Take notes on the sights, sounds, smells, and details; then write a vivid account of your adventure.

(Illusions of) Freshness for Sale

Martin Lindstrom

Excerpt from *Brandwashed: Tricks Companies Use to Manipulate Our Minds and Persuade Us to Buy* by Martin Lindstrom, copyright © by Martin Lindstrom Company, Limited. Used by permission of Crown Business, an imprint of the Crown Publishing Group, a division of Random House LLC and Random House Australia. All rights reserved.

As a child, Martin Lindstrom loved Legos. He built a miniature Lego world in his backyard that attracted so many visitors that executives from the Lego company visited his house. When Lindstrom was 13, they put him on their advisory board. Now an expert in consumer behavior and marketing, Lindstrom reveals in this article some of the secrets of "brandwashing," the tricks that companies use to brainwash us and make us want to buy, buy, buy.

1   As someone who has been on the frontlines of the branding wars,[1] I've spent countless hours with advertising executives, marketing mavens[2] and the chiefs of some of the biggest companies in the world. I've seen—and, honestly, been disturbed by—the full range of psychological tricks and schemes that some companies will use to prey on our most deeply rooted fears, dreams, and desires in order to persuade us to spend money on their brands and products.

2   A key lesson: Fear sells. I recall an early 20th century advertisement for lunchbox thermoses that bore an unforgettable tagline: "A fly in the milk may mean a baby in the grave." Advertisers have since become more subtle in their use of fear, but the underlying principle remains the same. The illusion of cleanliness or freshness is a particularly powerful persuader—and marketers know it.

3   To see all the tricks that marketers have for creating the appearance of freshness, there is no better place to go than Whole Foods, the giant US purveyor[3] of natural and organic edibles. As you enter a Whole Foods store, symbols—or what advertisers call "symbolics"—of freshness overwhelm. The first thing you see is flowers—geraniums, daffodils, jonquils—some of the freshest, most perishable objects on earth.

4   The prices for the flowers and other produce are scrawled in chalk on fragments of black slate, a tradition borrowed from outdoor markets in Europe. It's as

---

1. branding wars: competition among companies to sell their particular brands
2. mavens: experts
3. purveyor: supplier, seller

"A key lesson:
Fear sells."

if the farmer or grower had unloaded his produce (chalk and slate boards in hand), then hopped back in his flatbed truck and motored back to the country. But, in fact, while some of the flowers are purchased locally, many are bought centrally, and in-house Whole Foods artists produce the chalk boards.

This same strategy explains the coolers of chipped ice used by many super- 5 market chains. To our irrational, germ-fearing minds, tortillas, hot dogs and pickles must be fresher—and thus safer to eat—when they're sitting on a bed of ice. Likewise when soft drinks or juices perspire a little, a phenomenon the industry dubs "sweat" (the refrigerators in most juice and milk aisles are deliberately kept at the exact temperature needed for this "sweating" to occur). Similarly, for years now, supermarkets have been sprinkling select vegetables with little dew drops of water. Like ice displays, those drops serve as a symbol, albeit[4] a bogus[5] one, of freshness and purity.

You may think a banana is just a banana, but some growers have made the 6 creation of a banana a mini-science. US sales records show bananas with Pantone[6] color 13-0858 (otherwise known as Vibrant Yellow) are less likely to sell than those with Pantone color 12-0752 (also called Buttercup), which is one grade warmer, visually, and seems to imply a riper, fresher fruit. So these companies plant bananas under conditions most likely to produce the "right" color.

Knowing that even the suggestion of fruit evokes powerful associations of 7 health, freshness, and cleanliness, brands across all categories have gone fruity on us, infusing everything from shampoos to bottled water with pineapple, orange peach, passionfruit, or banana fragrances—engineered in a chemist's laboratory, of course. The same goes for baby soap, nicotine chewing gum, lip balm, teas, vitamins, cosmetics, and furniture polish. Will these products get your hair or your floors any cleaner than the regular versions? No, but the scent of fruit evokes strong associations of cleanliness for germophobic[7] consumers.

Shampoo companies also realise that the sheer volume of bubbles that their 8 shampoo generates can prompt thoughts of freshness and cleanliness—bubbles signal that the shampoo is strong and invigorating (just as the "sting" of an after-shave or the bubbles hitting our throat whenever we down sparkling water "inform" us that the product is fresh and uncontaminated). Some companies have gone so far as to create a chemical that accelerates the appearance of bubbles and increases their quality, making bathers feel as though their hair is getting cleaner faster. I have labelled this a "perceived justification"—a moment designed to reassure us that we made the right purchase.

Finally, a fish story from Spain's Canary Islands: A friend of mine was once 9 part of the crew that caught the day's supply of seafood for a harbor restaurant. Their catch was always transferred to a more traditional fisherman's boat (the kind that no one uses anymore). When customers arrived at the restaurant for lunch, the old boat would putter into the harbour and a grizzled old fisherman would deliver the fish, ostensibly[8] reeled in just moments earlier. It was all staged, but the customers ate it up.

At the end of the day, we want to buy into the illusions that the marketing 10 world sells to us—hook, line and sinker. And that may just be the scariest thing of all.

---

4. albeit: even though
5. bogus: fake, counterfeit
6. Pantone: an influential company that creates thousands of color formulas and picks "colors of the year"
7. germophobic: having an abnormal fear of germs
8. ostensibly: apparently, appearing to be

DISCUSSION AND WRITING QUESTIONS

1. What does Lindstrom mean when he says, "Fear sells" (paragraph 2)? Why does he refer to the old milk ad? Why do you think "the illusion of freshness" is a powerful persuader? What fears make us crave freshness and cleanliness?
2. Lindstrom provides many examples of marketing tactics used by Whole Foods. Do any of these tactics surprise or offend you? What other examples can you add based on the supermarkets or other stores where you shop?
3. Name one or two companies that, in your opinion, are very good at brandwashing. Why? Who is the target audience they are trying to reach in their ads? What specific tricks and tactics do these companies use?
4. The author concludes with the story about the fishing boat in the Canary Islands (paragraph 9). The arrival of the day's catch in an old fishing boat, transferred entirely behind the scenes from a commercial fishing vessel, delighted the watching diners. Are any illusions in addition to freshness being sold in this performance?

WRITING ASSIGNMENTS

1. Think and write about a product that has you "brandwashed." Perhaps you drink only Starbucks coffee or wear only Adidas sneakers. Can you account for your devotion to this product based on its genuine merits, or have marketers won you over with tricks and tactics?
2. Many companies aim their ads for candy, drinks, toys, and games at children, much to the frustration of parents. What can parents or schools do to counteract the effects of "brandwashing" on children?
3. You and several classmates have been asked to create the marketing campaign for a new sports drink, mascara, or laundry detergent (choose one). First, decide whether your tactics will appeal to "a fear, a dream, or a desire" in consumers (paragraph 1). Then write specifically what fear, dream, or desire you will connect with the product. Invent two or three ways that you will plant this connection in consumers' minds. Each of you should write up the proposed plan of action.

One Husband, Two Kids, Three Deployments

Melissa Seligman

Although recent wars in Iraq and Afghanistan are much debated in the American media, the public hears far less about the disruptive and even agonizing experiences of individual soldiers and the families they leave behind. In this article for the *New York Times*, a military wife explains how letters, not a Webcam, saved her marriage.

1   Five years ago, my new husband, David, swallowed his tears as he tried to find a way to say goodbye. He held our baby girl to his nose, inhaled her newborn scent and searched my eyes for understanding. "You know I have to go, right?" he asked. I nodded, trying to understand his leaving, his sense of duty. I imagined that I did as I watched him walk out our kitchen door toward a war in Afghanistan, but I didn't.

2   We talked—sometimes twice a day—ignoring the popping and snapping on the line and the long delays between our voices on the Webcam. And I fooled

A Gulf War soldier reading
mail from home

myself into believing a two-dimensional image could transmit and sustain a three-dimensional marriage. After all, I could see his eyes, hear his laughter. But he knew nothing of what I thought about our marriage, nothing of my postpartum[1] depression, and nothing of my anger at feeling lonely in a life that he chose.

How could I look at him on the Webcam and tell his sad eyes that I felt abandoned? How would I live with myself if, God forbid, the last words he heard from me were painful truths? The pressure to keep our conversations light controlled me, and it brought our marriage to a halt. When he returned from Afghanistan, I almost left him.   3

When he began packing for his second deployment, this time to Iraq, when he held our second newborn—a son, Elijah—my chest constricted just thinking of what might happen to us. To him.   4

"Let's not make the same mistakes," he said. "No secrets this time." I nodded, even though I knew full well that, faced with the Webcam, I would again hide my fears and anger.   5

With our daughter, Amelia, now 2 years old, the computer visits were more necessary than ever—she knew him now and longed for his attention. But they were harder than I could have imagined. Amelia would beg for days to see her daddy on the computer and then, when he appeared on the screen, ignore him. David pleaded with his eyes, but she walked away, defiantly—as only a toddler can do.   6

"On paper, our memories came to life."

"She's just tired," I'd say. He'd look down, hiding his emotions. I tried to hide mine as well. I wanted to be delighted, to drop everything when the instant messenger paged me, when he gave up badly needed sleep to be with us. But sometimes I couldn't help being annoyed at the interference. I needed unbroken routines in order to be both a mother and father to my children. At times, I wished he wouldn't call.   7

And then we found salvation in letters. I had always kept a diary, but growing frustrated with my inability to really connect with David through the Webcam and on the phone, I started sending him long letters from my journal. Before long,   8

---

1. postpartum: occurring shortly after having a baby

I was picking out stationery to match my moods and searching for the perfect pen to carry my thoughts. David responded with enthusiasm.

9   Writing allowed us to regain control of our marriage. On paper, our memories came to life. Through letters we could share our concerns without worrying that we'd be misinterpreted.

10   As I read David's words, I smelled his cologne, I heard him whistle while I cooked, I felt his hand on the small of my back. Amelia would stuff her daddy's letters into her pockets and take them with her to the playground. At night, she would beg me to read the letters again. Over and over until she felt content enough to sleep.

11   And the paintings that Amelia and Elijah sent to their dad allowed him to marvel at how his children were growing. He could run his calloused fingers over the bumps and grooves of their handprints. He could watch Amelia learn to form the letters in her name and guess what Elijah was eating from the bits of food that made their way onto the construction paper.

12   We poured our hearts into the letters, and there were no time delays in the way, no fears that an argument would be unfinished when the satellite dropped.

13   I know I'm not the first military spouse who has struggled to communicate with a loved one on deployment[2]—and I know I won't be the last. For those who came before me, the burden to overcome was communicating without technology—waiting months for letters to arrive. For me and those still to come, it's learning to communicate despite technology.

14   And now my husband is packing again, for another deployment to Iraq. The only balm[3] is that this time we can count on our letters to help heal our broken hearts.

DISCUSSION AND WRITING QUESTIONS

1. The author felt that she could not tell her husband the truth about her feelings on the Webcam (paragraphs 2 and 3). Why? What is it about the Webcam that made deep sharing difficult?
2. What qualities of letter writing allowed this military couple to "regain control of their marriage"? How do the details in paragraphs 10 and 11 help readers understand Seligman's argument? Why did the toddler Amelia react so differently to her dad's letters?
3. Today, many women serve in the military, as well as men. In fact, more than 100,000 mothers have been deployed to Iraq and Afghanistan. Are there any differences when a mother, not a father, is separated from the children?
4. Do you think that communicating by Webcam or letter writing is richer and more meaningful? Use examples from your own experience to support your stand.

WRITING ASSIGNMENTS

1. Have you or has a family member or close friend ever served in the military? What obstacles might keep a soldier from communicating honestly with people at home during his or her tour of duty? What obstacles might be there after he or she returns home? Explain.
2. All married or committed couples hit difficult times when the relationship either ends or must change. What positive or creative steps can couples take at times like this? Be specific.

---

2. on deployment: stationed and ready for combat
3. balm: something that soothes or heals

3. Write a letter to someone, living or dead, who is important to you (such as a relative, partner, mentor, or former teacher). In your letter, explain why you value your relationship with this person. You might wish to share things you were never able to tell this person face-to-face.

Quitting Hip-Hop

Michaela Angela Davis

Hip-hop music is "the talking drum of our time," declares Michaela Angela Davis in this article for *Essence* magazine. She wonders, however, whether too many hip-hop artists are beating out the wrong kinds of messages. In this article, Davis shares her personal struggle with this question.

1   I am a 40-year-old fly girl.[1] My 13-year-old daughter, Elenni, and I often look for the same next hot thing—that perfect pair of jeans, a she's-gotta-have-it shoe, the ultimate handbag, and the freshest new sound in music, which is, more often than not, hip-hop. Though we are nearly three decades apart in age, we both feel that hip-hop is the talking drum of our time; it teaches us and represents us. But, just as some of our African ancestors sold their people to European slave traders for a few used guns and porcelain plates, it seems as if the images of women of color in much of today's hip-hop music have been sold off to a greedy industry for a few buckets of "ice"[2] and a stack of "cheese."[3]

2   Recently while watching a new video in which yet another half-dressed girl gyrated[4] and bounced, Elenni turned to me and asked, "Why can't that girl just have on a cute pair of jeans with a halter top? Why does she always have to have on booty shorts? And why can't she just dance instead of grinding on the hood of a car? What does that have to do with the song?" I had no easy answers. Although the images of the women were both demeaning and predictable, the beats were undeniably hot. Therein lies the paradox[5] at the heart of my beef with hip-hop: songs that make you bounce can carry a message far and wide, irrespective of what that message is. And far too often the message is that most young women of color are "bitches" or "hoes." I was backed into a corner, forced to choose between my love for hip-hop and my need to be respected and to pass the ideals of self-respect on to my daughter. No contest.

"I was backed into a corner, forced to choose between my love for hip-hop and my need to be respected."

3   Look, I'm no finger-wagging conservative outsider. I was one of the founding editors of *Vibe*, the first national magazine dedicated to hip-hop music, style, and culture, so it's really hard for me to hate. I also worked as a fashion stylist, helping to create looks for everyone from LL Cool J to Mary J. Later I landed at *Honey*, a magazine for young urban women, and eventually became its editor-in-chief. I wouldn't have had my career if it weren't for hip-hop culture. And that goes for lots of black folks. In addition to its music, hip-hop has journalism, film, fashion, and other lucrative[6] by-products that have employed and empowered hundreds, if not thousands, of us. So clearly I'm not one of those out-of-touch mothers who

1. fly girl: slang for a pretty, stylish woman
2. "ice": slang for diamonds
3. "cheese": slang for money
4. gyrated: moved in a spiral
5. paradox: contradiction
6. lucrative: profitable

won't listen to current music or who espouse[7] corny clichés like "In my day, we knew what real music was."

4   Today is my day, too. And the danger with what's currently going on in hip-hop is not as simple as a mere generation gap. Increasingly, the male-dominated industry tends to view women as moneymakers (as in the kind you shake). Few of us are in a position to be decision makers. As a result of this imbalance, many popular hip-hop CDs and videos feature a brand of violence and misogyny[8] that is as lethal as crack and as degrading as apartheid.[9] And though I would love to maintain my "flyest mom ever" status, my daughter's self-esteem and that of every young sister in the world is at risk. I'm willing to risk my public image to help recover theirs. If there's not a shift in how the hip-hop industry portrays women, then our 20-year relationship is officially O-V-E-R.

5   I've since found creative ways to deal with my daughter's dilemma and my heartbreaking breakup: I ask Elenni why she likes a song, then I suggest alternative artists who might have a similar vibe. We look for videos that feature more progressive acts like Floetry, Jean Grae, and Talib Kweli. We listen to classics such as Public Enemy and MC Lyte, so she knows that hip-hop does have a positive history. We also participate in other urban-culture activities that affirm and satisfy us, like art exhibits, poetry slams, and yes, shoe shopping.

6   It's not going to be easy, leaving hip-hop behind. But I can no longer merely take what it dishes out and blame it on the boogie. The cost is just too great.

DISCUSSION AND WRITING QUESTIONS

1. What does the author like and respect about hip-hop music? What does she strongly dislike about it? Specifically, what caused the author's "heartbreaking breakup" with hip-hop (paragraph 5)?
2. Do you listen to hip-hop? Do you agree with Davis that much of today's hip-hop is degrading to women and often violent? If so, what effects might this have on young women and young men? Does this message prevent both genders from "dreaming big," as Diane Sawyer urges (page 438)?
3. An effective argument establishes the credibility of both the writer and any experts whose opinions are included. Is this author a credible authority on the subject of hip-hop? Where in the essay does she reveal her credentials?
4. Hip-hop artists in countries like Korea, Senegal, and Brazil don't rap about money and sex, as many American performers do. Instead, they use their music to fight oppression and encourage social justice. Do you think that American hip-hop music would be as popular if it focused on similar subjects?

WRITING ASSIGNMENTS

1. What kind of music do you enjoy? What do you like most about this style of music? What does it give you?
2. Michaela Angela Davis, like most parents, wants to nurture her child's self-esteem and protect her from the negative messages of pop culture. Choose one gender, describe the risks faced by young men or women today, and describe the best way that parents can nurture and protect them.
3. In paragraph 3, Davis credits hip-hop with providing careers for many black people. How, in your opinion, has hip-hop music and culture *positively* affected America? Use specific examples and details to support your argument.

---

7. espouse: adopt or follow
8. misogyny: hatred of women
9. apartheid: the official policy of racial discrimination that existed in South Africa before 1994

The Hidden Life of Bottled Water

Liza Gross

"The Hidden Life of Bottled Water," by Liza Gross, as appeared in Sierra. Reprinted by permission of the author.

Consumers buy more bottled water than ever, believing that they are satisfying their thirst with something healthy. In fact, they might be better off just turning on the tap, according to this writer for *Sierra*, a magazine devoted to conservation and the environment.

"Consumers spent more than $4 billion on bottled water last year, but is bottled really better?"

© Africa Studio/Shutterstock.com

1 Americans used to turn on their faucets when they craved a drink of clear, cool water. Today, concerned about the safety of water supplies, they're turning to the bottle. Consumers spent more than $4 billion on bottled water last year, establishing the fount[1] of all life as a certifiably hot commodity. But is bottled really better?

2 You might think a mountain stream on the label offers some clue to the contents. But sometimes, to paraphrase Freud, a bottle is just a bottle. "Mountain water could be anything," warns Connie Crawley, a health and nutrition specialist at the University of Georgia. "Unless the label says it comes from a specific source, when the manufacturer says 'bottled at the source,' the source could be the tap."

3 Yosemite brand water comes not from a bucolic[2] mountain spring but from deep wells in the undeniably less picturesque Los Angeles suburbs, and Everest sells water drawn from a municipal source in Corpus Christi, Texas—a far cry from the pristine[3] glacial peaks suggested by its name. As long as producers meet the FDA's[4] standards for "distilled" or "purified" water, they don't have to disclose the source.

4 Even if the water does come from a spring, what's in that portable potable[5] may be *less* safe than what comes out of your tap. Bottled water must meet the same safety standards as municipal-system water. But while the EPA[6] mandates daily monitoring of public drinking water for many chemical contaminants, the FDA requires less comprehensive testing only once a year for bottled water. Beyond that, says Crawley, the FDA "usually inspects only if there's a complaint. Yet sources of bottled water are just as vulnerable to surface contamination as sources of tap water. If the spring is near a cattle farm, it's going to be contaminated."

5 Let's assume your store-bought water meets all the safety standards. What about the bottle? Because containers that sit for weeks or months at room temperature are ideal breeding grounds for bacteria, a bottle that met federal safety standards when it left the plant might have unsafe bacteria levels by the time you buy it. And because manufacturers aren't required to put expiration dates on bottles, there's no telling how long they've spent on a loading dock or on store shelves. (Bacteria also thrive on the wet, warm rim of an unrefrigerated bottle, so avoid letting a bottle sit around for too long.) But even more troubling is what may be leaching[7] from the plastic containers. Scientists at the FDA found traces of bisphenol A—an endocrine[8] disruptor that can alter the reproductive development of

---

1. fount: source
2. bucolic: rural
3. pristine: pure
4. FDA's: Food and Drug Administration's
5. potable: a beverage that is safe to drink
6. EPA: Environmental Protection Agency
7. leaching: dissolving, draining away
8. endocrine: hormonal

animals—after 39 weeks in water held at room temperature in large polycarbonate containers (like that carboy[9] atop your office water cooler).

6   Wherever you get your water, *caveat emptor*[10] should be the watchword. If you're simply worried about chlorine or can't abide its taste, fill an uncapped container with tap water and leave it in the refrigerator overnight; most of the chlorine will vaporize. If you know your municipal water is contaminated, bottled water can provide a safe alternative. But shop around. The National Sanitation Foundation (NSF) independently tests bottled water and certifies producers that meet FDA regulations and pass unannounced plant, source, and container inspections. And opt for glass bottles—they don't impart the taste and risks of chemical agents and they aren't made from petrochemicals.[11]

7   To get information on bottled-water standards—or to find out what's in the water you buy—contact the Food and Drug Administration, (888) INFO-FDA, <http://www.fda.gov/>. For information on your tap water, call the EPA's Safe Drinking Water Hotline, (800) 426-4791, <http://www.epa.gov/safewater>.

DISCUSSION AND WRITING QUESTIONS

1. Why might tap water be safer than bottled water?
2. Even if bottled water meets all safety standards, what other problems can affect its quality?
3. According to the author, how can consumers ensure that the bottled water they buy is, in fact, safe spring water?
4. What is the author suggesting about the American public and bottled water? What is she trying to accomplish by writing this article? Does she succeed?

WRITING ASSIGNMENTS

1. Check a campus location that sells bottled water (vending machine, cafeteria, campus store). Which brand of bottled water is sold? Contact the Food and Drug Administration (see Gross's last paragraph) to find out what information the federal government has collected on that brand. Is it spring water? Tap water from another location? Safe to drink? What ingredients does it contain? Have any problems been associated with it? Report your findings in a letter to the campus newspaper.
2. Study the contents label of one of your favorite snacks. What are the ingredients? Consult a dictionary to "translate" those ingredients. Does your appetite diminish as a result? Describe the snack, including what you thought its ingredients were and what the ingredients really are. Conclude with a recommendation for other consumers.
3. Gross suggests that perhaps the public has been fooled by the bottled-water industry. What other products do people buy without really needing them? Find an ad for one such product and describe how it works—how it creates a need where there is none. Attach the ad to your description.

---

9. carboy: oversized bottle
10. *caveat emptor*: a warning in Latin meaning "buyer beware"
11. petrochemicals: compounds derived from petroleum or natural gas

Emotional Intelligence

Daniel Goleman

Excerpt from *Emotional Intelligence* by Daniel Goleman, copyright © by Daniel Goleman. Used by permission of Bantam Books, an imprint of The Random House Publishing Group, a division of Random House LLC, and Bloomsbury Publishing Plc. All rights reserved.

How important to a person's success is IQ—that is, his or her score on an intelligence test? According to a widely read book, other personality traits and skills are even more important than IQ. The author, Daniel Goleman, calls these traits and skills *emotional intelligence*. How would you rate your emotional IQ?

1. It was a steamy afternoon in New York City, the kind of day that makes people sullen[1] with discomfort. I was heading to my hotel, and as I stepped onto a bus, I was greeted by the driver, a middle-aged man with an enthusiastic smile.

2. "Hi! How're you doing?" he said. He greeted each rider in the same way.

3. As the bus crawled uptown through gridlocked traffic, the driver gave a lively commentary: there was a terrific sale at that store . . . a wonderful exhibit at this museum . . . had we heard about the movie that just opened down the block? By the time people got off, they had shaken off their sullen shells. When the driver called out, "So long, have a great day!" each of us gave a smiling response.

4. That memory has stayed with me for close to twenty years. I consider the bus driver a man who was truly successful at what he did.

5. Contrast him with Jason, a straight-A student at a Florida high school who was fixated[2] on getting into Harvard Medical School. When a physics teacher gave Jason an 80 on a quiz, the boy believed his dream was in jeopardy.[3] He took a butcher knife to school, and in a struggle the teacher was stabbed in the collarbone.

6. How could someone of obvious intelligence do something so irrational? The answer is that high IQ does not necessarily predict who will succeed in life. Psychologists agree that IQ contributes only about 20 percent of the factors that determine success. A full 80 percent comes from other factors, including what I call *emotional intelligence*.

7. Following are some of the major qualities that make up emotional intelligence, and how they can be developed:

8. **1. Self-awareness.** The ability to recognize a feeling as it happens is the keystone of emotional intelligence. People with greater certainty about their emotions are better pilots of their lives.

9. Developing self-awareness requires tuning in to . . . gut feelings. Gut feelings can occur without a person being consciously aware of them. For example, when people who fear snakes are shown a picture of a snake, sensors on their skin will detect sweat, a sign of anxiety, even though the people say they do not feel fear. The sweat shows up even when a picture is presented so rapidly that the subject has no conscious awareness of seeing it.

10. Through deliberate effort we can become more aware of our gut feelings. Take someone who is annoyed by a rude encounter for hours after it occurred. He may be oblivious[4] to his irritability and surprised when someone calls attention to it. But if he evaluates his feelings, he can change them.

11. Emotional self-awareness is the building block of the next fundamental of emotional intelligence: being able to shake off a bad mood.

> *"How could someone of obvious intelligence do something so irrational?"*

---

1. sullen: gloomy
2. fixated: rigidly focused
3. jeopardy: danger
4. oblivious: totally unaware

12   **2. Mood Management.** Bad as well as good moods spice life and build character. The key is balance.

13   We often have little control over *when* we are swept by emotion. But we can have some say in *how long* that emotion will last. Psychologist Dianne Tice of Case Western Reserve University asked more than 400 men and women about their strategies for escaping foul moods. Her research, along with that of other psychologists, provides valuable information on how to change a bad mood.

14   Of all the moods that people want to escape, rage seems to be the hardest to deal with. When someone in another car cuts you off on the highway, your reflexive[5] thought may be, *That jerk! He could have hit me! I can't let him get away with that!* The more you stew, the angrier you get. Such is the stuff of hypertension and reckless driving.

15   What should you do to relieve rage? One myth is that ventilating[6] will make you feel better. In fact, researchers have found that's one of the worst strategies. Outbursts of rage pump up the brain's arousal system, leaving you more angry, not less.

16   A more effective technique is "reframing," which means consciously reinterpreting a situation in a more positive light. In the case of the driver who cuts you off, you might tell yourself: *Maybe he had some emergency.* This is one of the most potent ways, Tice found, to put anger to rest.

17   Going off alone to cool down is also an effective way to defuse anger, especially if you can't think clearly. Tice found that a large proportion of men cool down by going for a drive—a finding that inspired her to drive more defensively. A safer alternative is exercise, such as taking a long walk. Whatever you do, don't waste the time pursuing your train of angry thoughts. Your aim should be to distract yourself.

18   The techniques of reframing and distraction can alleviate[7] depression and anxiety as well as anger. Add to them such relaxation techniques as deep breathing and meditation and you have an arsenal of weapons against bad moods. "Praying," Dianne Tice also says, "works for all moods."

19   **3. Self-motivation.** Positive motivation—the marshaling[8] of feelings of enthusiasm, zeal, and confidence—is paramount for achievement. Studies of Olympic athletes, world-class musicians, and chess grandmasters[9] show that their common trait is the ability to motivate themselves to pursue relentless training routines.

20   To motivate yourself for any achievement requires clear goals and an optimistic, can-do attitude. Psychologist Martin Seligman of the University of Pennsylvania advised the MetLife insurance company to hire a special group of job applicants who tested high on optimism, although they had failed the normal aptitude test. Compared with salesmen who passed the aptitude test but scored high in pessimism, this group made 21 percent more sales in their first year and 57 percent more in their second.

21   A pessimist is likely to interpret rejection as meaning *I'm a failure; I'll never make a sale.* Optimists tell themselves, *I'm using the wrong approach,* or *That customer was in a bad mood.* By blaming failure on the situation, not themselves, optimists are motivated to make that next call.

22   Your . . . positive or negative outlook may be inborn, but with effort and practice, pessimists can learn to think more hopefully. Psychologists have documented that if you can catch negative, self-defeating thoughts as they occur, you can reframe the situation in less catastrophic terms.

---

5. reflexive: automatic
6. ventilating: "letting off steam," raving
7. alleviate: reduce, make better
8. marshaling: gathering together, using
9. chess grandmasters: experts at the game of chess

4. Impulse Control. The essence of emotional self-regulation is the ability to 23
delay impulse in the service of a goal. The importance of this trait to success was
shown in an experiment begun in the 1960s by psychologist Walter Mischel at a
preschool on the Stanford University campus.

Children were told that they could have a single treat, such as a marshmallow, 24
right now. However, if they would wait while the experimenter ran an errand,
they could have two marshmallows. Some preschoolers grabbed the marshmallow immediately, but others were able to wait what, for them, must have seemed
an endless twenty minutes. To sustain themselves in their struggle, they covered
their eyes so they wouldn't see the temptation, rested their heads on their arms,
talked to themselves, sang, even tried to sleep. These plucky kids got the two-
marshmallow reward.

The interesting part of this experiment came in the follow-up. The children 25
who as four-year-olds had been able to wait for the two marshmallows were, as
adolescents, still able to delay gratification in pursuing their goals. They were
more socially competent and self-assertive, and better able to cope with life's frus-
trations. In contrast, the kids who grabbed the one marshmallow were, as adolescents, more likely to be stubborn, indecisive, and stressed.

The ability to resist impulse can be developed through practice. When you're 26
faced with an immediate temptation, remind yourself of your long-term goals—
whether they be losing weight or getting a medical degree. You'll find it easier,
then, to keep from settling for the single marshmallow.

5. People Skills. The capacity to know how another feels is important on the 27
job, in romance and friendships, and in the family. We transmit and catch moods
from each other on a subtle, almost imperceptible level. The way someone says
thank you, for instance, can leave us feeling dismissed, patronized, or genuinely
appreciated. The more adroit[10] we are at discerning the feelings behind other people's signals, the better we control the signals we send.

The importance of good interpersonal skills was demonstrated by psycholo- 28
gists Robert Kelley of Carnegie-Mellon University and Janet Caplan in a study at
Bell Labs in Naperville, Ill. The labs are staffed by engineers and scientists who are
all at the apex[11] of academic IQ tests. But some still emerged as stars while others
languished.[12]

What accounted for the difference? The standout performers had a network 29
with a wide range of people. When a non-star encountered a technical problem,
Kelley observed, "he called various technical gurus and then waited, wasting
time while his calls went unreturned. Star performers rarely faced such situations
because they built reliable networks *before* they needed them. So when the stars
called someone, they almost always got a faster answer."

No matter what their IQ, once again it was emotional intelligence that sepa- 30
rated the stars from the average performers.

DISCUSSION AND WRITING QUESTIONS

1. Goleman names five qualities that contribute to emotional intelligence. What
   are they?
2. Describe someone you observed recently who showed a high level of emotional
   intelligence in a particular situation. Then describe someone who showed a
   low level of emotional intelligence in a particular situation. Which of the five
   qualities did each person display or lack?

---

10. adroit: skilled
11. apex: top, topmost point
12. languished: stayed in one place

3. Did it surprise you to read that "ventilating" is one of the worst ways to handle rage (paragraph 15)? Instead, experts suggest several techniques. Suppose you are in the following situation, and your first reaction is anger: *You ask a salesperson for help in choosing an MP3 player. As she walks right past you, she tells you that the boxes and labels will give you all the information you need.* What might you do to calm yourself down?

4. In paragraphs 24 and 25, Goleman discusses a now-famous study of children and marshmallows. What was the point of this study? Why does Goleman say that the most interesting part of the study came later, when the children reached adolescence?

WRITING ASSIGNMENTS

1. Write a detailed portrait of a person whom you consider an "emotional genius." Develop your paper with specific examples of his or her skills.

2. Daniel Goleman claims that weak emotional qualities can be strengthened with practice. Choose one of the five qualities (self-awareness, people skills, and so forth) and recommend specific ways a person could improve in that area. Your audience is people who wish to improve their emotional intelligence; your purpose is to help them do so.

3. Review or read "The Gift" on page 460, and evaluate the emotional intelligence of Jermaine Washington. Washington saved a friend's life by giving her one of his kidneys after her two brothers and her boyfriend refused to be donors. Most people in their town still think Washington was "crazy" to make this decision. What do you think? Does he have a high level of emotional intelligence? A low level? Why?

Quotation Bank

This collection of wise and humorous statements has been assembled for you to read, enjoy, and use in a variety of ways as you write. You might choose some quotations that you particularly agree or disagree with and use them as the basis of journal entries and writing assignments. When you write a paragraph or an essay, you may find it useful to include a quotation to support a point you are making. You may simply want to read through these quotations for ideas and for fun. As you come across other intriguing statements by writers, add them to the list—or write some of your own.

Learning

Teachers open the door, but you must enter by yourself.

> —CHINESE PROVERB

Only the educated are free.

> —EPICTETUS

The mind is a mansion, but most of the time we are content to live in the lobby.

> —DR. WILLIAM MICHAELS

Pay attention to what they tell you to forget.

> —MURIEL RUKEYSER

Prejudices, it is well known, are most difficult to eradicate from the heart whose soil has never been loosened or fertilized by education; they grow there, firm as weeds among stones.

> —CHARLOTTE BRONTË

The day someone quits school he is condemning himself to a future of poverty.

> —JAIME ESCALANTE

The purpose of a liberal arts education is to liberate the human being to exercise his or her potential to the fullest.

> —BARBARA M. WHITE

Love

We can only learn to love by loving.

> —IRIS MURDOCH

So often when we say "I love you," we say it with a huge "I" and a small "you."

> —ARCHBISHOP ANTHONY

Choose your life's mate carefully. From this one decision will come 90 percent of all your happiness or misery.

> —H. JACKSON BROWNE, JR.

A divorce is like an amputation; you survive, but there's less of you.

> —MARGARET ATWOOD

Gold and love affairs are difficult to hide.

—SPANISH PROVERB

Marriage is our last best chance to grow up.

—JOSEPH BARTH

No partner in a love relationship should feel that she has to give up an essential part of herself to make it viable.

—MAY SARTON

Power without love is reckless and abusive, and love without power is sentimental and anemic.

—MARTIN LUTHER KING, JR.

Love doesn't just sit there, like a stone, it has to be made, like bread, remade all the time, made new.

—URSULA K. LE GUIN

To be loved, be lovable.

—OVID

Work and Success

The best career advice to give the young is, find out what you like doing best and get someone to pay you for doing it.

—KATHERINE WHILEHAEN

If there is any one secret of success, it lies in the ability to get the other person's point of view and see things from that person's angle as well as from your own.

—HENRY FORD

If you have built castles in the air, your work need not be lost; that is where they should be. Now put foundations under them.

—HENRY DAVID THOREAU

I think most of us are looking for a calling, not a job. Most of us, like the assembly line worker, have had jobs that are too small for our spirit.

—NORA WATSON

A celebrity is a person who works hard all his [or her] life to become well known, then wears dark glasses to avoid being recognized.

—FRED ALLEN

If at first you don't succeed, skydiving is not for you.

—FRANCIS ROBERTS

You've got to believe. Never be afraid to dream.

—GLORIA ESTEFAN

If you aren't fired with enthusiasm, you will be fired with enthusiasm.

—VINCE LOMBARDI

A good reputation is more valuable than money.

—Publius

Money is like manure. If you spread it around, it does a lot of good, but if you pile it up in one place, it stinks like hell.

—Clint W. Murchison

Measure a thousand times and cut once.

—Turkish Proverb

It is never too late to be what you might have been.

—George Eliot

Family and Friendship

Making the decision to have a child—it's momentous. It is to decide forever to have your heart go walking around outside your body.

—Elizabeth Stone

Govern a family as you would fry small fish—gently.

—Chinese Proverb

Nobody who has not been in the interior of a family can say what the difficulties of any individual in that family may be.

—Jane Austen

Everything that irritates us about others can lead us to understanding of ourselves.

—Morton Hunt

A true friend is someone who thinks that you are a good egg even though he knows that you are slightly cracked.

—Bernard Meltzer

The only way to have a friend is to be one.

—Ralph Waldo Emerson

Wisdom for Living

It is not easy to find happiness in ourselves, and it is not possible to find it elsewhere.

—Agnes Repplier

Regret is an appalling waste of energy; you can't build on it; it is good only for wallowing in.

—Katherine Mansfield

Smooth seas do not make a skillful sailor.

—African Proverb

Don't be afraid your life will end; be afraid that it will never begin.

—Grace Hansen

Flowers grow out of dark moments.

—CORITA KENT

Pick battles big enough to matter, small enough to win.

—JONATHAN KOZOL

A fanatic is one who can't change his [or her] mind and won't change the subject.

—WINSTON CHURCHILL

Take your life into your own hands and what happens? A terrible thing: no one to blame.

—ERICA JONG

My life, my *real life*, was in danger, and not from anything other people might do but from the hatred I carried in my own heart.

—JAMES BALDWIN

No one can make you feel inferior without your consent.

—ELEANOR ROOSEVELT

When you come to a fork in the road, take it.

—YOGI BERRA

Writing

Writing, like life itself, is a voyage of discovery.

—HENRY MILLER

I am a Dominican, hyphen, American. As a writer, I find that the most exciting things happen in the realm of that hyphen—the place where two worlds collide or blend together.

—JULIA ALVAREZ

I think best with a pencil in my hand.

—ANNE MORROW LINDBERGH

Writing is the hardest work in the world not involving heavy lifting.

—PETE HAMILL

I never travel without my diary. One should always have something sensational to read on the train.

—OSCAR WILDE

A professional writer is an amateur who didn't quit.

—RICHARD BACH

Parts of Speech Review

A knowledge of basic grammar terms will make your study of English easier. Throughout this book, these key terms are explained as needed and are accompanied by ample practice. For your convenience and reference, the following is a short review of the eight parts of speech.

Nouns

Nouns are the names of persons, places, things, animals, activities, and ideas.*

Persons:	Ms. Caulfield, Dwayne, accountants
Places:	Puerto Rico, Vermont, gas station
Things:	sandwich, Sears, eyelash
Animals:	whale, ants, Dumbo
Activities:	running, discussion, tennis
Ideas:	freedom, intelligence, humor

Pronouns

Pronouns replace or refer to nouns or other pronouns. The word that a pronoun replaces is called its *antecedent*.**

My partner succeeded; *she* built a better mousetrap!

These computers are amazing; order four of *them* for the office.

Everyone should do *his* or *her* best.

All students should do *their* best.

---

* For more work on nouns, see Chapter 22.
** For more work on pronouns, see Chapter 23.

Pronouns take different forms, depending on how they are used in a sentence. They can be the subjects of sentences (*I, you, he, she, it, we, they*) or the objects of verbs and prepositions (*me, you, him, her, it, us, them*). They also can show possession (*my, mine, your, yours, his, her, hers, its, our, ours, their, theirs*).

Subject:	*You* had better finish on time.
	Did *someone* leave a laptop on the chair?
Object of verb:	Bruno saw *her* on Thursday.
Object of preposition:	That iPad is for *her*.
Possessive:	Did Adam leave *his* sweater on the dresser?

Verbs

Verbs can be either action verbs or linking verbs. Verbs can be single words or groups of words.*

Action verbs show what action the subject of the sentence performs.

> Leila *bought* a French dictionary.
>
> Ang *has opened* the envelope.

Linking verbs link the subject of a sentence with a descriptive word or words. Common linking verbs are *be, act, appear, become, feel, get, look, remain, seem, smell, sound,* and *taste*.

> This report *seems* well organized and complete.
>
> You *have been* quiet this morning.

The **present participle** of a verb is its *-ing* form. The present participle can be combined with some form of the verb *to be* to create the progressive tenses, or it can be used as an adjective or a noun.

Geraldo *was waiting* for the report.	(*past progressive tense*)
The *waiting* taxis lined up at the curb.	(*adjective*)
Waiting for trains bores me.	(*noun*)

The **past participle** of a verb can be combined with helping verbs to create different tenses, it can be combined with forms of *to be* to create the passive voice, or it can be used as an adjective. Past participles regularly end in *-d* or *-ed*, but irregular verbs take other forms (*seen, known, taken*).

---

* For more work on verbs, see Unit 3.

> He *has edited* many articles for us.　　　　(*present perfect tense*)
>
> This report *was edited* by the committee.　(*passive voice*)
>
> The *edited* report reads well.　　　　　　(*adjective*)

Every verb can be written as an *infinitive: to* plus the *simple form* of the verb.

> She was surprised *to meet* him at the bus stop.

Adjectives

Adjectives describe or modify nouns or pronouns. Adjectives can precede or follow the words they describe.*

> *Several green* chairs arrived today.
>
> Collins Lake is *dangerous* and *deep*.

Adverbs

Adverbs describe or modify verbs, adjectives, or other adverbs.**

> Brandy reads *carefully*.　　　　　　　(*adverb describes verb*)
>
> She is *extremely* tired.　　　　　　　 (*adverb describes adjective*)
>
> He wants a promotion *very* badly.　　 (*adverb describes adverb*)

Prepositions

A **preposition** begins a *prepositional phrase*. A **prepositional phrase** contains a preposition (a word such as *at*, *in*, *of*, or *with*), its object (a noun or pronoun), and any adjectives modifying the object.***

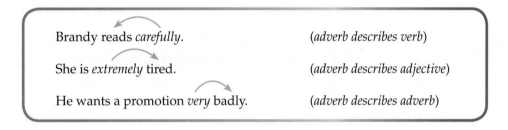

Preposition	Object
after	*work*
on	the blue *table*
under	the broken *stairs*

---

* For more work on adjectives, see Chapter 24.

** For more work on adverbs, see Chapter 24.

*** For more work on prepositions, see Chapter 25.

Conjunctions

Conjunctions are connector words.

Coordinating conjunctions (*and, but, for, nor, or, so, yet*) join two equal words or groups of words.*

Shanara is soft-spoken *but* sharp.

Ms. Chin *and* Mr. Warburton attended the technology conference.

He printed out the spreadsheet, *and* Ms. Helfman faxed it immediately.

She will go to Norfolk Community College, *but* she will also continue working at the shoe store.

Subordinating conjunctions (*after, because, if, since, unless,* and so on) join an independent idea with a dependent idea.

Whenever Alexi comes to visit, he takes the family out to dinner.

I haven't been sleeping well *because* I've been drinking too much coffee.

Interjections

Interjections are words such as *ouch* and *hooray* that express strong feeling. They are rarely used in formal writing.

If the interjection is the entire sentence, it is followed by an exclamation point. If the interjection is attached to a sentence, it is followed by a comma.

Hey! You left your wallet on the counter.

Oh, she forgot to send in her tax return.

A Reminder

REMEMBER: Sometimes the same word may be used as a different part of speech.

Terrance *thought* about the problem. (*verb*)

Your *thought* is a good one. (*noun*)

---

* For more work on conjunctions, see Chapters 16 and 17.

Guidelines for Students of English as a Second Language

Count and Noncount Nouns

Count nouns refer to people, places, or things that are separate units. You can often point to them, and you can always count them.

Count Noun	Sample Sentence
computer	The writing lab has ten *computers*.
dime	There are two *dimes* under your chair.
professor	All of my *professors* are at a conference today.
notebook	I carry a *notebook* in my backpack.
child	Why is your *child* jumping on the table?

Noncount nouns refer to things that are wholes. You cannot count them separately. Noncount nouns may refer to ideas, feelings, and other things that you cannot see or touch. Noncount nouns may refer to food or beverages.

Noncount Noun	Sample Sentence
courage	It takes *courage* to study a new language.
equipment	The company sells office *equipment*.
happiness	We wish the bride and groom much *happiness*.
bread	Who will slice this loaf of *bread*?
meat	Do you eat *meat*, or are you a vegetarian?
coffee	The *coffee* turned cold as we talked.

For more noncount nouns, visit <http://grammar.ccc.commnet.edu/grammar/noncount.htm>.

Plurals of Count and Noncount Nouns

Most count nouns form the plural by adding *-s* **or** *-es*. Some count nouns have irregular plurals.*

---

* For work on singular and plural nouns, see Chapter 22.

499

<table>
<tr><td colspan="2" align="center">**Plurals of Count Nouns**</td></tr>
<tr><td>ship/ships</td><td>video game/video games</td></tr>
<tr><td>flower/flowers</td><td>nurse/nurses</td></tr>
<tr><td>library/libraries</td><td>knife/knives</td></tr>
<tr><td>child/children</td><td>woman/women</td></tr>
</table>

Noncount nouns usually do not form the plural at all. It is incorrect to say *homeworks*, *equipments*, or *happinesses*.

PRACTICE 1

Write the plural for every count noun. If the noun is a noncount noun, write *no plural*.

1. mountain   mountains
2. wealth   no plural
3. forgiveness   no plural
4. student   students
5. generosity   no plural
6. man   men
7. assignment   assignments
8. homework   no plural
9. knowledge   no plural
10. bravery   no plural

Some nouns have both a count meaning and a noncount meaning. Usually, the count meaning is concrete and specific. Usually, the noncount meaning is abstract and general.

Count meaning: All the *lights* in the classroom went out.
Noncount meaning: What is the speed of *light*?

Count meaning: Odd *sounds* came from the basement.
Noncount meaning: The speed of *sound* is slower than the speed of light.

Food and beverages, which are usually noncount nouns, may also have a count meaning.

Count meaning: This store sells *fruits, pies,* and *teas* from different countries.
Noncount meaning: Would you like some more *fruit, pie,* or *tea*?

Articles with Count and Noncount Nouns

Indefinite Articles
The words *a* and *an* are **indefinite articles**. They refer to one *nonspecific* (indefinite) thing. For example, "a man" refers to *any* man, not to a specific, particular man. **The article *a* or *an* is used before a singular count noun.***

Singular Count Noun	With Indefinite Article
question	a question
textbook	a textbook
elephant	an elephant
umbrella	an umbrella

* For when to use *an* instead of *a*, see Chapter 35.

The indefinite article *a* or *an* is never used before a noncount noun.

Noncount Noun	Sample Sentence
music	*Incorrect:* I enjoy a music.
	Correct: I enjoy music.
health	*Incorrect:* Her father is in a poor health.
	Correct: Her father is in poor health.
patience	*Incorrect:* Good teachers have a patience.
	Correct: Good teachers have patience.
freedom	*Incorrect:* We have a freedom to choose our courses.
	Correct: We have freedom to choose our courses.

PRACTICE 2

The indefinite article *a* or *an* is italicized in each sentence. Cross out *a* or *an* if it is used incorrectly. If the sentence is correct, write *correct* on the line provided.

1. My friends give me *a* help when I need it. _____

2. The counselor gives her *an* advice about which courses to take. _____

3. *An* honesty is the best policy. _____

4. We have *an* answer to your question. _____correct_____

5. They have *an* information for us. _____

Definite Articles

The word *the* is a **definite article.** It refers to one (or more) *specific* (definite) things. For example, "the man" refers not to *any* man but to a specific, particular man. "The men" (plural) refers to specific, particular men. The article *the* also is used after the first reference to a thing (or things). For instance, "I got a new cell phone. The phone has a built-in MP3 player." **The article *the* is used before singular and plural count nouns.**

Definite (*The*) and Indefinite Articles (*A/An*) with Count Nouns

I saw *the* film. (singular; refers to a specific film)

I saw *the* films. (plural; refers to more than one specific film)

I saw *a* film. (refers to any film; nonspecific)

I enjoy seeing *a* good film. (refers to any good film; nonspecific)

I like *a* film that has an important message. (refers to any film that has an important message; nonspecific)

I saw *a* good film. *The* film was about the life of a Cuban singer. (refers to a specific film)

The definite article *the* is used before a noncount noun only if the noun is specifically identified.

Noncount Noun	Sample Sentence
fitness	*Incorrect:* He has *the* fitness. (not identified)
	Correct: He has *the* fitness of a person half his age. (identified)
	Incorrect: *The* fitness is a goal for many people. (not identified)
	Correct: Fitness is a goal for many people. (not identified, so no *the*)
art	*Incorrect:* I do not understand *the* art. (not identified)
	Correct: I do not understand *the* art in this show. (identified)
	Incorrect: *The* art touches our hearts and minds. (not identified)
	Correct: Art touches our hearts and minds. (not identified, so no *the*)

PRACTICE 3

The definite article *the* is italicized whenever it appears below. Cross it out if it is used incorrectly. If the sentence is correct, write *correct* on the line provided.

1. She dresses with *the* style.   _____

2. *The* beauty of this building surprises me.   _____correct_____

3. This building has *the* beauty of a work of art.   _____correct_____

4. ~~*The*~~ courage is an important quality.   _____

5. Alex has *the* wealth but not *the* happiness.   _____

Verb + Gerund

A **gerund** is a noun that is made up of a verb plus *-ing*. The italicized words below are gerunds.

> *Playing* solitaire on the computer helps some students relax.
>
> I enjoy *hiking* in high mountains.

In the first sentence, the gerund *playing* is the simple subject of the sentence.* In the second sentence, the gerund *hiking* is the object of the verb enjoy.** Some common verbs are often followed by gerunds.

---

* For more on simple subjects, see Chapter 9, Part A.

** For more on objects of verbs, see Chapter 23, Part F.

Some Common Verbs That Can Be Followed by a Gerund	
Verb	**Sample Sentence with Gerund**
consider	Would you *consider* **taking** a course in psychology?
discuss	Let's *discuss* **buying** a scanner.
enjoy	I *enjoy* **jogging** in the morning before work.
finish	Abril *finished* **studying** for her physiology exam.
keep	*Keep* **trying** and you will succeed.
postpone	The Brookses *postponed* **visiting** their grandchildren.
quit	Three of my friends *quit* **smoking** this year.

The verbs listed above are *never* followed by an infinitive (*to* + the simple form of the verb).*

> *Incorrect:* Would you consider *to take* a course in psychology?
>
> *Incorrect:* Let's discuss *to buy* a scanner.
>
> *Incorrect:* I enjoy *to jog* in the morning before work.

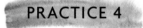 **PRACTICE 4**

Write a gerund after each verb in the blank space provided. Sample answers

1. Dave enjoys _____watching_____ television in the evening.
2. Have you finished _____studying_____ for tomorrow's exam?
3. T.J. is considering _____flying_____ to Mexico next month.
4. I have postponed _____celebrating_____ until I receive the results of the test.
5. We are discussing _____leasing_____ a car.

Preposition + Gerund

A preposition** may be followed by a gerund.

> I forgive you *for* **stepping** on my toe.
>
> Elena believes *in* **pushing** herself to her limits.
>
> We made the flight *by* **running** from one terminal to another.

A preposition is *never* followed by an infinitive (*to* + the simple form of the verb).

> *Incorrect:* I forgive you *for* **to step** on my toe.
>
> *Incorrect:* Elena believes *in* **to push** herself to her limits.
>
> *Incorrect:* We made the flight *by* **to run** from one terminal to another.

---

* For more on infinitives, see Chapter 15, Part E.

** For more on prepositions, see Chapter 25.

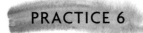

PRACTICE 5

Write a gerund after the preposition in each blank space provided. Sample answers

1. We have succeeded in _____finding_____ the DVD you wanted.

2. You can get there by _____turning_____ left at the next corner.

3. Thank you for _____buying_____ those striped socks for me.

4. I enjoy sports like _____canoeing_____ and _____kayaking_____ .

5. Between _____going_____ to school and _____working_____ , I have little time
   for _____relaxing_____ .

Verb + Infinitive

Many verbs are followed by the **infinitive** (*to* + the simple form of the verb).

Some Common Verbs That Can Be Followed by an Infinitive	
Verb	**Sample Sentence**
afford	Carla can *afford **to buy*** a new outfit whenever she wants.
agree	I *agree **to marry*** you a year from today.
appear	He *appears **to be*** inspired by his new job.
decide	Will they *decide **to drive*** across the country?
expect	Jamal *expects **to graduate*** next year.
forget	Please do not *forget **to cash*** the check.
hope	My nephews *hope **to visit*** Santa Fe this year.
intend	I *intend **to study*** harder this semester than I did last semester.
mean	Did Franco *mean **to leave*** his lunch on the kitchen table?
need	Do you *need **to stop*** for a break now?
plan	Justin *plans **to go*** into advertising.
promise	Sharon has *promised **to paint*** this wall green.
offer	Did they really *offer **to babysit*** for a month?
refuse	Haim *refuses **to walk*** another step.
try	Let's *try **to set*** up this tent before dark.
wait	On the other hand, we could *wait **to camp*** out until tomorrow.

PRACTICE 6

Write an infinitive after the verb in each blank space provided. Sample answers

1. The plumber promised _____to fix_____ the sink today.

2. My son plans _____to take_____ a course in electrical engineering.

3. We do not want _____to be_____ late for the meeting again.

4. They refused _____to begin_____ before everyone was ready.

5. I expect _____to see_____ Jorge next week.

Verb + Gerund or Infinitive

Some verbs can be followed by *either* a gerund *or* an infinitive.

Some Common Verbs That Can Be Followed by a Gerund or an Infinitive	
Verb	**Sample Sentence**
begin	They *began **to laugh***. (infinitive)
	They *began **laughing***. (gerund)
continue	Fran *continued **to speak***. (infinitive)
	Fran *continued **speaking***. (gerund)
hate	Juan *hates **to drive*** in the snow. (infinitive)
	Juan *hates **driving*** in the snow. (gerund)
like	My daughter *likes **to surf*** the Net. (infinitive)
	My daughter *likes **surfing*** the Net. (gerund)
love	Phil *loves **to watch*** soccer games. (infinitive)
	Phil *loves **watching*** soccer games. (gerund)
start	Will you *start **to write*** the paper tomorrow? (infinitive)
	Will you *start **writing*** the paper tomorrow? (gerund)

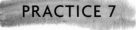

PRACTICE 7

For each pair of sentences, first write an infinitive in the space provided. Then write a gerund. Sample answers

1. a. (infinitive)   Ivana hates _____to wait_____ in long lines.

   b. (gerund)   Ivana hates _____waiting_____ in long lines.

2. a. (infinitive)   When will we begin _____to cook_____ dinner?

   b. (gerund)   When will we begin _____cooking_____ dinner?

3. a. (infinitive)   Carmen loves _____to sing_____ in the rain.

   b. (gerund)   Carmen loves _____singing_____ in the rain.

4. a. (infinitive)   The motor continued _____to rumble_____ noisily.

   b. (gerund)   The motor continued _____rumbling_____ noisily.

5. a. (infinitive)   Suddenly, the people started _____to clap_____ .

   b. (gerund)   Suddenly, the people started _____clapping_____ .

Subject Index

Index of Rhetorical Modes

This index classifies selected paragraphs and essays in this text according to the type of writing pattern, or rhetorical mode, they employ. Only passages with no or very few errors are included.

Index to the Readings

Rhetorical Index to the Readings

Notes

Notes

Notes